Nathaniel William Wraxal

The History of France

From the Accession of Henry the Third to the Death of Louis the Fourteenth. Vol. 2

Nathaniel William Wraxal

The History of France
From the Accession of Henry the Third to the Death of Louis the Fourteenth. Vol. 2

ISBN/EAN: 9783337070519

Printed in Europe, USA, Canada, Australia, Japan

Cover: Foto ©ninafisch / pixelio.de

More available books at **www.hansebooks.com**

THE

HISTORY

FRANCE,

FROM THE ACCESSION OF

HENRY THE THIRD,

TO THE DEATH OF

LOUIS THE FOURTEENTH.

PRECEDED BY

A VIEW

OF THE

CIVIL, MILITARY, AND POLITICAL

STATE OF EUROPE,

BETWEEN THE MIDDLE, AND THE CLOSE, OF THE SIXTEENTH CENTURY.

BY

NATHANIEL WILLIAM WRAXALL.

VOLUME THE SECOND.

DUBLIN:

Printed by William Porter,

FOR P. WOGAN, P. BYRNE, B. DUGDALE, AND J. POTTS.

1796.

CONTENTS.

BOOK THE FIRST.

THE REIGN OF HENRY THE THIRD.

CHAP. I.

CHAP. II.

CONTENTS.

CHAP. III.

CHAP. IV.

of

CHAP. V.

CHAP. VI.

BOOK

BOOK THE SECOND.

AGE OF HENRY THE THIRD.

CHAP. I.

CHAP. II.

CHAP. III.

THE

HISTORY

OF

FRANCE.

BOOK THE FIRST.

The Reign of HENRY THE THIRD.

CHAP. I.

Review of the French history, from the death of Francis the First, to that of Charles the Ninth.—Aspect of France, at the latter period.—Situation of the court, the capital, and the provinces, in 1574.—Regency, and measures of Catherine of Medicis—Execution of Montgomery.—Flight of Henry the Third, from Poland.—His reception at Vienna, Venice, and Turin.—Affairs of France.—Journey of the court to Lyons.—Political intrigues at Turin.—Return of Henry, and his entry into France.

CHAP. I.

THE French monarchy, from the period of the expulsion of the English, under Charles the Seventh, and the subsequent re-union of the great fiefs to the crown, was, for near a century, in a state of constant progression and advancement. The

CHAP. I.

successful irruptions of Charles the Eighth, and Louis the Twelfth, into Italy; and the conquests, made by those princes, beyond the Alps, however transitory, evinced how formidable France might soon become to the repose of Europe. Francis the First, with inferior forces, maintained a long, and almost perpetual conflict, during his whole reign, against the head of the empire, supported by the veteran bands of Italy, Spain, and the Netherlands. The compact and collected nature of his dominions; their happy position, in the center of his enemy's possessions; and the facility with which, from the extent of his prerogative, he could draw supplies from his subjects: these circumstances enabled him to balance, and even to limit, the unwieldy greatness of the house of Austria. Notwithstanding the defeat of Pavia, and the numerous disgraces or calamities experienced at various times, during his reign, which were principally owing to his negligence, profusion, or misconduct; he left the kingdom, at his decease, rich, flourishing, and capable of the greatest external exertions (1).

State of France, under Francis the First.

1547.

1552. Reign of Henry the Second.

The eastern frontier was extended and strengthened under his successor, Henry the Second, by the acquisition of Metz, Toul, and Verdun, dismembered from the German empire; and their capture was rendered peculiarly memorable by the siege which Francis, duke of Guise, sustained against the emperor, Charles the Fifth, in person. The victory of St. Quintin, where the constable Montmorenci, with the flower of the French nobility, fell into the hands of Emanuel Philibert, duke of Savoy; and which, if it had been improved, might have subverted the monarchy of France itself; was, in a great measure, rendered ineffectual by the procrastination, delays, and inaptitude of Philip the Second for con-

1553.

1557.

(1) Mezerai, passim.

ducting

ducting military affairs. The recal of the duke of Guise from Italy, not only dissipated the general consternation; but, diffused universal satisfaction, by the vigorous and successful attack of Calais, which the incapacity of Mary, queen of England, had exposed to danger. That valuable conquest was retained at the final treaty of peace, which soon afterwards took place between the two crowns of France and Spain: nor was even the evacuation and restitution of Savoy and Piedmont, so long occupied by the French arms, unaccompanied with advantage; as it precluded a renewal of the ruinous and expensive expeditions for the recovery of Naples and the Milanese, which, for more than sixty years, from the reign of Charles the Eighth, to that of Henry the Second, had impoverished, and exhausted the kingdom (2).

1558. January.

The premature and tragical death of Henry, which happened in the midst of the festivities consequent on the termination of thewar, by a splinter from the count of Montgomery's lance, may be regarded as the æra, from whence we date the calamities of France. His son, and successor, Francis the Second, though he had passed the age, at which the French monarchs were declared to be no longer in their minority; was, from inexperience, as well as from the very limited nature of his capacity, unequal to conducting in person the machine of government. Under these circumstances, the administration was rather assumed by, than delegated to, the duke of Guise, and cardinal of Lorrain; whose proximity of blood to Mary, the young queen of France and Scotland, sustained by their talents, ambition, and enterprize, enabled them to surmount all opposition. The unpopularity of their measures; their descent from, and alliance with, the house of Lorrain, which

July. Accession of Francis the Second.

(2) De Thou, Mezerai, passim.

CHAP. I.

might be regarded as foreign, if not hostile to the French interests; and more than either, the intemperate and persecuting spirit, evinced towards the followers of the reformed religion, who were numerous and powerful: these combined causes, operating on minds, already heated by controversy, produced the famous conspiracy of Amboise. Its object was, in some degree, equivocal and unascertained: but, the Guises, confounding any attempt to subvert their own authority, with the crime of treason, severely punished its authors, and displayed the full extent of royal, and ministerial vengeance, in the executions which followed. Intoxicated with prosperity, and stimulated by motives of personal safety, they determined to prosecute with equal rigor, the concealed abettors of the enterprize. Louis, prince of Condé, was justly regarded as such; and his high quality, which allied him to the crown, formed no protection against the machinations of his enemies. Seduced by assurances of security, to attend the convocation of the states-general at Orleans, he was seized, imprisoned, and, after a trial destitute even of the formalities of justice, he was sentenced to an immediate death. Anthony, king of Navarre, his elder brother, and first prince of the blood, whose more flexible and yielding character rendered him less an object of apprehension, was detained in confinement. But, at this critical moment, the sudden death of the young king, Francis, rescued the prince of Condé from his impending danger, and opened a new scene in France (3).

Conspiracy of Amboise. 1560. March.

1560.

December. Death of Francis the Second.

A minority, in name, as well as in effect, took place. Charles the Ninth, who succeeded to the throne, was still in his childhood, and it became indispensable to nominate a regent. Catherine of Medicis, the queen mother, who had hitherto re-

1561. Charles the Ninth.

Regency of Catherine of Medicis.

(3) Mezerai, De Thou, Davila.

mained

mained in a ſtate of comparative obſcurity; availing herſelf with promptitude and addreſs of the conſternation of the Guiſes, of the depreſſion of the princes of the blood, and of the abſence or diſgrace of the conſtable Montmorenci; procured her own elevation to the regency. If the rectitude of her intentions had equalled the extent and verſatility of her talents, it is probable, that her adminiſtration might have been equally pacific, and beneficial to the kingdom. But, regardleſs of veracity and honor, ſhe ſubſtituted artifice and diſſimulation in their ſtead; while, only intent on the preſervation and prolongation of her own authority, ſhe ſacrificed to it the great intereſts of the ſtate and monarchy. Incapable of cruſhing, or of coërcing by force the various factions, ſhe attempted to divide them, and to render herſelf the common arbitreſs: but, the effort exceeded her ſtrength, and the object eluded her graſp. The Guiſes, recovered from their firſt aſtoniſhment, and ſupported by their own intrepidity, formed a coalition with their antient rival, the conſtable, whoſe zeal for the ſupport of the Catholic religion prompted him to bury in oblivion all paſt animoſities. Marſhal St. André, one of the moſt powerful noblemen of the court, joined the confederacy; and France, like antient Rome, ſaw a triumvirate, in title as well as reality, form itſelf in her own boſom. The king of Navarre, fluctuating in his opinions, religious and political; allured by the ſpecious and illuſory promiſes of the Guiſes; and jealous of his brother's ſuperior conſideration, lent his aid to the triumvirs. Superior to all controul, they no longer obſerved even the forms of deference, or ſubmiſſion to the regent; and Catherine, deſtitute of any other reſource, embraced the dangerous expedient of calling to her aid the prince of Condé, who, with the admiral Coligni, commanded the forces of the Hugonots (4).

Syſtem of her adminiſtration.

1561.

Factions in the court.

(4) Davila, p. 420. De Thou, Mezerai.

From

CHAP. I.

1562. Commencement of the civil wars.

From this fatal measure originated the dissensions, by which France was long afflicted and desolated. Three civil wars, each more fiercely contested than the preceding one, extinguished all loyalty, obedience, or veneration for the laws. In their progress, the principal actors were swept off by various species of violent and premature death. The king of Navarre was killed by a ball, in the trenches before Rouen. St. André perished at the battle of Dreux; and the duke of Guise himself, who, with some defects of character, must ever be ranked among the most exalted and illustrious persons of the age, expired by the hand of an assassin, under the walls of Orleans. Montmorenci, at near fourscore years of age, fell, covered with honorable wounds, in the action at St. Denis; while the prince of Condé was put to death on the field of Jarnac, rather by deliberate assassination, than by the chance of war.

1562. November. December. 1563. February. 1567. November.

1569. March. Duke of Anjou, placed at the head of the army.

Catherine still survived among the ruins of the monarchy, and had placed her second son, Henry, duke of Anjou, for whom she early betrayed the fondest predilection, at the head of the royal armies, destined to exterminate the Hugonots. But, that party, far from being extinguished by the loss of their leader, seemed to acquire new vigor, under the guidance of the celebrated Coligni. A fourth battle, at Montcontour, in which the arms of Charles the Ninth were completely victorious, did not terminate the contest. Supported by his own resources, Coligni, after struggling with impediments, only to be surmounted by men who fight for their religious freedom, re-appeared in the ensuing year, at the head of a formidable body of forces; repulsed the troops sent to impede his progress; and even threatened to transfer the theatre of war to the vicinity of the capital (5).

October.

(5) Mezerai, passim. De Thou, Davila, D'Aubigné, Hist. Univ.

In

In ſuch a ſituation, peace became not only eligible, but indiſpenſable. It was concluded ſoon afterwards, and the conditions were highly favorable to the Hugonots (6). The meaſures of the court appeared to have undergone a total change, and to breathe conciliation. Coligni was invited to repair to the royal preſence; and Charles affected to liſten with eagerneſs and pleaſure, to his exhortations of employing the fiery and turbulent ſpirits, with which the kingdom abounded, in foreign expeditions of national glory, or advantage. The marriage of the young prince of Navarre, with Margaret, ſiſter to the king, was already ſettled; and every circumſtance ſeemed to enſure a long continuance of tranquillity. Theſe fallacious appearances preceded, and eventually terminated in the maſſacre of Paris: an event, which, whether we regard it as the joint act of Charles and Catherine his mother; as the ſeparate machination of the queen herſelf; or, as produced only by adventitious cauſes, unconnected with any deliberate ſyſtem of perfidy; ſtands equally alone, as the moſt flagitious and deteſtable violation of faith and humanity, commemorated in the annals of mankind. Its conſequences, neverthelefs, were not ſuch, as might naturally have been expected. The ſecurity, ſupineneſs, and inactivity of the government, allowed the Hugonots leiſure to recover from their firſt conſternation. Deſpair furniſhed them with arms; and Rochelle ventured to ſhut its gates againſt the forces of the Crown. Henry, duke of Anjou, after a long and fruitleſs ſiege, was compelled to withdraw his troops from the place; and eſteemed himſelf fortunate, that his election to the crown of Poland afforded him an honorable pretext for abandoning the enterprize. France was deſolated by a fourth civil war; and the mutual animoſity, manifeſted in

1570. Auguſt. Concluſion of peace.

1572. Auguſt. Maſſacre of Paris.

1572.

Siege of Rochelle.

1573. June.

(6) Mezerai, vol. ix. p. 49 and 50.

the

CHAP. I.

the courſe of it, bore a proportion to the circumſtances by which it had been produced (7).

1573. Election of the duke of Anjou to the crown of Poland.

The ambitious mind of Catherine of Medicis, perpetually occupied in viſionary ſchemes for the elevation of her children, had profited of the extinction of the race of Jagellon, to procure the Poliſh Crown for her favourite ſon, Henry. The levity and venality of the Poles; the political intrigues of Montluc, the French embaſſador; and the reputation which the duke of Anjou had acquired for military ſkill and valor, by his victories over the Hugonots; combined to produce the unexpected ſucceſs with which the attempt was accompanied. But, the new monarch did not betray the ſame alacrity to take poſſeſſion of his dominions, which he had manifeſted in their purſuit and attainment. The extenſive powers annexed to his quality of lieutenant general of France; the pleaſures of a licentious court; and the proſpect of the ſucceſſion itſelf, which Charles's ſtate of declining health rendered probable: all theſe motives tended to retard his departure. The interpoſition, and even the menaces of the king, his brother, were requiſite to propel and vanquiſh the reluctance of Henry (8).

October.

1574. New commotions in France.

His abſence was far from reſtoring a calm; and the concluſion of the reign of Charles the Ninth was marked with the ſame commotions, which had characterized its commencement and progreſs. The duke of Alençon, youngeſt of the four ſons of Henry the Second, and whoſe youth had excluded him from any participation in the counſels which led on the maſſacre of St. Bartholomew; expreſſed the warmeſt affection for the admiral Coligni, and the utmoſt indignation at his unmerited fate. Anxious to occupy the ſituation of lieutenant-general, left vacant by the king of Poland's election, and finding his demands

(7) Mezerai, vol. ix. p. 105. De Thou, vol. vi. p. 664. Davila, p. 390—3.

(8) Mezerai, vol. ix. p. 104—112.

eluded,

eluded, he projected to effect his escape, and to put himself at the head of the Protestants. He was to have been accompanied in his flight by the king of Navarre, who, after having been, not without long debates, excepted from the general carnage of his friends and followers, was, since that period, detained as a captive, together with his cousin, the prince of Condé. The irresolution of the duke of Alençon proved fatal to the enterprize, and conducted his adherents to the scaffold; while Charles the Ninth, after long struggling with a distemper, which the vigor of his constitution enabled him to resist, but, not to surmount; terminated his life and reign, in the flower of his age (9).

CHAP. I. 1574.

Death of Charles the Ninth.

May.

The aspect of France at the time of his decease, was widely different from the appearance which it exhibited under Henry the Second. In the interval of only fifteen years, the manners of the kingdom had suffered a complete alteration. The generous spirit of chivalry, characteristic of the age of Francis the First, and of which courtesy and humanity were the inseparable attendants, no longer existed. The people, habituated to scenes of civil war, were rendered ferocious and sanguinary. Almost all the arts, which tend to soften and polish society, were buried in the general confusion. Manufactures and industry languished; while commerce, become precarious, from the insecurity of the coasts, and hazardous, on account of the piracies which infested the narrow seas, annually diminished. Even agriculture, so indispensable to the existence of every state, was faintly and imperfectly carried on; while the peasants, plundered and massacred by a licentious soldiery, had neither any security for the possession of their lives, nor for the enjoyment of their property. Bands of foreign mercenaries, with

Aspect of France, at that period.

Anarchy, and insurrections.

(9) Mezerai, vol. ix. 124. Davila, 407. De Thou, vol. vii. p. 63.

which

CHAP. I. 1574.

which France was inundated, compleated the general desolation. Elizabeth, queen of England, whose generosity was always under the guidance of her policy, had early sent assistance to the prince of Condé; and had received from him the important town of Havre de Grace, at the mouth of the Seine, as a security for her repayment. The united efforts of the Catholics and Hugonots, had afterwards ejected her from the possession: but, her fleets continued to infest the coast of Normandy, to throw supplies of arms and provisions into Rochelle, and to molest the general trade of the kingdom. Philip the Second, king of Spain, whose zeal for the support of the Romish faith and church, served as a mark to conceal his purposes of interest and ambition, sent repeatedly supplies of troops to the aid of Charles; but, only attentive to prolong the calamities of France, and to avert the storm from his provinces in the Netherlands, he withdrew them, before they could render any effectual service to the royal cause.

Conduct of Elizabeth.

Of Philip the Second.

Switzerland, for near a century, since the reign of Louis the Eleventh, had constantly raised a body of stipendiaries, which was maintained by the French kings. To their fidelity, Charles the Ninth owed the preservation of his liberty, if not of his crown, at the famous retreat from Meaux to Paris; and in the battle of Dreux, their valor had not a little contributed to the victory, finally obtained over the Hugonots. The sovereign pontiffs, deeply interested in the contest between the adherents of the two religions, had unlocked the treasury of St. Peter, and dispatched not only pecuniary, but, military support, to the eldest son of the church. But, it was from Germany, the fruitful nurse of soldiers in the sixteenth century, that the most inexhaustible supplies of men were furnished. While the princes of Saxony, attached to the Catholic party,

Of the Switzers.

Of the popes.

Of the Germans.

party, aided the crown; the elector palatine, not less zealously devoted to the doctrines and followers of the Reformation, sent a numerous army to the assistance of Condé and Coligni. The Landskenets and Reitres composed a principal part of the forces on either side; and, though numbers perished in the repeated conflicts, the survivors returned to their native country, loaded with the spoils, and enriched by the treasures of France (10).

Policy and measures of the queen dowager.

These calamities, great in themselves, were not diminished, nor alleviated, by the probable prospect of any immediate, or beneficial change. The maxims and policy of Catherine of Medicis, which had plunged the kingdom into such accumulated distress, continued still to operate in all their force. That authority, which she had exercised during the minority of the late king, she retained after its termination, though no longer invested with the title of Regent. Her vast and capacious mind, fertile in the arts of destruction, had planned, matured, and executed, the massacre of Paris. The remorse, which Charles the Ninth felt from his reflections on it, heightened by his resentment at Catherine's predilection for her second son, Henry, had not only conduced to make him withdraw from her his confidence, but, even to menace her with the effects of his indignation. The progress of disease, and the diminution of his intellectual and bodily strength, as he approached the end of life, had effaced, or weakened, these unfavourable impressions. His apprehension of the duke of Alençon's design to impede the return of the king of Poland, and to infringe the order of succession, had even induced him, in his last moments, not without manifest signs of reluctance, to entrust the government to his mother, and to delegate to her the regency.

(10) De Thou, D'Aubigné, Hist. Univ. Davila, Mezerai, passim.

Those,

CHAP. I. 1574.

Those, who looked forward to futurity, anticipated with regret and apprehension, the augmentation of her influence, under the reign of a prince, who had always received from her, and evinced towards her, the strongest marks of reciprocal affection (11).

Duke of Alençon.

Francis, duke of Alençon, youngest of the four sons of Henry the Second, had not hitherto exhibited any endowments of disposition or character, which could justly excite the hopes, or awaken the expectations of his countrymen. Fickle and inconstant in his friendships; irresolute in his temper, timid and pusillanimous in adversity; seduced by favorites and flatterers; plunged in dissolute pleasures; and destitute of that elevation of sentiment, or generous ambition, which connects the public interests with its own; he acted only a subordinate part: and notwithstanding his high quality of presumptive heir to the crown, he was treated as a prisoner of state (12).

King of Navarre.

The king of Navarre, afterwards so distinguished under the name of Henry the Fourth, and who was reserved by Providence to restore tranquillity to his country; had displayed, under circumstances the most humiliating, a firmness of mind and magnanimity, which impressed even his enemies with respect and admiration. His valor, courtesy, and humanity, had endeared him to the nation. But, deprived of his patrimonial dominions; separated from his friends and adherents; compelled to abjure his religion; regarded by the queen-mother with jealousy and suspicion; destitute of resources, and detained in an inglorious captivity; all his great qualities were buried in obscurity, and did not unfold

(11) Ut supra, passim.

(12) Mezerai, vol. ix. p. 104 and 114. De Thou, vol. vii. p. 37. Davila, p. 396.

themselves

themselves till called into action, by the augmenting calamities of France (13).

1574. Prince of Condé.

His cousin, Henry, prince of Condé, occupied a greater portion of public attention, though removed by his birth to a more remote distance from the crown. Of a character severe, serious, and reserved; little addicted to the gratifications of pleasure; zealously attached to the principles of the reformed faith and worship; inflexible, brave, indefatigable, active, and formed for war; he had already assumed an ascendancy in the counsels of the Hugonots, and aspired to the rank of their chief and leader. Having effected his escape from Amiens, he had reached the frontiers of Germany; resumed the exercise of the Protestant religion, which Charles the Ninth had obliged him by menaces to renounce; and prepared to enter the kingdom with a formidable army (14).

Duke of Guise.

The place which the prince of Condé emulated as head of the Protestants, was possessed by the duke of Guise in the estimation of the Catholics. Nature had conferred on him almost all the qualifications, calculated to conciliate and retain the popular favor. Generous and munificent, even to profusion; affable and condescending in his manners; intrepid, to a degree of temerity; and adorned with every grace of exterior figure and deportment, he attracted universal admiration. His courage, at a very early period of his life, had been distinguished during the siege of Poitiers, as his father's had been at that of Metz. Descended from the family of Lorrain, and allied to the house of Bourbon; possessing an hereditary hatred for the Hugonots, and the most ardent zeal for the support of the antient religion, he was regarded as its best protector. Surrounded by a numerous and powerful band of adherents; guided

(13) De Thou, and Mezerai, passim.
(14) Mezerai, vol. ix. p. 122 and 139.

by

CHAP. I. 1574.

by the counsels of his uncle, the cardinal of Lorrain; and capable of the boldest projects of ambition; he seemed to be scarcely comprehended within the rank of a subject, and already inspired jealousy into the crown itself (15).

Family of Montmorenci.

The house of Montmorenci, which had formerly maintained so long a competition with that of Guise, for power and favor, was fallen into a state of depression and disgrace, towards the close of the reign of Charles the Ninth. The marshal Montmorenci, eldest son to the late constable, one of the most virtuous and incorrupt noblemen of the age, who had married the natural daughter of Henry the Second, was destitute of issue. Having been implicated in the attempt of the duke of Alençon to withdraw from court; his participation or privity in an enterprize, regarded as so criminal, had afforded a pretext for committing him to the Bastile, where he languished in confinement (16). Damville, his brother, not less odious to the government, owed his safety only to his absence and distance from the capital. He had been appointed governor of the province of Languedoc; and, aware of the machinations of Catherine of Medicis, who exerted every means to seize his person, he already began to concert measures with the Protestants, for their common preservation. The two remaining sons of the constable, Thoré and Meru, involved in the common ruin or persecution of their family, openly joined the insurgents, who, in various quarters of the kingdom, began to appear in arms (17).

(15) De Thou, Mezerai, passim.

(16) Davila, p. 399. Mezerai, vol. ix. p. 121 and 122. De Thou, vol. vii. p. 54.

(17) Davila, 395. Mezerai, vol. ix. p. 122.

Such

State of Paris.

Such was the general aſpect and ſituation of France, at the death of Charles the Ninth. Paris had not yet experienced in an extended degree, the calamities inſeparable from civil war. The Hugonot armies which had twice approached its walls, were neither ſufficiently numerous nor powerful, to affect it by famine; and they were ſpeedily driven from the vicinity of the capital, by the ſuperior forces of the Catholics. The frequent reſidence, and expenſive amuſements of a voluptuous court, kept alive the arts of luxury, and diffuſed a fallacious opulence. The maſſacre of St. Bartholomew, when the city was abandoned to all the enormities of a ſanguinary and ferocious populace, had been only temporary; and the extermination of the Proteſtants had produced an apparent uniformity in religious faith and worſhip, among the inhabitants. No ſymptoms nor indications of diſloyalty and rebellion had hitherto manifeſted themſelves: on the contrary, when the marſhals Montmorenci, and Coſſé, were ſent priſoners to the Baſtile, by order of Catherine, only a ſhort time before the deceaſe of Charles the Ninth; the Pariſians had exhibited every demonſtration of joy, and had even furniſhed a guard for the ſecurity and detention of the captives (18).

Condition of the provinces.

Normandy.

But, theſe appearances of order and proſperity in the metropolis, were contraſted with every ſpecies of misfortune in the provinces. Subordination and obedience had been ſubverted, by long habits of revolt and hoſtility. Normandy, peculiarly expoſed, by its ſituation, to the attacks of the Engliſh, was become the theatre of war. Montgomery, whoſe fatal dexterity had originally produced the calamities of his country; and who had eſcaped by flight from the carnage of his friends, at the maſſacre of Paris;

(18) Mezerai, vol. ix. p. 122. Davila, 399. De Thou, vol. vii. p. 54 and 55.

having

CHAP. I. 1574.

having landed with a naval force, not far from Cherburg, made a rapid progrefs. Invefted by the marfhal Matignon, in Domfront, after a brave defence againft fuperior numbers, he had furrendered upon a vague affurance of perfonal fafety, which was afterwards violated. Colombieres, another of the Hugonot leaders, perifhed in the breach, at St. Lo; and every part of the province experienced the fury, or feverity of the royalifts (19).

Brittany.

Brittany, protected, in fome meafure, by its almoft infular pofition, and its diftance from the interior parts of the kingdom, enjoyed a degree of comparative calm: but, from the mouth of the Loire, to that of the Garonne, comprehending an extent of near one hundred leagues, in the richeft, moft populous, and commercial diftricts of France, the Hugonots maintained a conflict with their enemies. Their principal power and refources were concentered in Poitou, Angoumois, and Saintonge, where their numbers far exceeded thofe of the Catholics. The battles of Jarnac and Montcontour had been fought in that quarter of the kingdom, which, during the third civil war, had been the principal theatre of military operations. Rochelle, open to the Atlantic, enjoying an extenfive trade, fupplied by England with arms and ammunition, inhabited by zealous adherents of the reformed religion, and elated by the recent advantage gained over the duke of Anjou; already began to arrogate and affume a fpecies of independence. It was to be apprehended, that a republic might arife within the monarchy of France, the moft inimical to its grandeur and repofe, fupported by foreign powers, and difficult, if not impoffible, to be reduced by force (20).

Rochelle.

(19) Davila, 403—6. De Thou, vol. vii. p. 57—60. Mezerai, vol. ix. p. 118 and 119.

(20) De Thou, vol. vii. p. 44 and 45. Mezerai, vol. ix. p. 116, &c. Comm. de Montluc, vol. iv. p. 344. Le Laboureur fur Caftelnan, vol. iii. p. 396 and 397.

Guyenne

CHAP. I. 1574. Guienne, and Gascony.

Guienne and Gascony, from the banks of the Garonne, to the foot of the Pyrenees and the frontiers of Spain, were scarcely more tranquil. Montluc, whose name has been transmitted by his writings, as well as by his actions, to posterity, had during many years, exercised over the Hugonots in those provinces, the most inhuman tyranny. Wounded at the storm of a little town in Bigorre, and incapacitated by age and infirmities, for the fatigues of a camp; he had been recently dismissed from the command of the royal forces: but his successor did not restore calm or order among the inhabitants (21).

Languedoc.

In the extensive government of Languedoc, Damville, to whom it had been entrusted, no longer professed any deference for the orders of the court. Irritated by the queen mother's attempts to involve him in the proscription of his family, he embraced a line of conduct, the most repugnant to his character and inclinations. Attached to the crown by gratitude and affection, he was reduced to the necessity of engaging in open rebellion: zealously devoted to the antient religion, he saw himself compelled to join with the Protestants. Having made himself master of Montpellier, and of some other places in the vicinity of the Rhone, he prepared to defend himself by force of arms: and he even peremptorily refused to lay down his office, notwithstanding repeated mandates of the sovereign (22).

Dauphiné, and Provence.

No part of the kingdom, during the whole course of the reign of Charles the Ninth, had suffered more severely from civil dissentions than the two provinces of Dauphiné and Provence. From the gates of Lyons, to those of Marseilles, every village was

(21) Montluc, Comm. vol. iv. passim.

(22) De Thou, vol. vii. p. 48. Mezerai, vol. ix. p. 119 and 120. Le Laboureur sur Castelnau, vol. iii. p. 397.

 fortified,

CHAP. I. 1574.

fortified, and every caftle was defended. All interior communication was fufpended by the exceffes and ravages of the contending parties. The mountainous and rugged nature of the country; the facility of efcaping into Savoy, or Switzerland; and the fuperior numbers of the Hugonots in Dauphiné, prolonged the conteft. The names of Montbrun, Mouvans, d'Acier, and des Adrets, on the fide of the Proteftants; and thofe of the count of Sommerive, and the grand prior of France, on the other, were become deteftable for their acts of wanton and deliberate cruelty. Humanity feemed to be extinct in the breafts of the chiefs; and mutual animofity knew no limits in the gratification of vengeance (23).

Burgundy. Champagne.

Burgundy, which after the deceafe of marfhal Tavannes, was committed to the care of the duke of Mayenne; and Champagne, the immediate government of his brother, the duke of Guife, were in a great meafure exempt from thefe calamities. But, the oppreffions and diforders, committed on the inferior claffes, by a foldiery deftitute of any regular pay, were fuch, as loudly to demand interpofition and redrefs. The weaknefs of the government rendered it neceffary to tolerate enormities, by which the peafants were reduced to poverty and ruin (24).

Interior provinces.

The interior and central provinces, Berry, Auvergne, and the Limofin, together with thofe on the banks of the Loire, though they had largely participated in the general defolation of the kingdom, were not marked by any characteriftic, or difcriminating features. Picardy, the government of which had been confided to the prince of Condé, was not lefs averfe to the reformed religion. The inhabitants, credulous, irafcible, and fufceptible of the ftrongeft

Picardy.

(23) De Thou, vol. vii. p. 85 and 86. Mezerai, vol. ix. p. 138.
(24) Memoires de Tavannes, p. 33—35.

impreffions

impreſſions of ſuperſtition, already gave indications of that ſpirit and temper, which ſhortly afterwards fitted them for the reception and commencement of the famous union, denominated "the League."

CHAP. I. 1574.

The firſt act of Catherine of Medicis, after the deceaſe of Charles the Ninth, was inſtantly to diſpatch meſſengers, who might convey, with the utmoſt ſpeed, intelligence of the event, to the king of Poland. In order to enſure obedience to her own authority, during the interval which muſt neceſſarily elapſe before his return from ſo remote a country, ſhe immediately addreſſed letters to the governors, magiſtrates, and great officers of the crown, throughout France, notifying the death of the late ſovereign, and his previous nomination of herſelf to the regency. The ſituation of public affairs demanded meaſures equally lenient and vigorous. The Proteſtants, who had already, in many provinces, taken up arms, encouraged by the vacancy of the throne, and the abſence of the legitimate ſucceſſor, were becoming daily more formidable. The prince of Condé hovered on the borders of the kingdom, ready to enter it, at the head of a numerous body of German forces. Even the Catholics had loſt their reſpect for the royal authority, and felt little attachment towards the perſon or character of the regent. But, Catherine, long accuſtomed to the toils and labors of government; miſtreſs of all the arts of diſſimulation; and having in her cuſtody, the firſt princes of the blood, as well as the other principal perſons of whoſe fidelity ſhe was doubtful, manifeſted no ſymptoms of apprehenſion. In compliance with the uſual maxims of her conciliating and temporiſing policy, ſhe began a negociation with La Noue, the chief of the inſurgents in Poitou; and anxious to ſuſpend all operations of a hoſtile nature, till the arrival of the new king, ſhe agreed upon a truce for two months, with the

30th May. Meaſures of Catherine, on her aſſumption of the regency.

Truce with the Hugonots.

CHAP. I. 1574.

the Hugonots. They were even permitted to hold a general aſſembly of their delegates, at Milhaud, in Languedoc, where meaſures might be concerted for a general pacification (25).

Trial of the count of Montgomery.

But, in the perſon of the count of Montgomery, her revenge, ſuperior either to the dictates of juſtice, or the conſiderations of honor, induced her to make a diſtinguiſhed ſacrifice. That gallant and unfortunate nobleman, having ſurrendered upon the aſſurances of perſonal ſafety and protection, given him by Matignon, commander of the royal forces; had been, nevertheleſs, by Catherine's expreſs command, transferred to Paris. The parliament, ſubſervient to the regent's wiſhes, became the inſtrument of her vengeance. Montgomery, upon pretexts equally frivolous and inſufficient, was condemned to ſuffer capital puniſhment, as guilty of treaſon; and he was previouſly put to the torture, in order to extort from him an avowal of the pretended conſpiracy, meditated by the admiral Coligni, againſt Charles the Ninth. His courage and magnanimity did not forſake him, under circumſtances ſo trying. He bore the rack, without uttering any exclamations, except thoſe of indignation for the breach of faith, committed againſt him; and though diſlocated in all his limbs, by the ſeverity of the torture, he preſerved an intrepid countenance to the laſt moment of his life. From the ſledge, on which he was drawn to the place of execution, he addreſſed the populace, and deſired their prayers. On the ſcaffold, he evinced the ſame unſhaken conſtancy and compoſure, terminating by the hand of the executioner, a career, which had been diſtinguiſhed in its courſe, by many brilliant atchievments. His real crime, for which he ſuffered,

His execution.

26th June.

(25) De Thou, vol. vii. p. 83 and 84. Mezerai, vol. ix. p. 134---137. Davila, p. 411---415.

was the unintentional death of Henry the Second; and Catherine offered him up as a victim to the memory of her husband. "Memorable example," says de Thou, "to teach us, that in the strokes "which attack crowned heads, misfortune is criminal, even though the will be innocent (26)!"

CHAP. I. 1574.

While these events took place in France, the king of Poland received, at Cracow, the news of his brother's death, and his own succession. Two very different modes of action presented themselves to him, and claimed his mature deliberation. The first, more honorable and dignified, was, to demand permission of the senate to return to his hereditary dominions, and to endeavour to procure the election of the duke of Alençon to the Polish crown. The other, more expeditious and secure, was, by a precipitate

Flight of the king of Poland, from Cracow.

(26) De Thou, vol. vii. p. 87. Mezerai, vol. ix. p. 135 and 136, D'Aubigné, Hist. Univ. vol. ii. p. 130 and 131.

D'Aubigné, who was a spectator of Montgomery's death, has left us the most circumstantial and interesting detail of that event. It may serve, in many particulars, to excite equal pity and indignation. "The count," says he, "wept, when he was informed of the decease of Charles the "Ninth, and from that instant regarded his own execution as certain. "The commissioners, before whom he was examined, would not exempt "him from the torture, though he did not attempt to disguise, or to con-"ceal any fact. He was conducted to the scaffold, in the "Place de "Greve," dressed in mourning; and after having complained, that his "executioners had broken his limbs, by the violence of the application of "the torture, he composed his countenance, in order to harangue the "spectators." D'Aubigné has preserved Montgomery's speech in this last, and trying situation. It breathes all the energy and elevation of a mind, sustained by a cause which appeared to him to be a good one, and for which he had sacrificed every consideration. He denied and reprobated the absurd pretexts, which Catherine of Medicis and his judges had used, in order to condemn him as guilty of treason. Having mentioned his involuntary crime in the death of Henry the Second, he enjoined the multitude assembled, to inform his sons, who had been involved in the penalties of his sentence, and degraded from the rank of nobles; that, "if "they had not the virtue to regain it, and to restore themselves, he con-"sented to their degradation." He protested that his only real guilt consisted in his steady adherence to a religion, proscribed by the government, and for which so many individuals had already suffered in France. Having requested the executioner not to apply any bandage before his eyes, he passed a short time in prayer, and then submitted to his sentence. De Thou, who is more concise in his narration, agrees in every important particular, with D'Aubigné, and condemns the injustice of the trial and execution.

CHAP. I. 1574.

cipitate retreat, or rather flight, to gain the frontiers of the Auſtrian territories, and regardleſs of every inferior conſideration, to preſent himſelf again in France. The latter advice, more analogous to the character, and gratifying to the inclinations of Henry, prevailed. After having made the neceſſary diſpoſitions for concealing his deſign, he quitted his capital under cover of the night, with only a few attendants; and was already on the borders of Sileſia, before his departure was univerſally known in Cracow. The Poles, irritated at ſo contemptuous a dereliction of the royalty to which they had recently elevated him, manifeſted their reſentment, by arreſting the principal perſons of his court, who remained in their hands: but, the ſenate being aſſembled, and having heard the reaſons for his conduct, ordered his equipage and ſervants to be honorably conducted to their maſter. A body of near four hundred horſe purſued, and overtook the fugitive prince, who had paſſed the Poliſh limits, and was no longer in danger of being re-conducted as a captive to his own palace. Count Tenczyn, at the head of a ſmall number of gentlemen, advancing, unarmed, towards him, endeavoured by exhortations and entreaties to induce him to return to Cracow. Henry received theſe marks of affection, with ſimilar demonſtrations of regard; promiſed to reviſit Poland, after having reſtored tranquillity to France; aſſigned the reaſons which had neceſſitated him to withdraw from a country and people, for whom he ſhould always preſerve the moſt lively attachment; and continued his journey to Vienna (27).

18th June.

His reception by the emperor Maximilian.

The circumſtances of his flight, which were, in ſome meaſure, ignominious, when contraſted with thoſe of his elevation to the throne of the ſame

(27) Solignac, Hiſt. de Pologne, vol. v. p. 453—473. De Thou, vol. vii. p. 72—76. Mezeraï, vol. ix. p. 140 and 141.

kingdom,

CHAP. I. 1574.

kingdom, only a few months preceding, were ſpeedily effaced from his mind, by the reception which he met with in the imperial court. Maximilian the Second treated him with every mark of deference and honor; advanced to meet him with a ſplendid retinue; and detained him ſome days, in his capital, among feſtivities and entertainments. That beneficent and enlightened monarch, whoſe maxims of toleration rendered his reign happy and proſperous, ſtrenuouſly exhorted Henry, on his return to France, to adopt ſimilar principles of government. He adviſed gentle meaſures towards the Hugonots, and beſought of him, to commemorate the æra of his entry into his hereditary dominions, by giving peace to his ſubjects, of every perſuaſion. Theſe arguments and entreaties, Maximilian enforced by the example of his own, and of his father, Ferdinand's experience; who after many ineffectual efforts to reduce the Germans by violence, had found, that in matters of faith, war, far from curing, only aggravated the evil. It would have been fortunate for Henry and the people, if the remonſtrances of the emperor had influenced his future conduct (28).

Magnificent treatment of Henry at Venice.

Unwilling to paſs through the territories of the elector palatine, from whom he had received ſo ſignal and humiliating an affront, on his former progreſs to Poland; the king determined on taking his courſe through Lombardy. The magnificence with which the Republic of Venice honoured his approach and arrival, far exceeded that which any other European ſtate could exert, in the ſixteenth century. From the inſtant that he entered the Venetian territories, to the moment of his final departure, every variety of ſuperb and diverſified amuſement was laviſhed, to gratify their royal gueſt. That cele-

(28) De Thou, vol. vii. p. 76. Solignac, vol. v. p. 475—476. Mezerai, vol. ix. p. 141 and 142.

brated

CHAP. I. 1574.

brated Commonwealth, though paſt its meridian, was ſtill the center of commerce, arts, and luxury. Its peculiar ſituation among the waves of the Adriatic, enabled the Senate to exhibit a ſpecies of pomp and ſplendor, not to be found in any other capital. During nine days which Henry paſſed in Venice, he beheld a perpetual ſucceſſion of ſhews, games, and recreations. Triumphal arches, raiſed on the deſigns of Palladio: combats, naval and military: illuminations, and balls, where the Venetian ladies, equally celebrated for their charms and their gallantry, endeavoured to captivate the young monarch: theſe varied pleaſures, which the policy of the Republic offered to its antient and moſt powerful ally, detained him, notwithſtanding the preſſing exhortations of Catherine, his mother, to haſten his return (29).

27th July.

Quitting with reluctance a city, which contained ſo many attractions, and accompanied by the dukes of Savoy, Mantua, and Ferrara, he proceeded towards Turin; remounted the river Po, and arrived in that capital, after having declined to viſit Milan, where Don John of Auſtria commanded for the king of Spain. France, during his abſence, had been torn by almoſt every calamity, incident to a ſtate where religion ſerved as a pretext, to conceal the projects of faction and ambition. In Poitou, the ſuſpenſion of arms, which had been concluded by the regent, was violated on her part; and the royal forces, under the duke of Montpenſier, profiting of the ſecurity of the Hugonots, after having captured Fontenoy, menaced Rochelle itſelf. Damville, after long irreſolution, iſſued a proclamation, avowing his junction with the Proteſtants; while, on the other hand, the prince of Condé publiſhed a manifeſto, from Heidelberg, in the Palatinate, accuſing the

24th Aug. His arrival at Turin.

State of France.

(29) Hiſt. de Veniſe, par Laugier, vol. x. p. 293—307. De Thou, vol. vii. p. 78—81.

evil

evil counsellors of the crown, with having produced the disorders under which the kingdom laboured. He preceded it, by letters addressed to the delegates, assembled at Milhaud, in which he demanded supplies of money, and promised to conduct to their assistance a military force. They, in return, elected him for their chief, though with very limited powers, of every kind. Throughout Languedoc, Guyenne, and Bearn, the Protestants were, universally, in arms: but, in Dauphiné, where Montbrun commanded against the royal army, hostilities were carried on with the greatest violence (30).

CHAP. I. 1574.

Catherine advances to Lyons. August.

In the midst of such complicated national misfortunes, which the regent fomented by her insidious and treacherous policy; that princess, after having caused the obsequies of the late king to be performed, quitted Paris, accompanied by her two prisoners, the duke of Alençon, and the king of Navarre. Passing through the province of Burgundy, she reviewed in person a body of six thousand Switzers, whom she had caused to be levied, and arrived at Lyons, where she impatiently expected the return of her favorite son (31).

Political intrigues at Turin.

The court of Turin, during the short residence which Henry made in it, was become the center of political intrigue and cabal. Margaret, duchess of Savoy, daughter of Francis the First, one of the most accomplished princesses of the age, endeavoured to enforce the exhortations, made to him at Vienna, by the emperor Maximilian; and she attempted, in conjunction with the duke, her husband, Emanuel Philibert, to reconcile him with the family of Montmorenci. Damville himself, whose loyalty and attachment to the crown had been shaken, but, not effaced, by the persecution of Catherine of Medicis;

(30) Mezerai, vol. ix. p. 138—140. De Thou, vol. vii. p. 85—95.
(31) De Thou, vol. vii. p. 95. Davila, p. 418.

dicis;

CHAP. I. 1574.

dicis; and who hoped to regain the interest which he had formerly possessed in Henry's esteem; ventured, under the engagement of the duke of Savoy, for his protection, to repair in person, to Turin. The king received him with demonstrations of affection. Bellegarde, who occupied a distinguished place in the royal favour, and Pibrac, joined their efforts to those of Damville, and appeared to have made a deep impression on the mind of the king. But, these auspicious beginnings were soon subverted and changed by the emissaries of the regent, who not only induced Henry to suspend every measure tending towards peace; but, instilled suspicions of Damville's fidelity. That nobleman, alarmed at the visible alteration in his sovereign's behaviour, and apprehensive of being arrested, left Turin with precipitation, and returned to his government of Languedoc, where he immediately signed an agreement with the Protestants (32).

Schemes of the duke of Savoy.

Emanuel Philibert, though he had failed in this attempt, was successful in another, which, as a sovereign prince, affected him far more deeply, and personally. Of the numerous garrisons, and extensive conquests, acquired by Francis the First, and Henry the Second, in Savoy and Piedmont, only Pignerol, Savillan, and the valley of Perouse, remained to France. All the others had been restored to the duke, by the treaty of peace, in 1559. The possession of these fortresses, not only gave to the French kings facility of penetrating at pleasure into Italy, by the passages of the Alps; but, from their vicinity to Turin itself, held the dukes of Savoy in awe, and kept them in a state of perpetual dependance. Every motive of sound policy dictated to preserve them with jealous attention. But, Henry, gained by the caresses of Emanuel Philibert, and

(32) De Thou, vol. vii. p. 131 and 132. Mezerai, vol. ix. p. 144 and 145.

neglectful

neglectful of the true interests of his crown, was prevailed on to promise their restitution (33).

CHAP. I.

1574.

The king soon afterwards quitted Turin, and proceeded towards the frontiers of his own dominions, attended by the duke of Savoy, at the head of his troops. This escort was not merely honorary, as the province of Dauphiné was infested by the Hugonot forces, who committed perpetual depredations on the confines of the two states. At the "Pont de Beauvoisin," where France and Savoy divide, he was met by the duke of Alençon and the king of Navarre, whom he received with marks of apparent civility and affection. On the following day, the interview between himself and his mother, took place; and the new king, accompanied by Catherine, and a vast train, made a public and magnificent entry into the city of Lyons (34).

Arrival of Henry at Lyons.

5th Sept.

(33) Mezerai, vol. ix. p. 145. De Thou, vol. vii. p. 132 and 133. Davila, p. 419.

(34) Davila, p. 420. De Thou, vol. vii. p. 133 and 134. Mezerai, vol. ix. p. 146 and 147.

CHAP.

CHAP. II.

Condition of the kingdom, and of parties, at Henry's assumption of the government.—Continuation of the war against the Protestants.—Restitution of Pignerol, Savillan, and Perouse, to Savoy.—Journey of the court to Avignon.—Death of the cardinal of Lorrain.—Inauguration, and marriage of the king.—Capture, and execution of Montbrun.—Inactivity, and vices of Henry.—Escape of the duke of Alençon.—Defeat of Thoré.—Truce with Alençon.—Entry of the German army into France.—Flight of the king of Navarre.—Negociation, and conclusion of peace.—Foreign affairs.—State of Flanders.—Election of Stephen Battori, to the crown of Poland.—Death of Maximilian the Second.—Aspect of Europe.

CHAP. II.

1574. September.

HENRY the Third, at the period of his return to France, was in the flower of his youth, having scarcely attained his twenty-third year. His figure was graceful and elegant: an air of majesty, tempered by sweetness, accompanied all his actions; and his eloquence was dignified, captivating, and calculated to persuade. He had been educated in habits of dissimulation, and initiated in his earliest years, to the fatigues of a camp. The reputation, which he had acquired by the victories of Jarnac, and of Montcontour, for which he was principally indebted to marshal Tavannes, his governor; had conduced in no small degree, to elevate him to the Polish throne. Europe expected from him, as he attained to manhood, a display of martial talents, and hardy virtue. He had been privy to, and active in all the counsels, which preceded the massacre of Paris, where he betrayed the most unrelenting barbarity

barity towards the Hugonots. The short period of his stay in Poland, had not allowed time for the exercise of any distinguished qualities; and the circumstances of his flight from that country, though inglorious, were, in some measure, excused, or palliated, by the necessity of his immediate appearance in France.

CHAP. II.

1574.

Character, and qualities of the new king.

Situation of France.

The situation of the kingdom, to which he was called by the decease of Charles the Ninth, though critical and alarming, was by no means desperate. Two powerful factions, irritated almost to frenzy against each other, by a long series of mutual injuries, violence, and war, persisted to maintain a desperate conflict. Religion added new incentives to their animosity, and aggravated the sources of discord. But, the leaders, on either side, continued to profess obedience to their common sovereign: the majesty of the throne, though defaced and violated, was not subverted; and the wounds which had been inflicted on the state, however deep and recent, admitted of a cure. Two great, and opposite lines of conduct, presented themselves for Henry's choice: either to signalize his accession by giving peace to his subjects; or, to continue the war, already begun, to the subjection and extermination of the Hugonots. Every inducement of humanity, wisdom, and policy, seemed to dictate the former measure. He had already evinced a disposition towards it; and its accomplishment must have been attended with consequences equally beneficial to his people, and happy for himself. But, the fatal counsels of his mother; the intolerant spirit of the age, which knew no limit to persecution; the desire of signalizing his zeal against those enemies, whom he had opposed and vanquished in his early youth; and the hope of triumphing over, and finally extinguishing both the Catholic and Protestant factions, when weakened by their dissentions: these fallacious reasons determined

CHAP. II. 1574.

determined him, after some hesitation, to command hostilities (1).

Vices, and defects of Henry.

From this improvident and ruinous step, originated all the subsequent misfortunes of his reign; and every part of his conduct evinced to the nation, that effeminacy, indolence, and luxury, had enervated his mind. Instead of acting with vigor to reform the abuses, which, under shelter of the commotions of the late government, had invaded the different departments; he had no sooner arrived in his dominions, than he resigned himself to inactivity. An enemy to fatigue, and incapable of application, he neglected all affairs of moment: surrounded only by parasites and favorites; difficult of access; entrenched in ceremonies and parade; or negligently reclined in a barge, richly decorated, on the river Saone, he appeared to have forgotten every duty annexed to his station. It was not possible to recognize the prince, who had been educated in the field, and trained to the hardships of a military life. The nobility, and the veteran officers of his army, disgusted at a change so unexpected, forsook the court, which became desert; and all the expectations to which Henry had given birth, when presumptive heir to the crown, disappeared from the instant of his accession (2).

Restoration of Pignerol and Savillan.

The contempt and alienation which so indecent a conduct excited among his subjects, were not diminished by the accomplishment of his engagement to the duke of Savoy, in restoring to him Pignerol, Savillan, and the valley of Perouse. Henry, more, as his enemies asserted, from facility and prodigality, than from any sentiment of equity or justice, ordered the immediate evacuation of those garrisons. All

(1) De Thou, vol. vii. p. 136—152. Mezerai, vol. ix. p. 153. Davila, p. 420—426. D'Aubigné, Hist. Univ. vol. ii. p. 132 and 133.
(2) De Thou, vol. vii. p. 134 and 135. Mezerai, vol. ix. p. 150.

the remonstrances of the duke of Nevers, to whose government they had been confided; joined to the opposition of his wisest ministers, were ineffectual (3). Emanuel Philibert repaid the generosity of the king, with neglect; and, liberated from so formidable a neighbour, assumed a higher tone in all his negotiations with France. It seemed as if the new sovereign, not content with the omission of the great duties exacted from him, desired to diminish the power, and to contract the limits of his dominions (4).

Renewal of the civil war.

While Henry, at the commencement of his reign, thus sacrificed his own dignity, and the esteem of his people, the kingdom became a prey to civil war. In Poitou, the duke of Montpensier, after a long siege, made himself master of Lusignan, and demolished that celebrated fortress. But, in the vicinity of Lyons, the Hugonots, unrestrained by any respect for the person of their sovereign, committed depredations with impunity, and refused to pay obedience to the royal mandate, enjoining them to lay down their arms. Montbrun, their commander, who had pillaged the baggage of Henry, on its passage from Savoy, treated with neglect his injunction to retire to his own home. Bellegarde, to whom the command of the Catholic forces had been committed, was repulsed in an assault upon the little town of Livron in Dauphiné; and every circumstance seemed to combine, to mark the æra of Henry's return to France, with ignominy and misfortune (5).

Dissipation of the court.

As if insensible to the national distress, the court, during these occurrences, was plunged in dissipation, and immersed in pleasures. Catherine of Medicis encouraged the propensity of her son to profusion

(3) Memoires du Duc de Nevers, folio, Paris, 1665, vol. i. p. 3—25, and p. 33—68.

(4) Davila, p. 419. De Thou, vol. vii. p. 154—157. Mezerai, vol. ix. p. 151 and 152.

(5) Mezerai, vol. ix. p. 153 and 154. De Thou, vol. vii. p. 159—164.

and

CHAP. II. 1574.

and indolence, with a view to engrofs a larger portion of authority, and to render her interpofition more neceffary. Indifferent as to the means by which fhe accomplifhed her objects, and reftrained by no principles of virtue in their profecution, fhe made gallantry fubfervient to all her projects. The ladies of her houfhold, initiated in the myfteries of their fovereign, aided and facilitated her views, by facrificing their honor, at her command; and fhe endeavoured to foften the captivity of the duke d'Alençon and the king of Navarre, who were ftill detained in an honorable confinement, by ftimulating their paffions, or fomenting their jealoufy, as circumftances feemed to follow.

Attachment of Henry, to Mary of Cleves.

The king himfelf, divided between various candidates for his affection, had determined to efpoufe Mary of Cleves, princefs of Condé, of whom, while duke of Anjou, he had been enamoured. The indecorum, if not criminality, of fuch a choice, and the obftacle interpofed by her marriage, were difregarded in the violence of his attachment. Religion afforded a favourable pretext for procuring a divorce; the princefs having adhered to the Catholic faith, fince the maffacre of Paris. All the exertions of the queen-mother; terrified at the afcendant which a beautiful and accomplifhed woman, raifed to the throne, might have retained over her fon; would have been ineffectual to prevent its accomplifhment, if death had not interpofed. The princefs was carried off by a fudden and violent diftemper, which naturally excited fufpicions, in an age and court, to which the ufe of poifons was familiar. Henry appeared to be inconfolable for this event: but, after betraying the moft extravagant fymptoms of grief, he, with equal rapidity, paffed to the contrary extreme, and even attempted to attribute to the effect of enchantment, his paffion and emotions for the death of his miftrefs (6).

(6) Mezerai, vol. ix. p. 155.

Under

Under the pretence of opening a negociation with marſhal Damville, governor of Languedoc, which would be rendered more practicable by approaching the confines of the province, Catherine ſoon afterwards induced the king to transfer his reſidence from Lyons to Avignon. During his ſtay in that city, which being a dependancy of the papal ſee, naturally preſented continual ſcenes of devotion and ſuperſtition, Henry firſt ſaw, and was deeply impreſſed by proceſſions of penitents, or flagellants, who publicly inflicted on themſelves the ſevereſt diſcipline. The inſtitution had originated about a century preceding, among the fervid and fantaſtic imaginations of the Italians, and had not yet penetrated into France. The king, who with effeminacy, and many of the vices moſt contrary to morals, had, notwithſtanding, a decided inclination for that factitious piety, which conſiſts in external ceremonies; eagerly caught at the ſhadow of religion; and partly from inclination, partly from policy, aſſiſted in perſon, followed by all his courtiers, at the proceſſions of Avignon (7).

Inſtitution of the penitents.

This devout extravagance proved fatal to the cardinal of Lorrain, who was carried off, by a violent fever, occaſioned by his attendance, barefooted, on one of the ceremonies of the penitents. Notwithſtanding the variety and ſplendor of his talents, he was neither lamented by the king, nor regretted by the nation. His arrogance in proſperity; the violence of his ambition; and the puſillanimity of his conduct under circumſtances of danger, or depreſſion: theſe defects and vices had impeded the greatneſs of his family, and rendered him generally unpopular. Even the clergy to whoſe intereſts he ſeemed to have been ſo much devoted, regarded him as the enemy of their order; and accuſed him of having ſacrificed the

December. Death of the cardinal of Lorrain.

(7) De Thou, vol. vii. p. 164 and 165. Mezerai, vol. ix. p. 156.

CHAP. II.

revenues of the church, to his desire of acquiring, or retaining, the favor of the crown. He was quickly forgotten in a court, engrossed only by dissipation (8).

1575.

Wearied with ineffectual efforts to conclude an accommodation with Damville, who, on his guard against the insidious artifices of the queen-mother, refused to accede to her propositions; Henry at length quitted Avignon, and began his journey back to Lyons. The Protestants, in possession of many places on either side of the Rhone, and not intimidated by his approach, defended themselves with equal courage and success. His presence in the camp before Livron, an inconsiderable town of Dauphiné, and the efforts made by the troops, under the eye of the king, to render themselves masters of it, only produced an aggravation of disgrace. They were repulsed; and the Hugonots, elated with so signal an advantage, outraged their sovereign, from the walls, by the most insolent and poignant reproaches. They even pursued the royal army in its retreat, cut in pieces the Switzers, and did not spare the sick, who had been left behind in the camp (9).

Royal forces, repulsed before Livron. January.

Under such an accumulation of ignominy, Henry proceed towards Rheims, where the ceremony of his inauguration was performed with the accustomed magnificence. On the following day, his nuptials were solemnized with Louisa, daughter of Nicholas, count of Vaudemont, a prince of the house of Lorrain. The king and court, plunged in excesses of every kind, appeared to have forgotten that the country was desolated by civil war. Prodigality compleated the ruin of the finances; and even an insurrection in the garrison of Mentz, one of the

15th Feb. Inauguration of Henry.

His nuptials.

(8) Mezerai, vol. ix. p. 155 and 156. Davila, p. 427. De Thou, vol. vii. p. 165—7.

(9) De Thou, vol. vii. p. 246.

most

most important frontier possessions of France, could not rouse to exertion a prince, sunk in sloth and luxury (10).

CHAP. II. 1575.

Long and ineffectual conferences were held, after Henry's return to the capital, between the delegates of the moderate Catholics, who acknowledged Damville as their head, and the emissaries of the prince of Condé as chief of the Hugonots, acting together on one side; and on the other, the council of state, at which the king himself was present, and assisted. No beneficial consequence resulted from their deliberations, which only produced new delays, and mutual distrust. In almost all the provinces, hostilities were commenced, and carried on with augmented violence: though not attended with any decisive consequence to either party, yet the principal advantages were gained by the Protestants. The city of Perigueux was taken and abandoned to pillage, by Langoiran, one of their commanders; while Damville extended his acquisitions in Languedoc. Montbrun, who had long been the terror of the Catholics in Dauphiné, and who had recently defeated their general in an engagement, felt in his turn the mutability of fortune. Having pursued with too much precipitation, a body of Catholic forces; his troops, imprudently occupied in pillage, were attacked by the enemy, who had rallied. He himself, after having performed every duty of a veteran and intrepid leader, was compelled in turn to retreat; and his horse falling under him, his thigh was fractured. In this situation, he surrendered prisoner of war, upon assurances of protection for his life. But, the court, mindful of the indignities received from him, anxious to inflict an exemplary punishment on so distinguished an officer,

Ineffectual conferences for peace.

May.

Defeat of Montbrun.

July.

(10) Mezerai, vol. ix. p. 157. De Thou, vol. vii. p. 248—250. Davila, p. 428.

and

CHAP. II. 1575.

and little attentive to the obſervation of any engagements; cauſed him to be interrogated before judges, like an ordinary criminal, accuſed of treaſon. He was condemned to die; and the ſentence was accelerated, from an apprehenſion of his eſcaping by a natural death, in conſequence of his fracture. When conducted to the ſcaffold, although debilitated in body, and ſcarcely capable of ſuſtaining himſelf, he exerted the moſt chearful and compoſed fortitude; harangued the ſpectators, and ſubmitted to his fate without a murmur. Like Montgomery, he was ſacrificed to the vengeance of the court; but, his execution, far from intimidating the Hugonots, only exaſperated them to new exertions. Leſdiguieres, at that time, in early youth, and who afterwards roſe by merit and talents, to the high dignity of conſtable of France, ſucceeded to Montbrun's credit and command. By the ſeverity of his diſcipline, he ſoon rendered his troops more formidable, and maintained his ſuperiority over the royal arms in Dauphiné (11).

His execution.

While

(11) De Thou, vol. vii. p. 268—272. Davila, p. 428 and 429. D'Aubigné, Hiſt. Univ. vol. ii. p. 133—137.

The leading circumſtances of Montbrun's capture and execution, are found in De Thou, and confirmed by D'Aubigné. Every exertion was made to obtain his pardon, or, at leaſt, that he might be treated as a priſoner of war. The prince of Condé, and Damville, ſent deputies to intercede, and to remonſtrate in his favor. Even the duke of Guiſe, whoſe powerful intereſt might have ſaved any other criminal, and who wiſhed to exchange him againſt Beſme, the aſſaſſin of Coligni, then in the hands of the Hugonots, could not prevail. The queen-mother, and Henry were inexorable. Montbrun had been the firſt ſubject, who had dared to take up arms againſt the crown: he had put to death numbers of Catholics; and when had recently plundered the royal baggage, he accompanied the act with a ſarcaſtic obſervation, that "war and play rendered all conditions equal." The court was alarmed leſt a natural death, in conſequence of his accident from the fracture of his thigh, ſhould rob them of their prey. His trial was indecently precipitated by the parliament of Grenoble. There is a ſtriking ſimilarity in the particulars of his death, to thoſe which accompanied Montgomery's execution. Though extenuated, and weakened to a great degree, his fortitude was unſhaken on the ſcaffold; and he ventured, in defiance of every prohibition, to harangue the people. He proteſted his innocence of rebellion, declared his ſatisfaction

1575. Indolence and effeminacy of Henry.

While these scenes of bloodshed and violence were acted in the different provinces of the kingdom, Henry, regardless of his own character, or of the public security, gave full scope to all his weaknesses and vices. Resigned to the dominion of rapacious favorites, to whom the people justly applied the odious denomination of minions, his profusion in heaping honors and emoluments on them, knew no limits. The most unmanly pleasures occupied his time, and left him neither leisure, nor inclination, for public business. Perpetual rivalities between the favorites of the king, and those of his brother, the duke of Alençon, transformed the palace into a theatre of quarrel, outrage, and dissention. Intrigues of policy and gallantry formed the only objects of serious attention. The duke of Guise, who had already conceived those projects of elevation, which he afterwards executed, stimulated the young queen to render herself mistress of her husband, and to aspire to the guidance of the state: but, Louisa did not possess sufficient energy and talents, to succeed in such an attempt. Educated in principles of an austere and melancholy devotion, she possessed few mental endowments, calculated to retain the affections of a dissolute and capricious prince. Her modesty and virtue secured the esteem, but never enabled her to acquire any ascendant over the mind of Henry. The queen-mother, with her usual dissimulation, fomented the jealousy, which from personal, as well as political causes, continually took place between the duke of Alençon and the king of Navarre. Those princes were still detained in a sort of confinement; and the court, careless of every ex-

tion in laying down his life for the cause of religion; and stretched out his head to the executioner. The Hugonots severely revenged his death on the Catholics, in the vicinity of Grenoble. De Thou strongly condemns the spirit of vengeance, by which the court was actuated on this occasion.

CHAP. II. 1575.

ternal concern, was immersed in pleasures, when an unexpected and alarming incident roused the king to a temporary exertion (12).

Escape of the duke of Alençon.

Francis, duke of Alençon, had hitherto been restrained from any effort to withdraw himself, or to form a party in opposition to the crown, by various motives. The expectation of his election to the Polish throne, which had been first held out to his ambition, had already proved fallacious; and the post to which he aspired of lieutenant-general of the kingdom, was too powerful and dangerous, to be conferred on any subject. Tired with fruitless solicitations; insulted by the minions of the king, who paid little regard to his dignity; and stimulated by his own adherents, who hoped to acquire consideration from their master's freedom; he determined to quit a court and capital, where he was subjected to continual mortifications. Having, on pretence of an affair of gallantry, gone into the suburbs, he instantly mounted on horseback; and, before the intelligence of his flight was publicly known, he reached the city of Dreux, on the confines of Normandy; from whence he issued a manifesto, calculated to conciliate the public favor. It enumerated the grievances under which the nation suffered; reprobated the number and severity of the pecuniary impositions; stated the necessity of a reform in the government, and finished by demanding an assembly of the states general (13).

15th Sept.

Consternation occasioned by it.

The consternation of the court, on this event, was equal to the security, by which it had been preceded. Henry, awaking from the lethargy in which he had been plunged, sent the duke of Nevers, at

(12) Mezerai, vol. ix. p. 161—163.

(13) Memoires de Nevers, vol. I. p. 82—86, and p. 92—94. Davila, p. 431—433. De Thou, vol. vii. p. 285—288. D'Aubigné, Hist. Univ. vol. ii. p. 176—179. Mezerai, vol. ix. p. 163-4.

the head of a body of troops, to pursue his brother; commanded the posts in the vicinity of Paris to be occupied; and made every preparation for defence. Meanwhile, the duke of Alençon, having continued his retreat, was met in Poitou, by many of the Hugonot chiefs, who expected protection and support from his junction with their party; and the consequences to the government were rendered more serious, by the certainty of the approach of a German army, conducted by the prince of Condé in person, which was ready to enter the kingdom. Terrified at such a prospect, destitute of resources, and ever ready from the impulse of his natural disposition, to have recourse to temporizing measures; the king, by the advice of his mother, opened a negociation for peace. Catherine, anxious to prevent hostilities between her two sons, and at the same time to render her interposition necessary; undertook to go in quest of the duke of Alençon, and to dispose his mind towards a reconciliation. In order to facilitate so delicate and arduous a work, she began by liberating the two marshals, Montmorenci and Cossé, who had languished in the Bastile since the conclusion of the late reign. Their influence with the duke of Alençon was great; and his manifesto had demanded, in specific terms, their emancipation from an unjust and cruel captivity. Accompanied by these noblemen, she immediately quitted Paris, and set out on her journey towards Champigny, in Touraine, the place appointed to manage a conference (14).

Efforts of the Queen Dowager, to prevent a war.

A considerable detachment from the army of the prince of Condé, commanded by Thoré, one of the younger sons of the constable Montmorenci,

(14) De Thou, vol. vii. p. 287—292. D'Aubigné, Hist. Univ. vol. ii. p. 178. Davila, p. 434. Memoires de Nevers, vol. i. p. 92—99.

CHAP. II. 1575. Combat of Dormans.

had already paſſed the Rhine, entered France, and advanced to the banks of the river Marne, on its march to join the duke of Alençon. At the town of Dormans, in Champagne, the royal forces, commanded by the duke of Guiſe in perſon, attempted to oppoſe their farther progreſs; and as their numbers were greatly ſuperior to thoſe of Thoré, it ſeemed to be imprudent in him to hazard an action. But, that nobleman, confiding in the bravery of his troops, did not decline the combat. After a long and deſperate engagement, he was defeated; the Germans, who compoſed a principal part of his force, were cut to pieces; and he himſelf, at the head of a few cavalry, eſcaped with difficulty. The victory, on the other ſide, was not purchaſed without bloodſhed; and the duke of Guiſe himſelf, in the purſuit, received a wound in the cheek from a private ſoldier, the ſcar of which he always retained, and which ſerved as an honorable teſtimony to the people, of his zeal in the defence of the Catholic religion (15).

November.

Truce concluded.

Notwithſtanding ſo ſevere a check, the duke of Alençon did not evince any eagerneſs to accept the terms offered him by Catharine, or to conclude an accommodation. The queen-mother, after ineffectually exerting every endeavour for the purpoſe, was reduced to the neceſſity of agreeing to a truce for ſix months between the two parties. Nor did Henry purchaſe even the ſhort and precarious ſuſpenſion of hoſtilities for ſo limited a period, without great conceſſions: the ſtipulation of payment for the Germans levied by the prince of Condé; places of ſecurity for the Hugonots; and a body of troops for the guard of the duke of Alençon. On theſe conditions, the truce was at length publiſhed by that

22d Decem.

(15) Davila, p. 435 and 436. De Thou, vol. vii. p. 292—295. D'Aubigné, Hiſt. Univ. vol. ii. p. 179—183.

prince

prince in his camp, and acquiesced in by his Protestant allies (16). It was evident, that, on the part of the king, as necessity alone had dictated so humiliating an agreement, there was no serious intention of carrying it into effect. Pretences were found for delaying, or evading some of the stipulations; and the governors of the places, which were to be surrendered to the confederates, encouraged by the court, refused to comply with the orders issued for their evacuation. Henry made preparations for war, and ordered a levy of six thousand Switzers to be instantly commenced. But, when he attempted to enact pecuniary supplies from the inhabitants of Paris, and convoked an assembly for the immediate object of raising them, he received a peremptory refusal. The parliament, clergy, and citizens of the capital, in the language of a free and indignant people, represented without disguise, and in the presence of the king, the abuses, malversations, and profusion, by which the treasury had been drained, and the country exhausted. Henry, far from punishing, did not even venture to mark his resentment at so bold a remonstrance; and having dismissed the assembly, he prepared to support the hostilities against his brother, from other, and more easy modes of contribution (17).

1575. Artifices of the court.

The German army, led by John Casimir, son to the elector Palatine, and the prince of Condé, which had so long hovered on the borders of the kingdom, at length began its march. Their numbers exceeded eighteen thousand; and as the royal forces, commanded, in the absence of the duke of Guise, by his brother the duke of Mayenne, were far inferior, no obstacle was interposed, effectually

1576. Entrance of the Germans into France. January.

(16) De Thou, vol. vii. p. 295. Davila, p. 437. Memoires de Nevers, vol. i. p. 99—104.

(17) De Thou, vol. vii. p. 296—299.

CHAP. II. 1576.

to impede their entry and progress into the interior provinces. Having passed through Lorrain and Burgundy almost unopposed, they crossed the Loire, and effected their junction near Moulins in the Bourbonnois, with the duke of Alençon. Previous to this event, Henry, king of Navarre, wearied with a confinement of near four years in the court of Charles the Ninth, and Henry the Third; disappointed in every hope of employment; odious to the queen-mother; and forgotten or neglected by the king himself; took the resolution of escaping from his captivity. Having deceived his guards, while engaged in hunting, he passed the Seine without delay, accompanied only by his chosen friends; arrived safely at Vendome; and having resumed the exercise of the Protestant religion, continued his retreat towards Guienne, of which province he was governor (18).

Flight of the king of Navarre.

23d. Feb.

Mean-

(18) D'Aubigné, Hist. Univ. vol. ii. p. 183—189. Davila, p. 438—440. Mezerai, vol. ix. p. 169. D'Aubigné, Memoires, p. 49—52.

The most minute relation of the escape and flight of the king of Navarre, is to be found in D'Aubigné, who has violated his customary brevity, in order to commemorate every circumstance which preceded and accompanied an event, so decisive in its consequences, and so hazardous in its execution. Six persons only were privy to it, who swore inviolable secrecy; and the king of Navarre, by affecting to believe that he should be constituted lieutenant general of France, confirmed the security of the court. On the evening preceding the day upon which he effected his escape, Fervaques, one of the six persons entrusted with the design, revealed it to Henry the Third. D'Aubigné having been present, and suspecting the treachery of his associate, charged him with it: and on his avowing it, instantly carried the intelligence to his master. The king of Navarre, after a day passed in hunting, accompanied by two gentlemen, his guards, who never quitted him; was at the town of Senlis, ten leagues distant from Paris. On receiving the information from D'Aubigné, that his intention was discovered, he instantly took a decisive resolution. Accompanied by a few adherents, he mounted on horseback, and having deceived his guards by an ingenious fiction, gained the banks of the Seine, which he passed near Poissi, on the following morning. Arriving, after numberless perils, at Alençon, he was there speedily joined by near two hundred and fifty gentlemen. Among these was Fervaques himself; who being warned by Grillon, that Henry the Third, notwithstanding the recent service which he had performed, was irritated against him, and had even determined to put him to death, as an accomplice with the king of Navarre; immediately contrived to leave Paris. As an excuse for his perfidy

CHAP. II. 1576.

Meanwhile, the chiefs of the confederate army, who unanimously acknowledged the duke of Alençon for their supreme head, assembled at Moulins, and presented articles to the king, on the acceptance of which, they professed a readiness to lay down their arms. Henry received their deputies with marks of regard, and promised a speedy answer to their demands. Notwithstanding the formidable nature of their forces, and the defenceless situation of the crown, many causes conduced to render their operations weak and languid. The German forces, ill paid and mutinous, were with difficulty retained under their standards, and insolently threatened to exact by force, their arrears. The leaders of the combined forces were of different nations, religions, and interests. Mutual jealousy and distrust prevailed among them; and the prince of Condé, who had, with equal danger and success, conducted so large a body of foreign troops into the center of the kingdom, saw himself supplanted by the duke of Alençon. The recent escape of the king of Navarre, introduced a new competitor, and increased the collision of opposite claims for pre-eminence. It became impossible to act with union and energy to one object; and the court availed itself of these circumstances. The duke of Alençon betrayed the strongest disposition to sacrifice his allies, to the acquisition of personal power; and the queen-mother, anxious to withdraw him from his new friends, gratified him on that favorite point. After a number of delays, the treaty of pacification was finally concluded by Catherine, and soon afterwards solemnly ratified by the king in person. It was, in almost

State of the confederates.

Conclusion of peace. 14th May.

fidy, he asserted that Madame de Carnavalet had previously revealed to Henry the Third, the plan concerted for the king of Navarre's escape; and his apology was admitted. D'Aubigné expressly says, that the soldiers, who guarded the king of Navarre in the Louvre, were placed about him by Catherine of Medicis herself; that they were zealous Catholics, and had, almost all of them, been active in the massacre of Paris.

CHAP. II. 1576.

almoſt all the articles, ignominious to the crown, and advantageous to the confederates (19).

Conditions of it.

The eſtabliſhment of the duke of Alençon was augmented by the addition of three of the richeſt provinces of France, Berry, Touraine, and Anjou: he himſelf aſſumed from that period, the title of duke of Anjou. Eight cities, in different parts of the kingdom, were ceded to the Proteſtants, for their ſecurity: every immunity or privilege, civil and religious, which could place them on an equality with the Catholics, was granted them: freedom of worſhip, the right of celebrating marriage, and of holding, under certain regulations, ſynods, or conſiſtories, were conceded. The king not only reverſed the attainders againſt Coligni, Montgomery, Montbrun, and their adherents; but, he renounced, on his own part, all participation in, or approbation of, the maſſacre of St. Bartholomew. Penſions and rewards were conferred on John Caſimir, who had raiſed the army which enabled the confederates to dictate to the crown; and a convocation of the ſtates-general was ſtipulated to be held within ſix months, in order to repreſent the grievances of the people, and to apply adequate remedies (20).

Affairs of the Netherlands.

While Henry, by a peace, which degraded his own dignity, and excited the indignation of his Catholic ſubjects, obtained a reſpite from his enemies; the Spaniſh provinces in the Netherlands exhibited a ſcene of anarchy and deſolation, ſcarcely paralleled in hiſtory. Requeſens, after a ſhort and troubleſome adminiſtration, diſtinguiſhed by his unremitting, but, unſucceſsful exertions, to reſtore order throughout the Low Countries, had been carried off by a violent diſtemper. His gentle and

(19) Memoires de Nevers, vol. i. p. 117—135.

(20) Mezerai, vol. ix. p. 169—174. Davila, p. 442—445. De Thou, vol. vii. p. 416—418. D'Aubigné, Hiſt. Univ. vol. ii. p. 215.

conciliating

conciliating character might, probably, have revived the allegiance of the Flemings for Philip the Second, if all possibility of reconciliation had not been precluded by the cruelties of his predecessor, the duke of Alva. The sudden and unexpected nature of Requesens' death, left him no time to execute the orders of the court of Madrid, in the nomination of a successor. In this defect of any legal governor, the council of state assumed the supreme authority, which was afterwards confirmed by the king of Spain. But, the revolt of the Spanish troops; their seizure of Alost; and the multiplied acts of outrage and violence, committed by them on the people, rendered any attempt to conciliate the minds of men impracticable. The sack of Antwerp, justly esteemed at that period, the most wealthy and commercial city in Europe, completed the calamities of Flanders, and drove the states of the province to the final necessity of uniting with those of Holland and Zealand, for their common protection. By the celebrated league, denominated the Pacification of Ghent, they agreed to make war upon the Spaniards, till they should be entirely driven out of the Netherlands. This treaty was notwithstanding made, and published in the name of Philip, from whom the states of Flanders had not withdrawn their obedience. But, the small number of his troops left in the country, and the augmenting progress of the Flemings, rendered the contest very unequal. The only adequate remedy to such accumulated evils, lay in the immediate nomination of a governor, whose talents and capacity might yet retrieve the royal affairs. Don John of Austria was selected by the king for the employment. The lustre of his birth; the attachment, entertained for the memory of the emperor, Charles the Fifth, his father, who was himself a native of Flanders; and the high reputation which

Death of Requesens.

Pacification of Ghent.

Don

CHAP. II. 1576.

Don John had acquired by the victory of Lepanto: these circumstances, it was hoped, might aid his efforts, and terminate the rebellion, which had so long rendered the Netherlands a theatre of war. The prince instantly obeyed the orders of his sovereign: having received directions for his conduct, he passed through France in disguise, and arrived safely at Luxembourg, the capital of the province of the same name, which had refused to enter into the general confederacy for the expulsion of the Spaniards (21).

Arrival of Don John of Austria.

Affairs of Poland.

After the precipitate departure of Henry from Poland, that kingdom remained for a considerable time, in a state of interregnum. The Senate and the other orders having met at Warsaw, drew up letters to him, which, though couched in terms of obedience and respect, evinced the resentment of the nation, for his contempt of their crown. They demanded his immediate return, to resume the functions of his dignity, as well as to protect them against external invasion; in case of his refusal or delay, they signified to him their resolution to declare the vacancy of the throne, and to proceed to a new election. Henry made only some faint and ineffectual exertions, to avert so decisive a measure. Pibrac, who was dispatched by him to Cracow, with instructions to propose to the diet, the union of the two kingdoms of France and Poland, found the sentence of deposition already issued, and the decree published in the capital. In so desperate and hopeless a situation, he, nevertheless, exerted every effort to prevent its accomplishment; addressed letters, in Henry's name, to the nobles; and urged all the motives which might be supposed to influence their deliberations. But, the Poles had irre-

Deposition of Henry by the Poles.

(21) Strada, de Bello Bel. vol. ii. p. 285—320. De Thou, vol. vii. p. 364—394.

vocably

vocably determined to elect another sovereign; and the two factions by which the kingdom was agitated, however adverse to each other, agreed in their common aversion to the French prince and nation. The emperor Maximilian the Second was chosen in the ensuing diet, by a considerable party; but, his delays proved fatal to his cause, and gave advantages to his rival, which could never be retrieved. Stephen Battori, a Hungarian nobleman, who had been elected prince of Transylvania, called in by his adherents, was raised to the throne. His vigor, capacity, and various endowments, rendered him worthy of so extraordinary an elevation; and Poland, under his reign, was equally tranquil at home, and respected by foreign powers (22.)

Election of Stephen Battori. May.

It was, notwithstanding, highly probable, that his election would be followed by a civil and a foreign war. The partizans of Maximilian were numerous and powerful: John Basilowitz, Czar of Muscovy, prepared to support him, and to invade the eastern provinces of the kingdom: Dantzic, the most opulent and trading city of Poland, refused obedience to Stephen; and the emperor himself, though neither of martial temper, nor disposed to engage unnecessarily in hostilities; yet, could not tamely submit to renounce a sceptre, which had been conferred on him by a considerable number of the suffrages of the nation. The Poles were exempted from this calamity, by the death of Maximilian, who expired at Ratisbon, in the fiftieth year of his age, after having held the Imperial dignity only twelve years. His loss was deeply and universally felt, by every denomination of his subjects. The benignity of his character; his enlarged principles of toleration; his love of peace; his application to business; and the desire by which he was animated of diffusing

Death of Maximilian the Second. October.

His character.

(22) De Thou, vol. vii. p. 272—285, p. 353—356. Solignac, Hist. de Polo. vol. v. p. 477—493.

happiness,

CHAP. II. 1576.

happinefs, rendered him inexpreffibly dear to his people. The houfe of Auftria, though not formidable to the repofe of Europe, as it had been under Charles the Fifth, his uncle, was ftill refpectable; and the Imperial office, which, in Maximilian's hands, infpired equal veneration and affection, fell into contempt, and almoft oblivion, under the adminiftration of his fucceffor, Rodolph the Second. The laft acts of Maximilian were exerted to maintain the civil and religious tranquillity of Germany; nor did the fixteenth century produce any fovereign, fo juftly entitled to the love of his contemporaries, and the efteem of pofterity (23).

State of Europe.

The other European ftates, at this period of time, offered few events which materially affected the general repofe.

England.

England, governed by Elizabeth, enjoyed a profound tranquillity; though that wife and vigilant princefs, who never, during her long reign, intermitted her provident attention, kept a conftant eye upon the concerns of the Netherlands, and already extended to them her indirect affiftance.

Spain.

Philip the Second, not lefs attentive, and ftill more deeply interefted, in the fate of the Low Countries, exhaufted the immenfe treafures and refources of his vaft dominions, in fruitlefs exertions to reduce the Flemings. Incapable of atchieving it by force, and apprehenfive of the interference of France, he began to move thofe fecret, but powerful fprings, in the interior fyftem of the French government, by which the throne of Henry the Third was fhaken, and nearly fubverted. Philip himfelf, occupied in vifiting the various provinces of Spain, in reforming abufes, and in reftoring juftice, difcharged with ability the functions annexed to his fituation; and he preferved an uninterrupted peace in the Spanifh monarchy, while Flanders was defolated by all the

(23) Schmidt, Hift. des Allemans, tranflated by de la Veaux, vol. viii. p. 384—390. De Thou, vol. vii. p. 358.

calamities

calamities of war (24). Portugal, at the summit of prosperity, approached the term of its greatness, and even of its existence, as an independant nation. Sebastian, intoxicated with views of conquest in Africa, was engrossed by that single object. In defiance of the remonstrances of his ministers, and even of Philip the Second, he was preparing to embark on the fatal expedition against Morocco, which terminated his life, and reduced his country to a state of servitude and degradation (25).

CHAP. II. 1576.

Portugal.

(24) Abregé Chronologique d'Espagne, et Portugal, vol. ii. p. 425.
(25) Abregé Chronologique d'Espagne, et Portugal, p. 423 and 424.

CHAP. III.

Origin, formation, and principles of "the League."—Assembly of the states general, at Blois.—Henry declares himself the chief of "the League."—Renewal of the war with the Protestants.—Peace.—Edict of Poitiers.—Conduct of the king.—State of the court.—Expedition, and death of Sebastian, king of Portugal.—Affairs of the Netherlands.—Duke of Anjou is called to the assistance of the Flemings.—Death of Don John of Austria.—Internal concerns of France.—Recommencement of the civil war.—Causes, by which it was produced.—Ill success of the Hugonots.—Conclusion of peace.—Affairs of the Low Countries.—Exploits of the prince of Parma.—Treaty, made by the States of Flanders, with the duke of Anjou.—Death of Henry, king of Portugal.—Conquests of that kingdom, by Philip the Second.—Death, and character of Emanuel Philibert, duke of Savoy.

CHAP. III. 1576.

Condition of France.

THE peace which Henry had recently concluded with the confederate princes, had disarmed and disunited that powerful combination; but, it had by no means secured either his own repose, or the tranquillity of his subjects. Conditions, such as the Hugonots had extorted from him, placed them on an equality with the Catholics, in every essential point; and might rather be esteemed the triumph, than the toleration, of the Protestant religion. Nor could the people persuade themselves, that these concessions were the result of wisdom, in a discerning and sagacious monarch, attentive to the great interests of his dominions, and watchful over the general felicity. The whole tenor of Henry's conduct exposed

exposed him to censure, and tended to render him odious and contemptible. Sunk in dissipation, his prodigality had already exhausted all the ordinary sources of revenue, and subjected him to the severe humiliation of a refusal, when he attempted to extort supplies from the capital. His attachment to the Catholic faith was unquestionable; and his antipathy to all innovation in religious concerns was equally ascertained. But his devotion had nothing elevated, or even rational, in its nature; and it consisted rather in monastic observances, or ecclesiastical ceremonies, than in a sincere obedience to the duties and precepts of piety and morality. The indignation excited among his Catholic subjects, at the terms of the late pacification, concurring with the disadvantageous impressions, which the king's general character and administration produced, were artfully fomented by the partizans of the family of Guise. They represented, and exaggerated, the vices of Henry; the danger to which he exposed the antient religion; and the urgent necessity of some speedy interposition, to protect from ruin the church and state. The dissimulation of the queen-mother, and her indifference to every mode of faith; the recent junction of the duke of Anjou with the Protestants; and the pernicious concessions made by the king, in order to detach him from that party: all these obvious topics of declamation were insisted on with asperity and malignity. The minds of men, irritated by so forcible an appeal to their passions, and exasperated by the arts of faction, were prepared for a daring effort; and as the crown had either abandoned or betrayed their cause, they began to look elsewhere for support and protection. (1).

Dissatisfaction of the Catholics.

In such a state of fermentation and discontent, no remedy was regarded as too violent for the dis-

Confederations, formed.

(1) De Thou, vol. vii. p. 422—429.

CHAP. III. 1576.

ease. Allegiance itself seemed to be withdrawn, where superior considerations stimulated to resistance; and it became requisite to combine, for the purpose of mutual preservation against a common enemy. During the turbulent and agitated periods of the reign of Charles the Ninth, indications of a disposition in the people to form confederations, or fraternities, had manifested themselves, in various parts of France. The avowed or ostensible object of them, was the maintenance of the purity of the Catholic faith; but, from many causes, they had hitherto been confined in their operations, and limited in their extent. The weakness of the throne under Henry, and the personal contempt into which he was fallen, encouraged the most timid, and impelled the most wavering. Picardy, a province, remarkable for the bigotry and fervour of its inhabitants, gave the first open example of an association for preserving the antient religion. By the articles of the late peace, the government of Picardy had been confirmed to the prince of Condé; and the town of Peronne was assigned for his peculiar residence. He was speedily expected to arrive there; and it was natural to suppose, that his presence must be attended with injurious consequences to the zealous Catholics. The apprehension of this impending danger, gave birth to the memorable confederation, known in history by the name of "the League;" which, spreading with rapidity, soon overshadowed, and at length overturned the throne; occasioned the assassination of Henry himself; and during near twenty years, involved the kingdom in all the misfortunes of civil war, confusion, and anarchy (z.)

Origin of the League.

Its favorable reception.

Humieres, governor of Peronne, was the first instrument and mover of so vast a machine, by encouraging the inhabitants of the place, and of the

(z) Davila, p. 446 and 447. Mezerai, vol. ix. p. 177—180.

neigh-

CHAP. III. 1576.

neighbouring country, to sign the association. The nobility of Picardy, with ardor, followed the example, which spread through various provinces: Champagne, and Burgundy, from the hereditary influence of the dukes of Guise and Mayenne, received it universally. In Poitou, Louis de la Tremouille, duke of Thouars, from apprehension of the Hugonots, who were numerous and powerful in the vicinity of his estates, introduced it among his vassals, and gave it credit by his support. Agents of an inferior description, chiefly selected from the private walks of life, were its promoters in the metropolis.— Paris, discontented, and easily inflamed by artful suggestions, embraced with enthusiasm, a proposition, which appeared to have no object except the preservation of civil and religious rights (3).

Its nature and principles.

The form and language of the League itself, did not, on a superficial view, seem to strike at any of the prerogatives of the crown, or to endanger the public tranquillity. The preservation of the monarchy, and even of the reigning sovereign, formed a distinguished article of the covenant. But, on a closer inspection, it was evident, that under so fair an appearance, designs the most destructive to the kingdom, and to Henry, were concealed. The oath of unlimited obedience to the orders of the chief or head, was clear and specific; and it extended to engage the contracting persons to support him against any and every power, which might oppose his commands. No exception, in favour of the crown, was inserted, or admitted; and it was palpable that another person than the sovereign might be named to that high and dangerous office. Those who were intitiated in the mysteries of the association, already understood, that the duke of Guise was designed for its leader; and that the king, far from

(3) De Thou, ut supra. Mezerai, ibid.

receiving

CHAP. III. 1576.

receiving protection, might become the victim of the League (4).

Protection extended to it by Philip the Second.

External assistance and support were not wanting to aid the internal efforts, made to spread so alarming a conflagration. Application was made, at a very early period, to the Papal see, for spiritual aid and approbation; while similar demands were conveyed to the court of Spain, for pecuniary supplies, and even, if necessary, for a military force. The answer to both these requests, was encouraging. Gregory the Thirteenth, who then filled the chair of St. Peter, a pontiff of zeal, but neither violent nor sanguinary in his character; though he approved the ostensible motives, yet, apprehensive of the consequences concealed under them, lent only an ambiguous and mitigated degree of sanction to the project. But, Philip, who dreaded the approach of the French arms towards the Netherlands, and already anticipated the application of the Flemings to the duke of Anjou, or to Henry, for succours; did not hesitate to promise the most unbounded assistance to the League, and even accepted the title of its protector (5).

Dissimulation of the king.

Information of the commencement and progress of this alarming attempt to overturn the principles of civil order and obedience, was conveyed, through various channels, to the government. An emissary, who had been dispatched to the court of Rome, was seized on his return to France, by the Hugonots; and the plan of the League in its greatest detail, being found upon him, they rendered it public. Corroborating proofs of the same nature were transmitted to the king, from his embassador at Madrid, in a manner to preclude any doubt upon the authenticity of the intelligence. But, numer-

(4) Davila, p. 448—452. D'Aubigné, Hist. Univ. vol. ii. p. 223—230.
(5) Davila, p. 452 and 453. Mezerai, vol. ii. p. 179 and 180.

ous

ous reaſons induced him to diſſemble, and to ſuſpend his reſentment. The Guiſes not only denied many of the charges made againſt themſelves perſonally, as entertaining ambitious views of elevation: thoſe princes were likewiſe popular, powerful, and dangerous to provoke. Henry was incapable of a ſteady, ſyſtematic exertion, and preferred temporizing, to violent meaſures, in every event or ſituation of his life. His policy, which always aimed at deſtroying one faction by another, dictated to him to encourage, rather than depreſs, the party of the Catholics; and as he never meant to accompliſh the conditions of the late peace, he was not ſorry that the general reſentment, manifeſted at the favorable terms granted to the Hugonots, afforded him ſo plauſible a pretence for not carrying it into execution (6).

CHAP. III. 1576.

He eludes the late treaty.

The intentions of the court were clearly manifeſted, by the infractions, openly authorized, or privately permitted, in defiance of all the complaints and remonſtrances of the Hugonots. Even the interpoſition of John Caſimir, who had not yet evacuated the kingdom, and whoſe forces lived at diſcretion in Burgundy, were ineffectual to obtain redreſs. The prince of Condé, far from being put in poſſeſſion of the government of Picardy, was refuſed entrance into Peronne. The admiſſion of Proteſtants into the parliaments and courts of juſtice was delayed, or eluded: their aſſemblies for purpoſes of devotion were inſulted; and every unqualified violation of the peace ſo recently concluded, was committed with impunity. Irritated at ſuch a breach of faith, and deſtitute of any retreat, in caſe of a recommencement of hoſtilities; the prince of Condé, without waiting for the iſſue of a negociation, which Henry had begun with him

Reſentment of the prince of Condé.

(6) Davila, p. 453 and 454.

for

CHAP. III. 1576.

for the exchange of St. John d'Angely in the place of Peronne, rendered himſelf maſter of the former city. It was ſituated in the province of Saintonge; and he ſhortly afterwards acquired a more important poſſeſſion in its vicinity. Brouage, a town, not diſtant from Rochelle, and open to the Atlantic, fell into his hands; and theſe valuable captures formed no inconſiderable equivalent for the loſs of Picardy (7).

Convocation of the ſtates general. December.

Under theſe circumſtances of public fermentation and animoſity, the aſſembly of the ſtates general met at Blois. They were opened by the king in perſon, who, accompanied by his brother, by the queen-mother, and the Catholic princes of the blood, in a long and eloquent harangue, depictured and deplored the condition of the kingdom. He repreſented the decay of loyalty, the diminution of commerce, the triumph of immorality, and the univerſal depravity which pervaded all orders of the people. He profeſſed his readineſs to liſten to their advice, and beſought their co-operation towards reſtoring the proſperity of France. Theſe gracious and conciliating aſſurances were anſwered by ſimilar demonſtrations of affection. But, the king, who had flattered himſelf that he ſhould be able to guide and controul the deliberations of the ſtates, was not long in diſcovering, that a more powerful, though a concealed cauſe, influenced all their deliberations. The boldeſt invaſions of his prerogative were attempted: a renewal of the war was loudly demanded; and the majority proteſted againſt the toleration or exiſtence of any religion, except the Catholic, throughout the kingdom (8). In ſo embarraſſing a ſituation, beſet with difficulties, and conſcious that the emiſſaries of the Guiſes were

Henry ſigns the confederation of the League.

(7) De Thou, vol. vii. p. 432—436. Mezerai, vol. ix. p. 176.
(8) Davila, p. 458—463.

maſters

1576.

masters of the assembly; Henry embraced an expedient, which, however the result of necessity, fully evinced his own weakness. Apprehensive that the League might dictate to him in the most peremptory terms, and even turn their forces against him: still more alarmed, that the duke of Guise might be named to the vacant place of chief; he resolved to assume that post himself. Having taken the resolution, he executed it immediately; signed the League in the most public manner, assumed the title of its head, and transmitted the confederation itself to Paris, with orders to receive it throughout the kingdom (9).

Measures adopted by the king.

So incontestable a proof of his adherence to the Catholic faith, and the prospect of those calamities which were inseparable from a renewal of war, began to produce a deep impression on the assembly. The members of the third estate, aware that on the body of the people, whom they specially represented, the pecuniary burdens must principally fall, betrayed symptoms of aversion to the assumption of arms. Henry augmented these proofs of repugnance, by a requisition of two millions of ducats, a sum not very far short of a million sterling, as indispensable for maintaining the armies to be employed; and he ventured to propose an alienation of the domain of the crown to a considerable annual amount, as the most eligible mode for raising the money, in the present exigency. The proposition was solemnly argued in the assembly; and after a long discussion, the virtue of the representatives of the commons, rejected it in a manner the most decisive. The king, anxious to reduce the Hugonots to a state of civil and religious dependance; but, more desirous to avoid engaging in a war for their extermination, still delayed, and avoided ex-

1577. Deputation sent to the Hugonots.

(9) De Thou, vol. vii. p. 458 and 459. Davila, p. 466.

CHAP. III. 1577.

tremities. He even ſent, with a view of deprecating hoſtilities, a deputation to the king of Navarre, and the prince of Condé, as well as to marſhal Damville. Its reception was different, according to the character and diſpoſition of the three perſons. From the firſt, an anſwer was received, which, though equivocal and ambiguous, breathed the ſpirit of obedience to the crown, and of moderation on religious concerns: but, the prince of Condé, more zealous, inflexible, and ſevere, refuſed either to acknowledge the validity of the ſtates, or to receive their delegates. Damville, while, on one hand, he profeſſed the ſtrongeſt adherence to the Catholic faith, reprobated the violation of the late edict, and declined entering into any negociation, excluſive of the other confederates (10).

Renewal of the civil war.

The irreſolution of Henry was overborne by the imprudence of the Proteſtants themſelves, who, incenſed at the revocation of a treaty, which had ſecured to them ſo many and important immunities, refuſed to admit of any innovation, or modulation of the articles. But, the event ſufficiently demonſtrated, how erroneous an eſtimate they had formed of their own ſtrength and reſources. Diſunited among themſelves; no longer conducted by the genius of Coligni, who had ſurmounted ſo many defeats; unſupported by a foreign force; and preſſed by the ſuperior weight of the crown, united to the Catholics; the conteſt was too unequal to be long maintained. Two armies, levied by the king, marched againſt them, and met with a feeble reſiſtance. The firſt was commanded by the duke of Anjou in perſon, who, from their ally, had become their moſt implacable opponent. Henry's jealouſy of the duke of Guiſe, excluded him from conduct-

March.

(10) De Thou, vol. vii. p. 471—474, and 478. Davila, p. 469 and 470.

ing

ing the ſecond, which was committed to his brother, the duke of Mayenne. An uninterrupted ſeries of ſucceſs attended both armies. La Charité, one of the moſt important military poſts in the kingdom, as it formed a paſſage acroſs the Loire, and might have facilitated the entry of a German army; ſurrendered, after a ſhort ſiege, to the duke of Anjou. His victorious troops, unoppoſed, penetrated into Auvergne, inveſted Iſſoire in that province; and having entered it at the breach, reduced it to aſhes. The garriſon was ſacrificed to the ferocity of the ſoldiers. Nor was the duke of Mayenne's progreſs in Poitou, leſs rapid. Brouage, which had been recently ſeized by the prince of Condé, capitulated after a long blockade: the Hugonot fleet, which attempted to throw ſupplies of proviſions into the place, was compelled to retire, after ſuſtaining a conſiderable loſs; and even Rochelle itſelf, regarded as the aſylum of the Proteſtant faith and party, appeared to be in a ſituation the moſt perilous. Damville, who had long fluctuated in his political connexions, alienated by ſome cauſes of miſunderſtanding, quitted the confederacy; and turned his arms againſt his late allies, in Languedoc. No effort, worthy their former reputation, was made by any of the Hugonot chiefs. The nobility, weary of the war, retired to their caſtles: the troops diſbanded; and the people, reduced to poverty by the rapacity of a fierce and licentious ſoldiery, loudly demanded a termination of their accumulated misfortunes (11).

1577. Succeſs of the royal arms. May. June. Auguſt. Feeble exertions of the Hugonots.

If Henry's policy, or inclinations, had permitted him to puſh his advantages over a party, broken, and already vanquiſhed; the Hugonots might have been reduced to accept any conditions, however ſevere, which he had thought proper to impoſe.

Policy of Henry.

(11) Mezerai, vol. ix. p. 191—196. Davila, p. 471 and 472.

But,

CHAP. III. 1577.

But, ſuch a triumph would have been more apparent, than real; and would have conduced more to the advantage of the houſe of Guiſe, as the concealed chiefs of the League, than either to the grandeur or ſtability of the throne. The Catholics themſelves, who preſerved their allegiance, and who were not diſpoſed to ſacrifice the public ſafety to the ambitious projects of the duke of Guiſe, betrayed the moſt anxious deſire for peace. Encouraged by theſe ſymptoms of the national approbation, Henry, after a ſhort negociation with the king of Navarre, concluded a treaty, which was afterwards ratified and publiſhed at Poitiers. It was the fifth, which had been made between the two parties, ſince the commencement of the civil wars, under Charles the Ninth. The articles, though far leſs favorable to the Proteſtants, than thoſe of the preceding one, eſtabliſhed and admitted, under certain reſtrictions, a toleration of religion. Its exerciſe was, however, interdicted within ten leagues of the metropolis, or, in the immediate vicinity of the court. Eight cities were ceded to the Hugonots, as a guarantee for the execution of the conditions: but, their reſtitution was ſtipulated, at the end of four years. Various regulations, calculated to introduce a degree of police, and to maintain order, were inſerted into the treaty (12).

Concluſion of peace. September.

Reflexions on that event.

The general ſatisfaction with which it was received by the majority of the nation, formed its beſt eulogium. The king, who regarded it as peculiarly his own work, denominated it, with complacency, *his* peace; and the prince of Condé did not manifeſt leſs impatience to publiſh it in the city of Rochelle. It may be eſteemed the wiſeſt and moſt judicious

(12) Davila, p. 473 and 474. De Thou, vol. vii. p. 529—531. Mezerai, vol. ix. p, 197 and 198. D'Aubigné, Hiſt. Univ. vol. ii. p. 327 and 328.

measure

CHAP. III. 1577.

measure of the reign of Henry the Third; and if that prince had improved the occasion which it presented him, of establishing a vigorous administration; the League, notwithstanding its prodigious resources, might have been crushed before it attained to maturity (13). But, the character of the king, as it became more fully unveiled, far from inspiring respect, excited contempt, and even aversion. His profusion anticipated and exhausted the revenues. A succession of favorites, characterized by the same rapacity, profligacy, and contempt of decorum, rendered the court a scene of indecent riot, or of scandalous dissipation. Catherine of Medicis, subservient to all the vices and weaknesses of her son, did not scruple to be present at these festivities; and Margaret, queen of Navarre, her daughter, lost to every sense of female honor, or chastity, constituted the principal ornament of her brother's palace and amusements. The prerogative of the crown became odious, from the abuse of its powers. Taxes, varied by the ingenuity of pernicious ministers, and multiplied in a thousand shapes; while they exhausted the patience of the people, were insufficient to suffice for the prodigality of the sovereign. The mixture of devotion, which Henry affected, and the pilgrimages or processions, in which he continually engaged, only served to render his enormities more conspicuous, and to call in question the sincerity of his attachment to religion itself. His brother, the duke of Anjou, however exempt from some of the imputations thrown on the king, was scarcely more an object of esteem. Like Henry, he was inconstant, capricious, and destitute of principles of virtue; plunged in excesses of libertinism; equally enslaved by favorites; and incapable of sustaining the majesty of the throne, to which his birth, and the

Mal-administration, and vices of the king.

Conduct of the duke of Anjou.

(13) Memoires de Nevers, vol. i. p. 289—307.

CHAP. III. 1577.

the king's want of issue, rendered it probable that he might eventually be called. These defects and vices, still more than the great qualities by which the duke of Guise was distinguished, gradually prepared the minds of the people for the convulsions that followed; and when matured by time, left the crown exposed to all the enterprizes of ambition, and the violence of rebellion (14).

1578. Internal commotions of France.

France, meanwhile, was far from enjoying the internal repose, which the peace concluded at Poitiers ought to have naturally produced. Religious antipathy, superior to the force of edicts, or the restraints of law, continued to arm the inhabitants against each other. The intolerance of the age could not allow liberty of opinion, or of practice, in matters of conscience; and the long habits of civil war, had rendered the people sanguinary, suspicious, and cruel. Damville, who exercised a species of independant jurisdiction in his government of Languedoc; on various pretences refused to disarm, and even maintained hostilities against the Protestants. Lesdiguieres, who commanded the Hugonot forces in Dauphiné, had not forgotten the recent execution of Montbrun, under whom he had carried arms; and he did not trust sufficiently either the faith of the king, or the sanction of edicts, to divest himself of his military protection (15). Many acts of outrage and violence were committed with impunity in the provinces. The court itself, after exhibiting every species of luxurious and dissolute entertainment, became a theatre of discord and of blood. These transitions originated in the king's misconduct, and excited little surprize. His brother, the duke of Anjou, dissatisfied with the treatment which he received, and apprehensive of being again arrested,

February. Retreat of the duke of Anjou from court.

(14) Mezerai, vol. ix. p. 199.
(15) Davila, p. 474.

withdrew

withdrew a second time, quitted Paris, and retired into Normandy; from whence he sent assurances of his loyalty and obedience to the crown. But, a more serious and tragical event, made a deep, though only a temporary, impression on Henry's mind. From the period of his accession, he had been governed by favorites, who succeeded each other with amazing rapidity. Bellegarde had been supplanted before his master's arrival at Lyons; and du Gua was assassinated within a year, during the plenitude of his power. The vacant places were quickly occupied by new candidates. Villequier, one of the most corrupt and profligate companions of the king's pleasures, presided over the department; and the royal favor was divided between those whom he presented, or recommended. As they were all in the bloom of youth, distinguished by the graces of person, and naturally elated with their good fortune; perpetual quarrels took place between them, and the adherents, or retainers of the nobility, who filled the court.

Royal favorites.

Quelus, one of Henry's minions, having challenged Francis d'Entragues, a young man of quality, attached to the duke of Guise, the combatants, each accompanied by two of his friends, met in one of the most public places of the capital, to terminate the dispute. The seconds engaged with the same ardor and animosity as the principals. Of the six, two were left dead upon the place: one expired on the following day; and Quelus himself, pierced with nineteen wounds, languished near a month, before he breathed his last. The indications of affection, exhibited by the king towards him, during the course of his malady; and the demonstrations of his sorrow for the death of Quelus, and of Maugiron, another of his favorites who had fallen in the duel, were equally indecent and unmanly. He embraced their dead bodies; ordered them

Duel of Quelus and Entragues.

April.

CHAP. III. 1578.

them a public funeral, at which all the courtiers assisted; received compliments of condolence, as for the loss of the princes of the blood; and appeared to be, for some time, inconsolable (16). Incapable of any permanent emotion, he soon recovered his gaiety, and obliterated the recollection of the deceased, in the society of new favorites. But, the injurious impressions, made by his conduct, on the minds of the people, were not effaced with the same facility. Proofs of contempt, and of indignation, appeared in many parts of the kingdom; and the profusion with which offices, dignities, and emoluments were conferred on the unworthy associates of his looser hours, while it exhausted the public treasure, encreased the general dissatisfaction. The states of Burgundy, in a high-spirited remonstrance, ventured, without disguise, to arraign in severe terms, the king's profusion; enumerated their grievances, and specified the adequate remedies. Henry dissembled his resentment at so bold an attack, which he attributed to the princes of the house of Guise; and he was even reduced to the necessity of employing the intervention of the duke of Mayenne, governor of the province, to allay the discontent of the nobility and of the states. These seeds of discontent were not however eradicated; and time gradually matured them to the most alarming degree (17).

General discontent of the kingdom.

November.

Affairs of Portugal.

While the vices of Henry, which a powerful faction placed in the most conspicuous and odious point of view, silently prepared a great convulsion in France; an ardent, and ill-regulated thirst of glory in Sebastian, king of Portugal, produced the destruction of that monarchy. Having determined

Enterprize of Sebastian.

(16) Etoile. Journ. d'Henry III. p. 92. De Thou, vol. vii. p. 725—728. Mezerai, vol. ix. p. 201 and 202.

(17) De Thou, vol. vii. p. 729—731.

on

CHAP. III. 1578.

on an expedition to the coaſt of Barbary, for the purpoſe of reſtoring Mahomet, who pretended to the ſovereignty of Fez, no obſtacles could prevent, nor remonſtrances diſſuade him from his reſolution. After ſurmounting, not without difficulty, numerous impediments, he, at length, embarked from the Tagus, at the head of a numerous ſquadron, and a conſiderable army. Muley Moluc, the reigning prince, againſt whom his efforts were directed, endeavoured to avoid the conteſt, and made offers for an accommodation. But, the temerity and imprudence of Sebaſtian rendered him incapable of diſcerning his own intereſt, or of liſtening to any conſiderations, except thoſe of conqueſt. Landing in Africa, he engaged in a general action near Arzila, where his troops, ill diſciplined, outnumbered by the enemy, and ſurrounded on all ſides, were either cut to pieces, or captured by the Moors. He himſelf, after having given proofs of the moſt deſperate valor, periſhed in the engagement. Mahomet, whom he had vainly attempted to place on the throne of Fez and Morocco, was drowned in his flight from the field of battle; and Muley Moluc, attacked by a mortal diſeaſe, expired in his litter, in the moment of victory, before the event of the day was fully decided. Hamet, his brother, ſucceeded to the ſupreme authority (18).

August. His death.

Reign of the Cardinal Henry.

The conſternation, occaſioned in Portugal by ſo lamentable a cataſtrophé, exceeded deſcription; and the preſent calamity, however great, was ſwallowed up in the view and contemplation of the more alarming conſequences of Sebaſtian's defeat and death. That young and unfortunate prince had left no iſſue; and the crown devolved to the only ſurviving

(18) La Clede, Hiſt. de Portugal, vol. ii p. 58—72. De Thou, vol. vii. p. 599—634.

CHAP. XII. 1578.

male descendant of their antient kings. Henry, cardinal of the Romish church, and archbishop of Evora, son to the celebrated Emanuel, had attained to his sixty-seventh year, when called to the throne. Adorned with many of the virtues which render a private station amiable, he possessed few of the qualities requisite in a monarch; and his advanced period of life, together with his declining health, promised only a short and precarious reign. The succession, uncertain, and claimed by many candidates, held up to the nation the prospect of a civil and foreign war; while the late disaster deprived them of the means of defence against an enemy. Philip the Second, king of Spain, who stood in the relation of uncle to Sebastian, by the marriage of Isabella of Portugal with Charles the Fifth, already displayed his pretensions; and the vast disparity between his force, and that of any other claimant, must necessarily decide the contest in his favour (19).

Transactions in the Netherlands.

But, neither the terrors of the Spanish power, which seemed to be on the point of receiving so vast an accession, by the probable conquest of Portugal; nor the presence and talents of Don John of Austria, could restore any degree of tranquillity in the Netherlands. The affairs of that country, and its final destiny, appeared to become annually more complicated, perplexed, and doubtful. Don John, far from adducing any remedy to the discontents of the Flemings, had, by his conduct, alienated and incensed them against the court of Spain. His first proceedings were, notwithstanding, calculated to conciliate universal affection.

Measures of Don John of Austria.

By the advice of Escovedo, his secretary and minister, he confirmed the pacification of Ghent, caused the Spanish troops instantly to evacuate Flanders, and received anew the

(19) La Clede, vol. ii. p. 72 and 73.

oath

1578.

oath of fealty and obedience from the States, to Philip the Second. His entry into Bruſſels, as governor general, was marked with demonſtrations of public joy; and for a ſhort time, his adminiſtration ſeemed to rival in popularity that of his ſiſter, Margaret of Parma. But, the ambition of Don John could not be gratified by ſo limited an authority; and he ſpeedily repented of his facility, in having diſmiſſed the veteran troops, which had fought under the duke of Alva, and Requeſens. Having ſeized on the citadel of Namur, he prepared to regain the power which he had unwillingly ceded, and to reduce the Flemings, by force of arms. Irritated at ſuch treatment, the States called to their aid the archduke Mathias, ſon to Maximilian the Second, and brother to the emperor Rodolph; while Don John, reinforced by the Spaniards, whom Alexander Farneſe, prince of Parma, conducted from Italy, attacked, and defeated the Flemings at Gemblours (20).

January.

The duke of Anjou embraces the protection of the Flemings.

An event, which ſeemed to threaten the entire reduction of the Netherlands to the obedience of Philip, and the extinction of all their privileges, afforded a favourable occaſion for the duke of Anjou to offer his aſſiſtance to the States. That prince, reſtleſs and ambitious; ill received at the court of Henry, who feared and ſuſpected him; odious to the Hugonots, whom he had abandoned; and anxious to obtain an eſtabliſhment beyond the limits of his brother's power; immediately ſent a deputation, to make propoſals for undertaking their defence and protection. His agents were received with gratitude, and treated with diſtinction. He himſelf, in order to accelerate the concluſion of the treaty, which promiſed him an entrauce into the

(20) Strada, de Bel. Belg. vol. ii. p. 321—404. De Thou, vol. vii. p. 545—573, and 649—661.

CHAP. III. 1578. August.

Low Countries, advanced to the city of Mons in Haynault, where all the conditions were finally settled. He engaged to conduct to their assistance an army of ten thousand infantry, and three thousand cavalry; in return for which, the States conferred on him the title of Protector of the Belgic Liberties; guaranteed to him certain places, as security for the execution of the articles; and promised to elect him for their sovereign, if they should eventually withdraw their alliance from the king of Spain (21).

He enters Haynault.

In consequence of this treaty, the duke of Anjou entered Haynault, at the head of a considerable military force; made himself master of several frontier towns; and excited the highest expectations of his future progress. But, he soon perceived the difficulties attending an enterprize, which demanded talents equally various and superior. His troops, composed of Catholics and Protestants, long accustomed to the licentiousness of civil war, refused to submit to the severity of discipline. The Flemings, disgusted and alienated by the excesses which the French soldiery committed, considered them as enemies, rather than as allies; and the places, stipulated to be delivered to him, shut their gates to oppose his entry. Incensed at the failure of the engagements contracted by the States, the duke of Anjou withdrew again into France; after remonstrating with them on their treatment of him, and assuring them of his return. He even sent a detachment of three thousand men to join the army of the Flemings. The remainder of his forces, no longer paid, immediately disbanded (22).

October.

etreats.

The ill success attending the enterprize of the duke of Anjou, together with the victory lately

(21) De Thou, vol. vii. p. 670 and 671.

(22) Mezerai, vol. ix. p. 207—209. De Thou, vol. ix. p. 688—690.

obtained

obtained by Don John of Auſtria at Gemblours, might have reſtored the Spaniſh affairs in the Netherlands, if Philip the Second had extended ſupport to his brother. But, that jealous and ſuſpicious monarch, alarmed at the ambitious and extenſive projects of Don John; far from ſupplying him with the requiſite force to reduce the Flemings, left him in a ſtate of total inability to maintain the war. The Spaniards were defeated in their turn, and compelled to retreat before the army of the States. Eſcovedo, who had been ſent by his maſter, to Madrid, to urge the diſpatch of troops and money, was aſſaſſinated in that capital, by the order, or conſent of the king of Spain. Don John himſelf, exhauſted by fatigue, and depreſſed by anxiety, did not long ſurvive. Having reſigned the command of the forces to Alexander, prince of Parma, he retired to Namur; where the ſtruggles of a high-ſpirited and indignant mind, aiding the advances of diſeaſe, he expired in the vigor of his age, having ſcarcely accompliſhed his thirty-third year. The affliction of his troops at the intelligence, was extreme; and his contemporaries compared him to Germanicus, as they did Philip to Tiberius. The circumſtances of his diſtemper and death, which were, though unjuſtly, attributed to poiſon; and the period of life at which he died, rendered the reſemblance with the Roman general more ſtriking, and the ſimilarity more complete. Philip confirmed the government of the Low Countries, to the prince of Parma; and his great endowments, military as well as civil, rendered him worthy of ſo arduous a ſituation (23).

CHAP. III. 1578.

Death of Don John.

1ſt October

Prince of Parma, made governor of Netherlands.

During this period of time, when the attention of all Europe was attracted towards the fate of Portugal, and of Flanders; France offered few events, which deſerve to be commemorated. Henry, who

1579. Indolence of Henry.

(23) Strada, vol. ii. p. 466—471. De Thou, vol. viii. p. 696—698.

might

CHAP. III. 1579.

might have improved the interval of repose, afforded by the peace with the Hugonots, to regain the esteem of his subjects, and to attack, while yet in their infancy, the dangerous designs of the League; made no exertions for his own preservation. Resigned to a life of indolence and pleasure, he abandoned the care of the state to his mother, and seemed to regard the royal dignity as only intended for the oppression of his people. Catherine of Medicis, whose virtues and whose vices were more active, visited, in the name, and by the authority of her son, the different parts of his dominions. She negociated with the king of Navarre, in Gascony, for the maintenance of the treaty of Poitiers; which, after a long discussion, was explained by a number of secret articles, calculated to prolong the public tranquillity. Having traversed all Languedoc, and endeavoured to appease, or to extinguish the seeds of commotion in the province, she arrived at Grenoble, accompanied by Damville; in which place she held a conference with Emanuel Philibert, duke of Savoy. That able and enterprizing prince had engaged deeply in projects, injurious to Henry. Not content with having already obtained from him, the restitution of Pignerol and Savillan, the duke meditated the seizure of the marquisate of Saluzzo. Catherine, anxious to preserve so valuable a possession, did not hesitate to pass the borders of France, in order to have an interview with Bellegarde, the governor, at Montluel, in the territories of Savoy. It was ineffectual; but, his death soon afterwards, suspended the execution of Emanuel Philibert's designs (24).

Activity of the queen.

March.

Creation of the order of the Holy Ghost.

While the queen-mother thus exercised the real functions of a sovereign, Henry performed the pageantries of royalty. The institution of the order of

(24) Mezerai, vol. ix. p. 217—220. De Thou, vol. viii. p. 75—84. Davila, p. 481—483.

of the "Holy Ghost," which took place at this period, was designed to replace that of "St. Michael," become venal and contemptible, under the late reigns. The celebration of so public and splendid a ceremony, gratified the king's passion for expensive exhibitions; and he flattered himself, that by associating to his new order, many of the highest nobility, he might attach to his person a number of adherents (25). Insensible as Henry appeared to every event of a public or national kind, he, nevertheless, betrayed, on various occasions, a degree of attention, or concern, which proved, that however indolence and flattery had corrupted him, his mind was not totally destitute of elevation. He manifested the deepest regret at the death of marshal Montmorenci, whom, from the purity of his virtue, his rectitude, and patriotism, the glorious title of "the last of the French," was conferred by his countrymen. During the rage of civil war, and the shock of opposite factions, he preserved his moderation, and exerted all his efforts to extinguish the flames of discord, by which France was desolated. Become suspected to Catherine of Medicis, in the last months of the reign of Charles the Ninth, on account of his supposed adherence, to the duke of Alençon and the Hugonots; he had been committed to the Bastile: during his detention in that fortress, Henry, at the instigation of his mother, had issued orders to Souvré, the governor, to strangle him; and he only owed the preservation of his life to the delays, interposed by Souvré. His imprisonment, and the hardships annexed to it, advanced his end; and he expired of an apoplectic seizure, at fifty years of age. His death, peculiarly in the circumstances of the kingdom, was a national misfortue. Dam-

May.

Death of marshal Montmorenci.

(25) Davila, p. 481. Mezerai, vol. ix. p. 214—217.

ville,

CHAP. III.

ville, his brother, succeeded to the title of Montmorenci (26).

1579. Henry takes under his protection, the city of Geneva.

Nor did the king evince less regard to the interests of the monarchy, on an occasion, which called for his interference, nearly at the same time. The little republic of Geneva, almost surrounded by the dominions of the dukes of Savoy, derived its best security, from the alliance of the Swiss cantons. It was believed, that Philip the Second and Emanuel Philibert had entered into a treaty, the object of which was the conquest and partition of Switzerland. To effect such an enterprize, it was indispensable to commence by the reduction of Geneva; and the ruinous consequences of the plan to France, if carried into execution, were too obvious, to need elucidation. Urged by the cantons of Berne and Soleure, in the name of the Helvetic confederacy, to take the city of Geneva under his protection, as an ally of the Swiss nation; Henry, after a considerable reluctance, complied. Articles, calculated for the defence of Geneva, against all external attack, were agreed on, and ratified by the king; who, in the troubles which he already anticipated from the adherents of the League, knew that he should derive his surest military support from the affection of the Switzers (27).

May.

Dissolute conduct of the king.

These transitory or capricious exertions were, unfortunately for himself and his people, preceded and followed by a complete dereliction of every public duty. The finances, committed to the most corrupt and profligate ministers, became annually more inadequate to the necessities of the crown; while the king expended in diversions, or festivities, the produce of accumulated taxes, under which his subjects groaned. The duke of Anjou, after again effecting

(26) Mezerai, vol. ix. p. 162 and 163. De Thou, vol. viii. p. 84 and 85.
(27) De Thou, vol. viii. p. 97—99. Mezerai, vol. ix. p. 221 and 222.

his

his reconciliation with Henry, had, in some measure, postponed, though he had not abandoned, his projects on the Netherlands. The brave and celebrated La Noue, a Protestant, conducted a body of about three thousand French, who were to act in conjunction with the states of Flanders; while the duke himself, excited by the hopes of marrying Elizabeth, queen of England, had passed over, with a very slender train, into that kingdom. His reception was so flattering, as to maintain him for a long time, in illusive expectation (28).

CHAP. III. 1579.

August.

Towards the close of the year, alarming symptoms of the intention of the Hugonots to renew the civil war, began to manifest themselves. At an assembly of the Protestant churches, held by the king of Navarre in person, at Maziere in Gascony, it was publickly agitated to take up arms. Various infractions of the last treaty, were assigned, as the cause and justification for their conduct; and after considerable difference of opinion, it was finally determined, that if immediate redress was not obtained from the crown, they would endeavour to extort it by violent means. No resolution could have been more imprudent, if not unjust. Henry had not evinced any hostile disposition towards the Hugonots; and the edict of Poitiers had been executed, if not with strictness, yet in as literal and rigorous a degree, as the tumultuous state of the kingdom, and the disordered nature of affairs, could permit. The Protestants themselves were divided, and almost defenceless. Neither the zeal, nor the union, religious and civil, which had rendered them so formidable under Charles the Ninth, continued to exist. Since the temporary combination into which they had entered with the duke of Anjou and Damville, num-

Internal commotions. November.

Hugonots project to renew the war.

(28) Davila, p. 483 and 484. De Thou, vol. viii. p.89. Mezerai, vol. ix. p. 221.

bers

CHAP. III. 1579.

bers of men, destitute of any principles of morals or religion, had united themselves to the party. The king of Navarre himself, though attached to his own faith by honor, and by conviction, yet did not, in his conduct, observe even the appearance of decorum and morality. The little court of Nerac, in Gascony, where he held his principal residence, was the center of pleasure, libertinism, and every species of gallantry. Margaret, queen of Navarre, his wife, who had been conducted thither by her mother, Catherine of Medicis, gave the example of these excesses, which were imitated by the courtiers; and she even condescended, on many occasions, to become subservient toher husband'samours, which she facilitated and conducted (29). The prince of Condé was almost the only person of distinguished rank among the Hugonots, who maintained the purity and fervor of the primitive reformers: but, his power, revenues, and influenee, were too limited, to produce any considerable effect. He derived, notwithstanding, a personal consideration from his intrepidity, activity, and indefatigable exertions. Impatient at the delays practised by the court of France, to prevent his entrance into Picardy, of which he was only the nominal governor; the prince anticipated the general resolution of his party, to take up arms. Having quitted the city of St. John d'Angely, in Saintonge, where he usually resided, he repaired in disguise to La Fere, in Picardy, which place he surprized, and immediately garrisoned (30).

State of the court of Navarre.

Prince of Condé.

November.

1580. Inactivity of the king.

Notwithstanding this demonstration of the discontent of the Protestants, Henry, relying on the promises and assurances of his sister, the queen of

(29) Mezerai, vol. ix. p. 222 and 223. D'Aubigné, Hist. Univ. vol. ii. p. 344—346. Hist. de Marguérite de Valois, p. 322 and 323.
(30) De Thou, vol. viii. p. 92.

Navarre,

Navarre, took no meaſures againſt the projects of his Hugonot ſubjects. But, Margaret, who had received the moſt contumelious and humiliating marks of her brother's averſion, on various occaſions; and whoſe vindictive diſpoſition ſtimulated her to revenge; far from allaying, or ſoothing the paſſions of her huſband, endeavoured to point them againſt the perſon by whom ſhe had been offended. Her exhortations were ſufficiently powerful, not only to prevail on the king of Navarre, but, to induce the principal perſons in his confidence, to embrace the hazardous expedient of renewing the civil war. Regardleſs of their own inability to ſupport ſo arduous an enterprize; and impelled only by pretences of the weakeſt nature, they began their operations. The king of Navarre, after diſpatching meſſengers to his adherents in Languedoc and Dauphiné, to acquaint them of his ultimate reſolution, inſtantly attempted to make himſelf maſter of Cahors, by ſurprize. That city, capital of the province of Quercy, conſtituted a part of the dowry of Margaret, his wife; but, the animoſity of the inhabitants, zealouſly devoted to the Catholic faith, had prevented his reception into the place. The garriſon, notwithſtanding the loſs of their governor, who was killed at the beginning of the conflict maintained a deſperate reſiſtance for ſeveral days; but, the aſſailants, ſupported by the preſence of their prince, who expoſed himſelf to every danger, were at length victorious. Cahors was reduced to aſhes; and every act of unreſtrained barbarity was exerciſed by the Proteſtants, in retaliation for the maſſacre committed there under Charles the Ninth, eight years preceding, of which the Hugonots had been the victims (31).

CHAP. III.

1580.

April.

King of Navarre takes up arms.

May.

Capture of Cahors.

(31) D'Aubigné, Hiſt. Univ. vol. ii. p. 350—353. De Thou, vol. viii. p. 374—379. Mezerai, vol. ix. p. 223—225. Davila, p. 478—489.

The

CHAP. III. 1580.

Measures of the king.

The astonishment of Henry, at receiving intelligence of the attack and capture of Cahors, was exceeded and lost in his indignation. Surmounting his habitual indolence, he made immediate and vigorous preparations for punishing the audacity of his rebellious subjects. At the same time, that he fitted out three considerable armies, destined to act against them in Dauphiné, Guienne, and Picardy; he embraced a measure, not less calculated to weaken and disarm their adherents. A declaration was published by the royal authority, confirming all the preceding edicts favourable to the Protestants, on condition of their remaining peaceable; and enjoining the civil magistrates to punish as traitors to their country, such as should molest them in any manner (32).

June.

Their effect on the Hugonots.

The effect of so wise and timely an act, was sensibly felt throughout the kingdom. Many persons, sincerely attached to the reformed doctrines, had, nevertheless, disapproved the resumption of arms; and their disinclination was augmented, as well as justified, by the declaration issued on the part of the crown. La Noue, one of the most virtuous and respected of their leaders, who was occupied at that time in hostilities against the Spaniards in the Netherlands, condemned the war, as manifestly unprovoked and unjustifiable. Rochelle refused to engage in it, and maintained a perfect neutrality. Other provinces declined to contribute towards, or to mingle in the controversy. Even, in those, where the Hugonots were the most numerous or powerful, feeble exertions were made, and few successful enterprizes effected. It must be avowed, that of all the civil wars, occasioned by religious animosity, since the conspiracy of Amboise under the reign of Francis the Second, this was begun on the most insufficient pretexts, and is the least to be vindicated (33).

(32) De Thou, vol. viii. p. 387 and 395.
(33) Mezerai, vol. ix. p. 225 and 226.

Its

1580.

Succefs of the royal forces.

Its fuccefs was perfectly correfpondent to the principles, on which it had been commenced, and forcibly evinced the decay of the Hugonot power. Lefdiguieres was reduced to retreat before the duke of Mayenne in Dauphiné, and fcarcely maintained himfelf among the defiles and mountains of that inacceffible province. The moderation and clemency of the duke towards his enemies, completed the progrefs of his arms. In Picardy, the prince of Condé, not venturing to fuftain a fiege in the city of La Fere, quitted France, and embarked for England, where he hoped to derive fupplies from the policy of Elizabeth. Fruftrated in his expectation, he croffed over into Germany; and returning through Switzerland into Dauphiné, after furmounting numerous impediments, he joined the forces of Lefdiguieres. Meanwhile, the marfhal Matignon, at the head of an army, invefted and befieged La Fere. The camp was filled with the young nobility, who, in crouds, arrived from the court to fignalize their prowefs. At their head, diftinguifhed by the fplendor of their appearance and train, were the two favorites of Henry, Arques, and La Valette; better known in hiftory by the titles of Joyeufe and Epernon. They had already attained to the preeminence in the king's affections, and were the channel of every grace or preferment. After fuftaining a fiege of fix weeks, the governor of La Fere capitulated on honorable conditions (34).

Siege of La Fere.

September.

King of Navarre is purfued by Biron.

The king of Navarre, who had imprudently engaged in a war fo much above his ftrength or refources, was not more fortunate than his confederates. Unable to collect under his ftandard, or to maintain in the field, any confiderable body of troops; compelled to retire before marfhal Biron, who had paffed the Garonne, and entered Gafcony;

(34) De Thou, vol. viii. p. 396 and 397. Mezerai, vol. ix. p. 227. D'Aubigné, Hift. Univ. vol. ii. p. 367—370.

deftitute

CHAP. III. 1580. September.

destitute almost of a guard for the protection of his person, he was necessitated to take refuge in Nerac. Biron approached the place, drew up his army, and even fired some vollies of cannon against the town; while the queen of Navarre, like Helen on the walls of Troy, attended by the ladies of her court, occupied the watch towers and battlements, as spectators of the action. But, it was not the intention of the king of France to reduce to the last extremities, a prince so nearly allied to him by blood and marriage, in whom he beheld the only counterpoise to the power of the Guises and the League. Biron, after displaying his force, withdrew from the vicinity of Nerac; and a fall, by which he was, for some time, rendered incapable of personally commanding the troops committed to his charge, tended to impede his further progress (35).

Conclusion of peace.

In this desperate extremity of his affairs, the king of Navarre was saved by the interposition of the duke of Anjou. That prince having already accepted the offers of the states general of the Netherlands, by which, on certain conditions, they agreed to delegate to him the sovereignty, of which they had deprived Philip the Second; and anxious to obtain the assistance of the Hugonots, mediated their accommodation. The queen-mother, willing to aid the ambitious views of her youngest son, joined her powerful intercession; and Henry, who only desired repose, easily consented to open a treaty with his brother-in-law.

November.

It was conducted at the castle of Fleix, in Perigord, and suffered little impediment or delay. The articles of the preceding peace were renewed with some variation; and France, after a war of only a few months, was restored to tranquillity (36).

(35) D'Aubigné, Hist. Univ. vol. ii. p. 364. De Thou, vol. viii. p. 389—393. Davila, p. 490 and 491.

(36) De Thou, vol. viii. p. 399. Davila, p. 491. D'Aubigné, Hist. Univ. vol. ii. p. 384. Mezerai, vol. ix. p. 230.

No

1580.

Affairs of the Low Countries.

No part of Europe, during this period, was so constantly desolated, or subject to such numerous and rapid revolutions, as the Netherlands. The Spanish affairs, which, at the decease of Don John of Austria, appeared to be almost beyond recovery, were speedily retrieved by the vigor and capacity of the new governor general. Not discouraged by the total want of pecuniary resources, by the general desertion of the provinces, or by the superior military force of the enemy; the Prince of Parma supplied every defect, by the energy of his mind, the promptitude of his movements, and the superiority of his genius. Equally fitted for the cabinet and for the field, his comprehensive talents embraced either department. Severe in the camp, he was mild and gentle in every act of private life; and his clemency was still more effectual in subduing, or regaining the Flemings, than his transcendent military capacity. The states of Brabant and Flanders having proceeded to form a new and closer union with the prince of Orange, for their mutual defence; the provinces of Haynault and Artois, apprehensive of the complete subversion of the Catholic religion, began to exhibit marks of a disposition to return to the obedience of Philip the Second. These favorable symptoms were encouraged and ultimately matured, by the wisdom and prudence of the prince of Parma. At the same time he undertook the siege of Maestricht, in order more effectually to preclude the future entry of German armies into the Low Countries; he continued, and concluded a treaty, by which, on condition of dismissing the Spanish troops, the Walloon provinces, comprehending Artois, Haynault, the city of Lisle, and several subordinate places, submitted anew to Spain. Maestricht, after a siege of four months, was entered by storm, the garrison and inhabitants, put to the sword, and the city completely reduced.

Character of the prince of Parma.

The Walloon provinces return to the obedience of Spain.

The

CHAP. III.

1580.

Progress of the Spanish general.

The progress of the Spanish commander was aided by the dissentions of the states of Flanders, caused by religious disputes; and his recent accommodation with the Walloons, shook the basis of the independence of the Flemings. Having, not without extreme reluctance, and many delays, completed the evacuation of the Netherlands by the Spanish soldiery, in compliance with his engagements; he formed a new army with incredible celerity. La Noue, who commanded the combined forces of the States of France, after performing the most distinguished services, was defeated, and taken prisoner. The Spaniards, who regarded themselves as invincible under the prince of Parma, carried terror thro' every part of the Netherlands; and if Philip the Second had not, in his ardor to attain the crown of Portugal, withheld the necessary supplies of money from his general in the Low Countries; an universal submission of those provinces to their antient sovereign, might, probably, have been effected (37).

June.

Treaty between the Flemings and the duke of Anjou.

Under these alarming circumstances, the prince of Orange strenuously exhorted the States, not to delay the conclusion of a treaty with the duke of Anjou, as the only competent barrier against the further inroads of the Spanish general. It was accelerated by the voluntary renunciation, on the part of the arch-duke Mathias, of the post of governor of the Netherlands, to which he had been called, and which he had, in effect, only nominally occupied. That prince, neglected by the Flemings, who had invited him; and possessing neither talents, authority, nor consideration, withdrew soon afterwards into Germany. The definitive treaty between the duke of Anjou, and the states of Brabant, Flanders,

August.

(37) Strada de Bel. Belg. vol. ii. p. 1—277. De Thou, vol. viii. p. 100—122, and 316—366.

Holland,

CHAP. III. 1580.

Holland, Zealand, and Friesland, with whom the cities of Antwerp and Mechlin were joined; was finally adjusted at the castle of Plessis, near Tours. The sovereignty of those rich and commercial provinces was conferred on him and his posterity, on the condition of being annexed to, but, not incorporated in, the French monarchy; and with a reservation of all their privileges and immunities. An army, to which the contracting parties agreed jointly to contribute, was to be immediately levied for their defence and protection. The peace between Henry the Third and his Hugonot subjects, was the consequence of this treaty; and the duke of Anjou exerted every effort, to carry it into vigorous execution. He obtained the indirect approbation of the king his brother, and issued orders to levy troops in every part of France (38).

Articles of the treaty.

If the capacity of the French prince had been equal to his good fortune, a considerable portion of those opulent and maritime countries, extending from the frontiers of Picardy and Champagne, to the mouth of the Weser, might have been transferred to the house of Valois. But, the duke of Anjou, like his predecessor, the arch-duke Mathias, only represented the pageant of a sovereign, and was unqualified to effect so vast and arduous an atchievement, as the expulsion of the Spaniards from the Netherlands. The essential authority resided always in William, prince of Orange, whose depth of policy, and superior talents, had already cemented his independant supremacy over the northern provinces, Holland and Zealand. Irritated against him to the highest degree, and justly regarding the measure of calling in the duke of Anjou, as his peculiar act, Philip the Second no longer imposed any

Impediments to the progress of the duke of Anjou.

(38) De Thou, vol. viii. p. 336. Mezerai, vol. ix. p. 228 and 229.

 restraint

CHAP. III. 1580. June. Manifesto of the king of Spain.

restraint on his indignation against his revolted subject. In a public manifesto, dispersed by his command throughout all Europe, he proscribed the prince of Orange; stigmatized him with the epithets of traitor, rebel, and heretic; exposed his estates to pillage; and finally offered a reward of twenty thousand ducats, to any person who should bring him dead or alive. William was neither terrified nor depressed by this proscription, to which he replied by the apology that bears his name, and which in energy of composition is not inferior to the most celebrated works of antiquity. It was transmitted to the different European courts, and covered Philip with opprobrium, by the severe display which it contained of his vices, crimes, and enormities (39).

December.

Affairs of Portugal.

While the fate of the Netherlands was still uncertain, that of Portugal was already decided. The insatiable ambition of Philip was gratified by the addition of a new kingdom, and of the rich colonies possessed by the Portugueze in Asia. All the discoveries made by Gama, and the conquests effected by Albuquerque, were carried into the house of Austria, and lost in the enormous mass of the Spanish monarchy. The reign of the cardinal Henry, who had succeeded to the unfortunate Sebastian, was of short continuance. He expired, after having nominally held the sceptre only seventeen months. The period was, notwithstanding, of sufficient length, to have secured the independance of his country; and to have named a successor, under whom Portugal might still retain her existence as a separate monarchy. But, the feeble age, and procrastinating or indecisive character of Henry, instead of terminating the contest between the various candidates, left it open to litigation. Catherine, duchess of

January.

Indecision of the cardinal king.

(39) De Thou, vol. viii. p. 362 and 363.

Braganza,

Braganza, daughter of a ſon of the great Emanuel, king of Portugal, appeared to poſſeſs a claim ſuperior to any other. It was, nevertheleſs, conteſted by Anthony, ſon to don Louis, ſecond ſon of Emanuel; and whoſe title would have been indiſputable, if his illegitimacy had not excluded him from the throne. Even this circumſtance, which was not poſitively eſtabliſhed, might have been ſurmounted, if Henry had not conceived for his nephew the moſt implacable averſion. The crown of Portugal had been worn by John the Firſt, notwithſtanding a ſimilar defect in blood; and the people, who pretended to a right of deciſion, where the claim was a doubtful one, were almoſt unanimouſly attached to Anthony. But, the great endowments of every kind, which had raiſed John the Firſt to the throne, and maintained him in it during a long and victorious reign, were not to be found in his deſcendant. Philip the Second, at the head of all the forces of the Spaniſh monarchy, prepared to enter the liſts, as a competitor; and he had, already, before the death of Henry, began to aſſemble troops upon the frontiers (40).

Condition of the Spaniſh monarchy at this period.

Unequal as was the conteſt, it could by no means be regarded as deſperate. The king of Spain, however powerful, had many impediments, internal and foreign, to prevent his exerting with vigor, the reſources that he poſſeſſed. In Arragon, and in Navarre, ſymptoms of diſaffection had appeared. Naples and Milan groaned under the Spaniſh tyranny; while the Netherlands, in open revolt, defied the power, and drained the revenues of Philip. If the Portugueze had been united under any one leader, they might have rendered the attempt to ſubject the kingdom, difficult; perhaps, impoſſible. The fron-

(40) La Clede, Hiſt. de Port. vol. ii. p. 72—89.

CHAP. III. 1580.

tiers towards Estremadura, where the Castilians must necessarily enter, were covered with fortresses, which would delay, or defeat their operations. The clergy, and the people, were zealously disposed to maintain the independance of Portugal; and the nobility, though corrupted and seduced by the promises, or presents of the Catholic king, did not want either valor, or patriotism. But, the dissentions of the kingdom prevented every effort for its preservation, and delivered it over, almost without resistance, to the invaders. The duke of Braganza, timid, and unpopular, tamely bartered the rights which his wife possessed, and opened a negotiation with Philip. That artful prince did not lose the occasion of disarming, and securing so dangerous a rival. The five administrators, or regents, to whom the deceased king had committed by will, the government, till the contested succession should be finally determined, either sold, or abandoned their trust. No effectual opponent appeared, except Anthony; whose title was disputable, and whose authority was not generally acknowledged. The duke of Alva, recalled from his castle, where he had been confined for some time, in a state of disgrace; assumed, at more than seventy years of age, the command of the army, destined to effect the conquest of Portugal. The high military reputation which he had acquired in Flanders; and, perhaps, the severity of his disposition, recommended him to a monarch, who, throughout the whole course of his reign, governed more by terror, than by affection. Wherever the Spanish commander appeared, treachery, fear, or disaffection, opened to him the cities; and he penetrated, almost unopposed, to the gates of Lisbon itself. Having taken St. Ubes, one of the most important fortresses in the kingdom; and, afterwards, by a masterly and rapid movement, having

Dissentions in the kingdom of Portugal.

Entrance of the duke of Alva into Portugal.

June.

His progress.

having crossed his forces over the Tagus, he prepared to invest the metropolis (41).

CHAP. III.

1580.

Under these circumstances of danger and depression, Anthony did not abandon the contest; but, of the many personal qualities indispensable to maintain him against so vast a disparity, he possessed only courage. He even manifested a character deeply tinged with cruelty, treachery, and the most odious, or degrading vices. Incapable of commanding the services, or compelling the attendance of the nobility; he trusted his cause to a licentious populace, who committed every act of violence with impunity, and desolated the capital by their excesses. His army, deficient in discipline, and entirely composed of the vilest of the people, inflamed by the exhortations of monks, scarcely waited to be attacked by the duke of Alva; and after a short resistance, fled on all sides. Lisbon instantly capitulated, and admitted the Spaniards; while Anthony, reduced to wander through the provinces, and concealed by his adherents, at length found means to embark from a kingdom, the misfortunes of which he had only aggravated, by an ineffectual opposition. After eluding every attempt which Philip made to gain possession of his person, and receiving the most incontestable proofs of the disinterestedness and attachment of his countrymen, who disdained the rewards offered by the court of Madrid, for his apprehension; he embarked with a few attendants, from St. Ubes, and landed safely in France (42).

Ineffectual efforts of the prior of Crato.

August.

His flight.

That country was liberated from one of its most formidable enemies, nearly at the same period, by the death of Emanuel Philibert, duke of Savoy. He expired in the vigor of his age, having only attained

Death of Emanuel Philibert, duke of Savoy.

(41) La Clede, vol. ii. p. 89—120. De Thou, vol. viii. p. 221—270.

(42) La Clede, vol. ii. p. 121—128. De Thou, vol. viii. p. 271—280.

CHAP. III. 1580. August.

tained his fifty-second year. Conscious that the indolence and mal-administration of Henry the Third, were rapidly preparing a great revolution in his dominions; Emanuel Philibert already made dispositions for profiting of the dissentions of the kingdom. The death of Bellegarde had frustrated, or, at least, postponed his designs, upon the marquisate of Saluzzo; but, he did not renounce his projects of still further augmenting, and aggrandizing his power, at the expence of France. All his political and ambitious views survived in his son, Charles Emanuel, who succeeded to his father's courage and genius, as well as to his territories. The sixteenth century, fertile in illustrious princes, did not produce any more distinguished, than Emanuel Philibert. His good fortune in re-establishing himself in Savoy and Piedmont, from both of which his predecessor had been expelled, was equalled by his magnanimity, elevation of mind, and talents for government. If we except the intolerant and persecuting spirit, which was more the vice of the age, than of the individual, and which stimulated him to undertake, by violence, the conversion of his Protestant subjects; he was free from almost every defect, which could materially affect the happiness of his people. His superior military talents did not render him less disposed to cultivate the arts of peace; and under his administration, uninterrupted tranquillity was preserved throughout his dominions, while France, the Netherlands, and many of the finest countries of Europe were involved in all the calamities attendant on war. We may regard his reign as the era from which Savoy dates its political existence; and the troubles by which France was soon afterwards agitated, enabled his successor to adopt, and nearly to execute, the most extensive projects of ambition (43).

His character.

(43) Guichenon, Hist. de Savoye, vol. ii. p. 696 and 697. De Thou, vol. viii. p. 230 and 231.

CHAP.

CHAP. IV.

Internal ſtate of France.—Profuſion, and mal-adminiſtration of the king.—Entry of the duke of Anjou into the Netherlands.—His firſt exploits.—He paſſes over into England.—Submiſſion of Portugal to Philip the Second.—The iſlands of Azores adhere to Anthony.—Return of the duke of Anjou to Flanders.—Attempt to aſſaſſinate the prince of Orange, by Jaureguy.—Conſpiracy of Salcede.—Naval expedition to the Azores.—Defeat of Strozzi.—Operations in the Low Countries.—Attempt of the duke of Anjou, upon Antwerp.—Conſequences of it.—Retreat of that prince into France.—Indolence and vices of Henry.—Inſtitution of the penitents.—Symptoms of an inſurrection in France.—Second enterprize againſt the Azores.—Progreſs of the prince of Parma in Flanders.—Death of the duke of Anjou.—Aſſaſſination, and character of the prince of Orange.

CHAP. IV.

1581.

State of France, and of the court.

WHILE, on one hand, the duke of Anjou, having ratified the treaty with the Flemings, aſſembled his forces, in order to enter the Netherlands; and while Philip the Second, in another quarter, prepared to take poſſeſſion of Portugal, already ſubjected; Henry, neither occupied by ſchemes of conqueſt, nor by ſyſtems of legiſlation, abandoned himſelf to a diſgraceful indolence. Equally inſenſible to the incitements of glory, or to the dictates of policy: neglectful of the intereſts, honor, and proſperity of France: improvident even of his own future repoſe, to the enjoyment of which, he made ſo many ſacrifices; he ſaw, without emotion, or effort, the formation of that ſtorm, in which

CHAP. IV. 1581.

which he was eventually ſwallowed up and loſt. The partizans of "the League," reſerving for a more propitious moment, the full diſcloſure and execution of their plan, ſilently laboured to cement and conſolidate all its component parts. The ſterility of the queen of France, and the general opinion diffuſed among the people, of the inaptitude of the king for the duties of marriage, rendered the proſpect of the ſucceſſion uncertain. The duke of Anjou was not yet married; and, even if ſucceſsful in his ſuit to Elizabeth, queen of England, the age of that princeſs made it highly improbable that ſhe ſhould ever have iſſue. Henry, king of Navarre, was equally deſtitute of any legitimate offſpring; and his religion formed, of itſelf, an inſuperable obſtacle to his aſcending the throne. Profiting of ſo many concurring circumſtances, the duke of Guiſe, whoſe ambitious views already ſeem to have embraced the future attainment of the crown itſelf, as a poſſible event; began to diſcloſe a part of his vaſt and extenſive plan. Among the princes of the blood, Charles, cardinal of Bourbon, younger brother of Anthony, and uncle of Henry, kings of Navarre, occupied a diſtinguiſhed rank. Of a limited capacity, and a ſuperſtitious diſpoſition, he was yet by no means inſenſible to the allurements or ſeductions of ambition. Sinking in years, and precluded by the priority of his nephew's pretenſions, from any expectation of attaining to the ſovereignty of France, in caſe of the entire extinction of the reigning houſe of Valois; he lent a ready ear to the ſuggeſtions of the duke of Guiſe, who flattered him, that his adherence of the Catholic faith, rendered him the only prince whom the nation would permit to ſway the ſceptre. Won by theſe artifices, he forgot the antient enmity of his family to the Guiſes, and ſuffered himſelf to be made

Projects of the duke of Guiſe.

He gains the confidence of the cardinal of Bourbon.

made the dupe and instrument of all their purposes (1).

1581. Profusion and misconduct of the king.

Amidst such various and augmenting sources of confusion, the king prosecuted his accustomed diversions, and encreased his ordinary expences. The court was no longer filled with counsellors of state, and antient nobility, as it had been under Henry the Second, and Francis the First. Young and insolent favourites, raised by Henry, and promoted to the highest dignities, military and civil, eclipsed, and expelled the natural attendants on his person. The indecent and unrestrained marks of affection, prostituted on these minions, excited indignation, and were attributed to the most disgraceful motives. Not satisfied with raising Arques and La Valette, to the rank of dukes, and attempting to establish their pre-eminence above the oldest peerages of the kingdom; he destined for them the two princesses of Vaudemont, allied to the house of Lorrain, and sisters to the queen. The first of the two matches was actually accomplished; and Henry presented to the bride, the same portion which was usually given to a princess of France, amounting to three hundred thousand ducats. The marriage of the duke of Epernon was delayed, on account of the youth of the princess, intended for him; but, Henry did not less, by anticipation, order a sum of equal magnitude to be paid to the future husband. Enormous as such prodigality appeared, it was lost in the still greater profusion, exhibited at the celebration of Joyeuse's nuptials, which exceeded twelve hundred thousand ducats (2), and were solemnized with more than royal magnificence (3).

Minions of Henry.

A dissipation of the public treasure, so odious in itself, and which seemed to impeach, not only the

Rapacity and oppression of the government.

(1) De Thou, vol. viii. p. 553.

(2) A sum equal to five hundred thousand pounds sterling.

(3) Etoile, Journ. d'Henry III. p. 130. De Thou, vol. viii. p. 550 and 551.

king's

CHAP. IV. 1581.

king's conduct, but, even the sanity of his intellects, could not be supported, without laying adequate burthens on the people. Every onerous, and oppressive imposition, which the pernicious ingenuity of Italian financiers could devise, was accumulated upon the subject. In defiance of the reluctance and opposition, manifested by the parliament of Paris, a number of new pecuniary edicts, not short of twenty-seven, were registered in one day. By a single edict of the list, twenty places of counsellors were created, in addition to those already existing. Henry was necessitated to appear in person, in order to vanquish the repugnance of the parliament to sanctify such violation of justice and good government. To supply his excesses, and the rapacity of his favourites, venality was openly introduced into the magistrature, the courts of justice, and all the dignities or offices of the kingdom. The patience of the nation, wantonly trampled on, began to be nearly exhausted; and even those, whose loyalty and attachment to the crown remained unshaken, yet foresaw with apprehension the necessary consequence of the vices and profligacy of the sovereign (3).

July.

Exploits of the prince of Parma, in the Netherlands.

During the transactions in France, the Netherlands exhibited a more animating and important scene, on which the attention of Europe was fixed. The superior talents and activity of the prince of Parma began gradually to re-establish on a solid basis, the Spanish power, in all the provinces to the south of the Schelde and the Maese. His inviolable fidelity to his engagements, added to the severity of his discipline, and his consummate military skill, rendered his troops invincible. Having taken Breda, and closely invested Cambray, the states of Flanders and Brabant, terrified at the rapidity of his

(3) Mezerai, vol. ix. p. 233—236. De Thou, vol. viii. p. 55[illegible].

progress,

1581.

progress, loudly invoked the duke of Anjou to accelerate his march to their assistance. That prince having, at length, assembled a body of near ten thousand infantry, and four thousand cavalry, entered Artois, and advanced to the relief of Cambray, which had already suffered the pressure of famine. At his approach, the Spanish commander, whose forces were very inferior in number to those of the French; after having remained for some hours in order of battle, decamped, and retreated towards Bouchain. The event justified this cautious measure, to which, in some degree, may be attributed the subsequent ill success of the duke of Anjou. His army, principally composed of volunteers, and adventurers, equipped for a short and vigorous expedition, and who received no regular pay, was unfit for enterprizes of duration. Licentious, undisciplined, and subsisting principally by plunder, they alienated the people, to whose aid they were arrived; and disbanded, when weary of the campaign (4).

Duke of Anjou enters Artois. August.

State of his army.

The first success of the duke of Anjou was, notwithstanding, such as to awaken the sanguine expectations of his new subjects. He made his triumphal entry into Cambray, as a conqueror, and was received by the inhabitants as their liberator from slavery. The command of the place and of the citadel was conferred by him on Balagny, one of his followers. Pursuing his advantages, he drove the enemy from Arleux and Ecluse, besieged and captured Cateau in Cambresis, and seemed to be ready to penetrate into Brabant. If he could have effected his junction with the forces of the States and of the prince of Orange, so great a superiority might have enabled him to give battle to the prince of Parma, under circumstances highly favorable. But,

His entrance into Cambray.

His troops disband.

(4) Mezerai, vol. ix. p. 238.

already,

CHAP. IV. 1581.

already, his soldiers, disgusted with the delays and impediments interposed to their progress; impressed with little respect, or confidence in their commander; and disdaining all subordination, had deserted their standards. Apprehensive in his turn of being attacked by an enemy, whose vigilance and promptitude were fully known; he retired towards the French frontiers, having lost more than half his cavalry, and nearly an equal number of infantry. Incapable of renewing the attempt on Flanders, and still occupied by his pursuit of Elizabeth, he quitted his army, and passed over into England; to which court Henry the Third had dispatched a magnificent embassy, in the view of facilitating his brother's nuptials. During his absence, the prince of Parma, no longer restrained by the operations of so formidable an opponent, invested Tournay, rendered himself master of the place, after a siege of two months, and spread consternation over every part of Flanders and Brabant (5).

September.

Duke of Anjou passes over into England.

November.

Reduction of Portugal to the obedience of Philip the Second.

Brilliant as was the success of Philip's arms in the Netherlands, conducted by his lieutenants; it was surpassed by the facility, with which, in his own person, he completed the subjection of the Portugueze. Wherever he appeared, the most profound obedience was manifested; and in the assembly of the states of the kingdom, held at Tomar, he was proclaimed king, with all the accustomed solemnities. The crown was declared to be hereditary in his family: an amnesty, from which Anthony, and his principal adherents were excluded, was published; and the privileges of the nation were confirmed. Continuing his progress, the new king entered Lisbon, was inaugurated with pomp, and received by the fickle and credulous populace, with

April.

June. Philip enters Lisbon.

(5) Strada, vol. iii. p. 278—358. De Thou, vol. viii. p. 519—521. Mezerai, vol. ix. p. 236—238.

loud

loud acclamations. His deportment, and meafures on his acceffion, were calculated to footh the difcontent, and to allay the apprehenfions of his fubjects. The duke of Braganza was treated with external marks of confideration: the univerfity of Coimbra, which had diftinguifhed itfelf by the warmeft oppofition to Philip's claims, received, notwithftanding, teftimonies of his protection and forgivenefs. Honors, and employments, were conferred, though with a fparing hand, on fome of the grandees; and the adminiftration was vefted in minifters of talents and difcernment (6).

Submiffion of the Portugueze colonies.

Throughout the vaft dependencies of Portugal, in Afia, Africa, and on the fouthern continent of America, no oppofition was made to a revolution, which reduced the kingdom to a province of the Spanifh monarchy. The numerous colonies on the coaft of Guinea; the garrifons on the fhore of Barbary; Madeira, and the iflands of Cape Verd, fubmitted without a murmur. Ataide, viceroy of the Indies, who might have repelled the utmoft efforts of Philip, acknowledged his title; and the rich fleet returning from Goa, entered the Tagus, and brought to the Spanifh monarch an immenfe acceffion of wealth, at a juncture the moft critical. Amidft fo aftonifhing and general a fubmiffion, the iflands of the Azores alone ventured to refufe obedience to Philip; and with the exception of only one, adhered inflexibly to his competitor. Their pofition in the Atlantic, nearly midway between the old and the new world; together with the utility derived from the refrefhments and fhelter, which they afforded to the fleets from the Indies and Brafil, on their homeward-bound voyages; rendered their poffeffion highly important. Philip, too wife not to be fully fenfible of their value; and too vigilant to

The iflands of the Azores remain firm to Anthony.

(6) La Clede, vol. ii. p. 129—132. De Thou, vol. viii. p. 482—489.

lofe

CHAP. IV. 1581.

lose a moment in attempting to reduce them; sent a squadron, commanded by Valdez, followed by a second, under Figueroa, to effect their conquest. But, the expeditions were completely unsuccessful.—

Repulse of Valdez.

Valdez, repulsed in an attack upon Angra, capital of the island of Tercera, was reduced to fly before the inhabitants, after having sustained a considerable loss. Elated by their victory, they proceeded to the most violent excesses of rage against the Spaniards; nor did Figueroa, discouraged by the recent defeat of his predecessor, venture to renew the experiment. He returned, therefore, to Lisbon, in order to demand supplies; while the insurgents dispatched messengers to Anthony, then in the court of France, to assure him of their inviolable adherence, and to press for instant succour (7).

1582. Consequences of the duke of Anjou's visit to England.

The visit of the duke of Anjou to England, was not accompanied with greater success, than had attended his former attempt to attain the hand of Elizabeth. She received him with every demonstration of amity and affection; permitted the articles respecting their future nuptials, to be discussed; and even proceeded so far as to present him with a ring, in token of her fidelity and consent. But, these deceptive appearances, calculated to answer the political purposes of the queen, and to retard, or prevent an alliance between the French prince and a daughter of Philip the Second; were laid aside, when the object was attained. Wearied, if not disgusted with perpetual procrastination; and pressed by the importunity of the prince of Orange, to revisit the Netherlands, where his presence was so necessary; he took leave of Elizabeth. Escorted by the English fleet, and attended by a number of the nobility, he set sail for the port of Flushing, in Zealand; and after having made a short stay at Mid-

He returns to Flanders.

February.

(7) La Clede, vol. ii. p. 132—135. De Thou, vol. viii. p. 490—494.

dleburg;

1582.

dleburg, capital of the province, he proceeded by sea, to Antwerp. In that city, he was solemnly invested with the dignity of duke of Brabant. The States swore allegiance to him as their rightful sovereign, and delegated to him the prerogatives exercised by their antient masters. He, in return, took an oath to govern by the established laws, and to respect inviolably all their privileges (8).

His investiture.

The general joy, diffused by this happy event, which promised their entire emancipation from the tyranny of Philip the Second, was, notwithstanding, interrupted, and nearly extinguished, by an attempt to assassinate the prince of Orange. Jaureguy, a young Biscayan, allured on one hand, by the rewards which the king of Spain offered; and stimulated by religious enthusiasm, on the other; undertook to execute so detestable a deed. Having chosen the moment when the prince, accompanied by his friends, had risen from table, and was preparing to withdraw into his own apartment, he discharged a pistol ball, which entering under his right ear, passed through his cheek. The wound, though severe, was not mortal: but, the assassin having been put to death by those who were present, in the first transports of their indignation; a suspicion that the French, and even the duke of Anjou himself, had authorized the commission of the act, spread universally through Antwerp. The citizens, who idolized the prince of Orange, ran instantly to arms, and were on the point of taking vengeance on the sovereign whom they had recently elected, before it could be ascertained from what quarter the blow had been aimed. Two accomplices of Jaureguy, Spaniards as well as himself, were either seized and executed, or took refuge in the prince of Parma's camp. The prince of Orange recovered of his

Attempt to assassinate the prince of Orange.

March.

(8) De Thou, vol. viii. p. 600—605. Mezerai, vol. ix. p. 240.

wound;

CHAP. IV.

wound; and the consternation, occasioned by it, insensibly disappeared (9).

1582.

Campaign in the Netherlands.

Meanwhile, the campaign which began to open, produced no events decisive of the fate of the Netherlands. The Spanish general, notwithstanding his consummate knowledge of the art of war, was restrained by the want of forces, from undertaking to attack the enemy. Nor did the duke of Anjou, whose troops were with difficulty retained under their standards, venture to hazard an engagement against a commander, whose reputation inspired terror and respect. In this situation, the prince of Parma, profiting with dexterity of the inroads made by the French on the provinces of Artois and Haynault, and of their inability to provide for their own defence without foreign assistance; obtained the consent of the nobility to demand from Philip the Second, the recal of the Spanish bands. Their request was eagerly granted by the court of Madrid; while the duke of Anjou, with equal impatience, expected a powerful reinforcement from France, under the conduct of the duke of Montpensier (10).

State of France.

That kingdom, since the treaty concluded with the Hugonots, continued to enjoy a fallacious and precarious repose, interrupted at intervals, by disturbances between the Catholics and Protestants, irritated against each other. The king, faintly actuated by sentiments of national glory, rather permitted, than approved, or supported, the enterprizes of his brother. Too indolent, and too timid, to venture on so decisive a measure as an open rupture with the Spanish monarch; he was still induced to lend an indirect assistance to every effort, which might impede, or overturn the course of

Indolence of the king.

(9) Strada, vol. viii. p. 366—370. De Thou, vol. viii. p. 608—614.
(10) Strada, vol. viii. p. 37[illegible]—377. De Thou, vol. viii. p. 607 and 608.

Philip's

Philip's profperity. Deftitute of pecuniary refources; devoured by rapacious favorites; and little inclined to facrifice his own tranquillity, to the gratification of the duke of Anjou's ambitious views in Flanders; Henry liftened with coolnefs to his folicitations, and affected to maintain a ftrict neutrality. But, the king of Spain was neither deceived by his proteftations, nor mollified by his conduct. Taxis, his embaffador at the court of France, had already entered into the deepeft and moft criminal intrigues, with the princes of the family of Guife; and an event, which took place at this period, difclofed in their full extent, the enormity and treafonable nature of their defigns.

Confpiracy of Salcede.

Among the numerous adventurers, whom the profpect of honor or advantage, attracted to the duke of Anjou's court, at Bruges in Flanders, was Nicholas Salcede. He was of Spanifh extraction, had been compelled to fly from France on account of his crimes, and might juftly be fufpected of adherence to the enemies of that country. But, Salcede having offered to the duke a regiment, levied at his own expence, and ready to join the French troops, was received with careffes, and treated with diftinction. The prince of Orange, whofe vigilant and penetrating mind was ever awake to the events that paffed around him; and who had difcovered that Salcede, on his way to Bruges, vifited the prince of Parma's camp; firft entertained doubts concerning his intentions. Enquiry confirmed them; and fome other indications of his guilt appearing, he was arrefted, committed to prifon, and ftrictly interrogated. His voluntary confeffion, made in prefence of the duke of Anjou, revealed a plot fo vaft, complicated, and which involved in it fuch a number of eminent perfons in the court of France, that it was judged indifpenfable to communicate the information to Henry

July. His confeffion.

CHAP. IV. 1582.

the Third (11). That prince, equally terrified and astonished at a disclosure, which so nearly affected his own safety, caused Salcede to be transported to Paris, with every requisite precaution. On the arrival of the criminal, the king directed judges to examine him, and was even present himself, concealed behind a curtain, when he was put to the torture. He varied at different times, in his depositions; denied, retracted, and again confirmed his original assertions; leaving the king and all his ministers, in a state of uncertainty as to the exact truth of many essential circumstances, respecting the conspiracy. But, the existence and reality of a plot, which had for its object the dethronement of Henry, the extermination of the royal family, the introduction of the Spaniards, and the complete destruction of the French monarch, was apparent and demonstrated. It was equally clear, that the Guises, in conjunction with the duke of Lorrain, were its immediate authors: that Philip the Second supported it with all his treasures: that many provinces of the kingdom were engaged in it; and that measures were embraced for carrying it into prompt and vigorous execution. Any other prince than Henry, after so minute a disclosure of the pernicious schemes of his domestic and foreign enemies, would have exerted some vigilance, in endeavouring to prevent their further progress. But, such was his credulous and supine security, that, when his first impressions of terror had subsided, he resumed his ordinary course of amusements, and took no measure for averting the danger with which he was menaced (12).

Security of Henry.

This

(11) Memoires de Nevers, vol. i. p. 569—573.

(12) De Thou, vol. viii. p. 621—636. Mezerai, vol. ix. p. 242—244. Busbeq. de Bong. letter 8th.

The most curious and interesting detail of Salcede's conspiracy, is to be found in De Thou. It is impossible, on a full consideration of all the circumstances,

This fatal and inexplicable apathy was the more censurable, as, notwithstanding his affectation of observing inviolate the peace with Spain, he had attempted to wound the Spanish monarchy in its most vulnerable quarter. Anthony, who claimed the crown of Portugal, after embarking from a

CHAP. IV. 1582. Enterprize against the Azores.

cumstances, to doubt that the duke of Guise had communicated to Salcede the leading facts, respecting the future projects of "the League." Not only a number of persons of the highest quality were enumerated by him, as acquainted with, or implicated in, the treasonable designs against the king, and kingdom: but, even several of those, who had been raised, and peculiarly favoured by Henry. Among these, was the duke of Joyeuse himself. Salcede's retraction may impugn the truth of some facts: but, cannot destroy the evidence of a deep and dangerous intention to subvert the monarchy, and deliver up France to Philip the Second. The conduct of the duke of Guise, and the subsequent disclosure of the principles of his adherents, bear the strongest testimony to the general veracity of Salcede's depositions. The advice given to Henry, by Christopher de Thou, father to the celebrated historian, and who, as first president of the parliament of Paris, was present at the examination of the criminal, was full of wisdom and sagacity. That virtuous and upright magistrate besought the king, to detain Salcede in confinement, and by no means to put him to death, "If," said he, "the intentions attributed to the duke of Guise and his partizans, are false, their future conduct will best evince their innocence: "but, if the allegations of Salcede are true, they will be retained "in awe, by the consciousness of a witness being alive, who is acquainted "with, and can divulge the extent of their criminal projects." Henry was incapable of feeling, or of following, so judicious a mode of action. His indolence, and aversion to trouble, made him desire to forget a subject of such unpleasing reflection; and those of his favorites, or ministers, who had been involved in the accusation, urged the punishment of a traitor and calumniator. He was torn in pieces by horses, and the king was present at his execution.

The death of the first president, de Thou, who only survived this event seven days, was accelerated, if not occasioned, by a deep and melancholy sense of the calamities, which he foresaw were about to overwhelm France; but, which he could not avert. It was in vain, that he warned Henry of the approaching and imminent danger: that infatuated monarch was deaf to his suggestions, or exhortations. De Thou, only a few months preceding, had, with a generous and manly boldness, withstood some of the oppressive taxes, continually imposed by the king; and he had the courage to warn him, that "if those ruinous experiments were repeated, a revolt would be "the infallible consequence." Henry, turning to his courtiers, by whom he was surrounded; said, with contempt, "the poor old man is in his "dotage." But, when, only a few years afterwards, the sedition of Paris began to manifest itself, he discovered the irreparable loss which he had sustained in de Thou. He deplored it with tears; and while, on every side, he only beheld treachery, rebellion, ingratitude, and perfidy, he was frequently heard to exclaim, "he was persuaded, if the first president had been alive, "and at the head of the parliament, an insurrection would never have "taken place in the capital."

 kingdom

CHAP. IV. 1582.

kingdom in which his affairs were desperate, obtained not only an asylum, but, a support, from the generosity of the French king. As his party still subsisted in the islands of the Azores, he earnestly solicited a naval and military force, to effect their complete reduction; and from thence, to make, with advantage, a new attempt to eject Philip from his recent conquest. Catherine of Medicis, whose predominant passion was ambition, and who had not even hesitated, on grounds the most absurd, to lay claim, herself, to the kingdom of Portugal, obtained leave from Henry, to equip, in her own name, an armament adequate to the enterprize. A considerable fleet, on board of which were five thousand soldiers, was fitted out from the harbours of France. The command was entrusted to Philip Strozzi, one of the most intrepid and accomplished officers in the French service; and not only Anthony himself, but, a number of the young nobility eagerly crouded to partake of the honor and danger of the expedition. Philip, attentive to all the motions of so formidable a squadron, instantly prepared to meet it with an equal or superior force. The marquis of Santa Croix sailed from the Tagus, at the head of a numerous and well-appointed fleet, nearly about the same period of time that Strozzi quitted the coast of Brittany: but, the French arriving first at the place of their destination, landed on the island of St. Michael, defeated a body of Spaniards, gained possession of the principal town, and drove the enemy to take refuge in the citadel. If the favorable moment had been vigorously improved, and the garrison, which was in want of provisions, had not been allowed to recover from their consternation, Anthony might have been master of the fortress. Its consequence and importance were beyond calculation; the island of St. Michael being the only one which remained attached to Philip; and the Spanish fleet possessing no other port, or

Naval force equipped, and sent to those islands.

Spanish fleet fitted out by Philip.

June.

15th July.

Success of the French.

or place of refreſhment and retreat. Unfortunately, the occaſion was loſt, while Anthony amuſed himſelf by liſtening to the acclamations of a populace, who ſaluted him king; and the arrival of Santa Croix, in a few days, ſoon changed the aſpect of affairs (13).

CHAP. IV. 1582. 22d July.

Naval victory of the Spaniards.

An engagement became unavoidable between the two fleets, and it was expected by both with equal impatience. The conteſt was long and obſtinate, as the prize was not leſs than the kingdom of Portugal. Strozzi behaved with the utmoſt valour; and if he had been ſuſtained with the ſame firmneſs, muſt have obtained a deciſive victory. But, the ſuperior magnitude of the enemy's ſhips, and the ſeverity of their fire, added to the treachery, or cowardice of ſeveral French commanders, who never came into action, determined the fate of the day. Strozzi, wounded in the knee, and incapable of reſiſtance, was preſented to the Spaniſh admiral, who had the inhumanity to order him to be diſpatched, and his body to be thrown into the ſea. Two thouſand of the French were killed, and eight of their veſſels were captured, on this memorable occaſion. But, the cruelty, exerciſed by the marquis of Santa Croix, on the priſoners, who ſurvived, and who fell into his hands; while it tarniſhed ſo brilliant an atchievement, ſtamped indelible infamy on his name and nation. Theſe unfortunate victims, to the number of near three hundred, among whom were many perſons of quality and reputation, were conducted to Villa Franca, in the iſland of St. Michael. A ſcaffold having been conſtructed in the town, they were all deliberately put to death, with no other diſtinction, except that the officers were beheaded, while the common ſoldiers ſuffered by the halter. To palliate, or juſtify

26th July.

Cruelties, exerciſed by the Spaniſh admiral.

(13) La Clede, vol. ii. p. 135—139. De Thou, vol. viii. p. 578—584.

CHAP. IV. 1582.

an act of such turpitude, the admiral pretended to consider the French as only pirates, or corsairs, acting without any legitimate commission, and wantonly infringing the peace subsisting between the two kings. Even his own troops could not acquiesce in so base and savage a proceeding: they demanded with importunity and tears, that the French might be treated as prisoners of war; but, Santa Croix, inexorable, delivered them over to the executioners; and Philip expressed neither horror, nor indignation, when he received the intelligence (14).

It was the first general engagement fought between any European nations, on the Atlantic, since the discovery of America, by Columbus; and its consequences were decisive of the fate of Portugal.

Incapacity of Anthony.

Anthony, who had not been personally present in the action, took refuge in the island of Tercera, which still adhered to his cause. Inconsolable on hearing the news of Strozzi's defeat, he only recovered from the transports of his grief, to plunge into the most degrading excesses of vice and sensuality. After remaining near two months in this state, irresolute as to his future conduct, and destitute of all resource, he embarked a second time for France: the Spanish admiral, satisfied with his victory, and cautious of remaining too long in an exposed situation, returned in triumph to Lisbon (15).

October.

Affairs of the Low Countries.

While these great events were performed upon the ocean, hostilities continued uninterruptedly in the Netherlands. Reinforced by the Spanish and Italian veterans, the prince of Parma took the field at the head of thirty thousand troops, and attempted to oppose the entry of the French, who, under Montpensier and Biron, having embarked from

(14) La Clede, vol. ii. p. 139—142. Mezerai, vol. ix. p. 247—249. De Thou, vol. viii. p. 585—593.

(15) Mezerai, vol. ix. p. 250.

Calais,

1582.

Hostilities.

August.

Calais, had joined the duke of Anjou, at Dunkirk. The reinforcement which they conducted, did not fall short of eight thousand infantry and cavalry, composed of Switzers and Germans, as well as of the forces of France. The Spanish general, nevertheless, did not hesitate to give them battle; and, even under the cannon of Ghent, to which they retired, he obtained a considerable advantage: but, the approach of winter, and the difficulty of subsisting two armies in a country already exhausted, produced an involuntary cessation of hostilities. Notwithstanding the exertions made by Philip, to enable the prince of Parma to push the war with vigor, and the great augmentations of soldiery which he had received, he found himself involved in almost insurmountable embarrassments. The court of Madrid, attentive to the preservation of Portugal, and occupied in the Azores, did not remit to the Low Countries, sufficient sums for the payment of the numerous forces acting in that quarter. The provinces of Haynault and Artois, from which the principal supplies of provisions were derived, could no longer furnish resources. Famine desolated the Spanish camp, and reduced its numbers; while the duke of Anjou, master of the rich tract extending from Ghent to Antwerp, and receiving constant succors from England and France by means of the sea, was not exposed to similar distress; and might open the ensuing campaign with a prospect of decisive advantages. But, all these flattering appearances, which would probably have been realized in a few months, were completely overturned by his own rashness, folly, and presumption (16).

Critical state of the Netherlands.

(16) Strada. vol. iii. p. 394—407. De Thou, vol. viii. p. 640. Mezerai, vol. ix. p. 252 and 253.

Henry

CHAP. IV. 1583.

Apathy of Henry.

Henry the Third, who, on account of the danger with which he was perſonally menaced by the conſpiracy of Salcede, rather than from public conſiderations, had evinced ſome degree of emotion, at that event; was little affected by the defeat and cataſtrophé of Strozzi. Inſenſible to national glory or ſhame, he neither betrayed reſentment, nor attempted to take vengeance for ſo cruel an outrage. Equally indiſpoſed to embrace the favorable occaſion which preſented itſelf, for diminiſhing the power of Philip in the Netherlands; he refuſed to liſten to the entreaties and ſolicitations of his brother, who implored his aſſiſtance. The duke of Anjou had already expended his revenues, and even contracted an immenſe debt, in the proſecution of his enterprize in Flanders. Every motive of affection, honor, and intereſt, dictated to the king to ſupport him in an attempt, ſo beneficial to France, and ſo injurious to Spain. He was well aware, that the court of Madrid, far from reſpecting either alliances of blood, or the faith of treaties, had kindled, and continued to feed the flame of civil diſſentions in his own dominions. Even the laws of nations, and of humanity, had been violated in the treatment of the unfortunate priſoners, taken at the Azores. Yet, ſo many conſiderations could not rouſe him to exertion, nor induce him to quit the diſgraceful and ruinous ſloth, in which he was ſunk. Far from extending the neceſſary aid to his brother, which might have enabled him to become maſter of the Netherlands, and to encloſe the prince of Parma between two ſuperior armies; his ſavorites dictated to him a language of inſult, in all his replies. The new duke of Brabant was adviſed to take warning by the fate of his predeceſſor, Mathias; who, after having been invited by the Flemings, to aſſume their government and protection, had been diſgracefully ſent back to Vienna. It was added, that when the duke had repreſſed the

His neglect of the duke of Anjou.

inſolent

CHAP. IV. 1583.

insolent audacity of his subjects, extended the narrow limits of his authority, and secured its permanency by the seizure of some fortresses or cities of Flanders; it might then be expedient and practicable, to mix the sovereign and kingdom of France in his quarrel (17).

Condition of that prince's affairs.

Insinuations and exhortations of such a nature, however originating in aversion or contempt, found too easy an access to the heart of a prince, corrupted by flattery, wounded by refusals, and stimulated by necessity. On repeated occasions, he had experienced the insolence of the Flemings; and at the assassination of the prince of Orange by Jaureguy, his own person, and those of all his countrymen, had been in the most imminent peril, from the suspicions entertained of his having authorized, or permitted the attempt. Continual disputes and altercations arose between the French and their allies, who, far from coalescing cordially, though engaged in one common pursuit, regarded each other almost as enemies. The duke himself, surrounded by unprincipled and profligate men, who continually held up to him the comparison between the unlimited prerogative of a king of France, and the contracted power delegated to him as duke of Brabant; inflamed and propelled him to encrease it by every means.

He determines to seize the principal cities of Flanders.

Yielding to these natural, but, pernicious suggestions, he, without communicating his design to Montpensier, or Biron, who might have dissuaded him from so treacherous a breach of faith; gave orders to seize, on the same day, a number of places in Flanders. The enterprize was facilitated by the confidence reposed in the French, as auxiliaries; and it was completely successful in the towns of Dunkirk, Dixmude, Alost, Menin, Vilvorden, and Dendermonde: but, at Ostend, and at Bruges, the conspiracy was

(17) Mezerai, vol. ix. p. 253 and 254.

rendered

CHAP. IV. 1583. 18th January. Attempt upon Antwerp;

rendered abortive. Having reserved to himself the conduct of the attempt upon Antwerp, as the most important and arduous, he marched out of the city on the day appointed, under the pretence of reviewing his forces, who were encamped in the neighbourhood. When he had reached the gate, the officers who accompanied him, began the onset; and the duke continuing his route to the camp, exhorted the troops to enter Antwerp, and to make themselves masters of the place. They obeyed with alacrity; and while their comrades seized on the cannon, they pushed forward to share in the pillage of so opulent a city. But, their own security was fatal to the enterprize; and some suspicions having been previously entertained of an intention to introduce the French, the citizens sounded the alarm, and rose in arms. The prince of Orange, who occupied the citadel, informed of the event, put himself at the head of a body of soldiers, attacked Fervaques, who commanded the duke of Anjou's troops, took him prisoner, and committed him to custody. Dispirited by the loss of their chief, his followers gave way on all sides; and as the croud was such at the gate by which they had originally entered, that it became impossible to retreat, a prodigious slaughter ensued. Numbers were suffocated by the pressure of their companions; and it was long, before the rage of the people, justly excited by such an act of perfidy, permitted any quarter to be extended. Yet, equally placable when all farther resistance had ceased, they evinced the utmost humanity in the treatment shewn to the wounded, and preserved the survivors from injury. About one hundred citizens fell in the affray; but on the other side, more than twelve hundred individuals perished, among whom were many persons of distinction (18).

unsuccessful

Carnage of the French.

(18) De Thou, vol. ix. p. 32—40. Mezerai, vol. ix. p. 255—258. Busbeq. de Bongars, letters 14 and 15. Strada, vol. iii. p. 412—425.

During

Conduct of the duke of Anjou.

During the commission of this tragical scene, the duke of Anjou, little prepared for its issue, remained at an inconsiderable distance from the walls, and already anticipated the possession of Antwerp. He was accompanied by his principal officers, many of whom highly condemned the proceeding, as equally dishonorable and destructive. The cannon of the city, pointed against him, and the sight of numbers of French, who precipitated themselves from the ramparts, in order to effect their escape, conveyed to the duke the first intelligence of the ill success of his attempt. Confused, and covered with shame, he instantly withdrew to his camp; from whence he dispatched letters to the States, extenuating the act; imputing it to the treatment which he had received, and the indignities that he had suffered; protesting his affection for the Flemings, and his repentance for the attack made on their freedom. No answer was returned; nor would the Senate, though urged by the prince of Orange to send supplies of provisions to the French army, permit any to be conveyed for several days. Such was their indignation, that they even caused the sluices to be opened, inundated the whole country, and thereby reduced the duke to the last extremity of danger and famine. He was compelled, by a circuitous and hazardous march, to gain Dendermonde, where he did not arrive, without having lost many of his soldiers (19).

He retreats to Dendermonde.

Consequence of these proceedings.

The consternation and resentment, excited in Flanders and Brabant, by so daring an invasion of their liberties, from a quarter to which the people naturally looked for protection and support, was general, and difficult to erase. Its effects were as subversive of the independance of those provinces, as they were ruinous to the newly-acquired dominion of the duke of Anjou. Mutual confidence between

(19) De Thou, vol. ix. p. 40—44.

the

CHAP. IV. 1583.

the two nations, was not only extinct; but, enmity and rancour subsisted in their place. The prince of Parma, relieved by so unexpected an interposition of fortune, from his pecuniary distresses, and from the difficulty of taking the field against superior forces; profited of the event, to open a negotiation with the revolted cities, and offered them, in the name of their antient sovereign, an amnesty for every offence, together with the most favorable conditions. These proposals, operating on minds inflamed by recent injury, and implacable against their late allies, were eventually productive of no inconsiderable effect (20).

Efforts made to effect a reconciliation.

Every effort was, notwithstanding, made to heal the wound, and to prevent the fatal consequences of a final rupture between the two parties. Henry the Third himself, alarmed at the effects which such an event might occasion, by the contumely and degradation in which it involved the name and nation of France, sent embassadors to mediate an accommodation. The prince of Orange, although included personally in the attempt of the duke of Anjou, which was levelled as much against him, as against the city of Antwerp; yet, displayed equal magnanimity and wisdom, in the advice given by him to the States. In a beautiful and masterly address, he enumerated the dangers annexed to every other mode of conduct; the impossibility of submitting anew to Philip the Second; the inability of the Flemings to sustain a contest with so powerful a monarch, unless assisted by foreign states; and the prodigious advantages derived from the co-operation and support of a French prince, presumptive heir to the crown. These weighty considerations, added to the danger of the duke's delivering up to the Spaniards the

(20) Strada, vol. iii. p. 426—433. De Thou, vol. ix. p. 43 and 44.

places

places of which he was in possession, if driven to despair, produced a treaty; but could not obliterate the recollection of so perfidious a breach of honor and humanity. It was stipulated, that he should repair immediately to Dunkirk, there to await a final reconciliation; and that Dendermonde, as well as Dixmude, should be surrendered to the States; who, on their parts, engaged to restore his baggage, and all the prisoners taken at Antwerp, without ransom. A mutual oblivion of every past event, formed the concluding article of the accommodation (21).

1583. 2d April. Treaty of oblivion concluded.

The terms were executed on the part of the duke, without delay; but, the States manifested in all their movements, a sentiment of insurmountable aversion to the French. They even permitted it to operate to the prejudice and ruin of their own affairs; which, no longer supported by any confidence in their allies, became daily more perplexing and alarming. Encouraged by such proofs of disunion, the prince of Parma recommenced his military operations, and acquired the most decisive advantages; while Biron, who commanded the troops of France, was impeded, or checked in every attempt. No cordial forgiveness took place; nor could any assurances of contrition and sorrow, on the part of the duke of Anjou, affect a reunion with his offended subjects. That misguided prince, dejected in mind, fallen from his elevation, abandoned in a great measure, by his brother, and become an object of derision to the Spaniards; after languishing near two months at Dunkirk, embarked for France. The city was immediately invested by the enemy, and surrendered in a few days. Biron, who might have compelled them to raise the siege, was not permitted to march to its rescue, from the jealousy and distrust

Resentment of the Flemings.

Return of the duke of Anjou into France. 28th June.

(21) De Thou, vol. ix. p. 45—54. Busbeq. de Bong. letters 15 and 16.

of

CHAP. IV.

1583.

Rapid progress of the prince of Parma.

of the Flemings. The prince of Parma rapidly made himself master of Dixmude, and Nieuport; menaced Ostend; besieged Ypres; and already approached Antwerp itself. Ghent, the inhabitants of which had been the most eager to invoke the assistance of the French; with the inconstancy always characteristic of their conduct, were the first to betray a disposition to return to the obedience of Spain. The people of Antwerp, irritated personally against the duke of Anjou, arose tumultuously on the slightest pretences, and were scarcely to be restrained from taking vengeance on those of his countrymen, who remained in Flanders. To augment their discontent, the Spanish general quartered his troops in their immediate vicinity, which had long been exempt from military ravage and contribution. The popularity of the prince of Orange himself, could not be maintained against the tide of obloquy and ill fortune; nor was he exempt from the severest animadversions, for his attachment to the French alliance. Warned by the symptoms of so serious a change in the opinions of the people, he determined to withdraw into Zealand; a resolution which he speedily executed. After his departure, he continued to exhort the Flemings to retain Biron, who still commanded a considerable body of troops; and he dispatched messengers to the principal cities, to enforce its expediency. But, all exertions were fruitless, to vanquish the resentment for injuries so deep and recent: a decree was issued, enjoining the French to quit the Low Countries: and Biron, in compliance with it, embarking his forces, joined the duke of Anjou soon afterwards in the neighbourhood of Cambray, where he attempted to re-assemble an army. Such was the unfortunate termination of an enterprize, which had for its object the transfer of the Netherlands to a prince of France; and which, conducted by a skilful and able hand, might have

Retreat of the prince of Orange into Zealand.

July.

August.

Evacuation of the Low Countries, by the French.

have materially affected and changed the face of Europe. The precipitation and treachery of the sovereign whom the Flemings had elected, overturned the foundations of his future grandeur; and by a natural transition, operated powerfully in facilitating the final return of the Low Countries, to the obedience of Philip the Second (22).

Fermentation in France.

While these sinister events took place in Flanders, the seeds of civil dissention, under the misguided and pusillanimous management of the king, were attaining rapidly to maturity in France. The exertions which he had made in order to extricate his brother, and to re-establish the harmony that had subsisted previous to the attempt upon Antwerp, had neither been produced by affection, nor esteem.

Incapacity, and misconduct of Henry.

On the contrary, Henry, only anxious to prolong his indolent and dissipated mode of life, regarded the projects of the duke of Anjou as subversive of his own repose, to which he sacrificed every consideration of public honor, or utility. Instead of correcting, and amending the errors, which had rendered him justly an object of aversion, or of contempt, to his people; all the vices of his character acquired force, as he advanced in age. Taxes, multiplied and augmented, far from enriching the royal treasury, left him needy, and incapable of opposing the designs of his enemies. The factions of his court and kingdom became annually more visible, and appeared to hasten to a crisis.

His feeble precautions, and measures.

Terrified at the prospect, and conscious that he had no refuge in the attachment or veneration of his subjects; he tried to find an asylum in the majesty of the throne itself. He encreased his guards; no longer appeared in public, as he had been accustomed, without attendants; and attempt-

(22) Strada, vol. iii. p. 435—452. Mezerai, vol. ix. p. 260—262. De Thou, vol. ix. p. 55—61. Busbeq. letters 17—24. passim. D'Aub. Hist. Univ. vol. ii. p. 475—477.

CHAP. IV. 1583.

ed, if he could not conciliate affection, to inspire fear, in all those who approached his person. Wearied, or disgusted, at the fetters imposed on his freedom by those precautions, he soon desisted from them, and plunged anew into amusements, or dissipation. Yet, anxious to acquire, or to retain some place in the love of the lower orders of the nation, he affected an exterior of devotion, and even gave a sanction, by his example, to the most absurd practices of superstition.

Institution of the confraternities of penitents.

The confraternities of penitents, which, in the beginning of his reign, he had seen at Avignon; and which the remonstrances of the magistrates of Paris, and of the most respectable members of the parliament, had hitherto prevented from finding an entrance into the metropolis; were introduced, and established. These pious mummeries, subversive of real piety, injurious to moral observances, and destructive of all obedience to the laws, became the perpetual occupation and entertainment of the inhabitants of the capital. The members, composing them, were, by the king's express authority, formed into a regular body; and statutes, published with solemnity, were framed for their regulation. Henry, in person, accompanied by the Papal nuntio, the princes of the blood, and the courtiers, assisted at the processions. The chancellor of France, the keeper of the seals, and the first magistrates, did not hesitate to mix in the cavalcade, covered with sacks, their faces concealed, and in the most inclement weather. Many disorders and irregularities, equally contrary to religion and to decency, found shelter under so convenient a disguise; and the people, instead of being edified, or amended, by such spectacles, grew more licentious, and manifested their contempt of civil order. Far from attaining the object, for which he had set on foot the confraternities, Henry became only more universally despised.

Processions. March.

spised. The contrast of debauchery and excess, which he had exhibited in the company of his minions, only a few days preceding, and before the eyes of the same people, served to expose him to the severest censure. Hypocrisy was added by his enemies to the list of all his other vices; and those who attributed to devout sentiments or impressions, his attendance on the processions of the Flagellants, did not less severely reprobate such conduct, as unbecoming his dignity and situation. Even the clergy, who might, from obvious motives, have been disposed to see his actions through a favorable medium, yet declaimed against his character; and the pulpits of Paris already resounded with the language of insolence and sedition (23).

CHAP. IV. 1583. Contempt of the royal dignity and authority.

Numerous symptoms of an approaching and serious insurrection began to appear; though such was the indolence and infatuation of the king, that they made little impression, and produced no change, in his system. Publications, derogatory to the title of his family, as derived from Hugh Capet; and calculated to impress the people with an opinion of the great validity of the pretensions of the house of Lorrain to the crown of France, as being descended from Charlemagne; were industriously circulated. The injudicious, and mistaken clemency of Henry, who did not punish the authors of such inflammatory, or treasonable productions, with the severity that they merited, encreased the evil. He even abased himself so far, as to authorize a refutation of the attack, made on his right to the crown of France; and by so undignified a mode of proceeding, he necessarily inspired his enemies with greater audacity (24).

Symptoms of popular commotion.

(23) De Thou, vol. ix. p. 66—69. L'Etoile, Jour. d'Henry III. p. 157 and 158. Mezerai, vol. ix. p. 262 and 263.

(24) L'Etoile, p. 162 and 163. De Thou, vol. ix. p. 70—72.

CHAP. IV. 1583.

Power and ascendancy of the minions.

The effect of so many causes, combining to shake his power, was heightened by the unlimited ascendancy obtained over him by his favorites. It seemed to partake of insanity, and was neither moderated by considerations of propriety, nor even of practicability. He was principally anxious to divide his bounty between Joyeuse and Epernon, with so equal a hand, that no degree of jealousy, or rivality, might interrupt their felicity, and diminish their mutual friendship. Joyeuse having conceived the design of acquiring the important and extensive government of Languedoc, possessed by Montmorenci; but, unable to procure his renunciation or dismission; ventured on a singular expedient, in order to attain his object. He went, in person, to the court of Rome, and endeavoured to induce Gregory the Thirteenth, to issue an excommunication against the marshal, as a protector and abettor of the Hugonots. His request was rejected by the pontiff, who penetrated the motives of Joyeuse's visit, and knew how to appreciate the conduct of Montmorenci, in forming connections with the Protestants. To compensate for the mortification attending the refusal, Henry, on his return, gave him the government of Normandy, which, from its magnitude and consequence, had usually been divided into four separate departments, and entrusted to lieutenants. Epernon received those of Boulogne, and of Mentz (25).

Journey of the duke of Joyeuse to Rome.

Ineffectual attempts to raise supplies.

Every measure, adopted by the king, in order to recover his popularity, or to impress the nation with a favorable opinion of his character and intentions, only served to evince his want of judgment, and was completely ineffectual. Under the plausible pretence of hearing and redressing the grievances of

(25) Mezerai, vol. ix. p. 264 and 265. De Thou, vol. ix. p. 74—80.

the

the people; but, in fact, with a view to derive supplies from their generosity, he dispatched commissioners into many of the provinces, selected from the nobility and clergy. They exposed the wants of the crown; magnified, and extolled the affection of Henry for his subjects; but, concluded with demanding contributions: their mission was equally fruitless and injurious. An assembly, composed of delegates, which was designed to point out remedies to the various evils in the courts of justice, and the administration of the finances, was not attended with more beneficial consequences. Propositions for abolishing venality in judicial employments, and for the diminution of taxes, were offered; but no alteration was effected (26).

Second expedition to the Azores.

Anthony, the titular and unfortunate king of Portugal, continued earnestly to solicit another enterprize for the reduction of the Azores, and his subsequent re-establishment in the throne from which he had been expelled. Henry, in compliance with the exhortations of his mother Catherine, and of the duke of Joyeuse; rather than from any inclination to undertake so perilous an attempt, permitted a squadron to be equipped at Dieppe. It consisted of a few ships, on board of which were embarked six hundred troops. They reached the island of Tercera, where Emanuel de Sylva still remained in the interests of the exiled king; and being joined by the survivors of Strozzi's army, added to a number of Portugueze and natives, they prepared for their defence. Philip, anxious to crush a rebellion, from which his new conquest might receive a fatal blow, dispatched the marquis of Santa Croix, at the head of sixty galeasses, gallies, and vessels of various dimensions. Near twelve thousand Spanish, Italian,

Fleet of Spain sent to those islands.

(26) Mezerai, vol. ix. p. 268—270. De Thou, vol. ix. p. 81 and 82.

CHAP. IV. 1583.

and German soldiers, accompanied him; furnished with every thing which could facilitate the entire accomplishment of the expedition. The event corresponded to the preparations. Disunion and jealousy impeded the operations of the French and Portugueze. Sylva, having separated from his allies, and even offered to betray them, in order to obtain his own pardon, no possibility remained of contending against so unequal a force. De Chatte, an officer of approved courage and fidelity, who commanded the troops of France, finding his situation desperate, capitulated on honorable terms; and Santa Croix, content with atchieving the great object of the war, did not violate the conditions. Sylva, delivered up by his own adherents, suffered the punishment of rebellion; and Philip exercised the severest vengeance on the inhabitants of Tercera, who had so long defied his power, and endangered his tranquillity. No further attempt was made in any part of the Portugueze dominions, to shake off the yoke of Spain; and the unsuccessful issue of the French armament, only tended to decry the administration, by which it had been fitted out and devoted to certain destruction (27).

August.

Complete reduction of the rebels.

1584.

Prosperous condition of the Spanish affairs in Flanders.

While Philip triumphed on the Atlantic, his arms were advancing rapidly in Flanders. The conspiracy of the duke of Anjou against the liberties of Antwerp, may be regarded as an æra, from which the affairs of the Netherlands constantly declined. Every endeavour to retard, or to avert its consequences, was rendered ineffectual by the resentment of the Flemings, and the promptitude of the prince of Parma. That celebrated commander improved his advantages, with vigor and celerity. Having invested Ypres, and compelled the place to capitu-

12th April.

(27) La Clede, vol. ii. p. 149—155. De Thou, vol. ix. p. 93—104.

late,

late, he ſoon afterwards became maſter of Bruges, which ſubmitted on favorable conditions. Ghent, ſhaken by inteſtine diviſions, already prepared to follow the example; and the navigation of the Scheld, which was greatly impeded, rendered the preſervation of Antwerp more than doubtful (28).

CHAP. IV. 1584. 26th May.

Negotiations opened by the Flemings, with the duke of Anjou.

In theſe diſtreſsful circumſtances, the States, yielding to the wiſe counſels of the prince of Orange, diſpatched deputies to wait on the duke of Anjou, with aſſurances of their diſpoſition to ratify a new treaty, and to ſubmit to his orders. But, that prince was no longer in a ſituation to liſten to the dictates of ambition. From the period of his quitting the Low Countries, a ſenſe of his miſconduct, and remorſe for its effects, had conſtantly purſued him. Oppreſſed with ſhame, and uncertain of his future operations, he avoided ſociety, and abandoned himſelf to dejection. After paſſing ſome months in retirement, he ſuddenly and unexpectedly appeared again at court, with a few attendants. A reconciliation was mediated between him and his brother, by Catherine of Medicis; and the duke returning to the caſtle of Chateau Thierry on the Marne, was ſoon afterwards attacked by ſymptoms of a very alarming nature. A violent effuſion of blood from all the paſſages of his body, cauſed by the effects of a cough, reduced him to ſo languid a ſtate, that he expired in a few weeks. The nature and circumſtances of his diſtemper, though probably natural, gave riſe to ſuſpicions of poiſon, in an age when that crime was familiar. His death was the ſignal of civil war, and liberated the partizans of "the League" from all further diſguiſe, or neceſſity of obſerving meaſures with the crown. Notwithſtanding the defects and weakneſſes of his character, he was not deſtitute of generous qualities; and during

11th Feb.

1ſt May.

His death.

10th June.

His character.

(28) Strada, vol. iii. p. 465—476. De Thou, vol. ix. p. 173—181.

his

CHAP. IV. 1584.

his last illness, he manifested a deep concern for the fate of those, who having contributed to enable him to undertake the enterprize of Flanders, were, by his decease, reduced to poverty and distress. He even, by his last will, addressed to the king, earnestly, though vainly, besought of Henry to discharge his pecuniary obligations, which were immense. Of all his acquisitions in the Low Countries, only Cambray remained; and he bequeathed it to his brother, as a bulwark to Picardy and Champagne against the Spanish power. But, Henry, fearful of giving to Philip a pretext for war, if he openly took the city under his protection, permitted his mother to retain it, as if devolved to her by inheritance. From similar motives, the council did not venture to qualify the deceased prince by the titles of duke of Brabant, and count of Flanders, at the solemnity of his funeral obsequies (29).

Assassination of the prince of Orange.

The duke of Anjou's death was speedily followed by a blow, still more alarming to the independance of the Flemings. The crime which Jaureguy had not been able to accomplish, was perpetrated by another assassin; and Philip, at length, reaped the detestable fruits of his proscription of the prince of Orange. That eminent and illustrious person, who had escaped the poniards of so many enemies, and the greater part of whose life had been passed in opposing the tyranny of Spain, fell by the hand of a desperate fanatic. He was shot with three balls, discharged from a pistol, as he rose from table, in the city of Delft, his most frequent residence. Balthazar Gerard, a subject of the king of Spain, and an emissary of the prince of Parma, was the murderer; and in the midst of the torments inflicted on him, he gloried in his crime. The prince survived

10th July.

(29) L'Etoile, Jour. p. 173 and 177—179. Mezerai, vol. ix. p. 274 and 275. De Thou, vol. ix. p. 181—184. Busbeq. letters 33, 34, 35, 37, 38, and 39. D'Aub. Hist. Univ. vol. ii. p. 422 and 423.

the

the wound only a few moments, and expired amid the tears and lamentations of his family, who were spectators of so tragical a scene.

1584. Character of that prince.

The desolation, occasioned by his loss, throughout the provinces of Holland and Zealand, was proportioned to the magnitude of the calamity. The people already anticipated their subjection to the Spanish yoke, and dreaded their own slavery, as inseparably connected with the death of their protector. In prudence, fortitude, moderation, firmness, and all the talents requisite to form the head of a vast and powerful combination, he exceeded any of his contemporaries. His military capacity was far inferior to that of the prince of Parma; but, the universality of his genius, and the depth of his resources, enabled him to sustain, and to surmount, all the efforts of the Spanish monarchy. Invincible under adverse fortune, he rose more formidable from his defeats; and to his unremitted exertions, the republic of Holland was indebted for its freedom, and its existence. The gratitude of the people whom he had saved from tyranny, was on the point of conferring on him the sovereignty of their country, when his death took place; and as the best proof of their veneration for his services, they elected his son, Maurice, although scarcely past the limits of childhood, governor of Holland, Zealand, Friesland, and Utrecht; to which was added the dignity of high admiral. By an instance of felicity, rare in the history of mankind, he inherited almost all the great endowments of his father; excelled him in talents for war; and during the course of a life, distinguished by brilliant atchievements, he confirmed and cemented the liberty, to which William, prince of Orange, had given birth (30).

Gratitude of the Dutch for his services.

(30) De Thou, vol. ix. p. 184—189. Strada, vol. iii. p. 480—487. Mezerai, vol. ix. p. 276.

CHAP. V.

State of France, at the time of the duke of Anjou's death.—Ineffectual attempt of Henry, to induce the king of Navarre to renounce his religion.—Preparations of the duke of Guise, for taking up arms.—Support, given by Catherine of Medicis, to his ambitious projects.—Irresolution of Henry.—Treaty of Joinville.—Sovereignty of the Low Countries, offered to the king of France—Rejected by him.—First enterprizes of "the League."—Timidity of the king.—Treaty of Nemours.—War, declared against the Protestants.—Manifesto of the king of Navarre.—Junction of the Protestants with Montmorenci.—Accession of Pope Sixtus the Fifth.—He excommunicates the king of Navarre.—Reply of that prince.—Commencement and progress of hostilities.—Unsuccessful attempt of the prince of Condé, on Angers.—Affairs of the Low Countries.—Surrender of Antwerp.—Queen of England accepts the protection of the Dutch.

CHAP. V.

1584.

Condition of France, at this period.

BEFORE we enter upon that portion of the reign of Henry the Third, at which the wars of "the League" may be properly faid to commence, it is indifpenfable to take a general view of the ftate of the court, and of the kingdom of France. Many caufes had hitherto conduced to retard, and to delay the operations of the confederacy, begun at Peronne in 1576; and the undoubted, though concealed, object of which, was the deftruction of the monarchy. Henry had, in fome meafure, difarmed it, at an early period of its exiftence, by adopting, and declaring himfelf its chief. The meafure, however unbecoming the dignity of the throne, and the character

character of the common father and protector of every denomination of his subjects; yet, had enabled him to guide and controul a machine, too powerful to be destroyed by open force. The Hugonots, feeble, disunited, and excluded from dignities and employments, excited little apprehension: while, their leader, the king of Navarre, banished to a distant province; deprived of authority, even in his own government of Guienne; and destitute of any prospect of succeeding to the crown, was neither an object of alarm to his enemies, nor of attention to the nobility and people. Almost all the youth of France, and the most turbulent or discontented spirits, had found occupation beyond the limits of the kingdom, during the expeditions of the duke of Anjou to the Netherlands. Even, in the event of Henry's death without male issue, the Catholic religion could not be endangered, while his brother, whose adherence to the faith of his ancestors was unimpeached, and who was only in the flower of his age, survived, to ascend the throne.

CHAP. V. 1584.

But, all these circumstances, so important to the preservation of general tranquillity, were completely overturned by the decease of the duke of Anjou. No barrier was any longer opposed to the eventual succession of the king of Navarre, which the nation regarded as certain, from the supposed inaptitude of Henry for the purposes of marriage. That prince, without waiting till his brother's eyes were closed, and during the state of extenuation which preceded his death, had already dispatched the duke of Epernon into Gascony. He was authorized to offer the king of Navarre the most advantageous conditions, if he would renounce his adherence to the Protestant religion, and repair to court without delay. A public declaration of his right to succeed to the crown, in case of Henry's failure of issue male, accompanied with every mark of

Consequences of the duke of Anjou's death.

May. Embassy of Epernon.

CHAP. V.

of regard and diſtinction, were the inducements propoſed, to obtain his acquieſcence (1).

1584.

Situation of the king of Navarre.

No ſituation could be more embarraſſing than that of the king of Navarre. Whether he accepted or rejected the propoſals made him, he beheld difficulties of no common magnitude. To abandon at once his religion, and thoſe faithful followers who had never forſaken him under every reverſe of fortune: to return to a capital and a palace, ſtained with the blood of his friends, and in which he had, himſelf, been ſo long detained a priſoner: to commit his life, his honor, and his intereſts, to the mercy of a prince, whoſe weakneſs, flexibility, and facility, he well knew; were alarming reflexions. On the other hand, the crown of France appeared to ſolicit his acceptance, and to juſtify, if not to demand, every ſacrifice, even of conſcience, for its attainment. His renunciation of the Hugonot faith and worſhip, could alone qualify him to wear it with ſafety; and would inſtantly remove the ſcruples of thoſe zealous Catholics, who might otherwiſe diſpute his title. Even the Guiſes and their partizans muſt be unable to oppoſe with effect his right of blood, when no longer weakened by the ſtain of hereſy; and the public felicity, paramount to every other conſideration, rendered his apoſtacy not only venial, but, in ſome meaſure, meritorious. If this important queſtion had been only decided on grounds of policy and expediency, it is probable that the latter alternative would have been predominant. But, in an age, when theological controverſy heated the minds of men, and when mutual injuries had rendered them tenacious of their opinions, arguments drawn from Scripture, were oppoſed to motives of ſtate neceſſity. The king of Navarre, after long heſitation, and mature delibera-

He rejects the offers of Henry.

July.

(1) Buſbeq. letters 37, 38, 39, and 40. L'Etoile, p. 176. De Thou, vol. ix. p. 198 and 199.

tion,

tion, rejected the proposition brought by Epernon: he qualified, at the same time, his refusal, by protestations of his duty and allegiance to Henry; by assurances of his gratitude for the mark of royal favor extended to him; and by the offer of all the forces of his party, to sustain the crown against their common enemies (2).

CHAP. V. 1584.

Although the result of Epernon's embassy was immediately rendered public by the Protestants themselves, yet it afforded a pretext to the adherents of "the League," to accuse Henry of intentions, the most hostile to the preservation and maintenance of the antient religion. They asserted, that, far from exhorting the king of Navarre to abjure his errors, Epernon had, on the contrary, been only dispatched, in order to conclude a treaty with him, for the extermination of all the adherents of the Catholic faith. Under this fictitious pretence, they proceeded to adopt measures, little removed from an avowed insurrection. Troops were silently collected in different provinces: chiefs were named and appointed, who, on a signal given, were to repair to their destination; and every movement of the confederates evinced a rebellion as imminent and inevitable (3). The feeble and pusillanimous conduct of the king, at a moment which demanded vigorous and decisive counsels, gave courage to his enemies, while it exposed the throne to insult and contempt. Far from meeting a danger that he could no longer disguise, or avoid, with firmness; he scarcely ventured to express his sense of its existence, or resentment at its approach. A proclamation, forbidding all confederations, or levies, on pain of treason, which he issued at this period, formed a

Conduct of the chiefs of the League.

Pusillanimity of the king.

December.

(2) Vie du Duc d'Epernon, vol. i. p. 85—91. Memoires de Villeroy, vol. ii. p. 77—175. De Thou, vol. ix. p. 198—200. Davila, p. 520—523.

(3) De Thou, vol. ix. p. 200 and 201. Mezerai, vol. ix. p. 280.

very

CHAP. V. 1584.

very insufficient barrier against a formidable faction, armed with the sanction of religion, supported by foreign powers, and conducted under leaders of equal intrepidity and talents.

Qualities, and character of the duke of Guise.

Henry, duke of Guise, the real chief of the League, and who exclusively directed all its motions, was supremely the object of popular idolatry. Concealing his personal ambition, under the mask of zeal: retaining in his own bosom the secret of his ultimate views and only divulging, even to his nearest relations, a portion of his intentions: rapid in his determinations, as well as in their execution; and conducted by the circumstances which he had originated, to the completion of his plans; he seemed to be formed for the scene in which he acted so distinguished a part. The superiority of his genius, more than the priority of birth, had given him an unbounded ascendant over his brothers, Louis and Charles. The first of these, already raised to the dignity of a cardinal, of an aspiring disposition, impetuous, and violent, continually urged and propelled the duke to the most daring and desperate counsels. On the contrary, Charles, duke of Mayenne, although distinguished by equal courage, yet more cautious, moderate, and phlegmatic, disapproved the rash projects of the head of his family; manifested a degree of reluctance to hazard their present greatness; and rather yielded to, than actively participated in, the resolution to commence a civil war (4).

Duke of Mayenne.

The cardinal of Bourbon joins the League.

Plausible as were the pretences on which the duke of Guise justified his opposition to the crown, they would not have been sufficient to enable him to escape the imputation of rebellion, or to seduce the affections and allegiance of the people, without other assistance. It was indispensable to cover

(4.) Davila, p. 502 and 503.

and

and conceal his ultimate plans, under the ſhelter of a prince of the blood; and the cardinal of Bourbon was the only one fitted to his purpoſe. This weak and ſuperſtitious prelate, deluded by the proſpect of ſucceeding to the crown, in preference to his nephew, the king of Navarre; and ſurrounded by emiſſaries, who exaggerated the danger to which the Catholic religion would be expoſed, in the event of a Hugonot aſcending the throne; reſigned himſelf implicitly to their ſuggeſtions. Incapable of diſcerning the ſnare, and flattered by the homage paid to his rank, he prepared to act a principal part in the ruin and ſubverſion of France (5).

Factions, and weakneſs of the court.

Nor did the Guiſes receive leſs ſupport at this critical juncture, from the internal diſſenſions, treachery, and intereſted views, by which the cabinet of Henry was ſwayed and actuated in all its deliberations. Catherine of Medicis, who had ſo long preſided in it, and whoſe influence or authority had been felt during near twenty years, was no longer in poſſeſſion of her former power. The minions of her ſon, who had engroſſed the royal favor, and alienated the king from his brother; ſucceeded in diminiſhing, if not annihilating, the queen-dowager's aſcendancy. She ſaw no probable means of reſuming it, except by rendering her interference neceſſary; and as her penetration enabled her clearly to perceive, that, in the ſituation of the Netherlands, Henry could only chuſe between a war with the king of Spain, or with his own ſubjects, ſhe deſired to involve him in the latter, where her mediation would be perpetually requiſite (6). Other motives concurred to induce Catherine to favor the family of Lorrain. Of her four ſons, three were already dead in the prime of youth; and no rational hope of legiti-

The queen-dowager.

Views and projects of Catherine.

(5) Davila, p. 510.—512. De Thou, vol. ix. p. 265 and 266.
(6) De Thou, vol. xi. 252.

mate

mate issue to inherit the crown remained, though Henry was still in the vigor of his age. Her detestation of the king of Navarre was inveterate and implacable; nor did she hesitate to declare, that she regarded his right of blood as chimerical, or, at least, as questionable and problematical (7). His marriage with Margaret, her daughter, solemnized at the time of the massacre of Paris, had neither been fruitful, nor productive of any conciliation between the two branches of Valois and Bourbon. The irregularities and libertinism of the queen of Navarre, unrestrained by decency, were so notorious, as even to excite the indignation of Henry the Third himself, though little attentive in his own conduct, to the rigid observance of the laws of decorum, or morality. That prince, incensed against his sister for having, as he believed, authorized the assassination of one of his messengers, charged with dispatches of a very secret nature, to the duke of Joyeuse, at Rome; had ordered her to leave the court, and to return to her husband. Not content with banishing her from his capital and presence, he had caused her to be treated with every possible indignity, and had publickly upbraided her with her infamy and debauchery. Neglected and despised by the king of Navarre, she soon afterwards quitted him, and took refuge among the mountains of the province of Auvergne (8).

Libertinism of the queen of Navarre.

Under these circumstances, the queen-mother, regardless of the Salic law, which excluded females from the throne, turned her views towards the descendants of her daughter Claudia, married to the duke of Lorrain. She even attempted to induce the king, whose aversion to the Hugonots rendered

Plan of Catherine, for altering the succession of the crown.

(7) Mezerai, vol. ix. p. 277.
(8) Vie de Marguerite de Valois, p. 341—348.

him

him susceptible of every impression to their disadvantage; to take measures for devolving the crown on the eldest son of his sister, the duchess of Lorrain. The duke of Guise, however disinclined to become subservient to the greatness of another, notwithstanding the connexions of blood which subsisted between them; yet, flattered the queen-dowager with his aid, and acquiescence in her project. In return, Catherine dissembled all his treasonable practices; deceived the king by plausible excuses for his daring conduct; extenuated his faults, and betrayed her son in the dearest interests of his throne and kingdom (9). That unfortunate monarch found no resources in his own character, against the perfidy of his ministers; who, desirous of conciliating the favor of Catherine, or corrupted by Spanish gold, were equally disposed to conceal, and even to advance the projects of "the League." His natural and habitual irresolution was encreased by the opposite opinions of his two favorites. Joyeuse, who, by his marriage, had contracted an alliance with the family of Guise, exhorted his master to temporise, and even to unite with the princes of that house, for the extermination of the Protestants. But, Epernon, by birth a Gascon, long attached to the king of Navarre, and one of those who accompanied him in his flight from the court, at the commencement of Henry's reign; urged him to have recourse to the friendship and assistance of a prince, who, though a Hugonot, was his rightful heir, and only legitimate successor in the throne of France. Uncertain of the course that he should follow; incapable of a vigorous effort; and ever disposed to consult his present ease, at the expence of his future glory, or safety; Henry allowed the period for action to elapse, in fruitless deliberations (10).

Irresolution of the king.

Opposite advice of his two favorites.

(9) De Thou, vol. ix. p. 252 and 253.
(10) De Thou, vol. ix. p. 253.

While

CHAP. IV.

1584.

Treaty between the League, and the king of Spain.

31st Dec.

While the king, by a timidity so pernicious, exposed his crown to the most imminent hazard; the chiefs of "the League," conducted by very different counsels, and conscious that they had already advanced too far to retreat with safety, signed their treaty with Philip the Second. It was solemnly ratified and exchanged at the castle of Joinville, belonging to the duke of Guise. He himself, in person, together with the duke of Mayenne, and a procurator who represented the cardinal of Bourbon, appeared in the names of the Catholics of France. Taxis, duped by the king of Spain, and fully authorized to conclude the negociation, stipulated on the part of his sovereign. By the articles, Philip took under his protection, and entered into an alliance, offensive, and defensive, with the contracting princes, for the maintenance and preservation of the Catholic religion in France, and in the Low Countries. In case of the demise of Henry the Third, the cardinal of Bourbon was declared to be the rightful heir to the crown; and a perpetual exclusion of all heretics, was specified. The restitution of Cambray was inserted; together with the co-operation of the French, to effect the reduction of the Flemish insurgents. Philip, in return, engaged, from the day on which war should be commenced against the Protestants, to pay to the Catholic princes fifty thousand crowns, monthly; and by another article, he promised to supply the duke of Guise with whatever number of men, or sums of money, might be requisite to enable him to carry the treaty into complete execution. For reasons of expediency, it was agreed to keep the secret, till a favorable moment for its disclosure should present itself (11).

Articles of it.

(11) Mezerai, vol. ix. p. 282 and 283. Davila, p. 513 and 514. De Thou, vol. ix. p. 272—275.

While

CHAP. V. 1585.

While, in France, every circumstance evinced the approach of civil war, the Flemings, divided among themselves, and pressed by the arms of the prince of Parma, were reduced to the greatest extremities. The death of the duke of Anjou, at a juncture when an obliteration of all past injuries was on the point of taking place; followed by the assassination of the prince of Orange, plunged them into accumulated distress. Ghent had already submitted on severe conditions, and was received into the obedience of its antient sovereign. Mechlin, and Brussels, invested by detachments from the army of Spain, and beginning to experience the effects of famine, could not make a long or successful resistance. The prince of Parma reserving to himself, as the most arduous and difficult atchievement, the siege of Antwerp; had commenced his operations, by completely intercepting all supplies, or reinforcements, which could arrive by means of the Scheld. In order to attain this object, without which all his efforts must be fruitless, he undertook to block the passage of the river below the city, notwithstanding the breadth and the rapidity of the stream. The work, which, in magnitude and difficulty, might be compared with the most sublime efforts of antiquity, was considerably advanced; and if perfected, the reduction of Antwerp became almost certain and inevitable. Urged by such alarming considerations, which admitted of no delay, the states of all those provinces where the Spanish power had not as yet penetrated, after mature reflexion, embraced the expedient of imploring the protection of the king of France. An embassy, composed of persons, selected for their wisdom and eminence, was empowered to offer the sovereignty of the Low Countries to Henry, on such conditions as might be stipulated for their mutual advantage. They sailed from the ports of Zealand; landed safely; and after remaining some time in the vicinity

Affairs of Flanders.

Siege of Antwerp.

Difficulty of the enterprize.

The Flemings implore the protection of Henry.

January.

CHAP. V. 1585. 12th Feb.

vicinity of Paris, were admitted, notwithstanding the remonstrances and menaces of Mendoza, the Spanish embassador, to an audience. Henry received them graciously, in presence of the queen-mother, and of his council of state; expressed his sense of the flattering proposition made him by the Flemings; gave them hopes of his acquiescence in their request; and signified his wish, that they would deliver a written copy of their offer, in order that he, in concert with his ministers, might deliberate fully on the subject (12).

Reasons for his acceptance of the offer.

Never did a more weighty and important discussion present itself to a king of France, nor one which involved in it consequences more deeply affecting his personal glory, and the general interests of his crown. The inhabitants of the richest and most commercial countries of Europe, sought to be received into the number of his subjects. Those provinces were contiguous to his own dominions; and a considerable portion of them had antiently been possessed by his predecessors. The tyranny of Philip the Second had driven them into a state of revolt; and greatly as their affairs had declined since the arrival of the prince of Parma, they were far from desperate. That commander, occupied before Antwerp, and engaged in an undertaking which demanded time and exertions, must be driven to a necessity of raising the siege under multiplied disadvantages, if a French army entered Flanders, or Brabant.

Provocations given him by Philip the Second.

The king of Spain had dissolved all the tyes which connected him with Henry; and had violated the peace of Cateau, concluded in 1559, between the two crowns, in a manner the most insulting. By his command, or with his approbation, the marquis of Santa Croix had ignominiously, and

(12) Strada, vol. iii. p. 491—495. Busbeq. letters 40, and 41. De Thou, vol. ix. p. 252—255. Davila, p. 524 and 525. Mezerai, vol. ix. p. 284.

in

in equal contradiction to the laws of nations and humanity, caused the unfortunate prisoners taken at the Azores to be massacred. Not content with so barbarous a revenge, Philip had conspired against Henry's domestic repose; inflamed his subjects to rebel; aided them with money; and concluded recently a solemn treaty with their chiefs, the avowed object of which was to involve the kingdom in an immediate civil war.

Debility of the crown, and monarchy of Spain.

These powerful inducements to awaken a generous resentment, were aided and sustained by motives of policy, and almost of necessity. Only the choice between a civil, or a foreign war, was, indeed, left to the king; and it seemed impossible to balance on the preference of the two alternatives. Nor was the power of the Spanish monarchy such, as to deter, or intimidate him from attacking it by open force. Philip, declining in years, and having only one sickly heir, still in infancy, to inherit his vast dominions, was, besides, involved in numerous embarrassments. Portugal was hardly subjected; and the Spanish treasury, unequal to the perpetual demands made on it by the prince of Parma, could not suffice to equip new fleets, and to pay the numerous armies which would be necessary to combat the French. Even, if the resources of the Catholic king were still greater than his adherents described them, it was more judicious to meet him in the field, than to permit the emissaries of Spain to kindle sedition, and to excite rebellion, by the secret distribution of arms and money (13). There were not wanting about the person of Henry, some incorrupt and honest ministers, who attempted to impress upon him a conviction of these facts, and to induce him to embrace a manly and a magnanimous part. That prince, who possessed penetration,

Henry rejects the proposition of the Flemings.

(13) De Thou, vol. ix. p. 298—312.

CHAP. V. 1585.

and who had a perfect knowledge of the interests of his crown, inclined to accept the offers of the Flemings. But, his aversion to engage in an enterprize of such magnitude, together with the opposition which it received from his mother, and the members of the cabinet, prevailed on him to reject the proposition. At the audience which he gave to the embassadors of the States, he endeavoured to temper the refusal by every conciliating expression; lamented, that the situation of his own affairs, and the troubles occasioned by the adherents of "the League," did not permit him to undertake their defence; assured them, that when he had pacified the commotions of France, he would extend his attention to the concerns of the Netherlands; and promised to recommend their cause to the protection of the queen of England (14).

March 30.

The League takes up arms.

The duke of Guise had not waited for the ultimate decision of Henry upon the proposals of the Flemings, to take up arms. No sooner had the intelligence reached the prince of Parma, that the embassadors, deputed by the States, had been admitted to an audience of the king of France, than he dispatched repeated couriers to Mendoza, the Spanish embassador at Paris. Convinced, that on the final event of the siege of Antwerp, depended the reduction of all the Netherlands to the obedience of Philip; he besought of that minister, to urge the partizans of "the League" to the immediate accomplishment of their late engagements with the crown of Spain. Guise himself, sensible that if a foreign war took place, he should not be able to retain under his standard the nobility and officers who were attached to him; did not hesitate to strike the blow. A second edict, published by Henry, in which he prohibited all assemblies of troops with-

Edict published by Henry. March 29.

(14) Busbeq. letters 44, 45, and 46. De Thou, vol. ix. p. 312—315.

out

out his exprefs command; and by which he diminifhed confiderably the ordinary taxes; made no alteration, nor occafioned any delay, in his refolution. Already, at the firft fignal given, the forces retained by him, began to collect in Lorrain; while the duke of Mayenne put himfelf at the head of a formidable body, in Champagne and Burgundy. Baffompierre, who had raifed a number of German cavalry; and Fifer, who had received a fimilar commiffion to levy infantry in the cantons of Switzerland, were ordered to advance with all poffible celerity. The firft attack was made on the city of Verdun, which, after a fhort defence, furrendered to the duke of Guife in perfon. Toul followed the example; but, Metz, of which Epernon was governor, and in which he had placed a numerous garrifon, remained firm in its adherence to the crown, and rejected all the offers of the rebels (15).

21ft April. Firft exploits of the League.

Previous to the commencement of hoftilities, the cardinal of Bourbon, acting in concert with the other chiefs of "the League," retired from court to his diocefe of Rouen; from whence, being invited by a deputation of the nobility of Picardy, he repaired to Peronne, in that province. On his arrival, he publifhed a manifefto, calculated to imprefs the nation with fentiments equally favorable to the caufe which he had embraced, and injurious to the character of the king. Every popular topic of declamation and complaint was enumerated, and placed in its moft confpicuous point of view. The indirect encouragement and fupport of herefy: the danger of the entire abolition of the antient faith and worfhip: the venality of offices; the abufes committed by favourites; and the intolerable pecuniary oppreffions exercifed on the people. To redrefs thefe grievances, it was ftated, that he, as

Manifefto of the cardinal of Bourbon.

March. 31.

(15) Davila, p. 535 and 536. De Thou, vol. ix. p. 275—283.

first

CHAP. V. 1585.

first prince of the blood, together with a number of other persons, of every order and condition, had taken up arms; which they were determined never to lay down, till they had obtained complete satisfaction and redress (16). Meanwhile, in every part of the kingdom, but, peculiarly, in the northern and eastern provinces, where the adherents of the house of Guise were numerous, they proceeded to throw off all subjection to the government. Lyons was secured to them by Mandelot, who having seized and demolished the citadel, declared in their favour. Bourges, Orleans, and Angers, three of the most important, and well fortified cities of France, were induced to revolt by their respective governors, who joined "the League." Mezieres, a frontier garrison of Champagne, was captured by the duke of Guise; while the duke of Mayenne rendered himself master of Dijon. Chalons, a place situate on the river Marne, and at no considerable distance from Paris, was fixed on for the magazine of arms; and the cardinal of Bourbon, whose presence and name were so useful in concealing, or in justifying their enterprize, was conducted thither from Peronne, with demonstrations of extraordinary attention and respect. (17).

Insurrections of the provinces.

Resources of the crown.

Notwithstanding so many proofs of disaffection and even of revolt, a prince of magnanimity might have found in the throne itself, and in the attachment of a considerable part of the nation, resources more than adequate to suppress the rebellion, commenced by the adherents of "the League." The specious pretences, under which the leaders attempted to palliate their insurrection, could only delude the multitude; and made no impression on the wise, or the

(16) Davila, p. 528—535. De Thou, vol. ix. p. 284—287. Memoires du Duc de Nevers, folio, Paris 1665, vol. i. p. 641—646.

(17) Davila, p. 538. Mezerai, vol. ix. p. 28. Busbeq. letters 48, 49, and 50.

moderate

moderate portion of their countrymen. In feveral places, their attempts had been completely fruftrated, and their partizans or accomplices punifhed as traitors. Marfeilles, after having been near three days in the hands of the infurgents, was recovered by the royalifts, and fecured in the obedience of the crown. At Bourdeaux, marfhal Matignon rendered ineffectual every effort to fhake the fidelity, or to gain the poffeffion of that important and commercial city. The proclamation of the king, declaring it treafonable to take up arms; weak as fuch a meafure muft be efteemed, had yet induced many perfons, who had been incautioufly induced to join the party, inftantly to return home. Others were ftill wavering and uncertain; the duke of Nevers, one of their greateft fupports, abandoned them from difguft, or from fcruples of honor and confcience. Even the cardinal of Bourbon himfelf, during a fhort abfence of Guife, had been powerfully fhaken, and almoft induced to return to a fenfe of his duty. It demanded all the eloquence and fophiftry of the duke, to obliterate the impreffion. Gregory the Thirteenth, notwithftanding the importunity and folicitation of the Spanifh cardinals, had pertinacioufly refufed to give any fanction to an enterprize, which, however decorated with the epithets of a holy union for preferving the Catholic religion, favoured of open rebellion. The fubfidies of Spain were fubject to many delays and contingencies: the Swifs and German troops had not yet arrived; and in feveral provinces, the forces of "the League" had been difperfed, or cut in pieces (18).

CHAP. V. 1585.

Failure of the plans of the League.

Obftacles to its fuccefs.

But, fuch was the inaptitude of Henry for any meafures of energy; fo infurmountable was his indolence, pufillanimity, and relaxation of mind, that

Weaknefs of Henry's conduct.

(18) Mezerai, vol. ix. p. 285—290. De Thou, vol. ix. p. 288—298, and 316—329.

CHAP. V. 1585.

all these circumstances did not rouse him to resistance. Neither indignation for the insulted majesty of the throne; nor a wise consideration of the calamities, which firmness and fortitude could alone avert, were of sufficient force to burst the habitual tameness of his character. It was in vain that the king of Navarre, by his agents, besought of him not to allow the menaces of the duke of Guise, to induce him to violate the peace subsisting with the Hugonots, and thereby plunge himself anew into civil war. Yielding to the suggestions of his mother, and to the interested, or perfidious advice of the same ministers, who had recently procured the rejection of the offers of the Flemings; he authorized Catherine of Medicis to open a negotiation with the heads of the confederates. It was begun at Epernay, near Chalons; and after some delays, was ultimately concluded at Nemours. The terms on which the duke of Guise agreed to lay down his arms, were not less destructive, than they were ignominious, to the sovereign, by whom they were accepted. Henry not only consented to commence hostilities on the Protestants, and to revoke every concession hitherto made for their protection; but, he submitted to the personal degradation of pardoning those by whom he had been insulted and injured, on account of the pretended zeal exhibited by them in defence of the Catholic religion. He even engaged to employ the troops of "the League," actually drawn out against his authority, for the extirpation of heresy; and to charge the chiefs, with the execution of the sentence pronounced against the princes of the blood, the presumptive heirs to the crown of France. In addition to these public articles, he was compelled to subscribe to private conditions, which cemented the power of the Guises, and levelled all the remaining barriers opposed to their encroachments. Twelve cities, situated in different provinces of the kingdom, were

He negotiates with the League.

7th July.

Ignominious articles of the treaty.

Secret conditions.

1585.

were granted them as places of ſurety: a company of guards, on horſeback, were allowed to the cardinal of Bourbon; to the dukes of Guiſe and Mayenne; to their brother, the cardinal, and to their uncles, the dukes of Aumale and Elbeuf. All the money belonging to the royal revenue, which they had intercepted and applied to their own purpoſes, was remitted; and the ſum of two hundred thouſand crowns, due to the German forces, raiſed by the duke of Guiſe, was agreed to be defrayed by the king (19).

Magnanimous behaviour of the king of Navarre.

While Henry thus purchaſed a precarious and diſgraceful ſuſpenſion of hoſtilities, at the expence of every prerogative of the crown, and by the ſacrifice of his own dignity and independance; the king of Navarre diſplayed a very different character. Conſcious that he muſt become the firſt victim to "the League," and that his perſonal ruin would open the way to the deſtruction of the monarchy itſelf; he did not heſitate to anticipate, and to expoſe, the treaſonable projects of his enemies. In a long, and ſpirited manifeſto, addreſſed to the nation, he exculpated himſelf from every injurious charge or imputation, which the malice of his opponents had invented; profeſſed his readineſs to ſubmit even his religious opinions, to the deciſion of a council, legitimately aſſembled; retorted the charge of rebellion and treaſon on thoſe who had, without provocation, taken up arms againſt their prince: reprobated their ambition, rapacity, and contempt of the laws; and concluded by beſeeching the king, that he would permit him to terminate a conteſt, in which ſo much blood muſt be ſhed, by a ſingle combat between himſelf and the duke of Guiſe, in whatever

10th June. His manifeſto.

(19) Davila, p. 557 and 558. Mezerai, vol. ix. p. 292. De Thou, vol. ix. p. 328—331. Memoires de Nevers, vol. i. p. 686—689.

place,

CHAP. V. 1585.

place, either within, or beyond the limits of the kingdom, he might think proper to appoint (20).

His letter to Henry.

10th July.

Finding, however, that all his efforts to prevent an accommodation between Henry and the adherents of "the League," were fruitless; and that the Protestants were on the point of being attacked at the same time, by their united forces; he addressed a letter to the king, in which was depictured all the heroism and magnanimity of an undaunted mind, struggling against oppression. He reminded Henry of his own orders recently issued, enjoining him, as head of the Protestants, to remain quiet; assuring him of protection; and protesting, that no menaces or artifices of their common adversaries, should ever induce him to infringe the toleration extended to the Hugonots, by the last treaty of peace. He remonstrated with Henry on the cruelty and impolicy of driving his unoffending subjects, to the necessity of defending themselves: he appealed to his own innocence, as the best justification; and professed his reliance on a just and superintending Providence, the avenger of crimes, and the shield of those who are oppressed. In conclusion, he declared his determination to perish with arms in his hands; and to oppose to his last breath, the unjust enterprizes of his own enemies, and of the crown and kingdom of France (21).

Union of Montmorenci, with the king of Navarre.

These spirited and generous sentiments were followed by measures equally decisive and efficacious. Although the ostensible preparations and menaces of "the League," armed with the sanction of the royal authority, appeared to be exclusively and solely levelled against the professors of heresy; yet, the duke of Montmorenci, well aware that his own ruin was inseparably connected with that of the

(20) De Thou, vol. ix. p. 320—325. Davila, p 358—362.
(21) De Thou, vol. ix. p. 326—328.

king

king of Navarre, did not hesitate to enter into the strictest union with him and the prince of Condé, for their mutual preservation. Having met near Lavaur, in the province of Languedoc, they framed, and rendered public a declaration, calculated to undeceive the nation on the motives of the war, ready to be commenced. They charged the family of Guise, with having been the authors of all the misfortunes, which, from the reign of Francis the Second, to the present time, had desolated and depopulated the finest country in Europe: that, after calumniating the princes of the blood, and endeavouring to render them odious to the people, they had not scrupled to take up arms against the king himself, and by the impressions of terror, to compel an equitable monarch, to wage war with his subjects. They protested, in their private and public capacities, against such acts of violence and treason; declared their readiness to take under their safeguard all Catholics who had not signed "the League;" and finished, by repeating their determination, with the means which God and Nature had put into their hands, to oppose such unprovoked, and unjustifiable violence (22).

CHAP. V. 1585.

10th Aug. Their joint declaration.

Tenor of it.

During the progress of these interesting events, Henry, irresolute, unable to recede, and irritated against the faction which was about to render him the reluctant instrument of their ambitious views, beheld before him the immediate prospect of a civil war. His discontent manifested itself, notwithstanding the presence of the cardinal of Guise, in the language and indirect reproaches, with which he loaded the Parisians; who, after engaging him in a rupture with the Protestants, from their antipathy to heresy, expressed no inclination to submit to the pecuniary burthens, necessary for carrying on hostilities. De-

Conduct, and discontent of the king.

(22) De Thou, vol. ix. p. 332—334.

CHAP. V. 1585.

firous to try all expedients, in order to avert fo great a calamity, of which he was the involuntary caufe, and of which he forefaw that he muft ultimately become the victim; he refolved to attempt anew, to fhake the conftancy of the king of Navarre, and with that hope, he again difpatched an embaffy to the court of Nerac. Every offer was held out, which could prevail upon him, if not to renounce his religion, and embrace the Catholic faith; yet, to fufpend, for a limited time, the exercife of the Hugonot worfhip in Bearn; and to furrender the places of fecurity, put into the hands of the Protestants, at the laft treaty of peace. In cafe of the refufal of the king of Navarre to confent to fo great conceffions, the embaffadors were ordered to infift, that he fhould iffue directions to ftop the march of the German auxiliaries, who were ready to enter the kingdom. But, that prince did not think proper to comply with any of the requifitions; and he befought the king not to expect, that whatever defire he might have to evince his allegiance, he could carry his obedience fo far, as tamely to prefent his neck to his implacable enemies. He adjured his majefty, not to abandon his own honor, by uniting with traitors; and he expreffed his readinefs to meet the queen-mother, for the purpofe of adjufting the terms of a final accommodation, provided that Henry would previoufly withdraw his forces from all the provinces fouth of the Loire (23).

25th Aug. Embaffy to the king of Navarre.

Propofitions rejected.

Death of Gregory the Thirteenth.

No alternative except war remained; and "the League," already poffeffed of all the authority of the crown, had received a further acceffion of ftrength, by the demife of Gregory the Thirteenth. That aged pontiff, who could never be induced to give his unqualified approbation to their fchemes,

(23) Davila, p. 573 and 574. De Thou, vol. ix. p. 337—340. Mezerai, vol. ix. p. 293.

expired

expired after a reign of thirteen years; and was succeeded by Felix Perretti, better known in history under the title of Sixtus the Fifth. He commenced his short, but memorable pontificate, by the severest punishment of the outrages and crimes, common in every part of the territories of the church; and from which the city of Rome itself was not secure, or exempt. The timid and moderate character of his predecessor had encouraged them, by the impunity with which they were attended; but, the inexorable severity of Sixtus, speedily restored order and submission to the laws. The arrogance and violence of his disposition, led him easily to comply with the entreaties, made to him by the emissaries of the house of Guise; and at their instigation, he soon after his accession to the chair of St. Peter, issued a bull, by which he declared the king of Navarre and the prince of Condé excommunicated, and incapable of succeeding to the crown of France. This political malediction was accompanied with epithets the most opprobrious, applied to the two princes themselves, who were stigmatized as apostates, heretics, and enemies of God and man. Their vassals, or subjects, were released from all obedience; and Henry was exhorted, in his capacity of the most Christian king, to extirpate the race of Bourbon, and to carry the Papal sentence into immediate execution (24).

CHAP. V.

1585. 10th April. Election of Sixtus the Fifth.

21st Sept. Bull, published by him, against the king of Navarre.

So indecent and insulting a display of the plenitude of the apostolic power, excited various and opposite emotions, on its promulgation in France. The partizans of "the League," elated at the favorable interference of the sovereign pontiff, expressed their satisfaction and triumph, by every possible means. Paris was inflamed, and the passions

Effects produced by it.

(24) De Thou, vol. ix. p. 368—371.

of

CHAP. V. 1585.

of the populace were irritated by seditious preachers; who, ascending the pulpits, harangued the multitude, and pointed their detestation not only against the Protestants, but, against Epernon, and other persons suspected of attachment to the princes of the blood. On the other hand, Henry, however servile and tame in his acquiescence with the requisitions of the duke of Guise, could not avoid feeling and resenting an outrage, which, though apparently pointed against heresy, did not less attack the majesty of the throne, and the independance of his crown. He well knew, that, under the minority of Charles the Ninth, twenty-three years preceding, when Pius the Fourth, who then occupied the Papal chair, had ventured to excommunicate Jane d'Albret, queen of Navarre; the ministers of his brother had not submitted in silence to the indignity. The constable Montmorenci, and the chancellor l'Hospital, who then presided in the cabinet of France, had compelled the see of Rome to revoke, and even to suppress the bull, as injurious to a princess so nearly allied to the royal blood. But, Henry, already engaged in a war for the purpose of exterminating the Hugonots, and apprehensive of giving any cause of offence to the adherents of "the League," contented himself with a more indirect mode of disapprobation, by only prohibiting its publication (25).

Conduct of Henry.

He indirectly opposes it.

The king of Navarre, restrained by no considerations of that nature, and following only the impulse of his indignation, took more efficacious measures for resenting the insult. Unawed by any terror of the pontifical power, he caused a reply to to the bull of excommunication to be published, and affixed in the most public places of Rome itself. Neither the person, nor the dignity of Sixtus,

Generous answer of the king of Navarre to the bull.

5th Nov.

(25) De Thou, vol. ix. p. 374—376.

tus, were respected in the composition. With the generous warmth of a high-spirited and injured prince, he gave to the successor of St. Peter the epithets of a calumniator, and a lyar; appealed from his sentence to that of a general council; and declared mortal and irreconcilable war against him, as the enemy of God, and as Antichrist. He reminded Sixtus, that his own ancestors of the family of Bourbon, had formerly repressed the arrogance and audacity of the bishops of Rome; and added, that, as he was no way inferior to his most illustrious predecessors, he trusted, by the divine aid, to exact a signal and exemplary vengeance for the late outrage. He concluded by appealing to all the allies of France, and to all the crowned heads or princes of Europe, against the tyranny of the see of Rome, and against the enterprizes of "the League," as the common foes of God, the king, and the state (26).

CHAP. V. 1585.

Approbation, which it excited.

An answer so magnanimous, made by a prince under circumstances the most adverse, excited universal admiration. All the moderate and dispassionate part of the nation, respected the courage and elevation of mind which could dictate it; and the Catholics themselves, far from approving the excommunication, saw with regret and concern, that its effects would be more beneficial, than injurious, to the party against whom it was directed. Even Sixtus himself, who knew how to appreciate the great qualities of an enemy, conceived from this specimen, the higheit opinion of the king of Navarre. He did not conceal his sentiments; expressed his esteem for a constancy and firmness, which no external accidents could depress; and uniformly refused to open the treasury of the church, or to contribute, in any manner, towards the war declared against the Hugonots.

(26) De Thou, vol. ix. p. 376—378. Davila, p. 574—576.

The

CHAP. V.

1585. New edict of Henry. 16th Oct.

The hostilities, which "the League," under the name and shelter of the crown, had been so long preparing, at length commenced. They were preceded by a new edict on the part of the passive and reluctant king, whom the Guises had compelled, against his inclination, to attack the king of Navarre. It reduced to the term of fifteen days, the remainder of the six months allowed to the adherents of the reformed religion, for quitting the kingdom; and enjoined the confiscation and public sale of all their effects, at the end of that period. The duke of Guise having signified to Henry his desire of commanding the forces, which were to be stationed on the eastern frontier, in order to oppose the entrance of the Germans into the kingdom; his brother, the duke of Mayenne, was appointed to conduct the army, destined to march against the king of Navarre, in Guienne. But, Henry, though he did not venture by open force to repress the enterprizes of that powerful family, took effectual precautions to impede their military operations. Matignon, a man devoted to the crown, was ordered to co-operate with Mayenne; but, in reality, his instructions were of an opposite nature; and the delays or obstacles which he continually framed, added to the advanced season of the year, prevented any enterprize of moment, on the part of the Catholics (27).

Conduct of that monarch.

Preparations of the Hugonots, for their defence.

30th Nov.

Meanwhile, the Hugonots, neither depressed by the late edict, nor dismayed by the vast disparity of force, prepared with vigor for their defence. The king of Navarre, after publishing a counter edict, justifying his resistance on the principle of necessity, and commanding the seizure of the effects of the inhabitants, in all the cities which had enforced the royal orders; assembled his troops, on the banks of

(27) Davila, p. 572 and 573. De Thou, vol. ix. p. 379.

the

1585.

the Garonne. In Dauphiné, Lesdiguieres obtained many advantages over the Catholics, and reduced to his obedience the greater part of the province. Another of their chiefs, the viscount of Turenne, penetrated into the Limousin; while the prince of Condé drove the duke of Mercœur out of Poitou, with considerable loss. Emboldened by his success, the prince, pushing his advantages, laid siege to Brouage; and he was on the point of compelling the garrison to capitulate, when he received the intelligence, that the castle of Angers had been surprized by a small number of his adherents. Elated at so unexpected and prosperous an event, which opened a prospect of transferring the theatre of war from Poitou, to the rich provinces beyond the Loire, and even of approaching Paris; he instantly determined to quit the prosecution of his present enterprize, and to advance, without delay, to the assistance of his friends. Many of his officers remonstrated with him on the danger, if not the temerity, of such an attempt: they represented the season, already far advanced; the difficulty of passing so broad a river as the Loire, swelled by autumnal rains; and the uncertainty of the castle holding out till his arrival. But, the prince, whose intrepidity qualified him for the most arduous exploits, and whom obstacles only irritated, remained firm to his purpose. He immediately began his march, at the head of a chosen body of his friends and soldiers; effected his passage across the Loire; and after surmounting many impediments, appeared before Angers.

Operations of the war.

Enterprize of Angers.

8th Oct.

The prince of Condé passes the Loire.

By a surprizing, and almost unparalleled series of accidents, in which fortune had a greater share than wisdom, or courage; the three officers who gained possession of the castle, had already perished. The soldiers, only sixteen in number, who remained; destitute of any chief, and of opposite religious per-

21st Oct.

 suasions,

CHAP. V. 1585.

ſuaſions, agreed to ſurrender; and on the day preceding the arrival of Condé, they had put the caſtle into the hands of the duke of Joyeuſe. Notwithſtanding ſo ſevere a diſappointment, which the prince did not receive, till he was in ſight of Angers, he perſiſted to attack the city. But, his troops, diſcouraged, and oppoſed by ſuperior numbers, gave way; and it became expedient to retreat. The attempt was arduous, and almoſt impracticable; as the Catholics, apprized of the expedition, had aſſembled to intercept his flight, or his paſſage over the Loire. Beſet by enemies, he reluctantly conſented to adopt the only means of extrication left; that of dividing his troops into ſmall parties, who might evade the vigilance of their numerous opponents. The expedient was embraced, and attended with uncommon ſucceſs; almoſt all the ſoldiers having rejoined their ſtandards, without loſs. The prince of Condé himſelf, whoſe capture was regarded as ſo certain, that the Pariſians already anticipated the ſpectacle of a prince of the blood brought priſoner to the capital; followed only by a few friends, took the route of Normandy; and paſſing over into the iſland of Guernſey, purſued his voyage from thence to the court of England (28).

He attacks Angers. His retreat and flight. He eſcapes to England.

While France was thus involved in all the calamities inſeparable from civil war, the prince of Parma had nearly atchieved the total reduction of Flanders and Brabant to the obedience of Spain. That great commander, profiting of the diſſentions of the Flemings, and of the death of the prince of Orange, puſhed his operations with augmented vigor. Bruſſels, reduced to the laſt extremities of famine, capitulated, and obtained honorable conditions.

Reduction of Flanders and Brabant. Bruſſels ſurrenders, March 13.

(28) D'Aubig. Hiſt. Univ. vol. ii. p. 440—452. De Thou, vol. ix. p. 385—398. Davila, p. 582—587. Mezerai, vol. ix. p. 294—296.

The

The Catholics, who formed the moſt numerous part of the inhabitants of Nimeguen, having expelled or overpowered the Proteſtants, opened their gates to the Spaniards. By this important acquiſition, Guelderland, and even the provinces of Holland and Utrecht, were, in ſome degree, laid open to the incurſions of the enemy. Mechlin, inveſted on all ſides, and hopeleſs of relief, ſurrendered at diſcretion. Antwerp alone continued, after near a year, to reſiſt the utmoſt efforts of the beſiegers. Aſſiſted by engineers of the moſt conſummate ſkill, and ſuſtained by their deteſtation of the tyranny of Philip; they not only rejected every offer of accommodation; but, repeatedly attacked the works, by which the prince of Parma had intercepted the ſupplies of proviſions. Exhauſted at length by fruitleſs endeavours to deſtroy the bridge conſtructed acroſs the Scheldt: repulſed in their ſallies; and beginning to experience the preſſure of famine; they opened a negociation with the Spaniſh general. It was ſoon terminated; and that celebrated city, which had long been the emporium of the north; but, which had experienced, during the laſt twenty years, every variety of deſolation, pillage, and misfortune, ſubmitted reluctantly to its former maſter. Philip, whoſe bigotry and violence had baniſhed order, tranquillity, and commerce from the Netherlands; after exhauſting the immenſe reſources of the monarchy of Spain in the attempt to reduce the Flemings, beheld himſelf again in poſſeſſion of the ten ſouthern provinces. But, the trade of Antwerp had fled with its civil and religious liberties; while Amſterdam, hitherto concealed by its own obſcurity, began to emerge; and all the ſources of wealth were irrecoverably transferred from the Scheldt to the Texel (29).

CHAP. V. 1585. April.

and Mechlin. 21ſt June.

Surrender of Antwerp. 17th Aug.

(29) Strada, vol. iv. p. 1—149. De Thou, vol. ix. p. 427—442.

CHAP. V.

1585.

Dutch implore the aid of the queen of England.

In this extremity, the Dutch, already united by the closest political tyes, and masters of the seven northern provinces of the Low Countries; far from yielding to despair, evinced an unshaken fortitude. Deprived of the assistance and co-operation of the Flemings; rejected in their application to the king of France; and on the point of being attacked by the victorious troops of Spain, conducted by the greatest general of the age; they determined to implore the aid of Elizabeth, queen of England. While Antwerp, reduced to extremity, though not surrendered, continued to resist an embassy, composed of the most illustrious persons from all the provinces yet unsubdued, arrived in London, and offered the sovereignty to her, on terms similar to those which had been proposed to Henry the Third. Following the dictates of the cautious and sagacious policy, which, during her long reign, had always tempered and restrained the natural magnanimity of her character; she declined the proposition in its full extent; but, assured the States of her immediate and efficacious protection. By a treaty concluded with them, she stipulated to send over five thousand infantry, and one thousand cavalry into Holland, under an experienced commander, to whom extensive civil and military authority should be confided. These troops, which the queen engaged to maintain at her own expence during the continuance of the war, were to be defrayed, after its conclusion, by the Dutch; and as pledges for their repayment of the money necessary to be disbursed, the towns of the Brille, and Flushing, together with the castle of Rammekins, were consigned to Elizabeth. Unterrified by the menaces and alarming preparations of Philip to invade her in her own dominions, she speedily accomplished the conditions. The English succours landed in Zealand; and though her partiality for an unworthy favorite,

6th July.

10th Aug. Treaty between Elizabeth and the Dutch.

December. English troops sent to Zealand.

favorite, induced her to commit so important an expedition, and so vast a charge, to the earl of Leicester, who abused his power, and tarnished the lustre of his sovereign's arms; yet the timely assistance extended to the Dutch, rendered ineffectual all the exertions of Spain, and finally established the existence and independance of the seven united provinces (30).

CHAP. V. 1585.

(30) Hume, Hist. of Eng. vol. v. p. 269—273. Strada, vol. iv. p. 176—185. De Thou, vol. ix. p. 447—452.

CHAP. VI.

Letters addreſſed by the king of Navarre, to the different orders of the kingdom.—Campaign in Guienne, and Poitou.—Conduct of Henry.—His journey to Lyons.—Audience, and anſwer, given by him, to the German embaſſy.—Operations of the duke of Guiſe.—Conference of St. Brix.—State of Paris.—Machinations of "the League."—Henry diſconcerts them.—Succeſs of Joyeuſe.—Entrance of the Germans and Switzers into Lorrain.—Inactivity of the king.—Duke of Guiſe defends France.—Battle of Coutras.—Progreſs of the foreign army.—Defeat of Vimory.—Second defeat, at Auneau.—Flight of the Germans and Switzers.—Treaty concluded with them, by Henry.—Exploits and perſonal glory of the duke of Guiſe.—Return of the king to Paris.—Foreign affairs.

CHAP. VI.

1586.

King of Navarre addreſſes letters to the different orders, 1ſt January;

DURING theſe important tranſactions in the Netherlands, where the interpoſition of Elizabeth rendered new efforts, on the part of Philip the Second, indiſpenſable; the king of Navarre, apprehenſive of being cruſhed by the confederacy of the crown with the forces of "the League," prepared to ſuſtain ſo ſevere a ſhock. Previous to the commencement of any military operations, he again addreſſed letters from Montauban, in Languedoc, to the different orders of the kingdom. In that to the clergy, he reprobated the ambition of the Guiſes, who, under the veil of religion, had not ſcrupled to involve France in civil war; had compelled the king to violate his own treaties with the Hugonots; and had ſacrificed all the liberties of the Gallican church, in order to obtain the protection of the ſee of Rome. His addreſs to the nobility, by the affectionate

fectionate and endearing manner, in which he implored their exertions to avert the calamities impending over their country; and by the reluctance which he expressed to shed the blood of a class of subjects, selected for the ornament and defence of the throne; was calculated to make a deep impression. In his letter to the third estate, he pointed out and lamented the heavy burthens about to be imposed on them, to gratify the malevolence and injustice of a powerful faction, who had made their sovereign the instrument of their own vengeance; and who prosecuted their private animosities, in the name, and at the expence of the nation. To the city of Paris, he recalled the recollection of their antient loyalty and adherence to their kings: he gave the just eulogiums to the reluctance which they had manifested, to contribute towards the support of hostilities so unprovoked; and he professed his readiness to submit all his opinions to the arbitration of a council, sanctioned and confirmed by the states general (1).

CHAP. VI. 1586.

and to the city of Paris.

Conscious, while he made his appeal to the nation, that neither eloquence nor arguments would decide the contest; he, at the same time, had recourse to arms. Too feeble in pecuniary resources, in numbers, and in all the requisites for a campaign, to venture to meet his opponent in the field; he embraced a system highly favourable to the protraction of the war. Having garrisoned his castles, situated along the banks of the Dordogne, and the Garonne, which formed a barrier difficult to force; he himself, accompanied only by a chosen body of cavalry, and unencumbered either with baggage or artillery, appeared wherever his presence was necessary. The celerity and uncertainty of his movements: the perfect knowledge which he possessed of

Military measures embraced by the king of Navarre.

(1) De Thou, vol. ix. p. 567—571. Chronol. Novenn. vol. i. p. 21—34.

the

CHAP. VI. 1586.

the country; and the decision of his natural character, prompt to conceive, or to baffle all the exertions of the enemy to force him to an action: These qualities were contrasted with the habitual caution and slowness which distinguished the duke of Mayenne, in every operation. That general laboured under numerous, and almost insurmountable impediments. His army, destitute of artillery, was distressed by the want of pay, and checked by the inclemency of the season. Matignon, jealous of his interference in a province, of which he himself was governor; and secretly prompted by the king to prosecute the war with languor; interposed perpetual obstacles and delays. After wasting nearly three months before they entered Guienne, during which time the troops were considerably diminished by distempers, an open misintelligence broke out between the commanders. When their operations at length commenced, they were limited to the siege and capture of some unimportant towns; and Mayenne, irritated with the difficulties opposed to his progress, only waited for the conclusion of the campaign, to demand his dismission from so inglorious and unprofitable a service (2).

Impediments to the progress of the royal army.

Feeble operations.

In every part of Poitou and Saintonge, where the principal strength of the Hugonots was concentered, the exertions were equally feeble and indecisive. The prince of Condé, returning from England, where Elizabeth had supplied him with money, and given him a squadron for his escort; repaired his late disaster before Angers, by redoubled vigilance and activity. Formed for the hardships and dangers of the field, his heart had, notwithstanding, been sensible to the attractions of Catherine Charlotte de la Tremouille; and motives of policy combining with his

Marriage of the prince of Condé.

16th March.

(2) Davila, p. 589—592. De Thou, vol. ix. p. 560—566, and 578—582, and 586—592. D'Aub. Hist. Univ. vol. iii. p. 24—32.

inclinations,

CHAP. VI. 1586.

inclinations, he soon after espoused her, at the city of Taillebourg. She was in the bloom of youth, sprung from an illustrious family, and sister to the duke de la Tremouille, who, having embraced the reformed religion, brought a vast accession of force to his new ally. Notwithstanding these circumstances, which seemed to promise so much felicity, no nuptials were ever more inauspicious, nor terminated by a more tragical catastrophé. Biron, meanwhile, at the head of a considerable body of soldiers, approached Rochelle, and laid siege to Marans, a town in its vicinity: but, hostilities in that quarter were shortly afterwards suspended by an armistice, agreed on between him and the king of Navarre. It was designed to facilitate a conference, which Catherine of Medicis, at Henry's entreaty, undertook to manage, with the view of concluding a final accommodation. Alarmed at the first intelligence of such a design, the duke of Guise, who was stationed at the other extremity of the kingdom, on the frontiers of Champagne, in order to oppose the entrance of the Germans; began to remonstrate, in terms approaching to menace. His efforts to prevent a treaty, which, he foresaw, must be fatal to all his ambitious projects, were powerfully supported by the Papal nuntio; and the discontent of the Parisians, which already threatened an insurrection in the capital, rendered a peace with the king of Navarre, a measure no less unpopular, than dangerous (3).

Armistice. August.

Opposition of the duke of Guise, to a pacification.

Amidst so many calamities, by which France was desolated; and with the prospect of still greater evils before him, Henry preserved all the indolence and supineness of his character. Concealed in the recesses of the Louvre, and besieged by rapacious minions;

Indolence of Henry.

(3) De Thou, vol. ix. p. 573—577, and 583—586. Davila, p. 592—594, and p. 600. D'Aub. vol. iii. p. 19—22. Mezerai, vol. ix. p. 300—304.

CHAP. VI. 1586.

nions; he emerged at intervals from his repose, only to render himself supremely odious, or contemptible. His recreations were as destitute of dignity, as they were proofs of an enervated and effeminate disposition. He was not ashamed to expose himself to the view of his people, surrounded with dogs, monkeys, and perroquets, at a time when the kingdom groaned under accumulated, and almost insupportable misfortunes. The expences incurred for objects so worthless and puerile, exceeded belief, and augmented the public indignation. It exhausted the treasury, to support them, and to maintain the armies acting against the Hugonots, notwithstanding the contributions levied from the clergy, and the alienation of a considerable portion of the royal domain. In this embarrassment, seventeen new edicts, imposing taxes, were sent to the parliament of Paris, by the royal order. But, the members, with a generous spirit of resentment at the abuse of the prerogative of the crown, refused to register impositions so oppressive. Henry was necessitated to appear in person, in order to surmount their opposition; and his presence was productive of submission. The murmurs, excited by such arbitrary and injudicious measures, were not less universal; and experience evinced to him, how dangerous it is, to exhaust the patience and loyalty of a great people.

His profusion, and oppressions.

16th June.

Monastic and superstitious practices of the king.

Passing rapidly from the extreme of luxury and dissipation, to the renunciations of a severe and monastic life; the king, not content with mingling in processions, and undertaking pilgrimages to various altars or shrines, renowned for their sanctity; abandoned frequently all the duties and functions annexed to his high station, in order to immure himself with Hieronimites, or Feuillans. These orders of Monks, introduced by himself, and the former of which he had caused to be brought from Spain, were placed in in the wood of the castle of Vincennes, in the immediate vicinity of Paris, where cells were constructed for their accommodation; or in the suburbs, close to the palace of the Louvre and the Tuilleries. After passing some days in the supposed exercise of mortification and abstinence among them, he suddenly re-appeared, in the habit of a penitent, followed by a number of Flagellants. He even carried his devotion, or hypocrisy, to so great a length, as to wear about his waist, a large chaplet, the grains of which were cut into the shape of skulls. Mixing a capricious taste for the elegant arts, with the practices of superstition; he amused himself with collecting, at whatever price, the most costly paintings upon vellum, executed by the greatest artists of Italy; and with these he ornamented the walls of his chapels. So many symptoms of a depraved, or alienated understanding, made a deep impression on the minds of the inhabitants of the metropolis; who, inflamed by seditious preachers, and no longer restrained by any respect for the person, or character of their sovereign, began to listen to the most daring proposals of insurrection and rebellion (4).

CHAP. VI. 1586

His amusements and recreations.

The Protestant princes of Germany having determined to send an embassy to Paris, in order to supplicate the king to terminate the war commenced against the Hugonots; he quitted the capital, and repaired to Lyons. Various motives induced him to undertake a journey of such distance, at so critical a juncture. By delaying to give audience to the German embassadors, he hoped to retain their sovereigns in uncertainty as to his intentions respecting peace; and he naturally concluded, that they would suspend their ultimate resolution of sending an army to the

He goes to Lyons.

23d July.

Motives for his journey.

(4) L'Etoile, p. 206. Mezerai, vol. ix. p. 310 and 311. De Thou, vol. ix. p. 594, and 599.

assistance

CHAP. VI. 1586.

assistance of the Protestants, till they should be convinced that it was indispensable. He was anxious to know the result of the intended conference between his mother and the king of Navarre, which might entail consequences of the last importance to his own repose, and to the general felicity of the kingdom. An inducement more powerful than any of a political nature; the desire to superintend, in some measure, the motions of his two favorites, Joyeuse and Epernon; impelled him to fix his residence at Lyons. Not satisfied with the acquisition of offices, dignities, and emoluments of every kind, the ambition of these minions aspired to the separate command of two armies; and the facility of Henry, which equalled his profusion, immediately accorded their request, though they possessed scarcely any other qualities requisite for the employment, except personal courage. Their views were likewise widely different, in soliciting the charge. Joyeuse, who had passed the zenith of his favor, and who leaned towards the interests of "the League;" entering the Gevaudan, directed all the force of his exertions against the Hugonots. As they had no regular troops to oppose him, he penetrated into that mountainous country, made himself master of several towns, and exercised the utmost violence against the unfortunate prisoners who fell into his hands. But, Epernon, whose influence continually augmented, and exceeded any limits; who had evinced his partiality to the interests of the king of Navarre; and who was not less odious to, than he, in turn, detested the Guises; was animated by very opposite inclinations. He had recently received from the bounty of the king, his master, the government of Provence, become vacant by the death of Henry, count of Angouleme, natural son to Henry the Second. Such was, however, the authority acquired by the partizans of the duke of Guise in that province,

Armies entrusted to Joyeuse and Epernon.

Conduct of Joyeuse.

Opposite inclinations of Epernon.

province, that it was doubtful whether the new governor could establish his power among a people disaffected to his person, and who had thrown off all respect for the orders of the crown. The entrance of Epernon was not a little facilitated by a signal victory which Lesdiguieres, at the head of the Protestants, obtained over the troops of the zealous Catholics, conducted by the baron de Vins, a steady adherent of "the League." Aided by so opportune an event, Epernon, with a well-appointed army, and a numerous artillery, found little resistance; and availing himself of the lassitude, or inferiority of the two parties, he surmounted all opposition (5).

Henry returns to Paris.

Wearied with the complaints of the German embassadors, who having arrived at Paris, waited with impatience for the king's return, in order to obtain an audience; Henry reluctantly repaired to the metropolis. The delegates, addressing him in the names of the three Protestant electors, of Saxony, Brandenburg, and the Palatine, as well as of many inferior states of the empire; caused their letters to be publickly read. Those princes represented, with a plain and hardy frankness, not only the calamities which he inflicted upon France, by persecuting his subjects; but, the dishonor and infamy annexed to an unprovoked violation of his own edicts of toleration. In the names of their respective sovereigns, they besought him to suspend the further progress of the war; and they offered him all the support which he might think proper to demand, or accept, if he would turn his efforts against such as had dared to excite commotions in his dominions, and to conspire against his dignity and repose. Henry was much more sensible to the severity of the former part of

12th Oct. Remonstrances of the German princes.

(5) Mezerai, vol. ix. p. 304 and 305, and 308 and 309. De Thou, vol. ix. p. 599—605, and 615—619. Davila, p. 602—604.

the

CHAP. VI. 1586.

the remonſtrance, in which his faith and honor were attacked; than he was touched by the entreaties, or affected by the offers of the German princes. In his reply, he adopted a tone, not only of reſentment, but, of indignation; and regardleſs of the conſequences, he diſmiſſed the embaſſadors with expreſſions of contempt and inſult (6).

Reply of Henry.

Meaſures of the duke of Guiſe.

Far from being mollified or diſarmed by theſe demonſtrations of his averſion to the Hugonots, the duke of Guiſe ſeemed to proceed with augmented boldneſs and celerity, towards the final execution of his deſigns. While, on one hand, he cauſed all the actions of Henry to be miſrepreſented by his emiſſaries, and attributed his recent treatment of the Germans, to profound diſſimulation; on the other, he employed the troops under his command in enterprizes unauthorized by the king, contrary to his orders, and injurious to his intereſts. As the territories of the duke of Bouillon, who profeſſed the reformed religion, might greatly facilitate the entrance of foreign forces into Champagne; it was determined to invade them, although no provocation had been given, nor act of hoſtility committed on his part. Donzy, and afterwards Rocroi, were attacked, and taken by the duke of Guiſe: who, continuing his incurſions, made himſelf maſter of Raucour, and menaced Sedan itſelf, the capital of the principality. He was diverted from the further proſecution of the enterprize, by the refuſal of the city of Auxonne in Burgundy, to receive a garriſon in the name of the duke of Mayenne. The place was inſtantly inveſted, and captured; while the duke of Aumale, another prince of his family, governor of Picardy, ſeized upon Dourlens, and the principal

He attacks the duke of Bouillon.

(6) De Thou, vol. ix. p. 6:6—610— Davila, p. 604—606.

towns

1586.

towns along the banks of the Somme. All the eastern provinces, including a vast proportion of France, extending nearly from the gates of Calais, uninterruptedly, to those of Lyons, were already in the dependance of "the League." The chiefs of the union, emboldened by Henry's timidity, and irritated at the obstacles which he had contrived to oppose to the military progress of Mayenne, met at the abby of Orcamp, near Noyon, in Picardy; where they proceeded to embrace resolutions subversive of all obedience to the crown. They agreed to continue the war undertaken against the duke of Bouillon; to render themselves masters of the whole duchy; and regardless of the king's approbation, whom they accused of indirectly sustaining the Hugonots, to push their operations with redoubled vigor, in every possible direction (7).

Power of the League.

30th Sept.

Resolutions of the chiefs.

While the duke of Guise was thus employed; the king, averse to a war which interrupted his habitual indolence; terrified at the prospect of a foreign army of Germans, which impended over his dominions; and incensed at the daring projects of a faction, no longer restrained by any remains of allegiance or duty; turned his whole attention towards the result of the conference between his mother and the king of Navarre. Catherine of Medicis, sinking in years, and oppressed by infirmities, did not decline an occasion of exerting her influence, and rendering her services necessary. If ever, in any of her negociations with the Hugonots, she can be regarded as having acted with sincerity, it was on this occasion. She saw the ruin into which her son was plunged, and to which she had, herself, been accessary, by the indirect support given to the projects of the Guises. An expedient presented itselff or unit-

Views and measures of Henry.

(7) Davila, p. 613—614. De Thou, vol. ix. p. 610—612. Mezerai, vol. ix. p. 304 and 307.

CHAP. VI. 1586.

ing the two kings, while it perpetuated the crown in her own descendants, and effectually crushed the pernicious attempts of the enemies of the state. Margaret of Valois, queen of Navarre, was not only destitute of issue; but, her abandoned conduct and dissolute life had rendered her unworthy to ascend the throne, or even to share her husband's bed. Sheltered among the mountains of Auvergne, she was already forgotten; and it could not be difficult to obtain from the see of Rome a dissolution of the marriage. Christina, the princess of Lorrain, grand-daughter of Catherine, and niece of Henry, might supply Margaret's place; and the beauty of her person was encreased by the modesty of her deportment. To give its full effect to the proposition, Christina accompanied the queen-mother to St. Brix, a small town on the Charente, near Cognac, in Angoumois; where, after many difficulties and precautions, the king of Navarre repaired. The interview commenced by mutual reproaches, calculated to conceal the real object of the conference; but, in the more private communications, Catherine, by authority of her son, offered him the young princess, together with a declaration of his right to the throne, in case of the death of Henry without male issue. She enforced it by every argument drawn from his own situation, and that of the kingdom itself, which so loudly called for an effectual remedy to its multiplied and encreasing misfortunes. His resumption of the Catholic religion, and his return to court, were the sacrifices demanded of the king of Navarre. Flattering as were the offers, he, notwithstanding, rejected them, after a delay of only two days. The same reasons, which had influenced his determination, when Epernon was dispatched to him by Henry, not only subsisted in their full force, but were even strengthened by the interval of time. He was well acquainted with the king's aversion to the Hugonots:

Interview of St. Brix.

18th Oct.

Offers of Catherine, to the king of Navarre.

Motives for their rejection.

Hugonots: he diſtruſted Catherine; and he was not ignorant, that negotiations with the Guiſes were carrying on, at the moment when the animoſity of the royaliſts and the adherents of "the League" ſeemed to render all reconciliation between them impoſſible. Above every other conſideration, he dreaded, with reaſon, to commit himſelf a ſecond time, to the mercy of a faithleſs prince, and of a tumultuous capital, deſtitute of obedience, inflamed by ſeditious demagogues, and the populace of which held his perſon and religion in equal execration. The queen-mother vainly attempted to ſurmount impediments of ſuch magnitude, by urging the impoſſibility of Henry's entering into new and indiſſoluble connections with a heretic. All her arguments were ineffectual; and the king of Navarre, after reiterating his profeſſions of loyalty to the crown, and of gratitude to his ſovereign, whom he offered to join, with his own and the German auxiliaries, in order to exterminate their common enemies; withdrew from the conference. It was continued for ſome time longer, in the name of the two kings, by the intervention of the duke of Nevers, and the viſcount Turenne; but, far from diminiſhing the difficulties oppoſed to an accommodation, they only rendered them more apparent and inſurmountable (8).

Ineffectual concluſion of the conference.

The

(8) Davila, p. 616—620. De Thou, vol. ix. p. 619—622. D'Aub. vol. iii. p. 22—24. Chronol. Novennaire, vol. i. p. 31 and 32.

Davila alone, of all the contemporary hiſtorians, ſeems to have been fully informed of the ſecret object of the conference of St. Brix, and of the offer of the princeſs Chriſtina of Lorrain, as the future wife of the king of Navarre. His relation of every circumſtance attending the interview, is too minute, and his authorities are known to have been too high, to call in queſtion his veracity. De Thou, who, in all reſpects, muſt be regarded as the moſt judicious and able writer of his age, does not appear to have been acquainted with the concealed nature of Catherine's propoſals, nor even to have known that Chriſtina herſelf was conducted to St. Brix. He omits her name, at leaſt, in his enumeration of the perſons of diſtinction, who accompanied the queen-mother, though he mentions Catherine of Bourbon, abbeſs

of

CHAP. VI. 1586. State of the metropolis.

The indefatigable exertions of the partizans of "the League" had, in no part of the kingdom been attended with such complete success, as among the inhabitants of the metropolis; where the personal weaknesses and vices of the sovereign being more intimately known, had withdrawn the obscurity, which veiled the throne from the rest of Henry's subjects, placed at a distance from the seat of government. His ill-timed clemency and lenity; if the inactivity and apathy of that prince, can be justly so entitled; towards all those who distinguished themselves by acts of daring outrage against him,

of Soissons, aunt to the king of Navarre. In D'Aubigné, are contained many curious, and interesting particulars concerning the interview; but, neither in his recital, nor in the "Chronologie Novennaire," is the offer of Christina specified. Those authors were probably ignorant of the fact. Sully passes over the conference of St. Brix; and there is no mention whatever of it, in the "Journal d'Henry III." Even, by the testimony of Davila, whose partiality towards his benefactress, Catherine of Medicis, renders him on that point, more deserving of credit; the king of Navarre was justified in not accepting the proposals made to him, however apparently brilliant. It appears, that, at the very moment when Henry commissioned his mother to urge their immediate acceptance, he was treating with the heads of "the League;" and that he had assured the papal Nuntio, the duke of Guise, and the Parisians, of his determination to conclude no treaty with the Hugonots, which would not be ultimately for the benefit of the Catholic religion. If we reflect on the similar protestations made by Charles the Ninth, to the Legate, before the massacre of Paris; and if we consider how little reliance could be placed on the oaths of so fickle a prince as Henry the Third, or so treacherous and fickle a woman as the queen-mother, secretly attached to the party of the Guises; we shall see ample reason for approving the determination of the king of Navarre; independant of every motive drawn from those sentiments of honor, decorum, and conscience, which must have opposed a renunciation of his religion.

D'Aubigné relates, that the duke of Nevers said to the king of Navarre, in the course of the conversations; "Sire, you would act better to make "your court to our common sovereign and master, than to the mayor of "Rochelle, from whom, in your greatest necessity, you cannot extort the "smallest assistance." "We do not (answered that prince) understand "the science of imposing contributions: for, we have no Italians among "us: but, at Rochelle, I do every thing that I wish, by only desiring to "do what I ought." Under Henry the Third, almost all the financiers, contractors, and persons who farmed the revenues, were natives of Italy.

It is somewhat singular, that De Thou fixes the conference, on the 13th of December; D'Aubigné, in the beginning of March; and Davila, on the 18th of October. As there were many interviews, and much time consumed in them, we must account for so extraordinary a contradiction of these three historians, from that circumstance.

seemed

seemed to secure impunity, and to provoke resistance. Every art, calculated to inflame a bigotted, sanguinary, and furious multitude, was practised in order to render the king odious, as well as suspected. Their credulity, proportioned to their ignorance, made them susceptible of any impression, and led them to swallow the most improbable fictions. Notwithstanding the incontestible proofs which, throughout his whole reign, the king had given of attachment to the antient religion, and of an equal aversion to the reformed doctrines; the Parisians considered him as privately leagued with the king of Navarre, for the extirpation of the Catholic faith. His retirements to Vincennes, for the ostensible purposes of maceration and devotion, were stigmatized, as only concealing the most enormous and profligate debaucheries. Even the clergy, with the exception of certain monastic orders whom he peculiarly favored and enriched; became the instruments to withdraw from him the allegiance of the people. In the confessionals, every treasonable and seditious principle was silently inculcated, and deeply impressed; while from the pulpit, the more eloquent and audacious preachers declaimed against their sovereign, and openly exposed his enormities, or arraigned his administration. Already, in almost all the various professions, trades, and obscure walks of inferior life, throughout the capital, persons selected for their activity and zeal, met, under cover of the night, to communicate their operations, and to compare their respective proceedings.

CHAP. VI. 1587.

Credulity of the Parisians.

Disaffection of the clergy.

Paris being divided into sixteen wards, or districts, a council, composed of as many men, chosen from each, was formed, in order to direct and superintend the movements of the subordinate actors. Many individuals, alarmed at the pretended danger of a subversion of the national religion, though not otherwise disaffected to the crown, were admitted to the

Plans for an insurrection.

CHAP. VI. 1587.

the nocturnal assemblies, and gradually initiated in their mysteries. Among the most distinguished leaders of the cabal, was Bussy le Clerc; who, after having been a fencing-master, had obtained a place of solicitor in the parliament of Paris. La Chappelle Marteau, a man of desperate fortune, pursued by his creditors, occupied likewise a high place in the seditious meetings. They all received their instructions from Mainville, the agent and minister of the duke of Guise; a young man of superior extraction, possessing eloquence, capacity, and an unbounded devotion to the cause in which he had engaged. These qualities were, however, contrasted with equal arrogance, insolence, and temerity (9).

Arts of the League to inflame the Parisians.

Many artifices were used, and numerous expedients devised, in order to sustain the flame of sedition among the multitude. The confessors denied absolution to such as refused to enter into the association: processions, not only of the inhabitants of Paris, but from Picardy, Lorrain, and other provinces; composed of persons of both sexes, dressed in white, and having crosses on their habits, continually kept alive the general ferment; while they were favorable to the designs of the chief conspirators. Emissaries of approved zeal and capacity, were sent into the country, to spread the tenets, and augment the proselytes of "the League." They artfully addressed themselves to those whose embarrassed circumstances, or profligate character, rendered their seduction easy; and they exaggerated the forces, military and pecuniary, possessed by the duke of Guise, who was the object of their supreme idolatry.

So numerous and ardent a body of men, was disposed to engage in schemes the most desperate; nor

(9) De Thou, vol. ix. p. 649—652. Davila, p. 606. Chron. Noven. vol. i. p. 12—15.

could

could they be restrained, without difficulty, from anticipating the cautious projects of the leaders, and proceeding to immediate extremities. As a prelude to greater and more decisive enterprizes, an attempt was formed against the city of Boulogne, of which Epernon was governor. Mendoza, the Spanish embassador, urged the execution of the plan, with a view of securing a port in the British channel, which, from its advantageous situation, might afford a safe and convenient place of refreshment or retreat, to the Spanish Armada, destined against England. In order to obtain the consent of the duke of Guise and the principal Parisians, he promised them, that Philip, when they were possessed of Boulogne, would openly join his forces, and act in concert with " the League." All the preparations for conducting the attack, were made with such secresy and ability, that its success seemed to have been certain, if it had not been revealed by one of the persons engaged in the design. Poulain, a subordinate officer of the police; although in indigent circumstances, yet moved by scruples of honor or loyalty, divulged it to Chiverny the chancellor. Precautions so effectual were taken in consequence, that the scheme was not only rendered abortive; but Vetus, the conductor of it, was made prisoner; and the duke of Aumale, governor of Picardy, who had advanced to support the assailants, escaped with difficulty from an ambuscade, placed to intercept his retreat. Notwithstanding the audacity of an enterprize so treasonable, Henry had the weakness, at the solicitation of the duke of Guise, to liberate Vetus, after a detention of a few months, and to bury in oblivion the whole proceeding (10).

CHAP. VI.

1587.

Enterprize against Boulogne.

It is divulged and prevented.

(10) Davila, p. 607 and 608. De Thou, vol. ix. p. 653—658.

Encouraged

CHAP. VI.

1587.

Project for seizing, and imprisoning Henry.

Encouraged by the king's pusillanimity, and almost secure of impunity, the leaders proceeded to acts of a more atrocious nature. Although the absence of Guise, and his exhortations not to precipitate affairs, in some degree, restrained their ardor; yet, on the arrival of his brother, Mayenne, from his campaign against the king of Navarre, the Parisians laid before him a project, of no less magnitude, than enormity. It had for its object, the seizure of the king, whom they proposed to confine in a monastery: the imprisonment, or massacre of his ministers and favourites: the capture of the Bastile, the Temple, the Arsenal, and the Louvre; and the formation of a government, composed of their own adherents. As the pillage of the metropolis might become an unavoidable consequence of the execution of the plan; and as their troops might disband, in order to plunder; measures of prevention were taken, by preparing barricades, composed of earth, and chains which could be stretched across the principal streets. Eight thousand armed men were asserted to be in readiness, for effecting the enterprize. Mayenne, naturally cautious, and little disposed to engage in schemes which must be committed to a tumultuous and ungovernable populace, was shocked at the atrocity, as well as overcome by the immensity of the proposition. He, notwithstanding, after some hesitation and repugnance, consented to avow and join the conspirators, if successful.

The king receives information of it.

Henry, warned of the design, by the same faithful spy, who had already frustrated the machinations of the Parisians; lost no time in taking effectual steps for his own preservation. The chiefs, ignorant of the quarter from whence they were betrayed, but, deterred by the king's precautions, postponed their measures: while Mayenne, terrified, and expecting hourly to be arrested, or executed as a trai-

tor,

tor, was reduced to the neceſſity of feigning indiſpoſition. Encouraged, at length, by the ſilence of the government; he ventured to withdraw from Paris, after previouſly repairing to the Louvre, to take leave of his ſovereign. Inſtead of ſeizing, and bringing him to puniſhment, Henry diſmiſſed him with a ſarcaſtic reprimand, calculated to incenſe, but, not to deter, him from repeating ſuch criminal attempts; and the leaders, whom he left behind in the capital, neither diſheartened, nor dejected, ventured to renew them, though with ſimilar ſucceſs. The remonſtrances and menaces of the duke of Guiſe, alarmed leſt ſuch premature efforts ſhould prevent the final accompliſhment, which time and occaſion could alone mature, with difficulty impoſed a reſtraint on their impetuous paſſions, and withheld them from open inſurrection (11).

Alarm of the duke of Mayenne, at its diſcovery.

While theſe appearances of popular diſcontent manifeſted themſelves in the metropolis; the proſpect was not leſs gloomy in every other quarter. The king, whoſe inſurmountable indolence had allowed the factions of his court to attain a degree of ſtrength which he could no longer controul; ſaw his dominions on the point of being ravaged by foreign, as well as by domeſtic enemies. On one hand, the German auxiliaries prepared to march to the aſſiſtance of the Hugonots, and might be ſhortly expected to enter France. On the other, he beheld the duke of Guiſe, at the head of a numerous and formidable party, ready to diſpute their paſſage, and to defend the monarchy, of which he himſelf, as ſovereign, was the natural guardian. His triumph, or his defeat, muſt even be alike fatal; ſince, in the former caſe, he would be left a prey to "the League;" and in the latter, he would be at the mercy of the Proteſtants. Unable to controul

Critical condition of the king.

(11) De Thou, vol. ix. p. 659—664. Davila, p. 608—614.

the

CHAP. VI. 1587. His indecision, and misconduct.

the events which were to decide on the cleareſt intereſts of his crown: impelled alternately by oppoſite and conflicting motives: betrayed, or abandoned by the ſavorites, whom his improvident prodigality had raiſed to the ſummit of greatneſs; and deſtitute of the vigor, or deciſion, requiſite to extricate him from the labyrinth in which he was bewildered, he ſuffered himſelf to be borne along by the current; and ſeemed to expect from time and accident, the means of ſurmounting or eſcaping from the accumulated dangers, which ſurrounded him on every ſide.

Joyeuſe marches into Poitou.

The duke of Joyeuſe, leſs ſenſible to the benefits received from Henry, than actuated by jealouſy at Epernon's pre-eminence in favor; and ambitious to fill the place which the duke of Guiſe had long poſſeſſed, as head of "the League;" was deſirous to approve himſelf deſerving of ſo high a ſituation. Having obtained the command of the army deſtined to act againſt the Hugonots in the weſtern provinces, he advanced into Poitou; ſurprized ſome troops of the king of Navarre, who were occupied in pillage; and, contrary to the terms of the capitulation granted them, as well as to the laws of humanity, he cauſed them indiſcriminately to be put to the ſword. Elated by his ſucceſs, which was followed with other advantages; and uneaſy at the decline of his intereſt with the king, he returned to court; where he was a ſpectator of the new and munificent marks of affection, ſhowered upon his rival, who had recently ſolemnized his nuptials with the rich heireſs of the houſe of Candale. Mortified at Epernon's triumph, and the rapid decreaſe of his own favour: irritated by ſome expreſſions, reflecting on his perſonal courage, that Henry let fall: and humbled by receiving intelligence, that the king of Navarre had, during his abſence, driven the royal forces into Touraine, and purſued them

August. He returns to court.

to

to the banks of the Loire; Joyeuſe perceived, that only ſome great and eminent exploit could maintain him in his preſent elevation. Under that conviction, he demanded, and obtained permiſſion from the king, to force the Proteſtants to a deciſive engagement. The young nobility, apprized that a general action was about to take place; eager to acquire glory; and captivated by the liberality and affability of the commander; flocked to his banner, with demonſtrations of the greateſt ardor: while Joyeuſe, impatient to acquire the laurels, which the ſuperiority of his force ſeemed to enſure him, loſt not a moment in quitting Paris, and by rapid marches advanced to ſeek the king of Navarre (12).

Reſumes the command.

If the fate of that prince, which drew to a criſis, powerfully attracted the national attention; the ſolicitude of the king was not leſs painfully awakened to the tranſactions on the frontiers of Lorrain and Alſace. The Proteſtant ſtates, offended at the contemptuous and indignant anſwer given to their embaſſadors, in the preceding year; had aſſembled a very conſiderable army, compoſed of various nations. The Cantons of Bern and Zurich, who profeſſed the reformed religion, animated by zeal, and in defiance of the general treaties ſubſiſting between Henry and the Helvetic confederacy, levied near twenty thouſand infantry. Germany furniſhed four thouſand foot, and twelve thouſand cavalry; which were joined by the duke of Bouillon ſoon afterwards, at the head of above two thouſand French troops. Regardleſs of the Imperial mandate, iſſued by Rodolph the Second, who enjoined them to diſband their forces; they aſſembled near Straſburg, and prepared to commence their march.

Germans prepare to invade France.

20th Aug.

(12) De Thou, vol. x. p. 5—10. Davila, p. 627—630. L'Etoile, p. 227. Mezerai, vol. ix. p. 314 and 315.

CHAP. VI. 1587.

So vast a body, if they had been properly conducted, might have speedily decided the contest in favour of the party whose cause they espoused. But, far from acting in union, or obeying any common head, they were deficient in military discipline, destitute of subordination, and easily inflamed to mutiny upon every occasion. Dhona, who exercised the supreme command, in the name, and by the authority of Casimir, uncle to the elector palatine, possessed scarcely any other requisites, except personal courage; and the duke of Bouillon's youth and inexperience disqualified him for so arduous an employment. Notwithstanding these vices in the original formation of the army, which did not manifest themselves till they were matured by various circumstances; their entrance spread universal consternation. No force which the duke of Lorrain could oppose to them, was adequate to impede their progress; and the king of France did not betray any extraordinary alacrity to risk his personal safety, and to endanger the monarchy, by attempting to stem the course of an inundation, which must swallow up the forces of "the League," before it could approach the throne. So convinced were the Germans and Switzers, of Henry's reluctance to dispute their passage, that they regarded themselves rather as his allies, than his enemies; and were deluded with the continual expectation, that, on their advancing towards the interior provinces, he would join them to crush their common opponents. Such a measure was not only justifiable, but, almost indispensable, after the open attacks made on Henry's authority; and must have rendered him the arbiter of "the League." But, his irresolution, his aversion to the Hugonots, and the habitual indolence which indisposed him for every exertion of magnitude, overcame all other considerations; and though during a short interview with Guise, which took place

Dissentions in the army.

They enter Lorrain.

Expectations formed by them, of assistance from Henry.

July.

place at Meaux, his suspicions had been awakened and augmented relative to the intentions of the princes of Lorrain; yet, he issued orders to assemble forces, and prepared to oppose in person the passage of the Germans across the Loire (13).

CHAP. VI. 1587.

Able conduct of the duke of Guise.

It must be confessed, that in no part of his life did the great endowments and superior capacity of the duke of Guise display themselves more eminently, than against the foreign army with which France was menaced. Uncertain of any effectual support from the crown, and conscious that he had injured his sovereign beyond the reach of pardon: reproached by the duke of Lorrain, with having produced the invasion and desolation of his dominions: unable to collect under his standard a body of forces adequate to meet the enemy in the field, and to try the issue of a battle: beset on every side with difficulties; the intrepidity of his character, and the decision which marked all his actions, supplied these numerous defects. Having advanced in person to reconnoitre the Germans, and being reduced to the necessity of retreating, or of engaging under manifest disadvantages; he preferred death to the appearance of flight. His firmness, and the skill of his movements, extricated him from the danger, while it augmented the confidence of his followers. Retiring before the invaders, as they penetrated into Champagne, he still contrived to harrass them in their march; while the duke of Mayenne having assembled troops in his government of Burgundy, and acting in concert with him, hung upon their rear, intercepted their convoys, and began to make them experience the inconveniencies of famine.

Magnanimity and courage of his measures.

Discord in the German camp.

Notwithstanding these obstacles to their progress, they might with ease have atchieved the great ob-

(13) De Thou, vol. x. p. 21—27. Davila, p. 631—635.

CHAP. VI. 1587.

ject of the expedition, and effected a junction with the king of Navarre. Chatillon, son to the celebrated Coligni, and who inherited no inconsiderable portion of his father's military talents, having been detached to meet and conduct them, earnestly exhorted the leaders to advance towards the sources of the Loire, and to cross the river without delay. But, neither Dhona, nor any of the other chiefs, were possessed of sufficient authority to enforce so salutary a counsel. The various and discordant parts of the army were animated by no common sentiment, except the desire of plunder. They dreaded the rugged and mountainous countries, through which they must, of necessity, pass, in order to avail themselves of Chatillon's advice; and, seduced by the defenceless, as well as fertile nature of the provinces which extend from the limits of Champagne to the gates of Orleans and Chartres, they demanded to be led into them, as abounding with provisions, and rich in the opportunities of pillage. To this injudicious measure, was entirely to be attributed their destruction. The duke of Guise, informed of their internal disputes, vigilant to take every advantage, and revolving in his mind the means of attacking them when too far engaged to retreat; continued to keep them constantly in sight. They were, nevertheless, sustained by the fallacious expectation, that the king would still declare in their favor. But, when they beheld Henry himself, at the head of a second army, occupy the banks of the Loire for a considerable extent, and take the most active measures to preclude them from entering Touraine, in which province they hoped to find a means of passing the river; their consternation exceeded any limit. Such was their perilous and almost desperate situation, at the period, when, in another quarter of the kingdom, the affairs of the Hugonots were completely re-

Misconduct and errors of the chiefs.

Perilous situation of the army.

established

establiſhed by the valor and fortune of the king of Navarre (14).

CHAP. VI.

1587. Battle of Coutras.

The victory of Coutras, which produced ſo beneficial a change, was principally due to the raſhneſs and imprudence of the duke of Joyeuſe. That favorite, whoſe ambition prompted him to hazard a general engagement; unwilling to divide the honor with Matignon, who was haſtening to reinforce him, and confident in the numbers and quality of his troops; felt no other apprehenſion, except that the enemy would not wait for his approach. But, the king of Navarre, far from avoiding an action, having aſſembled a ſmall body of hardy and experienced veterans, croſſed the river Dordogne; and the two armies faced each other near the town of Coutras, in Guienne. The contraſt was not leſs ſingular than was preſented by the Perſians and Macedonians, in the plains of Iſſus. Among the royal forces, every diſplay of magnificence and luxury was viſible; while the Proteſtants, caſed in armour, ruſty and defaced by the inclemency of the weather, exhibited a martial and rough appearance. Nor was the arrogance and want of ſubordination in the Catholic troops, leſs forcibly oppoſed to the diſcipline and ſevere obedience of the Hugonots. The effect correſponded to theſe cauſes; and never was triumph more rapid, or more compleat, than at Coutras. Above two thouſand of the royaliſts were left dead upon the field, and all the baggage, artillery, and ſtandards, fell into the hands of the conquerors. Joyeuſe himſelf, after having diſplayed the greateſt perſonal courage, was put to death, although he offered a prodigious ſum to obtain his ranſom. The Proteſtants, incenſed at the ſlaughter of their comrades in Poitou,

Aſpect of the two armies.

20th Oct.

Victory of the king of Navarre.

(14) Mezerai, vol. ix. p. 317—320. Davila, p. 637—646. De Thou, vol. x. p. 25—42. D'Aub. vol. iii. p. 62 and 63.

long

CHAP. VI. 1587.

long refused to grant quarter; and it required all the exertion of the king of Navarre to stop the carnage. His humanity towards the vanquished, and peculiarly to the prisoners who remained in his possession, was not less conspicuous than his valor in the action, and drew eulogiums from his enemies. The victory was rendered more memorable and conspicuous, from its having been the only one obtained by the Hugonots, during the course of more than twenty-seven years, since the conspiracy of Amboise, and the commencement of the civil wars. Henry received the intelligence, not only without any emotions of concern, but, rather with sentiments of pleasure. He wished to compel the king of Navarre to accept the conditions which had been tendered him; but, was no way desirous of his destruction, or of any event that could augment the power of their common enemies. The spoils of Joyeuse served to decorate his rival, who obtained from the king the government of Normandy, and the post of high admiral, notwithstanding the importunities and solicitation of Guise, who vainly exerted himself to obtain the latter employment for Brissac, one of his own adherents. To these ample gratifications, Henry's profusion, which seemed to know no bounds, added the governments of Saintonge and Angoumois; donations, only calculated to encrease the general detestation, in which Epernon was held by all the adherents of the family of Lorrain (15).

Sentiments of Henry, on Joyeuse's defeat and death.

Scarcely any advantage resulted to the Germans and Switzers, from so brilliant a victory, obtained by the king of Navarre. That prince, unable to retain under his banners the troops with whom he had conquered, or to prevent the nobility and gentry

King of Navarre returns into Gascony.

(15) D'Aub. vol. iii. p. 48—58. Mezerai, vol. ix. p. 320—322. De Thou, vol. x. p. 12—18. Davila, p. 646—651.

who voluntarily adhered to him, from withdrawing to their castles; instead of advancing towards the Loire, immediately returned into Gascony. Perhaps, his attachment to the countess of Grammont, at whose feet he deposited the trophies of his valour; and the facility with which, at every period of his life, he sacrificed his interests to the allurements of gallantry; might induce him to adopt a conduct, by which his glory was not a little obscured. It proved destructive to the foreign army, conducted by Dhona, for whose extrication, the greatest exertions would not have been more than sufficient, and who, thus abandoned, could neither proceed with confidence, nor retreat with safety. Embarrassed with plunder, incommoded by a prodigious quantity of baggage, and diminished by the diseases resulting from their intemperance, they no longer inspired the terror which had preceded and accompanied their entrance into France. As they continued their march, various bodies of troops, commanded by the princes of Lorrain, or by the king in person, straitened their quarters, and augmented their distress. The duke of Guise, anxious to engross the whole reputation resulting from their defeat, exerted equal vigilance in discovering, as he did promptitude in profiting of their errors. While, on one hand, he constantly placed himself between the enemy and the city of Paris, with a view to prevent their approaching the capital; he, on the other, waited to seize the first favourable opportunity of attacking them with advantage. Fortune soon presented him the occasion; and he instantly embraced it, in contradiction to the cautious advice of the duke of Mayenne, who was not induced without reluctance, to commit the fortune of their family to so imminent a hazard. Having obtained information, that a considerable number of the French and German cavalry, was lodged at the town of Vimory, he caused them to be

CHAP. VI.

1587.

State of the German army.

They are harrassed by the duke of Guise,

and defeated at Vimory.

CHAP. VI. 1587. 28th Oct.

be ſurrounded during the night; and after an obſtinate reſiſtance, during which, Dhona, their commander, eſcaped with difficulty, his troops were either routed, or put to the ſword (16).

They ſtill advance towards the Loire.

Notwithſtanding this defeat, which inſpired the troops of "the League" with as much confidence, as it diminiſhed the ardor of the confederates, they continued to advance, in hopes of penetrating through the intermediate provinces to the banks of the Loire, and paſſing it near Saumur. Their courage was not a little revived by the junction of the prince of Conti, Francis of Bourbon, whoſe high quality, and proximity of blood to the king of Navarre, ſufficiently demonſtrated the intereſt which he took in their ſucceſs. His arrival was celebrated by feſtivities and teſtimonies of public joy, which were augmented by the intelligence of the victory obtained at Coutras. But, all theſe premature demonſtrations of ſatisfaction were ſpeedily ſucceeded by a reverſe. Dhona having imprudently quartered part of his forces in the little town of Auneau, where they remained during ſome days, for the purpoſe of recovering their fatigues; Guiſe, who had encamped at Dourdan, found means to corrupt the governor of the fortreſs. In conſideration of a ſum of money, he promiſed to admit the duke's troops through the caſtle itſelf; and the enterprize was executed with the moſt complete ſucceſs. The enemy, unprepared for defence, and unapprehenſive of danger, were inveſted on every ſide, attacked, and cut to pieces before they could make any effectual reſiſtance. Two thouſand Germans periſhed in the action. Dhona, having effected his eſcape, at the head of a ſmall body of cavalry, ſafely reached the other diviſions of his army, who were ſtationed in the vicinity of Auneau. He inſtantly drew

Defeat of the Germans, at Auneau.

24th Nov.

(16) De Thou, vol. x. p. 43—45. Davila, p. 651—656.

them

them up in order of battle, and urged them to attack the victors, during the security of their recent triumph. The French auxiliaries, commanded by Chatillon, joined him in these entreaties, and represented the facility of the attempt. But, no arguments could prevail on the Switzers and Germans. Struck with terror, they refused to be led against an enemy, who had twice surprized and defeated them, nor were any efforts effectual to vanquish their repugnance. Retreat, or, more properly, flight, accompanied with all the calamities inseparable from a dispirited army, laboring under the accumulated evils of famine, cold, and sickness, became unavoidable. The Switzers, separating from their allies, concluded an accommodation with the duke of Epernon, and retired to their own country; while the Germans, exhausted, diminished, and sinking in the roads, began to listen to similar propositions. In this desperate emergency, Chatillon proposed to conduct them towards the province of the Vivarais, where they would be joined by fresh troops, and would find every refreshment necessary to recruit their force. He offered to be their guide during the march, which could not be long; and he represented, with energy and eloquence, the infallible destruction impending over them, if, deluded by a pretended negociation ratified in the name of the king, they trusted to the mercy of "the League," who had already thrown off all respect or obedience to the crown (17).

Retreat, and separation of the foreign troops.

Ineffectual exhortations of Chatillon.

His remonstrances being fruitless, and the spirit of mutiny which pervaded the army, rendering his stay dangerous to himself; he quitted the camp, attended by a few resolute and determined followers. Penetrating through the bodies of the enemy, who

He quits the army.

(17) Davila, p. 656—661. De Thou, vol. x. p. 45—60.

CHAP. VI. 1587. Capitulation of Dhona.

ſurrounded him on every ſide, he ſoon reached the provinces where the Hugonot forces maintained a ſuperiority: while Dhona, and his aſſociates, no longer reſtrained by any conſiderations of honor, or even of prudence, conſented to evacuate the French dominions, with their colours furled, and eſcorted to the frontiers of the kingdom. Conditions ſo ignominious did not ſecure their ſafe retreat; and the princes of Lorrain, regardleſs of the ſtipulations, waited for them beyond the confines. In the county of Burgundy, and even in the principality of Montbelliard, the miſerable relics of their once formidable army, were ſlaughtered by the duke of Guiſe's troops, or maſſacred by the peaſants. Not ſatisfied with nearly exterminating them, the ſoldiery of the duke of Lorrain exerciſed unprecedented cruelties on the inhabitants of the country of Montbelliard, and proceeded to the moſt enormous exceſſes of violence, rapine, and bloodſhed. Scarcely five hundred Germans, exhauſted with fatigue, and nearly in a ſtate of nakedneſs, reached their own homes in ſafety (18).

Destruction of the Germans.

Conduct of Henry.

Henry was little more than a paſſive ſpectator of a ſeries of victories, which covered his moſt inveterate enemy with ſo much glory. He received the intelligence of the defeat of the Germans at Auneau, without manifeſting any expreſſions of concern; and he accepted graciouſly, the trophies and ſtandards ſent him by the duke of Guiſe: but, he was not internally leſs wounded by the conviction that "the League," elevated with ſucceſs, would ſoon turn their arms againſt himſelf. The opportunity of cruſhing the houſe of Lorrain, which had preſented itſelf, was irrecoverably loſt; and it ſeemed difficult, if not impoſſible, to expect, that the duke of Guiſe, raiſed above the rank of a ſubject, would

His embarraſſments.

(18) D'Aub. vol. iii. p. 65—68. Mezerai, vol. ix. p. 323—326. De Thou, vol. ix. p. 61—63. Davila, p. 661—663. Chron Noven. vol. i. p. 37—41. Vie du Duc d'Epernon, vol. i. p. 170—178.

remain

remain long in a ſtate of repoſe. The recent events of the war, by an obvious and unavoidable compariſon, had conduced to humble the crown, in the ſame proportion that they gave ſtrength to its enemies; and the inhabitants of Paris, alienated more than ever from a king, whom they perſiſted to regard as ſecretly allied with the Hugonots; knew no bounds to their admiration for the deliverer and avenger of France. They even accuſed Epernon with favouring the eſcape of the foreign army, which muſt otherwiſe have been put to the ſword; and they conſidered Henry as participating in the intended crime of his favorite. Under theſe impreſſions, that prince, returning from the campaign, made his public entry into the metropolis, with the decorations of a conqueror: while the duke of Guiſe repairing to Nancy, the capital of Lorrain, and ſummoning a counſel compoſed of his neareſt friends, prepared to improve his late advantages, and to undertake more important enterprizes againſt the dignity and perſon of his ſovereign (19).

CHAP. VI. 1587.

He returns to Paris. 23d December.

N 2 During

(19) De Thou, vol. x. p. 63—65.

That Henry the Third not only expected his own extrication from the toils which "the League" had wrapt about him, by means of the German army; but, that he even favored the progreſs of thoſe invaders, as much as he could venture to do, conſiſtent with his own ſafety; are facts inconteſtible. There is an internal evidence of it, in his whole conduct; in the reluctance with which he took the field; in the poſition which he choſe, at a diſtance from the probable ſcene of hoſtilities, in the province of the Orleanois; in the coldneſs with which he received the intelligence of the duke of Guiſe's ſucceſs at Vimory and at Auneau; laſtly, in theterms of accommodation, by which he attempted, though vainly in a great meaſure, to ſave the remains of the Germans from the fury of the princes of Lorrain. Davila aſſerts it, and De Thou inſinuates it, throughout their whole narration of the events of that campaign. But, if any doubt could remain upon the point, it is completely done away, by the avowal of Henry himſelf, in the cleareſt and moſt unequivocal terms, contained in the curious and important diſpatch of the Engliſh embaſſador at Paris, ſir Edward Strafford, to queen Elizabeth, dated "the 25th February, 1588;" two months after the king's return to the capital. The letter is to be found in the "Hardwick State Papers," vol. i. page 251 to 264. In a ſecret interview with the Engliſh miniſter, managed with the utmoſt caution, and during the whole courſe of which there was no third perſon preſent, Henry unveiled his lamentable condition; beſought Elizabeth's friendly aid to extricate him; and particularly

CHAP. VI. 1587. Foreign affairs. Execution of Mary, queen of Scots.

During the course of so many internal events which occupied Henry's attention, he seemed to have lost sight of the foreign interests and concerns of the nation. The execution of his sister-in-law, Mary, queen of Scots, and dowager-queen of France, had been swallowed up in his own immediate embarrassments. The intimate connexion of blood and friendship between that unfortunate princess, and the family of Guise, necessarily diminished, if it did not extinguish the interest which he felt in her misfortunes; and it was doubted, whether the intercession made in her behalf by Bellievre, the French embassador, originated in affection and sympathy, or was only a piece of state dissimulation. It is certain that the remonstrance neither mollified Elizabeth, nor protracted the destiny of the Scottish queen. In the affairs of the Netherlands, which Leicester, the English commander, had embroiled, as well as greatly injured the reputation of the United States, the king of France took no part; and he appeared to view, with the same indifference, the vast preparations making in the ports of Spain and Portugal, where Philip the Second had long been occupied in fitting out his invincible Armada, designed for the conquest of England.

larly, entreated her to exhort the king of Navarre to embrace the Catholic religion, as the only means to disarm "the League." He clearly confessed to Stafford, that he had hoped for the destruction of the family of Lorrain, from the invasion of the Germans: that, in the expectation of it, and from no other motive, he had declined and refused Elizabeth's repeated offers, to stop the entrance of the foreign army: and that he purposely took his own station at a distance from them, and avoided, to the last moment, any attack upon their forces, till it became impossible for him longer to adhere to such a conduct. He bitterly, and with expressions of indignation, reprobated their cowardice, or incapacity, in not demolishing the feeble army, commanded by the dukes of Guise and Mayenne; or, at least, in not ravaging and desolating, as they might have done, the estates and territories of all the adherents of "the League," who must, in such case, have had recourse to his interposition, to rescue them from total ruin. He claimed, notwithstanding, the merit of having saved those of the Germans who escaped, by the treaty which the duke of Epernon concluded, for their safe return into their own country. No state paper, published in the present century, merits more attention, or lays open so much of the private feelings of Henry with respect to the duke of Guise, as the dispatch from Stafford to Elizabeth.

CHAP.

CHAP. VII.

State of France, after the defeat of the Germans.—Proceedings of the princes of Lorrain—Death of the prince of Condé.—Conspiracies against Henry.—Arrival of the duke of Guise, at Paris.—Insurrection.—Flight of the king.—Negotiations.—Treaty between Henry, and the duke of Guise.—Convocation of the states-general, at Blois.—Henry determines to assassinate the duke of Guise.—Measures adopted for its execution.—Assassination of the duke and cardinal of Guise.

CHAP. VII. 1587. State of France,

SUCH was the critical situation to which the affairs of France were reduced, that it was evident some great convulsion must speedily follow. The invasion of the Germans, which, if it had been conducted with vigor and capacity, must have driven the family of Guise to implore protection of Henry; had, in consequence of the errors and misfortunes of the expedition, thrown a prodigious weight into the opposite scale. Instead of advancing to form a conjunction with them, as had been concerted; the king of Navarre, terrified at the intelligence of their defeat, and expecting the united forces of the crown and of "the League" to overwhelm him; retired, notwithstanding his recent victory over Joyeuse, to the city of Rochelle. Henry, who had only acted a negative part in the operations of the late campaign, and who had derived from it neither security, nor reputation; returned to a capital, where his person and his dignity were equally exposed to perpetual insult. The populace, more than ever intoxicated with admiration of the duke of Guise, to whose valor and military skill, the expulsion of the foreign army was exclusively due, felt an augmented alienation

and of Henry.

CHAP. VII. 1588.

alienation and contempt for their ſovereign. All the treaſonable machinations and conſpiracies, which had been, in ſome meaſure, ſuſpended while the event of the recent tranſactions was uncertain, were renewed without apprehenſion. The king, agitated with continual ſears, diſtruſtful of his miniſters, doubtful of the adherence even of his own mother, who indirectly favored the houſe of Lorrain, and no longer able to fix on any ſyſtem which promiſed him a probable, or ſpeedy extrication from his embarraſſments; remained inactive and ſupine, at a moment which demanded the utmoſt energy and deciſion.

Deciſive meaſures of the duke of Guiſe.

On the other hand, Guiſe, conſcious of his advantages, prompt to improve them, and inclined from his character to embrace the moſt adventurous expedients for the completion of all his projects; proceeded inſtantly to avail himſelf of his augmented

January.

conſideration. In an aſſembly of the princes of his family, it was determined, notwithſtanding the reluctance manifeſted by ſome of them, who were inclined to more cautious or moderate counſels; that an attack ſhould be immediately made on the capital and territories of the duke of Bouillon. That prince was lately deceaſed at Geneva, without male iſſue; and as his contracted dominions devolved to his ſiſter, whoſe youth and ſex diſqualified her for making any vigorous defence, the occaſion of invading them was too favorable to be neglected.

Petition, preſented to Henry, by the League.

They reſolved, at the ſame time, to preſent a new petition to Henry in the name and behalf of "the "League," by which he was entreated to unite himſelf in cloſer tyes with the confederacy. The articles contained various requiſitions, calculated to degrade the throne, and to elevate on its ruins, the houſe of Guiſe. They demanded the eſtabliſhment of the inquiſition; the extirpation of hereſy; the ceſſion of new places of ſecurity, and the confirmation of thoſe already held by the adherents of "the League;"

4 together

together with an army, to be maintained by the king, in order to prevent the return of the Germans into France. Insolent and exorbitant as these propositions appeared, they were not rejected by Henry, who only sought by evasion and delays, to elude their accomplishment: while emissaries of the Guises, scattered over the metropolis, already began to reduce into order the tumultuous and discordant parts of which the faction was composed, and to prepare matters for the final catastrophé (1).

CHAP. VII. 1588.

He eludes it.

The affairs of the Hugonots, involved in distress by the defeat of the Germans, were rendered still more gloomy at this period, by the unexpected loss of one of their principal supports. Henry, prince of Condé, after having successfully encountered every danger in the field, was carried off by a death, no less sudden, than tragical. Incontestible symptoms of poison appeared during the progress of his disease, as well as after his dissolution. Suspicions, too well authenticated, fell upon the princess, his wife, who was seized, and imprisoned by order of the magistrates of the town of St. John d'Angely in Saintonge, the scene of the transaction. Her pregnancy, and the birth of a son, whom she brought into the world six months subsequent to her husband's decease; rather than any proofs of her innocence, preserved her from a more severe enquiry and punishment. She was, notwithstanding, detained in confinement above six years. Brillaud, one of the prince's domestics, convicted of having been accessory to his death, was torn in pieces by wild horses. Almost all the qualities which can combine to form an exalted, if not an amiable character, met in the prince of Condé. Exempt from the irregularities and gallantries of his cousin, the king of Navarre, he equalled him in valor, humanity, affability, prudence,

Death of the prince of Condé. 5th March.

Suspicions of poison.

His character.

(1) De Thou, vol. ix. p. 236—238. Davila, p. 669.

CHAP. VII.

1588.

dence, and liberality. Unfortunate in all his enterprizes; banished to an obscure place in a distant province: ejected from his government of Picardy: neglected by his sovereign: persecuted by the Catholics: driven, during the fury of civil war, in which he had been nourished from his infancy, to the severest extremities of poverty, exile, and hardship; his fortitude raised him above misfortune, but, could not surmount his evil destiny. He expired in the vigor of his age, at thirty-five years; and the intelligence of his melancholy fate excited various and contradictory emotions. The king of Navarre bewailed his loss, and undertook to avenge it, by a rigorous prosecution of his murderers. Henry, occupied in celebrating the funeral of his favourite, Joyeuse; and surrounded with dangers that menaced his own safety, scarcely appeared sensible to so affecting an event. The Parisians, by whom the prince was detested on account of his zealous adherence to the reformed religion, made public rejoicings to commemorate it: while, the duke of Guise, mindful of the uncertainty of human affairs, and who knew how to esteem the virtues even of an enemy; shed tears on receiving the news, and gave proofs of the most unfeigned concern (2.)

Different emotions, excited by his death.

These

(2) Mezerai, vol. ix. p. 330 and 331. De Thou, vol. ix. p. 242—247. Letters of Henry the Fourth, in Voltaire, vol. x. p. 232—235. Hist. de Bouillon, vol. i. p. 408. Mem. p. ser. à l'Hist. de France, p. 243, 244. D'Aub. Hist. Univ. vol. iii. p.72.

The prince of Condé's death is not to be ranked among those problematical, uncertain accounts of poison, with which every history abounds, and which may frequently be attributed to malignity, or credulity. By the unanimous, and undisputed testimony of all the contemporary writers, the prince died of poison: but, it is more difficult to determine, on whom the guilt of so atrocious a crime principally falls. Brillaud, who was executed, shewed marks of insanity; and his deposition, as de Thou asserts, was obscure, or defective in many particulars. Belcastel, page of the princess of Condé, and a valet de chambre, were accused of having administered the potion, which caused his death. They fled; and the former escaped out of France; but, the valet was seized at Poitiers, and brought to St. John d'Angely. It was pretended, that the page had been criminally intimate with the princess;

CHAP. VII. 1588.

Designs and irresolution of the duke of Guise. April.

These generous, but, transitory sensations, were speedily obliterated by the great and hazardous experiment which he was, at length, about to make; and on the success of which depended his honor, his fortune, and his life. Having dispatched a number of able, and experienced officers to Paris, who might make the necessary dispositions previous to his personal appearance: and having stationed five hundred cavalry under the command of the duke of Aumale, in the neighbouring villages; he advanced to Goneffe, in the vicinity of the capital, with intention to enter the suburbs. But, information being received, that the king had caused a body of four thousand Switzers to approach the metropolis, the duke, terrified, and apprehensive of being arrested, returned to Soissons. His adherents, nevertheless, continued their plots against Henry's person; and although constantly discovered, yet, as no exertion was made to seize and bring them to punishment, their audacity continually encreased. At the head of the most inveterate enemies of the king, was the duchess of Montpensier, sister to the duke of Guise. Irritated by some sarcastic and humiliating disclosures which he had made of her personal defects, she determined on revenge; and her implacable spirit animated

Projects of the duchess of Montpensier.

princess; and that she was pregnant by him, at the time of her husband's death. The king of Navarre, who went immediately in person to St. John d'Angely, and who must have known every circumstance which could elucidate the transaction; expresly accuses the princess of being privy to, and an accomplice in the prince's death. De Thou, who wrote under the reign of Henry the Fourth, and at a period of time, when the princess was declared to be absolved from the imputation, speaks guardedly respecting her; but, his opinion of her guilt, is evidently to be seen. Mezerai positively asserts it, at a greater distance of time. In 1596, she was liberated, by order of Henry the Fourth, and all the proceedings against her were burnt, as having been informal, and contrary to the privileges of her rank. L'Etoile, in his "Journal d'Henry trois," a contemporary work, makes no scruple of naming the princess, as the person, at whose instigation Belcastel poisoned the prince. She did not bring into the world a son, till the 1st of September, 1588, near six calendar months subsequent to her husband's death. He was afterwards Henry the Second, prince of Condé, and was father to the great Condé, so celebrated in the history of France.

CHAP. VII. 1588. 22d April.

mated the Parisians to the most desperate enterprizes. It was resolved to attack the Louvre by force, to cut in pieces the guards, and to imprison the king. When this plan became impracticable, in consequence of the precautions taken upon Poulain's deposition; a new project was set on foot, to seize him on his return from Vincennes, at which time he was usually accompanied only by a few of his guards. Henry received intimation of the design; and having sent to Paris for an escort of cavalry, was by them conducted in safety through the city. Driven to despair by so many unsuccessful attempts; expecting hourly vengeance; and unable longer to retain the numerous adherents who clamorously demanded to be employed; the heads of the enterprize sent a messenger to the duke of Guise, imploring him, as he valued the safety of all those who had embarked with him in the same common cause, not to delay his immediate appearance (3.)

Alarm of the malcontents.

Henry prohibits the duke of Guise from coming to Paris.

This event had long been foreseen by the king, as equally probable and alarming. With a view to prevent it, he condescended to an act unworthy the majesty of the throne, by dispatching Bellièvre, one of his ministers, to Soissons, where the duke then was, together with the cardinal of Bourbon, and his principal adherents. Bellièvre's message was rather to deprecate, than prohibit his arrival; and Henry adopted the language of supplication, instead of the requisition of authority. Far from yielding obedience to the royal injunction, the duke, in turn, had recourse to complaints and to excuses; leaving it uncertain whether he would obey, or disregard the order. New messengers were, therefore, sent to him from court, to reiterate the prohibition. But, Guise, who had embraced the final determination of appearing in per-

(3) Davila, p. 669—675, and 678. De Thou, vol. x. p. 247—251.

son

fon to extricate, or perish with his friends in the metropolis; contrived to elude them, by another road. Entering Paris with only seven attendants, he alighted at the residence of the queen-mother; who, amazed, and almost overcome by so unexpected a visit, betrayed her concern, notwithstanding the expressions of satisfaction with which she endeavoured to conceal her emotions. She instantly informed the king of his arrival, and signified her intention of bringing the duke to pay his respects to Henry at the Louvre.

CHAP. VII. 1588. 9th May. His arrival.

That infatuated prince, who had always deceived himself by an opinion that Guise would not presume, in contradiction to so many expressions of his will, to insult him in his own palace; was unable to resolve on the manner of his reception and treatment. In a hasty and disorderly consultation, held during the interval which elapsed between the intelligence of his approach, and his actual appearance, various propositions were debated. It was even agitated, to put him to death in the closet where Henry meant to give him audience; and the king did not appear to be averse from so violent an expedient: but the more timid, or more prudent part of his council induced him to reject the advice. Meanwhile, Guise, conducted by Catherine of Medicis, and followed by an immense crowd who pressed to give him marks of their attachment and devotion, proceeded on foot towards the Louvre. As he passed along, the inhabitants of the metropolis, and peculiarly, the women, loaded him with benedictions, and expressed the most unbounded veneration for his person. The affability and popularity of his deportment confirmed his empire over the people, and rendered them capable of every sacrifice, or exertion, to secure his safety. He was, notwithstanding, appalled at his entrance into the Louvre, when he found himself enclosed between the

Indecision of the king.

Reception of Guise by the Parisians.

CHAP. VII. 1588.

the Switzers of the royal guard, the archers, and other soldiers, drawn up, with Grillon at their head, and who received him in deep silence.

His visit to Henry.

Henry's reception of the duke was cold and even angry; nor did he seem to be either mollified or convinced by the excuses which were offered to justify so daring a measure. Guise, apprehensive of being detained, conscious that he was in the power of a sovereign whom he had insulted and incensed, surrounded by enemies, and aware that every moment of his stay might endanger his retreat; shortened the interview by pretending fatigue, and withdrew, unmolested, from the royal presence (4). The two succeeding days were passed in continual negociations, which only shewed their mutual distrust. A long conversation took place at the queen-mother's palace, between the king and the duke; where the latter, no longer restrained by the prudential considerations which had influenced his conduct in the Louvre, manifested his pretensions without disguise. They were so extensive and insolent, that, disposed as the king was to make numerous sacrifices in order to obtain peace, he rejected them, and prepared for defence. But, after having allowed his enemies to gain possession of the capital, to inflame the minds of the people, and to make provision of arms, leaders, and every requisite for commencing active war, it was not easy to reduce them within the limits of submission. Warned by the same vigilant and faithful spy, who had so often given him information, that nocturnal meetings were held at the duke of Guise's house, and that the conspirators were deliberating to proceed to the last extremities of violence and rebellion; he issued orders to introduce four thousand Switzers, under the command of Biron, and a con-

Demands of Guise.

Henry introduces the Swiss troops.

(4) Davila, p. 679—683. De Thou, vol. x. p. 253—255.

siderable

ſiderable number of his guards, who had been quartered in the villages near Paris. They entered early in the morning, were met by Henry in perſon at the gates, and marched to occupy the principal ſquares or places in the metropolis, without oppoſition.

CHAP. VII. 1588. 12th May.

Such was the conſternation occaſioned by the arrival and entrance of the royal forces, and ſo unprepared were the inhabitants for effectual reſiſtance; that if vigorous meaſures had been purſued before the firſt impreſſions of terror had ſubſided, the king might have diſarmed, or rendered himſelf maſter of the city. But, the ſame puſillanimous, and timid policy, which had enabled "the League" to continue their operations for many years againſt the crown, rendered ineffectual the only effort exerted for its preſervation. The exhortations of Catherine of Medicis, who was inclined to favor the Guiſes, and anxious to prevent a rupture; ſtrengthened by the advice of Villequier, governor of Paris; induced Henry to iſſue peremptory orders to the commanders of the troops recently ſtationed, to uſe no violence, and to remain entirely on the defenſive. Encouraged by the tame and paſſive behaviour of the ſoldiery, and after paſſing rapidly from the extreme of fear, to that of inſolence; the people, after ſome hours, began to aſſemble tumultuouſly. Conducted and directed by the officers whom the duke of Guiſe had purpoſely ſcattered among them, while he himſelf affected to remain quiet within his houſe; the populace drove the Switzers and guards from all their poſts. At the ſame time, advancing, as the others retired, they placed barricadoes at the end of every ſtreet, ſtretched chains acroſs, and ſecured their acquiſition (5).

His irreſolute conduct.

Inſurrection of the Pariſians.

(5) Davila, p. 684—690. De Thou, vol. x. p. 256—260.

On

CHAP. VIII. 1588.

They barricade the ſtreets.

On the firſt intelligence received at court, that the citizens having ſhut up their ſhops, and rung the alarm bells, had collected, with intent to oppoſe the troops; Henry ſent directions to Grillon to occupy certain places, calculated to give him poſſeſſion of the quarter in which the duke of Guiſe reſided; and from whence an inſurrection was moſt to be apprehended. But, the order arrived too late: the royal forces, reſtrained from reſiſtance, by the prohibition iſſued to fire upon the inhabitants, were already ſurrounded, and equally incapable of moving forwards, or of effecting their retreat: while, the barricadoes advancing regularly, were puſhed within a few paces of the Louvre, and the face of the body guard. Content with obliging the French troops to extinguiſh their matches, and to ground their arms; the populace ſpared their perſons. But, the Switzers, more obnoxious, as foreigners and mercenaries, being aſſaulted, were plundered; and near forty of them were put to the ſword. During ſo diſgraceful a proceeding, the king, inveſted in the Louvre, the gate of which was defended by about five hundred gentlemen and ſoldiers; beſieged by his own ſubjects; expecting to be attacked, and afraid to expoſe his perſon to the inſults of a furious and exaſperated mob; remained in a ſituation equally perilous and ignominious. The marſhals Biron, and Aumont, having ventured to harangue the people, and to perſuade them to diſperſe, were ſaluted with ſeveral muſket balls; and the king, incapable of long reſiſtance, might be conſidered as at the mercy of the inſurgents.

Dangerous and humiliating ſituation of the king.

Conduct of the duke of Guiſe.

No triumph could be more complete on the part of the duke of Guiſe, who, if he had profited of the ardor of the Pariſians, might have inſtantly, by force, or by negociation, ſeized on Henry himſelf. But, unprepared, or unwilling to proceed to the laſt extremity, he preferred a different mode of action. Quitting his houſe, in which he had hitherto choſen

to

to remain, as a paſſive ſpectator of the commotion; he appeared in the ſtreets, on horſeback, unarmed, with only a truncheon in his hand. His voice and preſence inſtantly ſuſpended the tumult. Satisfied with having excited the rage of the Pariſians, and directed it againſt the king; he checked and controuled its further progreſs. As he proceeded through the different quarters of the city, he cauſed the royal troops, who were every where diſarmed, to be ſet at liberty, and conducted in ſafety to the Louvre, bare-headed, and their arms trailed along the ground. But, attentive, while he gave this proof of his unlimited aſcendant over the people, to ſecure the great object of his exertions; he commanded the barricadoes to be maintained, and the moſt vigilant watch to be obſerved, in order to prevent the king's eſcape.

He pacifies the populace.

Negociations of the queen dowager, with Guiſe.

Under circumſtances ſo diſtreſsful, that prince had recourſe to his uſual expedient of negociation. Catherine of Medicis, continuing to mediate, viſited the duke of Guiſe, and endeavoured to accommodate matters between them. The populace, maſters of the capital, would not even permit her to paſs through the intermediate ſtreets in her coach; and ſhe was reduced to the humiliating neceſſity of being carried in a chair, while the barricadoes, opened to admit her paſſage, were immediately cloſed behind her. Nor did ſhe find in Guiſe any diſpoſition to treat, except upon conditions too inſolent to be accepted even by Henry, in his preſent abject ſtate. No alternative, therefore, except flight, was left; and it might ſpeedily become impracticable, if the Louvre, preſſed in front, and deſtitute of proviſions to hold out againſt the beſiegers, ſhould be inveſted from behind, towards the country. After a night of irreſolution, and alarm, the king determined to quit his palace, and effect his eſcape; while the queen-mother returning

a ſecond

CHAP. VII. 1588.

Terror of Henry.

a second time to the duke of Guise, attempted to mollify the terms demanded on the preceding day. Henry's departure was accelerated by the intelligence which he received, that measures were taken for surrounding him, and that eight thousand men were already on their march to cut off his retreat, while an attack was to be made upon the palace by the Parisians. Terrified at the prospect of remaining a prisoner, he quitted the Louvre; and having mounted on horseback, attended only by a few gentlemen, he took the road to Chartres, where he arrived on the following day. His courtiers, many of the magistrates, and the great officers of the crown, followed him in the utmost confusion (6).

13th May. His flight from Paris.

Such was the singular destiny of Henry the Third; raised to the throne of Poland by election, and to that of France by descent; yet, compelled to fly from the capital of each with precipitation; and to quit Paris, as he had done Cracow, near fourteen

(6) De Thou, vol. x. p. 260---267. Davila, p. 691---698. Chron. Noven. vol. i. p. 46---49. Memoires de Chiverny, vol. i. p. 102---108. L'Etoile, Jour. p. 244---246. Mezerai, vol. ix. p. 332---336. D'Aubig. Hist. Univ. vol. iii. p. 72---77.

Of all the contemporary historians, who have related the circumstances attending the duke of Guise's arrival at Paris, the day of the barricadoes, and the flight of Henry; Davila is the most minute, most interesting, and, perhaps, the most accurate. He recounts it from high authority, and with a perfect knowledge of the facts. De Thou contains, likewise, a number of very curious particulars. That great and virtuous magistrate was on the spot, an actor in, and a spectator of the scene. But, Davila seems to have known more of the secret springs, which actuated Henry's conduct.

Chiverny, who, from his high post of Chancellor, must have been acquainted with every transaction respecting it, is short, and destitute of any valuable matter. He asserts, that when the king left Paris, his intention was only to have gone to St. Germain; but, reflecting, that he should not be more in safety there, than in the capital itself, he resolved on retiring to Chartres. It appears from L'Etoile, that he had not a moment to lose; and that if he had delayed his flight for two hours longer, it would have become impracticable. We find by the "Chronologie Novennaire," that some soldiers, placed in the tower of Nesle, near the gate by which the king escaped, fired on him, and loaded him with the most abusive language. He slept in his boots, at Rambouillet, after having stationed guards on every side, to prevent surprize or attack.

years

CHAP. VII. 1588.

years earlier, under circumstances of disgrace, or of ignominy. His departure was not less unpleasing to the duke of Guise, who received the information, while he was still negociating with the queen-mother. Conscious that he had, by his want of vigilance, allowed his prey to escape; and aware of all the consequences which must ensue from so irreparable a fault, he exhibited marks of surprize, and even of consternation. But, recovering from his first emotions, he prepared to avail himself of his victory over the crown. Paris was completely in his possession, and he lost not a moment in securing so valuable a prize. Having caused the barricadoes to be removed, and restored universal tranquillity throughout the city; he summoned the governor of the Bastile to surrender that fortress. Henry had refused to entrust the defence of it to Ornano, one of his bravest and most faithful officers, who had offered, on pain of losing his head, to maintain it till the last extremity. The Bastile was immediately delivered up; and two days afterwards, the castle of Vincennes followed the example. New municipal magistrates were elected in the place of those who were attached to the king: Guise took possession of the arsenal; subjected almost all the places which command the course of the river Seine, and Marne; and omitted no precaution to ensure the safety, and encrease the attachment of the Parisians (7).

Emotions of Guise on that event.

He becomes master of the Bastile.

From the period of Henry's flight, the royal power may be said to have ceased, and to have been, in a great measure, transferred to "the League." Driven from his capital; abandoned, and betrayed by his ministers, who perceived his incurable supineness or incapacity: divested of the authority, and greatly diminished even in the external splendor annexed to the throne: compelled not only to gra-

Dissolution of the royal authority.

(7) De Thou, vol. x. p. 268—270. Davila, p. 699 and 700.

CHAP. VII. 1588.

tify his implacable enemies with every dignity and office; but, to complete his own humiliation by approving all their outrages: he continued merely to retain the title, without exercising the functions of a king. While Guise, elated with his success, addressed letters to the various cities of the kingdom, and to Henry himself, justifying the late transactions, and applauding their motives for taking up arms; that feeble prince scarcely ventured, in his manifesto to the nation, to express his resentment for the injuries which he sustained. Instead of assembling forces, and attempting to vindicate the insulted honor of his crown; he permitted Catherine of Medicis, who remained at Paris, to continue the negociations for peace. Insensible to the degraded situation in which he stood, he even prosecuted his accustomed pleasures, at the time that the adherents of his adversary rendered themselves masters of the most important cities of France. Epernon, who had been absent during the late insurrection, returning from his government of Normandy, met with a cold reception, and was ordered by Henry to retire to Angouleme. This step, whether the result of policy, or arising from his change of disposition, was followed by a treaty with Guise. The confirmation of all the various acts of rebellion and usurpation, committed by himself and his followers: the addition of new cities to those already ceded to "the League:" the post of commander in chief of the forces, with unlimited powers, conferred on the duke himself, besides the post of lord steward of the houshold, which he previously enjoyed: the re-commencement of war with the Hugonots: the exclusion of heretics from the succession to the crown: and the convocation of the states general in the ensuing month of October, to ratify all the preceding concessions in the name of the nation;

Feeble measures of Henry.

Treaty concluded with Guise.

21st July.

tion: these were the principal articles of the agreement accepted by the king (8).

1588.

So humiliating an accommodation was followed by the arrival of Guise in person at Chartres, where Catherine of Medicis presented him to her son. Henry, notwithstanding all the recent insults received from him, exhibited every mark of forgiveness, and even of affection, towards a man whom he justly feared, and whose destruction, it is probable, that he had already determined. The stipulations of the late treaty were fulfilled, though not without manifest repugnance; and the duke was invested with his new commission, conceived in terms the most ample. In order to gratify the cardinal of Bourbon, he was declared, by a separate edict, to be the nearest prince of the royal blood; and as such, to be entitled to all the privileges or exemptions usually accorded to the person possessing that high rank.

4th August. Guise visits Henry at Chartres.

During the course of these interesting events, the kingdom was far from enjoying tranquillity. In Poitou, the king of Navarre, who, by the death of his cousin, the prince of Condé, was compelled to assume the command, retook the important post of Marans, which had fallen into the hands of the royalists: while Lesdiguieres having joined his forces with La Valette, brother to Epernon, who acted as lieutenant for the crown in Provence, became by the junction, superior to the troops of "the League." Epernon himself, besieged in the castle of Angouleme by the inhabitants of the city, was reduced to the last extremity of famine; and only extricated himself from the danger by the most determined courage (9).

Commotions and military operations in the provinces. July.

August 13.

August 10.

(8) De Thou, vol. x. p. 323—326. Davila, p. 700—713. Memoires de Nevers, vol. i. p. 725—729.

(9) De Thou, vol. x. p. 328—343, and 352—367. Vie d'Epernon, vol. i. p. 230—273.

But,

CHAP. VII. 1588.

Projects of Guise,

But, all inferior interests or concerns were swallowed up in the consideration of the important scene which was about to open at Blois. The duke of Guise, notwithstanding his past success, regarded the concessions of the king as equally incomplete and insecure, till they were solemnly ratified by the assembly of the States; and he exerted, by himself and his emissaries, every endeavour to procure the election of delegates, favorable to his ambitious projects.

and of Henry.

Henry, on the other hand, had conceived the vain, and chimerical hope of resuming in that assembly, his antient authority. Having gratified the chiefs of "the League" by a compliance with all their demands, and by the pardon of their conduct in the insurrection of Paris; he flattered himself that they would rest satisfied with their acquisitions. Rendered distrustful by his experience of the infidelity of his ministers, whom he suspected of being either wholly devoted to the queen-mother, under whose protection they had risen; or, of being secretly attached to the Guises; he made a complete change in the members of his cabinet.

Change of ministers.

A new administration was formed, on whose adherence he believed that he could confide; and Chiverney, the chancellor, dismissed from his employment, was succeeded by Montholon, to whom the seals were delivered.

Convocation of the States General at Blois. October 16.

The convocation of the States, impatiently expected by both parties, was opened by the king in person; who harangued the three orders in the castle of Blois, exposed to them, in animated colors, the calamities of the nation, and besought of them to co-operate with him in applying instant, and adequate remedies. In order to give an incontestable proof of his sincerity in the late treaty with the duke of Guise, and of his intention to execute it with fidelity, he swore to its observance; caused the edict to be received as a fundamental law of the state, and the oath to be taken by every member of the aſſembly. He, nevertheleſs, ſoon perceived, that, inſtead of acquiring popularity by ſuch a meaſure; he had only degraded the throne, and augmented the confidence of his enemies. All the deliberations of the States were directed by them, and ſerved to convince him, that his expectations of aſſiſtance from the repreſentatives of the nation, were delu-ſive. The clergy, devoted to Guiſe, and peculiarly intereſted in the continuance of war with the Hugonots, conſidered him as their ſole protector: while the delegates compoſing the third eſtate, oppreſſed by the ſeverity of taxes, or corrupted by the money laviſhly expended to purchaſe their ſuffrages; received his commands with implicit obedience. Among the nobles alone, Henry maintained a conſiderable degree of influence; but, the crown was too weak to ſupport a conteſt with the other orders, or to render abortive the ſchemes of the powerful faction which preponderated in every reſolution (10).

Influence of Guiſe in the aſſembly.

Political, as well as perſonal motives, combined in urging him to adopt ſome vigorous meaſures for his ſafety and extrication. The duke of Savoy, Charles Emanuel, a prince of an aſpiring mind, and ambitious views, encouraged by the troubles of France; privately connected with the Guiſes; and availing himſelf of ſo favorable an occaſion; had attacked and conquered the marquiſate of Saluzzo, ſituated among the Alps, and the laſt remains of the French acquiſitions in Piemont. Henry was deeply ſenſible to the injury; and ſuch was the indignation of the States, that they proceeded inſtantly to declare war upon a prince, who had wantonly violated, without provocation, a long eſtabliſhed peace. The three orders, inſtigated by the duke of Guiſe, had

November.

Capture of Saluzzo, by the duke of Savoy.

Demands of the States.

(10) Davila, p. 719—726. De Thou, vol. x. p. 368—397.

CHAP. VII. 1588.

had moreover, unanimoufly, and clamoroufly, demanded the royal affent to a refolution, excluding the king of Navarre from his right of fucceffion; and though Henry had been able to delay an immediate compliance with their requeft, yet, it was evident that he muft eventually fanction the decree. From every quarter he received information of the duke's treafonable defigns, which had for their avowed objects, his imprifonment, and confequent depofition. Marfhal d'Aumont, one of the few perfons fincerely attached to his honor and interefts, had warned him, that not a moment was to be loft, as the States were already difpofed to infift on the nomination of the duke to the office of conftable of France; the powers annexed to which would render him equally independant of, and formidable to, the crown.

Motives to impel the king to adopt vigorous refolutions.

As if thefe public inducements were not fufficiently powerful to propel the indolence of the king, private infults and mortifications the moft humiliating, were added. Henry having defired to except the city of Orleans from the number of places ceded by him to "the League," his wifh was not only refufed; but, menaces were thrown out, if he fhould prefume to infift on the propofition. The duchefs of Montpenfier publickly fhewed the golden fciffars which fhe wore at her girdle; and owned, that they were deftined to give the tonfure to a king, whom fhe pronounced unworthy longer to wear the crown. Even from the adherents of the family of Guife, and, as it was generally believed, from the duke of Mayenne himfelf, whofe moderate temper rendered him averfe to his brother's ambitious views; Henry had received advice, that a defperate meafure was on the point of being taken againft his dignity and liberty, if not againft his life (11).

(11) Davila, p. 726—739. De Thou, vol. x. p. 422—449. Chron. Nov. vol. I. p. p. 95—103.

Roufed

Roused by so many concurring testimonies, that irresolute prince, driven beyond the bounds of patience, and compelled to have recourse to the most violent remedies, in order to preserve the remains of his authority; determined on immediate vengeance. Unable to arrest so powerful a criminal, or to condemn him by the customary forms of justice, he was necessitated to recur to assassination; and having embraced the resolution, it was not difficult to find instruments for the purpose. His terrors of "the League" had induced him to form a body guard, composed principally of Gascon gentlemen, chosen by Epernon; poor, faithful, and capable of any enterprize. They were forty-five in number, and commanded by Lognac, whose devotion was unquestionable. Having selected from among them, nine, of whose intrepidity he had the highest opinion, Henry distributed the poniards destined for the act, with his own hand; stationed them in the apartment adjoining to his cabinet; and recommended to them his honor and his crown.

Henry determines on causing Guise to be put to death.

He selects the instruments of his vengeance.

Notwithstanding the precautions taken to conceal the design, indirect and ambiguous notifications of it were transmitted to the duke of Guise, from various quarters. But, naturally incapable of fear, and audacious, even to temerity: too far advanced, either to retreat, or to fly, without sacrificing his projects and his adherents: relying on the timidity or indecision of Henry, whom he despised; and dissuaded by the archbishop of Lyons, one of his most confidential friends, from abandoning his plans at the moment of their completion; he disregarded all admonitions. The king having commanded his attendance alone, in order, as he pretended, to consult him on some affairs of a private nature; the duke, unaccompanied by his ordinary attendants, quitted the chamber in which the council was assembled. At the instant, when he entered the ad-

Audacity of Guise.

joining

CHAP. VII. 1588. His assassination. 23d Dec.

joining apartment, and while he was in the act of lifting up the tapestry which covered the door of the cabinet where Henry stood; the gentlemen, appointed to assassinate him, attacked him on every side. Overpowered by numbers, and incapable of making a long defence, he soon fell, and expired almost without uttering a single word (12).

Character.

Such was the fatal end of a man, who, in other times, and conducted by other principles, might have been equally the support, and the ornament of the throne. Nature had lavished on him many of the rarest and greatest endowments; peculiarly those

(12) Chron. Nov. vol. i. p. 103—109. L'Etoile, p. 257—259. De Thou, vol. x. p. 460—470, and p. 480. Davila, p. 741—747. Chiverny, vol. i. p. 121—123.

Every particular of this interesting catastrophé is to be found in Davila, L'Etoile, De Thou, and the "Chronologie Novennaire." They, in general, agree with each other, in the leading facts. It cannot be questioned, that the duke of Guise received repeated information of Henry's intention to assassinate him; nor does it seem that he altogether disbelieved or despised the admonitions: but, he could no longer retreat, without disgrace and ruin. L'Etoile says, that he received no less than nine billets on the morning of his death, to warn him of his fate; and, that he disregarded them all. He adds, that after his assassination, Henry, coming out of his closet, and regarding the dead body of his enemy, kicked it on the face; exclaiming, "Mon Dieu! qu'il est grand! Il paroît encore plus grand, mort, que "vivant." But, Davila, far better informed, expressly says, that "the "king, content with knowing that the duke was dead, would not even look "upon the corpse;" and, de Thou confirms it, by declaring, that, "so "soon as Guise's death was announced, Henry ordered the carpet upon "which he fell, to be laid over him, and came out of his closet." This conduct is much more analogous to the general character of the king, who was not cruel, nor vindictive. The last necessity alone had impelled him to anticipate the intentions of his enemies, which were levelled against his crown and liberty.

If it be true, as d'Aubigné asserts, that the door which communicated from the chamber in which Guise was killed, to the king's closet, was walled up, in order to prevent the possibility of his entering it; no circumstance can convey a stronger idea of the terror, inspired by him into Henry. The bodies of the duke, and of the cardinal his brother, were let down by ropes from the castle, on the night of the 24th of December, into the court yard; and there consumed by quick-lime, in order to prevent any relics of them from being preserved. By the seizure of Pelicart, secretary to the duke of Guise, and from the papers and letters in his possession, it was clearly proved, that a treasonable correspondence was carried on between Guise and Philip the Second, the king of Spain. The sums, asserted to have been remitted from Philip, during the ten years preceding 1588, did not fall short of two hundred thousand pounds sterling, as De Thou positively declares.

which

which are calculated to obtain, and to preserve an empire over mankind. In generosity, affability, and insinuation, he exceeded any of his contemporaries. His manners were popular and gracious; yet, dignified and elevated. Profuse of promises, of caresses, and of money, he acquired adherents in every class of society. His talents for war had been fully displayed; and his success in the late campaign against the Germans, by raising him to the pinnacle of public favor, prepared the way to his ruin. Patient of hunger, thirst, and every hardship, he was not less idolized by the soldiery, than by the people; and his incredible activity enabled him, without effort, or fatigue, to be present at, and personally to direct, every operation of the field, or of the cabinet. So many sublime qualities were, notwithstanding, obscured by an insatiable ambition, and sullied by a disregard to his promises, and a contempt of faith in all his transactions.

CHAP. VII. 1588.

At the same instant when the duke of Guise was assassinated, his brother, the cardinal, together with the archbishop of Lyons, were arrested in the council chamber. Henry, neither sanguinary, nor vindictive from natural character, was inclined to have spared the cardinal: but, the exhortations of those who surrounded him; the violent and implacable enmity, expressed by that prelate; and the menaces which even his present situation could not induce him to refrain from uttering; prevailed on the king to give orders for his execution. Four soldiers, to whom the charge was committed, dispatched him with their halberts: he met his fate with undaunted intrepidity. Satisfied with having sacrificed the two brothers, Henry did not shed any other blood; and he instantly granted the life of the archbishop of Lyons, to the entreaties of his nephew. The duchess of Nemours, mother to the duke and cardinal of Guise; the young prince of Joinville, son to the

Arrest of the cardinal of Guise.

His death.

24th Dec.

Imprisonment of various persons.

CHAP. VII. 1588.

the duke; together with the cardinal of Bourbon, who had been so long the instrument of "the "League;" and the duke of Elbeuf, another prince of the family of Lorrain, were committed to the castle of Amboise. Many of the inferior agents, or adherents of the Guises, were, likewise, seized; but, the injudicious, and ill-timed lenity of the king, soon restored them to freedom; and they abused it, by immediately proceeding to every act of violence against the crown. The duke of Mayenne, absent at Lyons, having received intelligence of the death of his brothers; and apprized, that if he lost a moment, he would be likewise arrested; precipitately left the city, and fled to Dijon, the capital of his government of Burgundy (13).

(13) Davila, p. 747—755. De Thou, vol. x. p. 471—479. D'Aub. Hist. Univ. vol. iii. p. 151—154.

CHAP.

CHAP. VIII.

Inactivity of the king, after the death of the Guises.—Emotions excited by that event, at Paris.—Death of Catherine of Medicis—Rebellion—Violent acts committed by the Parisians.—Duke of Mayenne constituted chief of the League.—Revolt of the principal cities of France.—Desperate situation of Henry.—Conduct of the king of Navarre.—Truce between him and Henry.—Excommunication of the king.—Interview of Plessiz les Tours.—Attack of Tours, by Mayenne.—Operations of the war.—Vigorous exertions of the king.—He marches to Paris.—Critical position of the affairs of the League.—Assassination of Henry.—His death.—Character.—General Reflexions.

CHAP. VIII. 1589. Escape of Mayenne. Consternation, excited by the late events.

THE consternation, excited by the death of the Guises, not only at Blois, but, throughout the kingdom, was such, that if Henry had availed himself without delay, and had acted with vigor, it is probable that no fatal consequences might have resulted, either to himself, or to his subjects. Notwithstanding the contempt into which his person and authority were fallen, the spirit of loyalty and obedience was not entirely extinct. The capital, and the provinces, were alike suspended, on receiving the intelligence, and waited in expectation of the events, by which so unexpected a blow would probably be followed. Orleans might have been saved by promptitude and dispatch; marshal d'Aumont having found means to enter the castle, which held out for the crown against the inhabitants of the city. In Poitou, the duke of Nevers commanded a considerable army against the protestants, and could have been recalled without

CHAP. VIII. 1589.

without difficulty. Sancy, who had recently been embassador to the Swiss cantons, urged the necessity of a levy of troops from that country, and offered to conduct them in person; nor was it possible for the adherents of "the League," unprepared, and scattered over the kingdom, to act with energy against their sovereign, when at the head of a formidable army, and followed by a numerous nobility.

Inaction of Henry.

But, all these advantages were rendered unavailing, by the inactivity and supineness of Henry. The emotions of resentment, which had excited him to revenge the insults offered to his dignity, having subsided, he relapsed into his former apathy and security. He had taken no measures for supporting the late violent act of severity; and he flattered himself, that the projects of the duke of Guise would be extinguished by his death. Instead of putting himself instantly on horseback, and marching his forces against Orleans and Paris, he appeared to be insensible to the situation of those cities; and he dreaded more the Papal excommunication for the murder of the cardinal of Guise, than the indignation of the people of France. His first attention was directed to deprecate the anger of the holy see; and after using every effort to mollify the legate, he dispatched the bishop of Mans, as his embassador to Rome, in order to appease the censures with which he was menaced from Sixtus the Fifth (1).

1589. Pernicious effects resulting from it.

A conduct so indolent and pusillanimous, was attended with the worst effects. The castle of Orleans, destitute of the necessary garrison, surrendered to the besiegers; and that important city, situated on the Loire, in the center of the kingdom, was lost by Henry's neglect. The royal army under the

(1) Davila, p. 777. De Thou, vol. ix. p. 483—485.

duke

duke of Nevers, infected with the general spirit of sedition and revolt, disbanded, and joined the enemy: while, the duke of Mayenne, who seemed irresolute and uncertain of the part which he should act, encouraged by the king's inaction, determined to revenge the death of his brothers. But, it was in the capital, that the most alarming events took place, on the arrival of the intelligence that the popular leaders had been assassinated. Apprehensive that their execution was only a prelude to greater displays of authority, and that Henry would soon appear in person to resume his prerogatives, and to punish the rebels who had insulted his lenity; the people betrayed scarcely any other emotions, except those of grief. Even the clergy, who had manifested the warmest devotion to the house of Guise, restrained their sorrow, or contented themselves with deploring the tragical end of two princes, so illustrious for their public services and virtues. The parliament of Paris, composed of persons, venerable from their age, character and judicial functions; was not inclined to adopt sentiments of a nature hostile to the repose of their country. Among the opulent classes of citizens in the metropolis, there was every disposition to aid and support the crown, if they had in turn, received from it, the natural and just protection. But, when, instead of hearing that Henry was on his march to restore order, they learned that he remained at Blois in a state of indolent repose; and when they beheld the example of Orleans, which ventured to resist with impunity, they gave full scope to their rage and violence. Having assembled tumultuously in the town-hall, they conferred the government of Paris on the duke of Aumale; came to a determination of sending immediate succours to the inhabitants of Orleans; and put the city into a state of defence. The fermentation was

Emotions of the Parisians, on the duke of Guise's death.

Fermentation and revolt in the capital.

CHAP. VIII. 1589.

was sustained by the popular preachers, who, enraged at the murder of the cardinal of Guise, confounded his punishment with the interests of the Catholic religion, of which they declared him the martyr; and branded their sovereign with the most opprobrious epithets (2).

Death of Catherine of Medicis.

While these symptoms of rebellion displayed themselves in Paris, an event took place at Blois, which, however lost in the turbulent and calamitous scenes presented on every side, at this period of Henry's reign, must forcibly attract the notice of the historian. Catherine of Medicis, at seventy years of age, during the last thirty of which she had directed, in a greater, or lesser degree, the affairs of France, expired, after an illness of a few days. At the time of the duke of Guise's assassination, she was indisposed with the gout; and her emotions on receiving information of an event, to which she might be said, in some measure, to have contributed by the protection of the Guises, accelerated the progress of her disorder. Her judgment, ripened by experience, enabled her to see, and to apprize the king, who, with marks of exultation, informed her of the duke's death, that only vigor and expedition could extricate him from the commotions, with which it must necessarily be followed. Her malady redoubled, in consequence of the severe reproaches made her by the cardinal of Bourbon, on her supposed participation in the violent measures adopted by her son; and the agitations of her mind aiding the attacks of disease, she survived only a short time. Few women have possessed a more exalted capacity, or have acted so distinguished a part on the theatre of the world. The strength of her genius, and the acuteness of her talents, enabled her to acquire, and to retain an

5th Jan.

Character of that princess.

(2) De Thou, vol. x. p. 485—490. Davila, p. 760—762.

ascendant

afcendant over her two fons, Charles the Ninth, and Henry the Third, after their confidence in her was totally extinct. Of a mafculine ambition, fhe defpifed the ordinary occupations and amufements of her fex, and was only intent upon more folid objects. Magnificent, liberal, affable, and capable of the clofeft application, fhe was never overcome by the magnitude, nor diftracted by the multiplicity of public affairs. Prodigal of human blood; faithlefs to her engagements; and regardlefs of the means by which fhe attained her ends; fhe was deftitute of principles of virtue. Continually employed in exciting the diffentions of the kingdom, in order to render her interference neceffary for their fuppreffion; fhe maintained her influence, at the expence of the national tranquillity and felicity. Mortified to behold her authority in a great meafure fubverted, by the favor to which Joyeufe and Epernon had attained; fhe had recourfe to the Guifes, in order to balance and preponderate the credit of Henry's minions. With that view, fhe facilitated, or fupported the meafures of "the "League:" but, her ability was unequal to extinguifh the conflagration which fhe had kindled; and fhe faw before her death the fatal effects of her inordinate thirft of power. Oppreffed at once by age and difeafe; reproached by thofe whom fhe had unintentionally precipitated on ruin; and no longer trufted by Henry himfelf; having outlived her influence, and involved her fon, as well as the monarchy of France, in almoft inextricable calamities; fhe might be efteemed fortunate in not furviving to witnefs the complete extinction of the houfe of Valois, and the transfer of the crown to the family of Bourbon, which fhe had always hated and perfecuted (3).

Support given by her to the League.

(3) Davila, p. 755—757. De Thou, vol. x. p. 500—503. L'Etoile, p. 261—263. Chron. Nov. vol. i. p. 124—133.

The

CHAP. VIII.

1589.

Dismission of the States General.

The king performed her funeral with all the solemnity and magnificence, which the distressed situation of his affairs and finances would permit. Inattentive to, and unaffected by the distracted condition of the kingdom, he continued at Blois, occupied in closing and finally dismissing the States.

16th Jan.

He executed it with the same tranquillity and complacency, which he would have exhibited in a time of profound repose; although every hour convinced him of the necessity of exerting his utmost efforts, to prevent the destruction impending over his crown and life. Previous to the dissolution of the assembly, he administered anew the oath, by which he bound himself never to tolerate any religion, except the Catholic; but, this proof of his zeal, only served to manifest his weakness, and to encourage his enemies. Mendoza, the Spanish embassador, had already taken his departure, and had repaired to Paris, in which city was concentered all the violence of "the League." Encouraged by Henry's feeble and dilatory proceedings, the inhabitants no longer observed any measures of respect towards him; and the spirit of revolt pervading all the classes of society, the remaining barriers which opposed their progress, were totally overthrown.

Insurrection at Paris.

Decree of the college of the Sorbonne.

The college of the Sorbonne, whose decrees in theology were regarded in that age as sacred, when consulted by the people, in the names of the municipal magistrates; solemnly determined, that the nation was freed from the oath of fidelity; and that arms might conscientiously be taken up against Henry, for the defence of religion. Such was the blind and furious attachment of the multitude to the duke and cardinal of Guise, that they saw in those princes only their devotion to the Catholic faith, and were insensible to the acts of treason and rebellion, by which they had merited and provoked their fate. From similar perversion of mind, a

prince,

prince, whose principal crime consisted in his insurmountable indolence, and who had with difficulty been roused to a single act of vengeance, necessary for his own preservation; was stigmatized by his subjects, with the imputation of a sanguinary tyrant, delighting in the effusion of human blood.

Powerful as the decree of the Sorbonne had been, in exciting the populace to throw off subjection to the government, it would have been ineffectual to produce their complete emancipation from all restraint, while the parliament of Paris continued to exercise its functions, and to retain its authority. It became, therefore, requisite to dissolve an assembly, whose presence and deliberations tended to keep alive a sense of duty and loyalty. Bussy le Clerc, a man whose audacity fitted him for the commission, undertook to arrest, and to conduct the refractory members to prison. Having surrounded the hall in which the parliament was met, and occupied all the avenues with his adherents; he entered, armed, into the great chamber, at the precise time when they were about to nominate deputies to wait upon the king at Blois. He instantly began to read the list of the obnoxious and proscribed members, among whom were the two presidents; when he was interrupted by the unanimous voice of the whole body, who declared their determination to follow their chiefs. They were conducted through the streets of the capital, accompanied by the lamentations and tears of the virtuous, or moderate part of the citizens; and were lodged in the Bastile. A new parliament, composed of individuals more subservient, was speedily constituted by the insurgents; who proceeded to administer a solemn oath, in the name of the princes, cities, and states of France, binding them to maintain the union, and to pursue the vengeance of the late assassinations. To inflame the passions of the peo-

Seizure, and imprisonment of the parliament.

16th Jan.

They are conducted to the Bastile.

CHAP. VIII. 1589.

ple, a ſpectacle calculated to awaken their pity, was likewiſe exhibited; that of the ducheſs of Guiſe, widow of the late duke, who, dreſſed in the deepeſt mourning, and accompanied by a train of weeping friends or relatives, preſented at the bar of the parliament, a petition, praying for redreſs againſt the authors of her huſband's death (4).

31ſt Jan.

Indeciſion of the duke of Mayenne.

Theſe important changes preceded the arrival of the duke of Mayenne, who remained, during a conſiderable time after his flight to Dijon, in a ſtate of indeciſion as to his future conduct. The natural moderation of his temper, added to the diſapprobation which he had felt, and expreſſed, at his brother's ambitious and criminal attempts, inclined him to liſten to the amicable propoſitions made him by Henry. But, the exhortations of his ſiſter, the ducheſs of Montpenſier; the invitation of the Pariſians; the ſucceſsful revolt of the city of Orleans; and the defenceleſs inactivity in which the king remained, at the moment which was to decide upon his greateſt intereſts: theſe conſiderations ſurmouuted the reluctance of Mayenne. Quitting Burgundy, he repaired therefore, to Orleans; was received into the city of Chartres, which declared for "the League;" and, after confirming the adherents of his partizans, he arrived in the metropolis, amidſt the acclamations of the inhabitants.

His arrival at Paris.

15th Feb.

His preſence diffuſed univerſal joy, and was followed by events which gave the laſt blow to the expiring influence or authority of the crown. The duke immediately conſtituted a council of the Union, compoſed of forty members, ſelected from among the clergy, nobility, magiſtrates, and citizens, for the ſupreme adminiſtration of all affairs;

18th Feb.

(4) De Thou, vol. x. p. 511—520. Davila, p. 76—765. L'Etoile, p. 264—271. Chron. Nov. vol. i. p. 117—121. Mezerai, vol. ix. p. 364—367.

the separate jurisdiction of Paris being still vested in the council of sixteen. Obedience to them was enjoined on pain of death; and from their hands, he soon afterwards received the investiture of his new office, denominated "Lieutenant-general of the "Royal State and Crown of France." Its duration was limited to the convocation of the States General, at Paris, in the following month of July; and the functions, annexed to it, were precisely those naturally and legitimately vested in the sovereign, whose person he was designed to represent. The duke swore, at the ceremony of his induction, to maintain inviolate the purity of the Catholic faith, the privileges of the nobility and clergy, and the laws of the kingdom. He likewise promised, in order to attach the people, a diminution of the taxes, and protection from all violence or oppression. This public act by which Henry was virtually deposed, aided by the inflammatory discourses of the Monks and preachers, carried the outrages of the Parisians to the last extremity. The populace, animated to a degree of phrenzy, listened with implicit credulity to all the absurd and monstrous fictions, invented to defame and traduce the king. In addition to the crimes of perfidy and assassination, were added the accusations of magic, impiety, and every profanation. He was no longer known by any denomination except that of Henry of Valois; and it was solemnly proposed, after his deposition from the royal dignity, to imprison him during the remainder of his life in the convent of the Hiéronimites, in the wood of Vincennes, there to expiate his past offences by penitence and prayer (5).

CHAP. VIII. 1589. 4th March. He is constituted lieutenant-general of the crown.

Fury of the Parisians.

The powerful example of the metropolis, operated with incredible force upon the other cities of the kingdom; and the greater number of them

Revolt of the kingdom.

(5) De Thou, vol. x. p. 523—529. Davila. p. 771—775.

 openly

CHAP. VIII. 1589.

openly embraced the party of the duke of Mayenne. From the northern frontier of Picardy, to the gates of Marſeilles, and the ſhore of the Mediterranean, ſcarcely a place of ſtrength, or importance remained firm in its allegiance to the crown. Amiens, and Abbeville, which, as well from their magnitude, as from their poſition on the river Somme, were of the firſt conſequence, joined "the League." Laon imitated their conduct; and Melun, the only town in the vicinity of Paris, which had refuſed to ſubmit, was loſt for want of aſſiſtance. Rouen, together with the whole of Upper Normandy, expelled the royal troops, and governors. The contagion ſpread with irreſiſtible rapidity. Chalons on the Marne, was the only city of Champagne, which adhered to Henry; and Burgundy was completely in the intereſts of the duke of Mayenne. Even the important and commercial city of Lyons could not be retained in its duty, by the exertions of Ornano; and Provence exhibited ſimilar proofs of diſaffection. The inhabitants of Toulouſe, after maſſacring, with circumſtances of uncommon ferocity, their firſt magiſtrates, renounced ſubjection to the king; and Narbonne followed the example. In the central and interior provinces, the defection was not leſs general. La Chatre, governor of Berri, induced the city of Bourges to revolt; and Mans was loſt, by the perfidy of Bois-Dauphin, one of the chiefs arreſted by Henry after the aſſaſſination of the duke of Guiſe, and whom he had afterwards imprudently releaſed upon his parole. Clermont alone, of all the cities in Auvergne, refuſed to throw off its allegiance. But, the defection of the duke of Mercœur more deeply affected the king, as in addition to the government of Brittany, he ſtood in the neareſt degree of connexion to the crown, by Henry's marriage with his ſiſter, Louiſa of Vaudemont. Among ſo many calamities, and amidſt ſo univerſal a revolt,

Rouen.

Lyons.

Toulouſe.

Brittany.

a revolt, Matignon retained Bourdeaux in its obedience, though not without difficulty. In Guienue, Languedoc, and Dauphiné, from the numbers and predominance of the Hugonots, "the League" had little power, and few adherents. The course of the Loire from the gates of Orleans, to those of Nantes, and the passages of that important river, were, likewise, principally occupied by the royalists; and Henry was still nominally obeyed in Tours, Saumur, and Angers (6).

Conduct of Sixtus the Fifth, towards the king.

Nor was the situation of that prince's affairs in the court of Rome, more favorable than the internal aspect of France. Sixtus the Fifth, naturally arrogant and irascible; inclined to profit of the anarchy of the kingdom, in order to extend the power and pretensions of the Holy See; and warmly solicited by the Spanish faction, who supported the duke of Mayenne; pertinaciously refused to grant the king absolution for the assassinations, committed by his orders. It was in vain, that he attempted by submissions and protestations of devotion, to mollify the pontiff; who demanded, previous to his forgiveness, that the cardinal of Bourbon, and the archbishop of Lyons should be set at liberty, and even transferred before the Papal tribunal at Rome. Sixtus, far from relaxing in his requisitions, menaced the king with excommunication, and appeared to have embraced with ardor the interests of his enemies; nor could the intercession of the embassadors of Venice and Tuscany prevail on him to adopt a conduct, more becoming the common father of the Christian world (7).

Deplorable condition of Henry.

Oppressed by foreign, and domestic calamities, the king's situation became every day more critical and desperate.

(6) De Thou, vol. x. p. 551—575. Davila, p. 765—768. Chron. Nov. vol. i. p. 139—148.

(7) Davila, p. 770—772. De Thou, vol. x. p. 530—550.

CHAP. VIII. 1589.

desperate. "The League" was in possession of almost all his dominions; while the Hugonots, relieved from the pressure of the royal forces under the duke of Nevers, advanced rapidly towards the Loire, and threatened to enclose him between two hostile armies. The exchequer was empty; the finances drained, or alienated; and he possessed no resources to supply the deficiency. His troops were neither numerous, nor could he rely on their attachment, in a moment of general desertion. The few places which still adhered to him, were shaken, and ready to revolt. Even his governors and commanders, whom he most trusted, opened their gates to the enemy, or compelled him to purchase their precarious fidelity, by presents and rewards. Spain and Savoy were unquestionably hostile; and he dreaded to ask, or to receive assistance from Elizabeth, queen of England, the protectress of heresy. Mayenne, master of the capital, and at the head of a formidable military force, prepared to commence active war; nor could the contest be either long, or dubious. It was already agitated in his council, to quit Blois, and to transport the court to Moulins, capital of the Bourbonnois. The condition of Charles the Seventh was not more deplorable, when the maid of Orleans appeared, and re-established the monarchy of France.

Edict issued by him.

Under these circumstances, the king, at length, issued an edict, in which, after justifying the late acts of severity against the Guises, as equally necessary and provoked, he commanded the rebels to return to their duty, on pain of treason. In order to give some efficacy to the proclamation, he published a second edict, transferring the parliament of Paris to

5th March.

Tours; in which latter city he fixed his residence, as more secure from insult than Blois. His presence prevented the inhabitants from following the general example; and Angers, which had already taken up arms against him, was kept in subjection by the firmness

firmness of Picheri, who commanded in the castle. Henry, having, on payment of a considerable sum, obtained from le Guast, the governor of Amboise, the delivery of the prisoners confided to his care, removed them to different prisons. The cardinal of Bourbon was confined at Chinon: the duke of Elbeuf was transferred to Loches; and the young duke of Guise was detained in the castle of Tours. (8).

CHAP. VIII. 1589. Transfer of the prisoners from Amboise.

Notwithstanding these exertions of vigor, aided by some advantages which the count of Soissons obtained over the troops of "the League," no solid hopes of success could be entertained, unless an accommodation took place with the king of Navarre. That event began already to be regarded as probable, if not imminent; and necessity dictated the measure. The count of Soissons, whose descent from the blood royal, rendered him deeply interested in effecting the reconciliation, and whose attachment to the Catholic religion was unquestionable; urged its expediency. Even the most bigotted servants of Henry, conscious of the danger which approached, and aware of Mayenne's superiority; admitted, that no other mode of extrication could be devised. The conduct of the king of Navarre himself, above all, tended to facilitate a re-union. As his troops advanced through Poitou, and made themselves successively masters of various places which surrendered, he prevented any insult, or injury, from being offered to the Catholics; respected their civil and ecclesiastical rights; and only restored to the Protestants the freedom of religious worship, previously enjoyed by the edicts of toleration which Henry had repeatedly issued. In addition to so beneficent and moderate a treatment of his enemies, he published a manifesto, dated at Chatelheraud in Poitou, calculated

Necessity of an accommodation with the king of Navarre.

Enlarged policy, and conduct of that prince.

4th March.

His manifesto.

(8) De Thou, vol. x. p. 575—583. Davila, p. 787 and 788.

CHAP. VIII. 1589.

lated to awaken the loyalty, while it conciliated the esteem and affection of every man, who retained any sentiments of patriotism, or public virtue. After deploring the calamities of their common country, and reprobating the traitors, who, under the mask of religion, had thrown off all subjection to their sovereign; he declared perpetual war and irreconcilable enmity with the adherents of the League. He concluded by beseeching of Henry to receive him again into favor; and protested in terms the most solemn, that whatever places should submit themselves either to the king, or to himself, he would maintain the inhabitants in the undisturbed enjoyment of all their privileges; peculiarly, in liberty of conscience (9).

Negotiation between the two kings.

So many concurring inducements, at length, overcame the king's repugnance; and he consented to open a negotiation. It was facilitated, and accelerated by the interposition of Diana, countess of Angouleme, natural daughter of Henry the Second. The conditions were speedily adjusted; the king of Navarre demanding only a place on the Loire, for the security of his retreat; and consenting to join the royal army with his own forces, amounting to two thousand foot, and twelve hundred cavalry. On these stipulations, a truce was concluded for one year, between the two princes; and after some delays, Saumur, one of the most eligible and commodious passages on the Loire, was ceded to the king of Navarre. Yet, at the moment of signing a treaty so advantageous to himself, Henry, actuated by his terrors of the Papal indignation, by his detestation of the Hugonots, and by his anxiety to obtain peace, on any conditions; commenced a negotiation with Mayenne. He even authorized the legate to offer the duke terms the most satisfactory, to-

3d April.

Treaty concluded.

Treatment of Henry, by Mayenne.

(9) De Thou, vol. x. p. 584—588. Davila, p. 785. Chron. Nov. vol. i. p. 159—165.

gether

gether with ample gratifications for all the princes of Lorrain, and the heads of the League. But, Mayenne, elated with the flattering aſpect of his affairs; and ſecure of the protection of Rome; rejected with diſdain, all propoſals of accommodation. He accompanied the refuſal, with expreſſions of contempt and averſion for Henry, whom he no longer treated, or affected to regard as king of France. Irritated at ſo inſulting a treatment, and conſcious that no hopes were to be entertained of reconciliation with his enemies; Henry conſented to the publication of the truce between him and the king of Navarre. It had been preceded by a ſimilar ſuſpenſion of hoſtilities, between Ornano, and Leſdiguieres, in Dauphiné, as chiefs of the Catholic and Hugonot armies (10).

Truce.

Violence of the Pariſians.

The intelligence of a treaty with the Proteſtants, and the conſequent reconciliation between the kings of France and Navarre, when it became known at Paris, carried the rage of its inhabitants to the utmoſt height. Libels, calumnies, and every kind of outrage, were circulated, or permitted, by which a furious and miſguided populace could expreſs their impotent reſentment: while the ducheſs of Montpenſier ſuſtained their courage, by falſe, or exaggerated accounts of pretended victories over the royal forces. But, Henry was far leſs ſenſible to theſe demonſtrations of the enmity of his own ſubjects, than to the effects of the Papal cenſures. Sixtus, convinced that the affairs of the crown were deſperate; incenſed at the king's refuſal to liberate the two priſoners, for whoſe freedom he had ſolicited; and yielding to the importunities of Mayenne's agents; iſſued a monitory, enjoining Henry to ſet at liberty, in ten days, the cardinal of Bour-

Monitory, iſſued by Sixtus. 24th May.

(10) De Thou, vol. x. p. 589—593. Davila, p. 786—790. Mezerai, vol. ix. p. 379—381. Chron. Nov. vol. i. p. 174—181.

bon,

CHAP. VIII. 1589.

bon, and the archbishop of Lyons. On failure of obedience, the pope declared him excommunicated, as well as all his adherents; and cited him to appear in person, or by his representative, before the tribunal of the Holy See, within the space of two months. The Italian powers, particularly Ferdinand, great duke of Tuscany, and the republic of Venice, were deeply sensible to so insolent a display of the pontifical authority; and warmly exhorted the king to resent and punish the affront. Ferdinand, in addition to this generous and high-spirited advice, assisted him with a very considerable loan, which enabled him to make new exertions, and to set on foot levies, within, and without his dominions. On the contrary, Sixtus, content with having anathematized him at the suggestion of the League, refused to open the treasury of St. Peter, or to aid Mayenne with the smallest pecuniary contribution (11).

Interview of Plessiz les Tours.

The personal interview between the two monarchs, which had been too long delayed by the scruples, or apprehensions of Henry, took place at length, in the park of the castle of Plessiz, near the city of Tours, amidst an incredible assemblage of people, who rent the air with acclamations. The king of Navarre, after rejecting the cautious and timid advice of those, who opposed his trusting to the honor of Henry; quitted his army, and advanced to throw himself at his sovereign's feet. He was received by that prince, as he merited, with demonstrations of extraordinary regard and affection. They embraced, exhibited marks of the most cordial reconciliation, and proceeded to concert measures for the vigorous prosecution of the war.

30th April.

The king of Navarre completed his first impression,

(11) Davila, p. 810 and 811. De Thou, vol. x. p. 594—600, and 603—614.

by

by returning, accompanied only with a single page, on the following morning, in order to prove his unbounded confidence in Henry's good faith and sincerity (12).

CHAP. VIII. 1589.

Exertions of Henry.

Roused from his habitual indolence, by so many incentives to action, the king dispatched Sancy to levy ten thousand infantry among the Swiss Cantons; and Schomberg, on a similar commission, into the empire, to raise a body of German cavalry. The war had already been commenced in Normandy, where the duke of Montpensier, at the head of the royal forces, obtained a decisive victory over the Gautiers; a community of peasants, who having been driven by oppression, to take up arms, had been seduced to join the party of the League. Surrounded, and repeatedly attacked, they were either put to the sword, or compelled to surrender at discretion. A prodigious carnage was made among them; and the survivors gladly accepted their lives, on condition of returning to their original occupation. An event so fortunate, at the commencement of hostilities, inspired the royalists with courage; and Henry's army was augmented by the arrival of the duke of Epernon, who, at this critical period, brought him a supply of twelve hundred troops from Guienne. The king of Navarre, having returned to his camp, was, likewise, on his way towards Tours, at the head of the Hugonot forces; and it was already in agitation to advance towards the capital of France (13).

Defeat of the Gautiers.

22d April.

8th April. Military operations of Mayenne.

During the progress of these events, the duke of Mayenne, with a numerous and well-appointed army, having quitted Paris, marched to Vendome; the governor of which city, by an act of the basest treachery,

(12) De Thou, vol. x. p. 618—622. Davila, p. 800. Chron. Nov. vol. i. p. 185 and 186.

(13) Davila, p. 794—799. De Thou, vol. x. p. 600—603. Chron. Nov. vol. i. p. 182 and 183.

CHAP. VIII. 1589.

treachery, received him immediately into the place. The archbiſhop of Lyons, who was confined in the caſtle of Amboiſe, found means to convey to him information, that the count of Brienne, with a conſiderable body of Epernon's cavalry, lay diſperſed, in a ſtate of negligence and ſecurity, not far from Blois. Mayenne, profiting of the intelligence, attacked him without delay, cut in pieces a great number of his troops, and made Brienne himſelf priſoner. Encouraged by ſo proſperous a beginning, and informed that Henry himſelf was not ſecure in the poſition which he occupied at Tours; the duke reſolved to make an attempt upon his quarters, before the junction of the Hugonots ſhould render him too formidable. Arriving unexpectedly, after a forced march, in the ſuburbs, his advanced body of horſe had nearly captured the king; who, unapprehenſive of danger, had rode out, accompanied only by a few officers, with an intention to reconnoitre, and fortify the poſt. If the general of the League had inſtantly availed himſelf of the ſurprize occaſioned by his appearance, and aſſailed the royal forces on every ſide; it is more than probable, that he might have obtained a deciſive victory: nor did he want adherents in the city itſelf, who, in ſuch a caſe, would have riſen, and completed the confuſion. But, the characteriſtic caution and prudence of Mayenne rendered him averſe to hazardous experiments, and allowed time to his opponents, for making a vigorous defence. Henry, on this occaſion, proved to his ſubjects, that, however his mind had been enervated by indolence and habits of effeminacy, he was not deſtitute either of perſonal courage, or of military capacity. Although unarmed, and unprepared for action, he betrayed no agitation; iſſued his orders with compoſure, and was every where preſent. During the ſubſequent part of the engagement, as the event was dubious, and

29th April.

8th May.

Attack of the ſuburbs of Tours.

Courage diſplayed by Henry.

CHAP. VIII. 1589.

and might be unfortunate; his judicious directions repressed the intemperate ardor of the nobility, controuled the seditious spirit of the inhabitants, and were highly instrumental to render ineffectual the designs of the enemy. The royal troops, animated by the presence and exertions of their sovereign, behaved with incredible bravery, under manifest disadvantages of number and situation. But, Mayenne, master of an eminence, from whence his artillery played upon the suburbs; and supplying with fresh soldiers, the places of those who fell; towards the evening completely gained possession of the post, notwithstanding the desperate resistance made by Chatillon, who arrived with the vanguard of the Hugonots. The two armies remained opposite each other, during the night; prepared to renew the contest on the ensuing day, if Mayenne, apprehensive of the approach of the king of Navarre in person with all his forces, had not decamped early in the morning, and taken the road towards Mans. He was pursued by a body of the royal cavalry; and towards noon, the arrival of the king of Navarre at Tours, diffused universal confidence. Henry received him as the best support of his future hopes and operations; committed to his charge the conduct of the army; and ordered him to march forwards to Beaugency on the Loire (14).

Mayenne decamps.

At the news of the duke of Mayenne's retreat, the nobility, who had regarded Henry's situation and affairs as desperate, finding that he was still able to make so vigorous a defence, flocked to the royal standard. The revolt of Poitiers, which declared for the League, was over-balanced by the success which, in other parts of the kingdom, attended

The nobility assist the king.

17th May.

(14) De Thou, vol. x. p. 622—628. Davila, p. 799—805. Chron. Nov. vol. i. p. 186—189. Sully's Memoirs, folio edition, vol. i. p. 65 and 66. Mezerai, vol. ix. p. 386—388.

him;

CHAP. VIII. 1589.

him; and only energy ſeemed wanting, to ſecure a prompt and happy termination of the war. Senlis, a city in the vicinity of Paris, having returned to its allegiance, and called in Thoré, brother to marſhal Montmorenci; was ſoon afterwards beſieged by the duke of Aumale, at the head of a numerous force, principally collected from among the inhabitants of the metropolis. He had been joined under the walls by Balagny, governor of Cambray, with four thouſand troops; and the place was reduced to the utmoſt extremities. In theſe circumſtances, the duke of Longueville, aided by the celebrated La Noue, who had acquired a high reputation during the civil wars of France, did not heſitate to attack the Leaguers, though inferior to them in numbers, artillery, and every preparation. They obtained a deciſive victory; cut to pieces twelve hundred of the beſiegers, and obliged Aumale to ſeek his ſafety in a precipitate flight. Senlis was not only relieved; but, the victorious royaliſts, purſuing their advantage, threw ſupplies of proviſions into the caſtle of Vincennes, and even fired ſome vollies of cannon againſt Paris itſelf. On the other hand, Chatillon, at the head of a body of cavalry, was not leſs ſucceſsful in a rencounter with Saveuſe and La Broſſe, two adherents of the League, whom he charged and defeated near Bonneval, in the province of Chartres. Both the chiefs periſhed in the action, together with above a hundred of the nobility of Picardy (15).

Siege of Senlis.

17th May. Victory of the royaliſts.

18th May. Subſequent advantages.

Alarm at Paris.

Such was the alarm occaſioned in the metropolis, by the diſaſter at Senlis, and ſo dejected were the boldeſt partizans of the family of Guiſe; that the council of the Union having met, determined in-

(15) Chron. Nov. vol. i. p. 204—212. De Thou, vol. x. p. 632—643. Davila, p. 805—808, and 810. Sully, vol. i. p. 66. L'Etoile, p. 280.

ſtantly

stantly to solicit the return of Mayenne. The duchess of Montpensier, who personally despised the duke of Aumale, and whose contempt was augmented by his recent defeat; urged her brother not to lose a moment in re-assuring the fickle and terrified inhabitants of the capital. That general, after his ill success before Tours, had made himself master of Alençon in Normandy; and he no sooner received the intelligence of La Noue's victory, together with the messengers from Paris, than he bent his march thither. His appearance appeased, though it did not extinguish, the popular emotion; and he prepared for a vigorous opposition. But, the tide of fortune appeared to have rapidly turned in favor of the crown; and Henry, after experiencing all its rigor, was on the point of resuming his nearly extinct prerogatives. No effective impediment was interposed to the progress of his forces, who successively stormed the few places that ventured on resistance. At Estampes, which was taken by assault, the king, irritated at the pertinacity of his rebellious subjects, abandoned the place to pillage, and caused the magistrates to be immediately executed. To augment his satisfaction, Sancy, whom he had dispatched to levy an army in Switzerland, succeeded beyond his most sanguine expectations. That faithful and zealous minister not only induced the Cantons to aid him with troops; but he obtained from them a supply of money, still more essential in the distressed condition of his sovereign's finances. After having carried an offensive war into the dominions of the duke of Savoy, in retaliation for his invasion and capture of the marquisate of Saluzzo; Sancy conducted the Swiss and German forces into Burgundy. Near Langres, in that province, La Noue and the duke of Longueville, by Henry's orders, met him, in order to superintend

CHAP. VIII. 1589.

22d May.

Return of Mayenne to the capital.

Rapid progress of the royal army.

Military operations.

CHAP. VIII. 1589.

perintend and direct his march towards Paris, the point of general union. So many fortunate events were chequered, but, in no degree, counterbalanced, by the ill success of the count of Soissons; who, having been sent to command in Brittany, was surprized, defeated, and made prisoner, by the duke of Mercœur, at Chateau Giron, near Rennes (16).

July.

The king, advancing rapidly towards the capital, unopposed by any enemy, was joined at Poissy, on the Seine, by Montpensier, at the head of a considerable body of men, from Normandy. With a view of reducing Paris to experience the distresses of famine, he laid siege to Pontoise, which surrendered, after a brave and obstinate defence. On the following day, Sancy having redoubled his speed, in order to arrive in the royal camp, passed the bridge of Poissy, with his numerous army, amounting to near ten thousand Switzers, two thousand German infantry, and fifteen hundred cavalry of the same nation. They were reviewed by Henry in person, who publickly returned his acknowledgments to their commander, for so signal a service, rendered still more important, by the critical emergency in which it was performed. The troops of the League were driven from St. Cloud, by the impetuosity of the royalists; and the pass which that village commanded on the Seine, being immediately occupied by the king in person, who established there the head-quarters, Paris began to be closely invested on every side. His forces exceeded thirty thousand in number, elated by success, and desirous of displaying their fidelity and courage. On the contrary, the affairs of Mayenne were declining, and nearly desparate. His troops scarcely amounted

24th July. Capture of Poissy.

Arrival of the Swiss auxiliaries.

Henry approaches Paris. 29th July.

State of Mayenne.

(16) De Thou, vol. x. p. 614—661. Chron. Nov. vol. i. p. 213—220. Davila, p. 808—812. D'Aub. Hist. Univ. vol. iii. p. 176—180.

to

to eight thousand foot, and about eighteen hundred horse, diminishing hourly and rapidly, in consequence of famine, discontent, and scarcity of subsistence. The succours, which the dukes of Lorrain and Nemours had undertaken to conduct, were distant, and could not avert the immediate danger. Mayenne himself, who had quartered his soldiers in the suburbs of the capital, vainly endeavoured to restore tranquillity, and to allay the terrors of the inhabitants. There were, besides, in the city, a number of persons, well affected to the royal cause, who only waited a favorable moment to declare, and to exert themselves in its behalf. All the exhortations of the duchesses of Guise, Nemours, and Montpensier, were ineffectual to sustain the Parisians, under the apprehension of a punishment, imminent and severe. It was generally known, that Henry, rendered inexorable by the insolence and atrocity of their conduct, had declared his determination to exact a cruel and memorable atonement, which might impress his rebellious subjects with awe, throughout the kingdom. Every measure was already taken for a general assault, the success of which could scarcely be doubtful. Mayenne, with a generous, though ineffectual despair, had embraced the resolution of putting himself at the head of four thousand of his choicest troops, devoted to death; of charging the enemy, and either cutting his way through them, or perishing on the field of battle. No situation could be more hopeless than that of the League; nor any triumph more assured, than that of Henry; when one of those events which mock all calculation, and decide the fate of nations, deprived the king of his crown and life, at the same time that it extricated Mayenne from manifest and almost inevitable destruction (17).

Danger, and consternation of the capital.

(17) Davila, p. 812—815. De Thou, vol. x. p. 661—666.

CHAP. VIII.

1589. History of Clement.

A Monk, ſcarcely twenty-three years old, of the Dominican order, by name James Clement, was the author of ſo extraordinary and important a revolution. Naturally ferocious, gloomy, and capable of projecting the moſt daring enterprize; he poſſeſſed the intrepidity and coolneſs requiſite for its execution. Diſſolute, ignorant, and eaſily excited to commit any act, however immoral or atrocious, when encouraged by the exhortations of his ſuperiors, he undertook, at the ſuggeſtion, and with the approbation of Bourgoing, the prior of his convent, to aſſaſſinate the king. Every artifice which cunning can practiſe upon credulity and fanaticiſm, was uſed to ſuſtain, and to inflame his purpoſe. Not only earthly rewards and honours; but, a celeſtial recompence was aſſured to the champion and the martyr of the Holy Union. The ducheſs of Montpenſier, menaced by Henry with the moſt exemplary and ignominious puniſhment, as ſoon as he ſhould be maſter of Paris; is even ſaid to have made ſacrifices, calculated to animate a depraved and ſenſual Monk, and to ſtimulate him to the perpetration of any crime, however flagitious. The manners of that age, and the magnitude of the impending evil, render it highly probable, that Clement was encouraged to the attempt by her, as well as by the duke of Mayenne himſelf. It is inconteſtable, that he was provided with letters of introduction, by the preſident of the parliament of Paris, Harlai, then a priſoner in the Baſtile; and by the count of Brienne, who was detained in the Louvre. Thoſe zealous adherents of the crown, were impoſed on by his aſſurances of loyalty, and of a deſire to repair with important intelligence, to the royal camp.

He undertakes to aſſaſſinate Henry.

31ſt July. He arrives in the royal camp.

Furniſhed with his credentials, the Monk quitted Paris; and being ſoon ſtopped by the advanced guards, was conducted to La Gueſle, the ſolicitor general. As he profeſſed to be charged with a meſ-

ſage

ſage to the king, of the moſt confidential nature; it being too late to procure him an audience on the ſame evening, he remained with La Gueſle, ſupped heartily, and during the night ſlept with perfect compoſure. Henry had received ſo many, and ſuch recent intimations, of perſons being employed to aſſaſſinate him, that it would have been difficult, if not impracticable, for any man, except an eccleſiaſtic, to have procured acceſs to him, without previous precautions. But his predilection for all individuals of the monaſtic order, exceed belief, and laid him open to the ſnare: a circumſtance, of which Clement's inſtigators were, unqueſtionably, well apprized. On the enſuing morning, at an early hour, when the king was ſtill undreſſed, Clement was brought into his preſence; and having preſented the letter from the count of Brienne, while Henry was attentively occupied in peruſing it, the Monk took a knife from his ſleeve, and with incredible quickneſs, plunged it into his belly. Feeling himſelf wounded, the king inſtantly drew the weapon, with which he ſtruck his aſſaſſin upon the forehead. La Gueſle, Lognac, and Mirepoix, who were preſent, not maſters of their indignation and horror, at the ſight of their ſovereign, bleeding, and as they imagined, expiring; fell upon the monk with their ſwords, and put him to death. His body was thrown out of the window, burnt by the ſoldiers, and his aſhes ſcattered in the Seine (18).

1ſt Auguſt. Aſſaſſination of the king.

Circumſtances accompanying it.

Henry's wound, though alarming, did not, on the firſt inſpection, appear to be mortal. But, when the ſurgeons had examined it anew, and had aſcertained, that the bowels were pierced, they announced to him his diſſolution, as certain. He received the information with calmneſs, ordered the doors of his apartment to be thrown open in order

Death of Henry.

(18) De Thou, vol. x. p. 667—671. Davila, p. 815—817.

CHAP. VIII. 1589.

to admit the nobility, and prepared, with resignation, for his approaching end. Having repeatedly embraced the king of Navarre, and conjured, as well as advised him to embrace the Catholic religion, if he ever hoped to reign over the French; he declared that prince to be his only, and legitimate successor. As such, he exhorted the officers and nobles who surrounded his bed, to regard him in the light of their future sovereign, notwithstanding his difference of religious persuasion. He expressed his deep concern at the unfortunate condition in which he left the kingdom; performed with marks of penitence and piety the ceremonies enjoined by the Romish church, and expired on the following day. By his queen, Louisa of Vaudemont, he left no issue; and at the time of his decease, he had not quite completed his thirty-eighth year, of which he had reigned above fifteen. His body embalmed with as much decorum, as the circumstances of the time would permit, was carried to Compiegne; and Benoise, one of his few faithful servants, interred his heart and his entrails, privately, in the church of St. Cloud (19).

His exhortations, and commands.

2d August.

Character of Henry.

The character of Henry the Third is strikingly pourtrayed, and faithfully delineated, in the events of his reign. No prince ever excited greater and more universal expectation, before he succeeded to the crown: none ever more completely disappointed the hopes entertained of his capacity and virtue. The lustre of his victories at Jarnac and Montcontour, where he commanded the armies of Charles the Ninth, gave him the highest reputation throughout all Europe, and facilitated his election to the throne of Poland. But, he was scarcely arrived in

(19) Chron. Nov. vol. i. p. 220—224. L'Etoile, p. 284—286, and 289—300. Sulli, vol. i. p. 67 and 68. Chiverni, vol. i. p. 140—143. Mezerai, vol. ix. p. 394—398. De Thou, vol, x. p. 671—674. Davila, p. 817—819. D'Aub. Hist. Univ. vol. iii. p. 180—183.

that

that country, when the death of his brother induced him to fly from his new capital, with circumstances of precipitation unbecoming his dignity, and injurious to his fame. Before he reached the frontiers of his hereditary dominions, his improvident liberality had already diminished the possessions, and contracted the territories of France, by the donation of Pignerol and Savillan to Emanuel Philibert, duke of Savoy. Instead of extinguishing the civil wars, and dispensing peace to all his subjects, upon his return, as policy and wisdom dictated; the pernicious counsels of his mother and of his interested or perfidious ministers, impelled him to persecute the Hugonots, who only demanded toleration and protection. Convinced by experience of the impossibility of tyrannizing over the conscience, or reducing the Protestants by the sword; he adopted more enlarged and humane maxims of government: the edict of Poitiers, which restored tranquillity, was his own measure, and always cherished by him as such. But, the Guises, whom Henry studiously depressed; mortified at the diminution of the power and consideration which they had enjoyed under the three preceding reigns; and incensed to see the elevation of favorites and minions to the highest offices of trust and dignity; counteracted his designs. In order to do it with effect, they knew that religion must be made the mask for concealing and advancing their schemes of ambition. The king, notwithstanding his disinclination to war, was reluctantly compelled to violate his engagements, to rescind his edicts, and even to become eventually the instrument of his own humiliation. Guise, master of the metropolis, drove his sovereign from thence; dictated the conditions upon which he consented to a reconciliation; and insulted the monarch, whom he had previously disarmed. Yet, such was the passive and indolent temper of Henry, and so rooted

His inclination to toleration.

Violence, exercised over him by the League.

was

CHAP. VIII. 1589.

was his antipathy to the Hugonots; that if Guise had not proceeded to acts which left no doubt of his intention to usurp the whole effective authority of the crown; the king would, probably, never have resisted. A rebellion was the consequence; not so much of the assassination of the Guises, as of the inactive security which followed, on the part of Henry; and it produced, by a necessary train of events, the reconciliation with the king of Navarre. At the moment when he justly anticipated the reduction of Paris, he perished by the hand of a private and obscure individual, whose order he had always protected and favoured. Throughout his whole life, he seems to have cherished those, who betrayed, or outraged him; and he was destined to experience the most cruel injuries, from his nearest connexions. Joyeuse, whom he had raised to the highest point of greatness, deserted his benefactor, to join the League. His brother-in-law, the duke of Mercœur, revolted, notwithstanding the distinguished favors received from the crown; and he attempted to render himself independant in the province of Bretagne. Catherine of Medicis, his mother, with a view to balance the credit of the minions, secretly instigated and encouraged the princes of Lorrain, in their treasonable projects of aggrandizement. Even his own queen, a princess of irreproachable manners, but, of a bigotted and melancholy disposition, was seduced to espouse the interests of her family, rather than that of her husband.

Fatality and imprudence of his attachments.

Endowments, and vices of Henry.

Henry possessed many amiable qualities, and some great endowments. To a graceful and majestic person, he added suavity of manners, affability, liberality, clemency, the love of justice, courage, and temperance. But, all his virtues degenerated into vices, or were enervated by indolence and pleasure,

to

to ſuch a degree, as to call in queſtion their very exiſtence. His munificence became profuſion; and ceaſed to attach thoſe who were the objects of it, becauſe they attributed his benefits more to facility and prodigality, than to generoſity. He degraded the majeſty of his high rank, and almoſt rendered queſtionable the ſanity of his underſtanding by his puerile, or unbecoming aſſociations with Monks and Penitents. Far from producing the effect which he intended, of acquiring popularity, ſuch a conduct completed his ruin. His diſſipation neceſſitated him to have recourſe to the moſt fatal expedients, to maintain his court, and to fill the exhauſted treaſury. The venality of charges, multiplication of offices, and accumulation of taxes, at length undermined the foundations on which reſted his throne, and enabled his enemies to achieve their pernicious purpoſes. At his deceaſe, he left the monarchy convulſed and nearly overthrown: it required the talents, heroiſm, and good fortune of Henry the Fourth, to reſtore it, and to diſperſe the chaos, into which the mal-adminiſtration of his predeceſſor had plunged the kingdom. The circumſtances in which he expired, and the atrocity of the crime that produced his death, rendered him, in ſome degree, regretted; and ſeemed to expiate, or obliterate, the ſeries of errors, faults, and vices, which render his reign one of the moſt melancholy and calamitous portions of modern hiſtory (20).

State of France at his deceaſe.

In his perſon, expired the branch of Valois, which, under thirteen kings, had reigned over the French nation, during the ſpace of two hundred and ſixty-one years. With the ſingle exception of Philip of Valois himſelf, ſource of the line, they were diſtinguiſhed by their love and protection of letters. Charles the Fifth, in wiſdom; Louis the

Retroſpect of the reigns of the princes of Valois.

Virtues.

(20) De Thou, vol. x. p. 674—678. Davila, p. 820.

Twelfth,

CHAP. VIII. 1589.

Twelfth, in paternal affection for his people; and Francis the First, in magnanimity, elevation of mind, and cultivation of the arts, have not yielded to any monarchs, of any period. Personal courage seems to have been hereditary among them; though its peculiar and characteristic quality was varied in different princes. It was rash and impetuous, in Philip and John: subdued to the dictates of policy, in Charles the Fifth, and Louis the Eleventh: unequal, in Charles the Seventh: adventurous, in Charles the Eighth; steady and temperate, in Louis the Twelfth: brilliant and captivating, in Francis the First: ferocious, in Charles the Ninth: indolent and passive, in Henry the Third.

Their virtues were eclipsed by their greater vices and misfortunes. Two of the number, John and Francis, were taken prisoners in the field, and conducted as captives to London and Madrid. It would be difficult to parallel the reigns of Charles the Sixth, of Charles the Ninth, and of Henry the Third, in every species of misfortune, resulting from civil and religious anarchy. Even the most prosperous and tranquil periods were clouded by intestine commotions, or stained by cruelty and tyranny. If neither of these descriptions will apply to the mild administration of Louis the Twelfth; yet, that beneficent reign, short in its duration, was marked by continual foreign war, and the greatest national losses and reverses. Louis the Eleventh stands nearly alone, in the list of monsters, who have trampled upon the rights of humanity; and the superiority of his talents, employed for purposes of destruction, only renders him more conspicuously an object of detestation.

Vices and misfortunes.

Neither their defects of character, fortune, nor administration, were, nevertheless, such, as to prevent the gradual and progressive augmentation of the grandeur, power, and dominions of France. Philip of Valois obtained by address and purchase, the

Progressive aggrandizement of France.

the important province of Dauphiné, with all its dependancies. To the valor and good conduct of Charles the Seventh, was due the expulsion of the English from the kingdom, of which they occupied so considerable a portion. Louis the Eleventh added the rich acquisition of Burgundy, by conquest, on the death of Charles the Bold; and of Provence, by conquest, at the decease of Charles the Third, the last prince of the Angevin race. Brittany was acquired by the marriage of Charles the Eighth, with Anne, the heiress of that duchy; confirmed by Louis the Twelfth's subsequent nuptials with the same princess; and finally incorporated into the monarchy, by Francis the First. The extinction of the house of Valois, and the elevation of that of Bourbon to the throne, forms a great and interesting æra in the history of France.

THE HISTORY OF FRANCE,

BOOK THE SECOND.

Age of HENRY THE THIRD.

CHAP. I.

Nature, limits, and extent of the royal power, under the laſt princes of Valois.—Function of the States General.—Inſtitution, and privileges of the parliaments.—Provincial aſſemblies.—Revenues.—Management of the finances.—Public funds.—Coin.—Military force.—Infantry.—Cavalry.—Arms.—Exceſſes of the ſoldiery.—Artillery.—Ranſoms.—Navy.—Gallies.—General ſtate of the French marine.

CHAP. I.

Prerogatives of the French kings.

THE prerogatives, enjoyed and exerciſed, as well by Henry the Third, as by all the kings of France, his predeceſſors, during the courſe of the ſixteenth century, might be ſaid to approach nearly to that ſpecies of power, which we juſtly denominate arbitrary and unlimited. Louis the Eleventh, who combined

CHAP. I.

combined in his character greater vices and greater talents, than were, perhaps, ever seen united on the throne in one man, had, by the oppression and destruction of the nobility, erected the despotism of the crown upon their ruins. The people were gainers by the exchange of a single tyrant, instead of many: for, it would be equally absurd and false, to suppose, that, at any period since the elevation of the family of Capet, and the formation of the feudal system; the nation collectively was possessed of civil liberty, guaranteed by laws against royal and aristocratic encroachment. Almost all the odious branches of prerogative, exercised in England by the princes of the houses of Tudor, and wrested from those of Stuart, were vested by long prescription in the French monarchs. The ablest civilians, the gravest writers, and the wisest magistrates, who flourished between the accession of Henry the Second and the death of Henry the Third, agreed in recognizing the unlimited powers of the crown. "The kings "of France," says Cayet, a contemporary author, "do not resemble the Polish sovereigns, and others "who swear at their election to observe the laws "made by those who have elected them; but, on "the contrary, they have the supreme and absolute "authority over their people. On their will, de-"pend all their deliberations of peace and war; the "taxes and tributes, the distribution of benefices, "offices, governments, and magistrates (1)." It seems scarcely possible to describe despotism in clearer colours. Charles the Ninth, when hardly past the limits of childhood, did not hesitate to say to the parliament of Paris, composed of the most respectable individuals for age, virtue, and talents; "It is for you to obey my orders, without pre-"suming to examine them; for I know better than "you

Unlimited power, exercised by them.

Language of Charles the Ninth,

(1) Chron. Novenn. vol. i. p. 4.

"you what is the custom of the kingdom, and "what order and decorum demand (2)." Whatever indignation such a speech might excite, it produced no remonstrance, nor reclamation on the part of the parliament.

CHAP. I.

When the Protestant princes of the German empire presumed, in 1586, to represent to Henry the Third the injustice of violating his own edicts, granting liberty of conscience to his Hugonot subjects; he replied, in presence of the whole court, in these words: "It belongs to me alone, to judge, "according to my prudence, of what may contri- "bute to the public welfare; to make laws for pro- "curing it; to interpret those laws; to change, or "to abolish them, as I shall judge proper: I have "done it hitherto, and I shall do it in future (3)." Even in the memorable assembly of the States General at Blois, two years afterwards, although he professed his readiness to abide by the determinations which he should embrace, in conjunction with the delegates of the nation; yet, he did not omit to state, that such a condescension was the pure effect of his own desire to contribute to the felicity of his people. He even apologized for so strong a deviation from the conduct of his predecessors; and obviated the reproaches which might be made him, for subjecting himself to the laws which he had previously ordained (4). Montluc, Davila, Chiverny, Villeroi, and almost all the other writers of that period, when speaking of the royal authority, regard it as paramount to law, and superior to any controul.

and of Henry the Third.

Among the branches of prerogative most frequently exercised, was that of arbitrary imprisonment.

Arbitrary imprisonment,

(2) Le Laboureur sur Castelnau, vol. iii. p. 27. Brantome, vol. iv. p. 34.

(3) De Thou, vol. ix. p. 609. (4) Ibid. vol. x. p 301.

CHAP. I.

ment. No rank, profeſſion, nor ſtation were exempt, or protected from it; and the cauſes, or pretexts upon which it was enforced, were ſo various, that they might be ſaid to include every ſpecies of offence. Treaſon or hereſy were the moſt ordinary; and ſuſpicion alone, independant of proof, was ſufficient to condemn to a long and ſevere captivity, any ſubject, however elevated, or illuſtrious. D'Andelot, colonel-general of the French infantry, and brother to the celebrated Coligni, being queſtioned by Henry the Second, reſpecting his belief of the real preſence in the Euchariſt; and having replied in a manner diſpleaſing to that orthodox monarch, was immediately ſent priſoner to the caſtle of Melun. He was, it is true, ſpeedily releaſed, at the powerful interceſſion of his uncle, the conſtable Montmorenci: but even the ſanctity of juſtice could not protect from a ſimilar treatment, various members of the parliament of Paris. The preſidents du Bourg, and du Faur, ſuſpected of holding heretical doctrines, were ſeized while exerciſing their judicial functions, in their ſeats; and three others were arreſted in their houſes (5). Under the following reign, in 1560, Louis, prince of Condé, though allied to the royal blood, and attending the convocation of the States General, to which he had been invited by aſſurances of ſafety; was, notwithſtanding, arreſted, and committed to cuſtody. The caſe was rendered ſtill ſtronger, by the conſideration, that Francis the Second, who authorized ſo violent an act of authority, had not attained to manhood; and was, in the ſtrict ſenſe of the term, a minor, when he ventured upon the meaſure (6). Charles the Ninth, or, more properly, Catherine of Medicis, availing herſelf of his power, as he lay expiring; did not ſcruple, in 1574, to ſend the mar-

Under Henry the Second.

Francis the Second.

Charles the Ninth.

(5) D'Aubigné, Hiſt. Univ. vol. i. p. 84. (6) Davila, p. 73.

ſhals

ſhals Montmorenci and Coſſé, to the Baſtile, on ſuſpicions, never clearly aſcertained, of their being privy to the deſign of the duke of Alençon to withdraw from court. Nor did the quality of that prince himſelf, who was, after the deceaſe of Charles the Ninth, preſumptive heir to the crown, preſerve him from experiencing the ſame treatment. He, as well as Henry, king of Navarre, firſt prince of the blood, were long detained captive in the Louvre, by Henry the Third, from motives only of ſtate precaution (7).

Henry the Third.

The inſtitution and creation of commiſſions for the trial of crimes, pretended or real, was another branch of the royal authority, conſtantly enforced; and which laid, at the mercy of the crown, the life and freedom of every ſubject. Numerous, and ſtriking inſtances of this practice, occur throughout the reigns of the laſt princes of the houſe of Valois. In many, the forms, as well as the eſſence of juſtice, were equally violated. Henry the Second, a ſhort time before his death, after arreſting the members of the parliament of Paris, named commiſſioners to form a tribunal for their trial. It was compoſed of ſeveral counſellors of that body itſelf, ſelected for their approved zeal, or devotion to the orders of the court; of the biſhop of Paris, and the inquiſitor of the faith. Du Bourg pleaded his privilege as a counſellor of the parliament and of the church, in order to exempt himſelf from their juriſdiction: but, his objections were over ruled (8). Under Francis the Second, in 1560, by the edict of Romorentin, a court was erected in every parliament of the kingdom, to which was excluſively confined the trial of heretics. Theſe tribunals, from their ſeverity, were denominated "Les Chambres Ardentes:" a title,

Creation of tribunals for the trial of offences.

Tribunals for the trial of heretics.

(7) Mezerai, vol. ix. p. 121 and 122. Davila, p. 399, 400.
(8) D'Aubigné, Hiſt. Univ. vol. i. p. 84.

which

CHAP. I.

which sufficiently denotes their destination. In the case of the prince of Condé, arrested towards the close of the same year, at Orleans, the crown, without any regard to his birth and privileges, named a tribunal to try him, composed only of three lawyers, taken from among the presidents and counsellors of the parliament of Paris; acting under the lord chancellor, as president. The attorney-general was plaintiff and accuser; the first notary of the court of parliament being appointed to take minutes of the proceedings on the trial. It will scarcely be matter of surprize, that such judges should declare the prince guilty of treason, and sentence him to lose his head. He vainly reclaimed the right of being tried before the parliament of Paris fully assembled, in the presence of the king, the peers of France, and all the great officers of the crown. No regard was paid to these demands, though founded on immemorial usage; and the royal pleasure supplied every deficiency in point of form (9).

Trial of the prince of Condé.

Right of levying taxes.

Nor did the power of the French kings, on a superficial view, appear to be less unlimited over the property, than over the lives and liberties of the subject. Louis the Eleventh, who sacrificed the nobility to his vengeance, did not venture to impose contributions on the people, without some form of law, and sanction of their representatives. It was not till the accession of Francis the First, that the French kings disdained to ask, and began to lay taxes on the nation, by the sole virtue and plenitude of their prerogative (10). Henry the Third, during the whole course of his reign, exercised it in its fullest extent; and he varied the modes of imposing them, and the contribution itself, in every possible way that ingenuity and oppression could

(9) L'Art de Verif. les Dates, tom. i. p. 645. Davila, p. 75.
(10) Memoires de Sully, vol. i. p. 428.

devise.

devise. In 1578, twenty-two new edicts, or taxes, were issued by him, and sent to the parliament of Paris to be registered and published (11). Seventeen more were added, at one time, in 1586; many of which were very onerous, and occasioned universal complaint (12). As if these impositions were not sufficiently heavy, arbitrary exactions, without the name of taxes, were forced from the people. In January, 1587, Henry demanded of the kingdom at large, the sum of three hundred thousand crowns; and of the city of Paris no less than three hundred and sixty thousand crowns, exclusively (13). Loans were another ordinary mode of raising supplies; and they were, as may be imagined, absolutely compulsory. In 1576, the counsellors, and advocates of the parliament of Paris, were commanded to repair to the Louvre, and ordered to lend his majesty, each, according to his ability, a certain sum. About four thousand pounds sterling were raised by this expedient (14). Similar exactions were practised on the wealthy citizens of the metropolis.

Compulsory loans.

The creation of posts and offices, for which the persons who occupied or exercised them, paid considerable sums, was one of the most intolerable abuses, issuing out of the arbitrary power of the crown. It was, indeed, more injurious to the people, than beneficial to the exchequer; and was carried, under Henry the Third, to an incredible height. In 1581, nine edicts of this nature were published; and in the following year, four more were issued, the profits arising from which were avowedly destined for the two powerful favorites, Joyeuse and Epernon (15). Villeroi expressly

Creation of offices.

Venality of places.

(11) L'Etoile, Journ. p. 31. De Thou, vol. vii. p. 729.
(12) De Thou, vol. ix p. 596. L'Etoile, p. 91.
(13) L'Etoile, p. 98.
(14) Memoires pour servir à l'Hist. de France, p. 65. L'Etoile, p. 17.
(15) L'Etoile, p. 42. Mem. pour ser. à l'Hist. de Fr. p. 152.

CHAP. I.

asserts, that fifteen, or sixteen hundred officers were employed in the collection of the revenues, all of whom had purchased their places, and the aggregate of whose annual appointments amounted to near a hundred thousand pounds sterling. Of these, above one hundred and eighty were entitled treasurers of France, and had each, a salary of five hundred crowns. He adds, as the strongest proof of the peculation and plunder committed in the management of the finances, that every piece of three livres, or half a crown English, levied on the subject, was reduced, in passing through so many hands, to less than three-pence halfpenny, before it entered the royal treasury (16). It is to be observed, that no higher, nor more incontestable authority than Villeroi, can be cited: he was secretary of state under Charles the Ninth, Henry the Third, and Fourth; by all of whom he was entrusted with the most profound secrets of government.

Royal letters of requisition.

It was customary to send letters, signed by the sovereign, or by his ministers, to corporate bodies, and even to individuals of reputed wealth, demanding either a free gift, or a loan of stipulated sums. Few persons dared to slight, or to refuse the requisition. Even ecclesiastics, who, in that age, were exempted under various pretences, from contributing, in due proportion, to the general wants of the state, were frequently taxed by Henry. In 1578, instead of the tenth and twentieth, which he demanded of the clergy, he thought proper to substitute mandates, subscribed with his own hand, desiring them to lend him certain sums. They were apportioned according to the faculties of the parties. The chapter of Paris "in Globo," was fixed at six hundred crowns: Mariau, a rich canon, at two hundred and fifty; and others, at inferior rates. This

(16) Villeroi, vol. iv. p. 425 and 426.

arbitrary

arbitrary substitution excited great murmurs, and does not seem have met with compliance in all instances (17).

CHAP. I.

Rapacious exactions from persons in trade.

Persons trading in the articles of wine and salt, appear to have been objects of royal rapacity, in a more than common degree. In December, 1582, all the wholesale wine merchants in the city of Paris were compelled to pay within twenty-four hours, on pain of imprisonment, sums from five hundred crowns, diminishing according to their supposed means, in a regular gradation. Similar demands were, at the same time, extended to the dealers in salt, throughout the whole kingdom (18). The people were every where obliged to purchase at the king's storehouse, such a quantity of this latter article, as the commissaries, instituted for the purpose, should estimate to be requisite for their private consumption. The edict, enjoining obedience to so cruel an act of oppression, was obtained from Henry, in 1581; but, it met with very general opposition in the provinces (19). About the same time, he doubled the imposition of ten sous, or five pence, antecedently levied upon every hogshead of wine, coming in or going out of all the cities of the kingdom, and their suburbs. It was necessary, in order to vanquish the repugnance of the parliament to publish this edict, that Henry should write a menacing letter with his own hand, commanding submission (20).

The people, compelled to purchase salt.

Duties upon wine.

Customs and duties.

The authority of the crown was not less arbitrary over the customs and duties, paid upon the importation, or exportation of every commodity into France. There were, however, treaties subsisting

(17) Memoires pour ser. à l'Hist. de Fr. p. 99.
(18) Ibid p. 154.
(19) Ibid. p. 127.
(20) Ibid. p. 127 and 128.

CHAP. I.

with foreign powers, particularly with England, by which the king was restrained from raising, or diminishing them, in all cases, at his pleasure. In 1577, upon the complaint of the English embassador, the augmented duties recently imposed upon goods from that country, were taken off by the French government (21). It seems, in the river Garonne, and probably, throughout the whole kingdom, these were two and a half per cent. on every branch of merchandize, imported, or exported (22). The right of pre-emption was exercised by the crown; and we find Charles the Ninth, in 1573, issuing peremptory directions to the governor of Bourdeaux, to take measures for securing all the best and finest wines made in its vicinity, for the use of Elizabeth, his ally, queen of England (23). Even over acts of a more private and personal nature, in which the revenue had no concern, immediate or remote, the royal interference was equally strict and universal. No person, of whatever quality, could pass the limits of France, without permission. Catherine of Medicis, when regent, after the death of Charles the Ninth, issued a prohibition to travel, unless after leave obtained (24). Marriages the most violent and compulsory, were celebrated between persons of the highest description and rank, in consequence of a peremptory injunction of the king.

Pre emption.

Inferior prerogatives.

Charles the Ninth, desirous to attach to himself Christopher de Bassompierre, and to fix him in the court of France, selected for him a young lady of noble birth, named Louisa de Radeval, niece to marshal Brissac. Her fortune amounted to the pro-

(21) Le Laboureur sur Castelnau, vol. iii. p. 529.
(22) Ibid. vol. iii. p. 536.
(23) Ibid. p. 367.
(24) Ibid. p. 417.

digious

digious sum of fifty thousand crowns. She expressed, as did all her relations, the most unqualified reluctance to contract a marriage with a German, who was unacquainted with the language and manners of France, and who was not possessed of any patrimonial inheritance, being only a younger brother. But, Charles's determination overcame every impediment, and procured the immediate celebration of the nuptials (25). It may be matter of surprize, that among the exertions of so undefined or unlimited a prerogative, we find no trace of two branches, possessed by the English princes down to Charles the First, and which were strong badges of servitude. These were purveyance, and wardships. If the former was ever enforced, it was only a temporary act of violence or oppression. No court of wards existed in France, at any period of the sixteenth century.

CHAP. I.

Barriers against the power of the crown.

Notwithstanding the enormous extent of the power vested in the French kings, the wisdom of the nation had erected bulwarks for its restraint, when too violently exerted. These were, however, it must be owned, rather intended for the protection of property, than calculated for securing their lives and freedom. In fact, we find by experience, that cruelty is directed towards a few individuals: rapacity extends over a whole people. The two great barriers between the crown and the subject, were the assembly of the States General, and the Parliaments; peculiarly, that of Paris. The States, which were, under various denominations, coeval with the monarchy itself; and, which bore an intimate resemblance to the parliaments of England; were composed of delegates from the nobility, clergy, and the third estate. The French monarchs, who did not, like the English princes of the family of Tudor,

The States General.

(25) Memoires de Bassompierre, vol. i. p. 15.

their

CHAP. I.

Rarely convoked.

their contemporaries, ſtand in need of the approbation of the repreſentatives of the nation, to confirm their ordinary acts of tyranny, or to impoſe ſubſidies; had ſuffered the aſſembly of the States General to fall into deſuetude, during a great part of the ſixteenth century. Francis the Firſt, in the courſe of a long reign of thirty-two years, marked by many reverſes, had never once convoked that body. They were tumultuouſly aſſembled, for a ſhort time, after the memorable defeat of St. Quintin, by Henry the Second, his ſon. But, when Francis the Second aſcended the throne, and the great factions began to diſturb the tranquillity of the kingdom, it was deemed neceſſary to have recourſe to the powerful engine of the States. They were held at Orleans, in 1560; interrupted by the deceaſe of the young king; and reſumed in the following year, by Charles the Ninth, his ſucceſſor. Henry the Third aſſembled them twice; in 1576, and in 1588. In order to form an accurate idea of the degree of influence which the national repreſentatives poſſeſſed, in reſtraining or tempering the authority of the crown, it is requiſite to follow the leading ſteps of their conduct.

Objects propoſed by Henry the Third, in aſſembling the States.

The oſtenſible motive of Henry, in convoking the States in 1576, was to determine on the meaſures to be embraced reſpecting the Hugonots. But, his concealed objects were, to induce them to grant him extraordinary aids of money, and to conſent to the alienation of a part of the royal domain. At their meeting, he promiſed them, in his harangue from the throne, to obſerve inviolably the regulations, which, in concert with him, they ſhould make; and to grant no diſpenſation nor privilege, that could derogate from them in any manner. When, however, he found, that the third eſtate was proceeding to adopt counſels calculated to diminiſh his prerogatives, and tending to render

render themselves independant in their deliberations; he changed his behaviour, and either eluded, or rejected their demands. The States, on their part, evinced a spirit of energy and freedom, which might have done honor to the representatives of any people. Far from consenting to the king's requisitions, they refused to grant the subsidies; and their language relative to the other proposition, was still more firm and inflexible. Undismayed by the apprehension of Henry's resentment, Hemar, president of Bourdeaux, in the names of the three orders, declared, that "the domain of the crown was "sacred and inalienable; that no case, however "extreme, could be stated, in which they could "permit of its being diminished; that the sovereign "was only the possessor and tenant during life; "and that the nation being the proprietors, it was "a fundamental law of the state, not to alienate "the smallest part of the domain." They not only resisted every artifice and blandishment of the court, which was exerted to shake their determination on this point; but, their remonstrance operated so powerfully on the king, as to induce him to relinquish his intention, and prevented the further prosecution of his plan for selling crown lands to the amount of fifty thousand crowns of annual revenue (26).

Energy of the States.

They refuse to permit the alienation of the royal domain.

Although Henry could not vanquish the meritorious pertinacity of the States on these points, he still retained, undiminished, his own prerogatives: but, in 1588, when they met again at Blois, he held a very different language. Pressed by difficulties; insulted by the Guises, who had driven him from his capital, and disgraced him in the estimation of all France; anxious to regain the confidence of his subjects, as the only means of triumphing

Submission of the crown to the States, in 1588.

(26) De Thou, vol. vii, p. 450, and p. 474—477.

over

CHAP. I.

over the powerful faction, by which he was beset; he laid the unlimited powers of the crown at the feet of the nation. All the abuses, malversations, and oppressions which had grown up by long prescription, and which seemed to be inherent in the very essence of the monarchical authority, he voluntarily and spontaneously subjected to the censure of the national delegates. He offered to revoke all reversions already conferred, without exception; and never to grant any in future. He referred to their wisdom, the laws which respected trials, appeals, and the expences attending courts of judicature. He submitted to them the state of manufactures and commerce: allowed them to examine the finances, and to make whatever regulations they might think proper for their management and amelioration; concluding by an assurance, that he would so regulate his own household in future, that it should serve as a model to all his subjects for imitation. To render the laws, which might be framed by the assembly, equally binding and permanent, he even condescended to become accountable, like the lowest subject, for any infraction of them, under the penalty of treason; and consented that they should be transmitted to the various parliaments of the kingdom, to receive the most universal sanction, as inviolable and unchangeable (27).

Magnitude of Henry's concessions.

It is difficult to imagine any concessions greater than these, or, on which it would have been more easy to have founded the basis of a free constitution. Henry pointed it out to them, himself; and such was his situation, that he must have yielded to any equitable proportion which the States had dictated. But, in that great body, consisting of near four hundred members, there was neither a spirit of patriotism, nor an enlarged comprehension of the in-

(27) De Thou, vol. x. p. 378—382.

estimable

eſtimable advantages attached to civil liberty. Europe contained ſcarcely any model of a limited monarchy. Spain, England, and Italy, might be ſaid to obey princes, poſſeſſed of very extenſive and arbitrary power. In the aſſembly at Blois, the individuals compoſing the States, were either bigotted Catholics, bent on the extermination of the Hugonots; or violent and factious men, corrupted with the gold of Spain, and devoted to the ambitious views of the duke of Guiſe. That enterprizing chief, far from deſiring to emancipate the people, or to diminiſh the royal authority, only aſpired to become himſelf the depoſitory of it, and to reduce the king to the ſhadow of a ſovereign. The favorable moment for affixing legal barriers to the deſpotiſm of the crown, was loſt: Guiſe himſelf ſoon became the victim of his criminal projects; and Henry, liberated from his apprehenſions, laid aſide his diſpoſition to deſpoil himſelf of his power and prerogatives.

Nature of the aſſembly at Blois.

The parliaments might be ſaid to form a ſecond bulwark againſt the tyranny and oppreſſions of the crown. At the cloſe of Henry the Second's reign, they amounted only to ſeven in number; and were, ſtrictly, no more than the ſupreme tribunals of civil and criminal judicature, throughout France. But, they poſſeſſed the advantage of being permanent; whereas the States were only convoked under circumſtances of national danger, for a limited and uncertain time. The parliament of Paris was, beſides, the organ and inſtrument, through which the edicts emanating from the throne, received the ſtamp of validity. It belonged to that venerable aſſembly to regiſter, verify, and publiſh every pecuniary edict, or impoſition, laid by the ſovereign on the people. Though this privilege was originally intended for no other purpoſe, than to give greater ſolemnity and publicity to acts of ſtate; yet, it enabled the parliament

The parliaments.

Their privileges.

CHAP. I.

Resistance to the royal will.

parliament to make frequent, and sometimes effectual oppositions to such taxes, as were by them considered to be oppressive, or unjust. Many striking examples of their patriotic and independant spirit, which occur under the reign of Henry the Third, sufficiently prove, that virtue and freedom were not extinct among the French. In 1578, the king having sent no less a number of edicts, instituting new contributions, than twenty-two, to be registered, the parliament refused to sanction them; and having selected some of the least exceptionable, returned the others. All the menaces of Henry could not induce them to publish those which appeared to be oppressive (28). A stronger instance of the right to oppose such acts of despotism, appears in 1581; when Birague, the chancellor, insisting on the immediate verification of nine new taxes; the first president of the parliament stood up in his place, and replied, in the collective names of his colleagues; that "according to the law of the king, "which is his absolute power, the edicts might "pass; but, that, according to the law of the "kingdom, which is reason and equity, they could "not, and ought not, to be published." Henry persisting, they forebore, however, from further opposition (29). It became necessary for that prince to come in person, and hold a bed of justice, in order to surmount the impediments, which the parliament threw in the way of the taxes laid on by him, in 1583 and 1586; and it required the exertion of all the powers vested in the crown, to enforce their promulgation (30). None of his measures tended so much to render him universally odious, and to produce the defection which he experienced towards the

Example of it.

(28) L'Etoile, p. 31 and 32.
(29) Ibid. p. 42 and 43.
(30) Ibid. p. 63 and 64, and p. 91. Chron.

close

close of his reign, as these compulsory exertions of arbitrary authority (31).

CHAP. I.

Provincial states.

Besides the States General and the Parliaments, there were other powerful obstacles to the unlimited exercise of the prerogative. Many of the provinces enjoyed the right of holding their own states, under the controul of the governor; and seem to have likewise possessed the faculty of laying on the particular taxes, requisite for raising the sums, demanded by the government (32). To be convinced of the weight and influence of the provincial assemblies, in controuling the inordinate abuse of the royal power, we need only peruse the request; or rather, the remonstrance; for such it may be justly termed; presented to Henry, in 1578, by the States of Burgundy, assembled at Dijon. It contains so severe a satyre on his administration, and speaks a language so nervous, bold, and independant, that we are astonished at its having been offered, or received. The delegates who carried it to the foot of the throne, demanded the reduction of the antient taxes, and the abolition of the new ones recently imposed: they recapitulated the many acts of prodigality committed by Henry; and desired that commissioners might be named, to ascertain the extent of his debts, to cancel such as were improperly contracted, and to liquidate those which were just, and well authenticated. They proposed, that the money necessary to be levied for discharging the incumbrances of the king, should be put into the hands of commissioners, and faithfully applied to the purpose for which it was destined.

Their manly and generous remonstrances.

Far from resenting a speech so uncourtly, Henry condescended to endeavour to mollify the delegates; dismissed them with many promises; and actually

(31) De Thou, vol. vii. p. 729.

(32) Montluc. Comman. vol. iv. p. 6. Memoires de Nevers, vol. i. 6:5—622.

exempted

CHAP. I.

exempted the province of Burgundy from the payment of the new taxes (33). It may be justly questioned, whether any house of commons, during the reign of Elizabeth, would have dared to offer a similar remonstrance to that princess; and we may boldly affirm, that notwithstanding the apparent limits imposed on her prerogative by the existence of parliaments, she was, in effect, as arbitrary as the kings of France of the sixteenth century. In 1583, Henry made an experiment, which forcibly evinced the impotence of the royal authority, when applied to the pockets of his subjects. He sent persons of the first rank and consideration, through the provinces, to expose to the people his wants, and to demand pecuniary assistance. They met every where with peremptory refusals, accompanied by complaints and reproaches, against the profusion of the king (34).

Inability of the crown to extort money, on many occasions.

Amount of the revenues.

It is difficult to state with any degree of accuracy, the precise amount of the French revenue, under Henry the Third. The domain of the crown was still very considerable; though it is certain that, before 1587, alienations had been made from it, notwithstanding the remonstrances of the States General, to the extent of sixteen millions of livres, in value (35). We may estimate that sum as equal to seven hundred thousand pounds sterling. The sale of the crown lands, which had remained untouched and undiminished during near five centuries, from Hugh Capet to Louis the Eleventh; began under the reign of Charles the Eighth, when that prince, in 1494, commenced his invasion of Naples (36). Previous to the expulsion of the English from France, under Charles the Seventh, the French kings sub-

(33) De Thou, vol. vii. p. 729—731.
(34) Busbeq. letters 15 and 27. De Thou, vol. ix. p. 81.
(35) Chron. Nov. vol. i. p. 28.
(36) Memoires de Sully, vol. i. p. 430, 431.

sisted

sisted principally on their domains. Grants of money were only made on urgent occasions, for a limited time, which was usually short; and such could only be accorded, or levied, by the consent of the three orders of the States, who were solemnly convoked for the purpose. Strengthened by the accession of power, which he received from the conquest of so many provinces occupied by the English, Charles the Seventh ventured to impose a permanent and annual taxation on his people. It was, nevertheless, assessed with such moderation, that no resistance was experienced from them; its whole amount not exceeding a million, eight hundred thousand livres (37), or about eighty-five thousand pounds sterling. But, under his successor, Louis the Eleventh, the taxes were raised to above four millions, seven hundred thousand livres. Charles the Eighth, before his decease in 1498, augmented them to more than five millions, eight hundred thousand livres. Even in the following reign, under Louis the Twelfth, whose paternal affection for his subjects inclined him to diminish their burdens; the impositions continued rapidly to advance. He levied in 1514, seven millions, six hundred and fifty thousand livres (38). If a prince of such oeconomy and benevolence, was necessitated to encrease the taxes, it may be naturally supposed, that Francis the First, profuse, magnificent, and continually engaged in expensive wars, could not fail to aggravate the evil. In fact, we find, that before the close of his reign, in 1547, he had more than doubled the amount of the sums levied by his predecessor. Francis raised them to fifteen millions, seven hundred thousand livres (39). Under Henry the Second, they were

(37) Memoirs de Sully, vol. i. p. 427, 428.
(38) Ibid. p. 428.
(39) Id. ibid.

still

CHAP. I. still progressive (40). But, a very considerable allowance must be made for the continual and rapid encrease in the price of all commodities, as well as for the diminution of the value of money, in consequence of the discovery of America, between the year 1492, and 1560. It would be difficult to calculate, or estimate, the prodigious influx of gold and silver into Europe, after the commencement of the sixteenth century.

Debts of the crown.

In the year 1587, Henry the Third exacted thirty millions of livres, which were insufficient to prevent his accumulating an enormous debt (41). Francis the First, at the time of his decease, in 1547, had paid off every incumbrance, and left near five millions of livres in his coffers: but, at the accession of Charles the Ninth, within fourteen years afterwards, the debts of the crown fell little short of three millions, five hundred thousand livres (42), or one hundred and fifty thousand pounds sterling. They were encreased during his reign; and Ronsard, the poet, in his satyre of the "Dryade violée," pathetically laments, that the necessities of the king had compelled him to sell a great part of the forests of the Vendomois. Among these, was the wood of Gastine, which Ronsard had consecrated to the muses (43). The civil wars, and the total mismanagement or neglect of the finances which followed, plunged the revenue into inextricable confusion, and added greatly to the embarrassments of the state. Henry the Third, in 1579, made an attempt to enquire into the state of the domain lands, woods, wastes, and other property of the crown, when he

(40) Discours de la Noue, p. 359.
(41) About a million, two hundred and fifty thousand pounds sterling. Hist. des Troubles de France, p. 39.
(42) Traduction de l'Hospital, vol. ii. p. 19.
(43) Vie de Ronsard, p. 144.

named

named commiſſioners to viſit the provinces of France. The recovery, amelioration, and augmentation of the revenue, was the firſt, and moſt important object of the deputation; and powers, almoſt deſpotic and unlimited, were conferred on the members (44). How deplorable was the condition of the ſovereign, and how ruined were the finances at that period, we may learn, from Henry's expreſſions in the letters patent, or commiſſion, which he iſſued. He expreſsly enjoins the perſons deputed, to demand entrance into the aſſembly of the States, in ſuch provinces as enjoyed the privilege of governing themſelves by their repreſentatives. "You are then," continues the king, "to repreſent to them, in the "ſtrongeſt language poſſible, my neceſſities, ariſing "from the magnitude of the debts of the crown, "incurred before my acceſſion. They are ſo en-"creaſed, from the conſequences of the civil wars, "that all the domain is ſold and engaged; and "almoſt all the aids, taxes, and other revenues, "are alienated. The remaining receipts not being "equal to one-third of the expences, indiſpenſable "for the preſervation of the ſtate; I have been "conſtrained, of late years, to my great regret, "to make many edicts and engagements very "injurious, in order to raiſe the neceſſary ſupplies "for the ſupport of my houſehold, and the offices "of the kingdom (45)." It ſeems hardly poſſible to depicture a more calamitous ſtate of the revenue. If we compare it with the deficit, in 1787, at the time when Calonne, as ſuperintendant of the finances, adviſed Louis the Sixteenth to call together the "Notables," we ſhall ſee how infinitely the pecuniary embarraſſments of Henry the Third exceed-

(44) Memoirs de Nevers, vol. i. p. 608—611.
(45) Ibid. p. 621, 622.

CHAP. I.

ed those of the late unfortunate and ill-fated sovereign.

Farmers general.

The pernicious practice of employing farmers, or partizans, as they were then called, in every department of the revenue, completed the ruin of the kingdom. It is difficult to conceive the extent and magnitude of this evil, which swallowed up all the resources of France. In 1577, Henry the Third was so egregiously defrauded, that, from taxes which produced twelve millions of livres, only eight hundred thousand ever entered the tresury (46). The greater part of the farmers were not natives, but, Florentines and Savoyards, who glutted themselves with wealth, and usually returned to spend it in their own country. Catherine of Medicis, herself an Italian, had contributed exceedingly to spread the disorder, by employing foreigners, as receivers or collectors of the revenue. So lucrative was the occupation, that people of all descriptions, noblemen, ladies, and members of the council, contrived to exercise it, and to participate in the general plunder (47). They were multiplied under Henry the Third, to such a degree, that Tavannes estimates them at thirty thousand (48). To render the calamity irremediable, they were accustomed to purchase of the king the new taxes, as soon as they came out, and to advance the money which it was calculated they might produce. But, as a recompense for prompt payment, the farmers seldom laid down more than a fourth, and often not a sixth part of the sum, levied by imposition on the people. We may see, in the Memoirs of Sully, a list of persons who were concerned and interested in the tax upon salt, in 1585. The name of the

Their numbers.

Sale of taxes.

(46) Memoirs de Nevers, vol. i. p. 197.
(47) Villeroi, vol. iv. p. 412.
(48) Tavannes. p. 313.

duchess

duchess of Joyeuse, sister to Louisa, wife of Henry the Third, is the first; and stands for no less a sum, than seventy-five thousand crowns. The aggregate amount of the money, thus advanced upon the mortgage of the duty on salt, exceeds a million, six hundred thousand crowns (49). Villeroi mentions as a fact well known, that two pecuniary edicts, obtained of Henry the Third by his favorites, were sold immediately afterwards to the financiers, for the sum of twelve thousand, and twelve thousand, five hundred crowns. The former produced fifty thousand; and the latter, sixty thousand crowns (50).

Grants of taxes to the courtiers.

Such was the facility and criminal prodigality of Henry the Third, that he did not blush to create taxes, which were exclusively meant to enrich his minions and servants. "It was common," says Villeroi, "to see ladies, gentlemen, even valets, "and persons of the vilest description, shamelessly "pursuing the verification of edicts which they had "obtained; soliciting their publication; recom-"mending them as productive, and calling them "*their* edicts (51)." Abuses could hardly be carried to a more astonishing point of indecency and enormity. The treasurers, who had the power of distributing, and apportioning the taxes, or impositions, throughout the kingdom, committed equal violations of justice. In order to spare some villages, of which they, or their immediate relations and friends, were the proprietors, they exacted unequal and severe contributions from others, to the oppression of the inferior classes of people. Numbers of wretched peasants, unable to pay the sums thus demanded, were thrown into dungeons, and devoured by vermin, or consumed by disease (53).

Inequality of their distribution.

(49) Memoires de Sully, vol. i. p. 334.
(50) Villeroi, vol. iv. p. 413 and 414.
(51) Ibid. p. 412.
(52) Ibid. p. 408 and 409.

CHAP. I.

Wealth of the financiers.

Cossé.

The prodigious fortunes, acquired by all those, who had, in any degree, the controul or management of the finances under Charles the Ninth and Henry the Third, excite amazement and incredulity. Marshal Cossé, who was raised to the post of superintendant, by the former of those princes, contrived in the course of only one year, to discharge a hundred thousand crowns which he was indebted, and to lay by fifty thousand crowns in reserve. His wife avowed the fact to Catherine of Medicis, in the midst of the court (53).

Adjacet.

Louis Adjacet, or Giacetti, a Florentine, and one of the contractors, or farmers general, amassed far greater wealth. He laid out a sum adequate to sixteen thousand pounds of our money, for the castle and county of Chateau Vilain, in 1578, and married Mademoiselle d'Atri, of an illustrious Neapolitan family, maid of honor to the queen-dowager. In addition to this landed property, he possessed rents or annuities, payable by the town-hall of Paris, to the amount of near forty thousand livres, or about sixteen hundred pounds sterling, annually; and his furniture alone was estimated at an immense sum. We may judge of the degree of intimacy and familiarity which subsisted between him and Henry the Third, when we find that he frequently entertained the king at his own house, in the most sumptuous manner; and that prince having several times ordered Adjacet to discharge a debt which he had incurred with a merchant, for pearls, to the amount of two thousand crowns, the financier turned a deaf ear to the solicitation, and would not comply with Henry's request (54).

(53) Brantome, vol. i. p. 189 and 190.

(54) Memoires pour ser. à l'Hist. de France, p. 99, and p. 131 and 132.

In

Molan.

In 1589, Molan, one of the treasurers of France, having quitted Paris when the party of the League took possession of the capital, concealed his wealth by burying a considerable part of it under his house. He joined the king in Touraine; but, under pretence of poverty, he constantly refused to advance to that monarch, any sum, however small, notwithstanding the state of distress, to which the crown was reduced. In his house at Paris, after a long search, were discovered above a million of livres in specie (55); which came most opportunely, to enable the duke of Mayenne to equip and pay his forces (56). Irritated at Molan's refusal to assist him, when possessed of such resources, Henry caused him to be arrested; and the unfortunate financier was glad to compound for his freedom and pardon, by the payment of fifteen thousand crowns to the king (56).

Impunity of the financiers.

The alliances which the opulent contractors formed with the greatest families in the kingdom, ensured their protection from research and punishment. Very ample powers of inquiring, suspending, and bringing to trial, all persons who appeared to have defrauded the revenue, were entrusted to the commissioners, sent in 1579, to discover abuses. Collectors, controllers, receivers, and treasurers, were rendered amenable to the tribunal, which institution seemed to promise a beneficial change in the finances (57). But, in 1585, Henry compounded at once with all the treasurers of France, and gave them a complete abolition of their past malversations, exactions, and oppressions. For this act of grace and oblivion, they presented him with only a hundred and twenty thousand crowns; a sum very in-

(55) About forty thousand pounds.

(56) Memoires de Bassompierre, vol. i. p. 18. Memoires pour ser. à l'Hist. de France, p. 274.

(56) Chron. Nov. vol. i. p. 176. De Thou, voi. x. p. 605.

(57) Memoires de Nevers, vol. i. p. 608 and 609.

CHAP. I.

adequate to the magnitude of their extortions, and which, at the same time, secured their future impunity. In order to levy the money, they imposed a contribution on the individuals composing their body; and Henry's necessities induced him gladly to accept a temporary aid, at the price of the felicity and property of his subjects (58).

Practice of funding.

The practice of funding was not unknown in France, under Henry the Third. That prince had contracted a debt of near a million and a half of pounds sterling, before the year 1577. Persons were found, who voluntarily advanced him sums of money, for which he gave them public security on the receipts of the revenue, or the domain (59). He paid them sixteen per cent. interest, and he even rejected the entreaties of the States, who exhorted him to break the contract, as usurious. Henry was the more meritorious in thus adhering to his engagements, as Philip the Second, king of Spain, had given him a recent example of the infraction of pecuniary faith, in his treatment of the Genoese, to whom he was indebted (60). Charles the Ninth borrowed money at twenty per cent (61). Yet, under Francis the First, a bank had been opened at Lyons, which lent money at only eight per cent (62). During the reign of that monarch, annuities had been granted, payable by and at the town-hall of Paris, for which the king was security. They subsisted under Henry the Third. Ten per cent. was the rate of interest paid to the holders, or lenders; and the majority of the inhabitants of the metropolis had scarcely any other property, or subsistance,

Interest of money.

Life rents.

(58) Tavannes, p. 313. Memoires pour ser. à l'Hist. de France, p. 191.
(59) Memoires de Nevers, vol. I. p. 925.
(60) Chron. Nov. vol. i. p. 231.
(61) L'Art de Ver. vol. i. p. 653.
(62) Ibid. p. 640.

independant

independant of their labour and professions, than that derived from the payment of the rents of the town-hall (63). It was, therefore, a most serious calamity, when, on the king's being compelled, against his inclination, in 1585, to make war against the Hugonots, he suspended the regular dividends, or payments (64). In order to ingratiate himself with the Parisians, the duke of Guise, in the course of the short negotiation which took place between him and the king, before the flight of the latter from the Louvre, in 1588; expressly proposed, as one of the articles of accommodation, that an assignment should be made on Henry's part, to secure the constant and certain payments from the town-hall (65). At the commencement of the war between the duke of Mayenne and Henry, in April, 1589, they were totally discontinued: but, such was the frenzy of the time, and so great the detestation borne to the royal name and dignity, that all private losses or distresses were swallowed up and forgotten in the enthusiasm of rebellion (66).

Suspension of their payment.

The coin of the kingdom, like every other institution of civil government, was in a deplorable state of confusion or debasement, during the reign of the two last princes of the house of Valois. In 1577, Henry the Third issued a celebrated edict, designed to regulate the value of the current money, and to reduce it nearly to its intrinsic weight. The custom of estimating and reckoning by livres, an imaginary coin, was abolished, on account of the inconveniencies arising from the fluctuation of its value. All effects were ordered to be estimated in sales and contracts, by the ecu, or gold crown of three livres,

Edicts relative to the current coin.

(63) De Thou, vol. x. p. 598. Davila, p. 571.
(64) De Thou, vol. ix. p. 336. Memoires de Nevers, vol. i. p. 907.
(65) Davila, p. 695.
(66) De Thou, vol. x. p. 598.

which

CHAP. I.

which from the firſt day of January enſuing, was to be taken at ſixty ſous, or thirty pence. They had previouſly riſen to nearly double that value, and were circulated in the common mercantile intercourſe, at five, and even at ſix livres, in ſome places. This edict was productive of the moſt beneficial conſequences to commerce (67). Previous to the acceſſion of Henry the Second, the effigy of the ſovereign was not engraven on the gold, or ſilver coin: but, in 1548, that prince cauſed it to be firſt ſubſtituted, inſtead of a croſs, which was more eaſily effaced. Soon afterwards, the year in which the piece of money was ſtruck; and the particular rank which the ſovereign held among thoſe of his own name, were added (68). Ecus, and teſtons, were the common money of France; but the doubloons and piſtoles of Spain were univerſally current (69).

State of the military force, before the acceſſion of Francis the Firſt.

Before the acceſſion of Francis the Firſt, in 1515, the French kings can ſcarcely be ſaid to have poſſeſſed any permanent, military force. The conqueſt of Naples, and the battle of Fornoua, under Charles the Eighth, were gained by the impetuoſity and valor of the cavalry, compoſed principally of nobility, who overbore the feeble and unwarlike Italians. Louis the Twelfth conquered the Milaneze, and beat the Venetians at Ghierra d'Adda, with troops formed upon ſimilar principles. But, when it became neceſſary to carry on war for ſeveral campaigns, in Flanders, Italy, and Germany, againſt the veteran, and formidable Spaniſh bands of the emperor Charles the Fifth; a new ſyſtem was adopted. The infantry, which antecedently had been neglected and deſpiſed, roſe into conſideration;

Infantry.

(67) De Thou, vol. vii. p. 531 and 532.
(68) L'Art de Ver. vol. iii. p. 644.
(69) Brantome, vol. iii. p. 199 and 202. vol. iv. p. 29.

though

though the cavalry ſtill continued to be the favorite service for the young nobility. Nothing could be more groteſque and ſavage than the dreſs and appearance of the antient foot ſoldiers, under Charles the Eighth, in 1495. They wore their hair long and floating on their ſhoulders, in order to encreaſe the fierceneſs of their aſpect; together with ſhirts, which had large hanging ſleeves, and which they continued to wear for ſeveral months, without waſhing. It was a diſtinctive mark of their profeſſion to go without ſtockings, or, at leaſt, with one leg bare. Even the officers and captains adhered to this badge of the infantry (70). They commonly carried their ſtockings tied, or hanging at their girdles. As late as the time of Henry the Second, in 1552, when the foot ſoldiers were dreſſed and diſciplined in a much ſuperior manner; it was cuſtomary for the officers and private men to cut their ſtockings at the knee, when going to the aſſault of a town. As their dreſs, from the waiſt to the ankle, conſiſted only of one piece, it facilitated their ſcaling a wall, or mounting a breach (71).

Their dreſs, and appearance.

Croſs-bows, with which the infantry were principally armed, till the cloſe of the fifteenth century, fell then into diſuſe; and the arquebuſs was ſubſtituted in their place, when powder became common: but, the French foot were, for a long time, far from attaining dexterity in the uſe of fire-arms (72). Under Louis the Twelfth, no intermediate military rank, or title between a captain and a general, was yet invented. Colonels and quarter-maſters were unknown. The famous chevalier Bayard commanded a thouſand foot in 1507, as a ſimple captain. But, eight years afterwards, in 1515, at the battle of Marignan, under Francis the Firſt, Claude, count of Guiſe, is ſaid to have commanded ſix

Arms and weapons.

Military ranks.

(70) Brantome, vol. iv. p. 43—45.
(71) Ibid. p. 46.
(72) Ibid. p. 50.

thouſand

4

CHAP. I.

Colonels.

thousand German auxiliaries, as colonel (73). It was not before the year 1542, at the siege of Perpignan, that the office of colonel began to be generally known. Brissac was then created colonel of the French infantry (74).

Quarter-masters.

Quarter-masters were soon after instituted, in imitation of the Spaniards. Montluc was the first, in 1545, and the only one in all France, before the accession of Henry the Second, in 1547; after which period, others were successively named (75). Charles the Ninth, or, rather, Catherine of Medicis, in 1562, divided the office, and created three quarter-masters for the French infantry (76). They seem to have remained at that number, under Henry the Third. The employment of colonel-general of the French infantry, originated towards the close of the reign of Francis the First; and the celebrated Gaspard de Chatillon, better known as the admiral Coligny, was the second who ever occupied the situation (77). Even his enemies admitted, that to his wholesome severity, and excellent regulations, was due the discipline introduced among the foot. Before his appointment, they subsisted by pillage, rapine, and every sort of violence. To correct the evil, he made some terrible examples; and in 1552, when Henry the Second undertook the expedition against Mentz, Toul, and Verdun, the trees were covered with soldiers, hung upon the branches for infraction of orders, and excesses committed upon the peasants (78). But, the commencement of the civil wars, about ten years afterwards, was the term of their discipline; and it soon became impossible for either Catholics or Protestants to restrain the enormous depredations, murders, and profanations,

Colonel-general of the infantry.

Contempt of discipline.

(73) Brantome, vol. iv. p. 50—57. (74) Ibid. p. 58.
(75) Ibid. p. 65 and 66. (76) Ibid. p. 85—87.
(77) Brantome, vol. iv. p. 220. (78) Ibid. p. 226.

committed

committed by the soldiery (79). Under Henry the Third, long habit had confirmed them, and rendered the evil almost irremediable.

Want of pay.

The principal cause, nevertheless, of these excesses, resulted from the want of regular pay. During the whole of the sixteenth century, and particularly, between 1560 and 1590, when the dissentions of France impoverished the crown, and exhausted the treasury, the army was frequently left unpaid for several months. The duke of Nevers seems to think, that soldiers who receive annually ten months pay, instead of twelve, have reason to be highly satisfied (80). The officers were equally deprived of their appointments; and the wretched people became the victims of the incapacity of the sovereign to maintain the national forces (81).

Consequences of it.

Even Philip the Second, though master of Peru, and possessing the treasures of the New World, in addition to his vast revenues in Spain, Italy, and Flanders, left his troops continually in arrears; and saw the fairest cities of the Netherlands desolated or pillaged by his own soldiers, driven to desperation from the detention of their pay (82). It cannot, therefore, excite wonder, that the kings of France should be unable to defray the expence of the armies, which they were obliged to retain, in a time of universal insurrection. How deplorable was the condition of the royal forces, employed against the Hugonots in Poitou, in December, 1588, we may see in the Memoirs of Nevers. "The men at arms," says he, "are not paid; "and their sufferings are extreme, from the rigour "of the season. Provisions, and even bread, are

(79) Discours de la Noue, p. 572—575, and p. 643. Brantome, vol. iv. p. 133, and 137.

(80) Memoires de Nevers, vol. i. p. 196.

(81) Montluc's Comm. vol. iv. p. 185, and 311, and 312. Memoires de Castelnau, p. 240.

(82) De Thou, vol. vii. p. 368.

"wanting.

CHAP. I.

"wanting. The greater part of the infantry are "without cloaths, ſhoes, or ſtockings; and the "men at arms ſay, that they are aſſembled for "their own deſtruction, not for that of the Pro-"teſtants (83)." To encreaſe the calamity, no proviſion or ſubſiſtence was allowed to the officers and ſoldiers, when age, wounds, and infirmities, had diſqualified them for active ſervice. Many, even among the former deſcription, at the ceſſation of a war, when a great proportion of the troops was diſbanded, either ſought foreign ſervice; or went over to the Turks, who gladly received them; or committed piracies on the ſeas; or, laſtly, embraced mechanical and mercantile profeſſions (84). Theſe laſt were, however, conſidered as degrading, by ſuch a conduct, the honorable profeſſion of arms.

The cavalry.

The cavalry was a far more ſplendid, expenſive, and faſhionable ſervice than the infantry, during the ſixteenth century. All the young men of the court ſerved in it by preference, and frequently at their own expence. Their armor, dreſs, and accoutrements were uſually ſuperb. When Strozzi brought a troop of two hundred horſemen to Francis the Firſt, equipped, mounted, and provided entirely at his own coſt, they were the admiration of the French monarch. Their helmets and corſlets were gilt, and every man had two horſes. Strozzi expended twenty-five thouſand crowns in forming this body, which he long continued to maintain without any aſſiſtance from the crown (85). During the reign of Henry the Second, when Savoy and Piemont were occupied by the French, that country was regarded as the ſchool for military education and improvement. The private ſoldiers became rich, by the plunder of the numerous towns and

Their dreſs and armor.

Riches acquired by plunder.

(83) Memoires de Nevers, vol. i. p. 874, 875.
(84) La Noue, p. 184.
(85) Brantome, vol. ii. Cap. Fran. p. 295—297.

caſtles,

castles, captured from the enemy; and they laid out the money acquired by their valor, in decorations of every kind, suitable to their profession. Fifty of them in one company had bonnets of red velvet, ornamented with gold; chains of the same metal round their necks, and velvet scarfs. A corporal, belonging to the colonel's own company, appeared at mass, dressed in green sattin, and having his drawers buttoned down to his shoes, with double ducats, angels, and nobles (86). All these marks of opulence disappeared after the beginning of the civil wars, which produced general poverty, relaxation of discipline, and dissolution of manners, not only among the soldiery, but, through every rank of society (87).

Change introduced in military weapons,

The arms, offensive, and defensive used, by the troops, underwent a considerable change, between the accession of Francis the First, in 1515, and the death of Henry the Third, in 1589. Pikes, the antient weapon of the infantry, gave place to the arquebuss: while, in the cavalry, lances were gradually and reluctantly changed for the pistol. Tavannes, about the year 1567, contributed principally to the latter alteration (88). Corslets were, likewise, in a great measure, abandoned by the infantry under Charles the Ninth (89). After the use of fire-arms became general, every part of defensive armor was fabricated in a manner so massive, that it was impossible for the youngest, or most vigorous soldiers, long to sustain its weight. Under Francis the First, the oldest officers supported the fatigue of a whole day, completely armed: but, before 1580, it was accounted a great exertion to remain two

and in defensive armor,

(86) Brantome, vol. iv. Cap. Fran. p. 331.
(87) La Noue, p. 223.
(88) Tavannes, p. 307. La Noue, p. 275. Montluc, vol. iv. p. 293.
(89) La Noue, p. 317.

CHAP. I. hours in a coat of mail (90). The art of destroying kept pace with the art of defending. Stuart, a Scottish gentleman, and a Hugonot, who is celebrated for having mortally wounded the constable Montmorenci; discovered a mode of fabricating balls of such a composition, that scarcely any armor, however exquisitely tempered, could resist their force, when discharged from a pistol. They were called "Stuardes," from the name of their inventor (91).

At the famous judicial combat, or duel, between Jarnac and La Chataigneraye, fought in 1547, under Henry the Second, the defensive arms were first delivered to the two combatants, and afterwards the offensive weapons, with the utmost solemnity, in presence of the king, the constable, and the whole court (92). It excites astonishment, that under the pressure of so vast a weight, they exerted such agility and dexterity. Morions, or hemlets, which were universally worn at that period, fell much into disuse, before the end of Henry the Third's reign (93). The arquebuss was the principal offensive weapon, which decided the fate of battles in the sixteenth century. D'Andelot first introduced them among the French infantry, about the middle of the reign of Henry the Second, on his return from Milan, where he had been detained during several years, a prisoner; and Strozzi, who become colonel-general of the infantry, in 1569, on D'Andelot's death, rendered them general. But as the best were fabricated at Milan, it was long before a sufficient number could be procured to arm all the foot soldiers (94). Brantome expressly says, that the arquebuss would kill,

Offensive arms.

Arquebusses.

(90) La Noue, p. 285 and 286.
(91) Brantome, vol. ii. Cap. Fran. p. 110.
(92) Le Labourer sur Castel, vol. ii. p. 557 and 558.
(93) Brantome, vol. iv. Cap. Fran. p. 299.
(94) Ibid. p. 290—296.

CHAP. I.

Musquets.

at the distance of four hundred paces (95). They were gradually supplanted by the musquet, which does not seem to have been known in France, before 1571, or the following year. To Strozzi was, in like manner, due their introduction; but, he found the utmost repugnance in effecting their reception among the troops. In order to overcome it, he himself, in 1573, at the siege of Rochelle, always had one carried by a page, or lacquey, wherever he went. His example soon vanquished, in a considerable degree, the reluctance of his men; more especially, when they saw him frequently kill even a horse, at five hundred paces distant, with a musquet (96). Henry, duke of Guise, likewise, by constantly using the same weapon, facilitated its progress among the troops. The principal objection to them was their weight, which so fatigued the soldier, that, among the Spaniards, every musqueteer was allowed a follower to carry it, during a march (97).

Guards. Their institution.

The first institution of guards, as distinct from the other forces, was due to Charles the Ninth, or to Catherine of Medicis, his mother; who, in 1563, formed one regiment, under the command of Charry, as quarter-master: they consisted of ten companies, and were, by the king's express direction, taken from under the controul or orders of the colonel-general of the infantry, in order to depend wholly and exclusively on the sovereign body-guard they constituted (98). In 1573, the same prince broke them; but, he issued directions to levy two companies anew, for his protection, in 1574; a short time before his decease (99). We find, from the Memoirs of the duke of Nevers,

(95) Brantome, vol. iv. Cap. Fran. p. 297.
(96) Ibid. p. 300. (97) Ibid. p. 302—304. (98) Ibid. p. 90.
(99) Ibid. p. 103 and 104.

that

CHAP. I.

that in 1577, Henry the Third kept in regular pay twelve hundred Swiss guards, two hundred archers, and a hundred gentlemen of his household (100). Yet, ten years afterwards, it appears, that there were only about three hundred men in the regiment of guards, which usually mounted at the palace of the Louvre, together with a few archers on horseback (101). In order more effectually to secure himself against the enterprizes of the League, he had, before that time, created the famous band of forty-five; so denominated from the number of which it was composed. They were all gentlemen by birth, of approved valor, and mostly Gascons, recommended by the duke of Epernon. Henry never moved without them; gave them, each, a hundred crowns of gold monthly, besides other gratifications; and entrusted his person entirely to their fidelity. During the night, they always were stationed in the anti-chamber of his apartment; and by their hands the duke of Guise was finally immolated to the resentment of their master (102).

Band of forty-five.

The nobility served from royalty.

During the course of the civil wars under the two last kings of the family of Valois, the nobility served, in a great measure, on both sides, either from loyalty, or zeal for their religion, or gratitude, or attachment to their respective leaders. Plunder supplied the want of regular pay, among the officers and men; who, inflamed by civil and religious animosity to a pitch of frenzy, were raised above considerations of a pecuniary and mercenary nature. On the side of the Hugonots, incredible instances of this spirit might be adduced. We need only recollect the memorable one which took place in 1568, when the German auxiliaries came to the

Example of zeal and enthusiasm.

(100) Memoires de Nevers, vol. i. p. 189.
(101) De Thou, vol. ix. p. 652.
(102 Vie d'Epernon, vol. p. 283 and 284.

assistance

aſſiſtance of the prince of Condé. Thoſe ſtipendiaries refuſed to join the Proteſtant army, notwithſtanding the ſimilarity of their faith, till they had received payment of fifty thouſand crowns. The prince was deſtitute of money, and the greateſt Hugonot nobles in his camp, had the utmoſt difficulty to provide a miſerable, and precarious ſubſiſtence. In this extremity, Condé and Coligni having chearfully ſacrificed all their plate and jewels, the example was imitated by the officers and ſoldiers. Even the pages and lacqueys tore the ear-rings from their ears, to augment the general maſs ; and a common footman had the incredible generoſity to contribute ten crowns. By this means, a ſum amounting to about four thouſand pounds ſterling, was raiſed, and immediately given to the Germans. No ſimilar act of diſintereſtedneſs and enthuſiaſm is to be found in the moſt ſhining periods of Greece and Rome (103).

Military ſervice, purely voluntary.

One natural and neceſſary conſequence of the voluntary ſervice performed by the nobility in the field, was, that they quitted the army at pleaſure, and could never be retained long under the ſtandard. No entreaties, nor commands, were ſufficiently powerful to compel their ſtay, when fatigue, or buſineſs, or attention to their domeſtic concerns, called them to their caſtles. To cite proofs of this fact, would be to relate the hiſtory of every campaign. Even Coligni, whoſe aſcendant over the Proteſtants, after the prince of Condé's death at Jarnac, was ſuch as to approach to deſpotiſm ; yet, could not cure an evil, inherent in the nature of the military profeſſion : nor was the effect of victory itſelf ſufficient to induce the conquerors to purſue their triumph. After the battle of Coutras, in 1587, gained by the king of Navarre over the duke of Joyeuſe ; inſtead of profiting of ſo ſignal an ad-

Inſtances of it.

(103 D'Aubigné, Hiſt. Univ. vol. i. p. 227 and 223.

vantage,

CHAP. I. vantage, that prince was instantly deserted by all the nobility of Poitou and Saintonge, who formed the principal strength of his forces. Far from marching, as he might be expected to have done, towards the Loire, he returned the very next day, into Gascony (104).

Infraction of capitulations.

A melancholy effect of the rancour subsisting between the Protestants and Catholics, during the course of the civil wars, was the continual infraction and shameless violation of the articles of capitulation, agreed on previous to the surrender of cities and garrisons. It would be endless to enumerate the examples of breach of faith, on both sides. Sometimes, the commanders themselves were either openly, or tacitly consenting to the plunder and massacre of the very enemy, to whom they had, a few hours or minutes preceding, granted and solemnly promised honorable conditions. More frequently, the brutal, and vindictive fury of the soldiers, was not to be restrained by any exhortations or commands. Among the great military characters of that period, Biron distinguished himself by his glorious and inflexible adherence to all his engagements with his enemies, and by his punishment of the slightest infraction of agreement. He gave a shining proof of it, at the surrender of St. John d'Angely in Poitou, in 1569, when the Protestant troops having capitulated, were pillaged by the Catholics, on quitting the town. Biron was no sooner informed of the outrage, than, drawing his sword, and rushing into the midst of his own men, who were occupied in plundering; he wounded numbers of them, and compelled the others to desist immediately from so scandalous a breach of honor and faith (105).

Conduct of Biron.

(104) D'Aub. Hist. Gen. vol. iii. p. 58. De Thou, vol. x. p. 19.
(105) Brantome, vol. iii. p. 364.

The

CHAP. I.

The deliberate murders, committed after the close of battles, or sieges, in that age, reflect greater dishonor on the nation, as they were commonly perpetrated on defenceless men, wounded, disarmed, and delivered over to the vengeance of some implacable, or vindictive individual. Such must be esteemed the murder of Louis, prince of Condé, at Jarnac, after he had presented his gauntlet, and while he was actually sitting on the ground, between his two sureties (106). A circumstance which rendered it more atrocious, was, that Montesquiou, who shot the prince through the head from behind, commanded the Swiss guards of Henry, duke of Anjou, and neither received any punishment, nor even reprimand, for so odious a crime. Stuart who, at the battle of St. Denis, had killed the constable Montmorenci, being taken prisoner at Jarnac, was, in like manner, stabbed in cold blood, by the marquis of Villars, brother-in-law to the constable, as an offering to his manès. This act was performed almost in the presence of the duke of Anjou, who expressed his reluctance, but consented, after some delay, to its commission. Chatelier, another gentleman, made prisoner on the same day, was butchered by the friends of Charry, whom he had assassinated in Paris, some years preceding (107).

Acts of atrocity and cruelty.

Prince of Condé.

Stuart.

In retaliation for these cruelties, the Protestants, on their part, immediately put to death two persons of rank, the Baron d'Ingrande, and Prune, who had fallen into their hands, by the chance of war (108). Carreliere, a Protestant gentleman, made prisoner at the engagement of Dreux, in 1562, was tied to a walnut tree, and shot with pistol balls, by the Catholic soldiery (109). After the great victory

Retaliations.

Instances.

(106) D'Aub. Hist. Univ. vol. i. p. 280.

(107) Brantome, vol. ii. Cap. Fran. p. 110—112. D'Aub. Hist. Univ. vol. i. p. 280.

(108) Brantome, vol. ii. Cap. Fran. p. 113.

(109) D'Aub. vol. i. p. 170.

CHAP. I.

of Montcontour, in 1569, many of the Hugonot prisoners were massacred from wanton barbarity, or revenge. La Noue, who was one of the captives, owed his life only to the interposition of the duke of Anjou (110). Charbonniere, a private soldier, having shot the count de Brissac, from the walls of Mucidan, during the progress of the siege; was, on the surrender of the place, ordered to be immediately hanged (111). Richard the First and Saladin could not carry on war with greater inhumanity and ferocity. Even those laws which have been esteemed sacred among nations the least polished, were trampled on in France, during the reigns of Henry the Third, and his predecessor. Tavannes declares, that, when he besieged Auxonne, the inhabitants poisoned the wells and fountains. Not content with contaminating the water, they sent him a letter, dipped in the morbid matter of the plague, in order to spread the contagion in his camp (112). The historians of that age contain many similar attestations and instances of the most ferocious malignity. They contrast wonderfully with the magnanimous clemency and humanity, which characterised the reign of Francis the First, and Henry the Second. The duke of Guise's beneficent treatment of the sick and wounded soldiers of the emperor Charles the Fifth, after his repulse before Metz in 1553, was more glorious than his preceding success. During the civil wars, quarter was rarely given on either side.

Poison.

Uniforms were unknown among the troops in the sixteenth century: the private men seem to have enjoyed the liberty of dressing, and arming themselves, according to their capacity or fancy; but, the nobility were all distinguished by their peculiar colours,

(110) La Noue, p. 689.
(111) Brantome, vol. iii. Cap. Fran. p. 418—420.
(112) Tavannes, p. 339.

during

CHAP. I.

during the civil wars. The Catholics wore crimſon jackets and ſcarfs: the Proteſtants were known by white ones (113). They are frequently called "Les Caſaques blanches." Henry the Third, in 1587, gave grey uniforms to the Swiſs guard, in alluſion to the colour, which he wore, himſelf, as a penitent of the order of the Hieronomites. The long continuance of hoſtilities, and the precarious intervals of repoſe, between 1562 and 1589, had rendered the nation univerſally acquainted with, and familiarized to, the uſe of arms. Even the peaſants, from neceſſity, more than choice, quitted the peaceable arts of huſbandry, and mixed in every fray. They were, unfortunately, victims to the rage of the ſoldiery, on many occaſions. Such was the fate of the Gautiers, in 1589. They were peaſants and labourers, who, driven to deſpair by the outrages of the royal forces, and by the ſeverity of the taxes, formed themſelves into a ſociety in Low Normandy, and were perſuaded to join the party of the League. Their numbers amounted to above ſixteen thouſand. We may judge to what a point of ferocity they had attained, and how much the oppreſſion which they experienced, had extinguiſhed in them all the emotions of humanity, by a circumſtance which De Thou commemorates. He ſays, that the Gautiers having made priſoner a royaliſt, who was occupied in pillage, they devoured him: no veſtige of his body was left; the women and children having drank the blood, while the men feaſted on the carcaſe (114). The horde was ſoon attacked by the duke of Montpenſier, who put three thouſand to the ſword, after a fierce reſiſtance. Four hundred were ſent to labour on the public works; and the remainder, compelled to ſurrender at diſ-

Familiarity with the uſe of arms.

Oppreſſion of the peaſants.

Gautiers.

Deſtruction of them.

(113) D'Aub. Hiſt. Univ. vol. i. p. 140. and p. 143.
(114) De Thou, vol. x. p. 600.

CHAP. I.

cretion, were allowed to return to their original occupation of tilling the earth (115).

Maſſacres of the peaſants.

After the defeat of Mouvans, a Hugonot commander, by Briſſac, in 1568; the peaſants of Perigord, in which province the action happened, cut in pieces a greater number of the fugitive Proteſtants, than had even fallen in the engagement. Coligni took an exemplary vengeance on them, for their attachment to the Catholics, Brantome declares, that in the caſtle of Chapelle Faucher, not a league from his own reſidence at Brantome, two hundred and ſixty were maſſacred in one room, by Coligni's expreſs orders; they had been detained a day in confinement, and the act was a deliberate one. He adds, that on his taking the liberty to remonſtrate with Coligni, becauſe the peaſants whom he had cauſed to be put to death, were not the ſame who had ſlaughtered the Proteſtants; he replied, that it was of no conſequence, ſince they were of the ſame province; and that the example would operate as a warning to their comrades (116).

Facility of raiſing troops.

In a country which had been ſo long the ſcene of war, it was not difficult to raiſe troops: every inhabitant of a village might be regarded as a ſoldier; and ſuch was the facility of levying them, that we find, in 1589, Thoré, brother to Henry de Montmorenci, procuring five hundred able and warlike peaſants, in the ſpace of a few hours. They were all vaſſals of the family and duchy of Montmorenci, and marched inſtantly to garriſon the city of Senlis, againſt the attack of the army of the League (117). It is difficult to aſcertain the amount of the French military force under Henry the Third. In 1577, marſhal Coſſé, in the council of ſtate, aſſerted, that there were a hundred and fifty compa-

(115) De Thou, vol. x. p. 600—603. Davila, p. 796—799.
(116) Brantome, vol. iv. Cap. Fran. p. 225.
(117) Le Labour. ſur Caſtel. vol. ii. p. 749.

nies

nies of men at arms in the kingdom, which, together with the archers, composed a body of twenty thousand, three hundred, and sixty-five men. "This "army," said he, "is sufficiently numerous, to "engage the largest foreign force, which ever "yet entered France." He, however, exhorts the king to form a separate body of six thousand Switzers (118). The science of fortification, in the modern acceptation of that term, was totally unknown in the sixteenth century; and it was reserved for the age of Louis the Fourteenth to re-model the Gothic towers and battlements of cities and castles. The most perfect production of the art, to be found in Europe, in the times of which we are treating, was the citadel of Antwerp, constructed by order of the duke of Alva, at an incredible expence. Mentz was accounted the second, and cost above forty thousand pounds sterling. The citadel of Turin was estimated to have cost near one hundred and fifty thousand crowns (119).

Science of fortification.

Under Henry the Third, the use, and practice of artillery, was not advanced beyond its infancy. D'Etrées, who occupied the post of master-general of the ordnance in 1558, at the siege of Calais, by Francis, duke of Guise; and who eminently contributed to its capture, was the first person among the French, who made any considerable progress in the construction of batteries. Anterior to D'Etrées, continual accidents took place, from the bursting of cannon; and it was customary to cool them with vinegar, in order to prevent those misfortunes (120). Armies were slenderly provided with artillery, which was considered as more requisite for sieges, than indispensable in the operations of the field. In 1562, when Louis, prince of Condé,

Artillery.

Slender provision of that article, in armies.

(118) Memoires de Nevers, vol. i. p. 252.
(119) La Noue, p. 335.
(120) Brantome, vol. i. Cap. Fran. p. 223.

marched

CHAP. I.

marched to invest Paris, he had only eight pieces of cannon, though his forces amounted to eight thousand infantry, and five thousand cavalry (121). At the siege of Chartres, in 1568, by the same general, he possessed no more than five battering cannon, and four light culverins (122). Even the duke of Anjou, commanding the royal army, which, in the subsequent year, gave battle to the Hugonots, and defeated them, at Jarnac, had only four cannon, and four culverins, with sufficient ammunition to fire them between two and three hundred rounds (123). Elizabeth, queen of England, sent, as a most ample and acceptable supply of artillery, to the prince of Condé, a short time preceding, six cannon, with powder and ammunition. It was done at the earnest solicitation of cardinal Chatillon, the Hugonot embassador; and Condé, grateful for the present, but unable to repay it in money, made a remittance to the queen, in bells, taken from the churches, and in wool (124).

Numerous examples:

When Coligni laid siege to Poitiers, a city several miles in circumference, and strongly fortified, he had, in his whole camp, scarcely more than thirteen battering cannon, besides culverins. His want of artillery was fatal to the success of the enprize (125). At the memorable battle of Montcontour, the royalists were much superior to their enemies in this respect. They had seventeen pieces of cannon: Coligni, only six (126). But, when that illustrious commander re-appeared at Arnai le Duc, in the ensuing year, 1570, and made an ad-

In the army of Coligni.

(121) D'Aub. Hist. Univ. vol. i. p. 163.
(122) La Noue, p. 633.
(123) Ibid. p. 670. Tavannes, p. 27.
(124) Memoires de Castelnau, p. 228.
(125) La Noue, p. 681. Memoires de Castelnau, p. 246.
(126) Memoires de Castelnau, p. 253. Tavannes, p. 356.—This latter author makes the disparity less considerable: he says, that the royal army had fifteen cannon; the Hugonots, eleven.

vantageous

vantageous peace with Charles the Ninth, he was destitute of even a single piece of artillery, of any size or description (127). Henry the Third, writing to his embassador in England in 1577, speaks of the train of battering cannon, which the duke of Alençon, his brother, conducted with him, at the head of the royal forces, as sufficient to reduce any town to obedience. It consisted of eighteen cannon, and six large culverins (128). We may judge of the usual proportion of artillery furnished in that age, by the terms of agreement between Henry, prince of Condé, and the count palatine, John Casimir, in 1575. It was stipulated, that to an army of eight thousand Germans, and six thousand Switzers, should be joined four large pieces of cannon, and twelve field-pieces, with suitable ammunition (129). Two years afterwards, in 1577, when the duke of Nevers exhorted Henry the Third to set on foot an army of six thousand infantry, two thousand, four hundred Switzers, and five hundred men at arms, besides twelve hundred cavalry; he proposed to join to that military force, as a just proportion of artillery, eight cannon, and twelve culverins (130). Eight hundred, or a thousand pioniers, were to be attached to the artillery. The monthly expence, including every article, ordinary and extraordinary, requisite to maintain an army of such magnitude, he estimates at only two hundred and fifty thousand livres a month, or about one hundred and twenty thousand pounds a year. It is not without astonishment, that, at the battle of Coutras, in 1587, we find the duke of Joyeuse had only two cannon. The Hugonots were superior in artillery; for, they were masters of two cannon and

Further proofs of the assertion.

(127) Mem. de Castel. p. 265. La Noue, p. 701.
(128) Le Labour. sur Cast. vol. iii. p. 506.
(129) De Thou, vol. vii. p. 289.
(130) Mem. de Nevers, vol. i. p. 189—191.

a culverin,

CHAP. I.

a culverin, which being placed on an eminence, did ſignal ſervice, and contributed greatly to the victory obtained by the king of Navarre (131). The largeſt battery of cannon, directed againſt any place, during the civil wars, ſeems to have been that which marſhal Matignon opened upon the town of St. Lo, in Normandy, in 1574. It conſiſted of eighteen cannon, and five great culverins (132). But, Brantome ſays, that the moſt furious, and well-ſuſtained fire ever remembered by the oldeſt officer, was kept up from thirty-ſix pieces of cannon, againſt Ivoy in Flanders, when Francis duke of Guiſe commanded the forces of Henry the Second, in 1552 (133).

Petards.

To the period of the civil wars, is due the invention of petards. They were firſt uſed by the Hugonots, in 1580, at the ſiege of Cahors, in Quercy; and they produced an effect proportionate to their novelty and violence (134). Montelimar, and Embrun in Dauphiné, were taken by Leſdiguieres, in 1585, principally by means of petards (135). Red-hot balls, which have been revived ſince 1782, at Gibraltar, were uſed by marſhal Matignon, during the ſiege of La Fere, in 1580 (136).

Ranſoms.

Ranſoms formed a very ſerious and lucrative object of attention, in that age. To the captors, they proved the means of enriching themſelves and their families: the captured were frequently impoveriſhed and exhauſted, by the neceſſity of raiſing large ſums, to procure their freedom. The prodigious prices, ſet on the enlargement of perſons of eminence, excite aſtoniſhment. At the ſtorm of

Their vaſt amount.

(131) D'Aub. Hiſt. Univ. vol. iii. p. 52. Sully, vol. i. p. 59.
(132) Letter of Cath. of Medicis, in the third vol. of Le Lab. ſur Caſt. p. 411.
(133) Brantome, vol. i. Cap. Etrang. p. 265 and 266.
(134) De Thou, vol. viii. p. 376.
(135) Ibid. vol. ix. p. 404 and 405.
(136) Pere Daniel, cited in L'Art de Verif. vol. i. p. 655.

Terouenne

Terouenne by the troops of Charles the Fifth, in 1553, Francis de Montmorenci, eldest son of the constable, was made prisoner on the breach. Twenty-five thousand crowns were exacted for his release (137). The liberty of Gabriel de Montmorenci, fourth son to the constable, taken captive at the age of fourteen, in the battle of St. Quintin, was fixed at ten thousand crowns (138); and that of the duke of Longueville, at forty thousand (139). Lord Grey, who commanded in the castle of Guisnes near Calais, when it fell into the hands of the French, in 1558, was given to marshal Tavannes, to recompense him for his exertions in the capture of the place. He carried his prisoner to Dijon in Burgundy, and did not release him till lord Grey had paid five thousand crowns (140). Brantome complains, that his family estate had been very considerably diminished by the necessity of ransoming his elder brother, taken by the Spaniards, at Hesdin, in Picardy, in 1553 (141). When we reflect, that private gentlemen served, in a great measure, at their own expence, or on a very precarious pay; and that, in case of being made prisoners, they were reduced to purchase their freedom by the sale of their property; we must allow, that a very high sense of loyalty and honor existed among that body of men. It cannot excite surprize, that the profession of arms was considered as more honorable than any other. The officers of high rank, taken in war, belonged

Impoverishment, caused by them.

(137) Le Lab. sur Cast. vol. ii. p. 350.
(138) Ibid. p. 85.
(139) Ibid, p. 656
(140) Tavannes, p. 203—This fact cannot reasonably be doubted, since Tavannes relates it himself. It is, however, very singular, that Brantome expressly declares, that lord Grey was given by the duke of Guise, to Strozzi; who obtained only four thousand crowns for his release, which were paid him by the count de la Rochefoucault, who had been made prisoner at the castle of St. Quintin, and whose ransom had been fixed at that sum. Brantome, vol. ii. Cap. Etran. p. 298.
(141) Brantome, vol. ii. Cap. Etran. p. 157 and 158.

always

CHAP. I.

Profit, derived from ransoms.

always to the commander in chief, as of right: inferior persons were retained by those, into whose hands they chanced to fall. Common soldiers frequently grew rich by these prizes. It was even customary for the general to purchase prisoners of his own men, at low sums; and afterwards to set their ransoms at very exorbitant ones. Philibert Emanuel, duke of Savoy, commanding the armies of Philip the Second, king of Spain, did not disdain this species of traffic; and he acquired not only glory, but profit, by his celebrated victory at St. Quintin, where so many illustrious captives fell into his possession (142).

A striking proof, and which places in a conspicuous point of view, the manners of the age, relative to captives, taken in war, is to be found in the writings of Ambrose Paré. Monsieur de Baugé, says he, brother to the count de Martigues, had been made prisoner by two Spanish soldiers, at Terouenne, in 1553. Vaudeville, governor of Gravelines, having seen him, conceived an opinion, that he was a man of rank. To satisfy himself on a point of such importance, he caused Baugé's stockings to be taken off; and remarking that his socks were neat, and his feet extremely clean, he became confirmed in his original apprehension. He, therefore, purchased him of the two soldiers, for fifteen crowns; who, being unable to maintain their prisoner, and ignorant of his quality, gladly accepted the sum offered. Baugé studiously concealed his name and condition, and patiently endured every hardship; sleeping on straw, and subsisting on bread and water. Vaudeville soon afterwards transmitted to him a list of the French killed at the capture of Hesdin by the Spaniards; and on reading his brother's name among them, his grief surmounted his prudence. He burst into

(142) Brantome, vol. ii. Cap. Fran. p. 157 and 158.

involuntary

involuntary tears and exclamations, which were heard by his guards; who no ſooner diſcovered the connexion between him and the count de Martigues, than they apprized Vaudeville of the value of his prize. By order of that officer, Baugé was immediately removed to an apartment hung with tapeſtry; he was ſerved with delicacy, and ſeven thouſand five hundred crowns were demanded for his ranſom. On his pleading inability to raiſe ſo conſiderable a ſum, Vaudeville obſerved, that it was poſſible he might not procure his freedom at a price ſo reaſonable; and the event juſtified the prediction. Mary, queen of Hungary, governeſs of the Low Countries, and the duke of Savoy, having been informed that a perſon of his quality was in Vaudeville's poſſeſſion, they diſpatched a meſſenger to him, to command that Baugé ſhould be forthwith delivered up to them; adding, that the morſel was too large for him, and that he had captives ſufficient beſides. Baugé's ranſom was immediately raiſed to twenty thouſand crowns (143).

Animoſity of the civil wars.

Frequently, animoſity, or revenge, more powerful even than intereſt, induced the captors to put to death on the ſpot, an enemy who was obnoxious, though he offered great ranſom. This circumſtance was peculiarly characteriſtic of the civil wars, when mutual rancour had extinguiſhed humanity, and even ſuſpended the love of gold itſelf. At Coutras, though the duke of Joyeuſe offered fifty thouſand crowns for his life, and threw down his ſword, he was ſhot dead immediately (144). The king of Navarre gained univerſal applauſe and popularity on that occaſion, by diſmiſſing the greater part of the Catholic gentlemen, who fell into his hands, without exacting, or accepting any ranſom (145).

(143) Œuvres de Paré, p. 794.
(144) D'Aub. Hiſt. Univ. vol. iii. p. 56.
(145) Ibid. p. 56 and 57.

Such

CHAP. I.

Such acts of renunciation and generosity were, by no means, common. The cruelties, exercised by the Spaniards, when they captured Hesdin, in 1553, in order to extort ransoms, can neither be perused without commiseration, nor related without wounding decency. The enormity of their conduct was greatly augmented, by the violation of the terms of surrender, which guaranteed to the French their lives. But, no articles of capitulation could restrain the ferocity, and merciless avidity of the Spanish soldiery. Those whom they did not stab, or massacre, were only reserved for more humiliating and lingering torments, of a nature too shocking to be described. Paré, who was an eye-witness to the facts, and who narrowly escaped with his life and liberty, gives a most affecting detail of every circumstance. It strongly paints the inveterate animosity, and savage fury, by which the most polished European nations, when at war with each other, were actuated and inflamed, in the sixteenth century (146).

Nature and composition of armies, in that century.

Francis the First, and Henry the Second, during their foreign wars, maintained very numerous armies, on a permanent footing. But, under the two last kings of the house of Valois, when their revenues were alienated or squandered, and when civil dissension depressed the throne, forces were only raised, and retained for a short time. The whole kingdom was in arms; but, the regular troops were few. The nobility led their retainers to the particular standard, which they chose to follow by preference. It became, under Henry the Third, an object of royal and ministerial contemplation, to change the nature of military service, and to commute, for a sum of money, the obligation, imposed on the vassal to attend his lord armed in the field.

(146) Œuvres de Paré, p. 791.

The

The duke of Nevers calculates, that by excluding all the holders of fiefs, who were bound on the publication of the "Arriere Ban," throughout France, to appear in arms, on paying an equitable fine to the crown, above twenty thousand pounds might be easily and speedily raised (147). Foreign auxiliaries from almost all the countries of Europe, composed a principal part of the soldiers on either side. Italians, Walloons, Spaniards, Switzers, English, and Germans, fought for one, or the other party. Even the Scots were desirous of tasting the pay, and plunder of France. In 1577, eighteen hundred Scots, who had served in Holland, and in Denmark, anxious for employment, offered their services to Henry the Third. James the Sixth, then a minor, does not seem, either by himself, or by his ministers, to have been acquainted with, or consulted in the transaction. Colonel Balfour, on the part of himself and his men, made the offer to Henry. That prince declined it, not without many acknowledgments (148).

Army of Henry the Third, how composed.

The largest army, seen during his reign, in France, was in 1589, when he besieged Paris, with near forty thousand troops. Of the number, fourteen thousand were Switzers and Germans, conducted by Sancy. Near four thousand, principally Protestants, were commanded by, and in the immediate employ of the king of Navarre. Epernon had brought to his master, a body of six thousand foot, and twelve hundred horse, raised at his own expence (149). The dukes of Montpensier, and Longueville, Givry, and many other noblemen, or gentlemen, led their retainers (150). But, this numerous body of forces, was not belonging to the

(147) Mem. de Nevers, vol. i. p. 193 and 194.
(148) Le Lab. sur Cast. vol. iii. p. 512.
(149) Vie d'Epernon, vol. i. p. 322.
(150) Davila, p. 813.

crown:

CHAP. I.

crown: no sooner was Henry dead, than the greater part immediately disbanded, or withdrew, under their respective leaders; leaving the king of Navarre to contest alone with his antagonist, the duke of Mayenne, for the sovereignty of France. We may judge how destitute was Henry the Third of any regular army, by his summoning, in the month of March preceding, the principal lords and gentlemen of his kingdom, to the number of one hundred and two, to join him, at the head of their troops (151).

Naval force. Gallies.

The French kings can scarcely be said to have possessed any navy, before the reign of Francis the First; the gallies of Louis the Twelfth which were stationed at Marseilles, being only calculated for the protection of the coast, or for expeditions of short duration. During the former part of Francis's reign, while the celebrated Andrew Doria commanded the marine, at the time that Genoa was subject to the French crown; they maintained a superiority in the Mediterranean, over the naval forces of the emperor Charles the Fifth. But, after the defection of Doria, and the revolt of Genoa in 1528, Francis having lost his ascendant, had recourse to an expedient, which rendered him odious to all Europe. He dispatched Poulin, a man who had risen by his merit and capacity in the marine, as embassador to Solyman the Second, emperor of the Turks, to negotiate for the junction of the Ottoman fleet with that of France. After surmounting many obstacles, Poulin succeeded in the object of his mission. Barbarossa, in 1543, at the head of a hundred and ten gallies, coasted the shore of Italy; arrived in the harbour of Marseilles; and having sailed from thence with the French fleet and forces, they laid siege to Nice. Notwithstanding their superiority,

Negotiation of Poulin, at the Porte.

Barbarossa joins the French fleet.

(151) De Thou, vol. x. p. 577.

periority, they were repulsed from before the castle; and Francis derived little benefit from an alliance so generally reprobated by the Christian powers (152). To recompence the zeal and ability of Poulin, he was raised, in the following year, to the rank of captain-general of the gallies; and he is commonly known in history, by the title of Baron de la Garde. In letters patent, issued on the occasion, the French navy is stated to consist of "gallies, fusts, brigan-"tines, and round vessels (153)." It is difficult to ascertain with certainty, their number, or force; but, we may rate the gallies below thirty, as only twenty-six, under command of the count d'Enghuien, joined Barbarossa in the expedition against Nice, when every effort was exerted to swell the French marine (154).

Creation of a captain-general of the gallies.

The war continuing between Francis the First and Henry the Eighth, La Garde conducted the fleet, composed of gallies and round vessels, through the straits of Gibraltar, across the Bay of Biscay, into the English channel. He even ventured to attack, in the month of August, 1545, the English fleet, stationed off the Isle of Wight; and, having, by the nautical skill of his evolutions, deprived them of the advantage resulting from a northerly wind, he extricated himself with honor, and sunk one of the largest ships of the enemy (155). It is probable that this was the first attempt made by any European power, to navigate gallies from the Mediterranean, across a portion of the Atlantic, into the northern seas; and it proves equally the progress of navigation, and the naval ability of the French commander. Encouraged by his predecessor's success,

Nautical skill and exploits of Poulin.

(152) Guichenon, Hist. de Savoye, vol. i. p. 651.
(153) Le Lab. sur Cast. vol. ii. p. 10.
(154) Gnichenon, vol. i. p. 651.
(155) Hume's Hist. of England, vol. iv. p. 250. Le Lab. sur Cast. vol. ii. p. 12.

Henry

CHAP. I.

State of the French marine, under Henry the Second.

Henry the Second, ſoon after his acceſſion, in 1547, diſpatched Leo Strozzi, one of the moſt ſkilful mariners of the ſixteenth century, with only ten gallies, to the coaſt of Scotland (156). The French marine was at its higheſt point, towards the termination of that monarch's reign; when, the grand prior, brother to Francis, duke of Guiſe, commanded at one time, upwards of forty gallies, well manned, armed, and equipped for battle (157). Under the three laſt princes of Valois, as the inteſtine troubles of the kingdom augmented, the navy ſunk, into neglect. Francis the Second, it is true, ſent ſome gallies to the aid of Mary of Guiſe, queen regent of Scotland, in 1560; and three years afterwards, Charles the Ninth diſpatched fifteen, to co-operate with the Spaniſh forces of Philip the Second, in the reduction of the Mooriſh fortreſs of Penon de Velez, on the coaſt of Morocco (158).

Its decline under his ſucceſſors.

But, theſe exertions were only temporary; and the French marine, in common with every other national, or public inſtitution, declined, from the exhauſted ſtate of the revenues. When it became requiſite, in 1572, to block up the port of Rochelle, in order to prevent ſupplies from being thrown into the place, while it was inveſted by land; the king, beſide ſending thither all his gallies, equipped eight "round veſſels (159)." They were ſo denominated from their circular conſtruction forwards, in contradiſtinction to the gallies, and other prowed veſſels, which were ſharp in the ſtern.

Equipment of ſquadrons for the protection of trade.

Charles the Ninth, and Henry the Third, fitted out, at different times, during the courſe of their reigns, ſquadrons of armed ſhips, for the protection of trade;

(156) Brantome, vol. ii. Cap. Fran. p. 357 and 358.
(157) Ibid. p. 396 and 397.
(158) Ibid. Cap. Etran. p. 36 and 37.
(159) Le Lab. ſur Caſt. vol. iii. p. 267.

3 parti-

particularly, in the English channel, which swarmed with pirates, or unauthorized and expatriated banditti, who plundered and interrupted all navigation. Elizabeth appears to have afforded them constant, though indirect, and concealed protection (160). In 1575, Henry the Third equipped, from the ports of Normandy and Brittany, twelve ships, for the purposes above-mentioned; but, he did it with every precaution, to prevent the alarm which, he apprehended, the queen of England might take, at such a measure (161). When the duke of Mayenne besieged Brouage, on the coast of Poitou, in 1577, the royal forces by sea amounted to eighteen round vessels, exclusive of the gallies, and tenders, or victuallers. The ships of war were fitted out from Bourdeaux (162). But, the most considerable naval equipment, made by Henry, or, rather by Catherine of Medicis, in whose name it acted; was the fleet which sailed to the islands of the Azores, in 1582, for the purpose of reducing them to the obedience of Don Antonio, titular king of Portugal. It quitted the river Garonne, under the command of Philip Strozzi, and consisted of thirty ships, and twenty-five pataches (163.) No French gallies durst undertake so distant and perilous a voyage upon the Atlantic: while, as a proof of the superior nautical skill of the Spaniards in that age, the marquis Santa Croce had, in his fleet, no less than twelve gallies. It was certainly the first effort of the sort; and would be regarded, even in the present age, when navigation has attained to such a degree of perfection, as a bold and hazardous experiment (164).

Expedition to the Azores.

Superior naval skill of the Spaniards.

(160) Le Lab. sur Cast. vol. iii. p. 299, and p. 390.
(161) Ibid. p. 458.
(162) D'Aub. vol. ii. p. 300. De Thou, vol. vii. p. 511. Le Lab. sur Cast. vol. iii. p. 512.
(163) D'Aub. vol. ii. p. 466. De Thou, vol. viii. p. 581.
(164) De Thou, vol. viii. p. 58.

Comparison of the fleets of the two nations.

The disparity between the naval force of France and Spain, is not less striking. Santa Croce commanded twenty large ships, of which the "St. Philip" alone might have encountered the whole fleet of Strozzi. She was a floating castle, of astonishing height, and eighteen hundred tons burthen; proportionably manned and armed. The largest vessel in Strozzi's squadron, on board of which he hoisted his flag, was only of six hundred tons; and he was obliged to quit her before he commenced the engagement with the Spaniards, as she was a very slow sailer, and unmanageable. The second ship, in which he actually ventured to attack the "St. Philip," was only of two hundred tons. Another difference, still more important, if possible, between the fleets of the two nations, was, that Philip the Second's vessels were all, in the strict sense of the term, men of war, built in the royal docks, at Seville; whereas, it would seem, that the far greater part of Henry's, were merchant vessels, hired expressly for the expedition (165). We can hardly be astonished, after considering these circumstances, that the issue of the enterprize was unfortunate to the French. It is difficult to form any estimate of the number of sailors who navigated Strozzi's fleet; or, of the amount of seamen which France could furnish in that age.

Jurisdiction of the general of the gallies.

The appointment of general of the gallies was equally honourable and extensive in its jurisdiction, though subordinate to the higher dignity of admiral of France: but, the latter was frequently only a simple title; whereas the former was a laborious, dangerous, and efficient office. He appears to have possessed considerable power, and to have decided by his supreme authority, in a summary manner, all

(165) D'Aub. Hist. vol. ii. p. 466—468.

questions

questions respecting prizes and captures (166). The salary annexed to the employment by Francis the First, was ample; being no less than five hundred livres, or above twenty pounds a month (167). Such was the elevation of mind, which distinguished the baron de la Garde, that, when at eighty years of age, and laboring under the symptoms of a mortal and incurable disease, Catherine of Medicis offered him the sum of fifty thousand crowns to resign his post, he had the magnanimity to decline it, and to prefer dying captain-general of the gallies. His death was correspondent with his other actions: the physicians having announced to him his dissolution as imminent and inevitable, he caused himself to be raised, placed in a chair, with his sword drawn in his hand, and soon afterwards expired in that attitude. The obscurity of his birth and origin rendered the heroism of his character more extraordinary. His parentage was so low, and so uncertain, as to baffle enquiry (168).

CHAP. I.

Salary.

Heroism of Poulin.

To La Garde was due the honor of some essential improvements and ameliorations in the mode of building and navigating gallies. We may judge of their materials and durability, from the instance of the "Reale," or admiral galley, constructed by him, which continued to keep the sea above thirty years (169). The greatest magnificence was displayed by the captains-general, in the decorations, ornaments, and other appendages of their vessels. The examples given by contemporary writers, and eye-witnesses, excite admiration. When, in 1573, a negociation of marriage was opened between Elizabeth, queen of England, and the duke of Anjou,

Durability of the gallies.

Their magnificence.

(166) Brantome, vol. ii. Cap. Fran. p. 387.
(167) Le Lab. sur. Cast. vol. ii p. 11—13.
(168) Brantome, vol. ii. Cap. Fran. p. 387 and 388.
(169) Ibid. p. 384.

CHAP. I.

afterwards Henry the Third; it advanced so far, that orders were issued to hold the gallies in readiness for transporting the prince to London. They were at that time before Rochelle, occupied in blocking up the harbour of the place. On receiving the intimation, La Garde made every preparation for convoying the duke, in a manner suitable to his high rank, and to the splendor of the occasion. He is said to have expended ten thousand crowns of his own fortune, in fitting up the admiral galley. All the slaves, who rowed her, were provided with jackets of crimson velvet, to be worne on their entry into the Thames. The state-room, or great cabbin, and the poop of the galley itself, were hung with the same materials, embroidered in gold and silver, having a Greek motto or device on the awning, which signified, that "however blown "about and agitated, I have never fallen, or "changed." The allusion was natural and obvious, to the fidelity and loyalty, evinced by La Garde, during a long life, checquered by many misfortunes and disgraces. The beds, furniture, benches, streamers, and flags, were either covered with, or composed of, velvet and damask in equal proportions, fringed with gold, or silver. All these superb preparations were rendered useless, by the rupture of the proposed marriage (170).

Splendor of the admiral galley.

Naval expeditions fitted out by private individuals.

Individuals appear to have possessed and exercised, in the sixteenth century, the right of fitting out, in time of peace, naval expeditions, at their own cost, without any leave obtained from the sovereign; and the object of which was either trade, or conquest, as accident and circumstances might determine. The only measure requisite to be observed, was, not to attack allies or confederates of the crown, to which

(170) Brantome, vol. ii. Cap. Fran. p. 385—387.

the

the adventurer owned allegiance. Henry the Third ſeems to acknowledge and admit this principle in all its extent, as equally juſt and generally recognized (171). Under Charles the Ninth's reign, a ſon of marſhal Montluc, having heard that great wealth was to be acquired on the coaſt of Africa, between Cape Blanco and the Cape of Good Hope; determined to ſhare in theſe ſuppoſed riches. Regardleſs either of the papal donation, or, of the long poſſeſſion acquired by the Portugueze; he publickly equipped two veſſels in the river Adour, employed ſix months in compleating their compliment of men, and ſailed from Bourdeaux. Arriving at Madeira, and being refuſed refreſhments by the governor, who had received intimation from his court, of the deſign of Montluc; the French landed, attacked, and carried the works; but, their commander being killed, they quitted the iſland. Great complaints were made by the Portugueze embaſſador at Paris, of this infraction of treaty (172). La Noue expreſsly ſays, that the piratical expeditions, undertaken by Frenchmen annually to the coaſt of Peru, did not drain the nation of a ſmaller number, than five hundred ſubjects a year (173).

Enterprize of Montluc.

Piracies.

Fire-ſhips were well known, and frequently uſed, under Henry the Third. Frederic Jembelli, an engineer, whom the Spaniards had diſguſted, threw himſelf into Antwerp, when beſieged by the prince of Parma, in 1584; and gave ſignal proofs of his capacity, by ſending down the Schelde, ſeveral fire-ſhips of prodigious magnitude. They had nearly demoliſhed the bridge, or mole, conſtructed by that great commander, acroſs the river, and on which he repoſed all his hopes of ſucceſs. Jembelli is

Fire-ſhips.

Their invention.

(171) Le Lab. ſur Caſt. vol. iii. p. 524.
(172) D'Aub. vol. i. p. 247 and 248. Brantome, vol. ii. Cap. Fran. 256—258.
(173) La Noue, p. 182.

CHAP. I.

regarded as their inventor (174): it is, however, incontestable, that they were used by the Hugonots several years earlier, in 1577, at the siege of Brouage, in Poitou. Clermont d'Amboise, who commanded the fleet of Rochelle, sent four fire-ships, to burn the royal squadron. De Thou very accurately describes their nature and destination (175). We find no mention of them among the English, before the invasion of the Spanish Armada in 1588, when they performed such signal execution.

(174) Busbeq. de Bong. p. 242. (175) De Thou, vol. vii. p. 518.

CHAP.

CHAP. II.

State of commerce, and navigation.—Bankers.—Attempts at colonization.—Manufactures.—Sumptuary laws.—Agriculture.—Condition of the peasants.—Oppression of the inferior orders of society.—Population.—State of Paris.—The Louvre.—Public edifices.—Courts of law, and of criminal judicature.—Venality of offices.—Corruption of justice.—Confiscation.—Torture.—Punishments and executions.—Sale of honors and dignities.

CHAP. II.

State of the French commerce.

IT is, by no means, easy, from the most accurate and laborious comparison of the materials, left us by the contemporary authors, to form any clear or perfect idea of the precise state of the French commerce under the last princes of the race of Valois. The information on that point, is usually short, obscure, and unsatisfactory; while, on subjects of far inferior importance, they frequently embrace a vast detail. We may, however, safely assert, that the true principles of trade were, at that period, little understood, or studied, either by men of speculative research, or by statesmen or financiers. A very precarious protection was extended by the state, to the merchant adventurer: navigation was dangerous, not only from the want of charts, which might direct the mariner; but from the number of pirates, with which the Mediterranean and the other European seas were infested. Ships were, besides, liable to detention, and even to confiscation, either from the rapacious spirit of the government, or from the impolitic and pernicious regulations, adopted in various countries, with a view

Impediments to trade.

CHAP. II.

a view to draw unreaſonable advantages from the affluence of foreign traders. Monopolies, or excluſive privileges, granted by the French kings, to favoured individuals, fettered, and oppreſſed the genius of commerce. Impolitic prohibitions, originating in narrow and contracted ideas of national benefit, prevented the exportation of many articles. Induſtry had not diſcovered and improved the numerous ſources of internal riches. Naval enterprize, and diſcovery, rather than the ſpirit of trade, characterized the age. Gold was the object of general reſearch, rather than the exchange of commodities, and the progreſſive acquiſition of wealth. The example of Spain and Portugal, whoſe ſovereigns had over-run and conquered the richeſt portions of the Old and New World with incredible rapidity; and whoſe ſubjects returned home with the ſpoils of India, of Africa, and of Peru; had contributed to awaken avidity, and to debauch the ſober genius of laborious application. Men preferred diſtant and precarious expeditions, in queſt of plunder, or in ſearch of mines, to the beaten track of limited profit. The effect of ſo many cauſes, operating to one point, was ſenſibly felt: and may account for the ſlender and contracted portion of trade enjoyed by France, at this period of her hiſtory.

Objects of commercial reſearch.

Objects of exportation.

The three great and principal articles of exportation appear to have been corn, wine, and ſalt, though it was frequently prohibited, under the ſevereſt penalties, to ſend any grain out of the kingdom (1). La Noue eſtimates the ſum annually received for theſe three commodities, from foreign nations; to which he adds a fourth, "Paſtel," or ſweet-meats; at twelve millions of livres, or about half a million ſterling (2).

(1) De Thou, vol. vii. p. 505. (2) La Noue, p. 356.

All

All the weſtern provinces, included between the Loire and the Garonne, but, particularly Poitou, were productive of corn, which the Spaniards and Portugueze gladly purchaſed, in exchange for the luxuries of the eaſtern and weſtern hemiſpheres. The port of Les Sables d'Olonne, ſituated in the little iſland of Olonne, on the coaſt of Poitou, was the uſual mart, to which the ſhips of thoſe nations reſorted, under Henry the Third. A fleet of twenty-five Portugueze veſſels, laden with corn, and ready to return home, was attacked and captured, in the harbour above-mentioned, contrary to the rights of nations, and on very inſufficient pretences, by a detachment of Hugonots, from Rochelle, in 1577, notwithſtanding the oppoſition of the prince of Condé. It was an act of lawleſs and unauthorized piracy, which ſtrongly proves the inſecure ſtate of property and commerce in that age, when the crown, ſcarcely able to defend itſelf, could afford little protection either to its own ſubjects, or to foreigners, who viſited the kingdom for the purpoſes of trade (3).

Wines.

Great quantities of corn were raiſed in ſome of the provinces near the Pyrenees, where the produce of eſtates was principally received in grain, and tranſported by the Garonne, to Bourdeaux (4). But, that city was more renowned for its wines, which, in the ſixteenth, as well as in the eighteenth century, were in the higheſt eſtimation, throughout Europe. It may be doubted, whether before 1589, any wines, the growth of Champagne or Burgundy, were exported by ſea, from France. We may form a very accurate judgment of the annual revenue which the crown derived from the commerce of the Garonne. It was eſtimated at more than a hundred thouſand crowns, in 1586, when Royan, a

(3) De Thou, vol. vii. p. 505—507.
(4) Comm. de Montluc, vol. iv. p. 165.

caſtle,

CHAP. II. castle, commanding the entrance of the river, was surprized by one of the adherents of the king of Navarre (5).

Salt. The Germans and English carried on a very considerable trade to Brouage, a town situate in the vicinity of Rochelle, and then possessing a commodious harbour. Salt was the principal, or only commodity, exported from thence; which was found in immense quantities, over the adjacent country. These salt-pits and works produced a great revenue, from the foreign, as well as domestic consumption (6). The Hugonots derived from them one of their best pecuniary resources, as they were enabled to repay, in salt, the various articles of commerce or of defence, received from England (7). How vast the resort of that nation was to Brouage, may be evinced by the circumstance of Lansac, who commanded the forces of Henry in 1577, when he made himself master of the place, having seized on near sixty vessels, belonging to the English, which were at anchor off the isle of Ré. Elizabeth, justly irritated at such an infraction of treaty between the two crowns, immediately caused an embargo to be laid on all the French ships in her ports; and it was not till after a negociation of some length, that matters were re-adjusted (8).

Brouage.

Trade to the Levant. Scarcely any branches of manufacture were exported by the French, in the period of which we are treating; and vast sums were annually sent out of the kingdom, for the purchase of various articles of luxury. The Levant trade drained France of above sixty thousand pounds sterling a-year; the Turks, in that age, as the Chinese, in the present, accepting only specie in return for the commodities which foreigners demanded (9). Spices, and many

(5) De Thou, vol. ix. p. 573. (6) Memoires de Cast. p. 261.
(7) Le Lab. sur Cast. vol. iii. p. 515.
(8) De Thou, vol. vii. p. 529. (9) Tavannes, p. 469.

other

other valuable productions of India, ſtill continued to be received by way of Alexandria, notwithſtanding the augmenting competition of the European nations who had diſcovered, or of thoſe who began to participate in the benefits of the paſſage round the Cape of Good Hope. The Ottoman miniſters appear even to have entertained the moſt enlarged conceptions of commerce, if we may judge of them from the propoſitions made by Amurath the Third, in 1582, to Francis, duke of Anjou, at that time ſovereign of the Low Countries. Emballadors were ſent by the ſultan, with offers to make Antwerp the ſole emporium for all the goods imported into Europe from Greece and the Turkiſh provinces in Aſia. They demanded permiſſion for eighteen merchants of their nation to reſide in the city of Antwerp, in order to conduct the ſales. It was projected to land the articles of merchandize at Marſeilles; to tranſport them acroſs Provence and Languedoc, to Bourdeaux; and to ſhip them from the river Garonne, to Flanders. We cannot ſufficiently admire a plan ſo extenſive in its principles and operations; and which, if it had been realized, might have produced a vaſt revolution in the commercial ſyſtem of Europe, before the lapſe of half a century. But, the anſwer returned to the propoſal, was inconcluſive; and the dominion of the duke of Anjou in the Netherlands was too ſhort, to permit of its being reſumed on either ſide (10).

Propoſal for making Antwerp the emporium of the Turkiſh trade.

The trade between France and the Baltic was very limited, if it can be properly ſaid to have had any exiſtence, before the reign of Charles the Ninth. The election of his brother, the duke of Anjou, to the Poliſh throne, in 1573, opened a proſpect of eſtabliſhing an advantageous traffic with Dantzic, which city conſtituted a part of the dependencies of

Trade to the Baltic.

(10) De Thou, vol. viii. p. 646.

Poland.

CHAP. I.

Poland. A ſociety of merchants, to the number of near thirty, in the beginning of the year 1574, fitted out ſome ſhips from Dieppe, in hopes, by the favor and protection of the new prince, to acquire a ſhare of the Baltic commerce; but, Henry's precipitate flight from Cracow ſoon afterwards, probably withdrew the principal incitement to the enterprize (11). It may excite ſome degree of ſurprize, that, notwithſtanding the impediments oppoſed by nature to any connexion between France and Peru, from the length and dangers of a navigation round Cape Horn; and in defiance of the jealous precautions embraced by the court of Madrid, to exclude all European nations from any participation in the benefits ariſing from their poſſeſſions in South America; yet, that ſhips from France viſited thoſe diſtant countries. We find in 1576, that a captain Nivelle, an experienced officer of the marine, on his return from Peru, was driven to take refuge with his veſſel in the ports of England, by the violence of a ſtorm. He was immediately arreſted by order of Elizabeth; his ſhip detained; and he himſelf was in imminent hazard of being treated as a criminal of ſtate. It is not eaſy to account for this conduct in the Engliſh miniſters, unleſs it was done to conciliate the good will of Philip the Second. That Nivelle was no unauthorized adventurer, is evident, from the preſſing ſolicitations made in his behalf, by the king of France: but, whether the object of his voyage had been plunder, or commerce, it is not poſſible to aſcertain (12).

To Peru.

Trade between England and France.

Between the French and Engliſh, there exiſted a very conſiderable mercantile intercourſe, under the two laſt kings of the family of Valois. It was, notwithſtanding, perpetually interrupted by diſputes,

(11) Le Lab. ſur Gaſt. vol. iii. p. 390.
(12) Ibid. p. 497 and 498.

ſeizures, confiſcations, and acts of violence, on the part of each crown, or nation. Elizabeth, whatever pretenſions of amity ſhe might affect, carried on a gainful traffic, by means of her ſubjects, with the Hugonots; and that able princeſs, conſcious of the embarraſſments with which the French monarchs were neceſſitated to ſtruggle, obſerved ſcarcely any meaſures, in her treatment of the individuals, who entered her ports. It is eaſy to ſee, that the Engliſh were commonly the aggreſſors, though they always demanded, and uſually obtained ſatisfaction. The depreſſion under which France laboured from 1560, to a period conſiderably later than the death of Henry the Third, has contributed to augment the luſtre of Elizabeth's reign. She may be ſaid, on many occaſions, to have almoſt dictated to the kings of France, in matters of policy, as well as of commerce (13). Numberleſs proofs of this fact are to be found in the contemporary writers.

Bankers.

The principal bankers who were eſtabliſhed in Paris before 1589, ſeem, as in London, at that time, to have been Italians, or Lombards. Very arbitrary and ſevere inquiries into their pecuniary tranſactions and remittances, were made by government, at pleaſure. Seizures of money, upon vague, or inſufficient pretences, often followed. Bankers were prohibited from having in their poſſeſſion, any gold or ſilver coin, except of France, or Spain, on pain of confiſcation (14). We may form ſome eſtimate of the ſtate of commercial intercourſe between Paris and London, in December, 1573, by the circumſtance of there not being a ſingle banker in the former city, who had a correſpondent in England. Charles the Ninth expreſsly aſſerts this

Intercourſe between London and Paris.

(13) Le Lab. ſur Caſt. vol. ii. p. 316; vol. ii. p. 316; vol. iii. p. 431 and 432, p. 515, and p. 535.
(14) Buſbeq. letter 8th.

extraordinary

CHAP. II.

extraordinary, and curious fact, in a letter to his embaffador at the court of Elizabeth, of that date. He adds, that there was no banker in Paris, who could furnifh letters of exchange on London, for fo large a fum as fifty thoufand crowns; and he refers it to his minifter to difcover a mode of making the remittance (15). Yet, a few months later, in June 1574, Chiverny, the agent of Henry the Third, and who was afterwards chancellor of France, fays, that he contrived, as foon as Charles the Ninth was dead, in the uncertainty of the rout which his mafter might take on his return from Poland, to tranfmit "letters of bank" to Augfburg, to Vienna, and to Venice. Twenty-five thoufand crowns were contained in each of the three remittances. It difplays the fuperior degree of facility in mercantile tranfactions with Germany, and the regular communication fubfifting between Paris and that country (16).

Remittances.

When Henry the Third borrowed a hundred thoufand crowns of Ferdinand the Firft, great duke of Tufcany, in 1589, a part of the fum was fent in fpecie, acrofs the Apennines and the Alps, from Florence to Augfburg, on the backs of mules. Ferdinand did not embrace this mode of remittance, from any difficulty of procuring letters of exchange; but, with an intention of keeping the affair concealed. Such was the publicity of bankers accounts, that, if conveyed through their medium, it muft have become univerfally known throughout Tufcany (17).

Mode of remitting money.

Colonies.

While Spain and Portugal, fortified by the Papal grant, quietly divided between them the vaft regions of Afia and America, France remained deftitute of

(15) Le Lab. fur Caft. vol. iii. p. 366—369.
(16) Chiverny, vol. i. p. 52.
(17) De Thou, vol. x. p. 630.

any

any colonies, or establishments, beyond the Cape of Good Hope, or the Atlantic. Francis the First was not insensible to so severe an exclusion. "I wish," said he, "to see the article in Adam's will, by "which the kings of Spain and Portugal are autho-"rized, in virtue of his bequest, to divide the New "World, without allotting me any share (18)." The baron de Levi having discovered Canada in 1518, Francis sent out Cartier, an able navigator of St. Malo, to ascertain the nature and productions of that inhospitable country. He arrived there in 1534, and returned to France with the expected information; but, no attempt seems to have been then made to plant, subject, or colonize Canada (19).

Attempts at colonization, under Henry the Second.

Under Henry the Second, in 1556, Villegagnon, a French gentleman, knight of Malta, having obtained the approbation of Coligni, admiral of France, to carry out a number of adventurers to Brazil, landed there, and constructed a fort. A reinforcement was sent him in the following year, principally composed of Calvinists, from Geneva. Many women embarked among them; and preparations were made for establishing a powerful colony. But, these prospects soon ceased: dissensions, arising from religious causes, produced the most destructive consequences; and the Portugueze, joined with the natives, having attacked Villegagnon, he was reduced to the necessity of leaving his artillery, embarking his followers, and returning to Europe (20).

Efforts of Coligni, to form colonies.

Not discouraged by preceding misfortunes, Coligni, whose vast and expanded mind was continually directed towards objects of national advantage; sent out, in 1562, Ribaud, in order to form an establish-

(18) Art de Verif. vol. i. p. 635.
(19) Ibid. vol. i. p. 635 and 636.
(20) Hist. Univ. D'Aub. vol. i. p. 41 and 42.

ment

CHAP. II.

ment in Florida. He was unsuccessful: nevertheless, in 1564, Lodoniere, a second adventurer, effected the object of the expedition, built a fortress, and entered into connexions of friendship and commerce with the Indians. Ribaud returning with seven ships in the following year, the two chiefs prepared to push their conquests, when a superior squadron of Spanish vessels appeared. Hostilities ensued, which were unfavorable to the French; and Ribaud, with five hundred of his followers, having, on the solemn assurances of safety, consented to a parley with the enemy, they were indiscriminately massacred, and their bodies reduced to ashes. Lodoniere escaped on board the vessels, and landed safely in France (21). History has scarcely ever commemorated a more complete, or extraordinary revenge, than was taken for this atrocious breach of faith. A Frenchman, named des Gourgues, descended of a respectable family at Bourdeaux, and who had been a galley slave, chained to the oar by the Spaniards, from which state of servitude he was redeemed, undertook to vindicate the wounded honor of his country, and to retaliate the cruelty of the Spaniards. Enraged at the relation of the events which had taken place in Florida, he sold his property, in order to fit out three vessels; the largest of which did not exceed two hundred and fifty tons, and the smallest was only fifty. About three hundred persons, of all descriptions, allured by hopes of gain or plunder, accompanied him on the expedition. Arriving on the coast of Florida, he took the forts by storm, which the Spanish commander, Melandez, had occupied; and after reproaching him with his perfidy and barbarity, he caused the whole garrison, amounting to near four hundred and sixty men, to be either hanged, or put to death.

Massacre of the French adventurers.

Retaliation on the Spaniards.

(21) D'Aub. Hist. Univ. vol. i. p. 248 and 249.

Melandez

Melandez had affixed labels to the dead bodies of Ribaud and the French, whom he massacred; signifying, that "they were so treated, not as French, "but as Lutherans." In imitation of this insult, des Gourgues attached a similar inscription to the slaughtered Spaniards, declaring, that "they were "not put to death as subjects of Philip the Second, "but, as perfidious miscreants." Having put all the artillery taken from the forts, on board his ships, he re-embarked, and landed at Rochelle in June, 1568, after a passage of only seventeen days. But, instead of receiving any marks of approbation from Charles the Ninth on his arrival at court, he had occasion to employ the intercession of his friends, to prevent his being capitally punished. The admiration, expressed by his countrymen, and by foreign nations, at so signal an act of vengeance, was his only reward (22). It strongly depictures the spirit of the age, in which the genius of chivalry was not yet extinct; and it still more forcibly demonstrates the abject situation to which France was reduced, after the death of Henry the Second, when Spain remained for near forty years, the most formidable power in Europe. From 1568, to the accession of Henry the Fourth, no further attempt seems to have been made, to form colonies, or establishments, beyond the Atlantic: a circumstance which cannot excite surprize, if we reflect on the calamitous condition of the kingdom between those two periods.

CHAP. II.

Behaviour of the French court.

If, from the consideration of commerce, we turn our attention to manufactures, we shall find that they were neither numerous, nor advanced to a state of any perfection, under Henry the Third. Articles of elegance and luxury were imported from foreign nations; and even such as were of general consumption, had not attained beyond their infancy.

Manufactures.

(22) D'Aub. Hist. Univ. vol. i. p. 354—356.

CHAP. II.

A fabrick of silk had been introduced under Francis the First; but, it met with many impediments, from the climate, from the ignorance of the artists, and above all, from the troubles of France. It was reserved for a happier and more tranquil reign, to awaken, and direct the industry of the French in this branch of art. Leather and parchment were prepared with considerable dexterity, at Troyes in Champagne; which was likewise renowned for the goodness of its dyes, in which occupation the inhabitants were principally employed (23). A manufacture of white paper was established at Brignolles, in Provence, about the beginning of Henry the Second's reign, and it was not the only one of the kind in the kingdom (24). The French in the sixteenth century, as in the present, appear to have discovered little ingenuity, or talents, for working in steel and iron. Fire-arms were far better fabricated in Lombardy. It was from Milan, that all the best arquebusses, corslets, helmets, and musquets, were procured. The science of gilding and inlaying armor was, likewise, practised with superior skill, beyond the Alps. Gaspard, an artist of Milan, was the favorite workman, who supplied Paris with every kind of arms, under Charles the Ninth, and his successor. Negroti, a Milaneze merchant, resided for the purpose, in that capital; where he acquired a fortune of above twenty-five thousand crowns, by the business, in the course of fifteen or sixteen years (25). We may judge how high a price was paid for armor in general, by the expence of a common morion, or head-piece gilt, and fabricated at Milan. It cost in Paris, seven crowns: but, encouragement having been held out to workmen in that branch, the secret of gilding was discovered

Fire-arms.

Milan supplied France with that article.

(23) De Thou, vol. x. p. 314. (24) Le Lab. sur Cast. vol. ii. p. 13.
(25) Brantome, vol. iv. Cap. Fran. p. 294.

and

and succesfully executed in France. Even then, the morions were purchased in Italy, and finished in Paris. Their price was, however, reduced to about four, to five crowns (26).

Musquets.

Charles the Ninth, in 1560, endeavoured to introduce among his soldiers, musquets, fabricated at Mentz, and Abbeville, where manufactures of arms were established; but, it was found impossible to accustom the troops to handle and carry them, on account of their enormous and oppressive weight (27). The finest musquets long continued to be brought from Milan. Gunpowder was made in France, under Henry the Third; but, not in sufficient quantity to dispense with the necessity of importing that article, as well as saltpetre, from foreign states. Genoa, in particular, supplied the French with gunpowder, on emergencies (28).

Sumptuary laws.

Sumptuary laws were enacted by the vigilance of the celebrated chancellor l'Hopital, under Charles the Ninth, with an especial view to discriminate the different orders of the people. Industry suffered little by the prohibition of articles of luxury, chiefly derived from foreign countries; and morals were benefited by the regulation. Princes, dukes, and their wives, were alone permitted the use of gold and silver stuffs. Silk, diamonds, and pearls, were interdicted to all except gentlewomen (29). In the beginning of 1581, these laws were renewed, and pecuniary penalties affixed to the breach of their observance (30). Henry the Third, while sunk in luxury himself, and indulging his minions in every refinement of an effeminate taste, affected to deprive the other sex of their natural ornaments, and to

(26) Brantome, vol. iv. Cap. Fran. p. 298 and 299.
(27) Ibid. p. 302—304.
(28) Memoires de Nevers, vol. i. p. 212, and p. 278.
(29) Traduction de l'Hop. vol. ii. p. 118. (30) L'Etoile, p. 72.

CHAP. II.

execute the new edict respecting dress, with the utmost severity. By an impolitic exercise of his power, he commanded the provost of the palace, an officer, whose jurisdiction extended indefinitely over the metropolis; to arrest, and to convey to prison, all such females as he should find, violating the sumptuary regulations. In obedience to the king's orders, he seized, and dragged into confinement, not less than fifty or sixty women, among whom were several of condition. They were even forcibly detained in the prison of the Fort l'Eveque, near Paris, till the next day, though offers were made to pay the penalty incurred, and to give security for their future compliance with the edict. But, Henry was not far from repenting of his indiscreet interference with the police of the capital. A sedition had almost taken place: the provost narrowly escaped the effects of the popular indignation; and the king condescended to repair in person to the prison, to release the captives, and even to pay the fees incurred for their confinement. This curious fact happened in November, 1583 (31).

Regulations respecting dress.

Agriculture.

Agriculture could not possibly have attained beyond its rudest state, in a country where the harvest was rarely reaped by the same hands which had sowed the grain; where the husbandman was at the mercy of the soldier; and where impolitic trade laws withdrew the necessary encouragement from the cultivator of the soil. The ravages of famine were frequently experienced in their utmost severity. At Paris, in May, 1586, such was the dearth of corn, that a peck of wheat sold from three to four crowns (32). It was even higher in the month of June, of the succeeding year, when the same measure of corn rose to five crowns, or thirty livres, in the

Famine. Its severity.

(31) Busbeq. letter 29. L'Etoile, p. 72 and 73.
(32) Memoires pour ser. à l'Hist. de France, p. 207.

metropolis; and to ſeven, or eight crowns, in the ſurrounding cities (33). We may judge of the miſeries which muſt have been experienced by the poor, at a time when, it would ſeem, no proviſion was made by the laws, for their maintenance. Contributions for the ſupport of the poor, were altogether voluntary, before the year 1587. During the famine of 1568, ſuch was the prodigious concourſe of beggars in the ſtreets of Paris, that it became indiſpenſable to adopt ſome meaſures for their ſubſiſtence. Two deputies from each pariſh, went from houſe to houſe, collecting charitable donations (34). This remedy being only temporary, and inadequate to the cure of the evil, it was enacted in an aſſembly held in Paris, on the 8th January, 1587, that the citizens ſhould raiſe at once, the aggregate ſum for three years, taken at the eſtimate of that which was weekly raiſed and appropriated to the relief of the poor. With ſo conſiderable a fund, which was actually collected, it was propoſed to clear the ſtreets of the numerous beggars; to compel thoſe who were able to work, and to feed the infirm (35). Notwithſtanding theſe beneficent and judicious meaſures, it was found neceſſary, only five months afterwards, during the ſcarcity of corn, to ſend two thouſand poor, to the hoſpital of Grenelle, without the city; where an allowance of five ſous, or twopence halfpenny, was made daily to each, by the king. Although ſuch a diſtribution muſt have been, if we conſider the relative value of money, extremely ample; yet, it became requiſite to withdraw it, and to place the poor in their former ſituation, becauſe, unreſtrained by the proviſion allotted for their maintenance, they could not be kept from returning to the capital, and reſuming their original profeſſion (36).

CHAP. II.

Police, Beggars.

Poor laws.

(33) Memoires pour ſer. à l'Hiſt de France, p. 222.
(34) Ibid. p. 207. (35) Ibid. p. 217. (36) Ibid. p. 222.

of

CHAP. II.

State of the peasants.

During the thirty years which elapsed between the death of Henry the Second, and the extinction of his posterity in the person of Henry the Third, the condition of the French peasants may, perhaps, be justly said to have been more deplorable than that of any other class of men, in Europe. The greater part of the period was passed in civil war; and the few intervals of nominal peace, were short, precarious, sanguinary, and cruel. The "ipsa etiam pace "sævum" of the Roman historian, might be applied with equal truth, to the French under the three last kings of Valois, as to the countrymen of Tacitus, during the dissensions and calamities which followed the accession of Galba. Neither the royal army, nor the forces of the Protestants being regularly paid, it became impossible for them to subsist, except by plunder; nor was any lenity shewn to friends and adherents, by a famished soldiery, undisciplined, fierce, and rendered obdurate by habits of violence. Even the cessation of actual hostilities, in consequence of the treaties which were repeatedly made between the two parties, was productive of little redress. We may be satisfied of this fact, by perusing the description given to Charles the Ninth, in one of the short truces, rather than times of peace, which took place under his reign, at the close of 1573. It was drawn by a nobleman of the first rank, the count de Tavannes; and he speaks only of the Burgundian peasants, who had suffered far less by the preceding disasters, than the inhabitants of almost all the other provinces. "They complain," says he, "to your majesty, that the gen-"darmerie not being paid, pillage, ransom, and "treat as enemies, the people in all the villages; "nor do they dare even to utter a complaint, lest "the soldier, irritated, should complete the desola-"tion of their families and properties, by instantly "reducing

Oppression of them.

Condition of the Burgundian peasantry.

"reducing their cottages to ashes (37)." If such was the treatment of the Catholic peasants, by men of their own persuasion, in a moment of peace; what must have been the enormities acted, when civil and religious enmity extinguished every emotion of humanity? Marshal Montluc did not blush to be called the "Bourreau Royal (38);" and his Memoires, in almost every page, bear bloody testimony to the justice of the appellation (39). We are struck with horror, on perusing in La Noue, and d'Aubigné, the incredible and wanton acts of flagitious cruelty, exercised upon the inferior classes of society, who were incapable of resistance, and whose sufferings do not excite more pity, than they awaken indignation (40). The "Gautiers," who were put to the sword in 1589, by Montpensier, were wretched Norman peasants, driven to despair by oppression, and rendered savage from the cruelty of the nobles and soldiery (41). Religion had no concern in their insurrection, which resulted from civil and political causes.

Cruelties exercised towards the Hugonots.

The Gautiers.

Nor was it only on the husbandman or cottager, that military ferocity exhausted its rage. All the lower orders, destitute of any efficacious protection, were alike victims to the despotism of their superiors. Strozzi, though, in many respects, an officer of high merit, and no way distinguished by a natural barbarity of disposition, yet, committed an act, to parallel which, we must have recourse to the annals of Domitian, or Caracalla, in antiquity. Unhappily, the present savage and infatuated race of republicans, if that epithet can justly belong to frantic and furious banditti, have outdone the most ex-

Barbarity of Strozzi.

(37) Tavannes, p. 34. (38) Montluc, vol. iv. p. 124.

(39) Ibid. p. 112, p. 313, p. 221 and 222, and p. 92 and 93.

(40) La Noue, p. 346. D'Aub. Hist. Univ. passim. Chron. Nov. vol. i. p. 9.

(41) De Thou, vol. x. p. 600.

travagant

CHAP. II.

travagant crimes of the Roman Cæſars; and have rendered credible the fabulous, or exaggerated enormities of the greateſt tyrants who have deſolated the earth. In 1570, after the concluſion of the peace between Carles the Ninth and Coligni, the army was, from its undiſciplined ſtate, accompanied by a vaſt number of proſtitutes, and common women. Strozzi, who had made many ineffectual attempts to purge the camp of them, cauſed above eight hundred of theſe unfortunate creatures, at a ſignal given, to be precipitated from the Pont de Cé, near Angers, into the river Loire, where they all periſhed. The ſtory is ſo extraordinary, that it would be incredible, if it was not related by Brantome, an eye-witneſs, Strozzi's intimate friend and panegyriſt (42). He, however, condemns it as a deteſtable act, and attributes it to the counſels of others. It appears inconteſtably, that no ſort of puniſhment was inflicted on the perpetrator of ſo abominable a deed, except the frowns and averted looks of the ladies of the court, incenſed at the cruelty ſhewn to perſons of their own ſex. But, a mutiny had nearly taken place among the troops themſelves, who beheld the objects of their affection ſwallowed up in the waves, and crying piteouſly for ſuccour. If any thing can augment the enormity of the fact, it is the conſideration, that it was a cool, and deliberate proceeding, done by the colonel-general of the French infantry, and perpetrated almoſt in the preſence of his ſovereign, who was at Angers when it was committed. The crimes of the duke of Alva, Strozzi's contemporary, were not reflective murders, wantonly acted; but ſanguinary executions, enjoined by Philip the Second, performed with ſolemnity, and in ſome meaſure palliated, or juſtified by the revolt of the Flemings.

Reflexions on that event.

Oppoſite conduct of the duke of Alva.

(42) Brantome, vol. iii. Cap. Fran. p. 416—418.

Flemings. Far from esteeming it necessary, in order to restore discipline among the Spanish bands, to cause the women who ministered to their pleasures to be murdered, the general of Philip permitted them in an ample degree. When he marched from Milan into Flanders, in the year 1567; during which march the severest obedience was enforced with rigor, and not a peasant was despoiled of his property in the slightest instance; twelve hundred courtezans accompanied the camp. Four hundred were of a superior description, and rode on horseback: the remaining eight hundred followed on foot (43).

Population of France.

Calculations of the population of extensive countries, are, in general, made upon very problematical principles, and are subject to great uncertainty. National vanity leads so obviously to exaggerate, that we must lend an academic faith to all assertions, unless supported by incontrovertible facts. It is difficult to form any decided opinion upon the number of people which France contained, at the period of which we are treating; and no contemporary writer has ventured to name their aggregate amount: but, we are justified in supposing, that, in an age when civil war had made such deep ravages, the kingdom could not, in proportion to its magnitude, have contained as many inhabitants, as it did before the late revolution in 1789. Yet, La Noue speaks of the multitudes who swarmed in every province; and compares the population in France to that of the county of Flanders, before the insurrections, produced by the tyranny of Philip the Second, had diminished the number of the Flemings (44). His testimony is respectable, not only

(43) Strada de Bell. Belg. vol. ii. p. 90. Brantome, vol. i. Cap. Fran. p. 81.

(44) La Noue, p. 356.

from

CHAP. II.

from the known integrity of the author; but, from its being written under the reign of Henry the Third, in a period of the greateſt national depreſſion. We are aſſured, that in 1581, the whole kingdom contained ninety-ſix biſhopricks, and one hundred and thirty-two thouſand pariſhes and hamlets (45). Four years earlier, in 1577, the duke of Nevers calculated, that in the dominions of France, there were three millions of hearths. If we eſtimate each of them at ſix perſons to a family, it will give a population of only eighteen millions. But, it muſt be remembered, that neither French Flanders, Artois, Alſace, Lorrain, the county of Burgundy, Rouſillon, Cerdagne, nor Bearn, were then included in the monarchy. It was ſuppoſed that by a poll-tax, levied equally on all the inhabitants, a ſum of twenty millions of livres might be raiſed annually (46), or about eight hundred and fifty thouſand pounds ſterling. On the number of inhabitants at Paris, we may form a more accurate judgment. It was found, that in 1588, there were in the capital, at leaſt twenty thouſand men in the ſervice of the League, capable of bearing arms; many ſtrangers having been recently introduced into the city, by the adherents of the houſe of Guiſe, in order to augment their ſtrength. The whole population exceeded two hundred thouſand (47).

Population of Paris.

Paris. Its ſtate.

The French metropolis, at the cloſe of Henry the Third's reign, was divided into ſixteen wards, or quarters, and was principally built on the northern bank of the Seine, and in the iſland of "Notre Dame." It had not as yet made any conſiderable progreſs to the ſouth of the river, where the "Faux-

(45) Cabinet des trois Perles, p. 5, cited in the Satyre Menippée, vol. ii. p. 70.

(46) Memoires de Nevers, vol. i. p. 197.

(47) Eſprit de la Ligue, vol. iii. p. 6. Mem. de Chiverny, vol. i. p. 163.

bourg

bourg St. Germain" is now ſituated. Strong walls, flanked with large towers, ſurrounded the city; and the keys of the gates were depoſited in the hands of the municipal magiſtrates, who took eſpecial care that they ſhould be carefully ſhut every evening. The citizens were regularly enrolled, diſciplined, and accuſtomed to the uſe and exerciſe of arms: they elected their own military officers; had their places of aſſembling, their banners, and their watch-words. If not formidable from their ſkill, they were ſtill reſpectable from their numbers (48). In general, the ſtreets were ſo narrow, that it was eaſy to leap from the tops of the houſes on one ſide, to thoſe on the other; and it was a common paſtime, during the carnival, for the young nobility to divert themſelves by this hazardous amuſement (49). That the principal ſtreets were paved, is undoubted; ſince we find that, at the preparations made for celebrating the unfortunate tournament in which Henry the Second was killed by Montgomery, in June, 1559, the ſtreet "Saint Antoine" was unpaved, converted into liſts, and adorned with theatres and triumphal arches (50). Other proofs of this fact might be adduced: but, the dirt and filth were notwithſtanding ſuch, as to render all paſſage exceedingly difficult, and to contribute, in an eminent degree, to the peſtilential and malignant diſtempers, by which the capital was frequently deſolated. In 1583, Montjoſieu, a man of talents, and peculiarly ſkilled in mechanics, undertook the execution of a plan which he had formed, for cleanſing the ſtreets; but, the expence ſo much exceeded the eſtimate made by him, that in endeavouring to accompliſh it, he conſiderably impaired his own private for-

Municipal government.

Mode of building.

Regulations of police.

(48) Eſprit de la Ligue, vol. iii. p. 3.
(49) Brantome, vol. iii. Cap. Fran. p. 326.
(50) D'Aub. Hiſt. Univ. vol. i. p. 84 and 85.

tune.

CHAP. II.

tune (51). At all the corners, were fixed heavy chains, commonly faſtened and ſealed; but, which could be, at the ſhorteſt warning, ſtretched acroſs; and by the additions of barrels filled with earth, they formed a barricadó, inſurmountable to infantry, or cavalry. Henry the Third experienced the formidable nature of theſe barriers, at the inſurrection of the Pariſians, in May, 1588 (52). The private houſes were conſtructed with ſalley ports, which rendered them more tenable and defenſible againſt an armed force (53). On the other hand, the Baſtile might be regarded at once, as the citadel of Paris, and as a priſon of ſtate. It was ſtrong; and the treachery alone of Tetu, who commanded in it, produced its ſurrender to the duke of Guiſe, immediately after the king's flight from the metropolis (54). Ornano had offered to maintain it, againſt all the forces of the League.

The Baſtile.

The Louvre.

The Louvre itſelf was rather a fortreſs, than a palace; and did not become the ordinary reſidence of the French monarchs, before the reign of Charles the Ninth. Francis the Firſt, and Henry the Second, occaſionally inhabited it; and the latter of thoſe princes made conſiderable embelliſhments, or augmentations; during which time he inhabited the Hotel de Maigrez, a houſe confiſcated to the crown, and preſented by him afterwards to the conſtable, Montmorenci (55). The palace of the "Tournelles," ſituated not far from the Baſtile, was the reſidence of Henry the Second, at the time of his unfortunate and premature death: but, Catherine of Medicis, ſtruck with horror at the recollection and

The Tournelles.

(51) De Thou, vol. ix. p. 78.
(52) Ibid. vol. x. p. 258. Davila, p. 690 and 691. Eſprit de la Ligue, vol. iii. p. 3.
(53) Eſprit de la Ligue, vol. iii. p. 3.
(54) De Thou, vol. x. p. 269.
(55) Le Lab. ſur Caſt. vol. ii. p. 510.

ſight

ſight of a place, which had been the ſcene of ſo tragical an accident, demoliſhed it to the foundations, and even cauſed the gardens contiguous, to be deſtroyed. We cannot wonder at her averſion to a palace, in the great hall of which, decorated at that time for balls and feſtivals, the dead body of her huſband lay in ſtate within a few days afterwards, ſurrounded with torches, altars, black cloth, and all the apparatus of funeral pomp (56). The aſpect of the Louvre, like that of almoſt all the palaces of kings throughout Europe, till the end of the ſixteenth century, inſpired terror, and partook more of the nature of a priſon, than of a royal reſidence, in many reſpects. It was compoſed of towers, conſtructed in a Gothic taſte, ſurrounded with a wide and deep ditch, acroſs which the entrance lay through vaſt gates, conſtantly guarded by archers. In 1574, Catherine of Medecis, as ſoon as Charles the Ninth had expired, cauſed all the doors and entrances to the Louvre, except one, to be cloſed up; and even of the remaining entrance, the gate was ſhut, and only the wicket left open, on each ſide of which were ſtationed the Switzers, who never quitted it by day or night (57). Theſe precautions were taken by the queen-mother, in order to prevent the eſcape of her ſon, the duke of Alençon, and of the king of Navarre, who remained, a long time, captives in the palace. Margaret, of Valois, in the year 1578, by an effort of courage and fidelity above her ſex, contrived to let down her brother, the duke of Alençon, by means of a rope, into the moat of the Louvre, whence he reached the abbey of St. Genevieve: but, ſhe deſcribes the attempt as of the moſt perilous nature (58).

Aſpect of the Louvre.

(56) D'Aub. Hiſt. Univ. vol. i. p. 85.
(57) L'Etoile, p. 4.
(58) Mem. de Marguérite de Valois, p. 164, 165.

There

CHAP. II.

There were few monuments of architecture in Paris, at the deceafe of Henry the Third. Catherine of Medicis, who, with the vices of the family from which fhe fprung, inherited, likewife, their tafte for the arts, began to conftruct the palace of the Tuilleries, in 1564, and fhe completed it before her death, in 1589. It was a magnificent edifice, raifed on the models of antient Greece, purified from the barbarity of the middle ages. Europe had hitherto feen no building, which could be placed in competition with it, beyond the Alps (59). Not content with fo fplendid a proof of her paffion for the elegant arts, fhe erected another palace in the parifh of St. Euftace, on which fhe expended immenfe fums, and at which fhe ufually refided (60). The fecond hotel in point of magnificence, in 1587, was that of the duke of Epernon, eftimated at only five thoufand crowns lefs value than the former (61). We may form an idea of the price given for houfes of the higheft defcription, in 1575, by the fum which Henry the Third paid for the one prefented by him to Chiverny, and in which he refided when chancellor of France. It coft twenty-fix thoufand livres, or about eleven hundred pounds fterling (62).

The Tuilleries.

Palaces.

Before the death of Charles the Ninth, there was not any bridge which croffed the river Seine in its whole extent: thofe previoufly exifting, only conducted from the northern bank, into the ifland of "Notre Dame." In the month of May, 1578, the foundations of the "Pont neuf" were laid by the king in perfon. It was compofed of hewn ftone; du Cerceau being the architect; and a tax

Bridges. Pont neuf.

(59) L'Art de Verif, vol. i. p. 648.
(60) De Thou, vol. x. p. 502.
(61) Vie d'Epernon, vol. i. p. 167.
(62) Memoires de Chiverny, vol. i. p. 62.

was

was imposed on the people expressly for its construction (63). The troubles which soon arose in the kingdom, interrupted its continuance; and it was not completed till their termination, under the succeeding reign. Quelus, the celebrated minion of Henry the Third, killed in a duel with Entragues, was interred with a pomp little short of royal, on the same day when the "Pont neuf" was begun; and the king, who was inconsolable for his loss, wished to have immortalized the memory of his favorite, by calling it the "Pont aux Pleurs (64)."

Paris began to be regarded as the royal residence.

Although Paris had, for ages, been regarded as the capital of the kingdom, it was not till after the year 1577, that it began to be the ordinary and general residence of the sovereign. Louis the Eleventh, and his two immediate successors, held their court more frequently on the Loire, at Tours, Amboise, or Blois. Chambord, under Francis the First, as well as Fontainbleau; the former of which he built, and the latter he re-constructed; were the favorite places of his abode (65). Henry the Second betrayed the same preference; and Charles the Ninth commonly divided his time between Monceaux, St. Germain, and Vincennes. At the last-mentioned castle, only about two leagues from the metropolis, he expired. But, Henry the Third, though he twice convoked the assembly of the States General at Blois; yet, from preference, resided during the greater part of his reign, at Paris. The city derived no small accession of opulence and splendor from the circumstance; and the king severely reproached the inhabitants for their ingratitude and revolt, after the numerous marks of predilection, which he had uni-

(63) L'Etoile, p. 29 and 30. De Thou, vol. vii. p. 727. Chron. Septennaire, p. 447.
(64) Vie de Mar. de Val. p. 258.
(65) Trad. de l'Hopital, vol. ii. p. 10—13.

formly

CHAP. II.

formly exhibited towards them (66). If it were permitted to the hiſtorian to indulge in ſpeculation, it might be curious to reflect on the deſtiny which awaited Paris, if Henry had not periſhed by the knife of Clement; and to conjecture what changes might have taken place in the metropolis of the French monarchy. Davila expreſsly ſays, that on the evening preceding his aſſaſſination, the king publickly declared, "within a few days, neither "houſes nor walls ſhould exiſt, and that only "the veſtiges of Paris ſhould be diſcernible." It is highly probable, that the threat would have been executed in its utmoſt rigor, and that the victorious troops, compoſed of different nations, would have vied with each other, in accompliſhing the vengeance of their maſter. The age was prone to acts of blood; and it muſt be admitted, that no ſovereign ever received from rebellious ſubjects, greater cauſe for indignation. Henry's death extricated the Pariſians from the awful, and imminent deſtruction (67).

Rigorous intentions of Henry the Third, towards Paris.

So perfectly was the king's determination of transferring his future court and reſidence to ſome other place, known throughout France; that in 1588, after Henry's flight to Chartres, the inhabitants of Tours and Lyons ſent deputations, to beſeech of him, to give the preference to their reſpective cities (68). It may be conjectured, that he would have fixed his abode, as well as transferred the courts of law, and other appendages of the metropolis, to the banks of the Loire. Philip the Second had given him a recent example of the kind, by quitting Toledo, the antient capital of Caſtile, and chuſing Madrid for the new ſeat of the Spaniſh monarchs.

Reflexions on it.

(66) Chron. Noven. vol. i. p. 66.
(67) Davila, p. 815. Memoirs pour ſer. à l'Hiſt. de Fr. p. 284.
(68) Chron. Nov. vol. i. p. 65.

There

Corruption, and venality of justice.

There is no circumstance which more strongly characterizes the period before us, than the universal corruption of justice. Francis the First had introduced the purchase and sale of employments among the members of the various parliaments of France, who instituted the supreme tribunals of civil and criminal judicature. His successors, peculiarly, Henry the Third, had augmented, in a vast proportion, the number of magistrates in every court; and as all the charges were venal, the persons who bought, had no other object in view, than to reimburse themselves for the expence incurred, by the most iniquitous perversions of equity. The sovereign himself, unrestrained either by the majesty and sanctity of the throne, or by a regard to the felicity of his people, did not blush to interfere in decisions of law, sometimes by solicitation, and, not unfrequently, by open violence. Examples of both continually occur. In 1578, at the entreaty of his minions, Henry condescended to prosecute, by personal importunity, the suit of Madame de Senneterre, a lady of the court, against La Chatre, a gentleman attached to his brother, the duke of Anjou; and of consequence, obnoxious to the king's favorites. So powerful a suitor did not exert his interest in vain; and La Chatre lost his cause (69). The royal guards, in May, 1582, broke open a prison, by the king's order, and rescued a follower of La Valette, detained for a capital crime (70). Some years afterwards, de Rusmenil, a gentleman of Picardy, accused of murder, having been conducted prisoner to the "Conciergerie," was taken from thence by force, at Henry's command, who was induced to commit the act, by the importunate request of the duke of Joyeuse (71). During the

Interference of the crown in decisions of law, and justice.

Creation of offices.

(69) Vie de Marg. de Val. p. 260.
(70) Memoires pour ser. à l'Hist. de Fr. p. 140.
(71) Ibid. p. 202.

 course

CHAP. II.

course of his whole reign, he seems only to have considered the creation of legal employments, as a mode of imposing taxes. The multiplication of them exceeded belief, and produced the most deplorable consequences. Even the highest dignities of the law became venal. In 1580, for the first time, Bellievre, on the resignation of his office of President of the great chamber of the parliament of Paris, rceived from his successor, the attorney-general, the sum of sixty thousand livres, or about two thousand five hundred pounds, as the price of the vacant post of attorney-general, by Faye, a master of requests; who sold his own to a third person, for near eleven hundred (72). The people became the victims of these iniquitous proceedings. So avowed was the traffic of charges to the courts of judicature, that the prices were public and notorious: they appear to have risen in value; no doubt, from the encreasing profits annexed to their exercise. In August, 1584, the place of counsellor in the parliament of Paris sold for three thousand five hundred crowns: those of the criminal court of justice, called the "Chatelet," for two thousand; and the masterships of requests and accounts, from four to five thousand crowns (73).

Sale of employments.

It was in vain, that the celebrated chancellor, l'Hopital, under Charles the Ninth, one of the greatest and most virtuous statesmen whom France ever produced; endeavoured, by his exhortations and personal example, to check the torrent of venality. In an age and a court so corrupt, his resistance could not effect a change in the national manners. All his writings prove the regret, as well as the indignation, which he felt, at the depravity of his countrymen. Placed on the highest eminence

Ineffectual efforts of l'Hopital, to reform these abuses.

(72) Memoires pour ser. à l'Hist. de Fr. p. 120.
(73) Ibid. p. 181.

of

of the law, and holding in his hand the great seal; neither the dignity of his office, nor the incorruptibility which was demanded from it, could protect the sanctuary of justice from invasion and pollution. "I am torn," says he, in one of his epistles, "by "the wolves and tigers who surround the king, who "carry off the patrimony of the state, break down "the most sacred barriers, and despise every consi-"deration, except their own interest (74)." The first nobility were not ashamed to tamper with the inferior ministers of the law, to solicit their favor, to buy their suffrages, and even personally to waste whole days in so disgraceful an occupation. "The "nobles," says L'Hopital, "forget the dignity of "their rank so far, as to place themselves, before "break of day, at the door of a vile secretary; "they accompany him to the court of law; remain "near him; expose themselves to the insults of the "croud assembled below the bar; and attend him "in the evening to his own house (75)." Nor did the men alone descend to these base and scandalous arts, to pervert the course of justice; ladies of the highest quality emulated them in rapacity, importunity, and solicitation. "The most obstinate con-"tests," exclaims the same virtuous magistrate, in another place, "which I am obliged to maintain, "are not against the men: the women resist much "more strongly, and do not so easily abandon the "struggle (76)."

Solicitation of the nobility.

Rapacity of the women of the court.

If it could be necessary to confirm a testimony so unquestionable, the Memoirs of Tavannes contain ample proof of the enormities committed in all the provincial tribunals, as well as in those of the capital (77). "The doctors in law," says he, "have

(74) Trad. de l'Hop. vol. ii. p. 235.
(75) Ibid. vol. i. p. 138.
(76) Trad. de l'Hop. vol. i. Eclairciſſements, p. 17.
(77) Tavannes, p. 34.

CHAP. II.

Tribunals of law.

"prolonged the period of ſtudy, requiſite for entering on the diſcharge of judicial functions, to ten years, in order to exclude the nobility from participating in their enormous depredations."—"The number of officers employed in the adminiſtration of juſtice and finance, do not fall ſhort of fifty thouſand."—"All the judges, having purchaſed their ſeats, make no ſcruple of receiving bribes circuitouſly, which clerks, ſolicitors, and others, preſent to their wives and ſervants (78)." Montluc pathetically laments, that the nobility, by diſdaining to occupy judicial and municipal offices, as they had done at the beginning of the ſixteenth century, had thrown away one very eſſential ſource of conſideration and power (79.)

Separation of the military, and judicial character.

It was not till the year 1560, in the States General held at Orleans, that a complete and total ſeparation was made between the long and the ſhort robe; or, in modern language, between the ſword and the gown. Previous to that æra, Bailiffs and Senechals, though not verſed in juriſprudence, or bred to the profeſſion of law as a ſcience, yet decided on queſtions of life and property (80).

Duration of ſuits at law.

The duration of ſuits was one of the moſt pernicious conſequences of the general corruption of juſtice; and the litigious ſpirit which diſtinguiſhed the times, rendered the evil more ſevere in its operation. All ranks of men were infected with it; and the chicane practiſed to protract deciſions, rendered the proceedings eternal. Families buried their whole eſtates in ruinous conteſts with each other, and paſſed their lives in ſoliciting, purchaſing, and corrupting the judges. L'Hopital draws a ſtriking and affecting picture of the extent of this

(78) Tavannes, p. 287.
(79) Memoires de Mont. vol. iv. p. 10.
(80) L'Art de Verif. vol. i. p. 648.

calamity.

calamity (81). Henry the Third, when he made the eloquent and pathetic harangue, with which he opened the States General, in 1588, insists at great length upon the magnitude and enormity of the evils, proceeding from the delays and procrastinations of courts of law; and recommends it as an object of the most serious attention to the national representatives (82). But, they were too deeply engaged in faction, to attempt the reformation of justice.

Forgeries.

Among the extraordinary crimes and abuses practised in that age, to corrupt or to pervert the course of justice, must be reckoned the fabrication of the great seal itself. A secretary of the court of chancery, named Mornat, aided by another accomplice, undertook to affix a counterfeit seal to the warrants issued. He executed it with so much dexterity and success, that in a very short space of time, he acquired between five and six thousand crowns. When discovered, he escaped the punishment due to his crime, by a precipitate flight into Germany; but, his confederate, less vigilant, was seized and executed. This event took place under Charles the Ninth, during the period when l'Hopital was chancellor (83).

Confiscations.

Confiscations were another of the modes by which wealth was obtained, more safely, but, hardly more honorably, under the last princes of Valois. Henry the Second presented to his mistress, Diana de Poitiers, all the effects seized or sequestered from the Hugonots, for heresy. It amounted to a prodigious sum; and the donation did not tend to retard or diminish the proceedings against the Protestants (84). Henry had given her, at his accession,

(81) Trad de l'Hop. vol. i. p. 137—144; and vol. ii. p. 56—62.
(82) De Thou, vol. x. p. 378 and 379, and p. 387.
(83) Brantome, vol. ii. Cap Fran. p. 83—85.
(84) D'Aub Hist. Univ. vol. i. p. 83.

CHAP. II.

in 1547, the money arising from the confirmation of offices throughout France, which were always renewed at the commencement of every reign (85). Under his son, Charles the Ninth, a new species of confiscation was introduced by Gondi, marshal de Retz, a Florentine; which long continued to be practised. Not only persons convicted of treason, or other crimes of state, but, men of every description, were liable, at death, to have their houses, property, and effects, seized on, by order of the crown, and lavished from their legal heirs, upon the slightest pretences. The old, rich, and infirm, were objects of unremitting attention to the rapacious courtiers; who often obtained a grant of their property, and kept a watchful eye upon their future prey. L'Hopital, at an early period of his life, introduces the cardinal of Lorrain, his patron, in one of his epistles, thus addressing him: "Observe "the houses of the dying, and on the first accident "write to me, or come to me in person: be assured in that case, of the royal favor, and of mine; "but, take care, that no one more alert, anticipate "you: don't lose sight of the beds of the sick (86)." When Mazille, first physician to Henry the Third, lay expiring, in 1578, the minions did not even wait till he was dead, to divide his spoils. Camus, a master of requests, was dispatched to take an inventory of his effects, which was done in the presence of the favorites to whom they were given. It does not appear, that Mazille had committed any sort of crime, unless the one of being suspected to lean towards the reformed religion. His only real crime consisted in his reputed wealth, which was estimated at ten thousand crowns (87).

Seizure of private effects.

Examples of this practice.

(85) Brantome, vol. ii. Cap. Fran. p. 9 and 10.
(86) Trad. de l'Hop. vol. i. p. 87.
(87) Mem. pour ser. à l'Hist. de Fr. p. 101.

The

CHAP. II.

Torture.

The torture was indiscriminately administered in the sixteenth century, to prisoners of every rank, in its utmost violence, and at the arbitrary pleasure of the magistrate. It was not even considered as any act of indecency, for sovereigns to be present at such a scene. Henry the Third, in 1582, assisted, behind a curtain, during the deposition of Salcede, who was put to the torture (88). Not only kings, but queens, and the ladies of the court, were accustomed to regard executions, as a spectacle of state, which excited little emotion. The genius of the age, sanguinary and ferocious, diminished, if it did not extinguish the horror, naturally produced by the apparatus of punishment and death. The public and magnificent entry of Henry the Second into Paris, in 1549, was solemnized by exhibitions of this nature. Several Hugonots expiated the crime of heresy; and Henry was a spectator of their sufferings. Florent Venot, one of them, had been previously confined for six weeks, in an engine, formed like a sugar-loaf, and pointed at its base (89). After the conspiracy of Amboise, Francis the Second; his brothers, who were still in a state of childhood; and all the princesses and ladies assisted, as at a pageant, when Castelnau, and his accomplices, were put to death. A platform was constructed under the windows of the castle, to facilitate the view of the ceremony (90). That the sentiments of compassion and terror, connected by nature with the sight of a barbarous execution, could not be entirely subverted by custom, or fashion, is, notwithstanding, evident, from the example of Leonora d'Humieres. She was the wife of William de Montmorenci, one of the younger sons of the constable; and having gone, in March,

Executions.

The court assisted at them.

(88) De Thou, vol. viii. p. 636.
(89) D'Aub. Hist. Univ. vol. i. p. 75.
(90) Ibid. vol. i. p. 94.

1563,

CHAP. II. 1563, together with the other ladies of the court, to see the execution of Poltrot, who was torn to pieces by horses, on the "Place de Greve," at Paris; she was so overcome with her emotions, as to faint away, and expire soon afterwards (91).

It is equally clear, that the fate of this lady, the result of sensibility, did not produce any alteration in the mode of frequenting punishments. When Salcede, in 1582, suffered by the same species of death, which had been inflicted upon the assassin of Francis, duke of Guise; an apartment at the town-house was fitted up, and ornamented expressly for the royal family (92). Henry the Third, his queen, and Catherine of Medicis, were present at the performance (93). The king not only regarded, but, directed the manner of it; and at the intercession of the duchess of Mercœur, who was allied to Salcede, he abbreviated that criminal's torments, by causing him to be strangled (94). His head was sent to Antwerp; as that of Coligni, in 1572, if we may believe D'Aubigné, had been carried to Rome (95). The embassador of Philip the Second having, with some acrimony, remonstrated with Henry, on his sending Salcede's head to be exposed in a city, where he had not the smallest right to command as sovereign; the king, somewhat embarrassed, replied, "I have forwarded it to my brother, to use his pleasure respecting it, if he pleases (96)." History has not disdained to commemorate, that the invention and use of gags is due to the age of which we are treating; and it is a characteristic circumstance. They were first known in 1560, and used in

Death of Salcede.

Gags.

(91) Le Labour. sur Cast. vol. ii. p. 220.
(92) L'Etoile, p. 55.
(93) De Thou, vol. viii. p. 636.
(94) L'Etoile, p. 54 and 55. Busbeq. letter 8th.
(95) D'Aub. Hist. Univ. vol. ii. p. 17.
(96) Busbeq. p. 64. letter 9th.

Dauphiné,

Dauphiné, to prevent the Hugonot minifters from exhorting, or converting the people (97).

Univerfal venality.

It was not only in the magiftracy, and all the courts of civil and criminal juftice, that venality was introduced and eftablifhed. It had pervaded every department, and polluted every charge, or employment. De Thou juftly attributes to fo nefarious a practice, which excluded merit, talents, and fervices, the univerfal depravity of manners under Henry the Third, and the final ruin of that prince's affairs. It had attained a pitch of enormity, beyond which it feemed impoffible to advance (98). The higheft offices of truft and dignity were publickly expofed to fale, without difguife; and the fovereign frequently purchafed them of his own fubjects and courtiers.

Examples. Joyeufe.

When Joyeufe was appointed governor of Normandy in 1583, he could not take poffeffion of the province, till he had bargained for the ceffion of the principal cities and fortreffes, with thofe, to whom they had been committed. Exhaufted by the fums requifite to be expended, and unable to fatisfy D'O, commander of the caftle of Caen; Joyeufe was neceffitated, befides paying a confiderable part of the purchafe in money, to place him in the poft of fuperintendant of the finances, from which he had been antecedently removed, for the moft criminal malverfation and incapacity. Henry confented to a transfer, fo pernicious to his people (99).

Mayenne.

In the following year, he condefcended to importune the duke of Mayenne, to part with the office of admiral of France; which he likewife conferred upon Joyeufe. Forty thoufand crowns were given for it; but Mayenne expreffed the utmoft reluctance to comply, and only did fo in the laft extremity.

Guife.

His brother, the duke of Guife, withftood all the folici-

(97) D'Aub. Hift. Univ. vol. i. p. 99.
(98) De Thou, vol. x. p. 676.
(99) Ibid. vol. ix. p. 80.

tations

CHAP. II.

tations of the king, and peremptorily refused to quit, or sell, on any conditions, the charge which he occupied, of lord-steward of the household (100).

Governments.

The inferior officers imitated the example of the great. Henry, king of Navarre, having demanded, in 1589, at the time of his treaty with the crown, a place of security upon the Loire, for the passage of his troops, it became requisite to cede to him either Saumur, or the Pont de Cé. But, Cosseins, who commanded in the latter fortress, refused to evacuate it, for a smaller sum, than a pension of fifty thousand crowns. De Lessart, governor of Saumur, was not so unreasonable; and in order to render him more accommodating, the king of Navarre did not hesitate to offer, nor De Lessart blush to accept, a bribe of three thousand crowns (101).

Prisoners.

Even the prisoners whom Henry had arrested at Blois, after the assassination of the Guises; and whom he had entrusted to Le Guast, a captain in his guards, governor of Amboise; he was reduced to purchase again of his own officer, within a few weeks. Such was the faithless and venal temper of the age. Fifteen thousand crowns were paid to Le Guast, from the royal treasury, for the persons of the cardinal of Bourbon, the prince of Joinville, son to the late duke of Guise, and the duke of Elbeuf. He was likewise permitted to retain, and to appropriate to himself, the ransoms to be derived from the liberty of the archbishop of Lyons, and several other captives, who remained in his possession (102).

Pernicious effects of those practices.

"I have seen," says Tavannes, "eight or "ten governments proposed to be sold, in order to "form a party against the sovereign himself: the "buyers felt no scruple in defrauding the soldiers of

(100) Davila, p. 500.
(101) De Thou, vol. x. p. 591.
(102) Ibid. p. 509 and 510.

"their

" their pay, and in laying exactions upon the mer-
" chants and people, in order to reimburse them-
" selves the interest of their money (103)." Such was the total dissolution of all authority, or obedience, that subjects presumed even to impose regular contributions in the provinces, by virtue of their mandate. Bussy d'Amboise, when commanding in the castle of Angers, in 1579, which constituted part of the establishment of the duke of Anjou, was accustomed to exact very heavy taxes from the citizens, and from the inhabitants of the duchy, frequently without consulting, or obtaining permission either from the duke his master, or from the king (104). It would be easy to cite similar instances of oppression, committed under a reign, when the facility, prodigality, and apathy of the prince, encouraged every abuse; when impunity accompanied the greatest crimes; and when the despotism of the crown was the smallest evil, to which the unhappy people were exposed.

Abuses and oppressions.

(103) Tavannes, p. 266.
(104) De Thou, vol. viii. p. 90.

CHAP.

CHAP. III.

State of the Gallican church.—Immunities of the clergy.—Revenues.—Taxes, levied on the ecclesiastical property.—Alienations.—Abuses.—Pluralities.—Sale of preferments.—Depravity of the great ecclesiastics.—Institution of the penitents.—Processions.—Seditious sermons.—Asylums.—State of the Hugonots.—Internal form of their civil government.—Numbers and resources.—Military, and naval force.—Commerce.—Intolerance of the age.—Mutual acts of violence and cruelty, between Catholics and Protestants.—Perversion of the human mind, on matters of religion.—Examples of toleration.—State of the king of Navarre.—His territories, power, and resources.—Court of Navarre.

CHAP. III.

State of the church.

THE Catholic church, in whatever point of view we consider it, with regard to its spiritual authority, its immunities, or its revenues, was an object of the first magnitude and consideration, during the sixteenth century. Notwithstanding the vast defalcation from the possessions of the see of Rome, occasioned by the revolt of Luther, the Papal power continued still to be extremely formidable, in all the countries which persisted to acknowledge its supremacy. The French hierarchy might be said, in some measure, to constitute a monarchy within the state itself; governed by its laws; amenable to its own jurisdiction; contributing from its proper and distinct resources; and professing obedience to a distant and superior sovereign. Although, from the resistance made by the Parliaments, the decrees of the council of Trent, which declared the independ-ance

ance of the clergy on the civil magistrate, and the inability of the crown to tax the ecclesiastical property, had never been published, nor recognized in France; yet, the validity of those regulations was not the less rigorously asserted by the Romish pontiffs. The age itself was by no means liberated from, or superior to, the influence of a superstitious veneration for the sacerdotal office and character; nor had the thunders of the Vatican ceased to unnerve the arm of princes, and to suspend their boldest determinations. It is difficult, or impossible to mark the precise limits of a power, which, in an especial degree, was founded on opinion, and maintained by religious terror; but, we may pronounce, that, however on its decline, it continued still to operate, and to affect the deliberations of the wisest and most vigorous cabinets. When Sixtus the Fifth, in the insolence of the apostolic authority, published an excommunication against Henry the Third, in 1589, that prince was so deeply wounded by it, that he could neither be induced to eat or drink, for more than forty hours. Universal sadness and dejection appeared in the army, even while advancing rapidly and prosperously towards Paris. Their operations were slackened; and all the efforts of the archbishop of Bourges to diminish the king's uneasiness, were ineffectual. He complained, that the emperor Charles the Fifth, who had impiously sacked Rome, and detained in prison the sacred person of the Pope himself, had not been so severely treated. "But, "sire," replied the king of Navarre, "that monarch was victorious: if we conquer, the censures will be revoked: if we are worsted by the "enemy, we shall die excommunicated (1)." Even in the article of death, Boulogne, Henry's chaplain, would not give him absolution, till he had solemnly

Ecclesiastical power.

Papal authority, and consideration.

(1) Davila, p. 811.

professed

CHAP. III.

professed his resolution to obey the Papal mandate, and to release the cardinal of Bourbon and the archbishop of Lyons, though their liberation should cost him his life and crown (2). Scarcely greater deference could have been manifested for the pontifical character and orders, in the darkest period of the middle ages.

Immunities of the clergy.

The immunities and privileges of the clergy were not only ample, but, a degree of sanctity surrounded, and protected them from invasion. Superstition, more powerful than any written law, withheld the sword of justice, and arrested the dagger of the assassin. Prelates and cardinals were regarded as beings separated from the mass of mankind, and as hardly amenable to any secular tribunal. When Henry embraced the determination of sacrificing the duke of Guise, instruments of his vengeance were readily found; but, it was much more difficult to procure men who would imbrue their hands in the blood of a member of the sacred college. Recourse was had to inferior ministers, for the purpose. Four common soldiers, each of whom received fifty crowns, dispatched him with their halberds, on the refusal of the band of forty-five, composed of gentlemen, to perpetrate a deed, esteemed so impious (3). It was not for the murder of the duke, but, for that of the cardinal, that the indignation of the holy see was manifested; and while Sixtus treated the former as an act of state, excused, if not justified by the circumstances which produced it, he affected to consider the death of one cardinal, and the detention of another, as a crime equally enormous and irremissible (4).

Their supposed sanctity.

Exemption from ordinary jurisdiction.

Nor were the great ecclesiastics protected only in their lives and freedom, by the privileges of the

(2) Davila, p. 818. De Thou, vol. x. p. 673.

(3) Davila, p. 751. Memoires pour ser. à l'Hist. de Fra. p. 259. De Thou, vol. x. p. 478. (4) Davila, p. 770.

order

order to which they belonged. They pretended to be exempt from appearing, or anſwering before any court, except that of Rome, even in caſes of treaſon. The archbiſhop of Lyons, arreſted as an accomplice of the Guiſes, in December, 1588, refuſed to anſwer interrogations, and pleaded his ſuperiority to any temporal, or ſpiritual juriſdiction in France. Henry aſſembled the privy council; and they determined, on the ſtrength of many weighty precedents, that as the crime laid to his charge exceeded the powers annexed to the eccleſiaſtical judges, he might be brought before the civil magiſtrate. The archbiſhop perſiſted nevertheleſs in his ſilence, and declined acknowledging the right either of the parliament, the peers, or the ſovereign, to bring him to trial (5). We may judge of the dangerous and unlimited nature of the clerical pretenſions, in that age, by the famous decree of the Sorbonne. A college compoſed of only ſixty doctors in theology, conſulted by the heads of the League, in January, 1589, had the audacity to declare the oath of allegiance void, and to authorize the aſſumption of arms againſt their legitimate prince. So bold and unanimous a deciſion had no inconſiderable effect in exciting, and confirming the rebellion, which took place throughout the kingdom (6).

College of the Sorbonne. Its weight.

Powers and pretenſions ſo vaſt and undefined, were ſuſtained by adequate revenues. It is difficult, if not impoſſible, to form any accurate eſtimate of the value of the lands poſſeſſed by the church, throughout France; but, we know that they included a large proportion of all the property of the country, together with extenſive feudal authority over their vaſſals. A Proteſtant writer of the time of

Revenues of the clergy.

(5) De Thou, vol. x. p. 480 and 481.
(6) Ibid. p. 511 and 512. Satyre Menip. vol. iii. p. 361, 362.

CHAP. III.

of Henry the Third, asserts, that they produced twenty millions of livres, or near nine hundred thousand pounds, annual income. He adds, that France contained six hundred and fifty abbies, of the orders of St. Bernard and St. Benedict; besides above two thousand, five hundred priories (7). In some instances, the episcopal jurisdiction seemed to have arrogated, or extinguished the functions most inseparable from royalty. The bishops of Mende in the province of the Gevaudan, enjoyed, by antient prescription and agreement, the right of parity with the sovereign. Justice was administered in their joint names, and the bishop struck money, as an independant prince (8). It is, however, unquestionable, that the French kings claimed and exercised the right of levying taxes from the clergy of their dominions; and it is equally certain, that the latter virtually acknowledged, by their submission, the validity of the royal prerogative. Four tenths, or "decimes," constituted the ordinary annual contribution, under the three last kings of the house of Valois (9). To what sum they amounted, it is hard to say; but, we may conclude, that they did not fall short of nine hundred thousand livres a year, or, about forty thousand pounds; because we find that between 1560 and 1575, including fifteen years, the crown had drawn from the order of ecclesiastics, full fifteen millions of livres (10).

Civil power.

Taxes levied on ecclesiastics.

Extraordinary aids.

Besides these regular impositions, extraordinary aids were frequently demanded, and obtained. Two, three, and even four "decimes" were, on particular occasions, exacted from the clergy, above the customary contribution, without any application being made to the see of Rome for its approbation;

(7) La Noue, p. 357. (8) De Thou, vol. ix. p. 601.
(9) Lettres de Paul de Foix, lettre 49, p. 539.
(10) Near six hundred and fifty thousand pounds sterling. De Thou, vol. vii. p. 296.

and

and without any attempt on the part of the church to refuse obedience, or to withhold payment (11). The Romish pontiffs, unable to prevent, did not the less resist and deny the right of the crown, to draw any pecuniary aid whatever from the clergy, even under the most pressing national calamities, unless by the Papal grant and permission. That the pretension, however arrogant and absurd, was not altogether visionary or destitute of existence, is not to be denied; since, in 1582, Henry the Third, having demanded and obtained one "decime" only, beyond the ordinary number; made, by his embassador at the court of Rome, the strongest exertions to obtain the dispensation of Gregory the Thirteenth, for thus invading the ecclesiastical property. He urged, that it was indispensable, as he was on the point of renewing the alliance with the Helvetic confederacy; and could not conclude it, without paying the arrears of the pensions due to the Switzers, and making the accustomed presents to the Cantons. These reasons, however plausible, or solid, produced no impression on the pontiff, who pertinaciously refused to give any sanction to a proceeding, derogatory to the power of the Papal see, and to the independance of the French clergy on the crown. He even founded his refusal, on the indirect approval, which his consent to levy a fifth "decime" might be construed to convey, of the right in the kings of France to exact the four, annually received. Henry, however, did not fail to levy the tax in question (12).

Resistance of the popes to the taxation of the clergy.

But, although the royal power was competent to compel the ecclesiastical body to contribute, like the other subjects, ordinarily and extraordinarily, towards the wants of the state; there was another species of contribution, sometimes demanded from

Alienation of the lands of the church.

(11) Lettres de Foix, p. 539.
(12) Ibid. p. 534—541, and 552—554.

CHAP. III.

the clergy, to which the crown was totally inadequate to enforce submission, without the express and formal consent of the sovereign pontiffs. Even the sanction of the Parliaments and States General could not give it efficacy, if the supreme head of the church withheld his permission. The alienation of the domain, or lands belonging to the clergy, was a resource, to which the calamities and poverty, produced by the civil wars, necessitated the French kings to apply, more than once. There were no less than five distinct and separate alienations of the temporalities of the church, between the accession of Charles the Ninth, in 1560, and the close of his brother's reign, in 1589; and we cannot estimate their aggregate amount, at a smaller annual sum than two hundred thousand crowns (13). It is not easy to ascertain the sum of money levied by the sale of lands; more particularly, as in the disordered state of the finances, every peculation was practised with impunity. A bull from the court of Rome was published, to give validity to each act of alienation; and Pius the Fifth, when he signified his assent, in 1568, to one, for selling lands to the value of twenty-five thousand crowns a-year, annexed to it the clause, that "the money could only "be employed against the Protestants (14)." His successor, Gregory the Thirteenth, peremptorily refused the duke of Joyeuse, deputed for that purpose, to allow of any diminution of the ecclesiastical property (15). Even, after the Papal approbation obtained by Henry the Third, in 1586, for alienating fifty thousand crowns of the church revenues; the clergy, by the mouth of the bishop of Noyon, as their representative, did not hesitate to

Papal approbation, indispensable.

Resistance of the clergy.

(13) L'Etoile, p. 89 aud 90. Le Lab. sur Cast. vol. ii. p. 293. Trad. de l'Hop. vol. i. p. 52 and 53.

(14) Trad. de l' Hop. ibid. (15) Busbeq. letter 24. p. 154.

make

CHAP. III.

make the boldeſt reclamations againſt the royal tyranny; and to ſtate as a crime, that the French princes, ſince the acceſſion of Francis the Firſt, had pretended to make the eccleſiaſtics tributary. The harangue was pronounced before the parliament of Paris; and though it excited the indignation of that court, yet no reſentment ſeems to have been expreſſed by the king, for ſo extraordinary a reſiſtance to his edicts (16).

Abuſes.

Enormous abuſes, of various kinds, had crept into the Gallican church, during the courſe of the ſixteenth century; and they naturally augmented under ſo profligate and licentious a reign, as that of the laſt of the princes of Valois. In 1579, no leſs than twenty-eight biſhoprics were vacant, the temporalities of which were poſſeſſed by laymen, and where the ſervice was altogether neglected. In ſome provinces, ſcarcely a biſhop was to be found, who reſided in his dioceſe; and the abbeys were in the ſame predicament (17). A commiſſion, armed with very ample powers of enquiry, and authorized to puniſh or to redreſs all miſconduct in eccleſiaſtics of every rank, was ſent from the crown, throughout France, in that year. But, it may be much doubted, whether the attempt was productive of reform or benefit (18). The practice of naming gentlemen, ſoldiers, and children, to church preferments, was not only common; but, ſanctioned by the ſee of Rome, in many inſtances. We find Gregory the Thirteenth, though otherwiſe a pontiff of decent, and even ſevere manners, yet permitting theſe nominations. In 1582, he confirmed the grand prior of Champagne, a knight of Malta, in the abbey of La Trappe (19). It is true, that he

Nomination of laics, to benefices.

(16) L'Etoile, p. 89 and 90.
(17) De Thou, vol. viii. p. 93.
(18) Memoires de Nevers, vol. i. p. 607.
(19) Lettres de Foix, p. 256 and 257.

CHAP. III.

objected to naming a monk, whom the French embassador recommended, to the bishopric of Agde in Languedoc, because it was notorious, that the revenues of the see had been, for many years, sequestered to the use of marshal Montmorenci. But, he voluntarily proposed to confirm the same monk in the episcopal dignity, and to assign a considerable portion of the temporalities to a natural son of Montmorenci (20). Brantome, so celebrated for his Memoirs, which sufficiently prove him to have been a dissolute courtier, destitute of morals, was provided by Henry the Second, with the abbey of his own name, in the province of Perigord. "The king "gave it to me," says he, "when I was very young, "in recompence for my brother's head, which was "carried off by a cannon ball, at the siege of Hesdin. "I have always governed it so well, that in three "changes of abbots, successively named by the kings "of France, and confirmed by the popes, no fault "has been found. It is only worth three thousand "livres annual revenue, of which I am obliged to "give considerably more than half to the abbot, "who is, likewise, compelled to pay very large "taxes, and to make considerable repairs. One of "my abbots, a most worthy man, was poisoned; "but, the king, understanding that I was still alive, "refused to dispose of the abbey (21)." These ecclesiastical preferments were considered by the sovereign, as a mode for providing for the gentlemen and officers, who grew old in the military service, or in attendance on the court. They were frequently conferred on men of letters. Philibert de Lorme, the architect of the Tuilleries, was rewarded with a donation of the abbey of Livry, in the vicinity of Paris (22). Ronsard, the poet, received from the

Instances.

(20) Lettres de Foix, letter 52, p. 580.
(21) Brantome, vol. i. Cap. Fran. p. 264—267.
(22) Vide de Ronsard, p. 144.

bounty

bounty of Charles the Ninth, the priory of St. Come in Touraine, at which he died (23). Desportes, who was equally beloved by Henry, his brother, possessed the three abbeys of Josaphat, Bonport, and Vanne (24). In 1588, Henry the Third recommended to the States, in his speech from the throne, the reformation of an abuse, which savoured so strongly of impiety (25).

Profanations.

Profanations far greater were committed, if we may credit the best contemporary writers. Ladies became possessed of dignities or benefices in the church. The council of state was not ashamed, in 1579, to adjudge a bishopric to a woman of distinction; and they were regarded as constituting a portion of inheritance, in families (26). Children received them, while still in infancy (27). In the first year of his reign, Henry the Third, on his arrival in France, from Poland, conferred the two episcopal sees, of Amiens and Grenoble, vacant by the death of the cardinal of Crequy, on du Gua, one of his favorites, who had the profligacy to dispose of them again by sale: for the former, he procured near thirteen hundred pounds; and for the latter, above seventeen hundred (28). The decency and dignity of religion were hardly less attacked, by the pluralities common among the great ecclesiastics. We cannot, without astonishment, read of the number of preferments held by one person, who was often a foreigner or resident in other countries. Hyppolito, cardinal of Ferrara, held eight abbeys in different parts of France (29). The famous cardinal du Bellay, who died at Rome, in 1560, was archbishop of Bourdeaux, and bishop

Sale of bishoprics.

Pluralities.

(23) De Thou, vol. ix. p. 413.
(24) L'Etoile, p. 88. Journal d'Henry IV. vol. i. p. 157.
(25) De Thou, vol. x. p. 387. (26) Ibid. vol. viii. p. 93 and 94.
(27) Memoires pour ser. à l'Hist. de France, p. 97.
(28) Ibid. p. 47 and 48. (29) Le Lab. sur Cast. vol. i. p. 795.

of

CHAP. III.

of Paris, Mans, and Limoges (30). Besides the archiepiscopal see of Rheims, and the bishopric of Mentz, the cardinal of Lorrain was possessed of many abbeys and inferior benefices (31).

Dissolution of manners.

The vices naturally connected with wealth, characterized the superior clergy, and completed, by their bad example, the general dissolution of manners. Louis, cardinal of Guise, who died in 1578, was notorious for debaucheries, epicurism, and gluttony (32). From his inordinate love of wine, he was commonly called in derision, "Le Cardinal "des Bouteilles." Of his nephew, the second cardinal of Guise, put to death at Blois, Sixtus the Fifth himself said, that "he had nothing of a car-"dinal, except the hat." Not satisfied with disgracing his profession by every species of profligacy and immorality; he did not hesitate to put himself at the head of four hundred lancemen, and to engage in enterprizes equally sanguinary and treasonable (33). The duke of Epernon reproached the archbishop of Lyons, in the presence of the king himself, with living in an open state of incestuous commerce with his own sister, and making a shameful traffic of every thing sacred in his diocese. So avowed were the facts, that the prelate did not even pretend to deny them, although he resented their disclosure (34). Du Perron, who rose by his talents and graces, to the highest dignities of the Romish church, made no scruple of prostituting his genius, to immortalize the profligate and adulterous amours of Margaret of Valois, queen of

Examples.

Du Perron.

(30) Trad. de l'Hop. vol. i. p. 18.
(31) Le Lab. sur Cast. vol. i. p. 278.
(32) De Thou, vol. vii. p. 645. Memoires pour ser. à l'Hist. de Fra. p. 91.
(33) Lettre du Car. de Joyeuse, dans les Mem. de Villeroi, vol. ii. p. 209—211. Chron. Nov. vol. i. p. 111.
(34) De Thou, vol. x. p. 238. Vie d'Epernon, vol. i. p. 183 and 184.

Navarre.

Navarre. In 1574, he composed some elegant verses, at that princess's request, in the nature of a monody, upon the death of her lover, La Mole, executed by order of Charles the Ninth (35). Nine years afterwards, in November, 1583, the same ecclesiastic, at the table of the king, where a croud of courtiers were present; maintained, by many solid arguments, the existence of a Deity, and demonstrated the folly of Atheism. Pleased with his discourse, Henry commended it with the warmest marks of approbation. "Sire," said du Perron, "I have, to-day, proved that there is a God: to-"morrow, if it shall please your majesty to grant "me audience, I will evince, by reasons equally "good, that there is none." Dissolute and relaxed as was Henry the Third in certain parts of his conduct, he expressed the utmost horror at such a proposition, and commanded du Perron instantly to quit his presence (36).

Impiety of his conduct.

We may see in the manifesto of marshal Montmorenci, published in November, 1574, to what a point the vices of the great ecclesiastics had infected the whole order, and how total was the abandonment and venality of the clergy throughout France (37). The depravity of the monastic orders was not less notorious. In 1577, a common prostitute was discovered in the convent of the Cordeliers, at Paris, who had remained ten years concealed among those holy fathers (38). Under the reigns of the three sons of Henry the Second, it was not uncommon to see prelates of the highest rank, who continued to retain their preferments, though well known to have renounced the Catholic religion. Brantome enumerates several, who did not cease to exercise the episcopal functions, after embracing

Depravity and abuses.

(35) Vie de Marg. p. 137.
(36) L'Etoile, p. 73.
(37) Le Lab. fur Cast. vol. ii, p. 134.
(38) L'Etoile, p. 26 and 27.

Calvinism,

CHAP. III.

Calvinifm, or Lutheranifm (39). Odet de Chatillon, brother to Coligni, a cardinal, archbifhop of Touloufe, and bifhop of Beauvais, not only perfifted to hold thofe dignities after he had become a Hugonot; but, he publicly folemnized his marriage with a lady of the court. She was even received as his wife, in the drawing-room of Catherine of Medicis; and was feated in the prefence of the queen-mother, as a peerefs, in her quality of countefs of Beauvais. The common people denominated her "Madame la Cardinale (40)." Thefe relaxations of difcipline, were, however, reluctantly tolerated by the French kings, from motives of policy, or neceffity.

Inftitution of penitents.

A phenomenon, referved for the time of Henry the Third, was the appearance and inftitution of the penitents. In the beginning of his reign, during his ftay at Avignon, in 1574, he firft faw, and affociated himfelf to the confraternity. There were three forts, diftinguifhed by their refpective colors. Thofe of the king, were white; thofe of the queen-mother, black; and the blue belonged to the cardinal of Armagnac. Catherine of Medicis, and even the young king of Navarre, afterwards Henry the Fourth, mixed in thefe cavalcades, covered with a fack. The cardinal of Lorrain loft his life by following their example, bareheaded, and barefoot; he was feized in confequence, with a violent fever on the brain, of which he expired (41). Notwithftanding the king's natural propenfity to encourage fuch mummeries, by his prefence and exhortations; yet, the manly and fpirited remonftrances of Chriftopher de Thou, firft prefident of the Parliament of Paris,

Oppofition made to them.

(39) Brantome, vol. ii. Cap. Fran. p. 262, and 263; and vol. ii. Cap. Etran. p. 258 and 259.

(40) Ibid. vol. i. Cap. Fran. p. 354—356. Trad. de l'Hop. vol. ii. p. 37.

(41) De Thou, vol. vii. p. 164 and 165. L'Etoile, p. 9 and 10.

Paris, prevented their complete reception and establishment, for several years. That able and upright magistrate represented to his sovereign, the pernicious tendency of ceremonies, only calculated to extinguish, among the lower orders, the spirit of real piety, discipline, and obedience to the civil authority. It was not till after his decease, that Henry, in the following year, 1583, yielding to his inclinations, instituted a confraternity of penitents at Paris; gave them rules; and rendered them permanent. It is hard to say, whether devotion, hypocrisy, or weakness of mind, were the predominant movements, by which he was influenced; but, it can admit of no doubt, that the institution tended to degrade and vilify him in the estimation of his subjects, and of mankind (42).

Prelates, noblemen, members of the long robe, and citizens, were all admitted and invited to become members of the society of Penitents. Their dress was a sort of sack, which concealed completely the wearer, leaving only two holes cut in the hood, in order to enable him to see his way. On the left shoulder was a cross of white sattin. White linen composed the materials of the sack itself, and it descended to the feet (43). Wrapt in this disguise, Henry the Third marched in slow procession, through the principal streets of his own capital, undistinguished from the other penitents. During the remainder of his reign, the ceremony was continually repeated; and it lasted during the greater part of the night, accompanied with music, and followed by multitudes of people. Cardinals, minions, magistrates, and persons of every description, composed the cavalcade, which was not exempt from many disorders and indecencies (44). It seems

Their dress.

Processions.

(42) De Thou, vol. ix. p. 68 and 69. L'Etoile, p. 64—67.

(43) Chron. Nov. vol. i. p. 32 and 33.

(44) Ibid. vol. i. p. 32—34. L'Etoile, p. 64—67. Le Lab. sur Cast. vol. iii. p. 46.

scarcely

CHAP. III.

ſcarcely credible, that the king ſhould voluntarily debaſe the majeſty of the throne ſo far, as to go on foot, in the habit of a penitent, from Paris to Chartres, and return in the ſame groteſque diſguiſe, accompanied by about ſixty of his companions. He performed this ſpecies of pilgrimage, in March, 1586 (45). Felix Perretti, who had raiſed himſelf from the condition of a private monk, to the chair of St. Peter; could not reſtrain the emotions of his contempt, at a conduct ſo unworthy of a great monarch. "I have done my utmoſt," ſaid he, "to "liberate myſelf from the monaſtic profeſſion; and "the king of France exerts his endeavours to enter "into it." Even the pages and lacqueys of the court were ſenſible to the ridicule attending the proceſſions of penitents; and Henry cauſed near a hundred and twenty of them, who had counterfeited the ceremony and the dreſs, to be ſeverely chaſtized in the kitchens of the Louvre (46.)

Pilgrimages.

Ridicule of them.

Superſtition of the people.

So contagious, notwithſtanding, was the example exhibited by the ſovereign, and ſo diſpoſed was the age to every ſort of ſuperſtition; that the people in the provinces ſpeedily imitated the model of the capital. Their paſſion for exerciſes of devotion and auſterity, was greatly encreaſed, by the ravages of a peſtilential diſtemper, which deſolated France in 1583. Crouds of penitents arrived at Paris, from the neighbouring diſtricts. On the 10th of September, between eight and nine hundred perſons, of both ſexes, many of whom had not attained to years of maturity, entered the metropolis. All of them were diſguiſed in ſacks, bearing in their hands, either lighted tapers, or wooden croſſes; and conducted by two gentlemen on horſeback, with their

Provincial proceſſions.

(45) L'Etoile, p. 90 and 91.

(46) Buſbeq. letter 8th, p. 116 and 117. Memoires pour ſer. à l'Hiſt. de Fr. p. 160.

wives

wives in a coach, habited in a similar manner (47). Five other companies of penitents followed, in the course of the same month; and such was the inconceivable frenzy, which manifested itself throughout the kingdom, that ten or twelve thousand are said to have visited the shrine of "our lady of Liesse," near Rheims, who were principally natives of the Ardennes (48).

Passion of Henry the Third, for these observances.

Notwithstanding the general contempt which Henry incurred by practices so unbecoming his station, he persisted in his adherence to them during his whole life. It was a mark of peculiar favor to be admitted, or allowed, to wear the uniform of the penitents; and the young nobility emulated the distinction, as an omen of their future elevation (49). The king, not satisfied with his public devotions, was accustomed to retire at stated intervals, to the convent which he had constructed in the wood of the castle of Vincennes; where, immured with his companions of the order of the Hieronimites, he seemed to lay down the functions of a prince, and to assume those of a recluse. He carried the monastic rage to such a length, as to deliver, himself, in person, the sermon, or exhortation, on particular occasions (50). When we reflect on these extraordinary marks of puerile or degrading superstition, we are almost led to question the sanity of his intellects; and it cannot excite amazement, that the League should have formed the project of immuring him for life, in a monastery. The vices of which he was too justly suspected, and which his retirements were calculated to favor or conceal, rendered him not only odious, but contemptible. It is well known, that the duchess of Moutpensier wore, when in the

Contempt, incurred by them.

(47) Memoires pour ser. à l'Hist. de Fr. [illegible] Etoile, p. 71. Busbeq. letter 25th, p. 158 and 159.

(48) Memoires pour ser. à l'Hist. de Fr. [illegible]

(49) Sully, vol. i. p. 40. (50) L'Etoile, [illegible]

royal

CHAP. III.

royal presence, a pair of golden sciſſars, at her girdle; with which ſhe did not ſcruple to declare, that ſhe hoped to perform the operation of the tonſure on the king, holding his head between her knees (51). He had aſſumed for his device, two crowns, in alluſion to thoſe of France and of Poland, with the motto,

"Manet ultima cœlo."

In deriſion, the League cauſed the following diſtich to be compoſed:

"Qui dedit ante duas, unam abſtulit; altera nutat;
"Tertia, tonſoris eſt facienda manu (52)."

Similar inſtitutions.

Beſides the order of penitents, Henry inſtituted, in May, 1585, a private confraternity, called "the "Society of the Brothers of Death;" of which he had ſeen the model among the Poles, during his ſhort reſidence in that country. Only twenty-one members, or brothers, were admitted into the company, named by the king: their dreſs was black; and the ſtatutes, compoſed by him likewiſe, betray a gloomy, eccentric, and diſordered imagination (53). Never was any period more deeply tinctured with ſuperſtition, or more deſtitute of real piety and morality.

Proceſſion of the penitents to Chartres.

But, the moſt groteſque and ſingular exhibition, preſented under this reign, was the proceſſion of penitents, deputed by the Pariſians, in May, 1588, to wait on Henry at Chartres, with a view of deprecating his reſentment, and perſuading him to return to the metropolis. The circumſtances are ſo incredible, that if we did not receive them from an eye-witneſs, and an hiſtorian of equal gravity and veracity, they could ſcarcely obtain belief. Nothing

(51) De Thou, vol. x. p. 445.
(52) Mem. pour ſer. à l'Hiſt. de Fr. p. 199.
(53) Le Lab. ſur Caſt. vol. iii. p. 47—51.

can

can more forcibly depicture the genius and character of the age, when such indecent and scandalous profanations were frequent, and excited neither horror nor disgust. Thirty-five brothers of the order of the penitents, followed by a vast croud of other persons, barefoot, were conducted by the count of Bouchage, brother to the duke of Joyeuse, killed at Coutras; and who had, in the course of the preceding year, embraced the monastic profession. He was induced, in order to awaken the sympathy or compassion of the king, to represent, on this occasion, the person of our Saviour ascending Mount Calvary. His head was encircled with a crown of thorns; and on his forehead were painted drops of blood. His hands were tied behind him; while on his shoulder he bore, or dragged, a long cross of painted pasteboard, under the oppressive weight of which he appeared to be sinking. At intervals, he threw himself upon the ground, uttering lamentable groans. Two young Capuchin Friars, on each side of him, appeared in the characters of the Virgin Mary, and of the Magdalen. Four others, wildly attired, held the cords, with which the principal actor was bound; and with their scourges, frequently inflicted on his back, a severe discipline. Accustomed as Henry was, and partial as he might be esteemed, to such spectacles, he felt the impiety and profanation attached to a mockery of one of the most sacred mysteries of religion: he even reproached Bouchage with his credulity and zeal, which rendered him an instrument in the hands of the League; many of whose adherents had the audacity to mix in the cavalcade, disguised under the penitential sack (54).

Description of that ceremony.

(54) De Thou, cited by d'Anquetil, in the Esprit de la Ligue, vol. iii. p. 30—33. Chron. Nov. vol. i. p. 61 and 62. Memoires pour ser. à l'Hist. de Fr. p. 248.

Processions

CHAP. III.

Religious processions.

Processions of every kind, intended either to conciliate the divine favor, or to deprecate its wrath, characterized the reign of the last of the princes of Valois. They were encouraged, and usually conducted, by the cardinal of Bourbon; a weak and superstitious prelate, who acted a distinguished, though only a subordinate part, in the troubles, caused by the ambition of the house of Guise. In July, 1587, he headed a procession at Paris, composed of persons of both sexes, and of every age, in which the seven shrines of St. Germain were carried by men in their shirts, without other dress. Torches of wax were borne by all the assistants. Henry, at a moment when cares of state ought to have occupied his whole attention, and when foreign armies conspiring with domestic enemies, were preparing to desolate his dominions; was not ashamed to mix in so motley a cavalcade, habited as a penitent, and to commend the order of its march (55). Crouds of devotees, from Champagne, Picardy, and Lorrain, dressed in white, and ornamented with crosses; quitting their occupations, and abandoning the cultivation of the country, continued to arrive in the capital. They were highly subservient to the designs of the duke of Guise, who, under shelter of the concealment, contrived to introduce his partizans, and to prepare for the insurrection which soon afterwards took place (56).

Political consequences of them.

During the period of about seven months, which intervened between the assassination of that prince at Blois, and the death of the king himself; when the minds of men were inflamed beyond measure, from the events of the moment; the rage for processions attained to its highest point. It seemed almost to partake of frenzy, among the Parisians,

(55) L'Etoile, p. 101 and 102. De Thou, vol. ix. p. 654.
(56) De Thou, ibid.

and

and to have perverted the exercise of reason. The people rose in multitudes, during the night; and, notwithstanding the severity of the season, clamorously compelled the priests and curates to lead them in procession. Even the rigor of the weather did not induce them to wear any clothes; and they paraded through the streets, in their shirts only, insensible to every impediment (57). The most libertine, and scandalous excesses, were committed with impunity, under the protection of the darkness, in these promiscuous assemblies, composed of men, women, and children. Ladies of gallantry found them too convenient, not to profit of the occasions; and so notorious were the debaucheries acted, that the few priests, who had not sacrificed every consideration of morals or of religion, to the spirit of rebellion, endeavoured, though fruitlessly, to stop such dissolute proceedings. We can hardly believe, that many thousand children of both sexes, carrying, each a taper in their hands, after traversing the capital, extinguished them at the same time, trampling them under foot, and exclaiming, "God extinguishes the race of Valois!" Scarcely any example of national madness, to be found in the annals of mankind, can equal that of the French people, at the conclusion of the reign of Henry the Third. The duke of Nevers, who flourished at that time, and whose Memoirs bear testimony to the enlargement of his understanding, considers the Parisians, as under the influence of a contagious delirium, or, an infectious distemper, only to be compared to the hooping cough (58). De Thou, a contemporary, and a spectator of it, seems to conceive, that nations, like individuals, are subject to paroxysms of frenzy, which visit them periodically;

CHAP. III.

Libertinism and debauchery.

Processions of children.

Sentiment of De Thou, on the madness of nations.

(57) Mem pour ser. à l'Hist. de Fr. p. 27?—272.
(58) Memoires de Nevers, vol. i. p. 935 and 936.

and

CHAP. III.

and the events of the present time, unparalleled in atrocity, precisely at the distance of two hundred years, might induce us to adopt the opinion of that sagacious and enlightened historian (59).

Declamations from the pulpit.

The year 1583, which saw the origin of the order of penitents, was likewise the era, from whence may be dated another characteristic feature of this period of general disorder and anarchy. By singular fatality, a prince, who had always loaded the ecclesiastics, and particularly, the monastic orders, with marks of affection bordering on weakness, found in them in his most dangerous, and implacable enemies. Poncet, a monk, possessed of a species of eloquence, adapted to the audience whom he was accustomed to address; and restrained by no sentiments of respect for the person of his sovereign, led the way, by the gross insinuations which he uttered, to the bolder invectives that followed, after Henry's flight from the metropolis. He did not scruple to accuse the members of the new confraternity, with hypocrisy and atheism. We may form an idea of the style of the pulpit declamation in that age, from Poncet's discoveries. "I have been informed," said he, "that after their procession, the spit turned "for the supper of these jolly penitents; and that "from devouring a fat capon, they proceeded to "complete their repast, by a delicate chicken kept "in readiness for the night. Ah! miserable hypo- "crites! It is thus that you jest with God under a "mask, and carry at your girdle a scourge. It is "not there, that it ought to be placed; but, upon "your backs and shoulders: there is not one of "you, who has not amply deserved it!" The only punishment inflicted on him, for a satire so insolent,

Lenity of Henry the Third, pernicious.

(59) De Thou, vol. x. p. 529. Esprit de la Ligue, vol. iii. p. 61 and 62. Chron. Nov. vol. i. p. 119. Memoires pour ser. à l'Hist. de Fr. p. 270—272.

and

and in which allusion was made to the king without any disguise, consisted in his temporary removal from Paris, by Henry's order, to the abbey of St. Peter, at Melun (60). Encouraged by so injudicious a lenity, the evil spread with prodigious rapidity. After the assassination of the Guises, no measures were observed by the preachers, who only seemed to vie with each other in the violent and treasonable appellations, bestowed by them on their sovereign. Many of them are too repugnant to our ideas of decorum, even to be transcribed. Regicide was publickly enjoined and recommended. Scriptural citations, of the most impious nature, were applied to the duchess of Nemours, mother to the duke and cardinal, recently put to death at Blois. She was compared to the Virgin Mary, as Henry was to Herod (61). Collects, and forms of prayer, or, rather of imprecation, were composed by the Sorbonne, invoking the vengeance of Heaven against their late king. Several of these are preserved, and forcibly demonstrate the virulence of the times (62).

Impiety, and indecency of the preachers.

Imprecations.

Reprehensible in the extreme, as were the excesses committed by the clergy of the League, they were, if possible, exceeded by the detestable doctrines, which the Catholic priests promulgated from the pulpit, in many of the provinces. There is an original letter still in being, written by Henry, king of Navarre, to his mistress, Corisande d'Andouins, dated the 17th of March, 1588, from the province of Saintonge, in which he expressly says: "The "Romish preachers, in all the cities of this country, "commend the act of poisoning the prince of

Detestable doctrines promulgated.

(60) Mem. pour ser. à l'Hist. de Fr. p. 159 and 160. De Thou, vol. ix. p. 69.

(61) L'Etoile, p. 113 and 115, and 123. Mem. pour ser. à l'Hist. de Fr. p. 272.

(62) Mem. pour ser. à l'Hist. de Fr. p. 269 and 270. Esprit de la Ligue, vol. iii. p. 82. Chron. Nov. vol. i. p. 118. De Thou, vol. x. p. 527.

CHAP. III.

"Condé; declare, that there is only one more, to "be desired; canonise the murder, and the murderer; nay, admonish every good Catholic, to "take example by so Christian an enterprize (63)." It is not possible more strongly to depicture the savage and sanguinary spirit, which pervaded every class of men in that age, when religious enmity had almost extinguished the sentiments of humanity. Tavannes accuses the Hugonots of having advanced similar tenets and principles, if not from the pulpit, yet, in their two famous publications, entitled the "Reveille Matin," and the "Tocsin des François," written at an early period of the civil wars (64).

Asylums.

Among the abuses produced by superstition, and tending, in an eminent degree, to spread through the lower orders of people, the contagion of vice, was the existence and sanctity of asylums. These institutions, originating in ignorance and barbarism, were perverted to purposes the most subversive of all justice, or good order. One of the most celebrated, in the period before us, was that of St. Romain, at Rouen. By the letters patent of Louis the Twelfth, confirming its privileges, persons guilty of treason, false coiners, and some others, were excepted from the right of protection. But, during the time when the see of Rouen was occupied by the cardinal of Bourbon, the asylum of St. Romain became a refuge for criminals of every description. Its vicinity to the metropolis, and the rigid support given by the archbishop, to the right of sanctuary, induced numbers to fly to it, in order to elude the purport of the laws. From a sense of gratitude to the protector, they readily entered into the great conspiracy,

St. Romain's, at Rouen.

Abuse arising from it.

(63) Letters origin. d'Henry IV. Œuvres de Voltaire, vol. x. p. 234 and 235.

(64) Tavannes, p. 217.

formed

formed by the League, againſt the royal authority and the ſtate, of which the cardinal became a voluntary inſtrument. The parliament of Rouen, deeply ſenſible of the impediments thrown in the way of juſtice, by the continuance of ſuch a privilege, made repeated, but, ineffectual applications to the king, for interpoſition. The careleſs apathy of that prince, rendered him inſenſible to their ſalutary remonſtrances. An aſſembly of princes and counſellors of ſtate having been convoked by Henry, in 1583, where the reformation of the courts of law formed a principal object of conſideration; La Gueſle, preſident of the parliament of Paris, harangued with eloquence and force, upon the pernicious nature and tendency of the aſylum of St. Romain. The cardinal of Bourbon, indignant at the attack upon the immunities of his ſee, inſtantly threw himſelf at the king's feet, and implored, that La Gueſle might be compelled to make ſatisfaction to himſelf, and to the church of Rouen, for ſo ſcandalous an outrage. The emotion of the prelate only excited ridicule; but, the abuſe, of which complaint was made, continued to exiſt in all its force (65).

Ineffectual attempt to procure its ſuppreſſion.

In no inſtance, does the credulity and folly of the vulgar ſeem to have been more abuſed, than in the article of relics. We find the ſame groſs deceptions, which had been practiſed, and expoſed among the Engliſh, at the time of the reformation under Henry the Eighth, ſtill ſubſiſting in France, at the commencement of the civil wars. It would be endleſs to cite examples of this fact. At the capture of Tours, by the prince of Condé, in 1562, the ſhrine of St. Martin, one of the richeſt and moſt celebrated in the kingdom, was plundered. Among other ſacred ornaments, was a gem, regarded as a

(65) De Thou, vol. ix. p. 83—86.

CHAP. III.

portrait of the Virgin Mary, and held in high veneration. Beza, on inspection, ascertained it to be an antique agat of Venus, weeping over the body of Adonis. A silver arm of a saint, found in the same place, on being opened, was discovered to contain a knave of spades, and a love song. At Bourges, the Hugonots broke to pieces a relic, within which was a small wheel turning on a piece of wood; and round it was a billet, containing these lines:

"Quand cette Roue tournera,
"Cette que j'ayme, m'aymera (66)."

State of the Hugonots, at this period.

In order to form a perfect idea of the political strength of France, during the period under our consideration, it is indispensable to take a survey of the state of the Hugonots. Notwithstanding the persecutions which they had suffered, the wars sustained by them, and the massacres repeatedly perpetrated by order of the court, or by the enmity of the Catholics; they still continued to be equally numerous and formidable. In the northern and eastern provinces, they were comparatively few; but, in Dauphiné, and along the shore of the Mediterranean, they constituted a large proportion of the inhabitants. Their principal force was concentered between the Loire and the Garonne; comprising a rich, maritime, and commercial tract of country, in which Rochelle, the capital, was situated. The genius of their government, civil and ecclesiastical, partook more of a democratic, than of any other form; tempered notwithstanding by a mixture of aristocracy, and greatly under the influence of their clergy, and municipal magistrates. Before the commencement of the first civil wars, in 1562, the cities of the Protestant communion, in imitation

Numbers.

Genius of their government, republican.

(66) Theod. Beza. Histoire Ecclesiast. liv. vii. p. 583 and 584. Confess. de Sancy, p. 463—465.

of

of Geneva, had formed the plan of excluding the nobility from any participation in the political power and authority. But, when, in consequence of the superior forces of the Crown and the Catholics, they found themselves ready to be crushed, it became indispensable to call to their assistance the princes of Bourbon. After the battle of Jarnac, in 1569, Coligni obtained over the whole Hugonot party, an empire the most unlimited, which he exercised till his death. His great endowments, age, and sincere attachment to the cause, joined to the perilous situation of their affairs, overcame all competition. The massacre of St. Bartholomew, in which Coligni, and so great a number of the Protestant nobility perished, emancipated the party from this servitude; and after successfully combating the Crown, they determined not to subject themselves voluntarily to any species of government, except a Republic (67).

Power of Coligni.

It was in vain that Francis, duke of Alençon, attempted, by affecting a regard for their interests, to acquire any permanent supremacy in their counsels. Even, while that prince headed the Hugonot armies against his brother, Henry the Third, his conduct was watched with jealous and suspicious attention. The city of Rochelle, in 1576, far from admitting him to exercise the slightest portion of authority, refused him the restitution of a few pieces of cannon, and rejected his request of aiding him by a pecuniary loan (68). During the whole period between 1576 and 1589, the king of Navarre and the prince of Condé, either openly, or in secret, exerted their endeavours to be respectively recognized protector of the Protestants. The former, as more nearly allied to the crown, seemed to have a superior claim: but, many circumstances inclined them to

Duke of Alençon.

Rivality of Navarre and Condé.

(67) Tavannes, p. 394. (68) De Thou, vol. vii. p. 431.

prefer

CHAP. III.

prefer the prince. The gravity of his disposition, and his aversion to every kind of libertinism, was more analogous to the spirit of the Hugonot religion, than the character of his cousin: his father's death at Jarnac pleaded in his behalf; and he possessed all the qualities requisite for so arduous a station. The king of Navarre, notwithstanding, obtained the preference; but, it was little more than a nominal supremacy (69). A pension was assigned to Condé, by no means ample; as the states of Flanders, nearly at the same period, had done by the archduke Matthias. It was not till after a long negociation, and many delays, that the magistrates of Rochelle admitted him to make his entry into that city, in November, 1756. He was only accompanied by a few followers, and he quitted the place soon afterwards, to retire to St. John d'Angely, his usual residence (70).

Independance of Rochelle.

The king of Navarre could not attain to any greater consideration, notwithstanding the numerous sacrifices which he made to his religious faith, and the zealous interest that he took in the welfare of the Hugonot-body. After his escape from Paris, in 1576, and his public resumption of the Protestant doctrines and worship, he could yet scarcely obtain permission to enter Rochelle, attended by fifty horsemen. The inhabitants, under arms, in great numbers, and reinforced by those of the neighbouring islands, Ré and Oleron, received him with apparent demonstrations of affection; while they took every precaution to secure themselves against any enterprize (71). A degree of competition and rivality constantly subsisted between the two princes of Bourbon, during the reign of Henry the Third, which might have

(69) Tavannes, ibid. Chron. Nov. vol. i. p. 88. Davila, p. 456.
(70) De Thou, vol. vii. p. 438—441.
(71) Ibid. p. 429 and 430.

produced

CHAP. III.

produced consequences fatal to the interests of both, if they had not been terminated by the premature and lamentable death of the prince of Condé. A short time only before that tragical event, after the victory at Coutras, in November, 1587, the duke de la Tremouille urged the prince to render himself independant sovereign in the provinces of Anjou, Poitou, and Saintonge: a scheme which he seemed not averse to have attempted without delay (72).

Struggle of Condé to supplant the king of Navarre.

The King of Navarre had foreign, as well as domestic competitors, for the title of Protector of the Hugonots. In a synod, held at Montauban, it was proposed to confer that dignity on John Casimir, son to Frederick the Third, elector palatine, who had repeatedly sent, or conducted troops to the assistance of the professors of the reformed religion. An annual donation of one hundred and twenty-five thousand crowns, was destined to accompany the office, in order to retain constantly the superior officers under the standard, besides a fund for paying the soldiery. The misconduct of John Casimir's ministers, deputed to negociate with the French Protestants, rather than any effectual opposition which it was in the king of Navarre's power to exert, seems to have rendered the plan abortive: but, it strongly displays the distrust entertained of that prince (73). If once any foreign chief had become the efficient head and protector of the Hugonots, the civil wars might have been prolonged and perpetuated without end. Even some months after the decease of the prince of Condé, in November, 1588, when the king of Navarre, as president, convoked, and opened the general assembly at Rochelle, he was menaced with a blow subversive of all his measures for retaining the protectorship of the Protestants. Many persons of quality, and even

Foreign competitors of that prince.

John Casimir.

(72) Sully, vol. i. p. 60 and 61. (73) Chron. Nov. vol. i. p. 88.

some

CHAP. III.

Attempt, to name protectors of the Hugonots.

some of the clergy, were desirous to name protectors of their religion in every province of France, which amounted to eighteen. In order to elude the blow, he consented to erect six courts or tribunals, in as many of the principal cities, to take cognizance of, and to pass sentence in all causes; peculiarly in those which respected his own officers, who had rendered themselves obnoxious and unpopular, by exacting contributions, on various pretences. A proposition so unobjectionable, met with universal approbation, and averted the impending misfortune (74). Such was the situation of the Hugonot Commonwealth; for so it may be justly denominated, at the close of Henry the Third's reign. The cities scarcely acknowledged any civil authority, except that of the mayors, or magistrates; paid few contributions; and resembled the free, imperial cities of Germany. It was not till after the termination of the civil wars, and the auspicious period of peace which ensued under Henry the Fourth, that an alteration took place in these important particulars (75).

Independance of that body.

Ecclesiastical polity.

In their ecclesiastical polity and tenets of faith, the reformed church of France followed the doctrines of Calvin. Lutheranism had made little progress among them; and the genius of Calvinism, repugnant to all gradations in spiritual preferment, tended to maintain the principles of civil equality. Provincial synods, and general assemblies, composed of delegates from the various orders, were frequently convened, to regulate their internal concerns, and to determine on the most important transactions of peace and war. In these meetings, the king of Navarre always presided, either in person, or by his representative (76). As early as the year 1555, un-

Synods.

(74) Chron. Nov. vol. i. p. 87.
(75) Tavannes, p. 394 and 395, and 227.
(76) De Thou, vol. viii. p. 87; and vol. x. p. 420 and 421.

der

der Henry the Second's reign, the Protestants began to establish places of religious worship, and to form societies for maintaining the purity of their faith. The first was made in Paris itself; and the example spread with amazing rapidity, in defiance of edicts and prohibitions (77). It would appear, that, at no period whatever of the reigns of Charles the Ninth and Henry the Third, was the exercise of their religion in private houses and families, altogether suspended, in the metropolis; although the penalty was capital for the offence (78).

Numbers of the Hugonots.

The numbers of the Hugonots, must be matter of conjecture, rather than of calculation. They never, probably, exceeded two millions, at their highest point. If we were to fix on the period when they were in the meridian of their power, and political strength, we should incline to date it, between the colloquy of Poissy in 1561, and the massacre of Paris, eleven years afterwards. During that interval, marked by all the calamities of civil war and religious discord, persecution sustained, and inflamed their enthusiasm. The name and aid of successive princes of the blood, the fortitude of Jane, queen of Navarre, the genius of Coligny, and the assistance of foreign powers, enabled them to dispute for pre-eminence with the antient superstition, and almost to subvert the throne itself. If the enterprize of Meaux had not been frustrated, by the promptitude and intrepidity of the Switzers, who protected the flight of Charles the Ninth to Paris, it is hard to say what barrier could have been affixed to the demands or inroads of the Protestants. How generally diffused were the tenets of the reformers, and how universally they were embraced or imbibed, even in the court, we may see in the Memoirs of

(77) Art. de Verif. vol. i. p. 644.
(78) Sully, vol. i. p. 57.

Margaret

CHAP. III.

Margaret of Valois. The duke of Anjou himself, afterwards Henry the Third, and who signalized his early youth by the victories which he obtained over them, had, nevertheless, previously caught the contagion. "All the court," says Margaret, "was "infected with heresy; and peculiarly, my brother "of Anjou, since king of France, whose childhood "had not escaped the impression of Hugonotism. "He incessantly teized me to change my religion, "throwing my prayer-books into the fire, and giving "me in their stead, psalms and Hugonot prayers, "which he compelled me to use. To these acts of "violence, he added menances, that my mother "would order me to be whipped (79)." We may judge from the force and simplicity of the queen of Navarre's description, how widely the reformed doctrines were spread, and how favorably they were received, among the highest orders of society. The Protestants continued still to be formidable, under Henry the Third, though their numbers were lessened; but, after the accession of the king of Navarre to the throne of France, they began rapidly to diminish. The desertion of that monarch, and his reconciliation to the church of Rome; together with the toleration granted them by him, tended insensibly to draw off all those, who were not animated with fervent zeal for the maintenance of the reformed religion.

Revenues.

It was impossible to ascertain the revenue of a body of men, whose contributions were, in a great measure, voluntary, and augmented or diminished according to the exigencies of the time. Their military resources were sufficiently demonstrated by the armies which they raised, and by the celerity exhibited in their levies. We cannot reflect without amazement, that, in 1568, the two provinces of

Forces.

(62) Memoires de Marguerite, Paris, 1658. p. 9, 10.

Dauphiné

Dauphiné and Languedoc only, conducted above twenty-five thousand men to the assistance of the prince of Condé, collected with surprizing facility. They were equipped, armed, and provided, in the amplest manner. D'Acier, their commander, had, in his own company, near two hundred gentlemen (80). Notwithstanding the defeats of Jarnac and of Montcontour, in the following year; the last of which actions cost the Hugonots not less than nine thousand troops; Coligni re-appeared in 1570, at the head of a new army, in Burgundy. No efforts of equal magnitude were made after the death of that celebrated chief; because the Protestants, disunited, no longer acted with the same promptitude and energy. The king of Navarre did not succeed to Coligni's power and influence; nor did Henry the Third betray the same sentiments towards his Hugonot subjects, which had animated him, when conducting the forces of Charles the Ninth. The edict of Poitiers, granting them toleration, was his own immediate act (81). It must be admitted, that the recommencement of war by the Protestants, in 1580, was a wanton and unjustifiable infraction of treaty, produced by the intrigues of the court of Nerac, where women and gallantry directed every measure. So sensible were the principal cities of the reformed religion to this fact, that Rochelle, and several others, refused to join in the insurrection (82). Before 1588, the violent enthusiasm of the Hugonots had greatly subsided: and they were no longer animated by the same spirit, which, under Charles the Ninth, had rendered them invincible, and superior to defeats, or massacres. The lapse of time had insensibly softened the asperity of

Renewal of hostilities in 1580, unjustifiable.

(80) Le Lab. sur Cast. vol. ii. p. 588 and 589.
(81) De Thou, vol. vii. p. 531.
(82) Mezerai, vol. ix. p. 225.

the

CHAP. III.

the two great factions, and calmed their rancour. The duke of Nevers, writing to Henry the Third, in August, 1588, says: "The Hugonots have "spent all their fire, and are only on the defensive. "Neither cities, nor provinces, follow them any "longer. The ardor of novelty is extinct, and "there is, in fact, nothing to be feared from them. "But, the League is in its first vigor, and all the "world is attracted to that party (83)." Towards the close of his reign, Henry can only be considered as acting under the impulse of the Guises, who compelled him, reluctantly, to take up arms against the princes of Bourbon, as the head of the Protestants.

Maritime force.

The maritime force of the Hugonots was principally maintained and stationed at Rochelle, or in the ports and islands of its vicinity. It bore no small proportion to the royal navy of France, and ventured, on various occasions, to contend with it, for victory. In 1573, the count of Montgomery commanded fifty-three vessels, when he appeared off the harbour of Rochelle, then closely besieged by the duke of Anjou. Several of these were, unquestionably, English; twelve were ships laden with stores; and, except two, the whole fleet consisted of vessels, not exceeding sixty tons burthen. We may judge of their size, by the number of men on board: there were eighteen hundred; of whom scarcely a thousand were sailors. They were very ill equipped, and still worse provided with cannon. Montgomery was unable to effect the object of the expedition, or to attack the royal gallies, anchored in the port (84). But, four years afterwards, in 1577, the Protestants possessed a more considerable naval strength. The prince of Condé put himself on board their fleet,

(83) Memoires de Nevers, vol. i. p. 855.
(84) D'Aub. Hist. Univ. vol. ii. p. 48.

composed

composed of seventeen upper-decked ships, and as many of inferior size. One of them was a Spanish vessel, of four hundred tons (85). Henry's admiral, Lansac, who had under his command no less than sixty sail, of different dimensions and descriptions, had been pursued by Clermont d'Amboise, only a short time before, at the head of the Hugonot squadron, and compelled to take refuge in the Garonne (86). The Protestants do not seem to have been masters of any gallies.

Commerce. Rochelle.

Their commerce, as well as their marine, was almost exclusively confined to Rochelle. That city, advantageously situated, open to the Atlantic, and inhabited by a hardy, industrious race of men, accustomed to brave the dangers of the ocean, enjoyed, even in the midst of civil war, an extensive and lucrative trade. In 1568, they reckoned ten thousand foreign merchants, who visited and carried on a traffic to Rochelle (87). Their complete independance on the crown, which took place in the following year: their civil and religious freedom: their mild internal government; and the spirit of naval or commercial enterprize, which characterised the inhabitants; all these combined causes conduced to render the city prosperous and opulent, notwithstanding the perpetual hostilities in which they were involved. The repulse, sustained by the duke of Anjou, under their walls, in 1573, at the head of a numerous army, inflamed, and exalted their courage. By means of Elizabeth, queen of England, they received continual supplies of military and naval stores, for which they made returns in corn and salt (88). Nor did they confine themselves merely

Its strength, and resources.

Naval enterprizes.

(85) De Thou, vol. vii. p. 513, and 516.
(86) Ibid. p. 512.
(87) Le Lab. sur Cast. vol. ii. p. 549.
(88) Ib. vol. iii. p. 515. Montluc, Comm. vol. iv. p. 344.

to

CHAP. III.

to the fair advantages, derived from a commercial intercourse with other states. They fitted out ships, which cruized in every direction, and captured numbers of trading vessels. In 1569, a large Venetian carrack, valued at fifty thousand crowns, was attacked near the coast of Brittany, by the vice-admiral of the Hugonot fleet, and carried into Rochelle. She was confiscated to the use of the cause, on very insufficient and slight pretences (89). Some years afterwards, a Portugueze ship fell into their hands, after an obstinate engagement, near the islands of the Azores; she was reported to have had on board a thousand pounds weight of gold, in bars (90). It was difficult to assign any cause for these acts of piracy and violence, except necessity, or convenience.

Captures.

Piracies and plunder.

We may judge how very productive were the naval expeditions, equipped for plunder, by the sum derived from them to the Protestant chiefs, or princes, in the course of only two years, between the commencement of the third civil war, in 1568, and its termination, in 1570. The share, appropriated to the admiralty, was one-tenth of all prizes; and it amounted, during that short space of time, to above three hundred thousand livres, or more than twelve thousand pounds (91). After the renewal of war in 1574, the admiralty portion was doubled, and one-fifth part of all captures was assigned to it, for the support of the common cause; yet, so considerable a diminution of profit did not deter or diminish the number of adventurers. Rapacity, and the hope of rapidly acquiring wealth, rather than any necessity, was the spur to these enterprizes. Crimes the most revolting and enormous, were frequently committed

Crimes perpetrated by the adventurers.

(89) Memoires de Cast. vol. i. p. 261.
(90) De Thou, vol. vii. p. 267.
(91) La Noue, p. 695.

by

by the Hugonot cruizers, who not only attacked, indifferently, almoſt all European nations, on the high ſeas; but, threw to the waves even the crews of their allies, in order thereby to conceal their depredations. This fact is not to be controverted, as we derive it from their own writers (92).

Intolerance, and cruelty of the age.

In an age like the preſent, diſtinguiſhed rather by indifference, than by zeal, in matters of religion, we cannot eaſily conceive the degree of enmity and intolerance, which characterized the period under our conſideration. It roſe to ſuch a height, that, when ſharpened by civil war, it overbore and extinguiſhed every ſentiment of private affection, or general humanity. Repreſſed in ſome meaſure, by the vigorous adminiſtration of Francis the Firſt, and Henry the Second, it burſt all limits under the three ſucceeding princes, and converted the kingdom into a vaſt burying-ground. Montluc does not ſcruple to acquaint us, that, after having agreed to admit the garriſon of a beſieged town in Gaſcony, to capitulate, he privately ſent an emiſſary to enjoin his troops to break into the place while the terms were adjudging, and to put every inhabitant to the ſword. The order was executed in its utmoſt rigor (93). "I can aſſert with truth," ſays he, "that there is "not a commander of the king in all France, who "has diſpatched more Hugonots by the knife, or "by the halter, than myſelf (94)." When wounded at the ſtorm of Rabaſteins, in Bigorre, and conceiving himſelf near his end, his only concern appears to have been, not to allow a ſingle perſon to eſcape the general carnage; and he iſſued peremptory directions for the purpoſe. Even the women were not ſpared; and the Catholic ſoldiery precipitated

Montluc.

Carnage of Rabaſteins.

(92) La Noue, p. 696.
(93) Montluc, Comm. vol. iv. p. 92—94.
(94) Ibid. p. 121.

fifty

CHAP. III.

fifty or ſixty of the inhabitants from a tower, as matter of amuſement (95). One of the moſt atrocious conſpiracies ever conceived by bigotry, and undertaken by ambition under the cloak of religion, was that of Philip the Second, king of Spain, in concert with the Guiſes, againſt Jane d'Albret, queen of Navarre. It was planned in 1565, and only failed in its execution, by the imprudence of one of the inferior agents. The intention was no other, than to ſeize a ſovereign princeſs, of irreproachable manners, and allied to the royal blood of France, in the midſt of her court, and in a time of profound peace, in order to deliver her over to the inquiſition. The pretext for an enterprize ſo flagitious, was the queen's attachment to hereſy. It was of ſufficient magnitude to juſtify any crime, however perfidious or cruel, in the opinion of zealous Catholics. Every detail of this abominable and extraordinary tranſaction, is to be found in Villeroy (96).

Conſpiracy, formed againſt Jane, queen of Navarre.

Its atrocious nature.

Even minds, naturally ſuſceptible of the moſt beneficent ſentiments towards mankind, became obdurate towards their own countrymen, when of a different perſuaſion in religion. Louis, duke of Montpenſier, a prince otherwiſe of a mild and generous character, who commanded the royal armies under Charles the Ninth and Henry the Third, was accuſtomed to put to death, by a ſummary proceſs, every priſoner accuſed of adherence to the Proteſtant doctrines, or to deliver them over to the brutal violence of his ſoldiers. When men were brought before him; "Friend," ſaid he, "you are a Hugonot; I recommend you to Monſieur Babelot." This inſtrument of his cruelty was no other than a monk of the Franciſcan order, who acted the part

Savage treatment of the Hugonots.

Montpenſier.

(95) Montluc, Comm. vol. iv. p. 221 and 222.
(96) Villeroy, Memoires, vol. ii. p. 39—58.

of

of judge and executioner. They were no ſooner interrogated, than condemned and maſſacred. The women were commonly reſerved for the ſavage embraces of his guidon, or ſtandard-bearer. Far from exciting horror, or indignation, theſe barbarities ſerved only for ſubject of converſation, and of indecent raillery, among the ladies of the court, and at the tables of the great (97).

Other inſtances.

John de Champagne, a nobleman of the ſame period, when reſiding at his caſtle of Peſcheſeul, on the river Sartre, uſed to throw all the Proteſtants who fell into his poſſeſſion, into the ſtream. He accompanied it with an inſulting piece of buffoonery, as performing an act of feſtivity, rather than a deliberate murder; nor did the laws take any cognizance of ſuch atrocious crimes (98). The chevalier Aumale, one of the princes of Lorrain, diſtinguiſhed for the ferocity and brutality of his manners, violated even the ſanctity of places of public worſhip; and committed every ſpecies of wanton debauch, or deliberate cruelty, in the Catholic churches. Nuns, and women of condition, were diſpoiled of their honor, before the high altar, to the foot of which they were dragged by the hair, in preſence of their huſbands, fathers, and neareſt relatives (99). But, it is in the writings of d'Aubigné, that we find the moſt accurate information upon a point, which ſo forcibly delineates the temper and ſpirit of the age. He is entitled to the greater credit, becauſe, being a zealuos Hugonot, he is, nevertheleſs, far from concealing the outrages committed by his own aſſociates, though he attempts to juſtify or palliate them, on the principle of retribution. St. Pont, a Catholic, com-

St. Pont.

(97) Brantome, vol. iii. Cap. Fran. p. 280—282. D'Aub. vol. i. Hiſt. Univ. p. 135.

(98) Le Lab. ſur. Caſt. vol. ii. p. 482.

(99) Satyre Menip. vol. iii. p. 333, 334.

CHAP. III. manding at Macon in Burgundy, in 1562, usually ordered a certain number of Protestants to be thrown from the bridge into the Soane, after the banquets with which he regaled the ladies, by way of pastime (100). We cannot peruse without disgust, as well as horror, the enormities committed at Tours, and at Orange, by the royal troops (101). Even Coligni himself, however naturally beneficent and mild, was propelled, by the sanguinary genius of the times, to permit, or to authorize acts of wanton severity. Retaliation, or vengeance, seemed to palliate these executions, which became unhappily necessary, in order to impose some restraint on minds, inflamed by religious animosity, to a pitch of mutual phrenzy.

In October, 1562, twelve monks of the order of St. Francis, at Chateau Vilain, having been accused of massacring the sick, or wounded Protestants of the army; Coligni caused them to be immediately hanged. Two of their own brotherhood voluntarily offered to become the executioners of the others. Ropes were delivered to both; and as an experiment of their respective capacity to perform the office of a hangman, one was ordered to dispatch the other. It afforded a cruel pastime to the spectators, to witness the efforts of these unfortunate men, to obtain the preference. "Never," says d'Aubigné, "did "the Retiarii, Laquearii, or Mirmillones of anti-"quity, display before the Romans in the amphi-"theatre, more address in vanquishing each other, "than did these Cordeliers. One of them having, "at length, dextrously contrived to strangle his "companion, put to death all the survivors." He was afterwards retained by the Hugonots, as executioner to the army, and grew very expert in his profession (102). The pre-eminence in cruelty of every

(100) D'Aub. Hist. Univ. vol. i. p. 145.
(101) Ibid. p. 130 and 146.
(102) Confession de Sancy, p. 492, 493, and p. 541.

species, was, notwithstanding, ceded, by the universal testimony of his contemporaries, to des Adrets, who long rendered his name proverbial for barbarity, in the provinces on the Rhone, where he was at the head of the Hugonot forces (103). His ordinary mode of dispatching the victims of his fury or enmity, was by precipitating them from a tower, and dashing them in pieces: a spectacle, in which he took a savage delight. He was, however, not inaccessible to pity, or to wit. Having ordered, after his dinner, thirty prisoners, taken at Montbrison, and whom he had purposely reserved, to precipitate themselves from the edge of the mountain; one of them, terrified, and unable to take the leap, stopt short on the extreme verge. "How," exclaimed des Adrets, "you take twice to do it?" "Sir," replied the soldier, "I will give you ten times, in "which to perform it." Charmed with an answer which evinced so much pleasantry and self-possession, in a moment of such peril, he immediately pardoned the man, and exempted him from the fate of his companions (104).

Des Adrets.

Anecdote of him.

From the determination of outdoing his enemies in cruelty, and of thus compelling them to carry on war with more humanity, des Adrets caused the hand and foot of three hundred Catholic gentlemen to be cut off, and sent them in that condition, on carts, to the royal camp. The expedient, terrible as it was, did not fail to produce the intended effect (105). Such was the ferocity and spirit of persecution, that it pervaded every rank and order of society. The princess of Condé, and her eldest son, were in the most imminent danger of being stoned to death by the peasants of a little village in

Severities of that commander.

(103) Brantome, vol. ii. Cap. Fran. p. 246—248.
(104) D'Aubigné, Hist. Univ. vol. i. p. 147.
(105) Ibid. p. 155.

CHAP. III.

Oblivion of the laws.

the neighbourhood of Orleans, for the sole crime of heresy (106). Obedience to the laws and the sovereign, were superseded by the detestation and antipathy of the two religions. When Rapin, a Hugonot gentleman, arrived at Toulouse, in 1568, charged with the dispatches from the king and from the prince of Condé, announcing the conclusion of a treaty of peace between the Crown and the Protestants; the magistrates and people instantly caused him to be executed without form of justice (107).

Massacres.

In the short interval which elapsed between that treaty and the renewal of war, not exceeding six months, more than ten thousand Hugonots were massacred in various parts of France (108). The bishop of Nevers, deputed by the prince of Condé, in 1562, to the emperor, Ferdinand the First, did not hesitate to assert, in his harangue, pronounced before the diet assembled at Frankfort, that in the space of only four months preceding the assumption of arms, thirty thousand persons professing the reformed religion were put to death by the populace, throughout the kingdom (109).

Even the most profound submission to the laws and magistrates, could not secure protection, nor preserve from violence. In 1572, eight hundred Protestants, who, in obedience to the injunction of the governor of Lyons, had voluntarily allowed themselves to be disarmed and confined, on receiving his assurance of safety, were massacred by the Catholics, within an hour afterwards. At Rouen, a still more enormous violation of faith was committed. More than eighteen hundred Hugonots, who had quitted the city, having returned to their houses, upon promise of security in the king's name,

(106) D'Aub. Hist. Univ. vol. i. p. 134.
(107) Brantome, vol. iii. Cap. Fran. p. 191. La Noue, p. 699.
(108) D'Aub. Hist. Univ. vol. i. p. 262.
(109) Le Lab. sur Cast. vol. ii. p. 35.

were

were indiſcriminately ſacrificed to the implacable animoſity of their enemies. Theſe facts were ſo notorious and ſo inconteſtable, that the deputies of Henry the Third, ſoon after his acceſſion, did not heſitate to ſtate them, in the moſt forcible language. Neither the king, nor Catherine of Medicis, attempted to controvert, or deny the aſſertions. They only tried to palliate their enormity, by accuſing the Hugonots of ſimilar acts of perfidy, or vengeance (110). In the review of this ſanguinary and ferocious period, we are perpetually reminded of the ſcenes of devaſtation and ſlaughter, which have been again acted on the ſame theatre, by a ſavage populace, ſince the revolution of 1789. It was criminal, only to lean towards toleration. The great chancellor l'Hopital, known to lament the ſanguinary maxims of Charles the Ninth, and to deplore the maſſacre of St. Bartholomew, was inſtantly marked for deſtruction. The guards of Catherine of Medicis could ſcarcely protect him from being torn in pieces by an enraged and furious people, who thirſted for his life, though paſſed in the diſcharge of every public duty, and every domeſtic virtue (111). Some years before, during the progreſs made by the court through the ſouthern provinces of France, it had become neceſſary to give him a guard, in order to ſecure him from outrage, on account of his avowed diſinclination to violent meaſures in matters of religion (112).

Danger of l'Hopital.

When we conſider how generally diffuſed was this intolerant ſpirit, we may, perhaps, incline to attribute to its influence, more than to any other cauſe, the calamities which mark the period. Neither the machinations of Catherine of Medicis, the ferocity of Charles the Ninth, nor the ambition and

Spirit and mode of thinking, in that century.

(110) Memoires de Nevers, vol. i. p. 339—341.
(111) Trad. de l'Hopital, vol. i. Eclairciſſements, p. 72 and 73.
(112) Brantome, vol. iv. Cap. Fran. p. 100—101.

CHAP. III.

revenge of the Guises, could have produced the massacre of Paris, if all the materials had not been previously disposed. It is more to the age, than to any individuals, however elevated or profligate, that we ought to look, for the explication of that memorable and unparalleled event (113). To shed the blood of Heretics, was esteemed meritorious. Marshal Tavannes, who fairly avows in his Memoirs, that he advised the massacre, and who justifies it on principles of necessity and policy, died in the following year, at an advanced period of life. He met the approaches of dissolution, with composure; exhibited marks of unfeigned piety; ordered his sons to restore to the crown, without touching the revenues, an abbey which he possessed; and made confession of all his sins without reserve. But, he did not include in the list, his advice to put to the sword two thousand Protestants who had repaired to Paris, on the faith of the royal protection, because he felt neither remorse, nor condemnation, for the act (114). Such was the genius of the century, and the perversion of the human mind on religious concerns. A degree of enthusiasm, which suspended and extinguished all the ordinary motives to human action, and which swallowed up even ambition, natural affection, and self-interest, pervaded the minds of men, on religious matters. A thousand proofs of it occur. The duke of Nevers says in his Memoirs, that he considered a war against Heretics and Hugonots, as a crusade, to which every man was bound to subscribe his private fortune. He gave the best proof of his sincerity, by lending immense sums to Henry the Third, in order to pay his forces, at various times, when employed to reduce, or to exterminate the Protestants. All his

Marshal Tavannes.

(113) Trad. de l'Hop. vol. i. Eclairciſſements, p. 67—69.
(114) Tavannes, p. 418—420, and 470.

writings,

writings, and the tenor of his whole life, evince, that the duke of Nevers was a man of ſcrupulous honor, unſhaken loyalty in an age of univerſal faction, and of real piety. He was carried away by the perſecuting ſpirit of the time in which he lived (115).

The cardinal of Bourbon, a prelate mild and humane in his own nature, but, ſuperſtitious and intolerant; declared in a council, held at Blois, in February, 1577, where Henry the Third was preſent, that not even a temporary toleration ought, on any pretence, to be granted to the Hugonots. "I "have," ſaid he, "more intereſt in the preſerva- "tion of that body of men, than any other indivi- "dual, ſince my two nephews are engaged in their "quarrel; but, I would myſelf become their exe- "cutioner, if they are Heretics (116)." Montluc, notwithſtanding the cruelties which he ordered or perpetrated againſt the Proteſtants, was not deſtitute of principles of devotion towards the Supreme Being, as is evident from all his writings. He regarded himſelf as no other than an executioner of the divine vengeance, and engaged in a holy vocation, when putting to the ſword perſons convicted of hereſy. "I have never," ſays he, "been in "any action, that I have not invoked the aid of "the Deity; and I have not paſſed a day in my "whole life, without having prayed to, and de- "manded his forgiveneſs (117)." The prayer which he ſubjoins, as that, which, from his earlieſt entrance on a military life, he had been accuſtomed to offer to God, is ſuch as Marcus Aurelius, or Socrates, might have dictated and approved. The concluſion is equally ſublime and reſigned: "I "aſk not for life: for I deſire only that which

Montluc.

His enthuſiaſm and conviction.

(115) Mem. de Nevers, vol. i. p. 170, 171.
(116) Ibid. p. 172. (117) Montluc, vol. iv. p. 332.

CHAP. III.

"pleases thee. Thy will be done: I submit all to "thy divine goodness (118)." It is in these contradictions and inconsistencies, that we see fully depictured the character of the age, in which superstition and intolerance were perpetually blended, and whose union was so productive of scenes of destruction.

Examples of liberality and tolerance.

It is, notwithstanding, matter of pleasing reflexion to all who desire to contemplate nature in an amiable point of view, to know, that even in a time so sanguinary, there were not wanting some mild and beneficent spirits, occupied in tempering the rage of religious discord. Every page of the works of

L'Hopital.

l'Hopital, breathes conciliation and forgiveness. He was not satisfied with lamenting and condemning the violent measures of the cabinet of Charles the Ninth: he opposed them with steady, though, ineffectual firmness. His epistle to the cardinal of Lorrain, in 1562; and that, addressed to du Ferrièr, the French embassador at Venice, in 1568; are two of the most enlightened and masterly productions of any period. They inculcate universal charity and toleration (119). It would have been happy for mankind, if maxims so benign had not been obliterated and rejected, in the frenzy of persecution.

Castelnau.

Castelnau, whose valuable Memoirs terminate with the peace, concluded between the Crown and the Protestants, in 1570, finishes by thus apostrophizing his son: "Thou mayst judge by what is "here related, that the spiritual sword, which is "the good example of the clergy, charity, ex-"hortation, and other good works, are more ne-"cessary to extinguish heresies, and to bring back "into the right path those who have wandered out

(118) Montluc, vol. iv. p. 332.
(119) Trad. de l'Hop. vol. ii. Epitres, p. 176—181, and p. 191—202.

"of

"of it, than that which sheds the blood of our "neighbours: more particularly, when the disease "has attained to such a height, that in proportion "as we attempt to cure it by violent remedies, we "only irritate the disorder (120)" The speech of Paul de Foix, archbishop of Toulouse, made in the cabinet and council of Henry the Third, on his return from Poland, in 1574, strenuously advising measures of lenity and toleration towards the Protestants, is full of the same enlarged and comprehensive sentiments. They were enforced by De Thou, first president of the Parliament of Paris, and by Harlay, his successor. But, Henry, for his own misfortune, and that of his subjects, was incapable of perceiving their beneficial tendency (121).

Paul de Foix.

Even marshal Damville, son to the constable Montmorenci, and who subsequently attained to the same dignity, though an unlettered soldier, more inured to the hardships of a military life, than competent to judge of scholastic and theological disputes; yet, felt the necessity of toleration. Experience supplied in him, the want either of expansion of mind, or benevolence of disposition. When the deputies of the States waited on him at Montpelier, in 1577, to acquaint him with their determination of renewing the war against the Protestants; he replied, that "the past calamities sufficiently demon-"strated, that to God alone it belonged, to dis-"pense faith, which cannot be the work of any "earthly power: that he could not enough express "his astonishment, at the resumption of projects "so fatal; and that all mankind must be convinced "of the necessity of permitting the exercise of the "two religions, as the only means of preserving, "or perpetuating internal peace (122)."

Damville.

(120) Castel. Memoires, vol. i. p. 266.
(121) De Thou, vol. vii. p. 137—149.
(122) Ibid. p. 478 and 479.

Henry,

CHAP. III.

King of Navarre.

Henry, king of Navarre, was a ſhining example of toleration, previous to, as well as after his aſcending the throne of France. In 1576, after his flight from Paris, and the renunciation which he made of the Catholic religion; far from attempting to force the conſciences of thoſe who adhered to it, he exerted all his endeavours, and not without ſucceſs, to obtain for them, the freedom of worſhip, in the city of Rochelle itſelf, the aſylum of the Hugonot faith and doctrines. At his requeſt, a chapel was permitted to be appropriated to the celebration of maſs; and his conduct in a point of ſuch importance and delicacy, acquired him, in no ſmall degree, the general eſteem and affection (123). In all his ſubſequent actions, we trace the ſame enlargement of mind. The ſeverity on religious concerns, which, if we may believe the teſtimony of Margaret of Valois, his wife, he exerciſed towards her at Pau, the capital of Bearn, during her reſidence in that city, ſeems to have ariſen more from private reſentment, than from a ſpirit of perſecution (124). When he over-ran Poitou, in 1589, and made himſelf maſter of a number of places in the province, he contented himſelf with reſtoring to the Proteſtants their civil and religious liberty, as granted them by the royal edicts; without attempting to moleſt, or, in any ſhape, to perſecute the Catholics (125). Even though we ſhould attribute to policy, a ſyſtem ſo replete with benefit to the State, we diminiſh little of its merit. The proſperity and repoſe, which diſtinguiſhed the laſt twelve years of the reign of Henry the Fourth, and which rendered the period one of the happieſt in the annals of the French monarchy, were eminently due to the benign influence of the maxims of toleration, embraced by that illuſtrious prince.

(123) Davila, p. 457. (124) Memoires de Marg. p. 172—174.
(125) De Thou, vol. x. p. 585. Chron. Nov. vol. i. p. 164.

It

CHAP. III.

Condition, and resources of the king of Navarre.

It is requisite for the completion of the picture before us, to trace, with some degree of accuracy, the condition and resources of the king of Navarre, previous to his elevation to the throne of France. He may be considered as the most interesting character of the period; and when we reflect, that, after having rescued the country from an abyss of calamities, he founded a new race of monarchs; no portion of his life can be matter of indifference, in the general delineation of the age and time. During more than three years immediately following the massacre of Paris, he remained a captive in the court of the two kings, his brothers-in-law; deprived of power, watched with jealous circumspection, compelled to profess a religion in which he did not believe, and not exempt from perpetual and imminent danger of his life. It is incontestable, that Charles the Ninth consulted Philip the Second, in 1574, upon the measure of putting to death his own brother, the duke of Alençon, and the king of Navarre (126). He could not better address himself than to a prince, justly suspected of having accelerated the end of his only son, Don Carlos, a few years preceding. If Margaret of Valois, queen of Navarre, had produced a son, the resolution to dispatch her husband, was already taken (127). Although he escaped from so many dangers, he was reduced to the lowest point of depression and insignificance. Catherine of Medicis compelled him, from his prison in the Louvre, to issue an edict, prohibiting, in all the territories of his obedience, the exercise of any other worship, except the Catholic (128). His subjects, encouraged by the court of France, and no

His captivity.

Danger.

State of depression.

(126) Deposition de Coconas, in Le Lab. sur Cast. vol. ii. p. 375, and p. 366.

(127) Deposition du Roi de Nav. in Le Lab. sur Cast. vol. ii. p. 361.

(128) Hist. de Marg. de Val. p. 117.

longer

CHAP. III.

longer controlled by the presence of a master, threw off all subjection or obedience (129). Insulted, or duped by the duke of Guise, who abused his confidence, and betrayed him to Henry the Third, he was considered as incapable of producing any disturbance, and he sunk into oblivion (130). Immersed in pursuits of gallantry, natural to his age, and which Catherine of Medicis artfully encouraged, in order to reconcile him to his captivity, he excited no apprehension (131). His emancipation from confinement, was the first moment of his political existence. During above thirteen years, which elapsed between his escape, and the interview of Plessiz les Tours, in 1589, he underwent the severest trials of his fortitude and virtue. Exiled to the distant province of Gascony: proscribed by the king, his brother-in-law; persecuted by the powerful faction of the League: declared by the States General, unworthy to succeed to the crown: excommunicated by the Romish pontiffs: attacked by the armies of Henry the Third; and dishonoured, as well as betrayed by his own wife, who was not only false to his bed, but engaged in enterprizes against his dignity and repose: he vanquished these numerous assailants, and sustained the throne, which he was destined to ascend, when on the point of being subverted by a powerful and triumphant faction.

Exile, and hardships.

The king of Navarre possessed little more of royalty, except the name and external honors. A small portion of the Lower Navarre, together with the principality of Bearn, at the foot of the Pyrenees, constituted the whole of his contracted dominions. Ferdinand the Catholic had usurped, and retained

His dominions.

(129) Deposition du Roi de Nav. in Le Lab. vol. ii. p. 363.

(130) Memoires pour ser. à l'Hist. de Fr. p. 26. D'Aub. Hist. Univ. vol. i. p. 186 and 187.

(131) Esprit de la Ligue, vol. ii. p. 162.

the

CHAP. III.

the far greater part of the antient kingdom of Navarre. The duchy of Albret in Gafcony, and that of Vendome, formed no inconfiderable addition to his patrimonial inheritance. In right of his queen, Margaret of Valois, he, likewife, exercifed the fupreme authority in the two provinces of the Agenois and Quercy, ceded to that princefs on her marriage, with every royal prerogative (132). The title of governor of Guienne, which he retained, was deftitute of political power or influence; nor would Bourdeaux, the capital, ever admit him within its walls (133). Limited as were the territories of the king of Navarre, his fovereignty was inconteftable and acknowledged. Jane, his mother, did not hefitate, in 1569, to caufe St. Colombe, Favas, Pordiac, and feveral other gentlemen, taken in arms againft her, to be executed as traitors; they being natural-born fubjects, and, of courfe, guilty of high treafon (134). The aggregate amount of the king of Navarre's revenues, was very inadequate to the fupport of his dignity. It appears, that in 1573, after the acceffion made to them, by the marriage portion of Margaret, they did not exceed, when the neceffary charges were deducted, the clear fum of one hundred and forty thoufand livres, or about fix thoufand pounds fterling; while the annual expence of his houfehold and eftablifhment rofe to double the fum (135). In the preceding year, when he arrived at Paris, previous to his nuptials, he was accompanied by eight hundred noblemen and gentlemen, all in mourning for Jane, queen of Navarre (136). His pecuniary difficulties were fuch, as to render it impoffible for him either to maintain

Patrimony.

Sovereignty.

Revenues.

Pecuniary diftrefs.

(132) De Thou, vol. viii. p. 375.
(133) Ibid. vol. vii. p. 436 and 437.
(134) Memoires de Caft. vol. i. p. 250.
(135) Le Lab. fur Caft. vol. ii. p. 777.
(156) Memoires de Margue, p. 29.

the

CHAP. III.

the decent ſplendor of his court, or to reward the ſervices of his followers and ſervants. He ſupplied the deficiency, in a great degree, by the affability, frankneſs, and amenity of his manners. When the duke of Epernon was ſent by Henry the Third, in 1584, to exhort him to a change of religion; the favorite far exceeded the king of Navarre, in the pomp of his retinue, and the grandeur of his attendants (137). "The whole court of Nerac "could not have furniſhed forty thouſand livres," ſays Sully, "in 1586, at my arrival (138)." In his way thither, he ſupped with the prince of Condé, who was ſerved in wooden platters (139). It appears, that the largeſt pecuniary appointments, given to any perſon in the court of Navarre, were thoſe enjoyed by Sully, in his double capacity of counſellor of ſtate, and chamberlain. They amounted together, only to the annual ſum of two thouſand livres, or about ninety pounds ſterling (140).

Military force.

A ſovereign ſo limited in his revenues, could maintain a very ſlender military force. He may be ſaid not to have had any regular troops under the ſtandard; and only to have compoſed a haſty aſſemblage of ill-diſciplined vaſſals, or retainers, when preſſed by the exigency of his affairs. His weakneſs was ſuch, that in 1577, during the war with Henry the Third, he found himſelf incapable of forming any army; and was repulſed before the inconſiderable town of Marmande, in Guienne, with loſs and diſgrace, though he was preſent in perſon, at the head of all the cavalry and infantry in his power to aſſemble. Such was his deficiency in every requiſite for a campaign, or a ſiege, that his whole artillery

(137) Vie d'Epernon, vol. i. p. 88.
(138) About ſeventeen hundred pounds. Sully vol. i. p. 45.
(139) Ibid. vol. i. p. 44.
(140) Memoires de Sully, vol. i. p. 414.

conſiſted

consisted in one large, and two small pieces of cannon (141). In the ensuing rupture of 1580, he betrayed still more evident marks of his inability to maintain a contest of duration, against the crown of France. Destitute of money and of troops, he was reduced to fly before Biron, who commanded the royal forces. The king of Navarre, shut up in Nerac, with only about four hundred horsemen, of whom the far greater number were in the service of the count of La Rochefoucault; beheld the enemy advance to the gates, and take post with four thousand foot, and six hundred cavalry, in the vineyards adjoining the city. He might have been compelled to surrender at discretion, and carried prisoner to Paris. But, Biron did not think proper to pursue his advantages; nor is it probable, that, at any period of his reign, Henry the Third could have desired, or approved, the entire destruction of the first prince of the blood (142). The largest body of forces which the king of Navarre seems ever to have commanded, before his accession to the crown of France, was at Coutras, where they amounted to four thousand foot, and two thousand five hundred horse: but, he was only the general; and far from being able to retain them after his victory, they immediately disbanded, or followed their respective leaders (143). At the accommodation between him and his brother-in-law, concluded at Tours, in 1589, it was stipulated, that he should maintain, at his own expence, two thousand infantry, and twelve hundred cavalry, to act against the League (144). Epernon brought a much more considerable force, levied and armed by himself, to the assistance of his master (145).

CHAP. III.

Slender resources.

Inability to resist the royal army.

His numbers at Coutras.

(141) Sully, vol. i. p. 16 and 18. Mezerai, vol. ix. p. 191.
(142) Memoires d'Aub. Remarques, p. 214 Mezerai, vol. ix. p. 226.
(143) De Thou, vol. x. p. 19. Mezerai, vol. ix. p. 322.
(144) De Thou, vol. x. p. 590.
(145) Vie d'Epernon, vol. p. 292.

We

CHAP. III.

We know, however, with certainty, from the testimony of Du Plessis Mornay, who negociated the treaty between the two sovereigns, that the king of Navarre was then at the head of five thousand infantry; besides five hundred gentlemen, and as many more harquebussiers, well mounted, and in the finest condition. Mornay even engaged, if orders for the purpose were issued by Henry the Third, that this body of troops should be doubled in less than two months. But, the Hugonot party, of which the king of Navarre was the chief, furnished the resources for levying, and maintaining them in the field. He was unable, from his own revenues, or dominions, to support so heavy a charge (146).

Court of Navarre.

Notwithstanding the poverty and distresses of the king of Navarre, his court was crouded, gay, and voluptuous. It was sometimes held at Pau, in the province of Bearn; but, more frequently, at Nerac, the capital of the duchy of Albret. At every period, but, particularly, when Margaret, queen of Navarre, was present, gallantry, diversions, and festivities of every kind, rendered it magnificent. The picture which she draws of it, in 1579, and 1580, is lively, and coloured with animation. "We passed," says she, "the greater part of our time at Nerac, where "the court was so brilliant, that we did not envy "that of France."—"There was not any thing to "regret, except that the greater part of the nobility "and gentlemen were Hugonots: but, of the difference of religious sentiment, no mention was "made; the king, my husband, and his sister, "going to their devotions, while I and my train "went to hear mass, in a chapel in the park. "When the service was ended, we assembled again "in a garden, embellished with avenues of laurels "and cypress, that bordered the river. In the after-

(146) Vie de Du Plessis Mornay. A Laide. 1647, p. 429.

"noon

"noon and evening, a ball was performed." She owns, that, far from imposing any restraint on the irregularities of the king of Navarre, she, on the contrary, aided, facilitated, and concealed his amours (147).

Margaret of Valois.

Abandoned to the most shameful excesses, and relying for impunity, on her descent from the blood of France, Margaret narrowly escaped from expiating her infidelities, by an ignominious death. Despised by her brother, Henry the Third, and become odious to her husband; after having been driven with ignominy and disgrace from the court of Paris, she only owed her life to the clemency and humanity of the king of Navarre (148). He himself, attached to the countess of Guiche, was disposed to make every sacrifice to his passion; and to have legitimated his connexion with her by marriage, if he had not been prevented by the firm and generous exhortations of d'Aubigné (149). The rough, but salutary remonstrances of Sully, at a subsequent period of his life, were alike effectual, when ready to give his hand to Gabrielle d'Estrées.

Number of his adherents.

Even in the most depressed state of his fortune, the courage, affability, and frankness of character which distinguished the king of Navarre, acquired him numerous followers. In 1576, at an interview which took place between him and the queen-mother, in the town of Thouars in Poitou, he seduced into his service, thirty-two gentlemen of the French court (150). At Pau and Nerac, he was constantly surrounded by Catholic, as well as Hugonot nobles; but, such was the animosity which subsisted between them, that they were more than once on the point of cutting each other in pieces. The king was accus-

(147) Hist. de Marg. p. 323. Memoires de Marg. p. 176, 177.
(148) D'Aub. Memoires, p. 105. Lettres du Roi de Nav. in the Œuvres de Voltaire, vol. x. p. 236 and 237.
(149) Memoires d'Aub. p. 123—129. (150) Ibid. p. 52.

CHAP. III.

tomed to say, that his obligations to the adherence of the Catholics, were much greater than to the Protestants; as the former served him upon principles more disinterested, and in contradiction to their religious prejudices (151).

Reasons for his refusal to abjure the reformed religion.

It may excite some degree of surprize, that, importuned as he was by Henry the Third, to resume the profession of the Romish faith, and tempted by the almost certain reversion of the greatest crown in Europe, he should yet have pertinaciously declined to adopt the measure. We must attribute his conduct partly to conviction, and partly to policy. The feeble character of the French king; the insidious enmity of Catherine of Medicis, and the dishonor, as well as danger, attached to such a step, deterred him, and delayed its consummation. But, he felt its necessity, if he ever attained to the throne of France; and though he refused, after a long struggle and much irresolution, to comply with Epernon's solicitations in 1584; yet, on that, and on every occasion, he professed his readiness to receive instruction, and prepared the minds of the nation for his final conversion. It may be fairly asserted, that whatever virtues or endowments he possessed, he never could have been peaceably and generally recognized for sovereign of France, if he had not assumed the religion of the people, over whom he was called to reign (152).

(151) Sully, vol. i. p. 17.

(152) Lettre de du Fresne, in the Memoires de Villeroy, vol. ii. p. 77—175.

CHAP. IV.

State of literature, the ſciences, and the fine arts.—Natural philoſophy.—Aſtronomy.—Pharmacy.—Juriſprudence.—Eloquence.—Hiſtory.—Poetry.—Polite letters.—Erudition of the age.—Imitation of the antients.—Protection of learning, and learned men.—Progreſs of the art of printing.—Libels.—Libraries.—State of the drama.—Paſſion for romances.—Mode, and ſeminaries of education.

CHAP. IV.

Glory, annexed to the protection of letters.

THE grandeur of ſtates and ſovereigns is not determined ſolely by their extent of dominion, by the magnitude of their fleets and armies, or even by the general riches and felicity of the people. To be entitled to the appellation of Great, it is neceſſary that the arts and ſciences ſhould be held in honor, and that polite letters ſhould be univerſally cultivated and diffuſed. It is the acknowledged privilege of genius, to immortalize not only its poſſeſſors, but even its protectors. The princes of Medicis, though, in fact, only the firſt merchants of Italy, and the firſt citizens of a ſmall republic, ſituated among the Apennines; have acquired a reputation far ſuperior to that of the moſt powerful monarchs, their contemporaries. Francis the Firſt, who emulated their fame, and followed their traces, diffuſed the luſtre of his name over Europe, more by the protection and cultivation of letters, than by his victories, or military atchievements. His exertions to awaken the dormant talents of his ſubjects, were not ineffectual; and in the courſe of a reign of more than thirty years, he had the ſatisfaction to behold the commencement of that light, which gra-

Protection, extended to them by Francis the Firſt.

CHAP. IV.

and by his successors.

dually spreading and augmenting, attained to its meridian, in the following century, under Louis the Fourteenth. His son, Henry the Second, however inferior in the enthusiastic love of arts and sciences, extended his munificence to their professors (1). Even Charles the Ninth, in the intervals of civil war and massacre, unbent himself by the softer occupations of poetry and music; in the former of which he did not disdain to compose (2). He was accustomed to hold an academy, twice every week, in his own cabinet, at which men of letters and ladies assisted, where questions of a literary nature were agitated and discussed (3). It is clear, by the expressions of d'Aubigné, that Hugonots were not excluded from this society. He may be regarded as a singular instance in the history of mankind, of a prince whose ferocity was not humanized by the study of letters. His brother and successor, Henry the Third, immersed in pleasures, or engaged in hypocritical exercises of devotion, found little leisure for the elegant researches of taste and genius: he was, notwithstanding, liberal in his donations to those who were distinguished by their talents in every branch of art; and Desportes, the poet, held the same rank in his affections, which Ronsard had enjoyed in the favor of his predecessor (4).

State of science.

When we consider the state of the sciences, at the period of which we are treating, we must be compelled to admit, that they were only in their infancy. Scarcely any thing was taught in the schools, except dialectics, and the Aristotelian philosophy. Such was the degree of idolatry paid to the Stagyrite, that Ramus, who perished at the massacre of Paris, was dragged through the streets, and his body

(1) Brantome, vol. ii. Cap. Fran. p. 55 and 59.
(2) De Thou, vol. vii. p. 64.
(3) D'Aub. Hist. Univ. vol. p. 184. (4) L'Etoile, p. 88.

afterwards

afterwards thrown into the Seine, by the ſtudents who followed the Ariſtotelian doctrines, which Ramus had combated and expoſed (5). Natural philoſophy, founded on experiments, was, in a great meaſure, unknown; and even aſtronomy had not advanced beyond its firſt rudiments. Copernicus had, indeed, from an obſcure and remote city of Poliſh Pruſſia, diſcloſed the ſyſtem which bears his name, and acquainted the world with the true poſition and revolutions of the celeſtial bodies, towards the cloſe of the reign of Francis the Firſt. But, that great truth, combated by the ſuperſtitious prejudices of the times, made its way ſlowly and progreſſively, through the European nations. France does not ſeem to have poſſeſſed any aſtronomer of eminence, before the deceaſe of Henry the Third; and both in Germany and Italy, far greater diſcoveries had been made in the ſiſter ſciences of aſtronomy and philoſophy. True chemiſtry was equally neglected; while aſtrologers and alchemiſts, availing themſelves of the ignorance and credulity of princes, filled every court, and were held in univerſal eſtimation. Henry the Third, without information, or examination, but, from deference to the Holy See, cauſed the Gregorian calendar and computation of time to be received among the French. It was, in ſome meaſure, ſurreptitiouſly regiſtered by the Parliament of Paris, in the abſence of the preſident, Harlay. Science had no ſhare whatever in its adoption, which took place immediately after its promulgation at Rome by Gregory the Thirteenth, on the 10th of December, 1582. That day was counted for the twentieth of the month (6). Similar motives of obedience to

Philoſophy.

Reception of the Gregorian calendar in France.

(5) Biograph. Diction. vol. xi. p. 28. Brantome, vol. ii. Cap. Fran. p. 55 and 56.

(6) De Thou, vol. viii. p. 662. Lettres de Paul de Foix, p. 611 and 616.

the

CHAP. IV.

the court of Rome, induced the duke of Anjou, then acknowledged as ſovereign of the Low Countries, to its introduction among the Flemings (7). Before the year 1563, the French were accuſtomed to reckon from Eaſter day, as the firſt of the year. The famous chancellor l'Hopital cauſed it to be altered to the firſt of January; but, the Parliament did not regiſter the edict till 1564 (8).

Pharmacy.

It may be juſtly queſtioned, whether pharmacy and ſurgery had attained to a much higher point of perfection, than the ſciences already enumerated.

Anatomy.

Anatomy was very imperfectly known, or ſtudied: ſcarcely had the prejudices which oppoſe themſelves to the diſſection of the human body, been overcome. Emetics were never adminiſtered; and ſome of the moſt powerful medicines, uſed in the cure of diſeaſes, were undiſcovered. The Peruvian bark, the only ſpecific in intermitting fevers, had not yet been imported from the New World, and lay concealed in the mountains of South America. Even the circulation of the blood was only ſurmiſed, and by no means aſcertained. Yet, the age produced ſome illuſtrious names, who drew from their contemporaries the moſt extravagant encomiums.

Fernel.

Fernel, phyſician to Francis the Firſt, was regarded as a man of conſummate ſkill. He received a penſion of two thouſand, five hundred crowns, for having rendered Catherine of Medicis, then dauphineſs, capable of producing children. Her ſterility had given riſe to reports of an intention to repudiate that princeſs, who was no longer ſuſtained by the credit of Clement the Seventh (9). Fernel's reputation was eclipſed by the fame of Ambroſe Paré, a Hugonot, whoſe talents exempted him from the

Paré.

(7) De Thou, vol. viii. p. 662 and 663.
(8) Trad. de l'Hop. vol. ii. Recherches, p. 119.
(9) Le Lab. ſur Caſt. vol. i. p. 284. Brantome, vol. ii. Cap. Fran. p. 55.

maſſacre

maſſacre of Paris, by the perſonal interpoſition of Charles the Ninth (10). With him, the ſcience of pharmacy, and the practice of ſurgery, may be ſaid to have ariſen among the French, from whom they were gradually diffuſed over the northern nations. His works, which appeared towards the concluſion of the reign of Henry the Third, and which were dedicated to that prince, bear teſtimony to the acuteneſs of his talents, the ſuperiority of his views, and the indefatigable attention paid by him, to ameliorate the mode of treating the objects of his care. In defiance of vulgar prejudices, and the remonſtrances of his countrymen, who were deſirous of concealing from the world, the myſteries of the medical profeſſion; Paré addreſſed his writings to mankind, not as his predeceſſors had been accuſtomed, under the veil of a learned language, but, in his own (11).

Before the year 1536, when he commenced his practice, as one of the ſurgeons attending on the army of Francis the Firſt, in Piémont; ſo ignorant were all the practitioners in that important branch of art, that the firſt elements of it were unknown. We can ſcarcely believe, that the preparation and ingredients of gunpowder were conſidered as poiſonous; and that it was univerſally cuſtomary, in order to deterge and cleanſe the wounds, cauſed by fire-arms, to apply to them boiling oil (12). John de Vigo, a celebrated phyſician, whoſe writings and opinions were received as oracular and infallible, had recommended this pernicious application, previous to every other dreſſing, or digeſtive. Paré ingenuouſly confeſſes, that, ſubdued and awed by ſo high an authority, he purſued it; and it was only from the failure of a ſupply of oil in the camp, that

(10) Brantome, vol. iii. Cap. Fran. p. 166.
(11) Œuvres d'Ambroiſe Paré, à Lyon, 1652, Au Lecteur, p. 4, 5.
(12) Œuvres de Paré, au Lecteur, p. 265—267.

he

CHAP. IV.

he was compelled to fubftitute a lefs deftructive application. "Yet, terrified," fays he, "at my own "boldnefs, in thus venturing to deviate from the "mode of practice; and apprehenfive, that I fhould "find the patients, whofe wounds I had not cauterized by the ufe of boiling oil, dead of poifon; "I was unable to fleep, and I rofe from my bed, at "an early hour, to vifit them. But, beyond my "hopes, I found thofe, to whom, from neceffity, "I had adminiftered a digeftive of a milder nature, "compofed of the yolk of eggs, oil of rofes, and "turpentine, free from pain, inflammation, or tumours, having repofed well during the night. On "the contrary, the perfons, whofe wounds had "been wafhed with hot oil, were in a ftate of "fever, with violent fymptoms of every kind. "From that time, I refolved never more to burn "thus cruelly the poor wretches, afflicted with "gun-fhot wounds (13)."

It was, therefore, in this inftance, as in almoft all the other difcoveries of art, only accident, which firft led the way to fo beneficial an alteration in the practice of furgery. We may eafily conceive, how prodigious muft have been the mortality in camps and armies, under the antient fyftem. Every page of Paré's works bears teftimony to it. To his laborious refearches, and unwearied exertions, was likewife due, the introduction and improvement of almoft all the principal inftruments, ftill ufed in furgery. Thofe for performing the operation of the trepan, were greatly perfected by him (14); and the accumulated honors, prefents, and emoluments, conferred on him, not only by the French kings, but by foreign princes and nobles, evince the high admiration entertained for his talents, all over Europe.

(13) Œuvres de Paré, au Lecteur, p. 263, 264, and p. 782, 783.
(14) Ibid. p. 787.

One

Surgery.

One of the moſt famous cures performed in ſurgery, during the period under our conſideration, was that of Francis, duke of Guiſe, wounded at the ſiege of Bologne, under Henry the Second. The ſtump of a lance which entered between his noſe and his eye, was extracted by Nicholas Lavernan, with ſo much delicacy and ſucceſs, as neither to impair his ſight in the ſmalleſt degree, nor to leave any unpleaſing ſcar. So deeply was it fixed in the duke's head, that, in order to draw it out, Lavernan was obliged to lay his foot upon the head of the patient, and to exert his utmoſt force (15). The operation was eſteemed a maſter piece of art and ſkill. We may judge how little the uſe of ſtyptics was known as late as 1582, by the inſtance of William the Firſt, prince of Orange. After the wound that he received from the piſtol ball of Jaureguy, which paſſed through both his cheeks, hot irons were immediately applied to cauterize the parts. That expedient appeared, at firſt, to ſucceed; but, on the tenth day, the cruſt which had formed, fell: the bleeding recommenced, and with ſo much violence, that no means could be diſcovered of ſtopping it, or of cloſing the veſſels. In ſo critical an emergency, Leonard Botal, an Italian of Aſti, in Piémont, phyſician to the duke of Anjou, adviſed, as the only means left, to ſtop the wound by the application of the thumb, and to employ men, who ſhould inceſſantly relieve each other, for the purpoſe. The advice was followed, and contributed to ſave the prince's life (16). Tavannes loudly arraigns and condemns the practice of ſurgery, as it exiſted in his time. He ſays, that it was cuſtomary to open all gun-ſhot, or other wounds, with ſuch indiſcretion, as to produce im-

Styptics.

(15) Brantome, vol. iii. Cap Fran. p. 121. Œuvres de Paré, p. 785.
(16) De Thou, vol. viii. p. 614.

posthumes

CHAP. IV.

posthumes or discharges, more fatal to the patient than the original wound itself. It would seem, that few persons recovered, or received a perfect cure. "The lancet," says he, "is more destructive than "the ball (17)."

Study of jurisprudence.

Notwithstanding the venality and corruption which polluted the courts of law, the study of jurisprudence was held in the highest honor, and the profession of a civilian was equally respectable and profitable. Cujas, a native of Toulouse, attained a vast reputation for his proficiency in the civil law, under the last princes of Valois. He was esteemed an oracle of knowledge; and he received from his own sovereign, as well as from foreigners, the most flattering marks of respect and consideration (18). Of the oratory of the bar, we have few specimens remaining; but, from the description given us by l'Hopital, of the celebrated pleading before the Parliament of Paris, under Henry the Second, in 1550; when the case of the Protestants massacred at Merindole and Cabrieres, was solemnly argued; we may judge that it had attained to no common degree of force, energy, and sublimity (19). That the profession of a lawyer, employed in civil and criminal causes, was a very lucrative one, is equally apparent. Fees seem to have been nearly as ample, if the relative value of money be considered, as in the present age; but, they appear to have been given, rather as the recompence of successful eloquence and exertion, than in every event of a suit. Under Henry the Second, we find a sum equal almost to two pounds sterling, offered by a rich client to his counsel, who had gained a cause of a slender pecuniary consequence, after a short pleading of less than two hours. The money

Oratory of the bar.

Fees.

(17) Tavannes, p. 66 and 67.
(18) Papire Masson. in vita Cujas.
(19) Trad. de l'Hopital, vol. i. Epitres, p. 29—31.

was

was refused and returned, as inadequate to the trouble and merit; not without expressions of resentment at so insufficient a reward (20).

CHAP. IV.

Eloquence.

Eloquence had not divested itself, in the sixteenth century, of pedantry, affectation, and the false ornaments of a corrupt and unformed taste. This style of oratory and declamation was long retained, and slowly abandoned. It is, notwithstanding, matter of curious remark, that in the two harangues of Henry the Third to the States General, in 1577, and in 1588, the purity of diction, simplicity, and energy of the composition, might vie with those of almost any period. The latter speech is long, pathetic, and dignified; disgraced by no unnatural allusions, or conceits; but, containing a clear exposition of the calamities of the kingdom, and exhorting, or pointing out the obvious, and necessary remedies. It might have been pronounced by Augustus, in the Roman Senate; or, by Louis the Fourteenth, at any period of his reign (21). But, when we peruse the speeches of Montholon, keeper of the seals, and of Renaud de Beaune, archbishop of Bourges, in the same assembly, we find ourselves transported to another century. Scripture, and mythology, profane and sacred history, are ransacked for matter. Joshua, and Solomon, and Asa, are mingled with Druids, and princes of the Merovingian and Carlovingian lines (22). The archbishop of Bourges compares the king, at the opening of his speech, to Nestor in wisdom, and to Ulysses in eloquence. After a compliment to the queen-mother, whom he denominates another Irené, he exhorts Henry to emulate the example and heroic actions of Hercules and Theseus; of Moses, Joshua, Nebuchadnezzar, Cyrus, David, Manasses, Augustus,

Style of Henry the Third's harangue.

Speeches of Montholon, and Bourges.

(20) Trad. de l'Hop. vol. i. p. 88 and 89.
(21) De Thou, vol. vii. p 448—451; and vol. x. p. 373—383.
(22) De Thou, vol. x. p. 383—389.

CHAP. IV.

tus, Vespasian, and Mithridates. He proceeds to draw a parallel between Solomon and the French monarch; concluding by a fervent wish, that he might exceed in longevity, Arganthonius, king of Gibraltar (23).

Harangue of Bellievre to Elizabeth.

If we would wish to form a perfect idea of the species of eloquence then used by statesmen and ministers, we have only to peruse the harangue of Bellievre, the French embassador, to Elizabeth, queen of England, pronounced in 1587. The motive of his address, was to deprecate and prevent the execution of the unfortunate Mary, queen of Scots. Bellievre, in order to prove that sovereigns are not amenable to any earthly tribunal, cites a hymn of Callimachus, who says, that Jupiter alone can judge kings. Having remarked from Plato, that the nature of ordinary men is composed of iron and lead, while that of princes is formed of gold; he proves by citations from Homer and Virgil, as well as by the example of Xenocrates, how sacred the rights of hospitality have been ever esteemed. He reminds her of Alexander's treatment of the Thebans, taken in the Persian camp; and of Totila's conduct towards Antistia, the wife of Boethius. Having compared the Scottish queen to Conradin, beheaded by Charles of Anjou, and to Saul, when in the power of David; he next talks of Regulus and Elius Verus. But, above all, he implores her to imitate the empress Livia, in her advice to Augustus, respecting the conspiracy of Cinna and Pompey (24). Elizabeth, who wanted no reasons, nor precedents, to justify a measure, on which she had long determined, heard the embassador patiently: opposed to the authorities and examples which he had so laboriously quoted, others

(23) De Thou, vol. x. p. 389—391.
(24) Ibid. vol. ix. p. 627—637.

favorable

favorable to her own intentions; and ſtruck off the head of her priſoner (25).

CHAP. IV.

History.

No great, nor eminent hiſtorian aroſe in France, during the period under our review. Comines belongs to the preceding age; and neither De Thou, nor Davila, had yet appeared; if, indeed, the latter can, with ſtrictneſs, be regarded as a French writer. Henry the Second, at the ſolicitation of the cardinal of Lorrain, had named a hiſtoriographer; annexed to the title a ſalary of about ſixty pounds ſterling; and even furniſhed materials for the hiſtory of his own reign and exploits: but, no progreſs was made in the work (26). We cannot ſufficiently regret, that the Memoirs, compoſed by Coligni, upon the events of his own time, and in particular, upon the civil wars, do not exiſt. The manuſcript, found after the admiral's death, was brought to Charles the Ninth, and burnt by advice of marſhal Retz (27). Montluc is only a plain, unlettered ſoldier, who commemorates his own military actions, under the name of "Commentaries." The "political and military Diſcourſes" of La Noue breathe the candour, veracity, and ſound reflexion, by which, in every part of his life, their author was diſtinguiſhed: but, they cannot emulate the praiſe of hiſtory. Tavannes's "Memoirs" contain much valuable and ſecret information on the events to which he was witneſs, and many of which he directed or adviſed. But, it is to be lamented, that his ſon, who gave them to the world, has mutilated, altered, and defaced them in numerous particulars. Caſtelnau muſt be eſteemed the fineſt writer of the four: he is modeſt, ſuccinct, clear, and perfectly well informed upon all the points which he relates, or diſcuſſes. He is, notwithſtanding,

Montluc.

La Noue.

Tavannes.

Caſtelnau.

(25) De Thou, vol. ix. p. 637.
(26) Brantome, vol. ii. Cap. Fran. p. 52—55.
(27) Ibid. vol. iii. Cap. Fran. p. 194 and 198.

ing,

CHAP. IV.

ing; inferior in every point of view, to his model, Philip de Comines.

French language.

The French language had not attained either to elegance, or purity, before the accession of Henry the Second. Men of taste and genius disdained to employ it as the vehicle of their compositions. Latin was commonly used by the poets; who found their own language too rough and unharmonious, for the fetters of verse. The finest productions of that kind, before the middle of the sixteenth century, were in Latin. Marot, who eclipsed the fame of all his predecessors, first quitted the language of Horace, to adopt that of his own country (28). The names and works of St. Gelais, Jodelle, Baïf, Belleau, Dorat, and Desportes, who formed the admiration of the court, under Francis the First and his descendants, are now in a great measure forgotten; or, only remembered by some happy lines, which have escaped the general oblivion. In all their writings, a redundancy of learning, and a servile imitation of the antients, is visible. Charmed with the great models of Greece and Rome, they dressed themselves in their borrowed ornaments, without reflecting that the grace and delicacy of the original, could not be transfused, or preserved in the copy.

Poetry.

Preference given to the Latin language.

Marot.

Marot may be regarded as the father and creator of the French verse. To him is due the invention of the Sonnet, the Rondeau, and the Madrigal, which were unknown before the sixteenth century, in France (29). He flourished during the reign of Francis the First, by whom he was caressed, protected, and rewarded; but, his religious opinions, which were supposed to be tinctured with heresy,

(28) De Thou, vol. ix. p. 412—414. Vie de Ronsard, par Binet, Paris, 1604, p. 128 and 175.

(29) Œuvres de Marot, 2 vols. Geneve, passim. Baillet, Jugement, sur les Poëtes, tom. iii. p. 206.

compelled

compelled him to quit the kingdom, and to ſeek an asylum at Geneva. He died in a ſpecies of exile, at Turin, in Piémont, which was then occupied by the French forces. This event took place in 1544 (30): Such was the elegance and beauty of his verſification in his native language, that none of the poets, if we except Ronſard, who formed the "Pleiad," or conſtellation of poetic genius, under the laſt princes of Valois, could equal him in thoſe endowments (31). La Fontaine, in the enſuing century, confeſſed his admiration for, and his obligations to Marot, as one of his maſters, and models (32). The indecencies, to be found in his compoſitions, are, in a great degree, to be charged to the taſte or manners of the period in which he lived; and may derive ſome apology, if not juſtification, from reflecting, that ſcarcely any of the greateſt Roman poets of the Auguſtan age, are free from the ſame blemiſhes. Nothing could exceed the vogue, which Marot's Tranſlation of the Pſalms into French, obtained, under Francis the Firſt. The emperor, Charles the Fifth, to whom he preſented them, rewarded him by a donation of near two hundred pounds ſterling; a ſum of very conſiderable magnitude in that century; and which, even in this, would not be eſteemed ſmall (33).

CHAP. IV.

St. Gelais.

St. Gelais was the contemporary, and the rival of Marot; but, with inferior talents and reputation. His verſes are eaſy, flowing, and ſometimes beautiful; ornamented with mythological alluſions, and a variety of learning. The greater part of his compoſitions are on ſubjects of a light and temporary nature, calculated for the amuſement of a gay and voluptuous court; ſuch as were thoſe of Francis

(30) Bayle. Dict. Art. "Marot," p. 154, 155.
(31) La Bruyere, Caracteres, p. 82.
(32) La Fontaine, Oüvrages Poſthumes, p. 107.
(33) Bayle. Dict. Article "Marot," p. 160.

the

CHAP. IV. the First, and Henry the Second. He surviv-ed his competitor Marot, and died in Paris, in 1558 (34.)

Jodelle. To Jodelle is due the revival of tragedy, as formed upon the models of antiquity. His "Cleopatra" was performed with incredible applause, by order of Henry the Second, at Paris (35). Belleau is principally known by his translations of the Odes of Anacreon. But, neither he, nor Dorat, could contest the pre-eminence of poetical fame and genius, with Ronsard. The invention of Anagrams, a passion for which, became universal among the French, is attributed to Dorat (36).

Desportes. Desportes may be said to terminate the list of poets, who flourished under the last kings of Valois. He was enriched by the profusion of Henry the Third, and even acted no inconsiderable political part, during the reign of Henry the Fourth. Desportes is the Tibullus of France, amorous, impassioned, and querulous. His elegies, though unequal in purity and elegance, to those of the Roman poet, are neither deficient in softness, nor in harmony. He accompanied his patron and master, the duke of Anjou, into Poland; and he gives, in one of his poetical compositions, a hideous picture of the Polish manners, country, and nobility (37). In order to sooth the distress of Henry the Third for the loss of his two minions, Quelus and Maugiron, killed in a duel, Desportes did not hesitate to prostitute his talents, by composing epitaphs to their memory, and exhausting panegyric in their praise (38). He was liberally rewarded for these

(34) Œuvres de St. Gelais, passim.

(35) Recherches de Pasquier, lib. vii. cap. vii. p. 618. Bayle. Dict. Art. "Jodelle," and "Belleau." Vie de Ronsard, p. 139.

(36) Bayle. Dict. Art. "Dorat," p. 618.

(37) Œuvres de des Portes, Antwerp, 1591, p. 427, 428.

(38) Ibid. p. 478—481.

servile

servile offerings of the muse, by a prince, whose munificence towards his favorites, knew no limits.

CHAP. IV.

The pre-eminence of poetical genius among the French, during the sixteenth century, is unquestionably due to Ronsard. The universality of his talents, the extent and variety of his compositions, the profound erudition scattered throughout his writings, and the splendor of his diction, eclipsed those of all his contemporaries. To him may be attributed the introduction of the higher and more sublime species of poetry. The "Franciad," dedicated to Charles the Ninth, in whose honor it is composed, was the first epic poem, strictly so denominated, that appeared in the French language. It was left imperfect, and unfinished, on account of the premature and early death of that prince (39). However inferior to the great models of antiquity, which he copied, the "Franciad" of Ronsard, is neither defective in grandeur of conception, luxuriancy of fancy, nor harmony of versification.

With him, arose comedy, likewise, in France. The "Plutus" of Aristophanes, which he translated, was the earliest production of that kind, given to the inhabitants of Paris. It was performed, under the reign of Henry the Second, at the theatre of Coqueret, with universal applause (40). The diversity of his compositions, in every branch of poetry, excites equal admiration and astonishment. If he was compared with Homer and Virgil, he may, with equal justice, be cited as the rival of Anacreon, Pindar, and Catullus. In many of his lighter pieces, which he entitles "Gayetez," we trace all the hilarity and wanton mirth of the Ionian poet. His "Dythirambics" contain the rich stream of harmony, and the unfettered grace of Pindar. The

(39) Œuvres de Ronsard, tom. iii. Paris, 1604, p. 1—213, passim.
(40) Vie de Ronsard, p. 125.

CHAP. IV.

poem, composed by him, to commemorate the festive offering of a goat, adorned with garlands, which was presented as a testimony of homage to the genius of Jodelle, is peculiarly beautiful (41). The "Sonnets" of Ronsard to his mistress, may be compared in warmth and tenderness, with those of Catullus, to Lesbia. Even inanimate objects derived celebrity, and attained immortality, from his pen. The fountain of "Bellerie," in the Vendomois, became scarcely less renowned, than the classical spring of Blandusia; and was one of his favorite subjects of poetic description. He frequently retired to it, as Petrarch did to Vaucluse, there to indulge his pensive meditations (42). Like Desportes, he did not refuse to commemorate the minions of Henry the Third. His epitaphs on Quelus and Maugiron, are elegant compositions, and models of courtly panegyric (43). If he is thought to have degraded the dignity of poetry, by composing an epitaph on the greyhound of Charles the Ninth, or the lap-dog of Madame de Villeroy; it may be remembered, that Pope, the proudest poet of the present century, who boasts perpetually of his independance, and who affects to carry his indifference for crowned heads almost to contempt, was not ashamed to write a distich for the Prince of Wales's dog at Kew. Ronsard consulted more the majesty of the weeping muse, in his epitaphs on the constable Montmorenci, and on Philip de Comines (44).

From his earliest years, he was the companion and attendant of kings. After having accompanied James the Fifth of Scotland, on his return from France to his own dominions, as one of his pages,

(41) Œuvres de Ronsard, "Gayetez," p. 333—346.
(42) Vie de Ronsard, p. 149, and p. 178.
(43) Œuvres de Ronsard, "Epitaphes," p. 87—89.
(44) Ibid. p. 47—55, and p. 60—61, and p. 87—103.

he

he paſſed into the ſervice of Charles, duke of Orleans, youngeſt of the three ſons of Francis the Firſt (45). Henry the Second aſſociated him to all his paſtimes, and peculiarly to the martial exerciſes and diverſions, in which that monarch excelled. The force and addreſs of Ronſard in theſe exhibitions of corporal ſtrength and proweſs, were not leſs conſpicuous, than the elegance of his intellectual endowments (46). Charles the Ninth expreſſed for him the moſt partial affection, commanded him not to quit the court, and enriched him by the donation of various abbies, and eccleſiaſtical preferments. The verſes of Charles, addreſſed to Ronſard, are to be found among the works of the poet; and if they do little credit to the talents of the king, they, at leaſt, diſplay his attachment to the muſes (47). Under his ſucceſſor, Henry the Third, Ronſard was choſen for one of the members of an academy, in which the principal men of letters met, to converſe, and to communicate their reſpective compoſitions. It was held at the palace of the Louvre, in Henry's preſence (48).

Nor was his celebrity confined to France. It extended to other kingdoms, and was only limited by the language in which he wrote. Elizabeth, queen of England, delighted in his writings, and expreſſed her admiration for their author (49). Even the unfortunate Mary, queen of Scots, to whoſe charms he had done homage during the tranſitory reign of her firſt huſband, Francis the Second; in her ſolitary impriſonment at Tutbury and Fotheringay caſtles, ſoothed her calamities, by the peruſal of

(45) Vie de Ronſard, p. 115, 116.

(46) Ibid. p. 119, 120.

(47) Œuvres de Ronſard, tom. iii. p. 217—223. Vie de Ronſard, p. 141—144.

(48) Œuvres de Ronſard, tom. iii. p. 176 and 147.

(49) Vie de Ronſard, p. 147.

Ronſard's

CHAP. V.

Ronſard's works. As a proof of her eſteem, ſhe ſent him, in 1583, by Nau, her ſecretary, a ſilver buffet, valued at a thouſand crowns, with this inſcription on it, "A Ronſard, l'Apollon de la Source des Muſes (50)." At the ceremony of the "Floral Games," inſtituted and held in the city of Toulouſe, the preſidents, parliament, and people, unanimouſly decreed the pre-eminence to Ronſard. Not ſatisfied with conferring on him a wreath of eglantine, the cuſtomary reward of the victorious poet, they ſent him a ſtatue of Minerva in maſſy ſilver, accompanied with the moſt flattering teſtimonies of their admiration (51). His funeral was attended by the moſt illuſtrious perſons in France, for rank, talents, and virtue. The dukes of Angouleme and Joyeuſe, together with the cardinal of Bourbon, and the principal members of the Parliament of Paris, did not diſdain to follow in the cavalcade, and to perform the laſt honors to ſo diſtinguiſhed a genius (52). Du Perron, who became afterwards a cardinal, and who had already diſplayed talents of various kinds, pronounced his funeral oration (53). Such was the reſpect and eſtimation in which his works were held by foreign nations, that they were read as models of poetic beauty, in all the French ſchools of Flanders, England, Germany, and Poland (54). Like Hadrian, when expiring, he compoſed ſome lines, addreſſed to his departing ſoul, which are not inferior in vivacity, to thoſe attributed to the Roman emperor; of which they may be eſteemed a parody (55). Criticiſm itſelf was ſilent, or converted to panegyric, when employed upon Ronſard; and Scaliger, whoſe pen inſpired ſo much dread among his contemporaries, dedicated

(50) Vie de Ronſard, p. 147, 148.
(51) Ibid. p. 137, 138. (52) Ibid. p. 159, 160.
(53) Oraiſon funebre de du Perron, p. 184—240.
(54) Vie de Ronſard, p. 168, 169. (55) Ibid. p. 151.

to

to him, his favorite Anacreontics. We may judge of the reverential awe which Scaliger felt for the French poet, by the language which he uses, in his address. It is such as Horace would have adopted, when speaking of Homer:

> "Quo te carmine, qua prece,
> "Quo pingui genium thure, adeam tuum,
> "Immensi sobolem ætheris,
> "Qui musis animi prodigus, imperas (56)?"

Notwithstanding the obligations which the French language owes to Ronsard, in whose hands it became copious, rich, and melodious, he is not exempt from defects. But, they are, perhaps, more the faults of the age, than of the poet. His productions are loaded with mythology and fable; nor can we acquit him of some degree of impiety and profanation, in comparing the labours of Hercules, to those of Jesus Christ (57).

Rabelais.

Rabelais and Montaigne, neither of whom were poets, are the only authors of the period, in the walk of polite letters, who can be said to have escaped the general fate of their contemporaries, and to be read, after two centuries, beyond the limits of France. Rabelais, notwithstanding the extreme indecency and low buffoonery of his writings, contains so much genuine and original humor, so much grotesque fancy, incidents so comic, satire so delicate and keen, mixed with learning so various and profound, that he must be for ever agreeable to mankind. It is probable, that the greater number of those who peruse the "History of Gargantua and "Pantagruel," see in the work, only its eccentric and extravagant outside. But, the ridicule of the church of Rome, of the Catholic religion, its cere-

His ridicule of the Romish church.

(56) Vie de Ronsard, p. 167, 168.
(57) Bayle. Dict. Art. "Ronsard," p. 895, 896.

monies

CHAP. IV.

monies and injunctions, escapes continually through the disguise, under which Rabelais found it requisite to conceal so hazardous an attempt. It may excite some surprize, that a man who evidently despised and disbelieved the most essential articles of the Romish faith, should, after practising medicine, have been promoted to a prebend in a collegiate church, and made curate of Meudon, near Paris (58). The cardinal du Bellai, his patron, who protected, and preferred him, was not more persuaded of the sanctity of the religion, which he professed. That prelate, in defiance of the injunctions of the Romish see, had not hesitated to contract a marriage with madame de Chatillon, though motives of convenience induced him to conceal the transaction (59). The veil of affected folly and absurdity, under which Rabelais aimed his shafts at popes and princes, saved him from punishment; while the Protestants, who gravely and morosely attacked the pontifical power and dignity, were seized and committed to the flames. Rabelais belongs to the age of Francis the First, and Henry the Second; under the latter of which kings he ended his days, at an advanced period of life.

Montaigne.

Montaigne flourished under the last princes of Valois, and survived the extinction of that family. His "Essays" are equally original, and not less amusing, than the writings of Rabelais. He was a man of condition; and the careless, but, graceful negligence of a gentleman, characterizes his style.

Genius of his writings.

Though he talks perpetually, and almost exclusively, of himself, his egotism never offends, and generally entertains. Ease and nature seem to guide his pen; which is, however, disgraced by equal transgressions of decency, with those to be found in Rabelais, and

(58) Œuvres de Rabelais, Vie, vol. i. p. 4.
(59) Brantome, vol. ii. Dames Gal. p. 177—180.

in

in Brantome. An intimate acquaintance with the Greek and Roman writers is visible throughout every page of Montaigne. He oppresses us with citations from all the poets; and he never disdains to fortify, or support his positions, by an appeal to their authority. He is a sceptic, and takes little pains to disguise it, though he chose to live and die within the pale of the Catholic church. We may judge of the avidity with which his Essays were devoured by the public, when we reflect, that even civil war, and every kind of internal calamity, could not impede their reception. They first appeared in 1580, under Henry the Third; and in 1588, a period of rebellion and anarchy, he published the fifth edition, at Paris, amidst the convulsions of the League (60).

Architecture.

Catherine of Medicis, descended from a family immortalized by their protection of all the arts, and desirous of transplanting them into France, constructed the palace of the Tuilleries, which she commenced in 1564, soon after the termination of the first civil wars. Philibert de Lorme, and John Bullan, were the architects whom she employed to raise that stately edifice, which she completed before her decease, notwithstanding the troubles of the kingdom, and the exhausted state of the finances (61). It was, unquestionably, the finest monument of architecture, then to be found, beyond the Alps. Louis de Foix, a native of Paris, began, in 1584, the celebrated tower of Cordouan, at the mouth of the river Garonne; designed as a pharos, or light-house, to direct the ships bound to, and from, the port of Bourdeaux. Its position was on a rock in the midst of the sea, exposed to the utmost fury of the elements. Three stories, ornamented with the

(60) Journal du Voyage de Montaigne, Disc. prelim, vol. i. p. 64 and 65.

(61) L'Art de Ver. vol. i. p. 648.

CHAP. IV.

different orders of architecture, and terminating pyramidically, formed the tower; whose solidity, proportions, and strength, have secured its duration to the present time. It was not entirely completed till the year 1611 (62).

Painting, and sculpture.

No regular school of painting, or sculpture, had appeared in France, before the extinction of the race of Valois. The exertions of Francis the First had nevertheless awakened the genius of the nation, in both those branches of art. John Gougeon, and Germain Pillon, were esteemed very expert sculptors, and had attained to a high degree of reputation, under Henry the Third (63). Leonardo da Vinci, who expired in the arms of Francis the First, was an Italian, and does not seem to have left behind him any eminent pupils. Scarcely a single statue of bronze, or of marble, ornamented the metropolis, in 1589. The monuments, erected by Henry, to the memory of his three minions, St. Megrin, Quelus, and Maugiron, in the church of St. Paul, which were composed of the most costly materials; had been demolished by the fury of the Parisians, on their receiving the intelligence of the assassinations committed at Blois (64). Medals, commemorative of great or auspicious events, were frequently struck, and scattered among the people, or distributed as marks of distinction. Considerable delicacy was displayed in their fabrication, as well as in the devices or legends with which they were ornamented. Jane, queen of Navarre, in 1569, presented gold medallions to the principal German commanders of the auxiliary army. On them were inscribed mottos, containing an allusion to their perilous situation, and

Medals.

(62) De Thou, vol. ix. p. 204. Dict. Univ. de la France, vol. i. p. 467—469.
(63) Satyre Men. vol. ii. p. 403.
(64) L'Etoile, p. 114.

religious union (65). Three years afterwards, at the nuptials of Henry, king of Navarre, with Margaret of Valois, gold and silver medals were thrown to the populace. The inscription, "Con-"stricta hoc discordia vinculo," was designed to signify the extinction of past animosities, to be produced by the marriage (66).

CHAP. IV.

Erudition.

The feature which peculiarly distinguished and characterized the age, was erudition. Letters, which had revived in Italy about the middle of the fifteenth century, did not penetrate into France till above sixty years later. It was Francis the First who cherished, patronized, and rendered their study general. The productions of Athens and of Rome, in poetry, history, eloquence, and philosophy, became known to the French; and all the beauties of the antients, were embellished by the charms of novelty. Captivated with graces so much superior to every other, and with which they had been hitherto unacquainted; they knew no limit to their enthusiastic admiration. All classes of society caught the infection: princes, nobles, soldiers, and even ladies, cultivated learning; and became familiar with the language of Cicero, and of Homer. Erudition was deemed necessary for attaining to employments of state; and ambition derived support from the study of letters. L'Hopital owed, in a great measure, his progressive elevation, through the various dignities of the law, to its highest eminence; not so much to his knowledge of jurisprudence, as to his reputation for science (67). Coligni, in the midst of civil war, found leisure to read the Roman writers, and conversed with fluency and elegance in Latin (68). Marshal Strozzi, though engaged

Enthusiasm for the literary productions of antiquity.

Examples.

Strozzi.

(65) Memoires de Cast. vol. i. p. 241.
(66) Vie de Marg. de Val. p. 87.
(67) Trad. de l'Hop. Eclairciss. vol. i. p. 9 and 10.
(68) Brantome, vol. iii. Cap. Fran. p. 197.

during

CHAP. IV.

during his whole life, in the tumult of a camp, translated the Commentaries of Cæsar into Greek, with notes and applications calculated for rendering the original more intelligible, or useful, to men of the military profession. "I have heard Ronsard and "Durant," adds Brantome, "express their amaze-"ment at the purity and eloquence of the Greek "translation, which, in their estimation, was not "inferior to the Latin of the Roman dictator (69)."

Henry the Third, and the king of Navarre.

It was the ordinary amusement of Henry the Third, to retire, after dinner, to his closet, with Baccio del Bene, and Corbinelli, two learned Florentines, who read to him the works of Polybius and of Tacitus, in their original languages (70.) Henry, king of Navarre, though naturally averse to sedentary and studious occupations; yet, was versed in Greek, and accustomed, from his infancy, to cite or repeat passages from their poets and historians. It is a well-known anecdote, that, while yet a child, he adopted for his motto, the words, "ἢ νικᾶν, ἢ ἀποθανεῖν," either conquer, or die: and that he refused to explain their meaning to the queen-mother, Catherine of Medicis, who was anxious to know their import (71).

Princesses.

L'Hopital addressed many of his Latin epistles to Margaret, daughter of Francis the First, duchess of Savoy; and that princess, to whom her father, when expiring, recommended the protection of the muses, improved herself by the frequent study of Cicero and of Horace (72). When the Polish embassadors, in 1573, arrived at Paris, to lay their crown at the feet of the duke of Anjou; the bishop of Cracow, one of the number, having harangued the young queen of Navarre, Margaret, in Latin;

(69) Brantome, vol. ii. Cap. Etrang. p. 261 and 262.
(70) Davila, p. 148.
(71) Chron. Noven. vol. i. p. 248.
(72) Trad. de l'Hopital, vol. ii. p. 123—134. Le Lab. sur Cast. vol. i. p. 706.

she

ſhe inſtantly replied in the ſame language, recapitulating, and anſwering every part of his ſpeech, with facility and preciſion (73). Catherine of Medicis, leſs ſkilled in the languages of antiquity, employed an interpreter on the ſame occaſion. Her ſelection fell on Catherine de Clermont, one of the moſt beautiful and accompliſhed ladies of the court; but, not more eminent for the graces of her perſon, than for her erudition (74). Jane d'Albret, queen of Navarre, and Renée, ducheſs of Ferrara, daughter of Louis the Twelfth, two princeſſes who embraced the reformed doctrines, were diſtinguiſhed by their proficiency in, as well as by their protection of learning.

Imitations of the antients.

To ſuch a point of perfection was the imitation of the antients carried, that many of the productions of l'Hopital, and of Morvilliers, biſhop of Orleans, were not diſtinguiſhable by the ableſt critics, from the writings of antiquity. The epiſtle of l'Hopital, to James du Faur, intitled "An Imprecation againſt "Suits at Law," deceived the learned ſo completely, as to be not only attributed to various Roman poets; but, to exerciſe ingenuity in pointing out the interpolations and alterations, introduced into the original text (75). We may ſee in d'Aubigné, how elegant were the Latin verſes, compoſed by the young nobility; and what facility they poſſeſſed in making them, upon every occaſion (76). Even from the pageants and amuſements of the court, the Latin language was not excluded; and females of the higheſt diſtinction recited Roman poetry, with equal grace and elegance. At a ſpecies of maſque, repreſented before Henry the Second, at St. Ger-

(73) Vie de Marg. p. 122.
(74) Ibid. p. 122. Le Lab. ſur Caſt. vol. ii. p. 102—105.
(75) Trad. de l'Hop. vol. i. p. 137—144 Le Lab. ſur Caſt. vol. i. p. 494, and p. 504.
(76) D'Aub. Mem. p. 85 and 89.

main,

CHAP. IV.

main, near Paris, in 1554; in which six ladies, or princesses, habited as Sybils, performed the principal parts; Mary, queen of Scots, then in very early youth, personated the Delphic Sybil. Addressing herself to the Dauphin, her destined husband, who was afterwards Francis the Second, she predicted in a distich, composed by St. Gelais, the poet, the future union, in his person, of the British and French crowns:

" Delphica, Delphini si mentem oracula tangunt,
" Britonibus junges regna Britanna tuis (77)."

A perfect acquaintance with the Latin language, was an indispensable qualification for embassadors to many of the European courts, and highly introductory to all foreign missions and employments (78). French had not then been adopted as a general medium of conversation. Spanish was much more generally used; and it was the language of the Imperial court, as well as that of Madrid, till the reign of Rodolph the Second (79). Montaigne was instructed in Latin, before he was permitted to learn his native language; and so perfectly did he possess it, that the celebrated Buchanan, who was one of his preceptors, confessed, that he apprehended conversing with his pupil (80). D'Aubigné says, that at six years of age, he could read Latin, Greek, and Hebrew: when only in his eighth year, he translated the "Crito" of Plato, into French (81). Military men composed their own epitaphs, or those of their friends, slain in action. "When la Case de Miram-

Universality and vogue of the Latin language.

(77) Œuvres Poetiq. de St. Gelais, à Paris, 1719. p. 12, 13.
(78) Le Lab. sur Cast. vol. ii. p. 776.
(79) Brantome, vol. ii. Dames Gal. p. 78.
(80) Essais de Montaigne, vol. i. p. 254—256. Voyages de Montaigne, Disc. Prelim. vol. i. p. 70 and 71. Biogr. Diction. vol. ix. p. 298.
(81) D'Aub. Mem. p. 4 and 5.

"beau was killed in 1574," says de Thou; "in his "boot was found the following distich, written with "his own hand, as if he had foreseen his end:

"Desine migrantem lugere, viator, et hospes.
"Non careo patria: me caret illa magis (82)."

Latin verses.

The satirical sonnets, which originated on a thousand trifling subjects, and which were circulated in the courts of Charles the Ninth, and Henry the Third, were rarely in French. Wits and satirists preferred the Latin, as more expressive, and equally intelligible. The six elegant lines, composed by a courtier, in 1577, upon the comet, which was then visible, and whose appearance impressed Catherine of Medicis with so much terror, as well as most of the epigrams upon the minions, or ministers of Henry the Third, were written in the language and spirit of Martial (83). Brantome, who is only a dissolute man of the world, is yet an accomplished scholar.

Munificence to men of genius.

Never was greater munificence extended to men of genius, in every branch of art and science, than by the princes of Valois. The bounties of Louis the Fourteenth were dispensed with more parade and ostentation; but, they were neither more general, nor superior in extent. Francis the First, not satisfied with encouraging and recompensing literary merit in his own subjects, exerted himself to discover and reward it among every foreign nation. He sent several learned men, at his own expence, to travel into Greece, and the countries of Asia Minor, in order to collect antiquities, manuscripts, and other monuments (84). Royal professors, with liberal

(82) De Thou, vol. vii. p. 45.
(83) L'Etoile, p. 25 and 26, and p. 37, and p. 80. and p. 108. Mem. pour ser. à l'Hist. de Fr. p. 111, and p. 192 and 193.
(84) Brantome, vol. i. Cap. Fran. p. 241.

pecuniary

CHAP. IV.

pecuniary ſtipends, were appointed, to teach in the colleges, which he founded, or endowed. Such was his predilection for perſons diſtinguiſhed by a knowledge of letters, that he uſually made choice of them for embaſſies to the European courts (85).

Jovius.

Paul Jovius, the famous hiſtorian, enjoyed a penſion of two hundred and fifty crowns, from the treaſury, during that monarch's life: but the conſtable Montmorenci, with whoſe character and actions Jovius had taken ſome unwarrantable liberties, retrenched and ſtruck it off, at the acceſſion of Henry the Second (86). Notwithſtanding this ſingle inſtance of reſentment, expreſſed by a miniſter, whoſe alienation to, and unacquaintance with letters, was well known; Henry diſplayed the ſame princely regard for them, which had characterized his father. He was ſo charmed with the "Cleopatra," a tragedy of Jodelle, as to give the author a preſent of two hundred and fifty crowns, beſides other gratifications (87). Henry the Third preſented the poets, Ronſard and Baïf, each, a thouſand crowns, as a recompence for the beautiful verſes, compoſed by them on the occaſion of his favorite, Joyeuſe's marriage (88). Even religious prejudices and antipathies, which were ſo powerful in that age, did not prevent Henry the Third from ordering five hundred crowns to be preſented to Henry Etienne, a Hugonot, who had written a work of much celebrity, upon the excellence of the French language (89). At the ceremony of the inauguration and inveſtiture of Francis, duke of Anjou, as ſovereign of the Netherlands, which was performed at Antwerp, in 1582; the deputies of the Proteſtants, in the act of

Jodelle.

Etienne.

(85) Brantome, vol. i. Cap. Fran. p. 241. Biog. Diction. vol. ii. Artic. Budaus.

(86) Brantome, vol. i. Cap. Fran. p. 231 and 232.

(87) Ibid. vol. ii. Cap. Fran. p. 59.

(88) L'Etoile, p. 46.

homage

homage and congratulation to their new prince, besought of him to take under his protection, letters, and their professors, and to honor them, according to the example left him by Francis the First (90). He promised to comply with the request. Prelates and cardinals expended the revenues of their ecclesiastical preferments, in the patronage of genius. The vices and irregularities of the cardinal of Lorrain were concealed and almost forgotten, in the munificent largesses with which he conciliated literary favor. He was the Mecœnas of the court of Henry the Second, and his two immediate successors (91).

Cardinal of Lorrain.

The art of printing, in the course of considerably more than a century, which had elapsed since its invention, had diffused very widely every species of knowledge, and penetrated among all orders of society. The Morels, and the Etiennes, celebrated printers, carried the art at Paris, to a pitch of eminence, before the death of Henry the Second, in 1559 (92). One of the former family, convicted of heresy, was burnt in the succeeding reign (93). Manutius, employed by the Venetians, and by various of the Romish pontiffs, had immortalized his own name, by giving to the world the most perfect and beautiful editions of Tully, as well as of many of the Greek and Roman writers. The fame of Aldus Manutius was sustained by his son, who died in 1574 (94). Fourteen years afterwards, in 1588, Metayer, the royal printer at Paris, gave to the world a magnificent work, executed by order of

Art of printing.

Manutius.

(89) Memoires pour ser. à l'Hist. de Fra. p. 193.
(90) De Thou, vol. viii. p. 605.
(91) Brantome, vol. ii. Dames Gal. p. 416. Trad. de l'Hopital, vol. i. p. 46.
(92) De Thou, vol. vii. p. 206.
(93) Trad de l'Hop. vol. i. p. 103.
(94) De Thou, vol. vii. p. 206. Biog. Dic. vol. ix. p. 52 and 53.

the

CHAP. IV.

the king. It contained the breviaries and prayers of the Romiſh ritual, in two folio volumes. The paper and the type were equally beautiful (95). With the benefits and advantages of printing, were proportionably diffuſed its evils. Under a reign ſuch as that of Henry the Third, when the royal conſideration and authority were ſo much relaxed, the preſs teemed with libels of the moſt inſolent nature. The Hugonots, after the death of Charles the Ninth, publiſhed ſeveral ſevere and ſatirical pieces againſt Catherine of Medicis, then regent during the abſence of Henry in Poland. She was exhorted by the council of ſtate, to puniſh the authors with rigor. But, her magnanimity diſdained the advice, and permitted an uninterrupted courſe to all the accuſations or calumnies of her enemies (96). Henry, on his return to France, did not imitate her in ſo ſhining a feature of her character. On the contrary, the only inſtances of rigor, which can be laid to his charge, which contraſt extraordinarily with the lenity, or apathy, demonſtrated in his general adminiſtration, were exerted againſt libellers. In March, 1577, while the court was at Blois, a ſatirical compoſition, in which the king, the queen-mother, and other perſons, were treated with extreme ſeverity, was laid under the bolſter of Catherine of Medicis's bed. It is not leſs ridiculous, than true, that for this crime, of which the author was unknown, all the poets about the court were immediately ſeized, and ſent to priſon (97).

Libels, numerous.

Severity exercifed towards libellers.

The faction of the League, from its firſt formation, ſeems to have been fully ſenſible of the importance of the preſs; and the leaders made bold and frequent application to the paſſions of the people,

(95) Satyre Menippée, vol. ii. p. 150, 151.
(96) Davila, p. 418.
(97) Memoires de Nevers, vol. i. p. 177.

through

Roziere.

through its medium. In 1583, before the great convulsions which marked the close of Henry's reign, Roziere, archdeacon of Toul, was brought before the council, to answer for having composed and published a book, entitled "Genealogy of the "dukes of Lorrain and Bar." The object of it was to prove, that Hugh Capet and his descendants were only usurpers; and that the dukes of Lorrain were the genuine representatives of Charlemagne. Some passages in the work were, likewise, of a nature personally insulting and injurious to the king himself. Roziere would have infallibly expiated his offence by a public execution, if he had not been extricated by the powerful interposition of the duke of Lorrain, and the queen-mother (98.) Belleville, a Protestant gentleman, having, in the following year, committed a crime of less political magnitude, but, to which Henry was deeply sensible; by writing a satire on his private debaucheries, was instantly arrested. Convicted of being the author, he was drawn in a sledge to the place of execution, hanged, and his body, together with the work, thrown into the flames. All his estates and property were confiscated (99). Even insanity formed no protection against the rigor of the laws, in cases of a libellous nature. Le Breton, a man of a heated and disordered imagination, bred to the bar, ventured in 1586, to stigmatize the magistrates and sovereign, with equally betraying the cause of the poor. Although in the course of his trial, he gave numerous indications of an alienated mind, and notwithstanding the intercession of the judges themselves, who besought of the king to remit his punishment, he was condemned and executed (100). These

Punishment of Belleville,

and of Le Breton.

(98) De Thou, vol. ix. p. 70 and 71.
(99) Ibid. p. 201 and 202. Mem pour ser. à l'Hist. de Fr. p. 184
(100) Chron. Nov. vol. i p. 33 and 34. De Thou, vol. viii p 613—615. Mem. pour ser. à l'Hist. de Fr. p. 213 and 214.

CHAP. IV.

exemplary chastisements did not deter the heads of the League from publishing a variety of pamphlets, calculated to withdraw the obedience of the subject from the crown. Such was the avidity of the people to peruse them, and so odious was the government, that no penalties could deter the printers or venders from circulating them through the metropolis. Impositions of the grossest nature, and invectives the most bitter, were not spared, and met with a ready belief. The universal defection which followed, evinced how powerful an engine was the press, in the hands of a desperate and unprincipled faction (101).

Powerful effect of the press.

Libraries.

Public and private libraries were already become common and general, before 1589. Francis the First began the celebrated one, at the palace of Fontainbleau, of which Budæus, one of the most learned men of the age, was constituted librarian. It had attained to very considerable magnitude, before that prince's death (102). Catherine of Medicis, who emulated and imitated him, in the cultivation of letters, augmented it by so many costly works, manuscripts, and books in every language, that, at her decease, it was accounted the finest collection in Europe (103). She was not satisfied with forming a library for the crown, but, exerted equal efforts to possess one, herself, at Chenonceaux, a castle in Touraine, to which she frequently retired. We may form some estimate of its size and value, by knowing, that at the death of marshal Strozzi, she added his collection of books, calculated to be worth above seven thousand crowns, to her own library (104). It is probable, that no private one in the kingdom, at that period, could compare in

Library of Strozzi.

(101) Chron. Nov. vol. i. p. 16 and 17.
(102) Brant. vol. i. Cap. Fran. p. 241 and 242.
(103) Chron. Nov. vol. i. p. 132.
(104) Brant. vol. ii. Cap. Etran. p. 263.

beauty,

beauty, or magnificence, with Strozzi's, who was of Florentine extraction, and had bought the library of cardinal Rodolfo at Rome, a prelate eminent for his taste and erudition (105). The great chancellor, l'Hopital, in 1573, only estimates his books, exclusive of memoirs, antiquities, and medals, at the sum of five hundred livres, or little more than twenty pounds; and he expresses great anxiety in his will, that they may suffer no diminution (106).

And of l'Hopital.

State of the drama.

The drama may be said to have been still in its infancy, during the whole period under our review. It was not till after the accession of Henry the Second, that any dramatic exhibition was performed in France. Only mysteries, and a sort of holy pageants or representations, were known under Francis the First, although Leo the Tenth had introduced them in Italy, before the year 1520. The cardinal of Ferrara, archbishop of Lyons, one of the most magnificent and accomplished princes of the age, first presented to the French court, the spectacle of a tragi-comedy, in 1549, at Lyons. The performers, male and female, were brought by him, at a great expence, from Italy; and the piece was represented in the language of that country, with so much grace and spirit, accompanied with interludes, that the king, queen, and spectators, expressed the utmost delight at the entertainment. It was said to have cost the cardinal five thousand crowns (107).

Tragi-comedy. Its introduction into France.

St. Gelais.

St. Gelais, a French poet, having translated the "Sophonisba," of Trissino, and ornamented or altered it in such a manner, as to accommodate it to the taste of his own country; it was performed by order of Catherine of Medicis, at Blois, soon after the commencement of Charles the Ninth's

(105) Brant. vol. ii. Cap. Etran. p. 263.
(106) Le Lab. sur Cast. vol. i. p. 492.
(107) Brant. vol. ii. Cap. Fran. p. 20—22.

CHAP. IV.

reign (108). We find, that in 1564, a comedy, the subject of which was borrowed from Ariosto, was represented by her command, at Fontainbleau; and that the duchess of Angouléme, natural daughter of Henry the Second, together with the principal ladies of the court, filled the parts (109). In 1571, at the festival of Nogent le Roi, where every species of diversion was exhibited, and where Charles the Ninth was present, it is expressly stated that a comedy was played by the king's comedians (110).

Dramatic amusements of the Hugonots.

A circumstance which may appear more singular, is, that the Hugonots, during the fury of the civil wars, had dramatic amusements. They were calculated to awaken, and to sustain religious enthusiasm. The duchess of Rohan composed a tragedy, called "Holophernes," drawn from the history of Judith, contained in the apocryphal writings of Scripture; and which was represented at Rochelle (111).

Comedies.

In 1569, comedies were played at Niort in Poitou, while the Protestant armies assembled; and it may be doubted, whether the loss of the battle of Jarnac ought not, in some measure, to be attributed to the negligence of the prince of Condé and the other commanders, who permitted the royal forces to collect in their neighbourhood, while they were engrossed by theatrical entertainments. Such, at least, was the opinion of the king of Navarre (112).

Indecency of the theatrical representations.

That the pieces represented before the court of France, were of a nature much too indecent to be exhibited before any modern audience, cannot be doubted, if we peruse the specimen given us by Brantome, of one which was

(108) Trad. de l'Hop. vol. ii. Recherches, p. 51. Brant. ibid.
(109) Ibid. p. 56.
(110) Manuscript de Bethune, N°. 8722, cited in the Trad. de l'Hop. vol. ii. p. 81.
(111) Trad. de l'Hop. vol. ii. Recherches, p. 23.
(112) Chron. Nov. vol. i. p. 250.

acted by order of Catherine of Medicis, and which was composed by Cornelio Fiasco, a captain of a galley. It was, indeed, in Italian; but, that language was perfectly familiar to the audience. The comedies of Mrs. Behn, under Charles the Second, are the only productions which can convey an adequate idea of Fiasco's composition (113). Political transactions were, likewise, frequently brought on the stage, under the disguise of pantomime, and presented with little refinement of conception or action. In 1579, upon the reconciliation of the Walloon provinces of Flanders with Philip the Second, that event was grossly figured, by the emblematical appearance of a cow, in one of the comic entertainments, exhibited at Paris. The king of Spain conducted the animal by a very slight string, which, as often as it broke, was mended by the prince of Parma. Elizabeth, queen of England, the duke of Anjou, the prince of Orange, and many other personages, approached, with design to liberate the cow: but, she rudely repulsed them, and, after many gambols, quietly delivered herself up to the Spanish monarch (114). The application was obvious, and the piece met with great applause.

Pantomimes.

Notwithstanding the favorable reception given to dramatic compositions, the predominant taste of the age was not directed towards the theatre. The national enthusiasm was awakened and concentered in the study of romances; and it is not easy to conceive the passionate admiration with which that species of writing was received. To the heated and eccentric imaginations of the Spaniards, was due the famous romance of "Amadis," which soon afterwards appeared in French, dedicated to Francis

Romances.

Amadis.

(113) Brantome, vol. ii. Dames Gal. p. 328.
(114) Strada, de Bello Belg. vol. iii. p. 93 and 94.

the

CHAP. IV.

the First (115). Its vogue continued unabated, during that, and the succeeding reign. When we reflect, that these unnatural productions were filled with passionate declarations of love, with magicians, warriors, enchantments, battles, and marvellous adventures of a thousand kinds; we shall not wonder at the fondness manifested for them by the French. All the predominant vices, or follies of the times, were artfully flattered in the romance of "Amadis of Gaul." Judicial combats, duels, amours, and magic, constituted the pursuits of the courtiers; who saw themselves agreeably reflected in the most polished, and flattering mirror. La Noue attributes to the rage for romances, many of the crimes and impieties, which distinguished the two last reigns of the princes of Valois (116).

Nature of those productions.

Education.

The difference in the education of youth under Francis the First and Henry the Third, may likewise, account, in a considerable degree, for the augmenting depravity of manners between those periods. We may judge of the severity and simplicity of the former, by the curious relation which De Mesmes has left us in the discourse upon his own life; where we see the exact detail of the studies of the young men of condition in 1545. "I was sent," says he, "in that year, to Toulouse, "being fourteen years of age, to study the laws, "with my preceptor and my brother, under the "superintendance of an antient gentleman, grey-"headed, and who had long wandered through the "world. We were, for three years, auditors; lead-"ing a much stricter life, and studying more se-"verely, than persons of the present time would "support. We rose at four o'clock in the morn-"ing; and having addressed our prayers to God,

Mode of education under Francis the First.

(115) Trad. de l'Hop. vol. ii. Recher. p. 24. La Noue, p. 134.
(116) La Noue, sixieme Disc. p. 133—146.

" began our ſtudies at five; our great books under " our arms, our ink-ſtands and candleſticks in our " hands. We liſtened to all the lectures till ten " o'clock, without intermiſſion; and then dined, " after having in haſte run over for half an hour, " the ſubſtance of the lectures, which we had taken " down in writing. After dinner, as a matter of " amuſement, we read Sophocles, or Ariſtophanes, " or Euripides; and ſometimes, Demoſthenes, " Cicero, Virgil, and Horace. At one o'clock, to " our ſtudies again: at five, home, to repeat, and " look out in our books, for the paſſages cited, till " after ſix. Then we ſupped, and read in Greek, " or Latin. On holy-days, we went to high maſs " and veſpers: during the remainder of the day, a " little muſic and walking (117)." But, the ſtrictneſs of the ſcholaſtic and collegiate diſcipline had diſappeared, with many other of the characteriſtic virtues of the age of Francis the Firſt, after the commencement of the civil wars. Profligacy, corruption, and debauchery, infected the aſylums of learning, and rendered the youth indolent or diſſolute (118). Maſters, or preceptors of ability, became rare. Almoſt all thoſe who excelled in teaching bodily exerciſes, were procured from Italy (119). Numbers of young men of family, from theſe cauſes, were annually ſent into foreign countries, as affording ſuperior advantages and facilities of improvement. Between three and four hundred youths were ſuppoſed to quit France every year, to receive their education abroad; of whom more than half periſhed by diſeaſes, or in duels (120). The moſt celebrated ſeminary of the kingdom, was the

Change under Henry the Third.

College of Navarre.

(117) Diſcours d'Henry de Meſmes, preſerved in Le Lab. ſur Caſt. vol. ii. p. 775.

(118) D'Aub. Memoires, p. 11 and 12. La Noue, cinq. Diſc. p. 119, and p. 122, and 125.

(119) La Noue, p. 129. (120) Ibid. p. 126.

CHAP. IV.

the college of Navarre at Paris, during the greater part of the fixteenth century. Henry the Third, Henry the Fourth, the duke of Mayenne, his brother, the cardinal of Guife, and almoft all the children of the higheft quality, received the firft rudiments of polite knowledge and letters, at that fchool (121).

College of Guienne.

The youth of the fouthern provinces were chiefly educated in the college of Guienne, at Bourdeaux, of which Montaigne fpeaks as the moft frequented, and beft regulated in France. Goveanus, the principal, was a man of uncommon abilities and learning. He flourifhed under Francis the Firft, and his fucceffor. The tragedies of Buchanan, compofed in Latin, and juftly regarded as productions of tafte and genius, were frequently performed by the ftudents. Montaigne tells us, that he had himfelf filled many characters. We may fee in his beautiful and mafterly effay, "de l'Inftitution des Enfans," addreffed to Diana of Foix; the nature, genius, and mode, as well as all the characteriftic vices and defects, of the fyftem of education in the fixteenth century. There is not any effay of that amufing and philofophic writer, which conveys a higher idea of the enlargement of his mind, his knowledge of man, and his fuperiority to the prejudices and errors of the age in which he lived (122).

Effect of the civil wars, on learning and the arts.

It may, however, be confidently afferted, that the civil wars, which defolated the kingdom for above thirty years, were not more injurious to the morals and general felicity of the people, than to learning, and the progrefs of the arts. The corrupt manners of Catherine of Medicis; the perfecutions

(121) Brantome, vol. iii. Cap. Fran. p. 129. Vie de Marg. de Val. p. 6 and 36.

(122) Effays de Montaigne, vol. i. p. 204—262, chap. xxv.

and

and maſſacres, cauſed by the antipathy of the two religions; and the ferocity produced by ſcenes of anarchy and bloodſhed; checked the growth of literature, debaſed the taſte of the nation, and plunged the country anew into barbariſm. From the æra of Henry the Second's death, in 1559, to the peace of Vervins, in 1589, France cannot be ſaid to have enjoyed any permanent tranquillity. During ſeveral years of that period, the monarchy itſelf ſeemed to be menaced with diſſolution. Far from wondering that ſcience was not more diffuſed, it may rather excite aſtoniſhment, that in a time ſo calamitous, we are yet preſented with many ſhining models of genius, in almoſt every branch of literature.

CHAP. V.

State of ſociety and manners.—Picture of the court, under Francis the Firſt.—Decline of its ſplendor, under the laſt princes of Valois.—Orders of knighthood.—Inſtitution of the order of the Holy Ghoſt.—Officers, and ceremonial of the court.—Palaces.—Caſtles of the nobility.—Dreſs.—Luxury of the table.—Furniture.—Carriages.—Litters.—Horſes.—Pages.—Lacqueys.—Buffoons.

CHAP. V.

State of ſociety and manners.

AFTER having conſidered the French people under ſo many different aſpects, it is ſtill indiſpenſable, in order to complete the picture, that we take a ſurvey of the national manners. Man, in a ſtate of ſociety, is more forcibly diſtinguiſhed and characterized by the modes, uſages, and cuſtoms univerſally received, than by any civil or political regulations. To the former, his ſubmiſſion is voluntary: to the latter, it is conſtrained and compulſory. The features of the nation, during the period under our immediate review, were uncommonly bold and prominent. A long period of inteſtine diſſenſion, approaching to anarchy, had liberated the ſubject from all reſtraint; and let looſe thoſe deſtructive paſſions, which, under a well-ordered government, are repreſſed by the vigilance of the magiſtrate, and the terror of puniſhment. The royal authority was become contemptible; the laws were deſtitute of vigor; and the facility of committing crimes was equalled by their impunity. All the majeſty which ſurrounded the throne under Francis the Firſt, and Henry the Second, had gradually

General diſſolution of manners.

dually disappeared under the three succeeding princes; and while luxury diffused itself among the inferior orders, the splendor of the sovereign diminished.

CHAP. V.

Court of France, under Francis the First,

The French court, before the death of Louis the Twelfth, in 1515, was like the nation itself, rude and unpolished. It was his successor, the young count of Angouleme, become king by the title of Francis the First, who introduced into it a magnificence, previously unknown in Europe. Ladies, released from the dungeons or castles, in which their husbands and fathers immured them from the world: prelates, liberated from the superintendance of their dioceses: men of letters, magistrates, and a vast train of nobility and gentry, crouded to pay their homage to a prince, who was so well able to appreciate, and to cherish or recompence, every species of merit (1). Manners may be said to have gained as much by the change, as morals were perverted and corrupted. The king himself, while he protected letters, and revived the arts, gave a mortal wound to the chastity, fidelity, and virtue of the female sex: his son, Henry the Second, imitated the example. But, those monarchs, respected by their subjects, and undisturbed, in a great measure, by civil commotions; maintained a becoming dignity even in their vices, and were careful to veil from popular inspection, the pleasures or debaucheries of the palace. Their successors, inexperienced, oppressed by misfortunes, plundered of their revenues, compelled to purchase loyalty and obedience, or prodigal of their treasures, were no longer able to sustain the preceding pomp and grandeur of the crown. At the close of Henry the Third's reign, scarcely any traces of the magnificence of his grandfather's court were to be discovered; and the uni-

and Henry the Second.

Change, under the last princes of Valois.

(1) Brantome, vol. i. Cap. Fran. p. 281.

versal

CHAP. V.

versal disorder of the times, levelled, in a considerable degree, the external distinction between the monarch and the subject.

We may judge how gross were the manners of the fifteenth century, when we know, that the kings of France admitted in their train a certain number of women of pleasure, who followed the court wherever it moved. Quarters were regularly assigned to them, and justice was administered by an officer, exclusively appointed to that employment (2). Women of honor and quality were unknown about the persons and residence of Charles the Seventh, and Louis the Eleventh. Anne of Bretagne began to assemble a select band of ladies, whom she retained near her, and whose conduct she vigilantly superintended: but, that assembly of persons of both sexes, held in the presence of the sovereign, and denominated in modern language, a drawing-room, originated with Francis the First. Every species of luxury in dress, tables, and furniture, soon followed. It may excite some surprize to find, that on occasion of marriages, Francis was accustomed to present dresses to the favorite ladies of his court, the materials of which were of the most costly kind (3). But, in no article was so much expence incurred, and such magnificence displayed, as in the provision made for the royal household. Not only the table of the sovereign, but, those of all the greater and lesser officers of state, who were extremely numerous, were served with the utmost profusion and delicacy. Nor was it confined to the residence of the court, when stationary in the capital. Wherever Francis moved, even in the midst of woods, or in villages, the same plenty was visible (4). The strongest testimony to the splendid hospitality of

Introduction of ladies.

Magnificence.

Hospitality.

(2) Brantome, vol. i. Cap. Fran. p. 282 and 283.
(3) Ibid. p. 270. (4) Ibid. p. 271 and 272.

that

that monarch, was borne by the emperor Charles the Fifth himſelf, during his viſit, in 1539. Having heard from the duke of Alva, how well the conſtable Montmorenci's table was covered, he determined to ſatisfy himſelf of the truth of the report. Diſappearing, therefore, unexpectedly, at the hour of dinner, he placed himſelf uninvited, as a gueſt, at the conſtable's ſide. His amazement was extreme, at finding the fact exceed the account which he had received (5).

Splendor of the court, under Francis the Firſt.

Beſides the immediate officers of the houſehold, the court of Francis was crouded with cardinals, biſhops, and eccleſiaſtics, who expended the revenues of their ſees, or benefices, in regaling the more needy courtiers and gentlemen. Above twenty members of the ſacred college, were frequently reſident at the ſame time, in the metropolis; and even the Roman pontiffs themſelves could rarely boaſt of ſo numerous an aſſemblage (6). Scarcely any diminution of the magnificence, or hoſpitality of the French monarchs, was viſible before the acceſſion of Charles the Ninth. Henry the Second maintained his father's inſtitutions, and ſucceeded to his propenſities. Catherine of Medicis, in every period of life, emulated the praiſe of munificence, and rendered her palace the ſcene of feſtivity, gallantry, and pleaſure (7). But, the beginning of the civil wars was the term of its real duration; and, whatever efforts might be exerted on particular occaſions, the dilapidation of the finances affixed inſurmountable obſtacles to the ſupport of the antient ſtate and majeſty of the crown. Retrenchments of every kind were made in the royal expence; and, far from being in a condition to maintain the hoſpitality or ſplendor of Francis the Firſt, it was often found dif-

Its decline, after the commencement of the civil wars.

(5) Brantome, vol. i. Cap. Fran. p. 273 and 274.
(6) Ibid. p. 286—288.
(7) Ibid. vol. ii. Cap. Fran. p. 42—50.

ficult

CHAP. V.

ficult under Charles the Ninth, and Henry the Third, to provide for the personal and most necessary expenditures of the king. Brantome draws a feeling picture of their distress, rendered, if possible, more poignant, by the comparison with preceding times (8). It attained, like every other national misfortune, to its highest point, during the reign of the last prince of the house of Valois. The garrison of Mentz, one of the most important frontier cities of the kingdom, was left for several months without pay, and was driven by necessity into a state of mutiny and revolt (9). Such was the poverty of the court in November, 1574, only three months after Henry's return to France, that, on the journey from Lyons to Avignon, the greater number of the royal pages were necessitated to leave their cloaks behind, as pledges, in order to procure bread. No salaries, or appointments, continued to be paid; and, if one of the farmers, or treasurers of the revenue, had not aided the queen-mother by a loan of about two hundred pounds, she would have remained unaccompanied by a single lady of any description (10).

Poverty under Henry the Third.

It affords, at once, a curious proof of the poverty of the crown, and of the difficulty of raising supplies, to see, that only two years afterwards, it was seriously proposed in council, by Catherine of Medicis, to apply to Muley Moluc, king of Fez, for a loan of money. If we did not know the fact from a person, who was present at its being agitated, and whose veracity is indisputable, we might justly call it in question. "On the 7th of February, 1577," says the duke of Nevers, in his Memoirs, "the "queen-mother proposed to dispatch the Abbé Gua-"dagni, to the king of Fez, to borrow two mil-"lions of gold." She likewise meant to authorize the envoy, to open a commercial treaty with Fez

(8) Brant. vol. i. Cap. Fran. p. 275 and 276.
(9) De Thou, vol. vii. p. 249.
(10) Mem. pour ser. à l'Hist. de Fra. p. 47.

and

and Morocco, which, ſhe conceived, might prove very lucrative to the Moors, and to the French. It was hoped, that he might return with a favorable anſwer from the Mahometan prince, in two months. The treaſures of that monarch were eſtimated to exceed two millions and a half, ſterling. It is hard to ſay, by what arguments he could be induced to lend any part of it to Henry the Third. So wild and chimerical a propoſition does not ſeem to have been proſecuted or adopted (11).

Army, unpaid,

In the ſame year, we find that the king was unable to pay even his embaſſador at the court of Elizabeth, queen of England; or to continue the uſual ſtipends, which he was accuſtomed to allow to various perſons, from whom he received intelligence of the motions and deſigns of that princeſs (12). The army was in the ſame predicament; and Sancy, who, in 1589, raiſed a body of Switzers, was reduced, after mortgaging the moſt valuable diamonds of the crown, to pledge his own patrimonial eſtates and property, for their ſupport (13). Without the pecuniary aſſiſtance of Ferdinand, great duke of Tuſcany, and of the canton of Bern, the troops could neither have been ſubſiſted, nor induced to march into France. The guards themſelves were left unpaid; and the archers who protected the perſon of Henry at Blois, applied to the duke of Guiſe, on the morning of his aſſaſſination, imploring him to intereſt himſelf in their behalf, as they muſt otherwiſe be neceſſitated to ſell their horſes, and return to their reſpective houſes (14). Similar diſtreſs had manifeſted itſelf, in the houſehold and troops of the duke of Anjou. In 1582, the unfortunate

and the guards.

(11) Memoires de Nevers, vol. i. p. 171.

(12) Letters 71 and 72, in Le Lab. ſur Caſt. vol. iii. p. 508—510. Lettres de Foix, p. 258.

(13) De Thou, vol. x. p. 647.

(14) Chron. Nov. vol. i. p. 106.

CHAP. V.

soldiers who had followed that prince's fortune into Flanders, were abandoned to such penury, as to solicit alms for their subsistence (15).

Institution of the order of the Holy Ghost.

In the midst of these accumulated and humiliating extremities, Henry the Third, whose passion for expence and ceremonies could not be controlled by any reflexions on his situation, instituted the order of knighthood of the Holy Ghost. It was designed to replace that of St. Michael, created by Louis the Eleventh, and which had been prostituted during the civil wars, in a manner that rendered it contemptible (16). The institutions of chivalry may be said to have expired, in a great measure, with Henry the Second. He was the last French monarch who received from the hands of a subject, the military honor of knighthood. Marshal Biez conferred it on him; as the chevalier Bayard had done upon Francis the First, before the battle of Marignan (17). We may judge how low the order of St. Michael was sunk in the general estimation, by the terms in which it is mentioned by the Viscount de Tavannes. "I have always disdained it," says he, "and repeatedly declined to accept it. In my own "company, I have often had three knights of the "order; and in my father, marshal Tavannes' "coffers, I found half a dozen blank patents, to be "given to whomsoever I should please (18)." Many persons, after having received it, laid it by, and concealed the honor. "Above a hundred gentlemen," says La Noue, "finding the expence and "stile of living inseparable from the distinction, "not only inconvenient, but ruinous, have chosen "to lock up the insignia of so pernicious a digni-"ty (19)." It was distributed to such numbers, as

State of the order of St. Michael.

Its degradation.

(15) De Thou, vol. viii. p. 645.
(16) Ibid. vol. viii. p. 73.
(17) Brantome, Les Duels, p. 304.
(18) Tavannes, p. 179.
(19) La Noue, p. 169.

to

to be denominated in derision, "Le Collier à toutes "Bêtes (20)."

Motives for the creation of the order of the Holy Ghost.

Conscious of this degradation, Henry the Third instituted the order of the Holy Ghost, on the last day of December, 1578. It was composed of only one hundred knights, at its commencement; and the king meant to have conferred on each of them four hundred crowns annual pension, taken from the revenues of the richest abbeys of his dominions. But, as the Papal consent was requisite, in order to make so material an invasion of the ecclesiastical property; as the clergy opposed it at Rome, the intention remained incomplete (21). Another object, proposed by its founder, was to attach the members of the new order, more strictly to himself; and to form, by its means, a counterpoise to the strength of the adherents of the League. But, he soon discovered how frail was the obligation of oaths, when counteracted by ambition. The order of the Holy Ghost was not long confined to the original number of a hundred. It was conferred indiscriminately, and incurred the same reproaches and contempt, which had been lavished on that of St. Michael (22).

Its prostitution.

Multiplication of offices and dignities.

A similar increase and prostitution of all the dignities or honors of the crown, characterised the reign of Henry the Third. Gentlemen of the bedchamber, esquires, and colonels, were augmented in a proportion with the other attendants of the court (23). "Monsieur d'Esse," says Brantome, "was made for his services in defending Landrecy "against the emperor, a gentleman of the bed-"chamber to Henry the Second, which was then a "great and honorable employment. They served

(20) Mem. pour ser. à l'Hist. de Fra. p. 103. Le Lab. sur Cast. vol. i. p. 356.

(21) De Thou, vol. viii. p. 73 and 74. Tavannes, ibid.

(22) Brant. Les Duels, p. 290.

(23) La Noue, p. 169.

CHAP. V.

" only ſix months, and received twelve hundred " livres, or about fifty pounds, of ſalary (24)." Under his ſons, the title was multiplied, and the appointments were withheld.

Houſehold of the duke of Anjou.

The eſtabliſhment of the duke of Anjou's houſehold, in 1576, of which a moſt accurate account is preſerved in the duke of Nevers' Memoirs, ſeems to have been more ſplendid and expenſive, if the comparative value of money be conſidered, than that of any prince of the family of Bourbon, before the late revolution of 1789. The aggregate amount of the appointments to all the officers and attendants, is no leſs than two hundred and ſixty-three thouſand, ſeven hundred and ten livres, annually (25). It is difficult to eſtimate the relative value of that ſum, at the diſtance of more than two centuries, in Engliſh money; but, perhaps, we ſhall not rate it too high, when we ſuppoſe that it was, in fact, equal to ninety thouſand pounds ſterling, at this time. It is extremely curious, and conveys a high idea of the magnificence of princes in that age, to ſurvey the number of offices, and ſalaries reſpectively annexed to each. Much of the genius and temper of the times, may be traced or diſcovered in them. The duke had no leſs than one hundred and ſix chamberlains, at ſix hundred livres, or about twenty-five pounds each; beſides one hundred and forty-eight gentlemen of the bed-chamber, whoſe ſalaries varied, from two hundred, to five hundred livres. There are fifteen almoners, ſeven chaplains, as many clerks of the chapel, and one preacher. Their appointments, in general, do not exceed two, to three hundred livres; and ſome are as a hundred ſous, or fifty pence. To the office of ſuperintendant of the houſehold, four thouſand livres, or, near a

(24) Brantome, vol. ii. Cap. Fran. p. 180.
(25) About eleven thouſand pounds.

hundred

hundred and eighty pounds, are annexed. The duke has ſixteen phyſicians, whoſe ſalaries gradually diminiſh, from ſix hundred, down to ten livres. The ſurgeons are eleven in number, and their appointments are exactly ſimilar, being, each, a hundred and eighty livres. There is only one apothecary, with four hundred livres ſalary. He has forty-ſix valets de chambre, and forty-one valets of the wardrobe, whoſe ſalaries are, in general, about two hundred livres. The firſt valet has eight hundred. It is amuſing to ſee, that he has five barbers, who receive the ſame pay as the ſurgeons, except the firſt, who is termed barber in ordinary, and has three hundred livres. Paré, in all his writings, ſeems to conſider the phyſicians, ſurgeons, and barbers, as exerciſing different branches of the ſame profeſſion of healing. He couples them together, and regards them as diſciples, or followers of one common maſter, Eſculapius (25). There are among the inferior officers, four tapeſtry hangers, and two helpers: clockmakers, embroiderers, and mercers. The council is very numerous; but, the office ſeems to have been little more than honorary and titular: the emolument is ſmall. To the chancellor, four thouſand livres. There are one hundred and eleven ſecretaries; and the laſt name in the liſt, is the duke's nurſe, with a ſalary of about eighteen pounds (26).

However ſplendid this eſtabliſhment appears on paper, it was far otherwiſe in reality. The duke, in his laſt will, dated the 8th of June, 1584, at Chateau Thierry in Champagne, owns with concern and expreſſions of the deepeſt diſtreſs, that the greater part of his officers and ſervants were unpaid. He pathetically and earneſtly recommends them to

(25) Œuvres de Paré, p. 568.
(26) Memoires de Nevers, vol. i. p. 577—599.

 the

CHAP. V.

the king, his brother's pity, or bounty; and declares, that he is, besides, indebted to various individuals, not less than one hundred and fifty thousand crowns (27).

Creation of a colonel-general of the infantry.

A creation which excited universal clamour, and which exposed to general censure, the unbounded partiality of Henry the Third towards Epernon, was the office of colonel-general of France. Henry, unable to induce the duke of Guise to lay down or to sell, on any conditions, his post of lord-steward of the household, erected a new charge for his favorite. The employment of colonel-general of the infantry, was declared to be henceforward an office, not of the king, but, of the crown of France. Prerogatives, little short of royal, were annexed to it: the power of filling up, and of naming to all vacant commissions in the infantry, without reserve, was added to the right of judging definitively, all causes which respected the life or honor of the troops, before a tribunal, composed of his own officers, in which he presided (28). It may be justly questioned, whether powers so vast were ever entrusted to any subject; and they degraded the sovereign who conferred them, in the same proportion that they elevated the object of his favor. In 1586, the post of grand-master of the ceremonies, unknown before that period, was instituted by the same prince (29). About two years earlier, he had the weakness, in consequence of a conversation which he had with the English embassadress at Paris, to issue a regulation respecting the ceremonial of the court. The forms, observed in approaching, and serving Elizabeth, queen of England, and her predecessors, in the sixteenth century, were more

Ceremonial of the court.

(27) Mem. de Nevers, vol. i. p. 601—603.
(28) Vie d'Epernon, vol. i. p. 100—102. De Thou, vol. ix. p. 202.
(29) L'Art de Verif. vol. i. p. 659.

pompous

pompous and befitting an arbitrary monarch, than those used in France. Henry, anxious to imitate, or exceed the English princess, in exacting marks of submission from his courtiers and ministers, published an injunction, specifying in the most minute detail, the hours, dress, and formalities, indispensable for all who wished to obtain audience, or to transact business (30). They were received with disdain, by the nation; and only served to render more contemptible a sovereign, who, while he was occupied with empty ceremonies, had squandered the revenues, diminished the power, and degraded the majesty of the throne. At the close of the reign of Francis the First, there were no peers in the kingdom, except the princes of the royal blood, and the collateral descendants of some sovereign houses, who were settled in France. The titles of duke, count, and marquis, were the only simple gradations and ranks of nobility. The first subject ever raised to the peerage, was the constable Montmorenci, by Henry the Second. Under Charles the Ninth, it became more common; and his brother, when he elevated to that dignity, his two minions, Joyeuse and Epernon, gave them precedence above every other gentleman, though of prior creation (31).

Creation of peers.

With Francis the First, magnificence and convenience in the style of constructing houses of every description, began to be known among the French. The castles of Plessiz les Tours, Amboise, and Blois, in which resided principally his immediate predecessors, were insulated, and almost inaccessible fastnesses, overhanging the Loire, and more calculated for defence against enemies, than becoming the majesty of a great monarch. Chambord and Fontainbleau were the first palaces, properly so denominated,

Constructi-on, and mode of building.

Improve-ments, in-troduced by Francis the First.

(30) De Thou, vol. ix. p. 202 and 203.

(31) Memoire au Depôt de Bethune, cited in the Trad. de l'Hop. vol. ii. Recherches, p. 94.

CHAP. V.

minated, that Europe had beheld beyond the Alps since the destruction of the Roman empire (32). Neither strength, nor safety, constituted their characteristic: they retained, indeed, the moat, and the castellated appearance, more in compliance with the established mode, than from any other cause. Pavillions, groves, statues, and all the ornaments of a softened and cultivated taste, were to be found in the residence of Francis. The example spread with rapidity, among the nobility. Ecouen, and Chantilly, constructed by the constable Montmorenci, were palaces of pleasure, and not fortresses, though they still presented a frowning, and embattled mien. The antient dungeons and turrets, in which the gentlemen and barons had immured themselves for so many ages, began to be re edified on the principles of a more splendid, or convenient architecture (33).

Elegance of palaces.

We may judge, from the description of Meudon, and of St. Maur des Fossés, (the villas of the cardinals of Lorrain, and of du Bellai,) which are to be found in the epistles of l'Hopital, how great a progress the art of embellishing a seat, had already made, before 1550. Plantations, grottos, terraces, and gardens, adorned with antique busts and statues from Rome, were to be found in the voluptuous retreats of those prelates (34).

Castles of the nobility.

It is not, however, by any means, to be understood, that the nobility in general, resembled them; or that the castles, in the most literal acceptation of the term, ceased to be maintained and inhabited by the gentry. For a long time subsequent to the period under our examination, the draw-bridges were regularly raised every evening, and only lowered in the morning, to receive the necessary supplies of provisions, brought by the peasants for sale. It was requisite to besiege a

(32) Brantome, vol. ii. Cap. Fran. p. 277—279.
(33) La Noue, p. 164—167.
(34) Trad. de l'Hopital, vol. i. p. 17—19, and 83—85.

refractory,

refractory, or rebellious gentleman, who from the battlements of his castle, bid defiance to the sovereign himself, and often maintained an obstinate conflict against the forces of the crown (35). Henry the Third was so convinced of the magnitude of the evil, and so desirous of stopping, or controlling its further progress, that, in 1579, he expressly enjoined the commissioners, who were sent to enquire into abuses, throughout the provinces, to render it an object of their peculiar attention. "You will make diligent search," says he, "after those "who have fortified, or may "hereafter fortify, "their houses with ditches, towers, bastions, or other "works, without having obtained our permission, or, "that of our predecessors (36)." How numerous were these castles, and embattled, or castellated houses, we may judge, when we find, that in 1588, the duke of Nevers, who commanded the royal forces, made himself master of thirty-six, only in Lower Poitou, and within the space of a few weeks (37). They were the receptacles and asylums of petty despots, who insulted the crown, and who plundered the miserable peasants of the neighbouring country.

CHAP. V.

Dress.

Splendor of it.

Dress is, perhaps, the strongest and most interesting feature, by which national manners are characterised. It was carried, like every other article of expence or taste, to a pitch of almost unlimited extravagance, under Henry the Third. The rapidity and fluctuation of fashion, kept pace with the costliness of the materials. Such was the general demand for gold and silver stuffs, or brocades, that the effect was sensibly felt, by the diminution of the quantity of specie throughout the kingdom (38). In 1571, at the entertainment of Nogent, in honor of the

(35) Le Lab. sur. Cast. vol. ii. p. 601.
(36) Memoires de Nevers, vol. i. p. 607.
(37) Ibid. p. 875 and 877.
(38) L'Art de Verif. vol. i. p. 659.

duchess

CHAP. V.

duchefs of Bouillon, the king, Charles the Ninth, his two brothers, and the duke of Lorrain, were all dreffed in the fame manner. Their habits were of filver ftuff, with an embroidery of pearls, and edged with gold (39). "Formerly," fays la Noue, "it was "ufual to wear the fame drefs, for a confiderable "time; but, at prefent, we may pronounce, that, "among the courtiers, their ordinary duration does "not exceed three months, for a common fuit; for "a more expenfive one, fix months: and among "the other nobility, fomewhat longer (40)." "Such has been the depravity of the age," adds he in another place, "that our pages and lacqueys have "been habited in filver ftuffs (41)." All diftinctive marks, by which the different orders of fociety might be diftinguifhed, feem, in a great meafure, to have been broken down under Henry the Third. "A cobler," fays la Noue, "who has followed "arms for a couple of years, will wear a gilt fword, "which our anceftors would fcruple to have "done, unlefs they had received the honor of "knighthood: he will put on filk ftockings; a "piece of elegance which Henry the Second never "knew during his whole life (42)." It is hardly poffible to mark the progrefs of luxury, in more expreffive terms. At the nuptials of Joyeufe, in 1581, when the feftivities and entertainments lafted feventeen days, and at which the dreffes were expenfive and fpendid beyond defcription; all the noblemen and ladies who were invited, changed their drefs every day, by the king's exprefs command (43).

Rapidity of fafhion.

Progrefs of luxury.

The hat, and turban.

The hat, decorated with feathers, and precious ftones, worn by Francis the Firft, was converted into

(39) Manufc. de Bethune, in the Trad. de l'Hop. vol. ii. Recherches, p. 81.
(40) La Noue, p. 163. (41) Ibid. p. 162. (42) Ibid. p. 194.
(43) L'Etoile, p. 45.

a bonnet,

a bonnet, or cap, by Henry the Second, and his two fucceffors. Henry the Third fubftituted in its place, the Italian "toque," or turban; not only as a more effeminate ornament, but, in the view of more effectually concealing his want of hair (44). It was compofed of velvet, adorned with jewels, and faftened or bound over one ear, leaving the other expofed, in which was hung a pearl, or diamond (45). When Sully was fent by the king of Navarre, in 1587, to treat with that infatuated and diffolute prince, he was prefented by Villeroy to him, at St. Maur, near Paris. "I found him," fays Sully, "in his clofet, a fword by his fide, a fhort "cloak on his fhoulders, his little turban on his "head; and about his neck, in form of a fcarf, "was hung a bafket, fuch as the venders of cheefe "ufe, in which there were two or three little "dogs, not larger than my fift (46)." It may be curious to oppofe to this portrait of Henry the Third, the defcription left us by a writer of equal veracity, of the king of Navarre, as he appeared at the memorable interview of Pleffiz les Tours, in April, 1589. It ftands fingularly contrafted with the preceding picture. "He paffed the river Loire," fays Cayet, "at the head of his guards. Of the whole "troop, not one, except himfelf, had either a cloak, "or a plume. All wore white fcarfs. The king "was clothed like a foldier; his doublet, worn "away over the fhoulders, and on the fides, with "the perpetual ufe of a cuirafs. His loofe breeches "were of fillamot velvet; his cloak, fcarlet. He "had on a grey hat, ornamented with a large white "plume, and a very handfome medal (47)."

Drefs of Henry the Third,

and of the king of Navarre.

(44) Mem. pour fer. à l'Hift. de Fra. p. 272.
(45) L'Art de Verif. vol. i. p. 659.
(46) Sully, vol. i. p. 48.
(47) Chron. Noven. vol. i. p. 185.

During

CHAP. V.

Ruffs.

During the reigns of Francis the Second and Charles the Ninth, ruffs, curiously plaited, were universally fashionable. Every gentleman wore them; and the men of dress took great pains, and passed much time, in adjusting them with elegance. "After the action near Perigueux, in 1568, where "the Hugonots were defeated," says Brantome, "the body of their leader, Pierregourde, was dis-"covered: he had on a clean white shirt; but, "above all, a very handsome ruff, most delicately "crimped and plaited, as they were then worn (48)." Soon after the accession, in 1575, Henry the Third quitted the mode, of which he had previously been extravagantly fond; and adopted the little Italian bands, or collars, turned down on the neck (49).

Bands.

Ear-rings.

How general was the use of ear-rings among the men, we may collect from d'Aubigné; who says, that when the Hugonots, in 1568, made a collection for paying the German auxiliary army, the pages and lacqueys tore their pendants out of their ears, in their anxiety to contribute towards the general supply (50). Henry the Third usually wore ear-rings; and among the many marks of indecent and unmanly fondness, with which he bewailed the death of Quelus, one of his minions, killed in a duel; he took out of that favourite's ears, the pendants, which he had previously fixed in them with his own hands (51).

Gold chains.

Gold chains were rather an honorary mark of distinction, than an ordinary appendage of dress. Sovereigns, and great personages, often conferred them for eminent services, or presented them to embassadors and foreign ministers. It was accounted

(48) Brant. vol. iv. Cap. Fran. p. 194.
(49) Mem. pour ser. à l'Hist. de Fra. p. 59.
(50) D'Aub. Hist. Gen. vol. i. p. 228.
(51) Mem. pour ser. à l'Hist. de Fra. p. 92. Mem. de Nevers, vol. i. p. 171.

a display

CHAP. V.

a display of magnificence in the famous constable of Bourbon, which excited the envy of Francis the First; that, at the ceremony of his son's baptism, to which the king was invited, he had five hundred gentlemen, his retainers, present, every one of whom wore a triple chain of gold round his neck (52). The Swiss deputies, twenty-six in number, who came to Paris in 1583, to renew the treaty with the crown of France, received from Henry the Third, before their departure, each a gold collar, valued at two hundred and fifty crowns (53). In 1568, Louis, prince of Condé, charmed with the valor of Schomberg, who had attacked and dislodged some of the Italian soldiery in the service of Charles the Ninth; and unable otherwise to express his sense of the courage displayed in the enterprize, put round the neck of Schomberg, at the head of the army, a gold chain worth a hundred crowns (54). That so honorable a testimony of merit, or mark of eminence, was sometimes prostituted and degraded by conferring it on improper subjects, is evident. We find Henry the Second, at the peace of Cateau, in 1559, presenting to the buffoon of Philip the Second, a chain of gold of considerable value (55).

Honorary marks.

In a court so voluptuous, as that of Catherine of Medicis, where pleasure was usually rendered the veil or vehicle of policy, it may be naturally supposed, that all the arts of luxury and elegance had made a progress not less universal, among the female sex, than in the other. Marriage portions, before the extinction of the family of Valois, were already increased, among the opulent part of the inhabitants of Paris, to such a point, that a young woman was

Arts of luxury.

(52) Brant. vol. i. Cap. Etran. p. 245.
(53) Busbeq. letter 12, p. 74.
(54) D'Aub. Hist. Univ. vol. i. p. 228 and 229.
(55) Brant. vol. ii. Cap. Etran. p. 293.

not

CHAP. V.

not esteemed an object of interested attention, unless she possessed at least from four to five hundred pounds sterling in ready money, and full twenty pounds of annual rent. This fact would appear incredible, or, at least, exaggerated, if it was not asserted as notorious and incontrovertible, by a contemporary author of credit (56). We may trace in Brantome, who had passed his life in the court of the three last princes of Valois, the gradual refinement, expence, and profusion of ornament, by which the ladies were distinguished. Margaret, queen of Navarre, a princess eminent for the beauty of her person, as much as for the depravity and libertinism of her manners, influenced greatly, by her example, the dress and modes of the period.

Female ornaments.

We find her attired or decorated with almost all the attributes and accompaniments of modern coquetry. False hair, masks, paint, both red and white; fans, black velvet shoes, white slippers pointed at the toe, hair powder, feathers, crape, white silk stockings, ear-rings, pearls, tooth powder, and a variety of subservient articles, composing her toilet, leave us no room to doubt the magnificence of her appearance (57). Many of these had been recently introduced into France, from Venice and other cities of Italy.

Modes.

As early as 1574, we find the earl of Leicester, who well knew all the foibles and weaknesses of his royal mistress, dispatching a gentleman of his household to Paris, to bring over false hair and edgings of the newest fashion, for Elizabeth (58). That

(56) Satyre Menip. vol. iii. p. 198, 199.

(57) Œuvres de St. Gelais, p. 108. Brant. vol. i. Dames Gal. p. 380—389, and 396—399; and vol. ii. Dames Gal. p. 131 and 159. Vie de Marg. de Val. p. 236, 243, and 284. Le Lab. sur Cast. vol. iii. p. 407. Œuvres de Ronsard, tom. viii. liv. i. p. 10, 11. Œuvres de Paré, p. 739—741.

(58) Le Lab. sur Cast. vol. iii. p. 407.

capital

capital began already to be regarded as the arbitress of taste and mode.

CHAP. V.

Masks.

Masks became universal among the ladies of every rank, under the reign of Charles the Ninth: they were particularly worn in travelling, in order to prevent the injuries of the air and sun (59). Margaret of Valois, on her two journeys to Spa, and to Nerac, performed in 1577, and 1583, is constantly masqued (60). When Henry, duke of Guise, arrived at Paris in 1588, a young lady, seated in a shop, in one of the principal streets through which he passed, attended by crowds of people, lowering her masque, said to him, "Good prince, since thou art here, we "are all saved (61)."

Sattins.

Sattin was principally used in the dresses of persons of quality of both sexes; or, still more frequently, velvet. Charles the Ninth, his brothers, and the king of Navarre, were all habited, at the nuptials of Margaret of Valois, in 1572, in uniforms of pale yellow sattin, covered with embroidery in relief, enriched with pearls and precious stones (62). The enormous expence of female dresses in that age, may be guessed at, when the queen of Navarre informs us, that she presented the countess of Lalain, at Mons in Hainault, with one of her gowns. "It was," says she, "of black "sattin, covered with embroidery; which had cost "from four to five hundred crowns (63)." A sum, almost incredible, if we consider the relative value of money; and much exceeding the most costly gown, worn by queens, or princesses, in the present time.

Female dress.

The petticoat was made very long, so as to conceal the feet entirely in walking; but, as a sort of com-

(59) Vie de Margue: de Val. p. 236 and 343.
(60) Mem. de Margue: p. 44 and 129.
(61) Mem. pour ser. à l'Hist. de Fra. p. 244.
(62) Vie de Marg. p. 85.
(63) Vie de Marg. p. 244. Mem. de Marg. p. 136.

pensation

CHAP. V. pensation of this mark of modesty and bashfulness, the ladies displayed their necks in an immoderate degree. To Margaret of Valois, was, likewise, due the introduction of the mode; and she continued to expose that part of her person, at a period of life when it was no longer calculated to excite admiration, in defiance of the admonitions and reprehensions, levelled at her from the pulpit (64). It excites entertainment, to know, that inventions for increasing the size of the female figure behind, as well as for augmenting it before; and both of which have been renewed in the present age; were common under the last princes of Valois. As early as 1563, treatises were written, and satires composed, on the "Basquines," and "Vertugalles;" the two articles of dress, destined to the above-mentioned purposes. They were, not without reason, considered as being subservient to, and productive of greater depravity of manners; particularly, from the concealment which they afforded to pregnancy. In 1579, under Henry the Third, the use of them was so general, that they were commonly called by the name of the part, which they covered, or protected. Ladies, before they went out, were accustomed, says a contemporary writer, to call to their maid-servant, "Apportez moi mon cul (65)."

Pattins.

With a view to increase their height, short women used a sort of pattins, composed of cork, and which, if we may judge by Brantome's account, were equally cumbrous and destitute of grace. However extraordinary it appears, he repeatedly asserts, that these pattins raised the person who wore them, near twelve inches from the ground (66). We feel no little surprize, and some degree of ridicule, at reading in

(64) Vie de Marg. p. 401.

(65) Biblioth. Exotica, p. 207. H. Etienne, Dialogues, p. 202, 203. Satyre Menip. vol. ii. p. 387, 388.

(66) Brant. vol. i. Dames Gal. p. 381, and 396—399.

so

ſo grave an author as Ambroſe Paré, at leaſt twenty different receipts, or preſcriptions, for making white paint, and rouge. The title of the chapter, in which he diſcloſes, and details the modes of painting the female face, without injury to the health, is denominated, "Des Fards, pour decorer et embellir la Face des Femmes (67)." He divides them into diſtinct ſpecies, applicable to various purpoſes; and the fineſt lady of the preſent age, might, probably, find ſome valuable hints, or make ſome important acceſſion to her knowledge on this delicate ſubject, by conſulting Paré, who wrote more than two centuries ago.

Mourning.

Mourning began already to be rendered ſuſceptible of ornament and elegance, under Henry the Third. Widows never appeared in any dreſs, except white or black. Their petticoats and ſtockings were ſcrupulouſly confined to grey, violet, and blue. Precious ſtones were only worn by them on their fingers, and on their girdles; but they might, without violation of propriety, ſubſtitute pearls on the neck and arms (68). Females of diſtinction were accuſtomed to wear pendants in their ears, made in the ſhape of human ſkulls. We find a ſonnet of Deſportes, addreſſed to Mademoiſelle de Chateauneuf, the celebrated miſtreſs of Henry the Third, on her appearing with theſe funereal ornaments (69). Small ebony, or ivory ſkulls, ſtrung as a chaplet, and hanging at their waiſts, were likewiſe commonly worn by ladies, not only, as it ſeems, for the loſs of their huſbands, but for the death of their lovers (70). The mourning of the kings of France, was always violet. In 1584, contrary to

Royal mourning.

(67) Œuvres de Paré, p. 739.
(68) Brant. vol. ii. Dames Gal. p. 131 and 132.
(69) Œuvres de Deſportes, p. 430.
(70) Brant. vol. i. p. 148.

received

CHAP. V.

received custom, Henry the Third put on black, to express his concern for the decease of his brother, the duke of Anjou (71): but, he only appeared in violet, when he accompanied the funeral procession of his mother, Catherine, four years afterwards (72). It is a circumstance not unworthy of attention, as it characterizes the age, that green was regarded as the colour for mourning for fools or lunatics. No sooner was the intelligence of Henry the Third's death, in consequence of the wound which he had received from Clement, divulged at Paris, on the second of August, 1589, than the people universally put on green, in derision. The duchess of Montpensier distributed scarfs of the same colour, to all the principal adherents of the League (73).

Funerals.

Funerals were commonly solemnized with great magnificence. We find Elizabeth, queen of England, though a Protestant, performing a service for Charles the Ninth, with the utmost pomp, in the cathedral of St. Paul, at London, in 1574. All the great nobility attended: the banner of France was displayed, and the bishop of Hereford made the funeral oration. It is to be presumed, that he took care to omit any mention of the massacre of St. Bartholomew (74).

Luxury of the table.

The luxury of the table kept pace with the elegance of dress, if it did not even exceed it, during the period before us; and it is highly probable, that the cookery of France was much more delicate than that of England, and the northern nations. We find mention made in Brantome, of many culinary articles, as common, which were certainly unknown among the English, under Elizabeth. The most exquisite sauces, meats, and vegetables, seem to

(71) Busbequius, letter 38, p. 203.
(72) Chron. Nov. vol. i. p. 124.
(73) Mem. pour ser. à l'Hist. de Fra. p. 287.
(74) De Thou, vol. vii. p. 66 and 67.

have

have been ferved at the tables of the great, in the utmoft profufion. Sallads, artichokes, afparagus, morelles, truffles, and many other delicacies, continually occur (75). The chancellor, l'Hopital, when enumerating the productions of his farm and garden, at Vignai near Eftampes, includes among them, beans, peas, and turnips (76). Orange trees had been brought from the Levant, and were fuccefsfully cultivated by the conftable of Bourbon, in his gardens at Moulins, before 1524 (77). The entertainments, and the deferts, given by the "vidame" of Chartres, to Edward the Sixth, and his court, when he was fent over as embaffador from Henry the Second, in 1551, were far more fplendid and coftly, than had ever been feen before in London (78). On the 26th of January, 1580, cardinal Birague received Henry the Third, his queen and mother, attended by a great train of noblemen and ladies, in the gallery of his houfe at Paris. A collation was there ferved, upon two long tables, confifting of between eleven and twelve hundred difhes, compofed of confectionary, and dried fweetmeats of various kinds, conftructed in the form of caftles pyramids, and other elegant figures (79). The original eftimate of the fum, requifite for maintaining the table of the duke of Anjou, as commander in chief of the royal forces before Rochelle, in 1573, was above two thoufand pounds a-month. Marfhal Tavannes reduced it to about four hundred (80). Even the latter allowance muft be confidered as very ample. Ronfard, enumerating the fruits common at the tables of the

CHAP. V.

Vegetables.

Banquets.

(75) Brant. vol. i. Dames Gal. p. 268—270.
(76) Trad. de l'Hop. vol. i. Epitres, p. 109.
(77) Ibid. vol. ii. p. 282.
(78) Brantome, vol. iv. Cap. Fran. p. 341.
(79) Mem. pour fer. à l'Hift. de Fra. p. 112.
(80) Tavannes, p. 448.

CHAP. V.

opulent, ſpeaks of peaches, mulberries, apricots, pears, quinces, raſberries, cherries, and ſtrawberries (81). Few of theſe delicacies were known, or produced among the Engliſh, before the reign of James the Firſt: a period later by near half a century.

Style and expence of tables.

We may ſee in Buſbequius, the conſumption of Don Antonio, titular king of Portugal, when reſiding at Rüel, not far from Paris, in 1583. "He conſumes," ſays that author, "every day, the fourth "part of an ox, two ſheep, and a hundred and "fifty loaves." It is to be obſerved, that Antonio was then ſinking faſt into poverty and oblivion (82). The Swiſs embaſſadors, who came to ratify the treaty between the Helvetic Union and Henry the Third, received daily, from the corporation of Paris, thirteen Mentz ham paſties, thirty quarts of red and white wine, and forty wax torches (83). The uſual hour of ſitting down to dinner was eleven o'clock, under Charles the Ninth. Catherine of Medicis, in a long letter which ſhe addreſſed to that prince in 1563, and which forcibly diſplays the enlargement of her mind, as well as her knowledge of the arts of reigning; ſtrongly exhorts her ſon never to dine at a later hour (84). It is a circumſtance worthy of remark, that Francis Montmorenci, eldeſt ſon of the conſtable, when taken priſoner, and confined at Liſle, in 1557, writes to his father, to inform him, that "his daily expences amounted to three half "crowns a-day, as every article of life coſt at leaſt "double the price paid for them in France (85)." The chancellor l'Hopital alone, appears to have adhered to the primitive ſimplicity of earlier times, in the article of his table. Brantome, who had dined

Hours.

Simplicity of l'Hopital.

(81) Œuvres de Ronſard, tom. iii. p. 58.
(82) Buſbeq. letter 20, p. 122. (83) L'Etoile, p. 61.
(84) Le Lab. ſur Caſt. vol. ii. p. 451.
(85) Depôt de Bethune, N° 8673, cited in the Trad. de l'Hop. vol. ii. Recherches, p. 106.

with

with him, expressly says, that only boiled meat was served at it, according to his regular custom (86). That great magistrate, who emulated the poetic fame of Horace, equally imitated the frugality of the Roman poet. It was always customary to present water to the guests, to wash their hands, before they sat down to table, and again at their rising (87).

CHAP. V.

Furniture.

Magnificence in furniture may be said to have been totally unknown among the French, before the reign of Henry the Second. Marshal St. André, a voluptuous and dissolute nobleman, who acquired an immense property from the favor of that monarch, gave the first example of rich furniture, at his castle of Valeri. It was said to exceed in beauty, any thing to be found in the royal palaces. Persian carpets, wrought with gold; and tapestries of exquisite workmanship, were among the ornamental pieces. He was justly denominated the Lucullus of France (88). Francis the First possessed two suits of tapestry, regarded as the most superb in Europe. Both were of Flemish manufacture. One represented "the continence of Scipio," and was, on great festivals, used for decorating the principal halls of his palace. "It cost," adds Brantome, "eleven "thousand crowns, at that time: at present, I have "been assured, it could not be procured for twenty-"five thousand, it being entirely composed of gold "and silk (89)." The second suit was, likewise, historical; but, the subject was taken from Scripture, and it was appropriated to the royal chapel. As a proof how much more universally commerce had diffused wealth and all the arts of luxury, among the Italians of the same period; Brantome owns, that in the house of a private banker at Genoa, he

Tapestries.

Their splendor and value.

(86) Brant. vol. ii. Cap. Fran. p. 80.
(87) Ibid. p. 183. Le Lab. sur Cast. vol. ii. p. 503.
(88) Ibid. vol. iii. Cap. Fran. p. 307. La Noue, p. 168.
(89) Ibid. vol. i. Cap. Fran. p. 271.

CHAP. V.

had seen a tapestry hanging, representing the exploits of Achilles before Troy, scarcely inferior in any respect to those of Francis. It was valued, by the owner, at fifteen thousand crowns (90).

Margaret of Valois, in her Memoirs, describes the tapestries and the furniture, with which Don John of Austria fitted up the apartments, occupied by her at Namur, as infinitely more costly than any that she had ever beheld in France. The tapestry was composed of velvet, or sattin, ornamented with columns, woven in embroidery of gold and silver. A Bashaw, whose sons Don John had made prisoners at the victory of Lepanto, and whom he had restored without ransom, presented him with the materials. He caused them to be made up at Milan, in which city were found the most expert workmen of Europe, in that branch of luxury (91).

Commonly removed from one palace to another.

It was common to remove the principal tapestries of the crown wherever the sovereign went, and to hang them on the walls of the chief apartments. At the precise moment of time when the duke of Guise was assassinated at Blois, a workman was occupied in unhooking and taking down the hangings of the room, in order to transport them to Clery, near Orleans, to which place the king was about to transfer his residence. A piece of the tapestry was, by Henry's command, laid over the dead body (92). We may judge of the value and splendor of the hangings used on great occasions, in the palaces of noblemen of high rank, by the description of that which was put up in the hall of the constable Montmorenci's house at Paris, when he lay in state after his decease, in 1567. It was crimson velvet, bordered with pearls, mixed with embroidery of gold thread. The floor was covered

Hangings.

(90) Brant. vol. i. Cap. Fran. p. 271 and 272.
(91) Memoires de Marg. p. 112, 113.
(92) Chron. Nov. vol. i. p. 109.

with

with Turkey carpets; and in the middle was raised a bed of state, over which was spread a quilt of thirty yards square, composed of cloth of gold, edged with ermine, and surmounted with a canopy of the same costly materials. The benches, pillows, and cushions, were covered with gold tissue or brocade (93). That great luxury in furnishing the castles of prelates and bishops, had displayed itself, even in provinces very remote from the capital, before the close of Henry the Second's reign, may be clearly inferred from the terms in which l'Hopital mentions the reception and entertainment given to Margaret, duchess of Savoy, in 1559, at Rousillon, in Dauphiné. The mansion belonged to the cardinal of Tournon, who was absent at Rome; but, the honors were performed by his brother. "Our tables," says he, "were splendidly served; "and delicious wines were poured into vases of "gold and silver. Nothing could equal the beauty "of the linen, the furniture, and the number of "rich carpets from Sidon and the coast of Asia "Minor (94)."

Luxury, in the castles of the great ecclesiastics.

It is curious to see, that, with all their magnificence, the nobility of France in that age, were by no means possessed of the virtue of cleanliness in their dwellings. La Noue severely reproaches them with this characteristic defect. "No sooner," says he, "has a gentleman constructed a house, than he "must, of necessity, furnish it with tapestries "from Flanders, and beds from Milan."—"But, "when we see how neatly, and at how small an "expence, the houses of simple citizens and mer- "chants are fitted up, the nobles ought to be "ashamed to keep their rooms so filthy (95)."

Want of cleanliness.

(93) Le Lab. sur Cast. vol. ii. p. 502 and 503.
(94) Trad. de l'Hop. vol. ii. Epitres, p. 288.
(95) La Noue, p. 167 and 168.

Plate

CHAP. V.

Plate.

Plate began to be common among the higher orders of society. At the departure of the English embassador from Paris, in 1585, who had brought to Henry the Third the order of the garter; the plate, presented to him by the king, was estimated at five hundred pounds value (96). One hundred crowns a day had been allowed him during his residence in the metropolis, for the support of his household. His stay did not exceed three weeks (97). The collation, given by cardinal Birague, to Henry, in 1580, of which mention has already been made, was not served in plate, but, in the Italian porcelain of Faenza, which was exceedingly beautiful. A circumstance not to be omitted, is, that the greater part of the dishes, amounting to above eleven hundred in number, were broken in pieces by the pages and lacqueys in attendance (98). Under the same reign, it appears that the use of glass at meals became common. Ronsard, in one of his poetical compositions, entitled "Le Verre," lavishes the warmest encomiums on the introduction of an article, at once so elegant and so clean. He peculiarly praises their substitution in the place of those massy goblets of gold and silver, which were antecedently in general use at the tables of the great (99).

Porcelain.

Want of domestic convenience.

Notwithstanding the magnificence displayed on particular occasions, by the nobility, and the ostentatious parade of wealth or grandeur; it is certain, that general comfort or convenience were unknown. Almost all those inventions of domestic ease and enjoyment, so familiar in the present age, and so universally diffused, did not then exist, even in the palaces of princes. Chairs were scarcely known; and only coffers, or benches, were to be found in the houses of the wealthy. We find no better fur-

Chairs.

(96) Busbeq. letter 48, p. 235. (97) Ibid. letters 46 and 48.
(98) Mem. pour ser. à l'Hist. de Fra. p. 112 and 113.
(99) Œuvres de Ronsard, 2d Bocage Royal, p. 130—134.

niture

niture in the queen-mother's chamber, at Bourdeaux, in 1566; or, in the royal apartments of the Louvre, in 1572 (100). Brantome ſeldom, if ever, mentions any other kind of ſeats, except cheſts (101). Under Henry the Third, arm-chairs were invented; but, their uſe was confined to the court, and almoſt the ſovereign (102). In the enumeration of the pieces of furniture, expoſed at the ceremony of the conſtable of Montmorenci's funeral, we find only one chair, covered with velvet, which was that belonging to the deceaſed, and in which he was uſed to ſit at table (103). So valuable was furniture, that kings themſelves conſtantly removed it from one palace to another, or inhabited apartments almoſt deſtitute of any. In 1584, Catherine of Medicis, finding her ſon, the duke of Anjou, in a hopeleſs ſtate of health, at Chateau Thierry upon the river Marne, ſtripped the caſtle of its moſt coſtly moveables, which ſhe cauſed to be put into boats, and tranſported to Paris by water. She executed this act, which appears to us ſo indecent, on the firſt of June; and the duke expired nine days afterwards (104). It would, however, ſeem to be evident, from the compariſon of all the accounts left us by the contemporary writers, that furniture, in the ſixteenth century, was principally compriſed in the three articles of tapeſtry, beds, and carpets; and it is to be obſerved, that of theſe, none were fabricated by the French themſelves. Milan furniſhed the beds; Flanders, the hangings, long known by the name of Arras; and the carpets were imported from the Levant. We find, that on the deceaſe of great perſonages, the tapeſtries were uſually taken down, as a mark of

Mode of ſtripping the houſes of the dying.

Furniture moſtly imported.

(100) Brantome, vol. ii. Cap. Fran. p. 200. Memoires de Marg. de Valois, p. 59.
(101) Brantome, vol. i. Dames Gal. p. 273.
(102) Art. de Verif. vol. i. p. 659.
(103) Le Lab. ſur Caſt. vol. ii. p. 103.
(104) Mem. pour ſer. à l'Hiſt. de Fra. p. 177.

ſorrow

CHAP. V.

sorrow or mourning. In 1589, Henry the Third, to express the depth of his affliction for his mother's loss, caused the walls of all the apartments of state at Blois, to be painted black, sown with tears (105).

Carriages.

Carriages, an essential component of modern luxury, were unknown in France at the end of Henry the Second's reign; but, we see them mentioned almost immediately afterwards. Christina of Denmark, duchess of Lorrain, who attended the ceremony of Charles the Ninth's inauguration, in 1561, at Rheims, is one of the first persons stated to have been drawn in a coach. Brantome describes the vehicle accurately, as an eye-witness. "It was," says he, "very magnificent, and entirely covered "with black velvet, on account of her widowhood. "Four white Turkish horses drew it, the most beau-"tiful that could be chosen, and harnessed all four "abreast, like a triumphal chariot. The duchess "was at one of the doors, habited in a gown of "black velvet; but, her head was superbly dressed "in white. At the other door, sat one of her "daughters (106)." It may be a matter of doubt, whether, at that time, Catherine of Medicis herself had any coach. Brantome expressly asserts, that they did not exist under her husband's reign (107). Before 1573, they were become so common, that Sir Francis Walsingham returned from Fontainbleau to Paris, on his way to England, in a chariot of Charles the Ninth, which the king had ordered for him, as a mark of attention to Elizabeth's embassador (108). In the following year, coaches are mentioned as the ordinary conveyance of the queen-mother; and, in 1575, in order to prevent the

Coaches.

(105) De Thou, vol. x. p. 503.
(106) Brant. vol. ii. Dames Gal. p. 123.
(107) Ibid. Cap. Etrang. p. 288.
(108) Letter of Catherine of Medicis, dated the 29th April, 1573, in Le Lab. sur Cast. vol. iii. p. 330.

escape of the duke of Alençon and king of Navarre, they were transported in carriages, from Lyons, across France, to Rheims (109).

Chariots. Their encrease.

Nearly about the same period, Margaret, queen of Navarre, describes her chariot, as being "gilt "on the outside, and within, lined with a yellow "velvet, edged with silver (110)." Towards the close of Henry the Third's reign, persons of eminence, all over the kingdom, travelled in carriages. Chiverny, in 1588, talks of his coach, as a part of his establishment (111). They were become so general in the metropolis, before 1589, that, as we learn from a contemporary writer, citizens of rank and consideration, kept one, or even two coaches, for their own use (112). The first president of the parliament of Toulouse, Duranti, was returning in his coach, through the streets of the city, to his house, in January, 1589, when he was attacked, and at length murdered, by the populace (113).

Litters.

Litters continued, notwithstanding, to be long used, as the most commodious and indulgent mode of conveyance. They were usually borne by mules (114). Henry the Third, on his return to Savoy, across the Alps, in 1574, was carried in "a glazed litter;" while Emanuel Philibert, duke of Savoy, proceeded on horseback, at the head of his troops (115). Coaches were not only unwieldy, but, rough; and, independant of the ornaments used to decorate them, the carts of the present age may be pronounced a far more agreeable vehicle. When Margaret, queen of Navarre, undertook her celebrated political journey to Spa, in 1577, she preferred a litter; and

Description of the queen of Navarre's litter.

(109) Le Lab. sur Cast. vol. iii. p. 400. Sully, vol. i. p. 15.
(110) Vie de Marg. p. 144. Mem. de Marg. p. 49.
(111) Chiverny, Mem. vol. i. p. 114.
(112) Satyre Menip. vol. iii. p. 199.
(113) De Thou, vol. x. p. 567.
(114) Brant. vol. i. Cap. Fran. p. 224.
(115) De Thou, vol. vii. p. 133.

sent

CHAP. V.

sent her attendants in coaches, or chariots: for, she uses the term indifferently. Her description of the cavalcade, is equally entertaining and curious. "I "went," says she, "in a litter constructed with pil-"lars, and lined with scarlet Spanish velvet, em-"broidered with gold and silk. The litter was en-"tirely glazed (116)."—"It was followed by those "of the princess of la Roche sur Yonne, and of "Madame de Tournon; by ten young ladies on "horseback, with their governesses; and by six "coaches, or chariots, in which went the remain-"ing ladies and female attendants (117)."

Horses.

There is scarcely any circumstance which excites more astonishment, than the enormous prices paid for horses, particularly, for chargers, during the period under our review. They appear to have been chiefly reserved for war, or for parade. Mules were used on ordinary occasions, even by sovereigns. Ladies commonly rode a small breed of horses, called haqueneys (118). Francis the First had twelve mules, for his own immediate use. When the cardinal of Lorrain went to Brussels, in 1559, to ratify the peace between the crowns of France and Spain, he had with him, thirty sumpter mules, covered with crimson velvet, on which were embroidered his arms and cardinal's hat, in gold or silver (119). The joint establishment of Charles the Ninth, and Henry the Third, when only dukes of Orleans, and of Angouleme, in their childhood, consisted of six mules; four little haqueneys for their own mounting; and six nags for their esquires (120).

Mules.

Progress of luxury.

"I perfectly remember, as a boy," adds Brantome, "that Margaret, sister of Francis the First, that

(116) Mem. de Marg. p. 98.
(117) Vie de Marg. p. 201 and 202.
(118) Brant. vol. i. Cap. Fran. p. 112.
(119) Ibid. p. 213.
(120) Ibid. vol. ii. Cap. Etrang. p. 234.

"great

"great queen of Navarre, had only three sumpter "mules, and six for her two litters. She had, it is "true, three or four 'chariots' for her females. "At present, neither men nor women, are content "with so small a number (121)." Noblemen, general officers, and magistrates, when riding out for pleasure or business, were mounted upon mules (122). In 1581, the price of a common one, was, it seems, about forty-five crowns (123). Montaigne had purchased three short-tailed nags, a few days before, for a hundred crowns (124). Brantome says, that the price of that breed of horses had doubled, in his time, having risen from thirty to sixty crowns (125). But, it is in Montluc and in Sully, that we see, with amazement, the sums given for fine horses. From a hundred, to a hundred and fifty crowns, are the smallest, of which they make mention. It is, however, to be remarked, that they always speak of chargers and coursers, used in war. Only strong horses could carry the immense weight of a man cased in complete armor. The animal himself was frequently barded or covered with iron mail, in front. One of that description, Montluc estimates at above seventy pounds sterling (126). Sully assures us, that he sold two horses; one to the "vidame" of Chartres, for three hundred crowns; and the other, a beautiful creature, of a Spanish breed, to the duke of Nemours, for six hundred. Such a sum, allowing for the difference in the value of money, would be esteemed high, even for a racer of the first reputation, in the present age (127). A very considerable traffic was

Augmentation of the price of horses.

Trade in horses.

(121) Brant. vol. ii. Cap. Etrang. p. 235.
(122) Brant. vol. ii. Cap. Fran. p. 204. Ibid. vol. i. Dames Gal. p. 149.
(123) Voyages de Montaigne, vol. iii. p. 459.
(124) Ibid. p. 452, 453.
(125) Brant. vol. iii. Cap. Fran. p. 319.
(126) Montluc, Commentaries, vol. iv. p. 228—230.
(127) Sully, vol. i. p. 43.

carried

CHAP. V.

carried on between the German empire, and France, in the article of horſes. Men of quality did not, it ſeems, diſdain to become dealers; and we find, that Sully made prodigious profits, by buying up ſmall horſes in Germany, where they were to be procured at low prices; and afterwards ſelling them for large ſums, in Gaſcony. He owns, that he, in a great meaſure, maintained the expence of his houſehold, by this lucrative commerce (128).

Pages.

It was one of the principal modes of providing for youth, to place them as pages in the families of the great. Gentlemen of ſlender fortunes had recourſe to the protection of the wealthy nobility, to receive their children. Fidelity, obedience, and adherence, were exacted on one ſide: patronage and ſupport were extended on the other. Sovereigns maintained a vaſt number about their perſons, and in their court; who, after a few years, when they attained to a proper age, were incorporated in the cavalry or infantry. They were divided into diſtinct claſſes, or departments; of the bed-chamber, the great ſtables, the royal hunt, the falconry, and other branches of the houſehold. Henry the Second uſually retained above a hundred and twenty pages, of whom he annually diſpatched at leaſt fifty, to the wars (129). How ſevere was the diſcipline, and how abſolute the power arrogated over them, may be judged, from the entertaining deſcription given us by Brantome. "My father, and "Monſieur d'Etrées," ſays he, "had, both, been "brought up pages of the queen, Anne of Bretagne, and they rode upon the mules of her litter. "I have often heard them ſay, that ſhe cauſed them "to be ſeverely whipped, whenever they did not "properly guide the mules, or if they ſtumbled the

Their numbers.

Severity of their treatment.

(128) Sully, vol. i. p. 41.
(129) Brantome, vol. ii. Cap. Fran. p. 43.

"leaſt

" least in the world. My father rode upon the " foremost; and Monsieur d'Etrées, upon the " second. When their time was expired, she sent " them both into Italy, to the army (130)." The correction of the whip, or of the rod, so much disused among us in the present times, was not, by any means, confined to boys, in the sixteenth century. Young women of high condition were frequently subjected to that humiliating punishment. " Catherine of Medicis," says Brantome, " caused mademoiselle de Limeuil, and two others of her " companions, all of them maids of honor, to be " most severely flogged, for having written a pasquinade upon the court (131)." So numerous were the pages, about the palaces of kings, that they composed a formidable body; more especially, as they were in the first fire of youth, and enthusiastically attached to their respective lords. A quarrel having arisen in the castle of Blois, during the convocation of the States, in November, 1588, between the pages of the duke of Montpensier, and those of the duke of Guise, in which a page of the latter was left dead upon the spot; the whole court took the alarm. All the nobility, princes, and the king himself, having armed themselves, repaired to the place; and if the duke of Guise had shewn the smallest inclination to bring matters to an issue, a general carnage would have commenced between the two factions of the Royalists and the League. Henry, after so serious an outrage on the majesty of the throne, and the respect due to the residence of the sovereign, issued an order, prohibiting every page, or footman, from presuming to enter the court of the castle with arms, on pain of chastisement with the whip (132).

Danger arising from their numbers.

(130) Brantome, vol. i. Cap. Fran. p. 224.
(131) Ibid. vol. ii. Dames Gal. p. 421.
(132) De Thou, vol. x. p. 415—417. Davila, p. 737.

Such

CHAP. V.

Respect paid by pages, to their masters.

Such was the respect borne by gentlemen towards those under whom they had been brought up as pages, that no length of time, or elevation, however great, could cancel and obliterate the obligation. " Monsieur d'Esse," says Brantome, " who " had been page to Andrew de Vivonne, my grand- " father, although he rose to the highest military " and civil dignities, yet, when he came to visit " my grandmother, would never permit himself to " wash his hands at the same time with her, on " sitting down to table; declaring, that it was im- " possible for him to lose the becoming recollection " of his having been a domestic servant in her " house (133)." It is evident, that much of this reverence had been lost, after the commencement of the civil commotions, which deeply affected and changed the national manners. In 1563, Catherine of Medicis, writing to her son, Charles the Ninth, and exhorting him to follow the examples of his father and grandfather, in the manner of holding, or regulating his court, thus expresses herself: " Under the two last reigns, the archers of the " guard were usually in the apartments, on the " stair-cases, and in the court-yards, to prevent " the pages and lacqueys from gaming, as they " presume to do at present; nay, to hold regular " gaming tables in the castle itself where you are " lodged, with oaths and blasphemies: a thing " execrable (134)!" La Noue, who discusses the advantages, derived from the custom of placing the youth, in quality of pages about the great nobility; and who exposes, with energy, the characteristic vices inseparable from that mode of education; informs us how relaxed the superintendance was become under Henry the Third. " We have seen

Dissolution of manners, under Charles the Ninth.

Consequences of it.

(133) Brant. vol. ii. p. Cap. Fran. p. 183.
(134) Le Lab. sur Cast. vol. ii. p. 452.

" princes

3

"princes and noblemen," says he, "who received "such a number of pages, that they abandoned all "care, not only of their instruction, but even of "their cloathing. Instances have been known of "pages, who were without breeches, and who "were left to play at bowls with lacqueys and "stable boys (135)." It cannot, however, be questioned, that the institution, in itself, was a beneficial one; and peculiarly, as a resource to the inferior gentry, who thus provided for their numerous sons. It may be considered as a nursery, from which the military service was, likewise, furnished with continual recruits; and many of the ablest commanders in the sixteenth century, had been in the condition of pages. Cheleque, and Klinquebert, two German youths, in that employment, under Francis, duke of Guise, and who were, unfortunately, too active in the memorable massacre of Vassy, in 1562, rose to a very considerable degree of military eminence, as well as to an uncommon share of royal favor. One of them constantly carried the duke's fowling piece; and the other, his pistols (136).

Benefits arising from the custom of having pages.

Besides pages, the great entertained in their service a prodigious number of domestics, or lacqueys, who were commonly armed, and ready on every occasion, to espouse the quarrels, or to aid the resentment of their master. We find, that in 1584, Henry the Third, when reforming his household, dismissed at once, near a hundred and thirty valets. They were reduced from a hundred and fifty, to twenty-four (137). Even Don Antonio, the exiled king of Portugal, kept about sixty servants, after his defeat at the Azores, and his return to France (138).

Lacqueys.

Their numbers.

(135) La Noue, p. 117—119, and p. 124.
(136) Brant. vol. iii. Cap. Fran. p. 88.
(137) Busbeq. letter 31, p. 181.
(138) Ibid. p. 122.

They

CHAP. V.

They were armed.

They were frequently ſelected and retained, more for their courage and ſkill in managing weapons of offence, than from any other motive. Montluc tells us, that he knew a gentleman, who never took any ſervant into his employ, till he had put a ſword into the man's hand, and aſcertained, by actual proof, that he was maſter of the ſcience of fencing. By this means, he drew to him a number of reſolute, and ſkilful guards for his protection, or devoted miniſters of his revenge (139). The marquis of Meilleraye having killed Livarot, one of the minions of Henry the Third, in a duel, was murdered by the lacquey of his antagoniſt, as he returned from the place of action (140). How dangerous was it to moleſt them, and how formidable were their numbers, we may collect from many inſtances.

Danger of moleſting them.

The duke of Orleans, youngeſt ſon to Francis the Firſt, having, in a juvenile frolic, attacked the lacqueys, who were in poſſeſſion of the bridge of Amboiſe, at the head of a band of the young nobility, during the night, was received by them in ſo reſolute a manner, that he ran the moſt imminent hazard of his life. Caſtelnau who interpoſed, and received the thruſt made at him, fell dead upon the ſpot (141).

Buffoons.

Buffoons, or jeſters, performed the part of no inconſiderable perſonage in the court of ſovereigns, during the period under our conſideration. If we may believe the ſtory related by Brantome, and which bears in it the ſtrong marks of authenticity, they ſometimes were entitled to a more reſpectable appellation, and might rather be denominated monitors. Louis the Eleventh, ſays he, was overheard by his fool, in the act of confeſſing the murder of his brother, the duke of Guienne, and im-

(139) Montluc, Commentaries, vol. iv. p. 290 and 291.
(140) Brant. Les Duels, p. 110.
(141) Ibid. vol. i. Cap. Fran. p. 345 and 346.

ploring

ploring the interposition of the virgin, to procure from the Divine Being, his forgiveness for the crime. The king was on his knees, before the altar of "our "lady of Clery," when he made a disclosure of so much consequence; and paid no attention to the buffoon, as conceiving him too contemptible and destitute of comprehension, either to hear, or to retain the fact. But, the jester, who had been in the service of the murdered duke, and who bore an affection to his memory, reproached the king, as he sat at table, with his guilt, and accused him, from his own confession, with having dispatched his brother. It may be well supposed, that a prince less flagitious than Louis the Eleventh, could not digest so unexpected a reprimand. The author of it expiated with his life, the imprudence, or honesty of his conduct; which, probably, in the estimation of the courtiers, might pass for an incontestible proof of folly (142). His successors appear to have taken warning by his fate, and to have occupied themselves rather in amusing, than in troubling their masters.

CHAP. V.

Anecdote of Louis the Eleventh.

The buffoon of Henry the Second, Brusquet, who attained to some celebrity in his profession, seems to have been a cunning, rapacious, sagacious knave, who was allowed to divert the king, in any way, and at the expence of all those who frequented the court. He was made post-master of Paris, and amassed very considerable wealth, partly by pilfering, and partly by benefactions, or donations of various kinds. If we may judge of his powers of exciting mirth, from the numerous specimens given us by Brantome, he would not, in the present age, have been thought sufficiently witty, or expert, to have played the part of a Merry Andrew, in a country fair. Yet, he certainly contributed greatly to enliven the drawing-room of Catherine of Medicis (143). It is, how-

Brusquet. His rise, and history.

(142) Brantome, vol. i. Cap. Fran. p. 30—32.
(143) Ibid. vol. ii. Cap. Etrang. p. 266—286.

CHAP. V.

ever, to be obſerved, that a thouſand tricks were played with him, as well as by him; and that, provided the king and queen were only amuſed, it was a matter of little conſequence how ſeverely Bruſquet ſuffered. The cardinal of Lorrain, when going on an embaſſy to pope Paul the Fourth, could not diſpenſe with the ſociety of ſo agreeable a companion, whom he, therefore, carried with him to Rome (144). It is not a little entertaining, to ſee, that at the peace in 1559, between the crowns of France and Spain, the firſt interchange of amity between the two monarchs, is the reciprocal preſent of their reſpective jeſters. But, the Spaniſh fool was a mere "Buffo "Magro," ſays Brantome, compared with ours, who preſerved over him a vaſt ſuperiority (145). Philip the Second relaxed from his Caſtilian gravity, in his treatment of Bruſquet; and Henry the Second, not to be behind-hand in munificence, or politeneſs, loaded the foreign jeſter with preſents (146). Brantome, after enumerating all the eminent buffoons of five ſucceeding reigns, gives the decided preference to Bruſquet's jeſts; and only laments, that, at laſt, he became ſuſpected of a ſerious attachment to the reformed religion. For this crime, one of the moſt heinous which he could have committed, he loſt his place, was plundered, and driven to take refuge with the ducheſs of Bouillon, where he ſoon after died in obſcurity and indigence (147).

Credit enjoyed by him.

His diſgrace.

Jeſters.

Great perſonages ſeem never to have travelled without at leaſt one jeſter, to diſſipate the melancholy of their own reflexions, or to enliven the converſation. Margaret, daughter of Francis the Firſt, when on her journey into Savoy, in 1559, was al-

(144) Brantome, vol. ii. Cap. Etrang. p. 283.
(145) Ibid. p. 291. (146) Ibid. p. 292.
(147) Ibid. p. 293 and 294.

lowed

lowed two buffoons, to disperse her chagrin. The provision was not too ample; for, the chief jester being seized with a fever at Rouane, not far from Lyons, the second was compelled to exert all his talents to divert the princess. L'Hopital, who accompanied her, and who has left us a poetic Latin journal of the route from Paris to Nice, which may vie with the fifth satire of the first book of Horace, describes the nature of the efforts made by Margaret's jester. They betray neither extent, nor variety of abilities. "Having covered himself," says l'Hopital, "with a fox's skin, and besmeared his face with "flour, he began the satire's dance, mimicking at "the same time the silly and ridiculous movements "of the peasants. Gradually augmenting his address, he contrived to seat him elf upon a large "stick, while he embraced both his thighs. Every "one who attempted to imitate him, fell down; "and their fall only increased the laughter of the "spectators (148)." It must be owned, that such a diversion does not convey any very elevated idea of the taste of the age.

Nature of their wit and humour.

Cardinals, and great prelates, had always jesters in their train. "The constable Montmorency," says Brantome, "was so fond of Thony, the "buffoon, that he usually had him at dinner, and "placed him on a joint-stool near himself, treating "him like a little king. If the pages or lacqueys "displeased him, they were whipped (149)." It appears, that the profession was by no means exclusively limited to men: there were female jesters; and Brantome cites the repartees of mademoiselle Sevin, who occupied that employment in the household of the queen of Navarre (150). When the famous

Thony.

Female jesters.

(148) Trad. de l'Hop. vol. ii. Epitres, p. 283.
(149) Brant. vol. ii. Cap. Fran. p. 126.
(150) Ibid. Dames Gal. p. 181.

CHAP. V.

countess of Guiche, mistress of the king of Navarre, went to mass, in 1584, at Nerac, in Gascony, d'Aubigné assures us, that she was regularly accompanied by a running footman, a buffoon, a Moor, a lacquey, an ape, and a water spaniel (151). We must confess, that the manners of those times, were very essentially different from our own.

Watches.

Among the ornaments, or inventions, become common under Henry the Third, may be reckoned watches. The first, ever seen in France, was found among the spoils of the marquis del Guasto, the Imperial commander, after the battle of Cerizoles, in 1544. It was sent by the duke of Enghien, to Francis the First, and formed an object of admiration to his courtiers (152). They were commonly worn, hanging from the neck, in 1588 (153). The introduction and use of snuff among the French, is, likewise, due to this period. John Nicod, a master of requests, on his return from an embassy to Portugal, brought some of it to Paris. It was at first denominated from him, "La Nicodine;" but, Catherine of Medicis liking the herb, and taking it herself, it received the name of "L'Herbe à la Reine," by which it was long distinguished (154).

Snuff.

(151) D'Aub. Memoires p. 102.
(152) Brant. vol. i. Cap. Etrang. p. 390.
(153) L'Etoile, p. 108.
(154) Lettres du Card. d'Ossat, vol. i. p. 5, note.

CHAP.

CHAP. VI.

Paſſion for martial exerciſes.—Tournaments, and combats at the barrier.—Judicial combats.—Relation of that between Jarnac and La Chataigneraye.—Defiances.—Diverſions.—Entertainments.—Sports.—Occupations.—Colours.—Devices.—Rage for gaming.—Theatrical repreſentations.—Falſe coiners.—Retainers.—Spies.—Duels.—Aſſaſſinations.—Murders.—Study and practice of magic.—Demoniacs.—Enchantments.—Aſtrology.—Horoſcopes and calculations of nativity.—Tranſmutation of metals, and alchymy.—Pilgrimages and jubilees.—Roads.—Inns.—Frequency, and ravages of the plague.—Diſtempers.—Review of the characteriſtic vices and virtues of the period.——Concluſion.

CHAP. VI.

Paſſion for martial exerciſes.

ONE of the ſtrongeſt features which characterized the period under our review, was the paſſion for martial exerciſes. It pervaded every ſpecies of diverſion or amuſement, and rendered them fierce, dangerous, and ſanguinary. The genius and ſpirit of chivalry, however rapidly on their decline, were yet far from being extinct; and the fatal accident, by which Henry the Second loſt his life, though it checked the rage for tournaments, did not produce their ſuppreſſion or abolition. A knowledge of fencing in all its extent, and a perfect acquaintance with the ſcience of offence and defence, was not merely the accompliſhment of a gentleman: it was indiſpenſable for the abſolute preſervation of life and honor. Every weapon had its reſpective maſters, or profeſſors, who excelled in their uſe, or management; and in order to be prepared for occurrences, it was neceſſary to be equally ſkilful with the

CHAP. VI.

Practice of arms.

with the harquebuss, the sword, the dagger, and the lance. Rome, Milan, and Ferrara, supplied the most expert gladiators, for the instruction of the French youth; who usually passed a considerable portion of their early life, in acquiring such a degree of dexterity in the practice of arms, as to extricate themselves with success from the frequent quarrels, which arose upon the slightest occasions (1). The young men of condition were occupied during whole days, in fencing; and the lower chambers of the Louvre, which were the scene of their pastime, might be regarded as a sort of school, or academy, for those exercises of the body (2). D'Aubigné describes the court of Nerac, as filled with gentlemen, employed in the same diversion (3).

Running at the ring.

Of the various species of martial amusements, frequent under the last princes of Valois, the only one which displayed the utmost vigor and address without any mixture of personal danger, or hazard, was the running at the ring. It was commonly exhibited either during the carnival, or some occasion of festivity; as the persons were masked, and disguised by grotesque dresses, calculated to heighten the singularity of the spectacle. Female ornaments and attire were always preferred. "I saw," says Brantome, "a course at the ring, under Francis the "Second at Amboise, where the performers were "the grand prior of Lorrain, and the duke of "Nemours, two of the best cavaliers in France. "The grand prior was mounted on a barb, dressed "very elegantly as a Gipsey woman. On his head, "he wore the large round Gipsey hat; his gown "and petticoat were composed of velvet and taffety, "made very full. Within his left arm, he held,

Grotesque dresses worn.

Description of a course, at Amboise.

(1) Brantome, vol. iii. Cap. Fran. p. 427.
(2) Esprit de la Ligue, vol. ii. p. 107.
(3) D'Aub. Memoires, p. 101.

"instead

CHAP. VI.

" instead of a little child, a small, female ape,
" swaddled precisely like an infant. But, after the
" fourth course, he was obliged to disembarrass
" himself of the animal. The duke of Nemours was
" habited as a tradesman's wife, with a hat and a
" gown of black cloth: at his waist was a house-
" wife's bag, and a large silver chain, to which was
" fastened a ring, with above a hundred keys hang-
" ing on it. The noise made by the multitude of
" keys, was very amusing. Both the performers
" were masked: they made ten courses; and at the
" eleventh, the grand prior carried off the ring (4)."

Other instances.

We find Henry the Third engaged in the same diversion at Paris, in 1576, when he wore the dress and arms of an Amazon (5). The king of Navarre excelled in every military, or manly exercise; and never, during his whole life, omitted any occasion of displaying his ability and prowess. He, and the prince of Condé tilted, and ran at the ring, in honor of d'Aubigné's nuptials, in 1581 (6).

Tournaments.

Tournaments, and combats at the barrier, were diversions of a much fiercer species, and accompanied with personal danger, notwithstanding all the precautions used to prevent their mischievous consequences.

Danger and severity of those amusements.

We cannot sufficiently express our amazement at the pertinacity with which not only the French, but, all the European nations, adhered to them, in defiance of catastrophes the most tragical, frequently repeated. In 1549, Henry the Second published through Italy, Germany, and Spain, the celebration of a great tournament. He himself, with the princes of the blood, were assailants, against Francis, duke of Guise, and others. Marshal Tavannes was among the number. Every ceremony of

(4) Brantome, vol. ii. Cap. Fran. p. 399—401.
(5) L'Etoile, p. 19.
(6) D'Aub. Memoires, p. 92. Chron. Noven. vol. i. p. 156.

chivalry

CHAP. VI.

chivalry was religiously observed. Tavannes assures us, that he was the only one of the noblemen, maintaining the barrier, who escaped unwounded; that the diversion lasted eight days; and that he ordinarily broke sixty lances, every day (7). The death of Henry the Second, an event so productive of calamity, and so calculated to impress with lasting apprehension, could not prevent a renewal of the same games at Orleans, in the presence of Francis the Second, only a year afterwards. A youth of the royal blood, Henry of Bourbon, son to the prince of La Roche sur Yonne, was also killed, at the age of fourteen, by the shock which he received from the count of Maulevrier's horse (8). Those who only lost an eye, or received a severe wound, might be esteemed fortunate (9). In 1571, at the festival of Nogent, was held a combat at the barrier, which continued during two nights, and was performed by the light of torches. Henry, duke of Guise, maintained the barrier, on the first evening, against Charles the Ninth, and other assailants. The king was wounded in the foot, by his antagonist's sword, which broke, and caused a great effusion of blood. Catherine of Medicis, who had seen her husband perish in a tournament, had reason to be alarmed for the life of her son (10). One of the most magnificent exhibitions of this kind, was given before the Louvre, in August, 1572, in honor of the king of Navarre's nuptials, and only a few days preceding the massacre of St. Bartholomew. Charles the Ninth, and his brother were habited as Amazons: the king of Navarre, together with his attendants, assumed the Turkish dress, and were clothed in long robes of brocade, with turbans on

Examples.

Combats at the barrier. Festival of Nogent.

Combat of 1572.

(7) Tavannes, p. 127.
(8) L'Art de Verif. vol. i. p. 648. Brant. vol. iii. Cap. Fran. p. 304.
(9) Brant. vol. i. Cap Fran. p. 215.
(10) Manusc. au Depôt de Bethune, N°. 8722, cited in the Trad. de l'Hop. vol. ii. Recherches, p. 85.

their

their heads. The combatants encountered with lances, in presence of the queens, and all the ladies of the court (11).

CHAP. VI.

Arts used.

We may see in the Memoirs of Marshal Tavannes, with what pains the nobility and gentlemen endeavoured to harden their bodies, and to inure themselves to support the shocks and injuries, so commonly received in these fierce amusements. He tells us, that at the tournament of 1549, he used every night to plunge his right arm into oil of sweet almonds, and to tie ligatures round it; by which means, while many of his companions had their arms entirely black with contusions, he preserved his vigor and freshness (12).

Taste of the diversions.

If we wish to form an estimate of the taste and elegance, which accompanied the diversions of the sixteenth century, we may see them fully displayed in the entertainments exhibited by Elizabeth, queen of England, in honor of her lover, Francis, duke of Anjou. On New Year's Day, 1582, a combat at the barrier was given, in the court of the palace of Westminster; where the duke, accompanied by several noblemen, French and English, of the highest quality, defied all comers. He entered the lists, in person, upon a carriage, constructed in form of a rock. His hands were fettered with golden chains, and he was conducted to the feet of Elizabeth, by love and destiny, who sung alternately sonnets composed in French, descriptive of the violence of his passion, and supplicating the queen to raise him to her throne and bed. The combat lasted till an hour after midnight, in presence of two or three thousand persons; and the device chosen by the duke of Anjou for the occasion, was,

"Serviet æternum, dulcis quem torquet Eliza."

(11) Vie de Marg. p. 94. (12) Tavannes, p. 127.

His

CHAP. VI.

in England.

His presents on that day, to different noblemen, and ladies of the English court, amounted in value, to near ten thousand crowns. To Elizabeth, he presented a ship, composed of precious stones, which she accepted with public testimonies of pleasure and attachment. The queen even gave him more personal and flattering marks of her predilection, by kissing and toying with him, before all the spectators. She afterwards condescended to conduct him to his apartment, and to visit him next day in his bed. Delicacy was not the distinguishing characteristic of female manners, in that century; and the sensations which ladies of her exalted rank experienced, they conceived themselves at liberty to express, without any reserve. It ought not to be forgotten, that this amorous princess was full forty-eight years of age, and her lover not more than twenty-seven. Masquerades, in which Elizabeth danced with the duke, succeeded to the combats at the barrier. Magic and enchantments were called in, to the aid of music and festivity. Imprisoned knights, detained by sorcery in the dungeons of a castle, were liberated by the interposition of "a "prince the most magnanimous, and constant in "love, and of a queen the most chaste, virtuous, "and heroic, who existed on earth." After extinguishing the Necromancer's lamp, which constituted the charm, Elizabeth, and Francis, advanced, and restored the captives to freedom. Every circumstance, attending these gallant, and magnificent diversions, may be found in the Memoirs of the duke of Nevers (13).

Decline of tournaments.

Under Henry the Third, it may be said that tournaments finally expired. The last memorable one, of which history makes mention, was given by the duke of Mayenne, at Grenoble, in Dauphiné.

(13) Memoires de Nevers, vol. i. p. 557—559.

Having

Having invited the nobility of the province, and even the Proteſtants, againſt whom he was about to make ſerious and effective war, to break a lance in honor of the ladies; many gentlemen, Catholic and Hugonot, relying on his honor, complied with the ſummons. Leſdiguieres himſelf, the general of the Calviniſt party, was among the number. Mayenne received him with every mark of reſpect and diſtinction; nor had any of thoſe who repaired to Grenoble on the aſſurance of protection, reaſon to repent of their confidence. This event took place in 1580 (14). Such was the fondneſs for tournaments, that they were varied in every ſhape, and not confined to a ſingle element. The water, as well as the land, became the ſcene of them. In 1568, Charles the Ninth exhibited to the Pariſians the ſpectacle of a combat on the Seine, in front of the palace of the Louvre. He himſelf, in perſon, defended a boat againſt his brother, the duke of Anjou, who was the aſſailant. Brantome, ſo celebrated for his Memoirs, which have preſerved a number of curious and intereſting anecdotes, highly elucidatory of the manners of that age, was an actor in the entertainment. He informs us, that he ſaved with difficulty, one of his comrades, the baron de Monteſquieu. from being drowned, by plunging into the water, and dragging him to the veſſel (15).

Combats on the water.

With what fatal conſequences, the tournaments of the ſixteenth century were attended, at an earlier period of it, may be collected from numberleſs inſtances. The marquis of Peſcara, during the wars between France and Spain, having ſent a defiance to the duke of Nemours, the French commander, challenging him to an encounter with lances, each ac-

Fatal conſequences of them.

(14) De Thou, vol. viii. p. 388. Trad. de l'Hop. vol. ii. Recherches, p. 85.

(15) Brant. vol. iii. Cap. Fran. p. 221 and 222.

companied

CHAP. VI.

Numbers killed.

companied by three chosen followers; the offer was instantly accepted. They met on the day appointed, under the walls of Asti, in Piémont; and the leaders, after breaking their lances on each other's armor, without receiving any personal injury, raised their vizors, and interchanged embraces, with the utmost courtesy. But, on the part of their attendants, it did not end in so bloodless a manner. Two of the French, and one of the Spanish gentlemen, were mortally wounded, and either expired upon the spot, or only survived a few days (16).

Judicial combats.

The particular species of combat, denominated "judicial," from its being an appeal to the immediate justice and interposition of the Supreme Being, in favor of innocence, had not totally disappeared before the progress of reason, during the period under our examination. Francis the First permitted, and was present at several, in the course of his reign; rather, as it would seem, in compliance with the barbarous prejudices of preceding times, than from conviction or real approbation of their principle (17).

Combat of Jarnac, and La Chataigneraye.

The most celebrated combat of this kind, fought under the kings of the family of Valois, was between Jarnac and La Chataigneraye, in 1547, immediately after the accession of Henry the Second. The cause of quarrel originated during the reign of Francis the First; but, that prince, superior to the age in which he flourished, and grown parsimonious of the blood, as well as of the property of his subjects, prohibited the two parties from proceeding to extremities, on pain of his indignation (18). He had the enlargement of mind to say, in his privy council, when the matter was under debate, that "a sovereign ought never to sanction or permit an

(16) Brant. vol. iii. Cap. Etran. p. 10—12.
(17) Brant. Les Duels, p. 35 and 36.
(18) Brant. Ibid. p. 169 and 170.

"act,

" act, from which no public benefit could possibly " result." His successor did not imitate him in so judicious and beneficial a line of conduct. He was, even, in some measure, implicated in the subject of dispute, and personally interested in its issue; having asserted, that Jarnac had, in confidence, confessed to him, when dauphin, a criminal intimacy with his own mother-in-law. La Chataigneraye, who maintained the truth of the allegation, was, therefore, the royal champion. He was, besides, in the flower of his age, a distinguished favorite of the new monarch, and remarkable above every nobleman of the court, for vigor, address, and courage. Jarnac laboured under many disadvantages; but, his own exertions, and the presumption of his enemy, decided the contest in his favor.

Origin and cause of it.

Every circumstance attending this combat, which may be said to have been the last memorable one of its kind, is so highly characteristic of the modes of thinking and acting, at the period when it happened, that they claim attention. The scene chosen, was the park of St. Germain, near Paris, in presence of Henry the Second, surrounded by all the lords and ladies of his court. It was preceded by every ceremony and solemnity, usual in the darkest ages; and the two combatants swore, " on the Evangelists, on " the true Cross, and on the Faith of Baptism, that " they had not any charms, words, or incantations; " but, trusted wholly to God, their right, the force " of their body, and their arms (19)." Brantome, whose testimony on this occasion may be regarded as, in some measure, partial to his uncle, La Chataigneraye, asserts, that he owed his misfortune, to Jarnac's adopting a piece of defensive armor, not usually worn; but, which the contempt of La Chataigneraye for his antagonist, induced him to over-

Circumstances attending it.

Ceremonies used.

(19) Le Lab. sur. Cast. vol. ii. p. 558.

look

CHAP. VI.

look and admit (20). It was invented by one of those Italian masters of the science of arms, who were then in such reputation, and of whom Jarnac received instructions, previous to the onset. The heralds having proclaimed silence, and enjoined every spectator "neither to cough, spit, nor presume to make any manual sign whatever," the weapons of offence were lastly delivered. They consisted in a sword, and two daggers; besides two other swords of reserve, which were held by the constable, as a supply, in case of accident. One of the heralds then gave the signal, by saying, "Let them go, the good combatants (21)."

Weapons.

Issue of the combat.

The contest was soon decided: Jarnac, by a dextrous and unexpected back-stroke, cut the tendons of his adversary's left leg, and repeated the blow, till he fell. It was in his power to have terminated all further hazard, by putting La Chataigneraye to death. But, conscious of the king's partiality towards him, and satisfied with the advantage acquired, he used his victory with the utmost moderation. Leaving his wounded antagonist on the ground, he approached the place where Henry sat; and putting himself on one knee, he besought of his sovereign to accept La Chataigneraye's life, and to restore him his own injured honor. It was not, however, till after three separate requisitions, made at distinct intervals; and till no hope remained of the combat being renewed, that Henry, solicited anew by Jarnac, exhorted by the duke of Vendome, and assured by the constable Montmorenci, of La Chataigneraye's desperate condition, consented to accept the proffered and forfeit boon. He afterwards embraced and commended Jarnac, declaring him restored in honor. La Chataigneraye, unable

(20) Brant. Les Duels, p. 50 and 51.
(21) Le Lab. sur Cast. vol. ii. p. 558. Sully, vol. i. p. 346.

to

to survive so public and humiliating a misfortune, tore the dressings from his wounds, and expired (22). The mixture of religion with gallantry, is not the least singular circumstance of this extraordinary transaction. Jarnac, finding his enemy extended on the ground, and incapable of resistance, immediately fell upon his knees, and returned thanks aloud to God, lifting his hands and eyes to Heaven. He beat upon his breast with his gauntlet, exclaiming in Latin, "Lord, I am not worthy." Then, approaching the scaffold, on which the ladies were seated, among whom was one to whom he particularly addressed himself, he said, "Madam, you "always assured me that it would terminate "thus (23)."

Spirit of gallantry, and of devotion.

The conqueror did not venture to use any of the privileges, allowed by the laws of chivalry to those who vanquished their adversaries. How extensive, as well as ignominious they were, we may judge from Brantome's account of a combat which took place at Sedan, beyond the limits of the French territories, soon after that between Jarnac and La Chataigneraye. Henry, equally shocked and chagrined at the disastrous fate of his favorite, swore, never again, during his reign, to permit of a second appeal to Heaven, by the mode of arms. Two gentlemen of his court, between whom a difference arose, had, therefore, recourse to the duke of Bouillon, who, as an independant prince, instantly complied with the request. But, one of the combatants, the Sieur de Fandilles, would not enter the place marked out for the lists, till he had first seen a fire lighted, and a gibbet erected, on which he intended to hang, and afterwards consume to ashes, his antagonist's body (25). The regret of Henry

Privileges of the conqueror.

(22) Brant. Les Duels, p. 48.
(23) Le Lab. sur Cast. vol. ii. p. 559.
(24) Brant. Les Duels, p. 4.

the

CHAP. VI.

Decline of judicial combats.

the Second for La Chataigneraye's loss, added to the progress of reason, gradually extinguished, and insensibly abolished these absurd and ridiculous appeals, which savoured not more of folly, than of impiety. They may still, however, be traced under Henry the Third; who was present at a judicial combat, between de Luines and Panier, in the commencement of his reign: but, the vogue which had antiently attended them, had completely ceased, before its close (25). The embassador of Solyman the Second, who had been a spectator of Jarnac's success, expressed his astonishment and disapprobation, that a sovereign should thus publickly permit an act of deliberate murder to be performed in his presence (26). So much more justly did a Mahometan and a Turk appreciate right and wrong, than the first monarch of the Christian world; and so faint were the efforts of the human mind, in opposition to established prejudices, little more than two centuries ago, among the most civilized people in Europe.

Sentiments of the Ottoman embassador, on the institution.

Defiances.

Solemn defiances, and challenges to single combat, continued still to characterize the age, and seem to have been as frequent as in the heroic times, when chiefs entrusted to their personal prowess the fate of armies and nations. Previous to a general action, while the forces on either side were preparing to engage, it was customary for the most intrepid, or adventurous individuals, to quit the ranks, and riding forward, to demand of their adversaries a stroke of a lance, in honor of the ladies (27). In 1577, we find the duke of Mayenne sending to defy the prince of Condé, either singly, or with a chosen number of attendants. But, the answer returned

Instances of them.

(25) Le Lab. sur Cast. vol. ii. p. 418.
(26) Brant. Les Duels, p. 206 and 207.
(27) Memoires de Marg. p. 183.

by

by the prince, was, that whatever inclination he might feel to accept the challenge, it was a received principle, that combats never took place, except among equals (28). Yet, the king of Navarre, some years afterwards, by a declaration, addressed to Henry the Third, requested permission to equal himself with the duke of Guise, in order to decide the quarrel of the house of Bourbon with the League, by a combat between them, with arms used among knights (29). The most singular encounter of this nature, happened on the second of August, 1589, only three or four hours after the decease of Henry the Third. L'Isle Marivaut, a royalist gentleman, stung with grief and rage at the assassination of the king, his master, and desirous to avenge it, defied the troops of the duke of Mayenne, and demanded, if any one would engage him, according to the laws of chivalry. Claude de Marolles instantly accepted the defiance; and the combatants, completely armed, met, in the presence of the two armies, under the walls of Paris. They were mounted on horseback, and rushed forward at the same instant. Marivaut's lance was shivered on the cuirass of his adversary, without effect: but, the spear of Marolles entered the eye of the royalist champion, who had neglected, from a presumptuous confidence in his prowess, to fasten his vizor. He expired immediately; and the preachers of the League, animated by so auspicious an omen, predicted the infallible destruction of the party of the king of Navarre, against whom Providence seemed to manifest its anger. The event did not, however, justify the prediction (30).

Combat of Marolles and Marivaut.

Event of it.

(28) De Thou, vol. vii. p. 510.
(29) Chron. Noven. vol. i. p. 8.
(30) Ibid. vol. i. p. 257. Journal d'Henry IV. vol. i. p. 1 and 2. Brant. Les Duels, p. 63—64.

Taste and elegance of the diversions.

If we reflect upon the diversity, taste, and magnificence of the amusements exhibited among the French, during the reigns of the four last princes of Valois, we shall find ample subject for admiration. In delicacy of conception, and even in the splendor of their execution, it may be pronounced that they were not greatly inferior to the boasted pageants of Louis the Fourteenth, given near a century afterwards. As early as 1549, at the public entry of Henry the Second into Lyons, games, in imitation of the gladiatorial, and naval spectacles of the Romans, were presented to that monarch (31). We may see in the Memoirs of Margaret of Valois, how superb, and how varied were the entertainments, imagined by Catherine of Medicis, to divert the leisure, and to enliven the interview of her daughter, Elizabeth, queen of Spain, at Bayonne, in 1565. She chose for the scene of one of her most sumptuous festivals, the little island, in the river Bidassoa, which separates the kingdoms of France and Spain; afterwards rendered memorable by the peace of the Pyrenees, in the succeeding century, between Louis the Fourteenth, and Philip the Fourth. Tables were disposed for the courtiers and nobility, male and female; that of the royal family, under a canopy, at one extremity of the apartment, being raised above the others by an ascent of four steps, composed of turf. Companies of shepherdesses, dressed in cloth of gold and sattin, and habited according to the dresses of the various French provinces, waited on the guests. They then performed the dances of their respective countries, in an adjoining meadow. On their passage by water, from Bayonne to the mouth of the Bidassoa, the splendid barges, in which the king, the queen-mother, and other attendants

Public games.

(31) Brantome, vol. ii. Cap. Fran. p. 13—22; and vol. i. Dames Gal. p. 383—392.

embarked,

embarked, were accompanied, or furrounded by marine deities, finging, and reciting verfes in honor of the occafion. The banquet was terminated by a "ballet" of nymphs and fatyrs, executed with equal delicacy and tafte.

Mythological, and allegorical reprefentations.

The mythology of antiquity was rifled and exhaufted, in the mafques and entertainments which accompanied the nuptials of the king of Navarre, in 1572. The impending deftruction of the Hugonots at the maffacre of St. Bartholomew, feemed even to be pourtrayed in the enigmatical reprefentations performed before the court. It is difficult to fuppofe, that Catherine of Medicis could intend thus to warn them of their danger: it is equally difficult not to admit, that the application was fo clear and obvious, as to ftrike the leaft fufpicious, or difcerning. The fcenery reprefented the Elyfian Fields, or the Paradife of Mofes: for, the fables of Homer and Virgil were mixed, by a fpecies of profanation, with the relation given in Scripture, of the Garden of Eden. A river, the Styx, traverfed the theatre, on which appeared the boat of Charon. Behind the Elyfium, was conftructed an "Empyreal Heaven," containing within a piece of machinery, which had an orbicular motion, the twelve figns of the Zodiac, the feven planets, and an infinity of ftars. Twelve nymphs, ftationed in the Elyfian Fields, were protected by Charles the Ninth and his two brothers, who defended the entrance, armed from head to foot. On the other fide of the Styx, appeared Hell, or "Tartarus," with its proper attributes. The king of Navarre, the prince of Condé, and the Hugonot nobility, who affailed the Elyfian Fields, were overcome, and precipitated into the infernal regions. Mercury and Cupid then defcended on the ftage; and after different dances, the captives were releafed. The reprefentation terminated by fire-works, which con-

Scenery.

CHAP. VI.

fumed to afhes the whole machinery and decorations (32). The Heaven, vainly attacked by the king of Navarre; the precipitation of himfelf and his followers into Hell; and the flames which clofed the exhibition; all appeared to have an allegorical allufion. Four days afterwards, the maffacre of Paris took place.

Splendid entertainments of the French court.

Magnificent as were the entertainments of 1572, they were excelled by thofe of the following year, at the reception of the Polifh embaffadors, who came to offer the crown of their kingdom to the duke of Anjou. In one of them, the Poles beheld with pleafure and aftonifhment, a prodigious mafs of rock, encrufted with filver, which was moved by concealed mechanifm. On the fummit, were placed fixteen of the moft beautiful women of quality, emblematical of the fixteen provinces of the kingdom of France. After finging, and repeating fome verfes compofed for the occafion, by Ronfard and Dorat, they defcended; prefented to the new monarch various offerings or teftimonies of homage; and concluded by performing a dance (33). It is not eafy to reprefent to ourfelves, even in the prefent age, any thing, conceived with more elegance of fancy. At the nuptials of the duke of Joyeufe, which were celebrated in 1581, the queen, Louifa, exhibited in the Louvre, a "ballet" of Circé and her nymphs, executed with incomparable grace, by the ladies of the royal houfehold (34). We can fcarcely credit, notwithftanding the well-known prodigality of Henry the Third, and the teftimony of contemporary writers, that he expended in various feftivities and diverfions, on the above-mentioned marriage, a fum of not lefs than a hundred and fifty

Expence attending them.

(32) Vie de Marg. de Val. p. 90—92.
(33) Ibid. p. 123.
(34) Memoires pour fer. à l'Hift. de Fr. p. 134.

thoufand

thousand pounds (35). Many of the masques, or dances, given at court, were celebrated by Desportes, the poet, who composed stanzas for the principal characters. We find in his works, the names of these diversions, which are taken usually from some mythological, or romantic fable. There is the masquerade of the "Chevaliers fideles," and of the "Chevaliers agitez." In another, denominated the "Masquerade of Visions," Night and Morning appear, and repeat verses in honor of the newly-married pair. They are ingenious, melodious, and full of grace (36). Ronsard introduces the most fantastic and ideal beings, or personages, in his masques. The four elements, personified, come forward in one of them, to defy the four planets, who accept the challenge (37). Syrens, and mermaids, predict the future destiny of the French monarchs (38) Charles the Ninth, habited one while as the Sun, and at another as Hercules, pronounces a cartel to love, which is sent by a dwarf. Such was the genius and taste of the entertainments of that age.

Puerile amusement.

The indecent puerility, or contempt of public opinion, manifested by Henry the Third, rose to such a pitch, that he did not blush to appear commonly in the streets of his own capital, playing with a "Bilboquet." The fashion became general; Joyeuse and Epernon imitated their master; and in a short time, all the gentlemen, pages, and even domestics, were seen every where in public, with the same appendage (39). It must be owned, that if rebellion was ever venial, it might plead some excuse, when provoked by such profusion, folly,

(35) Mem. pour ser. à l'Hist. de Fra. p. 130.
(36) Œuvres de Portes, p. 460—470.
(37) Ibid, de Ronsard, Mascarades, p. 127—129.
(38) Ibid.
(39) Mem. pour ser. à l'Hist. de Fra. p. 195.

and

CHAP. VI.

and abuſe of power. De Thou himſelf aſſures us, that the king expended above twelve thouſand pounds annually, in the ſingle article of little dogs; beſides the ſums conſumed on monkeys, parroquets, and other animals (40). The ball given by him to the Engliſh embaſſadors, in 1585, coſt him ten thouſand crowns (41). Two years afterwards, at Epernon's nuptials, he danced in public, with every indication of mirth, while, at his waiſt hung a large chaplet of ivory ſkulls (42). Like Heliogabalus, he affected the ornaments and dreſs of a woman. The accounts given us by Dion and Herodian, of the indecent appearance of the Syrian emperor of Rome, were realized by the French monarch. In 1577, he commonly frequented public entertainments, in a female attire; his doublet open, and his boſom bare; with a necklace of pearls, and three little capes, as they were then worn by the ladies of the court (43).

Balls.

Effeminacy, and indecorum.

It would, however, be unjuſt, to appreciate the general character of the age, even in its paſtimes, by the conduct or actions of ſo relaxed and effeminate a prince. The ſports of the period were not only manly; but rough, hazardous, and daring, to a point of temerity. Marſhal Tavannes was accuſtomed, when young, to amuſe himſelf with his companions, in leaping acroſs the ſtreets of Paris, from the roof of one houſe to that of another (44). In preſence of the court, at Fontainbleau, he undertook, and performed a leap on horſeback, of twenty-eight feet, from rock to rock (45). Frolics the moſt adventurous and deſperate were common, particularly in time of carnival, when every indiſcre-

Rude diverſions of the age.

Examples.

(40) De Thou, vol. ix. p. 599.
(41) L'Etoile, p. 85.
(42) Ibid. p. 102. (43) Ibid. p. 21.
(44) Brant. vol. iii. Cap. Fran. p. 326.
(45) Le Lab. ſur Caſt. vol. ii. p. 527.

tion

tion ſeemed to be ſanctioned by the ſeaſon. Henry the Second, in 1558, accompanied by the princes and youth of his court, on Shrove Tueſday, a day peculiarly diſtinguiſhed for extravagant demonſtrations of conviviality, rode through the ſtreets of Paris, maſked, committing the raſheſt actions. In a fit of wild emulation, the whole company mounted the great ſtair-caſe of the hall in which were held the courts of juſtice, and galloped furiouſly down again, without incurring any accident (46). We find Henry the Third himſelf, in the carnival of 1583, and the following year, performing the ſame mad exploits, followed by his brother, the duke of Anjou, and his minions (47). They rode at full ſpeed through the capital in maſks, overturning, beating, and ill-uſing every one who fell in their way. On the night of the maſſacre of St. Bartholomew, when the aſſaſſins came to the door of the count de la Rochefoucault's apartment, and demanded entrance; he had ſo little ſuſpicion of any deſign againſt his life, that he imagined it to be Charles the Ninth himſelf, at the head of a band of young courtiers, bent on ſome juvenile frolic. Impreſſed with this idea, he roſe, and dreſſed himſelf, exclaiming all the time, "Theſe "are the tricks of the late king, your father; "but, you will not catch me thus." The door was no ſooner opened, than he was inſtantly murdered (48).

Henry the Second.

Charles the Ninth.

Occupations the moſt ſevere and laborious, were conſidered as paſtimes, and practiſed by ſovereign princes for their diverſion. Charles the Ninth beheaded animals, diſſected them, and performed the functions of an executioner and a butcher, with ſingular addreſs (49). The preſent age, however

Occupations and amuſements of the great.

(46) Brantome, vol. ii. Cap. Fran. p. 401.
(47) L'Etoile, p. 62 and 75.
(48) Brant. vol. iv. Cap. Fran. p. 9 and 10.
(49) Le Lab. ſur Caſt. vol. iii. p. 25.

refined,

CHAP. VI

refined, has not been wanting in a similar example of a crowned head, one of whose greatest enjoyments consisted in opening, and embowelling the deer, or other game, which he had previously killed.

Forging armor.

It was common for Charles the Ninth to work at the forge, and even to make with his own hands the barrels of musquets and harquebusses (50). Brantome says, that Philibert Emanuel, duke of Savoy, constantly amused himself at the same robust exercise; and, that he had seen the duke practise at his forge, in the garden of the palace, at Turin (51).

Coining.

There was not any piece of coin, either gold or silver, which Charles the Ninth had not learnt to strike so exquisitely, and to counterfeit so perfectly, as to deceive the nicest eye. It was one of his favorite recreations to fabricate them, and to shew them to his courtiers (52). We can still less reconcile to our manners and ideas of royal decorum, his introduction of ten thieves and common cutpurses, into the drawing-room of the Louvre, during a crouded ball and festival; with orders to them to exercise their address, at the expence of the company. He gave them assurance of impunity; watched their feats of dexterity; reviewed the amount of their plunder, which exceeded in value fifteen hundred crowns; permitted them to retain it; and then dismissed them with menaces of being instantly hanged, if ever they ventured to repeat their depredations (53). It must be confessed, that such a conduct was not much calculated to amend the morals, or effect the reformation of that class of his subjects.

Bear-hunting.

Bear-hunting was one of the sports of the court of Navarre. How hazardous was the pursuit of those

(50) Le Lab. sur Cast. vol. iii. p. 25. Brant. vol. iv. Cap. Fran. p. 28.

(51) Brant. vol. ii. Cap. Etran. p. 164 and 166.

(52) Ibid. vol. iv. Cap. Fran. p. 29.

(53) Ibid. p. 29—31.

animals,

animals, and how fatal the accidents which continually attended the chace, we may fee in Sully. In 1578, during the courfe of one given by the court of Navarre, in the province of Foix, at the foot of the Pyrenees; a bear, purfued by the hunters, and driven to madnefs by the number of lances fixed in his body, feized feven or eight foldiers ftationed on the point of a rock, and precipitating himfelf with them, dafhed them to pieces (54). Thefe tragical adventures neither diminifhed the ardor of the fportfmen, nor tended to humanize and foften the genius of the diverfions.

Colors and devices.

The period of time under our review, may be juftly called the age of colors and devices. The former were worn, in honor of their miftreffes, by kings, noblemen, and gentlemen of every rank. Marriage impofed no reftraint in this particular. At the naval games exhibited before Henry the Second and his queen, by the city of Lyons, in 1549, the gallies which obtained the honors of triumph, were decorated with black and white, in compliment to the king and his miftrefs, Diana of Poitiers. Thofe which were vanquifhed, difplayed green; the color always affected by Catherine of Medicis, before her hufband's death (55). No umbrage whatever appears to have been taken by her, at fo public a mark of homage to her rival. On the day when Henry was killed by Montgomery, in the lifts at Paris, he was diftinguifhed by the fame livery. The three other princes, who maintained the barrier with the king, againft all affailants, and who were the dukes of Guife, Nemours, and Ferrara, each appeared in the colors of their refpective miftreffes (56). "Buffy d'Amboife wore," fays Brantome, "two 'favors,' given him by his miftrefs; one in his hat,

Univerfally worn.

(54) Sully, vol. i. p. 23.
(55) Brant. vol. ii. Cap. Fran. p. 20. (56) Ibid. p. 39.

"the

CHAP. VI.

"the other about his neck. When he was ordered "to quit the court of France, by Henry the Third, "whose minions he had insulted and defied, he "besought of me to assure the lady whom he serv-"ed, that those favors would infallibly induce him "to put to death the favorites, who had produced "the affront received by him (57)." It was well known, that the lady in question was the queen of Navarre. Colors were assumed, not only as marks of devotion and gallantry towards the ladies; but, as badges of friendship and adherence. At the judicial combat of Jarnac and La Chataigneraye, the band of gentlemen who were in the interests of the latter nobleman, amounted to five hundred, all habited in his colors, white and red. Those attached to Jarnac, did not exceed a hundred, dressed in white and black (58). On all occasions of danger or glory, lovers never failed to decorate themselves in the colors, or favors, bestowed by the object of their affection (59).

Badges of gallantry, and friendship.

Devices.

The imagination was tortured in the invention of devices, anagrams, and mottos, assumed by persons of both sexes. Margaret, the second queen of Navarre of that name, speaking of her litter, says, "there were, either in the lining, or in the windows "of it, forty different devices, the words of which "were in Spanish or Italian, upon the Sun and its "effects." She had chosen a Sun for her emblem (60). In 1568, Crussol, one of the Hugonot commanders, upon his standard, caused to be represented a Hydra, all the heads of which were ornamented with the dresses of cardinals, bishops, and monks. He himself, in the character of Hercules, was depictured as employed in their extermination.

(57) Brant. vol. iii. Cap. Fran. p. 404.
(58) Brant. Les Duels, p. 60.
(59) Ibid. vol. ii. Dames Gal. p. 316; and vol. ii. Cap. Fran. p. 402.
(60) Vie de Marg. p. 2[illegible]2. Memoires de Marg. p. 112.

The

The motto, "Qui casso, crudeles," and was anagram on his name, Jacques de Crussol (61). When Francis the First quitted his mistress, the countess de Chateaubriant, and attached himself to the duchess of Estampes, he demanded of the former his "devices," which he had caused to be inscribed, or engraven on all his presents to her. They were of the invention and composition of his sister, Margaret of Valois, and were regarded as the most delicate productions of female taste (62).

CHAP. VI.

Rage for play.

The rage for play may be justly reckoned among the characteristic features of the age. It was carried to a pernicious height, under the reign of Henry the Third; and tended eminently to produce a general depravity of manners. That monarch established in the Louvre itself, in 1579, a gaming-table for cards and dice, open to all comers, and at which he gave the example of playing constantly, in person. A company of Italians, who profited of his permission, won from him fifteen thousand crowns, in the course of a month (63). Epernon imitated the model set him by his master. On the evening previous to his departure for Gascony, in 1584, on the embassy to the king of Navarre, he lost above three hundred pounds sterling, to marshal Retz (64). The rapid progress of so destructive a vice, may be ascertained from Brantome. "The parties at tennis," says he, "under "Henry the Second, were for one, two, and three "hundred crowns at most, even when the king "played himself. At present, they are for two, "three thousand, and even double that sum (65)." Mary of Guise, queen-dowager of Scotland, lost

Examples of it.

(61) Le Lab. sur Cast. vol. ii. p. 589.
(62) Brant. vol. ii. Dames Gal. p. 455 and 456.
(63) Memoires pour ser. à l'Hist. de Fr. p. 105.
(64) Ibid. p. 176.
(65) Brant. vol. ii. Cap. Fran. p. 64.

CHAP. VI.

three thousand crowns, in one evening, to Monsieur d'Esse, a French gentleman, then resident in her court (66). It seems to have been her whole stock of ready money, as she continued the game, upon honor, without any stake. We may see the price of a pack of cards, purchased at the manufactory itself, in Montaigne. He says, that in 1581, he paid for ordinary ones, at Thiers, in Auvergne, where they were fabricated, only one sous, or a halfpenny, the pack. But, for finer ones, they demanded above six sous, or three-pence (67).

Cards.

Theatrical exhibitions.

Italian comedians.

Theatrical exhibitions began to be known under Henry the Third, as a public diversion. In February, 1577, a company of Italian comedians, who entitled themselves "Li Gelosi," and whom that prince had invited from Venice, arrived in France. On their way to the court, they fell into the hands of the Hugonots; and the king, in order to procure their deliverance, was necessitated to pay a considerable ransom. They began to perform dramatic pieces, by his permission, in the great hall, usually appropriated to the convocation of the States General, in the castle of Blois, where he then resided (68). The remonstrances of the clergy, and of the cardinal of Bourbon himself, could not induce Henry to delay the commencement of the comedies, or pastorals, as they were denominated, till the end of Lent (69). On his return to Paris, in the month of May of the same year, the comedians opened a theatre in the palace of Bourbon, near the Louvre, where they renewed their exhibition. It would seem, that there was no distinction of places, in the theatre allotted to the spectators; as the price of all seats indiscriminately was fixed at four

(66) Brant. vol. ii. Cap. Fran. p. 191.
(67) Voyages de Mont. vol. iii. p. 455.
(68) Mem. pour ser à l'Hist. de Fra. p. 78.
(69) Memoires de Nevers, vol. i. p. 173 and 177.

sous,

ſous, or two-pence. The concourſe of people to partake of ſo novel a ſpecies of entertainment, was immenſe (70). But, in the following month, the Parliament iſſued a prohibition to continue a diverſion, which the magiſtrates conceived to be of a nature extremely injurious to national manners. From this ſentence, the Italians appealed, and preſented the royal letters patent, authorizing them to perform, in defiance of the mandates of Parliament. It was in vain that the preſident and members of that body impoſed a fine of four hundred pounds on the comedians, if they preſumed to obtain or plead the king's ſanction. Henry interpoſed; and, by his expreſs command, the foreigners reſumed and continued their performances, under his immediate protection (71). Nothing can more forcibly prove, how low was the ſtate of the French drama, than the exiſtence of an Italian theatre in the metropolis, at a time that a national one was unknown.

Suſtained by the king, againſt the Parliament.

Among the evils, to which anarchy and contempt of the laws had given birth, after the commencement of the civil wars, may be reckoned the practice of counterfeiting the current coin. It is difficult to conceive how univerſal it had become, and to what a degree the money in common circulation was debaſed. Towards the concluſion of Henry the Third's reign, France was inundated with falſe coiners, who ſubſtituted the baſeſt metals, in place of gold and ſilver. Tavannes aſſures us, that gentlemen retained in their caſtles and houſes, perſons ſkilled in the art of fabricating money, whom they dignified with the appellation of philoſophers; and who, after quitting the laboratory, eat at the tables of their employers. He adds, that thoſe gentlemen who only counterfeited dollars and florins, which were German coins, and who abſtained from ſtriking

Counterfeit coin.

Practice, general.

(70) Memoires de Nevers, vol. i. p. 79.
(71) Mem. pour ſer. à l'Hiſt. de Fra. p. 81 and 82.

French

CHAP. VI.

French money, regarded themſelves as free from all criminality (72). Salcede, who was put to death in 1582, for having conſpired againſt the State, had merited an exemplary puniſhment by his preceding crimes. Notwithſtanding the penalty annexed to falſifying the coin of the kingdom, which was no leſs than throwing the culprit into boiling oil; he had fabricated ſuch a quantity of baſe money, as to enable him to make with it, the purchaſe of an eſtate (73). It was not till the final termination of the diſſenſions of France, and the reſtoration of vigor in the execution of the laws, that ſo pernicious an abuſe was aboliſhed.

Retainers.

The practice of keeping retainers among the great; one of the moſt powerful ſupports of the feudal ſyſtem, and which the policy or tyranny of the two firſt princes of the houſe of Tudor had totally extinguiſhed in England, continued ſtill to exiſt among the French. It even derived ſtrength, and became more confirmed, from the diſorders of the court and kingdom, under the reigns of the three laſt ſovereigns of Valois. Every nobleman had his followers, whoſe numbers bore a proportion to the power and conſequence of their patron. Tavannes ſays, that at the death of Henry the Second, the conſtable Montmorenci, on his retreat to his own houſe, was abandoned by at leaſt a hundred gentlemen, who had always been accuſtomed to follow in his train (74). The greater number of theſe, ranged themſelves under the protection of the Guiſes, who were then poſſeſſed of authority. We may judge how much the royal dignity was obſcured and enfeebled, by the adherence of ſo many individuals to their reſpective lords, from the relation left us by Brantome. "At the deceaſe of Francis the Second,"

Numbers of them, about the nobility.

The Guiſes.

(72) Tavannes, p. 132 and 133. (73) Buſbeq. letter 8th.
(74) Tavannes, p. 220.

ſays

ſays he, " I was at Orleans, and was a witneſs to " the devotion of the whole court to the duke of " Guiſe. Seven or eight days after that event, he " went on a pilgrimage to Clery, on foot: he " was accompanied by almoſt all the nobility and " courtiers; the new king remaining nearly " alone, chagrined, and jealous at ſuch a pre- " ference (75)."

Entrance of the duke of Guiſe into Paris.

Even in the following year, 1561, after the duke's retreat from court to his caſtles in Champagne; when, at the earneſt ſolicitation of the queen-mother, he re-appeared at Paris, it was at the head of a band of followers, which impreſſed reſpect and terror. Brantome, who was one of the number, and who attended him to the levee of Charles the Ninth, deſcribes his dreſs, arms, and behaviour on that occaſion. They were ſuch as Sylla, or Cæſar, might have adopted, when entering Rome; and bore no reſemblance to the humility of a ſubject, approaching the foot of the throne. " Beſides his " ſword," adds Brantome, " I ſaw him order three " daggers to be brought into his cloſet, of which " he ſelected the ſharpeſt."——" He was mounted " on a black gennet, and accompanied by three " or four hundred gentlemen (76)." It muſt be confeſſed, that ſo formidable a train ſeemed more calculated to ſhake, than to confirm the crown, on the head of the young king.

Poverty and dependance of the retainers.

Many of theſe unfortunate retainers ſtarved in the ſervice of the princes or grandees, to whom they devoted themſelves. Coconas, who was put to death in 1574, for a ſort of conſpiracy to procure the eſcape of Francis, duke of Anjou; ſays, in his confeſſion, that " he had been eight years a retainer of " the duke, without having ever received from him, " in the courſe of that time, wherewithal to pur-

(75) Brant. vol. iii. Cap. Fran. p. 77. (76) Ibid. p. 85.

" chaſe

CHAP. VI.

"chase himself even a hat (77)." Henry the Third became, from the sovereign of a great people, only the head and chief of a band of gentlemen, who filled the court with continual disputes, caused by their insolence and temerity. His brother, the duke of Guise, and all the principal nobles, had, in like manner, their partizans. It was deemed an object of triumph, to seduce those of each other. Epernon, who rose to such a point of favor and grandeur, towards the end of Henry's reign, was originally in the service of the duke of Anjou; as were Maugiron, Livarot, and others of the minions (78). When a forced reconciliation took place in the royal presence, between Bussy d'Amboise and a gentleman named St. Fal, in 1577; the former had the audacity to enter the palace of the Louvre itself, attended by above two hundred determined and devoted friends. Henry the Third expressed his indignation at it; but, did not venture to attempt its repression, or punishment. Bussy even augmented the train of his followers, during his stay in the capital, as his best protection and security against the vengeance of his sovereign, whom he braved and defied (79). It was, in fact, the only effectual preservative from assassins and murderers (80). We find the duke of Epernon, in 1585, on his setting out to visit the king of Navarre, carrying with him above five hundred gentlemen; and at his appearance before the king, his master, at Chartres, after the flight of Henry from Paris, he was surrounded by as numerous a band (81). The great nobles became almost independant of the crown, and maintained each, a sort of separate court, protected by their armed followers.

Their insolence.

Bussy d'Amboise.

Epernon.

(77) Le Lab. sur Cast. vol. ii. p. 371.
(78) Vie de Marg. p. 232.
(79) Brant. vol. iii. Cap. Fran. p. 399 and 400.
(80) Vie de Marg. p. 166.
(81) Vie d'Epernon, vol. i. p. 86 and 198.

lowers. In 1588, the duke of Nevers offered to arm, and pay one hundred gentlemen, at his own expence, for three years, to serve against the Protestants (82). Henry the Third was equally incapable of carrying on war with vigor, or of supporting his own authority in time of peace.

Spies. Their numbers.

The treachery and violation of faith which characterized the age, gave birth to a race of men who infested society, and who derived a subsistence from betraying the secrets of those with whom they lived. Spies became one of the principal engines of state, under Catherine of Medicis; and she expended considerable sums for their maintenance about the persons of all those whom she distrusted. So pernicious an invention tended eminently to destroy mutual confidence, friendship, and fidelity. We find that no rank, birth, or situation, elevated the possessor above assuming the odious office of a spy. Bellegarde, a marshal of France, condescended to act the part of one, about Damville, at the persuasion of the court (83). The queen-dowager usually retained in her immediate pay, from twenty to thirty; all of whom were, as might be naturally expected, the most depraved and abandoned of mankind (84). She even entertained them in the household of her own sons; and Cosmo Ruggieri, a Florentine, who pretended to a knowledge of magic, served her in that capacity, near the duke of Alençon. He betrayed her to the duke, divulged all her secrets, and was involved in the conspiracy of la Mole and Coconas, in 1574 (85). Charles the Ninth employed a lady of the queen of Navarre, to watch her actions, and received from her a regular information of his sister's conduct. Many of

Ruggieri.

(82) Chron. Nov. vol. i. p. 75.
(83) De Thou, vol. vii. p. 528.
(84) D'Aub. Memoires, p. 45.
(85) Le Lab. sur Cast. vol. ii. p. 376.

the

CHAP. VI.

the original letters, addressed by her to the king, are yet preserved (86). Margaret informs us, that she herself, at the pressing solicitation of her brother, the duke of Anjou, afterwards Henry the Third; undertook, and executed the employment of a confidential spy over her mother and Charles the Ninth. It ought not to be forgotten, that when she accepted the task, she had scarcely completed her seventeenth year (87). Nor were these agents of a perfidious and unprincipled policy, confined to France. All the courts and cabinets of Europe were filled with the emissaries of Catherine and Henry the Third. In 1574, we find her writing to the French embassador in England, enjoining him to send over a spy, named Jannoton, to the camp of the prince of Orange, in Flanders; and specifying his annual appointments, which were fixed at twelve hundred livres (88). It appears from the letters of the king to the same minister, in 1577, that he maintained numbers of secret agents and pensioners in the court of Elizabeth (89).

Margaret of Valois.

Foreign spies.

Duels.

Frequency of them.

One of the greatest scourges of the time, was the rage for duels, which prevailed universally among the men of quality and condition. The continual practice of arms, the facility of obtaining pardon, and the debility of the laws, carried the evil to its utmost height. La Noue declares, that if a calculation had been made of the number of gentlemen who perished every year in these encounters; it would be found, that many battles had been fought, with less effusion of generous blood (90). Under the predecessors of Henry the Third, duels, however frequent, or fatal, were, at least, limited to the

(86) Depôt de Bethune, Manuf. 8676, cited in the Trad. de l'Hop. vol. ii. p. 102.

(87) Vie de Marg. p. 18—22.

(88) About fifty pounds. Le Lab. fur Caft. vol. iii. p. 419.

(89) Le Lab. fur Caft. vol. iii. p. 508.

(90) La Noue, Douzieme Dif. p. 244.

two

two perſons between whom cauſe of quarrel had ariſen. But, during his reign, originated the mode of involving in the effects of the diſpute, the ſeconds and friends on either ſide. The firſt introduction of ſo abſurd and deſtructive a cuſtom, was exhibited in the memorable duel between Quelus and Entragues, in 1578. The former gentleman repaired to the place of action, near the Baſtile, attended by two others of the royal minions, Maugiron and Livarot. With Entragues, came Schomberg and Riberac. "Theſe ſix champions," ſays De Thou, "met at break of day, and engaged in "deep ſilence (91)." Four of the ſix expired either on the ſpot, or, in a few days afterwards. They wore no defenſive arms, and fought with the ſword and dagger. Brantome, who has left us a minute relation of the event, compares it to the combat of the Horatii, and the Curiatii, in the fabulous ages of Rome and Alba. He aſſerts, that Entragues, who killed his antagoniſt Quelus; and who alone of the two ſurvivors, eſcaped unwounded, owed his advantage and preſervation to the circumſtance of having armed himſelf with a dagger; whereas his adverſary was deſtitute of any weapon, except the ſword (92). Inſtead of exerting the force of the laws, to repreſs and puniſh ſo audacious an infraction of them, in his own capital; the king abandoned himſelf to the emotions of grief for the loſs of his favorites (93).

Seconds.

Quelus and Entragues.

Impunity of duels.

This extraordinary combat was not the only one of its kind, which diſtinguiſhed the period before us. Biron, ſon to the firſt marſhal of that name, and who ſuffered capital puniſhment for his treaſonable conſpiracies, in the beginning of the ſeven-

Biron, and

(91) De Thou, vol. vii. p. 726.
(92) Brant. Les Duels, p. 99—101.
(93) L'Etoile, p. 28. Brant. Les Duels, ibid.

teenth century; fought, at an early period of his life, a similar duel with the prince of Carency. Two seconds, on either side, who not only were completely unconnected with the dispute between the principals; but, who were intimately acquainted, and in habits of general friendship; joined in the fray, and betrayed equal animosity. We may judge of the mutual fury which animated them, when we find that they met at day-light, in the midst of a storm of snow, which drove with so much violence as almost to intercept the sight. The precautions taken by them to prevent a discovery, were such, that they had no spectators, except some accidental passengers. Biron and his two seconds having, with great address, taken their ground in a manner to avail themselves of the snow, which was driven in the faces of their adversaries, laid them all three dead on the ground. No legal proceeding or prosecution, seems to have been instituted against the victorious survivors (94). The slightest causes; a word, carelessly or unguardedly uttered, a look, or a gesture, were sufficient to produce a challenge. No age or rank exempted from their acceptance. La Chasnaye, who was killed by Sourdiac, in a duel, under Henry the Second, was eighty years old (95). To prevent every kind of deceit, and to obviate the suspicion of wearing concealed armor, it was customary to fight in their shirts only. In 1579, Bussy d'Amboise, and Angeau, for a trifling difference, fought two gentlemen, at Alençon: they were all four destitute of any dress, except shirts (96).

Carency.

Circumstances of that duel.

Other instances.

History of Vitaux.

The most formidable duellist of the age, was the Baron de Vitaux. He was equally dexterous, expe-

(94) De Thou, vol. ix. p. 592 and 593. Brant. Les Duels, p. 102—104. La Noue, p. 246 and 247.

(95) Brant. Les Duels, p. 259—261.

(96) Mem. pour ser. à l'Hist. de Fra. p. 105.

rienced,

rienced, and intrepid. Numbers of gentlemen, in every part of France, had fallen victims to his superior skill. His vengeance knew no limit; and even Henry the Third trembled at the prowess and desperate resolution of one of his own subjects (97). His renown was such, that it spread over all Europe; and foreigners who visited France, were anxious to see a champion so fortunate and celebrated (98). After having been compelled to fly into Italy, in order to escape the punishment ready to be inflicted on him for the various lives which he had destroyed; he ventured to return to Paris, in 1573, on a new project of revenge. To facilitate it, he lay concealed, suffered his beard to grow to an unusual length, and put on the disguise of a lawyer. Millaud, a gentleman, who had murdered the baron's brother, was then resident in the metropolis. Vitaux, accompanied by two brothers of the name of Boucicaut, who were called his lions; watched the moment when his enemy was passing through one of the principal streets, attended by five or six men; attacked him, left him dead on the spot, and escaped. He was taken and confined; but, by the powerful intercession of his friends, obtained a pardon (99). Ten years afterwards, the son of Millaud, who had attained to manhood, and who nourished an ardent desire to avenge his father's death, demanded reparation of Vitaux. They met, without the walls of Paris, naked in their shirts only, armed with a sword and a poniard. There the baron, abandoned by his good fortune, and rendered careless, by his contempt for so young an adversary, received a mortal wound, and expired immediately (100).

His exploits,

and death.

(97) Busbeq. letter 22, p 140.
(98) Brant. Les Duels, p. 119.
(99) Ibid. p. 120—124.
(100) Mem. pour ser. à l'Hist. de Fra. p. 165. Brant. Les Duels, p. 116—118. Busbeq. p. 138—141.

It

CHAP. VI.

Rage for duels.

It is in the Memoirs of d'Aubigné, that we may see in the strongest colors, the extravagancies and acts of temerity, by which the gentlemen of his time were characterized. They cheerfully incurred the greatest expences, and made the longest and most toilsome journeys, in order to meet in their shirts, and decide their differences with the sword. D'Aubigné rode from the vicinity of Orleans, to Castelgeloux in Gascony, across half of France, to fight la Magdelaine; with whom his chief reason for quarrelling, appears to have been, on account of the reputation acquired by the latter. La Magdelaine had dispatched eight gentlemen in single combat, without losing a drop of blood. This passion for duels, by one of the inconsistencies so common in human nature, was not incompatible with fervent piety. D'Aubigné, on the point of meeting la Magdelaine, says, that he rose early, and prayed devoutly to God. It is certain, that his inflexible adherence to his religious principles and professions, was highly injurious to his fortune and elevation in life (101).

Mixture of religion and revenge.

Under Francis the First, duels were comparatively unknown: the manners of the nation, more simple, were far more pure; and the royal authority, sustaining the laws, repressed the licentiousness which afterwards grew under three reigns of minority, conspiracies, and civil war (102). Some weak, and ineffectual efforts, to set limits to so pernicious a practice, were made by Henry the Third, in 1579; but, as they were rather calculated for reconciling, than for punishing the parties engaged in quarrels, little advantage accrued from the attempt (103). In 1588, at the convocation of the States by Henry

(101) D'Aub. Memoires, p. 75—77.
(102) La Noue, p. 244 and 245. Brant. Les Duels, p. 182.
(103) Memoires de Nevers, vol. i. p. 608.

the

the Third, Montholon, keeper of the seals, in his speech to the assembly, enumerating the national evils that called for redress; insisted strongly upon the impiety and destructive consequences of the practice of duelling. But, no measures were taken to produce a reformation, or to punish those who persisted in the open infraction of the laws (104).

Supineness of government.

The gratification of revenge, one of the strongest passions of the human mind, when not controlled by the terror of punishment; was not even restrained in every instance, by the finer ties of honor. Assassination and murder, tacitly, if not openly sanctioned by the sovereign, exhibited scenes of horror, over which, from their publicity, it is not possible to draw a veil, and the bare narration of which excites equal abhorrence and incredulity. It is one of the most hideous, as it is one of the most prominent features of the time under our contemplation. We are only at a loss, in the multitude of facts, which present themselves, to select those, calculated to depicture the spirit and temper of the age in its strongest point of view. Can we, in fact, be surprized that individuals should gratify their resentment, jealousy, or hatred, without limit, when we know that Charles the Ninth, encouraged, and employed assassins (105)? Catherine of Medicis, and her son, the duke of Anjou, afterwards Henry the Third; did not hesitate to suborn, and to instruct Maurevel, who, under their immediate directions, aimed the balls at Coligni, by which he was wounded, in 1572, previous to the massacre of Paris. Five thousand crowns were stipulated as the reward for the assassination of the admiral, which Maurevel undertook, some years earlier, at the personal solicitation of Charles the Ninth himself. Unable to find

Assassinations.

Maurevel.

(104) De Thou, vol. x p. 386. Chron. Nov. vol. i. p. 92.
(105) Vie de Marg. p. 31 and 48.

a favora-

CHAP. VI.

a favorable occasion for his purpose, and continually baffled by the precautions which Coligni took for his security; he determined to merit the protection of the court, by a service of importance, though of inferior magnitude. Having joined the Hugonot army, he was there received, and protected by Vaudré, Sieur de Mouy, one of the bravest and most distinguished officers of the Protestant forces. That generous and unsuspecting friend divided with Maurevel, his bed, his table, and his purse. But, so many acts of hospitality and affection neither made an impression on him, nor delayed the execution of his design. Having availed himself of the same opportunity which enabled Martialis to stab Caracalla, he fired a pistol-ball into his benefactor's reins, and immediately effected his escape to the Catholics, mounted on a horse which Mouy had presented him. The most debased and depraved period of the Byzantine annals, when human nature seems to have sunk to the lowest ebb of degradation, scarcely presents features more horrid, than the reigns of the last princes of Valois (106).

Assassins employed by sovereign princes.

In the extraordinary confession made by Henry the Third, when king of Poland, to one of his confidents, at Cracow, relative to the causes of the massacre of St. Bartholomew, which is preserved in the Memoirs of Villeroy; we read with amazement, that he himself, having caused to be brought into his presence a Gascon officer, addressed him in these words: "Captain, the queen my mother and I "have selected you from among all our good servants, as a man of valor and courage, proper to "conduct and execute an enterprize which we meditate: it only consists in directing a determined

Confession of Henry the Third.

(106) Memoires de l'État de France, sous Charles 9me. tome ii. p. 32. Confession de Sancy, p. 511—513.

"blow

" blow at a perſon whom we will name to you. " Conſider, therefore, whether you have the bold- " neſs to undertake it. Favor, and means, ſhall " not be wanting; and, beſides, a recompence " worthy the moſt ſignal ſervice which can be ren- " dered us (107)." Maurevel was, notwithſtanding, afterwards, preferred, as a more cool, and tried aſſaſſin. The relation of Henry's converſation with the Gaſcon captain, is, perhaps, the only authentic record of ſuch a propoſition, made by a ſovereign to an individual, preſerved in modern hiſtory. Its enormity is augmented, when we conſider that Catherine of Medicis was preſent at, and a party to ſo deteſtable a machination. It ſeems ſcarcely poſſible to carry further, depravity and crime. The king of Navarre, when examined before the queen-dowager, and the council of ſtate, aſſembled in the Louvre, on the 18th of April, 1574, declared, that he had received certain information of the king of Poland's having ordered du Gua, to kill him at all events (108).

Reflections on it.

We find that Charles the Ninth, in 1570, when irritated at the duke of Guiſe's pretenſions to the hand of his ſiſter, Margaret of Valois, ordered his natural brother, the count of Angouleme, to be called, and ſaid to him: " Of thoſe two ſwords " which thou ſeeſt before thee, one is deſtined for " thy own execution, if to-morrow, when I go to " the chace, thou doſt not ſtab the duke of Guiſe." The count cheerfully undertook the employment; but, he had not the courage requiſite for its execution; and the duke, by retiring from court, averted the fury of the king (109). Lignerolles, a gentleman of the houſehold of the duke of Anjou, whoſe only crime was

Duke of Guiſe.

Lignerolles.

(107) " Diſcours d'Henry III. à un Perſonnage d'Honneur," in the ſecond volume of the Memoires de Villeroy, p. 59—66.
(108) Le Lab. ſur Caſt. vol. ii. p. 373.
(109) Vie de Marg. p. 31.

that

CHAP. VI.

that of having been entrusted by his master, with the destructive intentions of Charles the Ninth respecting the Hugonots; was murdered in open day, by the command of his own sovereign, while on a party of amusement (110). Even when expiring, in 1574, that ferocious prince, with the advice and approbation of his mother, dispatched two famous assassins, St. Martin and Maurevel, into Poitou, on the specific commission to murder La Noue, one of the Protestant leaders, who had survived the carnage of St. Bartholomew (111). Brantome owns, that Maurevel was commonly designed by the appellation of "Le Tueur du Roi;" the king's murderer (112).

Encouragement, given by Henry the third to crimes.

Henry the Third, become king of France by the decease of Charles the Ninth, though less furious in his rage, was not restrained by any sentiments of virtue, or by any principles of honor. The most enormous crimes found not only protection, but, encouragement from a monarch, abandoned to dissolute pleasures, and corrupted by examples the most flagitious. If he did not, like his brother, command, he secretly instigated, to their commission.

Instances.

The count of Montsoreau, who assassinated Bussy d'Amboise in 1579, was indirectly exhorted to revenge himself. The most complete impunity followed the perpetration of the murder (113). Some years before, he had sent a detachment of his own guards, to seize, and drown Madame de Thorigny, a lady belonging to the court of his sister, the queen of Navarre. She was rescued from the hands of the assassins, at the instant when, having bound her,

(110) Vie de Marg. p. 31.
(111) De Thou, vol. vii. p. 55.
(112) Brant. vol. iii. Cap. Fran. p. 165.
(113) De Thou, vol. viii. p. 90. L'Etoile, p. 37—39. Le Lab. sur Cast. vol. ii. p. 498.

they

they were about to fulfil their orders (114). To the generous delays and expoſtulations, interpoſed by Souvré, it was owing, that the order, iſſued by Henry, in 1575, to ſtrangle the marſhals Montmorenci and Coſſé, then priſoners in the Baſtile, was not inſtantly executed (115).

Henry the Third received poſitive information, that his own brother, the duke of Alençon, had attempted to deſtroy him, ſoliciting his valet to ſcratch him on the nape of the neck with a poiſoned pin, at the time when he was adjuſting the king's ruff (116). Being ſoon afterwards ſuddenly ſeized with a violent and acute pain in his ear; and doubting, that it proceeded from poiſon adminiſtered by his brother's order, or with his approbation; Henry, in a paroxiſm of rage, commanded the king of Navarre, who was afterwards Henry the Fourth, to put Alençon to death. But, that generous and magnanimous prince, refuſed to execute the commiſſion, though it would have removed the only obſtacle to his eventually aſcending the throne of France. Henry the Third ſpeedily recovered; but, his deteſtation of the ſuppoſed author of his late attack, remained too deeply rooted, to be ever eradicated. Of theſe particulars, it is not poſſible to doubt, becauſe they depend on the teſtimony of Henry the Fourth himſelf, whoſe veracity was never impeached, even by his enemies. They convey a faithful, though a diſguſting picture, of the manners of that age (117). The accuſation of poiſon was ſoon afterwards retorted on the king, by his brother (118). Eteocles and Polynices, in the Theban hiſtory, were not inflamed with a more inextinguiſh-

(114) Vie de Marg. p. 160.

(115) De Thou, vol. vii. p. 292. Memoires de Nevers, vol. i. p. 81, 82.

(106) Mem. de Nevers, vol. i. p. 79.

(117) Ibid. p. 79—81. (118) Ibid. p. 106, 107.

able

CHAP. VI.

able antipathy and animosity towards each other, than were Henry the Third, and the duke of Alençon.

Chiverny.

The chancellor Chiverny assures us, that in 1575, the duke of Alençon gave directions to one of his most confidential captains, to assassinate him on the road from Paris to Chatelherault in Poitou: he adds, that he owed his life to the accidental circumstance of the murderer arriving too late to execute the commission (119). It is not the only instance which might be produced, of that prince's guilt and criminal intentions. Even parricide did not restrain him, when irritated, or incensed. Catherine of Medicis, his own mother, declared to the cardinal of Bourbon, that she feared to approach her son's bed, on the night when La Mole, his favorite, was executed, lest he should plunge a dagger in her breast (120). He was surpassed in atrocity, by his sister, Margaret of Valois. De Thou positively asserts, that she persuaded and induced, by her eloquence, the celebrated baron de Vitaux to perpetrate the murder of du Gua, the favorite of Henry the Third, in 1575.——The crime was rendered more detestable, from the cruelty with which it was accompanied. Du Gua, unarmed, and employed in reading in his bed, fell an easy victim to the vengeance of his implacable enemy (121). It is a circumstance which ought not to be omitted, because it paints in all its horror, the savage spirit of the times; that, the murderer having executed the object of his commission, was descending the staircase, in order to effect his escape, when he was met by a lady, who lived in a criminal intimacy with du Gua. He had the barbarity to

Du Gua. His murder.

(119) Memoires de Chiverny, vol. i. p. 63.
(120) Memoires de Nevers, vol. i. p. 177.
(121) De Thou, vol. vii. p. 300—302.

wipe

wipe his ſword, ſtill reeking with the blood of her lover, on the apron of the unfortunate miſtreſs (122).

CHAP. VI.

Enormities of the queen of Navarre.

Even though we ſhould incline to acquit the queen of Navarre of having inſtigated the aſſaſſination of du Gua; it is not poſſible to doubt of her having ſent perſons to murder a meſſenger of Henry the Third, who was on his way to Rome, with diſpatches from the king to his favorite, Joyeuſe, in 1583 (123). Indignant at ſo audacious an enterprize, executed upon a royal courier, Henry drove her from his court and capital, with public marks of ignominy. But, her future life was diſtinguiſhed, even to a late period, by a repetition of ſimilar enormities. Such was the contagion of the times, that even Henry the Fourth himſelf was not, it would ſeem, entirely free from its influence. He is accuſed, though perhaps unjuſtly, of having propoſed to the duke of Alençon to ſtrangle Catherine of Medicis, in the Louvre, with their own hands. This propoſition is ſaid to have been made in 1574, at a time when the two parties regarded their own execution as imminent, on account of La Mole's conſpiracy (124). D'Aubigné aſſerts, that the king of Navarre, incenſed againſt him for the freedom of his remonſtrances, embraced the reſolution of cauſing him to be poignarded, and thrown into the river Gave, at Pau. If there be no exaggeration in theſe facts, it may ſerve to prove how univerſal was the depravity of manners, and how difficult it was to eſcape the infection (125).

Henry the Fourth.

In 1578, St. Megrin, one of the minions of Henry the Third, was attacked and murdered, cloſe to the

St. Megrin.

(122) Vie de Marg. p. 165—169. Mem. pour ſer. à l'Hiſt. de Fra. p. 106—109.
(123) Vie de Marg. p. 342. Buſbeq. letter 22. p. 135.
(124) Le Lab. ſur Caſt. vol. ii. p. 352.
(125) D'Aub. Mem. p. 62 and 63.

palace

CHAP. VI.

palace of the Louvre, by a band of aſſaſſins, whom the duke of Guiſe had employed to revenge the honor of his bed, which it was ſuppoſed St. Megrin had attempted with ſucceſs. The duke of Mayenne did not heſitate to put himſelf at the head of this troop of ruffians, and to lend his perſonal aſſiſtance in ſo foul a tranſaction (126). Some years afterwards, in 1587, he committed an act ſtill more de-

Sacremore.

teſtable, by ſtabbing Sacremore, one of his own officers and adherents, who demanded with too much warmth, the reward promiſed to his long and faithful ſervices (127). Wherever we turn our view, we find only ſimilar crimes, and ſimilar impunity.

Ornano. His Hiſtory, and Crimes.

It cannot excite ſurprize, that the nobility and people ſhould imitate the example of the ſovereign. San Pietro Ornano, a Corſican in the ſervice of France, equally renowned for his courage and his brutality; having married a Genoeſe lady of quality, whoſe rank was not inferior to her virtue, put her to death, on a pretext the moſt unjuſt. Approaching her with every external demonſtration of reſpect and humility; after entreating her pardon on his knee, he deliberately applied the cord to her neck, and ſtrangled her with his own hands. Quitting Marſeilles, where he had committed the act, he arrived at court; diſplayed his breaſt, covered with ſcars and wounds received in battle; treated the murder as a private tranſaction, with which public juſtice had no concern; and obtained his pardon from Charles the Ninth (128). During the reſidence of Henry the Third at the caſtle of Poitiers, in 1577, a ſcene, if poſſible, ſtill more inhuman, was

Villequier.

acted. The count de Villequier, firſt gentleman of

(126) L'Etoile, p. 30 and 31.

(127) Lettre d'Henry IV. in the tenth vol. of Voltaire, p. 231. L'Etoile, p. 106.

(128) A'Aub. Hiſt. Univ. vol. i. p. 231.

the king's bed-chamber, and who had been his governor; having received information of his wife's infidelity, ſtabbed her at her toilet, while ſhe embraced his knees, and ſupplicated forgiveneſs. The crime was conſidered as peculiarly indecent, from the circumſtance of its having been committed in the perſonal reſidence of the ſovereign; and no leſs deteſtable, as the unfortunate counteſs was far advanced in her pregnancy. Villequier obtained not only his immediate pardon; but, the king was accuſed of having inſtigated, or, at leaſt, approved of the murder (129). In the long liſt of aſſaſſinations, with which the annals of that prince's reign are crouded; we find ſcarcely a ſingle inſtance of the criminal being brought to juſtice, except in the ſolitary one of La Bobettiere, a Hugonot gentleman of Poitou, who was beheaded in 1579, for having put to death his wife and her lover, with circumſtances of peculiar treachery and malignity. He was beheaded in the Place de Greve, at Paris (130). Thoſe who were not even ſecure of impunity and pardon in the court of France, found an aſylum in that of Navarre. In 1578, Laverdin having killed his rival in cold blood, was received with open arms, at Nerac (131).

Impunity of murders.

La Bobettiere.

A crime, if poſſible, ſtill more odious, though from its nature and ſymptoms, more ambiguous and equivocal, followed in the train of aſſaſſination. Poiſon began to be known, and even to be ſtudied as a ſcience, after the commencement of the civil wars. It would be endleſs to enumerate the perſons of the higheſt condition and quality, ſuppoſed to have periſhed by this means, between the acceſſion of Francis the Second, and the concluſion of the reign

Poiſon.

(129) De Thou, vol. vii. p. 749. Mem. pour ſer. à l'Hiſt. de Fra. p. 82 and 83. Le Lab. ſur Caſt. vol. ii. p. 756—758.

(130) Mem. pour ſer. à l'Hiſt. de Fra. p. 107 and 108.

(131) Ibid. p. 93.

of

CHAP. VI.

of Henry the Third. Jane d'Albret, queen of Navarre; Charles the Ninth; the prince of Condé; Mary of Cleves; the cardinal of Lorrain; Francis, duke of Alençon; Henry, prince of Condé; marshal Bellegarde; and a number of other illustrious personages, were believed by their contemporaries, to have been dispatched by poison. Malignity and credulity invented, or exaggerated, the symptoms of their diseases, in the majority of these instances. Counterpoisons, preservatives, and antidotes, were eagerly sought after by the great, and commonly vended by the needy, or the profligate. The Bezoar stone was long believed to possess the virtue of expelling, or counteracting the most violent poisons. Paré was among the first, who exposed and confuted that pretension, by causing the Bezoar stone to be applied, and administered internally to a criminal, who had previously swallowed a dose of sublimate. The experiment was made at Clermont, in Auvergne, by order of Charles the Ninth, in 1565, to whom a Spanish nobleman had brought a Bezoar stone. The unfortunate culprit, already sentenced to die, gladly accepted the commutation of his punishment, in order to produre a chance of life. The antidote was given him almost immediately after the poison; but, ineffectually. He expired, within seven hours, in violent agonies; and the king, convinced by so incontestable a proof, of the inefficacy of the medicine, commanded it to be thrown into the fire (132).

Magic.

The credulity of the age gave encouragement to numbers of persons who pretended to a knowledge of magic and judicial astrology. The art was even reduced to rules, and privately taught as a branch of education. D'Aubigné informs us, that while at Lyons, in 1565, being then about fifteen years

Study of it.

(132) Œuvres de Paré, p. 506, 507.

old,

CHAP. VI.

old, he applied to mathematics, and to the first elements of magic, though with a resolution never to avail himself of the latter (133). It is difficult to guess what he means by "the first elements of "magic:" they are certainly unknown in the present times. Ambrose Paré, though one of the most enlightened men of the age in which he lived, and superior to many of the vulgar superstitions, then received; yet, expressly admits the existence of magic, and the invention of evil spirits. He classes the magicians under their respective heads, enumerates many instances of their communication with demons; and in particular, one, to which he was an eye-witness, in the presence of Charles the Ninth. These facts tend to prove how widely diffused, and how universal was that belief, in the sixteenth century (134). Cosino Ruggieri, the celebrated Florentine, who was sentenced to work in the gallies, for his participation in the plot of 1574; if he did not obtain his liberty, drew, at least, to himself, the utmost consideration and respect, from his supposed acquaintance with magical secrets. Instead of being, like his companions, chained to the oar, he was permitted to enjoy his freedom, with only a guard of honor; and even to open a sort of academy for judicial astrology in Marseilles, which attracted pupils of every description (135). Catherine of Medicis, from her anxiety to penetrate into futurity, or to ward off imaginary dangers, extended her protection to every pretender to occult and supernatural powers. The capital, and the kingdom, were inundated with them; and their credit eclipsed that of the wisest, or most pious theologians. They were said to amount, in 1572, to thirty thousand (136).

Ruggieri.

Numbers of pretenders to skill in magic.

(133) Memoires de d'Aub. p. 17.
(134) Œuvres de Paré, p. 673.
(135) Le Lab. sur Cast. vol. ii. p. 377.
(136) L'Etoile, p. 98. La Noue, p. 9.

CHAP. VI.

Cabalistical words.

Cabalistical words, or characters, were commonly worn, as preservatives against sickness or attack (137). Medals, of magical virtue to produce, or, to preserve friendship, were equally supposed to exist. We find la Mole, the favorite of the duke of Alençon, constantly wearing one, which he was assured would perpetuate the affection of his master (138).

Charms used in surgery.

Medicine and surgery, professions which do not seem to have any connexion with magic, were not less open to its supposed influence. "My brother," says Brantome, "was wounded at the siege of Metz, "with three balls, two in the neck, and one in the "arm; of which he would probably have died, if "it had not been for the aid of Doublet, the duke "of Nemours' surgeon. He was regarded as the "most expert practitioner in France, and every one "had recourse to him, notwithstanding that Ambrose Paré, so celebrated since, was then in Metz. "Doublet performed all his cures with only bandages of clean linen, and plain water: but, to "those he added sorceries, and charmed words, as "numbers of persons now alive, who saw him, can "affirm (139)."

Death of Francis, duke of Guise.

When Francis, duke of Guise, lay without hope of life, in the royal camp before Orleans, from the consequences of the wound inflicted by Meré Poltrot; St. Just d'Alegre, as Brantome informs us, undertook and offered to effect his recovery. He was brought to the duke, and proposed to begin his dressings; which consisted in applications precisely similar to those of Doublet. But, the duke, conscious that he was beyond the reach of art, refused to have recourse to an expedient which he regarded as impious. He did not, by any

(137) Le Lab. sur Cast. vol. i. p. 284.
(138) Ibid. vol. ii. p. 377.
(139) Brant. vol. iii. Cap. Fran. p. 324 and 325.

means,

means, despise, or call in question the ability of d'Alegre to restore him by the help of magic: he only expressed his readiness rather to die, if such was the will of God, than to prolong his life by enchantments. Brantome declares, that he was present at the circumstance (140). In 1582, Sancho d'Avila, one of the most renowned captains of the sixteenth century, died of a wound, which might have been easily healed by skilful applications. But, having had recourse to charms and sorcery, he fell into a languishing disease, of which he expired (141).

CHAP. VI.

D'Avila.

Ambrose Paré relates many similar instances to which he was a witness, and which he exposed to public derision, in the manner that such impostures merited. During the siege of Metz, in 1552, he was sent to visit a gentleman, whose leg had been fractured by a cannon ball. "I found him," says Paré, "in bed, his leg crooked and bent, without "any dressing on it, because a person had promised "to cure him, only by using certain words, taking "his name and belt. He had lain during four days "in exquisite pain, neither sleeping by day or night, "crying piteously. I laughed at the pretended "mode of cure, and immediately dressed his leg. "He recovered, and is now alive (142)." The most curious recital of this kind, is to be found in another part of Paré's works. "At the siege of Hesdin, in 1553, the count de Martigues, a nobleman of the highest distinction, received a ball in the lungs, of which he languished, with mortal symptoms. Emanuel Philibert, duke of Savoy, who commanded the Spanish forces, exerted every endeavour to prolong his life, and caused him to be at-

Count of Martigues.

(140) Brant. vol. iii. Cap. Fran. p. 113 and 114.
(141) De Thou, vol. viii. p. 599.
(142) Œuvres de Paré, p. 787.

CHAP. VI.

tended by the most eminent surgeons of the two armies, after the surrender of Hesdin. But, the wound was incurable. When it had been so pronounced by Paré, and all the other practitioners, a Spaniard presented himself, and engaged, on pain of death, to operate his recovery, provided that neither surgeon, apothecary, nor physician, were permitted to approach his patient. They were instantly dismissed; and the duke of Savoy sent a gentleman to notify to Paré, that, as he valued his own life, he should not presume to interfere further with the count de Martigues. He gladly obeyed; conscious that no efforts of art could effect the cure. The Spaniard, then advancing, thus addressed his patient: "My Lord, the duke of Savoy has commanded "me to come and dress thy wound. I swear to "thee, by God, that, within eight days, I will enable thee to mount on horseback, lance in hand; "provided no other person approach thee, except "myself. Thou shalt eat and drink every thing "which is to thy taste: I will perform abstinence "for thee; and of this, thou mayest be assured, on "my promise. I have cured many, who had worse "wounds than thine." The noblemen present, answered: "May God give thee grace!" He then desired to have a shirt of the count de Martigues, which he tore into little shreds, in form of crosses, mumbling, and muttering certain words upon the wounds. Having dressed them, the Spaniard permitted him to eat and drink whatever he chose; repeating, that he would observe the requisite regimen in his stead. He did so, only eating six small plumbs, and six bits of bread at his meals, and drinking simply beer. Nevertheless, two days afterwards, count Martigues died; and the Spaniard, seeing him in the agony, made off with the utmost expedition. I believe, if he had been

Mode, used for his cure.

His death.

been caught, the duke of Savoy would have ordered him to be ſtrangled (143)." Nothing can more ſtrongly diſplay the ignorance, credulity, and unacquaintance of the age with the principles of medicine, than their committing to bold and obſcure empirics, the care of perſons in extremity, when abandoned as hopeleſs by regular practitioners.

During the ſiege of Jametz by the duke of Lorrain, in 1588, almoſt all the priſoners who fell into the governor's hands, were found to have about their bodies, cabaliſtical words, or prayers, written on vellum. They were believed to poſſeſs the virtue of protecting the wearer from wounds, or ſhot (144).

Brantome ſays, that he had known an infinite number of perſons, who wore ſuch charms: "with "ſome," adds he, "they ſucceeded; with others, "they had no effect (145)." As there were protecting, ſo there were deſtructive charms. Small waxen images, pricked, or pierced about the heart, with magical words and ceremonies, were ſuppoſed to produce death. Such having been found in the houſe of la Mole, which, it was aſſerted, he had procured from Ruggieri, in order to accelerate the progreſs and final effect of the diſeaſe, under which Charles the Ninth laboured; the unfortunate culprit did not deny, that they were magical images: but, he maintained, that their virtue was to excite love, and not to deſtroy life. He appealed to the teſtimony of the figures themſelves, which were female; and proteſted his innocence. The court did not the leſs condemn him to expiate his imprudence on a ſcaffold (146).

Deſtructive charms. Waxen images.

During the frenzy of the Pariſians, and their hatred againſt Henry the Third, after the aſſaſſination

(143) Œuvres de Paré, p. 792.
(144) De Thou vol. x. p. 226.
(145) Brant. Les Duëls, p. 90. Mem. de Nevers, vol. i. p. 73—75.
(146) Le Lab. fur Caſt. vol. ii. p. 378 and 379.

of

CHAP. VI.

of the Guises, in 1589; they had recourse to forcercy, in order to rid themselves of a prince, whom they considered as a tyrant. Their profane and impious rage was so great, that even the priests did not scruple to place upon the altars images, which, at every mass, they pricked; accompanied with incantations and invocations to destroy the king. Magical torches were extinguished, with similar ceremonies (147). The chiefs of the League employed a more effectual instrument; the knife of Clement. Such was the credulity of the populace, that two candlesticks of costly workmanship, and ornamented with the figures of satyrs, which had belonged to Henry, were produced and shewn to the audience by one of the popular preachers, as the demons whom he was accustomed to invoke. The imposture, however gross, was not less successful (148). So much had the licentiousness of the times produced impunity, that sorcery became, under the two last princes of Valois, a profession, exercised without apprehension or disguise. We find, notwithstanding, that, in 1587, an Italian, named Dominique Miraille, seventy years of age, and his mother-in-law, were hanged, and their bodies consumed to ashes, before the church of "Notre Dame," at Paris, for the pretended crime of magic. The punishment excited astonishment, not from its injustice or absurdity, but, because it was novel and singular (149).

Magical torches.

Credulity of the Parisians.

Horoscopes, and calculations of nativity, were so common, that it was usual to draw them on the birth of all princes and sovereigns. The predictions of Michael of Salon, known more universally, under the name of Nostradamus; were peculiarly celebrated in the sixteenth century. They were read

Horoscopes.

Calculations of Nostradamus.

(147) Mem. pour ser. à l'Hist. de Fra. p. 270.
(148) Ibid. p. 272 and 273. (149) Ibid. p. 218.

and

and ſtudied with the moſt implicit credulity; and as, like all oracular writings, they were couched in dark and ambiguous expreſſions, men ſaw, or fancied that they ſaw in them, every event which afterwards took place. Jerome Cardan, who died at Rome in 1576, had filled Italy and Europe, with his aſtrological fame. The merit of his other writings, however eminent, was loſt in that of his calculations. He had even the abſurd impiety to draw the horoſcope of Jeſus Chriſt, and to ſubject him to the chimerical laws, or motions of the celeſtial bodies, by which he explained, and to which he referred, every ſublunary event (150). The moſt philoſophic and enlightened minds of that period, were not altogether ſuperior to theſe vain and viſionary ſtudies. Aſtronomy and mathematics were implicated with aſtrology; and ſciences the moſt ſolid, lent their aid to ſuſtain ignorance and fiction. We may ſee in many parts of the hiſtory of de Thou, that he had not been able to reſiſt ſo general an infection (151). La Noue, though he treats the ſtudy and practice of magic, or aſtrology, as deteſtable, ſpeaks of it as not the leſs real and unqueſtionable (152). Comets and meteors, or phenomena of the Heavens, which our knowledge of aſtronomy enables us to explain, or to view without apprehenſion; ſpread terror over whole kingdoms, and alarmed princes, who conſidered them as preſages of their own approaching diſſolution (153). Catherine of Medicis was, during her whole life, the victim of her apprehenſions; and avoided with anxious ſolicitude, every place, where ſhe fancied that her deſtiny awaited her (154). De Thou aſſures us, that having been admoniſhed

Univerſality of a belief in predictions.

Comets. Terror produced by them.

(150) De Thou, vol. vii. p. 362.
(151) Ibid. p. 134; vol x. p. 215 and 667.
(152) La Noue, p. 8—11.
(153) De Thou, vol. vii. p. 593. Brant. vol. iv. Cap. Fran. p. 27.
(154) De Thou, vol. vii. p. 639; vol. x. p. 502.

CHAP. VI.

"to distrust St. Germain," she never could be induced to make other than a short stay at the royal castle of that name; which she quitted precipitately, on the first symptoms of indisposition. She even carried her alarms to such a point, that the palace of the Louvre being situated in the parish of St. Germain l'Auxerrois, she abandoned it; and constructed a palace for herself, at a vast expence, in another quarter of the capital. De Thou betrays his own conviction of the reality of the fact, by acquainting us that the prediction was accomplished at her death, because a theologian of the name of St. Germain, was called in to assist her in her last moments (155).

Catherine of Medicis.

Compacts with the evil spirit, whom we denominate the devil, were regarded as not only possible, but common. The confessions of ignorant and credulous, or timid and superstitious wretches, who avowed such pretended communications, were considered even by the magistrates, as juridical proofs, and punished with exemplary severity (156). The profession of a demoniac, was at once lucrative and celebrated. The persons, selected for personating the part, were usually women of obscure extraction, ignorant, and afflicted with violent nervous disorders, by which they were convulsed in a frightful manner. These fits were mistaken by the credulous, or superstitious spectators, for the infallible proofs of demoniacal possession. In 1565, a young woman of Vervins, in Picardy, named Nicola Aubry, and known in history by the title of "the Demoniac of Laön," was believed to be possessed by no less a number of devils than thirty. Three of the most refractory, who could not be expelled by any ordinary exorcisms, were publicly compelled to evacuate their tenement, in presence of a prodigious

Compacts with evil spirits.

Demoniacs.

Nicola Aubry.

(155) De Thou, vol. x. p. 502.
(156) La Noue, p. 9.

multitude,

multitude, aſſembled on the occaſion. The ſcene of deception; for ſuch, it can only be eſteemed; was the cathedral of the city of Laön, where Nicola Aubry was exhibited on a theatre, expreſsly conſtructed to facilitate the view of the ceremony. She appears to have received a complete cure (157).

CHAP. VI.

Other inſtances.

About ten years afterwards, in 1575, a woman of the looſeſt life and moſt abandoned manners, was ſelected by Marſhal Fervaques, as a proper ſubject for pretended poſſeſſion. She was inſtructed by the prieſt of the village of Bellouet, near Liſieux, in Normandy, how to act the part; and her deliverance from the ſuppoſed power of the infernal ſpirit was magnified into a ſpecies of miracle. The ſhrine, before which this ſpiritual interpoſition was performed, became ſo famous, as to draw to it an incredible number of votaries, devotees, and pilgrims, from every part of France. It is hardly credible that in the ſhort ſpace of three years, near eighty houſes, and fifty inns, for the reception and entertainment of thoſe pious ſtrangers, were conſtructed at Bellouet. When we conſider the pecuniary advantages, which muſt have reſulted from the concourſe of ſuch gueſts, we ſhall no longer wonder at the frequency and repetition of the impoſture (158).

It was generally ſuppoſed in the ſixteenth century, that inviſible beings, or demons, practiſed upon human weakneſs, aſſumed the ſhape of men and women, and under that form, might have the moſt intimate and criminal communication with perſons of either ſex. Fancy and terror amuſed themſelves by decorating and perſonifying the creatures, which they had originally invented. The Succubus, and the Incubus, were not only believed to exiſt, by the vulgar: men of the deepeſt learning, and of the

(157) Confeſſ. de Sancy, p. 180, 181.
(158) Ibid. p. 171, 172, and 180.

moſt

CHAP. VI.

most acute talents, equally regarded them as real. "The Incubus," says Ambrose Paré, "are demons, who transform themselves into the shape of men, and cohabit with sorceresses. The Succubus are demons, who, in like manner, assume the appearance of women (159)." He cites, or relates examples of the fact. But, in another place, he seems only to consider them as a species of the night-mare (160). His understanding, and his prejudices, were evidently at variance, and left him under a degree of uncertainty and indecision.

The Incubus, and Succubus.

Nuptial spells.

The nuptial couch was, in like manner, believed to be invaded by supernatural agents, or rendered sterile, by the operation of sorcery and magic. Numerous instances of this opinion might be produced, if the nature of the subject did not render it improper. Paré not only owns and maintains the existence of such charms and spells, as would debilitate, and incapacitate for the functions of marriage; but, he declaims against them and their authors, in the most forcible language. He declares the persons, capable of having recourse to such diabolical arts, in order to frustrate the purposes of wedlock, enemies of God and man. Overborne by the universality of the belief, and deceived by some equivocal or doubtful examples, he did not permit himself to examine, whether they might not either be wholly fictitious, or, the natural result of physical causes. Montaigne is far more philosophical in his opinions on the subject, though at the expence of decency (161).

Familiar spirits obtained equal belief, not only among the vulgar; but, among people of every description (162). Catherine of Medicis consulted

(159) Œuvres de Paré, p. 672.
(160) Ibid. p. 675, 676.
(161) Ibid. p. 676. Montaigne, Essays, chap. xx. p. 120—136.
(162) Brant. vol. ii. Cap Fran. p. 325.

Simeoni,

Simeoni, an astrologer, on the choice of a happy and auspicious day for Charles the Ninth's inauguration (163). Papyre Masson assures us, that Nostradamus having drawn his horoscope, predicted that his reign would be sanguinary and unfortunate (164). It is certain that Henry the Second sent that astrologer to Blois, in order to ascertain the destinies of his children. In the four lines, composed by Nostradamus, and which were considered as prophetic, or descriptive of Henry the Second's death by the lance of Montgomery, it is impossible to discover any thing, except a vague and fanciful allusion to a combat between two lions, in which one of them loses his eyes. But, as the imagination of his contemporaries was struck with the sudden and deplorable catastrophé of that monarch, which was the signal of the calamities of France; they eagerly seized on any casual resemblance between the verses of Nostradamus, and the fate of the French prince (165). Ronsard, though he doubts of the source from which Nostradamus derived his prophetic powers, and leaves it undetermined whether the Deity, or the demon, inspired him in his predictions; yet, professes his perfect conviction of the supernatural assistance extended to that impostor (166).

Celebrity and vogue of Nostradamus.

Prediction of Henry the Second's death.

Margaret of Valois, like her mother Catherine, was immersed in magical pursuits and studies. She is described by a lady of her own household, in 1573, as Canidia is in Horace, surrounded with spells, and invoking the aid of supernatural beings. A spy, placed by Charles the Ninth, about his sister, writes to him: "The queen of Navarre has been "three days shut up, with only three of her women.

Spells.

Margaret of Valois.

(163) Trad. de l'Hop. vol. ii. Recherches, p. 102.
(164) Le Lab sur Cast. vol. iii. p. 21.
(165) Biograph. Dict. Art. "Nostradamus," vol. ix. p. 535.
(166) Œuvres de Ronsard, tom. ix. p. 36, 37.

"One

CHAP. VI.

"One of them holds the two-edged ſword; ano-"ther, the paſte; and a third, the iron. She is "conſtantly in water, and burning incenſe like a "ſorcereſs (167)." Such were the occupations of the human mind in that age.

La Broſſe. His predictions to Sully.

Sully founded his inviolable adherence to the king of Navarre, among other reaſons, upon the poſitive aſſurances of la Broſſe, his preceptor, who early revealed to him, that the deſtinies had decreed the elevation of that prince to the throne of France. Nay, La Broſſe had, by his art, aſcertained, that, as Henry and Sully were both born on St. Lucia's day, they would be inſeparably attached to each other, during their lives. Sully made no ſecret of ſo pleaſing a piece of intelligence to his maſter; who, on his part, owned to him, that an aſtrologer, having calculated the nativity of the duke of Alençon, had, not without reluctance, denounced to that prince, a premature and inglorious end; while he had acquainted him, that the crown of France was reſerved for the king of Navarre. Sully lays the ſcene of this converſation as early as 1580, at a time when the events foretold were only, at moſt, probable (168). It is certain, that a general opinion prevailed throughout France, during the reign of Henry the Third, that the ſceptre would paſs into the family of Vendome, or Bourbon (169).

Expectation of the extinction of the houſe of Valois, general.

This expectation was founded on more ſolid foundations, however, than horoſcopes and nativities. The debaucheries of Henry the Third, and of his brother, the duke of Alençon: the virtue, and the ſterility of Louiſa, wife to the former prince: the preceding deceaſe of Francis the Second, and Charles the Ninth, without male iſſue: and the heroic, or amiable qualities of the young king of Navarre: theſe circumſtances, when combined, operated forci-

(167) Trad. de l'Hopital, vol. ii. Recherches, p. 102.
(168) Sully, vol. i. p. 31—33.
(169) Chron. Nov. vol. i. p. 242.

bly

bly on the minds of the nation, and attracted their attention towards the event, which took place by the assassination of Henry the Third, in 1589.

Transmutation of metals.

The transmutation of metals, and the discovery of the philosopher's stone, was another of the characteristic pursuits of that credulous age. Brantome informs us, that Castelnau de Mauvissiere, a French gentleman of distinction, defrauded Emanuel Philibert, duke of Savoy, of above fifty thousand crowns, in the prosecution of the research (170). We may see the implicit faith lent to the assurances of these alchymists, in the depositions of the principal persons concerned in the conspiracy of 1574. Grantrye, who had been the embassador of Charles the Ninth to the Grisons, was to have been appointed superintendant of the finances of the duke of Alençon, "because he promised by his art, to convert silver into gold, and by that expedient to pay the duke's army (171)." It is true, that he stipulated at the same time for his retreat into Switzerland, where he was to produce the transmutation. Grantrye being examined before commissioners named for that purpose, declared, that, "while he was resident among the Grisons, he had employed himself in distilling and transmuting metals; that he was possessed of the secret, which he would not communicate to any one except the king, or those whom his majesty should please to name. He added, that he could produce a million of crowns every year; the king only depositing fifty thousand crowns in silver, in order to gain five hundred thousand, annually; and that the profit might be drawn out monthly, or even weekly, if it was thought proper (172)." These pretensions, added to some interest at court,

Alchymists. Grantrye.

His offers.

(170) Brantome, vol. iii. Cap. Fran. p. 112.
(171) Le Lab. sur. Cast. vol. ii. p. 376.
(172) Ibid. p. 368.

exempted

CHAP. VI. exempted Grantrye from the fate of his associates, who perished on the scaffold (173). It would be easy to select many similar proofs of the belief given to pretenders to chymical secrets.

Pilgrimages. Pilgrimages were in the highest vogue under Henry the Third, who, as well as the queen his wife, had recourse to them, with a view to obtain issue. In 1579, he made a journey of this nature, to the shrine of the virgin, at Chartres, which had attained an extraordinary reputation in cases of sterility. In order to assist the effect of his prayers, he received likewise, two shirts, denominated from their virtues, "Chemises de nôtre Dame," which he carried to Paris, for the queen and himself. They were commonly esteemed infallible recipés. (174). As they proved, however, of no effect, the king, after making vows to various saints, invoking their aid or intercession; in November, 1582, had recourse to "our Lady of Liesse" in Champagne, who was supposed to preside over, and to shed her benediction, in an especial degree, upon the nuptial couch. He went thither as a pilgrim (175). Louisa of Vaudemont still continuing without issue, their majesties repaired twice in the following year, to the virgin at Chartres. Supplications having been found ineffectual alone, they next tried the force of presents on her. An image of silver gilt, representing the virgin herself, and weighing a hundred marks, was offered by them (176). They continued nine days in devotion; and repeated the experiment some months afterwards, when they presented a lamp of silver, weighing forty marks, together with lands to the amount of above twenty pounds sterling annual rent, for the purpose

Shirts of our Lady.

Remedies for sterility.

Presents to the virgin.

(173) De Thou, vol. vii. p. 54.
(174) L'Etoile, p. 35.
(175) Busbeq. letters the 5th and 9th.
(176) Mem. pour ser. à l'Hist. de Fra. p. 136.

of

of keeping it alive, day and night (177). As the virgin persisted to reject the royal supplications, we find the king, in 1584, going with forty-seven companions, all on foot, and in the habit of penitents, to Chartres, and to Clery, another celebrated shrine (178).

By a profanation, which strongly characterizes the manners of that dissolute age, religion was made a vehicle for coquetry; and relics were worn by ladies, in order to counteract the ravages of time, or to renovate the attractions of beauty. It is not without astonishment, that we can reflect on the use to which some of them were applied. D'Aubigné assures us, that the maids of honor belonging to Catherine of Medicis, expressed the utmost anxiety to redeem from the sacrilegious hands of the count de la Rochefoucault, a Hugonot, the girdle of St. Catherine of Sienna. It was kept at Tours, from whence the Protestants carried it off during the civil wars, under Charles the Ninth. Its virtue was of a singular and precious kind; far surpassing any of the empyrical remedies, so common in the present time. It was fondly believed by those who used it, that it could restore to the most beautiful part of the female form, its original loveliness, when lost by the effects of age and disease (179). The cestus of the Queen of Love, so famous in antiquity, was not more powerful.

Despairing of effectual relief from any application of his own to the virgin, Henry had recourse, in 1582, to the sovereign pontiff, and demanded the publication of a jubilee, in order to procure him offspring. Gregory the Thirteenth, who, as we may see in the letters and dispatches of De Foix, the French embassador, was frequently very inflexible

Jubilees.

(177) Mem. pour ser. à l'Hist. de Fra. p. 144.
(178) Ibid. p 175.
(179) Confess. de Sancy, p. 205.

on

CHAP. VI.

on ecclesiastical or pecuniary matters, expressed the utmost readiness to oblige the French monarch on this point. He even offered, voluntarily, to join his own entreaties and prayers, to those of the king and the nation. To render them more beneficial, the third week in Lent was selected, as peculiarly fitted for pious mortification; and the bull, promulgated for the purpose, enjoined every subject of France to unite in fervent addresses to Heaven (180).

Harangue of the archbishop of Bourges.

In 1588, at the convocation of the States General, the archbishop of Bourges, as president of the clergy, observed in his harangue to the three orders, that "they ought all to implore of the Divine goodness to withdraw from the royal house, the opprobrium of barrenness; to cast a favorable look upon the queen, as he had formerly done upon Anne, the mother of Samuel; and to grant the king a numerous posterity to inherit his dominions (181)." It would seem that the "shirts of our Lady" were apprehended to diffuse a protecting, as well as a generative virtue over their wearers; for Brantome gravely discusses, whether a champion going to engage in a judicial combat, might, or might not, be allowed to wear one of them. He treats them as a species of charm, or pious magic; and concludes by declaring, that if one of the combatants be permitted to avail himself of their assistance, the advantage should be rendered common to both (182). So little progress had the human mind made, at the close of the sixteenth century, even among men of liberality, rank, and education.

Efficacy of charms.

Impediments to travelling.

We may naturally suppose, that during a period so agitated by every calamity of civil and religious dissension, the intercourse from one part of the king-

(180) Lettres de Foix, p. 252 and 258, lettre 28.
(181) De Thou, vol. x. p. 396.
(182) Brant. Les Duels, p. 90.

dom

dom to another, muſt have been difficult, perilous, and interrupted. Poſts, and poſt-horſes, were, indeed, eſtabliſhed throughout France; but, the impediments to travelling were, nevertheleſs, very conſiderable. All communication with foreign countries, was frequently ſtopped by order of government, in time of profound peace; nor were even letters and couriers allowed to paſs, or ſecure from arreſt and inſpection (183). Henry the Second appointed Bruſquet, his buffoon, poſt-maſter of Paris, which was a very lucrative employment. Brantome informs us, that he had commonly near a hundred horſes ſtanding ready for uſe, in the ſtables. It appears, likewiſe, that the price paid by foreigners for them, was one-fifth part higher, than that given by Frenchmen (184). No aſſertions, however poſitive, can ever perſuade us, that the intelligence of the maſſacre of St. Bartholomew was carried from Paris to Madrid, in three days and three nights. Yet, Brantome, a contemporary, declares it in terms the moſt preciſe, and relates every circumſtance attending the reception of the news by Philip the Second (185). The weſtern, and ſouthern provinces, in which lay the principal ſtrength of the Hugonots; and where, of conſequence, even during the intervals of civil war, the inhabitants remained always on the watch; were, in fact, hardly to be paſſed without an eſcort. Epernon, who was ſent from Bourdeaux, with diſpatches to Henry the Third at Blois, in 1576, with difficulty found means to penetrate through the intermediate country, which owned neither ſovereign, nor laws, nor police (186). D'Aubigné, when diſpatched by the king of Navarre to the ſame prince in 1584, during a period

Poſts. Their eſtabliſhment.

Difficulty of paſſing from one part of France to another.

(183) Buſbeq. letter 8, and letter 15.
(184) Brantome, vol. ii. Cap. Etran. p. 289.
(185) Ibid. vol. iii. Cap. Fran. p. 169.
(186) Vie d'Epernon, vol. i. p. 26.

CHAP. VI.

of nominal tranquillity; yet was fo apprehenfive of being attacked, or plundered, on the road, that he did not venture to carry with him his mafter's commiffion. Having caufed it to be copied, he took only the duplicate, leaving the original in his own houfe (187).

Banditti, and outlaws.

The frontiers were infefted by troops of outlaws and banditti, whom perfecution had driven to feek fubfiftence among the mountains or defiles of Savoy and Germany. It was unfafe even for embaffadors, or men of the higheft quality, to venture beyond the limits of France, unlefs protected by an armed force. In 1575, Pibrac, on his embaffy to Poland, from Henry the Third, was befet by a band of robbers near Montbelliard; his equipage was plundered, two of his attendants were murdered, and he narrowly efcaped with his life (188). Henry, prince of Condé, fome years afterwards, returning from Geneva into Dauphiné, was, in like manner, ftopped and pillaged by ruffians, who, ignorant of his rank, did not detain his perfon (189). It is, notwithftanding, certain, that the northern and eaftern provinces of the kingdom enjoyed, at intervals, a comparative ferenity; and that travelling was not only fafe, but commodious, in thofe diftricts. We may fee with what fafety, and even convenience, Montaigne travelled in 1580, through Champagne, from La Fere, in Picardy, to Plombieres, in Lorrain; as well as in the following year, from Lyons, acrofs all the interior provinces, to his caftle on the Dordogne, in Perigord. He feems to have neither fuffered hardfhip, nor apprehended danger; though it is evident that his attendants were few, and only fuch as every man of condition

Their numbers.

Facility of travelling in fome provinces.

(187) Memoires d'Aub. p. 98.
(188) De Thou, vol. vii. p. 276.
(189) Mezerai, vol. ix. p. 228.

would

CHAP. VI.

would carry with him on a journey (190). It would probably have been difficult, even before the late revolution in 1789, to have discovered at Chalons on the Marne, so good an inn as Montaigne found in that town, above two centuries earlier, in 1580. "We lodged," says he, "at the Crown, which is "a handsome house, and they serve in silver plate: "the greater part of the beds and coverlids are of "silk (191)." This description, and some others, may tend to make us doubt, whether, in the parts of France where civil war had not banished the arts and comforts of life, accommodations, and places of reception for travellers, were greatly inferior to those found in the present age. Montaigne appears to have performed the journey on his own horses; and to have been accompanied or followed by mules for his servants and baggage (192).

Inns, and accommodations.

Among the disorders frequent during the period under our review, and whose ravages were peculiarly destructive, must be reckoned the plague. That scourge of the human race seemed to have succeeded to the leprosy, which the Cruzaders had brought from the coasts of Syria, as early as the twelfth century. It is clear, that France was scarcely ever altogether free from pestilential diseases; sometimes lurking in the provinces, among the poor inhabitants of obscure towns; sometimes laying waste the capital, and extending their fatal effects over the whole kingdom. No wise and vigilant precautions, such as are adopted by modern states, were taken to prevent its entrance, or to arrest its progress. The insalubrity of cities, the want of air, cleanliness, and police, contributed to nourish or perpetuate it, among the inferior orders of people. To that class, were usually confined its principal attacks, though

Distempers. The plague.

Want of police, and precautions.

(190) Montaigne, Voyages, vol. i. p. 1—23; and vol. iii. p. 452—460.

(191) Ibid. vol. i. p. 12. (192) Ibid. p. 3.

CHAP. VI.

it ſometimes entered the houſes of the great, and the palaces of kings. In 1562, thirty thouſand perſons were carried off by the plague, in the city of Orleans alone (193). We ſhall not wonder at ſo vaſt a mortality, when we conſider, that the infected were heaped together in rooms, where they communicated the malady to each other. D'Aubigné ſays, that at Orleans, the ſurgeon, and four other perſons of the family, died in the chamber where he himſelf lay at the point of death, of the ſame contagious diſeaſe (194). The plague of 1580, was the moſt memorable and deſtructive of any which took place under Henry the Third. We may ſee in De Thou, all the ſymptoms by which it was preceded and accompanied. In the beginning of June, a diſtemper manifeſted itſelf at Paris, which he denominates "La Coqueluche," or, the hooping cough; but, which, if we may judge from his deſcription, was far more ſerious than the diſorder ſo termed in the preſent age. "It ſhewed itſelf," ſays he, "by an aching at the extremity of the "back-bone; by a ſhivering, followed with heavi-"neſs in the head; and by weakneſs in all the "limbs, joined with a violent pain in the breaſt. "If ſuch as were affected with it, were not cured "by the fourth or fifth day, the malady degenerated "into fever, which almoſt always carried off the "patient. Thoſe who neglected the diſorder, did "well: on the contrary, ſuch as were either bled "or purged, generally died (195)." Henry the Third himſelf, the duke of Guiſe, and many of the firſt nobility, were attacked with this diſtemper, which was immediately followed by the plague (196). "There never," ſays De Thou, "was ſeen a "finer autumn, nor a greater abundance of every

Numbers, carried off by it.

Hooping cough.

Deſcription of it.

Plague at Paris. Its ravages.

(193) D'Aub. Memoires, p. 11. (194) Ibid.
(195) De Thou, vol. iii. p. 401 and 402.
(196) Mem. pour ſer. à l'Hiſt. de Fra. p. 117.

"ſort

" sort of fruit; insomuch that the contagion was " believed to proceed, rather from the influ- " ence of the stars, than from a corruption of " the air (197)."—" The plague carried off, in " about six months, forty thousand persons, of " whom the greater number consisted of the lowest " of the people. It rendered Paris almost desert; " and the houses of the rich, whom fear had in- " duced to fly from the capital, were in great dan- " ger of being pillaged by robbers, who, during " the nights, armed themselves, infested the streets, " and committed disorders with impunity. All " the vigilance of the provost of the merchants, " aided by the magistrates, was scarcely effectual to " repress their outrages (198)." The king, after first retiring to St. Maur, only a league from the metropolis, withdrew precipitately to Blois, in order to secure himself from infection. In this crisis, the intrepid and magnanimous conduct of Christopher de Thou, first president of the parliament of Paris, and father to the celebrated historian, just cited, eminently conduced to preserve that city from complete anarchy and desolation. Though he was arrived at a very advanced period of life, and was accustomed annually to repair to his country-house during the autumnal season; he refused to consult either his own safety, ease, or gratification, at the expence of his public duty. He even appeared every day in his coach, in the streets, to convince the people how much he despised the danger, and to animate them by his example. We must own, that such a character would not have disgraced the consular ages of Rome.

Magnanimity of president De Thou.

Precautions and exertions, for diminishing the violence of the contagion, seem to have been made by the magistrates of Paris, in 1580. An officer,

Exertions made to check its progress.

(197) De Thou, vol. viii. p. 401 and 402.
(198) Ibid. p. 400. Œuvres de Paré, p. 568.

intitled

CHAP. VI.

intitled from his functions, the provost of health, was created, who caused the sick to be transported to hospitals, where they appeared to be unable to procure proper assistance in their own houses. Tents were pitched without the walls, for their reception; and a contribution for supporting these extraordinary expences, was raised upon the inhabitants (199). Malvedy, mathematical instructor to the king, and who possessed an equal knowledge of medicine, undertook to attend the diseased; but, it does not seem to have been with any eminent success. The pestilence raged for six months, and diminished as the winter approached. It is not unworthy of remark, that so awful a visitation of Providence, far from amending, rather augmented, the depravity of manners, among the people. Such was the solitude and depopulation of the capital, that the tradesmen not only played bowls upon the bridge of "Notre "Dame," and in the great hall where the courts of law were accustomed to be held; but, games of chance and tables for play were established in the streets (200). A circumstance very similar is related by Boccace, relative to the effect of the great pestilence, in 1348, upon the manners of the Florentines (201). Almost all the towns and villages in the vicinity of Paris, caught the infection. At Laön, in Picardy, it was so violent, as to carry off six thousand persons (202).

Dissolution of manners, produced by it.

Notwithstanding these destructive ravages, so little had the malignity of the distemper ceased, or so inattentive were the magistrates to effect its total extinction, that we find it re-appearing in the capital and in the provinces, during the greater part of the

Re-appearance of the plague.

(199) Mem. pour ser. à l'Hist. de Fra. p. 118.
(200) Ibid. p. 119. Chron. Nov. vol. i. p. 67.
(201) Decameron, vol. i. p. iv. Preface.
(202) De Thou, vol. viii. p. 400. Lettres de Foix, p. 46.

years

years 1583 and 1584. One of the ladies of the queen's houſehold having been ſeized with it, and carried off ſuddenly at Blois, the court fled to St. Germain (203). We may ſee in the Memoirs of Sully, what havoc was made by the plague in that age, and what terror it inſpired (204). In 1587, having obtained permiſſion to viſit his wife, who had remained at Roſny; he learnt on his arrival, that the greater part of the inhabitants of the town were already dead of the plague; and that in the caſtle, where ſhe reſided, two of her women, and three of her domeſtics, had been carried off by the ſame malady. Such was the violence of the contagion, that ſhe was reduced to quit the caſtle, and to remain two days and two nights in the adjoining foreſt, in her coach, as no perſon would open their houſe for her reception." "I found her lodged," ſays he, "in a caſtle named Huets, lent her by my aunt, "Madame de Campagnac, with no other attendants, "than one young lady, a maid-ſervant, a coachman, "and a lacquey. When I arrived, ſhe repeatedly "refuſed to open the gates; imploring me from "a window, with her hands claſped, and tears in "her eyes, not to approach her for at leaſt a month." Sully's affection and impatience ſurmounted, notwithſtanding, his terrors, and induced him to enter the caſtle (205).

Account given of it by Sully.

It is difficult for the imagination to conceive a picture more terrible, or affecting, than that drawn by Paré, in his medical works, of the plague. He had been converſant with it, and preſent at its ravages, throughout a long life. He deſcribes its operation on the human mind, on ſociety, and on the affections of the heart, in colors the moſt glowing and

Deſcription of it, by Paré.

(203) Buſbcq. letters 20, 22, 27, and 43.
(204) Sully, vol. i. p. 34.
(205) Ibid. p. 53 and 54.

awful.

CHAP. VI.

awful. All the charities, ties, and connexions of life, ſeemed to diſappear and extinguiſh before it. Far from extending aid to thoſe who were attacked by its malignant ſymptoms, they were inſtantly abandoned, or driven out to periſh, by their own neareſt relatives. The terror of receiving the infection ſurmounted every emotion, and ſteeled to pity the moſt benevolent, or generous minds. Populous cities became ſuddenly deſert; and every habitation was ſhut, or quitted, by its owners. Bands of deſperate malefactors, or robbers, availing themſelves of the general conſternation, entered the houſes of the dying, plundered their effects, and even accelerated their end, by ſtrangling them in their beds (206). It would be incredible, if we did not know the fact from the ſame inconteſtable authority, that theſe wretches even endeavoured to ſpread the peſtilential and malignant influence of the diſtemper, by beſmearing the doors and window-ſhutters of thoſe houſes where the infection had not hitherto penetrated, with the virulent and infectious matter, taken from the bodies of perſons already dead of the plague. The preſence of Charles the Ninth himſelf did not reſtrain, or prevent, theſe flagitious enormities, at Lyons, in 1565 (207). No ſpiritual aſſiſtance could be procured for the ſick; but, in the houſes of the opulent, a ſurgeon was uſually ſhut up with the family, and compelled to adminiſter help, while any remained alive (208). The calamity attained to its utmoſt point of horror and deſtruction, by the incapacity of burying the dead, whoſe bodies remaining in a ſtate of putrefaction, ſpread the infection to the ſurvivors. "Even "the phyſicians themſelves were purſued," ſays

State of thoſe infected.

(206) Œuvres de Paré, p. 567, 568.
(207) Ibid. p. 536 and 570. (208) Ibid. p. 570.

Paré,

Paré, " when they appeared in the ſtreets, by the " inhabitants, who attempted to murder them with " ſtones, like mad dogs; exclaiming, that they " ought only to come out by night, leſt they ſhould " communicate the diſeaſe to ſuch as had hitherto " eſcaped its malignity (209)."

The practice, common during a great part of the ſixteenth century, of leaving, uninterred, the corpſes of thoſe who fell in battles, contributed, in no ſmall degree, to ſpread, and to produce the moſt peſtilential maladies. We cannot read without amazement and diſguſt, the recital made us by Paré, of the ſpectacle which the field of St. Quintin exhibited, ſome few days after that celebrated engagement, in the ſummer of 1557. " Several gentlemen," ſays he, " who were ſent to endeavour to find the body " of Monſieur de Bois-Dauphin, who had been " killed in the late action, requeſted me to accompany " them. Their ſearch was unſucceſsful; the putre- " faction which had univerſally taken place, having " ſo disfigured the corpſes, as to render them no " longer recognizable. We ſaw the earth covered " with human bodies, for more than half a league " round us; and our ſtay was ſhort, on account of the " cadaverous ſtench, iſſuing from ſuch a multitude " of men and horſes. Our arrival diſturbed the " flies, which were ſettled on them: they were of a " monſtrous ſize, with green and blue backs. " When they roſe into the air, ſuch were their " numbers, as to darken the ſun; and they buzzed " in a marvellous manner. I believe, that they " were ſufficient to produce the plague, in the place " where they ſettled (210)."

Cuſtom of leaving the dead, unburied.

If the ravages of the plague were, in a great degree, limited to the inferior orders of ſociety, there was another diſtemper frequent in that age, whoſe

Other diſtempers.

(209) Œuvres de Paré, 568. (210) Ibid. p. 795.

attacks

CHAP. VI.

attacks were hardly lefs fatal, and which feemed to be directed againft fovereigns, in common with the meaneft of their fubjects, It is remarkable, that Paré, who has written on the nature, fymptoms, and cure of this fcourge of the human race, and whofe authority muft be regarded as fuperior to any other of the period, does not feem to confider it as imported from America. On the contrary, he fays, that it was denominated by the Romans, "Pudendagra;" and, in another place, he afferts, that it refembled, in many of its fymptoms, the difeafe called "Mentagra," with which, under Tiberius, the Roman empire was afflicted (211). The recital given by him of the effects, produced from its attacks on the body, cannot be perufed without horror. Yet, he admits, in the moft pointed terms, that, at the time when he wrote, under Charles the Ninth and Henry the Third, it was infinitely diminifhed in violence. "The diforder of the prefent time, is much lefs "cruel, and eafier of cure, than it was, at its firft "commencement, in time paft; for, it evidently "becomes mitigated, from day to day. Aftrologers "attribute this fact to the influences of the fky."— "Phyficians rather chufe to refer it to the invention "of a number of excellent remedies, which men "of talents have diligently fought, in order to op-"pofe fo cruel an evil (212)."

Remedies.

Four different modes of treating the diftemper, were known and practifed, when Paré wrote, between 1570, and 1585. "The firft," fays he, "is "the decoction of gum-guaiacum: the fecond, by "unctions: the third, by mercury: the fourth, by "perfumes (213)." But, he repeatedly and decidedly maintains, that the only fpecific and fovereign remedy, is mercury. He denominates it the

(211) Œuvres de Paré, p. 444 and 446.
(212) Ibid. p. 446. (213) Ibid. p. 447.

true

true antidote; and compares it to a ferret, which chases and expels the malady, however concealed, or inveterate (214).

CHAP. VI.

The disease which Columbus is accused of having brought from the New World, was not felt in any of the royal houses of Europe, in so severe a manner as in France. One of the most accomplished princes of the sixteenth century, Francis the First, expired in the vigor of his age and talents, from its incurable effects. It was in vain that Henry the Third addressed his prayers to the Virgin, or obtained jubilees from the sovereign pontiffs. He had met with an accident, amidst the splendor of his reception at Venice, in 1574, which had incapacitated him for perpetuating the family of Valois (215). His brother, the duke of Alençon, youngest of the four sons of Henry the Second, and last descendant of so many monarchs, was even, if possible, more unfortunate. His face, disfigured and hideous, exposed him to universal pity, or derision; and his premature death was probably caused by the same complaint, which had abridged the life and reign of his grandfather (216). After the lapse of near a whole century since the introduction of that disease, we may judge how malignant it was still esteemed, and how little progress had been made in its extirpation or cure; by the regulations established at the public baths of Plombieres, in Lorrain, as late as 1581. All women of pleasure or disorderly conduct, were prohibited, by order of the dukes of Lorrain, not only from presuming to enter the baths; but, from approaching within five hundred paces of them, on pain of being whipped at the four corners of the town (217).

Francis the First.

Henry the Third.

Duke of Alençon.

(214) Œuvres de Paré, p. 444 and 449, and 555.
(215) Davila, p. 598.
(216) Busbeq. letter 19. Le Lab. sur Cast. vol. i. p. 701.
(217) Voyages de Montaigne, vol. i. p. 32.

Inter-

CHAP. VI.

Intermitting fevers.

Intermitting fevers and agues appear to have been general among armies and ſoldiers. It would be endleſs to cite examples ; nor can we wonder at their frequency or obſtinacy, when we recollect, that the only ſpecific for thoſe diſorders, the bark of Peru, was not imported into Europe before the reign of Louis the Thirteenth (218). It may excite a ſmile in the preſent age, to know that the French monarchs laid claim to the ſame ſupernatural power of curing the ſchrophula, or king's evil, ſo long arrogated and exerciſed by Engliſh princes. It was performed by touching with the right hand. Paré informs us, that in 1564, when Charles the Ninth, then ſcarcely fourteen years old, viſited Bayonne, Spaniards of condition came, to receive the benefit of his touch. He tacitly confeſſes, at the ſame time, its inefficacy, when he adds, that he afterwards treated them according to the principles of art, and effected ſeveral cures (219). Henry the Third ſeems, very prudently, to have declined exerting its virtue on Epernon, his favorite, who, in 1584, was attacked with the diſeaſe ſo immediately ſubjected to his maſter's power and controul. The pretenſion ſeems, indeed, to have excited among men of liberality and education, not leſs ridicule in the ſixteenth, than in the eighteenth century (220).

King's evil.

General review of the period.

Before we finally diſmiſs the period under our conſideration, it may be proper to take a general review of the great characteriſtic vices and virtues by which it was marked ; and which ſtrongly diſcriminated it, as a portion of time, either from the age of Francis the Firſt which preceded it, or from that of Henry the Fourth, and Louis the Thirteenth, by which it was followed. Unhappily, the liſt of vices,

Characteriſtic vices.

(218) Brant. vol. ii. Cap. Etrang. p. 182. Trad. de l'Hop. vol. ii. Recherches, p. 106.

(219) Œuvres de Paré, p. 800. (220) Buſbeq. letter 43.

includes

includes many of the moſt deformed, or diſguſting features of human nature; whereas the virtues may be compriſed in a narrow compaſs. In both, we trace the genius of the nation, as it then exiſted; violent, intemperate, and carrying even its laudable qualities to a cenſurable exceſs. At the head of the vices, may be placed the practice of mingling oaths and imprecations in ordinary diſcourſe. It is well known, that Francis the Firſt, however diſſolute in his pleaſures, yet carefully abſtained from every ſpecies of profaneneſs of language. His common and peculiar atteſtation was, "on the faith of a gentleman," which he piqued himſelf on preſerving unſullied (221). So different were the habits of Charles the Ninth, that all his converſation was mingled with blaſphemous and indecent oaths. Catherine of Medicis was, herſelf, the cauſe of it, by placing him under the tuition of marſhal Retz, a Florentine, who infuſed into his pupil, the moſt odious principles. "He taught the young monarch," ſays de Thou, "to ſwear, never to ſpeak the truth, "and always to diſguiſe his thoughts (222)." Can we wonder at the pernicious effects of ſuch a ſyſtem of education? The cuſtom was become univerſal, and excited ſo little animadverſion, that even children and peaſants, as well as gentlemen and ſoldiers, permitted themſelves an unbounded freedom of imprecation (223).

Imprecations.

Education of Charles the Ninth.

Univerſality of imprecations.

It will ſcarcely be credited, that "legends of "oaths," containing every mode and variation of blaſphemy, were publiſhed, as if to circulate and facilitate their uſe (224). We find that the practice excited, by its enormity, the attention of govern-

(221) Brant. vol. i. Cap. Fran. p. 229.
(222) De Thou, vol. vii. p. 740.
(223) La Noue, premier Diſcours, p. 6 and 7. Hiſt des derniers Troubles de Fra. liv. ii. p. 38.
(224) Eſprit de la Ligue, note, vol. ii. p. 103.

ment.

CHAP. VI.

ment. Henry the Third was, himself, exempt from the reproach, if we may believe Chiverny (225): yet, Sir Edward Stafford, in his famous dispatch to queen Elizabeth, of the 25th of February, 1588, expressly repeats the great oaths which the king swore during his discourse (226). In his harangue to the States at Blois, in December, of the same year, he strongly insisted on the necessity of prohibiting blasphemies, under severe penalties; and on the propriety of punishing, without distinction, all such as should be guilty of the practice (227). He was followed by Montholon, the keeper of the seals, in the same assembly; who warned the nobility from provoking and drawing down the divine vengeance, by their execrable, and familiar custom of swearing (228). But no effectual exertion was made for the reform of so general and disgraceful a vice. The king of Navarre, in his declaration from Saumur, dated in April, 1589, warmly exhorts the Catholic clergy to interpose their efforts for checking and suppressing it. The admonitions of a Hugonot and an excommunicated prince, were not, it must be owned, likely to awaken the zeal, or to stimulate the fervor of the Romish ecclesiastics (229). We may see in Brantome, what strange and eccentric imprecations were common among military men, who generally affected one peculiar to themselves, and made use of it as their special form of attesting, or assuring any fact (230).

Ineffectual attempts of government, to repress the practice,

and of the king of Navarre.

Libertinism.

Never, perhaps, was libertinism and debauch carried to a greater height, than under Henry the Third. It had gradually augmented since the accession of Francis the First, and it attained to an enormous

(225) Chiverny, vol. i. p. 148.
(226) Hardwick State Papers, vol. i. p. 251—264.
(227) De Thou, vol. x. p. 378. (228) Ibid. p. 385.
(229) Chron. Nov. vol. i. p. 177.
(230) Brant. vol. i. Cap. Fran. p. 104.

pitch

pitch during the reign of his laſt deſcendant. Catherine of Medicis, deſtitute of ſentiments of virtue, and conſulting only intereſt or policy in all her ſteps, did not heſitate, throughout her whole life, to ſacrifice the chaſtity and honor of her female attendants, to the completion of her objects. Every negociation was facilitated, and every treaty was cemented, by ſome victim, ſelected from among the numerous and brilliant circle of ladies, who attended her wherever ſhe moved. It was denominated the "Eſcardon volant (231)."—"The impudicity of the young women of the court in "general," ſays a contemporary writer, "but, "peculiarly, of the attendants of the queen-mother, is ſo notorious, that among all the cour-"tiers, not a teſtimony could be found in their fa-"vour (232)." Mademoiſelle de Rouet, who was ſacrificed to Anthony, king of Navarre, and who attended him even to his laſt moments; Mademoiſelle de Limeuil, who, by the expreſs command of Catherine, permitted the criminal aſſiduities of Louis, prince of Condé, and was brought to bed in the queen-dowager's apartments; together with a long train of others, commemorated by Brantome and d'Aubigné, leave no room to doubt of the depravity of the court. An example ſo pernicious did not fail to produce the worſt effects on the morals of the court, and of the nation. If we wiſh to read the deſcription of the former, as it exiſted in 1572, under Charles the Ninth; we may ſee it in the ſtrongeſt language and colors, by the pen of the queen of Navarre, Jane d'Albret, in a letter to her ſon, the prince of Bearn, afterwards Henry the Fourth. It is dated from Blois, where the French

CHAP. VI.

Diſſolute conduct of Catherine of Medicis.

Letter of Jane d'Albret to her ſon.

(231) Eſprit de la Ligue, vol. ii. p. 165 and 166, and p. 298. Trad. de l'Hopital, vol. ii. Recherches, p. 55.

(232) Tocſin des Maſſacres, p. 49, cited in the Confeſſion de Sancy, p. 461.

court

CHAP. VI.

court then resided, and merits to be universally known. The duplicity, and treachery of the king and his mother, are exposed without disguise. We trace in every line, the apprehensions of a parent for her child, whose morals, she dreaded, might be corrupted by the contact with so dissolute a society, from which not only religion, but decorum itself, was banished. "It is not," says she, "the men "who solicit the women here: the women corrupt "and solicit the men (233)."

Margaret of Valois.

Margaret of Valois, wife of Henry the Fourth, realized in her conduct, every thing related of the Messalinas and Faustinas of antiquity. Abandoned from her earliest years to the most shameless libertinism, she rendered the court of Navarre a theatre of intrigue; and did not even hesitate to aid her husband's amours, by every possible subserviency (234). She had scarcely attained her twenty-first year, when she successfully undertook, in concert with the duke of Guise, and the cardinal of Lorrain, to shake the nuptial fidelity of Mary of Cleves, princess of Condé, who was conducted to the duke of Anjou's bed, by Margaret (235). Even to its latest period, her life was a perpetual scene of sensuality and prostitution. She was imitated by the ladies of that voluptuous court, who blended libertinism even with the most pious exercises and acts of devotion. "The duchesses of Guise, and "of Nevers," says d'Aubigné, "had the portraits "of their two lovers, Roquemont, and the baron "de Fumel, painted as on the cross, in their prayer-"books, and closets. They, in a similar manner, "had the likenesses of their mistresses, under the "character and dress of the Virgin." Such a pro-

Her profligacy, and debauchery.

(233) Le Lab. sur Cast. vol. i. p. 869—601.
(234) Vie de Marg. p. 314. Vie d'Epernon, vol. i. p. 56.
(235) Vie de Marg. p. 126.

fanation

fanation of the moſt ſacred myſteries of religion, excites not more amazement, than it impreſſes with horror.

CHAP. VI.

Depraved and looſe education.

How looſe was the education beſtowed on young women of condition, and how licentious were the manners, we may ſee in the writings of l'Hopital. "The firſt leſſon of a mother to her daughter," ſays that ſevere and virtuous magiſtrate, "is to inſtruct her how to diſtribute with grace, the edifice "of her hair; to ſpoil by art the luſtre of her natural attractions; to adorn her head with diamonds, and her boſom with a necklace of gold. "She next carries her to the ſuppers of our prelates, ſo prolonged, and ſo licentious. The unfortunate girl is loſt at her return (236)." Brantome declares in the cleareſt and leaſt ambiguous language, that there was hardly a young woman, married or ſingle, who, on her firſt arrival at court, did not fall into the hands of the cardinal of Lorrain, and was not ſeduced by his preſents. "Few, or "none," ſays he, "quitted the court, with their "honor (237)."

Its effects.

Encouragement given to vice by Henry the Third.

Henry the Third, not content with exhibiting in his own conduct, a model of the moſt depraved and effeminate debauch, endeavoured, by precept and exhortation, to encourage vice, and to render female chaſtity ridiculous. Either deſtitute of inclination or of ability to practiſe his own maxims, he delighted in defaming and expoſing the weakneſſes with which he became acquainted. "Never," ſays a contemporary writer, "did the court of our kings, "in which formerly the French nobility learnt the "exerciſe of virtue, overflow ſo much with every "kind of diſorder, luxury, and exceſs, as under "the reign of Henry the Third; peculiarly, in the

(236) Confeſſ. de Sancy, p. 234. Trad. de l'Hop. vol. i. Epitres, p. 128.

(237) Brant. vol. ii. Dames Gal. p. 418.

CHAP. VI.

" years 1586 and 1587. It may be ſaid that " every thing was then permitted, except to be " virtuous (238)." Brantome did not heſitate to dedicate his work, denominated, " The Lives of " the Women of Gallantry of his own Time," to the duke of Alençon: a production, which, in depravity of ſentiment and of language, may rank with the worſt age (239). It ſeems difficult to form an idea of a more abandoned court, than that which he depictures. " I knew," ſays he, " a Venetian painter, by name Bernardo, who " kept a ſhop at Paris: he has ſworn to me, that " within the ſpace of a year, he had ſold more than " fifty ſets of Aretino, to ladies, married and un- " married (240)." He aſſerts in another place, that women of beauty were commonly ſent by their huſbands, to ſolicit the judges in all cauſes of moment; and that it was notorious, how much the decrees and ſentences were affected by the compliances of female ſuitors (241). La Noue, and Le Laboureur, confirm, in the fulleſt manner, all the aſſertions of Brantome (242).

Works of Brantome.

Depravity of the court.

Entertainments and banquets of Henry the Third.

In the more ſelect and private pleaſures of that age and court, decency itſelf was withdrawn. In 1577, we find the king giving an entertainment to his brother, the duke of Alençon, at the caſtle of Pleſſiz les Tours. The company was numerous, and all the gueſts of both ſexes were habited in green. It is hardly credible, that the ladies who aſſiſted at it were dreſſed in men's clothes, half naked, having their hair looſe and floating on their backs, as it was then commonly worn by brides.

(238) Hiſt. des derniers Troub. de Fra. liv. ii. p. 39.—" à Lyons, " 1597."
(239) Brantome, vol. i. Dames Gal. Dedication.
(240) Ibid. p. 60.
(241) Brantome, vol. i. Dames Gal. p 224 and 225.
(242) La Noue, p. 14—16. Le Lab. ſur Caſt. vol. ii. p. 102.

In this disorderly attire, they served at table, and brought up the dishes. It appears, that the queen-mother herself, though then in a very advanced age, was not ashamed to assist, and to preside at so indecent a banquet (243). The amours of Henry became the opprobrium of mankind, and were supposed to be of a nature, which the purity and dignity of history cannot mention, without contamination. His minions subjected him to the contumely and abhorrence of his own subjects. They were young men, whose dress and manners partook more of a feminine, than of a manly beauty. An author of that period, describing them as they commonly appeared in 1576, says, "that they wore their hair long, "frized to a great degree, and turning up over "their little velvet bonnets, precisely like wo-"men (244)." Allusions to the apprehended nature of his attachment towards them, were made in all the satirical verses or epigrams of the time.

Minions of that monarch.

Satires.

We find in D'Aubigné, who, though a Hugonot, is a writer of veracity, and who had access to the highest information; that the king contracted a marriage with Quelus, and afterwards with another of his minions. The contract of this abominable union was even signed by Henry, in his own blood; and the Marquis d'O, superintendant of the finances, witnessed it in the same manner, having opened one of his veins, for the purpose. After the death of Maugiron, the king lavished marks of fondness and affection on his corpse, which are not to be reflected on without astonishment, nor related without debasing the dignity of the human species, and staining the English language. It is only in the effeminate and monstrous vices of the Syrian, Heliogabalus, that we can find in antiquity, any pa-

Vices.

(243) L'Etoile, p. 21.
(244) Memoires pour ser. à l'Hist. de Fra. p. 70.

 rallel

CHAP. VI.

rallel to those of Henry the Third. The younger part of the members, deputed to the States General, convoked at Blois, in 1588, complained publicly, in their letters to the provinces by whom they were sent, that attempts were not only made to corrupt their principles, and to gain their suffrages; but, to subject them to the pleasures of their sovereign (245).

Profanations.

By a refinement in vice and impiety, which excites horror, he made even the exercises of devotion subservient to his detestable gratifications. The most skilful artists were employed in adorning his missals and prayer-books, with the portraits of his minions, habited in the monastic dress of St. Francis, or of St. Jerome. We can scarcely believe, if it was not asserted by contemporary writers of the best authority, that several of the most favoured, were represented on the cross, with the attributes of our Saviour; and others, depictured and dressed in the character of the Virgin Mary (246). To render this monument of impious sensuality still more singular, it was consecrated to vengeance, as well as to pleasure. At the end of the prayers, were similar portraits of the individuals, who had rejected and disdained his solicitations. Among them, was peculiarly distinguished the head of Francis de Chatillon, son to the admiral Coligni, with his sleeves turned up, in order to display his arms. Round it was this inscription: "Non per amor, "mà per vendetta (247)." It is difficult to conceive, or to convey an idea of greater depravity; nor can we wonder at the indignation and contempt which such a conduct excited, not only in the court, but throughout the country.

(245) Confess. de Sancy, p. 201, 202, and 219.
(246) D'Aubigné, Histoire Gen. vol. iii. p. 362. Confess. de Sancy, p. 213, 214, and 223—225, and 234, and p. 236.
(247) Confess. de Sancy, p. 204.

Tavannes

Tavannes does not hesitate to say, that the institution of the order of the Holy Ghost, in 1579, was only designed to commemorate the amours of the king with his two minions, Quelus and Maugiron, who had been recently killed in a duel; and, that he celebrated by it, their funeral games, in imitation of Alexander and Hadrian, who had thus immortalized their favorites, Epheſtion, and Antinous (248). It is true, that he mentions this extraordinary fact, as, possibly, only a calumny; but, he allows, that Henry the Fourth altered the cyphers and devices worn by the knights, which implies the truth of the report (249).

Order of the Holy Ghost.

Public honor and principle did not survive the extinction of private virtue and morality. Corruption found its way into the highest departments, and every thing became venal. Under Henry the Second, the constable Montmorency did not blush to accept the estate and castle of Chateaubriant, from the count of that name, in recompence for the order of St. Michael, obtained through his interest (250). But, though he forgot his own dignity in such a transaction, he would have been incapable of betraying his master to his foreign enemies. After the accession of Charles the Ninth, ministers occupying the first employments of state, were so base as to sell their sovereign and their country to Spain. In 1565, when Philip the Second meditated his detestable project of seizing and delivering over Jane d'Albret, queen of Navarre, together with her two children, to the Inquisition; intelligence of the design was communicated to the French court, by Elizabeth, queen of Spain, sister to Charles the Ninth. The Spanish officer, who was charged with dispatches, containing not only

Corruption and venality.

Examples of those vices.

Ministers, sold to Spain.

(248) Tavannes, p. 179.
(249) Le Lab. sur Cast. vol. iii. p. 41.
(250) Brant. vol. ii. Cap. Fran. p. 124.

the

CHAP. VI.

the particulars of that plot; but, of the machinations of Philip againſt the repoſe of the French monarchy, might have been eaſily apprehended on his road to Paris, or on his return to Madrid: but, the king of Spain had already found means to corrupt, and to purchaſe ſome of the moſt confidential ſervants of his brother-in-law, who averted the blow, and permitted the courier to perform his journey, unmoleſted. L'Aubeſpine, firſt ſecretary of ſtate, was Philip's penſioner; and ſo notorious was his corruption, that the conſtable Montmorency no ſooner knew of L'Aubeſpine's having been acquainted with the tranſaction by Catherine of Medicis, than he inſtantly predicted the conſequence; and foretold, that the courier would be allowed to quit Paris without injury (251).

L'Aubeſpine.

Villeroy.

During the reign of Henry the Third, it was not even doubted, that Spaniſh gold pervaded the inmoſt receſſes of the cabinet. In 1587, the duke of Epernon reproached Villeroy, then ſecretary of ſtate, in preſence of the king himſelf, with betraying to the League and to Philip the Second, every ſecret of importance. So rude an inſult was ſuppoſed to have been committed with the royal participation and concurrence. Epernon accuſed him of receiving a penſion of double piſtoles (252). It is, however, certain, that Villeroy, in his Memoirs, while he avows the corruption of the age and of the miniſtry, juſtifies himſelf, in a ſatisfactory manner, from having taken money, or accepted any pecuniary bribe (253). The treaſonable correſpondence and connexion between the Guiſes, as heads of the League, and the king of Spain, was ſo undiſguiſed, that ſcarcely even a veil was drawn over the tranſac-

The Guiſes. Their connexion with Philip the Second.

(251) Villeroy, Memoires, vol. ii. p. 56 and 57.
(252) Memoires pour ſer. à l'Hiſt. de Fr. p. 228.
(253) Villeroy, Mem. vol. i. p. 122—126.

tion.

tion. We may judge, of what nature, and how momentous, were the ſervices to be rendered on the part of the princes of Lorrain, by the magnitude of the ſums received from Philip. After the aſſaſſination of the duke, at Blois, in 1588, it was aſcertained, that he carried on a regular intercourſe with Spain and Savoy. The amount of the money tranſmitted him by the former power, during ten years, ſince the death of Don John of Auſtria, did not fall much ſhort of two hundred thouſand pounds (254). It muſt be owned, that Philip paid dear for the alliance and friendſhip of the Guiſes. In return, they convulſed, and had nearly overturned, the French monarchy. The remittances from Madrid, enabled them to ſhake the fidelity of many of the royal governors. Villars, to whom Havre-de-Grace had been entruſted, ſold the place, together with himſelf, in 1588, to the League, for fifteen thouſand crowns (255). His conduct was, by no means, ſingular.

Vaſt ſums expended by that prince.

It is curious to ſee, that the ſame venality which ſo ſtrongly marked the French court and miniſters, was practiſed by Charles the Ninth and his ſucceſſor with ſimilar induſtry, if not with ſimilar ſucceſs, in other kingdoms. We cannot doubt, from the original letters ſtill exiſting of thoſe two monarchs, addreſſed to the embaſſador of France in England, that they diſpenſed continual largeſſes and penſions, to perſons occupying the higheſt public ſituations about Elizabeth. The great object of both princes, was to effect the marriage of the duke of Alençon with the Engliſh queen. In order to compaſs it, no promiſes, engagements, or preſents, were ſpared: but, the two former were more liberally beſtowed than the latter. Ladies, who could facilitate, or

Corruption in foreign courts.

England.

(254) De Thou, vol. x. p. 480. Villeroy, Mem. vol. iii. p. 123.
(255) Davila, p. 676.

accelerate

CHAP. VI.

accelerate the proposed match, found reason to be satisfied with the liberality and attention of the queen-dowager. Catherine of Medicis, writing on the 29th of April, 1573, to the embassador at London, says: "I shall cause to be presented to the "Sieur de Walsingham, as he passes through Paris, "on his return home, two pieces of fine black silk "cloth for his wife, and two others in colors, with "gold and silver intermixed, for her daughter; in "order to gratify him as much as possible, on account of the hope that I have in his promises, to "do all in his power towards accomplishing the "said marriage (256)." Sir Francis Walsingham was at that time going over to England, from his embassy in France. That the earl of Leicester should accept of pensions, or gratifications, from a foreign prince, cannot excite surprize. His rapacity and his other vices, justify the imputation. But, that the lord-treasurer Burleigh, condescended to receive the gold of Charles the Ninth, and to bargain for the surrender of his mistress to the duke of Alençon, is more difficult to believe. If, however, the dispatches of the king of France, and his mother, of "the 18th of January, 1574," do not absolutely prove this fact; it must be owned, that they afford strong presumptions of its existence (257). We find the earl of Leicester, four years afterwards, in 1578, expressing his discontent to the French embassador, at the non-performance of the promises of money, which had been made to him, on the part of Henry the Third. That prince renews his assurances of being liberal in future, and relies on the earl's best exertions to cultivate the friendship between the queen and himself (258).

Letter of Catherine of Medicis.

Lord Burleigh.

Earl of Leicester.

(256) Le Lab. sur Cast. vol. iii. p. 330.
(257) Ibid. p. 373. (258) Ibid. p. 551.

It

It cannot excite wonder, that in a period so corrupt and dissolute, religion was overborne by the torrent of immorality. True piety could not exist in so contagious an atmosphere. Infidelity, impiety, and even atheism, were characteristics of the nation, and had made a general progress among every rank of men. The long continuance of the civil wars, had tended to render the two parties equally indifferent to that very cause which originally produced them (259). Such was the open contempt of the Catholic troops of the duke of Mayenne, for the ordinances of the Romish faith, that, in 1589, they not only transgressed against one of its most peremptory injunctions, by eating flesh publicly during Lent; but, they added to it mockery and profanation. By menaces of death, they compelled the priests to baptize sheep, pigs, and other animals, and to call them by the names of various kinds of fish. The duke of Mayenne was obliged to tolerate these enormities, which strongly prove the universal dissolution of manners (260). We may close the list of vices, by one of a nature more immediately destructive than any hitherto enumerated; but, which has been already described in its effects. The unlimited scope and exercise of vengeance desolated private life; armed individuals against each other, produced assassinations, duels, and murders; and converted the kingdom into a vast charnel house.

Irreligion, and impiety.

Profanations, committed by the Catholic soldiery.

Exercise of private vengeance.

The characteristic virtues of the period were few; and, far from dispelling, they scarcely illuminate the darkness. Some illustrious examples of inflexible integrity; of loyalty and public virtue; and even of a magnanimous dereliction or contempt of

Virtues of the period, few.

(259) La Noue, p. 5—7. Hist. des der. Troub. de Fra. p. 38.
(260) Mem. pour ser. à l'Hist. de Fra. 282 and 283.

private

CHAP. VI.

private intereſt, when oppoſed to the general welfare, may, indeed, be produced. The names of Olivier, and of L'Hopital, ſucceſſively chancellors of France, and of Chriſtopher de Thou, firſt preſident of the Parliament of Paris: thoſe of Francis of Montmorency, of marſhal d'Aumont, of Sancy, of Souvré, and of ſeveral others, might diffuſe a luſtre over the worſt age: but, ſuch are to be found under Domitian, and under Commodus, and can only be conſidered as ſhining exceptions to the national character. It is with difficulty, that among a people ſo corrupt, we diſcover ſome amiable or elevated qualities allied to virtue, and challenging our eſteem or admiration. The ſame impartiality which ſtigmatizes vice and crime, demands the commemoration of whatever is laudable and generous. Even the ſhadow may be pourtrayed, if we cannot graſp the ſubſtance; and it is pleaſing, after the ſurvey of ſo depraved a time, to conſider man under a leſs diſguſting form.

Filial piety, and obedience.

Examples of it.

Parental authority and filial reſpect ſeem to have ſurvived the extinction of general philanthropy, and to have been held in the higheſt honor, even by thoſe who did not affect a regard for any other ſpecies of reputation. Francis of Montmorency, eldeſt ſon to the conſtable of that name, long after he had attained to manhood, and when married to the natural daughter of Henry the Second; yet addreſſes his father with a humility and reverence, which recals the idea of the primitive and patriarchal ages of the world (261). Margaret of Valois herſelf, though one of the moſt diſſolute women who ever diſgraced her ſex, far from being deficient on this point, appears to have ſcrupulouſly

Margaret of Valois.

(261) Manuſc. de Bethune, Nº 8673, cited in the Trad. de l'Hop. vol. ii. Recherches, p. 105.

fulfilled

fulfilled her filial duties. We may ſee in her own Memoirs, with what awe and implicit deference, ſhe receives and obeys the orders of her mother, even after ſhe became queen of Navarre, and ſeemed to be by that circumſtance, emancipated, in a great meaſure, from a ſtate of ſubjection. The ducheſs of Lorrain, her elder ſiſter, expreſſes ſimilar ſentiments towards Catherine of Medicis; who uſes the moſt authoritative language, and is obeyed in ſilence, without a murmur (262). "I have always "preſerved," ſays ſhe, in another part of her Memoirs, "that reſpect to the queen, my mother, "that whenever I have been with her, whether "married or ſingle, I never went to any place, "without having aſked her leave, and obtained her "permiſſion (263)." We trace in Sully, Chiverny, Tavannes, and D'Aubigné, the ſame humility on one ſide, and the ſame exertion of parental authority on the other.

Courage, and contempt of death.

Courage, which is not improperly defined to be rather a happy quality than a virtue, has been found in every period, and among every people. It has, notwithſtanding, from the effect of natural, political, or moral cauſes, been heightened, or depreſſed; and we do not conſider the degenerate Romans under Conſtantine and Juſtinian, as equal to the legions who ſubjected Macedonia, Carthage, and Gaul. The ſpirit of chivalry raiſed and ſublimed the valor of the Gothic nations, who over-ran Europe in the middle ages. Under the laſt princes of Valois, continued ſcenes of ſlaughter and civil war had produced a familiarity with death, and bereaved it of the terrors which accompany the laſt act of life. Men became accuſtomed to contem-

Cauſes of it.

(262) Memoires de Marguerite, à Paris, 1658, p. 19 and 36.
(263) Ibid. p. 54.

CHAP. VI.

plate it under every form, and to regard it as continually imminent, or probable. They looked on it with a ſteady eye, and awaited it with a ſort of ſullen intrepidity, whether on the ſcaffold, in a dungeon, or in a field of battle. Education, habit, and enthuſiaſm, all conſpired to ſteel the mind, and to pronounce a diſregard of peril and diſſolution.

Genius of the age.

D'Aubigné.

D'Aubigné tells us, that in the year 1560, when he was ſcarcely nine years old, his father carried him to Paris. On their way through Amboiſe, they beheld the heads of the Hugonots, who had been recently executed for the conſpiracy againſt the Guiſes, planted upon the poles, and which were ſtill eaſy to be recognized. "At ſo lamentable a "ſight, my father," ſays he, "was deeply moved, and his agitation was viſible on his countenance. When we had left the town, he laid his "hand upon my head, and addreſſing me, ſaid; "My child, thou muſt not ſpare thy head after "mine, to avenge thoſe honorable chiefs whoſe "remains thou haſt juſt ſeen; and if thou ſpare "thyſelf, thou ſhalt have my malediction (264)." We may naturally conceive what muſt have been the effect on a young mind, of ſuch an exhortation. D'Aubigné's whole life was paſſed in fulfilling his father's inſtructions. We muſt not imagine that the romantic honor inſpired by chivalry, was totally extinct, even in the times which we have reviewed. Some traces of it appear, and excite admiration. D'Aubigné ſays, that when on the point of commencing a ſkirmiſh, having remarked, that no other of his comrades was covered with mail on their arms, except himſelf; he diſdained an advantage which was not common to the whole

Traces of the ſpirit of chivalry.

(264) D'Aub. Memoires, p. 5 and 6.

troop,

troop, and immediately threw away those pieces of defensive armor (265).

CHAP. VI.

Friendship.

Friendship seems to have been cultivated with uncommon ardor, and the demonstrations of it to have been frequently carried even to a pitch of excess, during the time under our consideration. The duke of Alençon, flying from Paris, in 1575, first clothed himself in the doublet of his unfortunate favorite and friend La Mole, whose attachment had conducted him to a scaffold, under Charles the Ninth (266). It was not uncommon to neglect every species of dress or ornament, and even to allow the hair and beard to grow, in sign of regret for the temporary loss or absence of a companion.

Romantic testimonies of grief.

When D'Aubigné, in 1583, was dispatched by the king of Navarre, to demand reparation of Henry the Third, for the treatment shewn to the wife of the one, and the sister of the other; St. Gelais, his friend, penetrated with grief, fell into a state of dejection, and permitted his appearance to display the melancholy which he felt at the event. "On my return," says D'Aubigné, "to Pau, the king was walking in "the garden of the castle; and he no sooner "saw me, than he instantly said to one of his "gentlemen; Go, tell St. Gelais to shave him-"self and to cut his hair, since his friend is safely "arrived (267)."

Conclusion. Reflexions.

This list of virtues, short as it may appear, includes all those which can be properly said to discriminate and characterize the age. There are, however, many softer features, of a doubtful or equivocal nature, which necessarily, from their minuteness, escape the research of history. It

(265) D'Aub. Memoires, p. 61.
(266) Vie de Marg. p. 164.
(267) D'Aub. Memoires, p. 99.

suffices

CHAP. VI. ſuffices to have marked the outline with an impartial hand; and to have endeavoured to convey a juſt, though an imperfect and defective idea, of a period of time, which, notwithſtanding the vices that deformed and debaſed it, will ever, from the magnitude of the events with which it is crouded, powerfully awaken the attention of the moſt remote poſterity.

INDEX.

INDEX.

A.

The

B.

C.

Chantilly,

D.

Dauphiné,

Duranti,

G.

H.

Assists

J.

K.

L.

M.

N.

O.

P.

Q.

R.

Strozzi,

V.

W.

END OF THE FIRST VOLUME.